The Biblical story comes alive in this novel retelling! The threa[...] man is sustained throughout, despite man's continuing rebellion a[...] Pikkert has done an excellent job of weaving the Biblical narrative int[...] hand and purpose unfolds. The lives of Biblical characters and their s[...] and dynamic way as the Epic unfolds chronologically. The story is very enlightening for both the first time reader and for the theological student of the Bible.

Henry Bell, *Deputy International Director, WEC International, Singapore.*

I highly recommend "The Epic" as a chronological summary of the Old Testament for both the serious and first time Bible reader in order to understand what laid the stage for the arrival of Jesus the Messiah. Dr. Peter Pikkert uses his years of cross-cultural experience to bring insightful explanations to the cultural background of the stories. My personal favorite is the summary of the book of Job, where the author unlocks some insights that have escaped me for years. I look forward to the New Testament sequel.

Ken Benson, *Director, MissionPREP, Toronto, Canada.*

Few things are more important for developing a Christian worldview than grasping the grand Biblical narrative from which it arises. Pikkert's thoughtful and detailed retelling of the Biblical story draws the reader into the story episode by episode in understandable language. It also provides a Christian theological interpretative touch with short comments and cross-references as the story unfolds, unobtrusively helping the reader to see the point of each scene in light of the whole. Highly recommended both for those who have never read through the whole story and for those who know it well, but want a fresh encounter with the real story of God and humanity. This first volume covers the entire Old Testament narrative, leaving us with the hope that the second volume will soon follow.

Dr. George Bristow, *Hasat Church Services, Istanbul, Turkey.*

There are more Bible study resources than ever before, and yet there is widespread ignorance regarding the book's plotline—even among those who profess to believe it and claim to live by it. The tendency for many preachers to whimsically hop between the Old and New Testaments, giving micro-attention to textual minutiae without giving due weight to the macro-context and purpose does little to enable their listeners grasp the Bible's overarching "Big Story": Creation-Fall-Redemption-Restoration. Without some understanding of the sweeping 'epic' from Genesis to Revelation the glorious focus and climax of the story, the Gospel of Jesus Christ, will be misunderstood and perhaps a tad disappointing. Written primarily for those with little understanding of the Bible story, Pikkert's superb retelling of it is an excellent introduction that helps one see how all the dots of countless stories of generations, of battles won and lost, of failed leaders and broken promises, join to point towards the true prophet, priest and King, Jesus. Peter has stayed faithful to the Biblical text: no embellishments or reimagining conversations simply to hold readers' attention. Rather, he uses his lifetime of careful, scholarly and devotional study, along with insights gained from years living in the Middle East, to illuminate those episodes having bearing on the larger metanarrative which might easily have been overlooked. For those who wish to know what the Christian faith is about; for families with older children to read together; for those who want to become more familiar with the Bible storyline. This is a great book about the greatest Story of the greatest Truth ever told. As you read it may you come to know the One that this Story is all about: Jesus.

Rev. Mark Goudy, *Minister, Macosquin Presbyterian Church, Northern Ireland.*

Despite the growth in literacy levels and the advent of the worldwide web, biblical illiteracy is as much a problem today as it has been in other periods of church history. In many of those eras the issue was actual illiteracy. Today, it is an inability to focus upon and digest both the overarching narrative of the Bible as well its details. Enter *The Epic of God and Man*, an excellent resource for quickly understanding the flow, structure, and finer points of the Bible's story. Its accessibility and narrative simplicity make it a wonderful resource for both comprehension and teaching.

Dr. Michael Haykin, *Professor of Church History & Biblical Spirituality, Southern Baptist Theological Seminary. Louisville, Kentucky, USA.*

In *The Epic of God and Man* Peter Pikkert has, in narrative form, clearly presented the epic story of God's relationship with man as depicted in the Old Testament. Written to help those who may not be conversant with the Bible or its stories it will, I am convinced, help them develop a better understanding of the story. It is recounted in a manner which is easily read and with historical details clearly identified and explained.

This book is also a valuable tool for those who well understand the Biblical narrative. The fact that the entire story is relayed so naturally as a unified whole enables the reader to better understand the scope and flow of this "epic". As such the book serves as a valuable companion to the myriad of commentaries which focus on the details of the various components of the story

Peter has done a marvelous job in relaying this history in such a readable manner and yet staying faithful to the Biblical account. I, personally, enjoyed reading this "epic" and had my personal insight increased. I would heartily recommend *The Epic of God and Man* to the novice, the biblical scholar and the many of us who fall somewhere in between.

Paul Hooper, *former Vice-President of Personnel, Wycliffe Bible Translators, Canada.*

A well told story always appeals to the human soul and mind. In *The Epic of God and Man* the author has produced a wonderfully flowing narrative that successfully combines historicity, biblical authority, spirituality and an overall sense of the sovereignty of God. The entire account is suitably accentuated with many cultural explanations and clarifications that help us better understand the ancient eastern world. Intended primarily for those with no background with the Bible, it will also be of inestimable help to those who simply wish for a better grasp of the chronology and inter-connectedness of the Word of God.

Mark Hudson, *General Coordinator, Fellowship of Sovereign Grace Baptist Churches, Canada.*

There is a desperate need today, especially in this post-Christian era, for God's people to understand the ways and the dealings of God with mankind. Many Christians have only a "bits and pieces" understanding of the Bible and of the historical flow of God's purposes for nations and individuals. Peter Pikkert's book, covering the flow of Biblical history prior to Christ's coming, is written in a clear and lucid way, in story format, with great readability. For growth in confidence in God's love and care for you as expressed in the lives of people of old, get this book and read it through. It will encourage you and give you new understanding of our wonderful God.

Dr. John Kayser, *Faculty and Educational Consultant, Bethany Global University, USA.*

In this book Dr. Pikkert has provided an easily-intelligible narrative that comprehends the entire story-line of the Bible and communicates it in simple language to the reader (or listener). In a world where even the rudiments of the Christian worldview are often not known at all this project is timely and valuable.

Dr. Duane A. Miller, *St. Mary's University, San Antonio, Texas, USA.*

Christians believe that the Bible is the actual Word of God. They also believe that whilst the Bible is clear on the essentials of the faith, God has also provided us with teachers to help us understand the glorious message of Sacred Scripture. Peter Pikkert is one such teacher. With care appropriate for one handling the Word of God, Pikkert unfolds the narrative and proves to be a sure-footed guide down the winding road of the Biblical story. His retelling of the great story is clear and succinct, and he summarizes lengthy accounts with consummate ease. He helps us to see the flow of the story and keeps pointing us forward to the coming of the Christ, who is so eagerly anticipated by Old Testament characters. Even the time stamps at the head of each chapter are helpful. But the best thing about this book is its faithfulness to the Book. Pikkert has accurately and faithfully set before us the Biblical story and surely God will bless this work to the enlightening of many a heart!

Rev. Carl Muller, *Minister, Trinity Baptist Church, Burlington, Ontario, Canada.*

The chronological sweep through the Old Testament, aptly entitled *The Epic of God and Man,* is a thoroughly engaging read. Peter's interests as a theologian shine through as he wonderfully traces the thread of God's covenant relationships. His thorough understanding of Middle Eastern culture deeply enriches the whole narrative by adding valuable background information. The Epic is easy to read yet profound, with the Old Testament narrative placed in its historical context. Particularly helpful is the story of David, which places many of the Psalms in their original setting.

Elizabeth Stewart, *Principal, Cornerstone Bible College for Mission Training, The Netherlands.*

In a day when the greatest story of all time has slipped from view, *The Epic of God and Man*, by Peter Pikkert, is a welcome publication. Tracing God's plan of redemption through the Old Testament from Genesis to Malachi, this missionary-scholar skillfully retells the older biblical narrative that sets the stage for the ministry of Jesus Christ. Pikkert's prose is easy to read, his ability to summarize complicated material is exemplary, and his articulation of major biblical and theological themes is very helpful. I can heartily recommend this book to anyone who wants to better understand what God has done for human beings as that story comes to us in the scriptures of the Old Testament.

Kirk Wellum, *Principal, Toronto Baptist Seminary, Canada.*

The Epic of
God and Man

The Old Testament

The Epic of God and Man

The Old Testament

Peter Pikkert

The Epic of
God and Man

The Old Testament

Peter Pikkert

85 Miller Dr.
Ancaster, ON
Canada L9G 2H9

www.alevbooks.com
www.the-epic.org

ISBN-13: 978-0-9881252-7-8
ISBN-10: 0988125277

All profit from the sale of this book goes towards its translation and publication into other languages.

To those whose faithful support over many years has enabled

my wife and me to give our lives to serving Christ cross-culturally.

The secret things belong unto the LORD our God,
but those things which are revealed belong unto us and
to our children for ever, that we may do all the words of this law.

Deuteronomy 29:29

Contents

Preface

WE ARE STORY-telling creatures, and will pay big money to those who can tell a good tale. We buy their books, watch their movies, pay for their theater tickets and reward the best of them with prizes: Man Bookers, Nobels, Pulitzers, Oscars, Emmys, Golden Globes....

As much as we like a good tale, all of us are also characters in the various interlocking and overlapping stories of our families, communities, nations, and religion. In fact, much of our identity is derived from the narratives with which we identify ourselves. Sadly, many peoples' stories are flawed and confused, or they make themselves the main character. That leads to all kinds of problems.

For many years I was a Bible teacher—a teller of the Biblical story—in a Middle Eastern country. Most of the Christians in this country are converts from Islam. They have grown to love God as He revealed Himself in Jesus Christ, and often make great sacrifices for their new-found faith. They often find it difficult, however, to re-forge their identity in line with the all-important story of God's dealings with man in the course of history. Often their grasp of God's unfolding revelation and its relevance is almost non-existent. I have also taught at theological institutions in North America and Europe where my students also love Jesus Christ, but who can be as Biblically illiterate as ex-Muslims. This volume seeks to deal with this problem with respect to the Old Testament narrative. It attempts to retell that story in chronological order and in its historical context, thus allowing its teachings and doctrines to unfold as they did in the course of history.

It is, of course, impossible to write a book like this without betraying one's own theological convictions, so let me state those up-front: I believe that the Bible is the divinely inspired story of God's progressive revelation of Himself, a story which culminates in the person and work of Jesus Christ. Hence I have tried to be clear when I have incorporated extra-biblical historical data into the narrative.

With respect to salvation from the holy God's eternal revulsion of sin I hold that without His antecedent grace people will not accept the redemption He made available through Jesus Christ's substitutionary atonement.

I believe that true faith is life-transforming, that it creates a desire to glorify God, and is evidence that one has—to use the Bible's own terminology—been "born again to newness of life" (John 3:3-8; Rom. 6:3-4) by God's Spirit.

With respect to the end of history I am a historical premillennialist. This means that I believe that after a period of great tribulation Christ will return bodily to this earth to inaugurate the ideal kingdom that both the Old Testament prophets and the New Testament apostles foresaw.

Having said all of that, however, I would like to think that this retelling of the Bible story would have resonated with sincere Christians from the 2nd century onward. Thankfully our Biblical theologies are usually more alike than our systematic theologies!

The work is pitched at the level of an inquisitive young adult and written in an easy-to-translate style—something I am sensitive to as a missionary. Any profit this book generates will go towards its translation into other languages. Hopefully the illustrations by Julius von Carolsfeld will help stimulate the readers' imagination.

I have many people to thank, but none more than my wife Anna. Her editing skills combined with her rigorous focus on keeping the narrative flowing kept the story from getting mired in the historical details I love. I also thank Jeremy Johnson and William Kennedy for proof-reading the manuscript before it went to press.

By retelling the Biblical narrative and its implications as it unfolds in its historical and cultural context my hope and prayer is that its inherent power will touch your heart and mind, and that you will be more firmly established in your Christian identity.

Peter Pikkert

Introduction

THE BIBLE is a large volume of 66 books written over a period of about 1500 years. The twists and turns of the story are sometimes confusing but its basic message is clear: people are sinners who stand condemned before a holy God. In His mercy God made a series of covenants[1] in which He revealed the essence of His character, and promised a Saviour to redeem mankind from the devastating results of their sin and bring them back into a right relationship with Himself.

The Bible breaks this story into two parts: the Old Testament and the New Testament. "Testament" is the Latin word for "covenant". Most of the Old Testament relates how God's covenants with Abraham and his descendants, the people of Israel, were played out in the course of their history. When they submitted to its stipulations He blessed them, but when they were disobedient He punished them according to the terms agreed upon. In the course of that history He progressively revealed more and more of His plan of salvation for humanity through their prophets. Around the year 250 B.C., 39 of their books were compiled into a single volume that came to be known as the TANAKH by the Jews and, later, as the Old Testament by Christians.

The series of remarkable promises God gave the Jewish people in the course of time were eventually fulfilled in Jesus Christ. His sinless life, atoning death, and resurrection from the dead reconciled the perfectly righteous, holy God with flawed, sinful humanity. The story of Jesus Christ's unique conception, birth, life, death and resurrection in the first half of the first century, and the implications of all of that for the world, are described in the New Testament. This volume retells the preparatory part of the divine narrative, the Old Testament.

---

[1] In the Bible the word "covenant" refers to a binding arrangement—either conditional or unconditional—between God and people.

"The Lord said to him, 'Take your sandals off of your feet for the place where you stand is holy ground."

Genesis 1-2   *Date: prehistory*

GOD EXISTS, He is the creator of all things, He is eternal and He is separate from His creation. These are the basic presuppositions of the creation story.

Initially God's creation was formless, empty and dark, but with God's Spirit present over it. No one knows how long creation remained in that state. At a certain point in time, however, God chose to impose His will on the raw matter He had created.

"Let there be light," He said, and light came into being. The separation of light from the primordial darkness for a specific period of time was the first day[2]. When the light returned the next day God spoke the sky, the atmosphere—the air we breathe—into existence.

On the third day God willed the separation of land from sea. He also created the countless species of vegetation which covers much of the world's landmass: colorful flowers, towering hardwoods, luscious fruit trees and vegetable bearing plants—everything needed to sustain animal life.

On the fourth day God spoke the heavenly bodies into being: the sun, the moon, and the countless stars that dot the night sky. From that day the sun has warmed the earth and sustained life while the gentle lights of the moon and myriads of other heavenly bodies soften the utter darkness of the original night.

On the fifth day God created the various species of fish and fowl, and on the sixth day he spoke the rest of the animal world into existence.

Although not specifically mentioned in the creation story, at some stage God also created the hosts of heavenly beings, including the angels who inhabit heaven, the place He created to most fully reveal himself. After each creative act God looked at His handiwork and declared it to be good. As originally created, the world was without blemish, wholly in harmony with God's perfect will.

---

[2] People have wondered if the days of Genesis 1 were really 24 hours long. After all, they argue, the 24 hour day wasn't created until day four when the heavenly bodies were created, and Genesis uses the word "day" in different ways: as a 12 hour period, a 24 hour period, and with respect to the whole period of creation (Gen. 2:4). By arguing for long periods of time they try to harmonize the biblical narrative with geological evidence suggesting that the earth has been around for billions of years. Others maintain that the earth is quite young, pointing out that God created a fully developed universe, thus making it impossible to trace its age. Others have noted how the story beautifully balances the 1st and 4th, the 2nd and 5th, and the 3rd and 6th days: the separation of light and darkness of day 1 corresponds with the creation of the sun, moon and stars on day 4, the separation of the sky from the water on day 2 is balanced with the creation of birds and fish on day 5, and the separation of dry land from the sea along with the creaton of vegetation on day 3 is balanced with the creation of animals and man on day 6. The Genesis story, they hold, is a revelation of essential truths we need to know to relate rightly to God. Although they may differ in their interpretation of certain aspects of the narrative, all Bible-believing Christians accept that God created a universe which is distinct from yet dependent on Himself, that He did so to show His glory, and that He declared it to be good.

God rested on the seventh day, not because He was tired but to derive pleasure from all He had accomplished and to set a pattern for people to follow ever after: six days of work followed by one of rest.

The Bible records the creation of man two times. Genesis 1 focuses on the creation of the material, physical world, and summarizes the fact that God created man on the sixth day, along with the rest of the animal world. It also reveals that He blessed man and gave him authority over the rest of creation. Genesis 2 expands this story, giving us important details about both the creation and the first era in the lives of the first man and woman. In this chapter God refers to Himself as Jehovah (YHWH in the Hebrew text), which was to become God's covenant name with Israel.

Unlike the rest of creation, which God simply spoke into being, God personally crafted man's body from the dust of the earth before breathing life into it. Man was the apex of God's creation, fundamentally different from, and vastly superior to, the animal world—so much so that the Bible states that man was created "in God's image".

The Bible calls the first man "Adam", the Hebrew word for "man". God gave Adam a mandate over the rest of creation: he was to care for it but could also use it to meet his personal needs. As Adam explored the stunningly beautiful and complex creation around him he developed a system for classifying and naming the animal world. The system he devised is now lost to us; the Bible merely states that God brought the birds, livestock and the other beasts of the field to him so that he could name them.

As he went about this task Adam couldn't help but notice that the animals lived in pairs of males and females. He, on the other hand, was the sole human on the face of the earth. There was no creature in the animal world with whom he could be intimate. God then declared that it was not good for man to be alone. He caused Adam to fall into a deep sleep, removed one of his ribs and formed it into a suitable helper for him: a woman. When Adam woke he recognized that the woman was "bone of his bones and flesh of his flesh" and accepted her as his wife. She received the name Eve, which is probably an old Hebrew word meaning "living". She became the mother of all other human beings.

God had prepared a beautiful garden for Adam and Eve's enjoyment that came to be known as Paradise, or the Garden of Eden. No one knows exactly where the Garden of Eden was located, but we do know that a river flowed through it. We also know that this river divided into four headwaters. Two of these, the Pishon and the Gihon, no longer exist but the other two, the Euphrates and the Tigris, still flow across the Middle East.

The Bible states that Adam and Eve were naked but not ashamed to be so. This was true in a physical sense, but also in a deeper, spiritual sense. There was nothing hidden or secret which they wanted to hide from each other or from God. They knew each other intimately, and both fully accepted and loved each other as God had created them. In Eden they stood before God as two complementary creatures who drew their sense of identity, security and purpose from their relationship with their Creator God.

When God created Adam and Eve he didn't create robot-like creatures programmed to behave a certain way. He gave them a free will. They could choose to either obey or disobey God and this obedience—or disobedience—would reveal the depth of their commitment to Him. As long as they remained obedient to God they, along with the rest of creation, would not experience the consequences of disobedience: alienation from God resulting in fear, pain, want, shame, and spiritual and physical death.

The test of obedience was unambiguous. God placed two trees next to each other in the middle of Paradise. The fruit of the first tree, the Tree of Life, gave them immortality; eating from it would prevent them from dying. The fruit of the second tree, the Tree of the Knowledge of Good and Evil, would infect them with sin and lead, ultimately, to their death. Adam and Eve were free to eat of every fruit tree God had placed in paradise with the exception of that latter tree. "The day that you eat of it, you will die," God told them.

▪ 2 ▪ The Fall

Genesis 3   *Date: Prehistory*

WHEN GOD completed His creative work He declared the result to be "very good". Angelic beings worshipped and served Him in heaven. In a middle-sized galaxy in a constantly expanding universe there existed a small but stunningly beautiful place called earth, home to two very special creatures, a man and a woman. Adam and Eve walked in voluntary fellowship with their creator and ruled as God's viceroys over the countless species of life that shared the planet with them.

We don't know how long this glorious state continued. One day, however, something went terribly wrong: Adam and Eve broke the one, simple command God had given them—and the results were catastrophic. Sin and evil entered the world, and everything changed. Nothing remained the same.

It happened as follows: Satan embodied a snake and addressed Eve through it. "Did God really say, 'you must not eat from any tree in the garden?'" he asked.

Eve must have been surprised and intrigued when she heard an animal talking. Drawn to the strange spectacle she found herself answering back. "We may eat the fruit of all the trees in the garden except the Tree of the Knowledge of Good and Evil. If we touch it we will die," she responded.

"No, you won't die if you eat from that tree," the serpent replied smoothly. "In fact, God knows that when you eat its fruit you will become like Him! Your eyes will be opened and, like Him, you will know good from evil!" Satan, who had Himself rebelled because he had wanted to be like God, now tempted Adam and Eve to do the same.

Instead of resolutely telling it that she would never disobey God, instead of running from this strange creature that tempted her to disobey her creator, she studied the forbidden fruit. The animal had piqued her curiosity, and it suddenly looked very appealing! She thought about the serpent's promise: it would reveal to her a new, mysterious area of knowledge called "evil". She stretched out her hand, plucked a piece of fruit and took a bite… She then offered Adam some of it as well.

The Bible tells us that Satan deceived Eve (1 Tim. 2:13-14). Adam, however, was not deceived. In fact, he faced a terrible dilemma. He must have realized that Eve's disobedience would lead to her physical and spiritual death. Her act of disobedience would cause him to be separated from the sole creature with whom he enjoyed human fellowship and intimacy. He was forced to choose between God and his human companion. It must have been an agonizing decision but, in the end, he chose for Eve. He took the fruit from her hand and bit into it.

The results were instantaneous and calamitous. They suddenly realized they were naked and, feeling shame for the first time, struggled to sew some fig leaves together to cover themselves. That evening, when they heard the Lord approaching, fear filled their hearts. They used to stand before him confidently, with nothing to hide. They used to love His companionship! Now, suddenly, they were alienated from Him, from each other, from their own selves and from nature. Terrified, they tried to hide from their Creator.

"Where are you?" God's voice rang out.

Realizing the futility of hiding, Adam answered: "I heard you coming into the garden. I was afraid because I was naked, so I hid from you."

"Who told you that you were naked? Did you eat from the tree that I forbade you to eat from?" God asked.

"The woman you gave me gave offered me some of its fruit and I ate it," Adam replied, blaming both Eve and God. "The woman *you* gave me…" he said. Sin was already affecting all he did and said, even how he addressed God.

God turned to Eve. "What have you done?" He asked. She too sought to shift the blame. "The snake deceived me, so I ate," she responded.

God then cursed the snake. Most of that curse, however, was really addressed to Satan. "You are cursed more than all the livestock and animals in the world! You will crawl on your belly and eat dust all your life. I will put enmity between you and the woman, and between your descendants and hers. He will crush your head and you will bite his heel." In the ancient Middle East the phrase "to make someone crawl on their belly" was a way of saying that their downfall was certain (see, for instance, Micah 7:17). In other words, God was saying to Satan that his downfall was only a matter of time. God then promised that a descendant of Eve would, one day, crush Satan's head. This promise is the second of God's covenants with mankind. It went into effect the day they had broken the first covenant God had made with Adam and Eve about not eating from the Tree of the Knowledge of Good and Evil.

After cursing Satan, God turned back to Eve. He told her that she would bear children, but that giving birth and raising them in a world full of sorrow and sin would be painful. He also told her that her desire would be for her husband, but that he would rule over her. This enigmatic statement probably refers to the fact that instead of deriving her sense of identity, purpose and meaning from her relationship with God, these things would largely be defined by her relationship with her husband. She would seek to usurp his divinely appointed headship, which he would fight to retain. Love would give way to struggle, manipulation and domination. Sin had spoiled their relationship with God and with each other.

God told Adam that the world was now cursed. The beautiful creation would be marred by thorns and thistles and Adam would have to work hard to procure the food needed to sustain him and his family. He then drove them from Paradise into a suddenly ominous and dangerous world. To keep them from re-entering the garden, where the Tree of Life still beckoned, He placed angels called cherubim with a flaming sword to block its entrance.

God had told them that the day they ate from the Tree of the Knowledge of Good and Evil they would die. Their relationship with God was broken and so, on that fateful day, they died spiritually. Physically too their bodies began to break down until, many years later, they died physically as well.

But there was more to it than that. God regards humanity as an organic whole. Adam represented the human race, and his progeny was "made in his image" (Gen. 5:1-3). All of mankind, therefore, inherited Adam's fallen, spiritually dead sin-nature. From now on every person would be mortal and possess a corrupted nature that would alienate them from the holy God and, like Adam, become an object of His wrath (Rom. 5:12-21). The only person who would ever be born whose nature was unaffected by that of Adam's was Jesus Christ. He would be born of a virgin. With no earthly father he would not be created in Adam's image and therefore did not possess Adam's sin nature.

In spite of Adam and Eve's awful fall into sin God did not desert them. His promise of a Savior gave them hope. God also killed some animals and used their skins to make a suitable set of clothes for them. That act has often been interpreted as the first sacrifice. It would take the shedding of the blood of an atoning sacrifice[3] to cover the guilt and shame mankind had brought on itself.

▪ 3 ▪   Cain and Abel

Genesis 4:1-16   *Date: Prehistory*

AFTER THEIR expulsion from the Garden of Eden, Adam and Eve either found a cave to live in or built a shelter for themselves. They learned to plow, sow, weed and reap, even as their once perfect bodies began to break down. God had, however, promised that the "seed of the woman" would, one day, overcome the curse of sin and death. So God blessed them with children. Adam and Eve named their first son Cain and their second son Abel.

Adam and Eve would have told their children everything that had taken place: Satan's temptation of Eve, how Adam had decided to follow their mother's act of disobedience and how that had led to their expulsion from Paradise and brought misery and death into the world. They may have showed their sons the guarded entrance to the Garden of Eden. They also explained that God's curse had been tempered by the tremendous promise that, one day, a person would be born who would defeat the great deceiver, Satan.

In the course of time Cain learned to till the soil and became a farmer while Abel domesticated sheep and became a shepherd. They also married. At this early

---

[3] To "atone" means to satisfy or appease someone you have offended. In the Bible the term "atoning sacrifice" refers to that which is offered to God in order to satisfy or appease His righteous anger at disobedience.

point in human history there were no other families. However, the Bible states that Adam and Eve had more sons and daughters (Genesis 5:4) so; odd as that seems today, Cain and Abel must have married their sisters.

One day the two brothers decided to offer a sacrifice to God. They each built a platform of large rocks on which they placed some of the results of their labor. Cain burned some fruits and vegetables from his fields while Abel brought the fat portions of a choice sheep from his flock. As the smoke rose heavenward, however, they both sensed that God was pleased with Abel's, but not with Cain's offering. This was because Abel's offering was an expression of his faith (Heb. 11:4). He evidently realized that he was a sinner who stood in need of God's promised savior. Cain's offering, on the other hand, was not a reflection of his faith in God's promise. He apparently thought that the ritual itself would improve his standing with God, and became angry when this was not acceptable.

"Why are you angry?" the Lord asked. "If you do the right thing your sacrifice will be accepted as well." The Lord then warned him: "Be careful: sin is lurking at your door! It wants to dominate you. You must overcome it!"

Instead of heeding the warning Cain let his jealousy master him. One day he invited his brother Abel to go out into the fields. There he attacked and killed him.

Once again the Lord spoke to Cain. "Where is your brother Abel?"

"I don't know," Cain lied. "Am I supposed to look after my brother?"

"Your brother's blood cries out to me from the ground," God responded. "From now on you are cursed. The land, which absorbed your brother's blood, will not produce food for you anymore. You are going to be a restless wanderer." Cain learned the hard way that God is omniscient, that He knows everything. However, he still refused to repent.

"You are punishing me too harshly," he complained. "If anyone finds me, they will try to kill me..."

"No," the Lord replied. "I will severely punish whoever kills you." The Lord then put a protective mark on Cain, the nature of which is not described in the Bible.

Cain took his wife and fled eastward, towards the land of Nod. The word "Nod" is Hebrew for "wandering".

▪ 4 ▪ Early Civilization

Genesis 4:16-26; 5, 6   *Date: Prehistory*

CAIN BUILT a small "city" in the land of Nod. The word city at this early stage in history refers to a simple settlement, possibly with a palisade around it to protect its inhabitants from wild animals.

Cain had a descendant called Lamach, a strong, godless brute who killed a young man who had injured him, and then boasted about it. Adam and Eve's initial sin had triggered such a downward spiral that murderers now boasted about their feats. This Lamach had three remarkable sons. Jabal became a Bedouin. Instead of slash and burn farming, he opted to live in a tent, roam around and raise livestock. Jabal's brother Tubal was musical. He invented the first instruments: a simple harp and some kind of flute. The third brother, Tubal-Cain, became a smith able to forge tools from metals.

After Cain and Abel the Lord blessed Adam and Eve with a third son, Seth. Seth grew up, married and had children. People back then lived to be around eight or nine hundred years old, so Adam and Eve were able to tell many generations of Seth's descendants about creation, paradise, and their fall into sin, subsequent expulsion from the garden, and God's promise of a Savior.

One man called Enoch, a descendent of Seth, only lived to be 365 years. This is less than half the average age of people in that era. Enoch had a very intimate relationship with God. God so loved him that, one day, He simply lifted him directly up to heaven so that he did not have to experience death (Heb. 11:5). Before that, however, the godly Enoch had a number of children. One of them, Methuselah, would become the world's oldest man, dying at the age of 969 years. Methuselah called his firstborn son Lamech and he in turn had a son called Noah. Noah had three sons, Shem, Ham and Japheth who were destined to play a very important role in world history.

During this early era at least two separate civilizations developed on earth: the descendants of Cain, a generation of godless people, and the descendants of Seth, a generation through which God's promise of a Saviour would be realized.

▪ 5 ▪   Noah and the Great Flood

Genesis 5-10   *Date: Prehistory*

GOD GRIEVED deeply over humanity's rapid descent into sin. One man, however, was an exception. Noah, a descendant of Adam's godly son Seth and grandson of the godly Enoch, sought to live righteously and in communion with God.

One day God told Noah that He would destroy the earth by means of a great flood. To save himself and his family Noah was to build a huge, three-decked boat, 450 feet long and 75 feet wide. It took Noah and his family 120 years to construct the massive vessel. It became known as the "ark".

The undertaking must have been a cause of mirth to onlookers. Imagine building a huge boat many miles from the nearest body of water! Nevertheless, Noah persevered. The Bible calls him a "preacher of righteousness" (2 Pet. 2:5) who tried to warn people of the judgment to come. His warnings were to no avail.

By the time Noah finished building the ark he was 600 years old. God then spoke to him a second time, saying, "Seven days from now I am going to send rain on the earth. It will rain for forty days and forty nights. I will wipe every living creature I have made from the earth." During the week prior to that judgment, however, something amazing happened. All kinds of animals and birds made their way to Noah's ark and entered it: seven pairs of all the clean animals and one pair of all the unclean animals. Clean animals were those people were allowed to eat, such as sheep and cows, while unclean animals were those that they were to refrain from eating, such as dogs and lizards (Lev. 11). After these animals had entered the ark, Noah, his wife, his three sons Shem, Ham and Japheth and their wives—eight people in all—also climbed aboard. God himself closed the hatch after them.

Then it began to rain. A torrential deluge lashed the earth and underground springs of water burst to the surface. The cataclysmic storm lasted for 40 days and 40 nights. Eventually the highest mountains were submerged to a depth of more than 20 feet. All non-aquatic life drowned.

The dreadful catastrophy etched itself on the memories of the eight people inside the ark as they and the animals floated safely on the huge waves of judgement. It was a story they would tell their children and grandchildren again and again so that it became part of almost every culture's remembered past.

After 150 days God sent a wind over the earth causing the water to recede. It gathered into oceans or was reabsorbed into the earth. Those aboard the ark eventually saw mountain peaks emerging like islands from the sea. The ark floated between those peaks until it came to rest on a plateau on Mount Ararat while the water continued to recede.

One day Noah released a raven. Ravens are strong birds that feed off carrion, of which there must have been plenty floating around. The bird flew back and forth, feeding on the carrion without returning to the ark. A week later Noah released a dove. Doves don't have the stamina of ravens nor do they feed on carrion. It returned to the ark.

After seven days Noah released the dove again. When the bird returned that evening it carried a freshly plucked olive leaf in its beak! The earth had dried up and vegetation was sprouting again! After seven more days Noah let the dove loose a third time. This time it did not return. After that Noah opened the hatch and saw that the earth in his vicinity was dry. However, they still had to wait for more than a month before God finally gave them permission to leave the ark. Eventually, 371 days after they'd entered the ark, they were allowed to disembark.

The first thing Noah did was build an altar upon which he sacrificed some of the clean animals. The Lord was pleased with Noah's offering and responded with a third covenant, or divine promise: He promised to never again destroy humanity with a flood, and instituted the rainbow as a reminder of this promise. He also promised that the cycle of seasons would continue as long as the earth endured. He further commanded the death penalty for murder. That, as we saw with Cain and Lamach, was not the case before the flood. This stiffening of the law was designed to hold the human potential for evil in check. God then instructed Noah and his family to multiply and be fruitful.

After the flood Noah's family turned to farming. Noah himself planted a vineyard. When the harvest was in he turned some of the grape juice into wine and became drunk. When his son Ham discovered him lying naked in a drunken stupor he went and told his brothers about the spectacle. Instead of mocking their father, however, Shem and Japheth took a garment and, walking backwards so that they would not see their father naked, covered him. When Noah learned what had happened he blessed Shem and Japheth and their descendants and cursed Ham's son Canaan and his descendants. Canaan, according to Noah's curse, would become his brothers' slave, while Japheth's territory would increase.

Why would Noah curse his grandson and not his son? He could not curse Ham, the actual offender, for in doing so he would have passed judgment on himself. Ancient society held the father responsible for the son's behaviour (Deut. 6:6-9, 20-25; Prov. 22:6, 15; Eph. 6:4). The Bible makes clear that children suffer because of their parents' misdeeds. This, in itself, is not surprising. Parents' actions are often reflected in their children's behavior, though this does not absolve those children of their own moral culpability (Ex. 20:5).

Noah's curse was fulfilled when the Jews enslaved the Gibeonites, a Canaanite people, and killed many of the remaining Canaanites during their conquest of Canaan. Archeological artifacts show the Canaanites to have been exceedingly sexually immoral. The sins of parents had, indeed, a very negative downward effect on their children.

Noah lived for 350 years after the flood, to die at the ripe old age of 950 years. Although genealogies in the Bible sometimes skip generations, Abraham, the father of the Jews, is listed as only nine generations removed from Noah's son Shem.

· 6 ·   The Tower of Babel

Genesis 11:1-8   *Date: Prehistory*

NOAH'S SON Shem's great-grandson was named Peleg. The word "Peleg" means "division". The Bible tells us that the boy was given this name "because in his time the earth was divided" (Genesis 10:25). This is apparently a reference to the confusion of languages that took place early in the history of the world.

Noah's descendants settled the Plain of Shinar in ancient Mesopotamia, between the Tigris and Euphrates rivers. Obviously, they all spoke the same language. As the population increased and social organization developed they sought ways to maintain their unity to better control their destiny. To accomplish this they decided to build a city with an imposing tower as its centerpiece. Since stone was scarce on the sandy Mesopotamian plain they used mud bricks and tar. The tower was probably an early ziggurat, a type of square-based, stepped, temple-tower with a shrine and zodiac at the top. The zodiac probably explains the reference that the tower "reached to the heavens". Instead of worshipping God, mankind started looking to the stars for guidance.

God intervened. His solution for early mankind's attempt at "one-world" government was simple: he confused their language. Suddenly people were unable to communicate with each other, and in the ensuing chaos and frustration were forced to give up their lofty ambitions. They divided into mutually intelligible groups and broke away from those with whom they could not communicate. As a result mankind scattered all over the earth. The half-built city and its tower came to be known as "Babel", which in Akkadian, one of the world's oldest languages, means "Gateway to God", but which also sounds like the Hebrew word for "confused".

Some people continued living on the site after the confusion of languages. In time the place would develop into the city of Babylon, which continued to feature as a symbol of false religion.

· 7 ·   God's Covenant with Abram

Genesis 12   *Date: circa 2000 B.C.[4]*

LIFE MUST HAVE been sad for Noah's family. Even with the memory of God's judgment fresh in their minds, people once again forsook the worship of their creator. If the Biblical genealogy is complete then Noah's son Shem would have witnessed the building of the tower of Babel and the dispersion of the nations. He would have recognized that in spite of the flood man's essential nature had not changed. It remained at enmity with God. How would God henceforth relate to His creation? When would His patience run out again? Would He then destroy the people and nations of the world once and for all?

When Adam and Eve fell into sin God made a promise about the seed of the woman one day crushing Satan. A milestone in the realization of this promise was a special covenant God made with a man named Abram. This was such a major turning point that from now on the story focuses primarily on the realization of this divine promise to Abram and his descendants, the people of Israel.

Abram lived about 2000 years before Christ. He was a descendant of Eber, the father of Peleg—whom we met in conjunction with the scattering of human languages. Since people did not have last names back then they were often identified by the name of one of their ancestors.

---

[4] Based on non-biblical references in ancient king lists the dates of Solomon's reign can be established with reasonably certainty as 971-931 B.C. According to 1 Kings 6:1 the construction of the temple began in the 480th year after the Exodus, in the 4th year of Solomon's reign. In other words, if the construction of the temple began around 966 B.C. then the exodus took place in 1445 or 1446 B.C., a date which harmonizes with other biblical evidence (i.e. Judges 11:26). If that were the case the Pharaoh of the Exodus would be Thutmose III. Other scholars believe the exodus took place later, around 1280 B.C. during the reign of Ramses II when, they hold, the historical conditions in Egypt as described in the narrative were more similar. They suggest that "480 years" is really a stylized way of stating 12 generations, each of which could range anywhere from, say, 20 up to 40 years. The dating followed in this book is the former, not the latter.

A complicating factor with respect to later dating is that the kingdoms of Judah and Israel calculated the beginnings of their respective kings' reigns differently: Judah began counting a particular king's reign at the beginning of the calendar year while Israel began counting from the day his reign began (with the exception of one period during which both kingdoms applied the same system). Furthermore, the two kingdoms began their calendar year six months apart. Another complicating feature was that at times there were co-regencies, when the reign of two kings (father and son) overlapped. All this to say that establishing dates for most biblical events is complex but not impossible.

Abram became known as "Abram the Hebrew"; the word "Hebrew" comes from the name "Eber".

Abram's family lived in a Sumerian city called Ur. Terah, Abram's father, was a pagan (Joshua 24:2), probably a moon-worshipper. Terah had three sons: Haran, Nahor and Abram. One of these sons, Haran, died quite young, though not before he had married and had a son called Lot.

Terah decided to leave Ur and move northward, to settle in a place called Haran. (Although the name of this place sounds like the name of Terah's son Haran, the two words are spelled differently in Hebrew). The reason for this move was probably because Terah was not a true settled Sumerian farmer but a sheep-herding Semite (descendant of Noah's son Shem). Haran was a thriving caravan town on the northern reaches of the Mesopotamian plateau. It was surrounded by grassy plains and was ideal for raising sheep.

Although Terah was an idolater, his son Abram became restless for a relationship with the Creator himself. He must have heard the stories passed on by Shem and the other ancients about creation, the fall into sin, and of God's judgments, stories that would be passed orally from one generation to the next until Abram's great-great-great grandson Moses finally wrote them down.

One day God spoke directly to Abram, telling him to leave Haran for an undisclosed location, a land He would show him in due course. God then promised that if Abram did so He would make him into a great nation, bless him, bless those who blessed him and curse those who cursed him. Last but not least God promised to make Abram a blessing to all people on earth! This amazing set of promises came to be known as the Abrahamic covenant. It also came to be called God's promise, His pledge, His declaration, His blessing and His oath to the people of Israel, as it was clarified in the course of the centuries and as its consequences were played out in the ups-and-downs of their history. It found its final fulfillment in Jesus Christ.

▪ 8 ▪　Abram's Travels

Genesis 12:4-20   *Date: circa 2000 B.C.*

ABRAM WAS 75 years old when God first spoke to him. Although he owned herds, servants and slaves, he packed his possessions, said farewell to his brother Nahor and other relatives and friends and set off for… well, he had no idea! His nephew Lot, the son of his deceased brother Haran, decided to join his uncle on the new adventure. Lot too owned flocks, which he probably inherited from his father.

After the final farewells Abram directed his caravan westward, in the opposite direction of Ur, the pagan city they had originally come from. Week after week they plodded along slowly, steadily, until they reached northern Syria, and then they headed south, following the curve of the Fertile Crescent. Traveling parallel to the eastern Mediterranean Sea they entered territory inhabited by descendants of Shem's son Aram. They passed the Aramaic city of Damascus and headed further south-west, past Sidon, a Canaanite city named after the cursed Canaan's firstborn son. They skirted Mount Hermon and entered Palestine's rolling hills and fertile valleys.

Abram reached Palestine, then known as Canaan, around the year 2000 B.C. At that time the region was inhabited by lots of little tribes of Canaanite descent such as the Jebusites, Amorites, and Girgashites who lived in culturally backward little city-states under chieftains they called kings. They survived by farming, raiding each other and trading honey and sheep with Egypt.

The Egyptians were descendants of Ham's son Mizraim. Mizraim means "two Egypts", referring to Upper and Lower Egypt. They had developed a sophisticated civilization on the banks of the Nile River ruled over by a "Pharaoh", which was the title they gave to their rulers. The highly cultured Egyptians despised the immoral, uncouth Canaanite tribes and avoided interacting with them as much as possible.

Abram continued traveling until he came to a place called Shechem, a town right in the middle of Canaan. The place boasted a huge oak tree associated with a Canaanite shrine. Right there, in the middle of Canaanite territory, next to a pagan shrine, God ordered Abram to stop traveling and told him that this was the land He would give to him and his descendants! Abram's heart must have sunk. Who would want to raise a family among these uncultured, ungodly people in this cultural backwater? Also, Abram wasn't getting any younger—and he still had no children. The whole undertaking began to look like a fool's enterprise. Nevertheless Abram built his own altar to reaffirm his faith in God's covenant promise. Soon afterwards, however, he moved to the hill country. He would live in Canaan as God commanded him, but not among the ungodly tribes inhabiting the valleys. His little tribe was less likely to be tainted by the Canaanites' idolatrous ways in the less densely populated, agriculturally less desirable hills.

After Abram had been in Canaan for some time a severe famine plagued the land. Abram struck his tents and moved his caravan southward, to Egypt. There his faith failed him...

Abram was married to a strikingly beautiful woman named Sarai. Abram worried that the Egyptians might kill him in order to get her, so he told Sarai to say that she was his sister, not his wife. This was a half-truth. They were both children of Terah, but from different mothers. In that culture it was acceptable to marry a relative; it ensured that the clan would not be weakened by the loss of a member.

Pharaoh's officials laid eyes on Sarai and sang her praises to him. He then had her brought into his harem as one of his concubines, paying Abram a huge bride price for her in the form of slaves and livestock. God, however, would not allow anything to thwart His promise to Abram that through a descendant of a child to be born to his legitimate wife Sarai all nations would be blessed—not even Abram's sinful, callow act of surrendering her to save his own skin. God inflicted a series of serious diseases on Pharaoh and his household. Pharaoh soon realized that the unfortunate events striking his household were related to the beautiful woman he had accepted into his harem. When he discovered her true identity he summoned Abram, chided him, gave Sarai back to him, and let them go—even letting them keep the bride price.

Abram left Egypt and wandered aimlessly in the Negev Desert. His faith had failed him, and now it seemed that he didn't know what to do. Eventually, however, he travelled back to Canaan, the place God had promised him, and recommitted himself to his Creator.

▪ 9 ▪   Abram, Lot and Melchizedek

Genesis 13 and 14; Hebrews 7   *Date: circa 2000 B.C.*

PROGRESS BRINGS its own problems. Abram became very wealthy in Canaan, both in terms of livestock and in silver and gold, in part because of the bride price Pharaoh had paid for Sarai. His nephew Lot's flocks also increased steadily so that he too became very wealthy. Their joint herds became so large that the hill-country where they had settled couldn't support them both. That, in turn, led to infighting and quarreling between their herdsmen over choice pastures and access to water.

One day Abram led Lot to the top of a high hill. "Instead of quarreling," he said to his nephew, "let's part company. If you decide to go left, I'll go to the right; if you go right, I'll go to the left." Lot's eyes lingered on the lush, well-watered fertile plain of the Jordan River valley. He could see the Canaanite towns of Zoar, Sodom and Gomorrah where he could market his cattle. He knew his business would flourish much more on the Canaanite plain than in the shrubby hills. It didn't take him long to make up his mind; soon he was leading his caravan down to the fertile plain while Abram remained in the hills.

God comforted Abram by reaffirming His promise. "Look in every direction," God said. "Eventually your descendants will receive all this land forever. You are going to have so many children they will be like the dust of the earth—you won't be able to count them! Go ahead, walk the length and breadth of the land, for I'm giving it to you!"

Abram traveled westward, to a stand of large trees known as "The Great Trees of Mamre", named after their owner, Mamre the Ammorite. There Abram built another altar to reaffirm his commitment to God. In time Abram and Mamre became friends.

Back on the plains of the Jordan River things didn't turn out the way Lot had hoped. Soon after his split with Abram he decided to give up his nomadic life-style and moved with his family into the town of Sodom.

Sodom and the surrounding Canaanite towns were subject to the king of Elam. After 13 years of subjugation to this distant despot the towns rebelled. Their hopes for independence were short-lived, however, because the following year the king of Elam defeated the rebelling cities. He seized the entire population and goods of Sodom and Gomorrah to carry them off to his distant homeland on the Arabian Gulf. Lot and his people and possessions were also seized.

Fortunately one of Lot's men managed to escape. He hurried to Abram's encampment and reported on the catastrophe that had befallen his nephew. Abram, his bodyguard of 318 personal armed retainers along with his ally Mamre and his militia set off in pursuit. They caught the Elamite king by surprise and managed to recover all the loot, including Lot, his family and possessions.

After Abram returned from this battle two local kings came to offer their respects. The first was the king of Sodom, who tried to strike a deal. He suggested Abram keep the plunder and cattle but give him back his captured people. Abram gave him both the people and their possessions. He didn't want this evil man to be able to boast that he was responsible for Abram's wealth. When the King of Sodom took his stuff and returned to his city, Lot, who still hadn't learned his lesson, went back with him.

The second king who came to meet Abram was called Melchizedek. He was the king of Salem. Salem is short form for Jerusalem, the name by which the city would later become known. Melchizedek, though not involved in the recent war, realized that Abram and his men would be hungry and thirsty, and kindly supplied them with bread and wine.

Melchizedek was more than a king. He was also a priest of the one, true Lord God. Abram and Melchizedek were kindred spirits; both had rejected idols to worship the Creator God of Adam, Enoch and Noah. In fact, Abram recognized Melchizedek as his spiritual superior and gave him a tenth of all his goods.

▪ 10 ▪ God Renews His Covenant with Abram

Genesis 15   *Date: circa 2000 B.C.*

IT HAD BEEN 15 years since, at God's command, Abram left Haran for Canaan. 15 eventful years during which he had grown richer... and older. The one great grief in Abram and Sarai's life was the fact that they did not have a child, and this increasingly worried them. In spite of the divine promises on which he had staked his life he had neither a son nor any land to call his own. He was now 85 and his wife Sarai was 75—long past child-bearing age. What if he'd been wrong? What if he'd merely imagined his encounters with God? His whole life would be a sham and, worse, the God he'd dedicated his life to would turn out to be a liar, no better than a Canaanite idol. If that were the case there was no hope for mankind: no promised savior, no forgiveness of sin.

One evening as Abram was mulling over these things the word of the Lord came to him again saying, "Do not be afraid, Abram. I am your shield and your great reward."

"O Sovereign Lord You have given me no children. What good is everything else? I had hoped that a son would inherit my estate. Instead, it will go to my servant Eliezer of Damascus," Abram responded dejectedly.

"Your own son, not Eliezer, is going to be your heir," the Lord said. He then invited Abram outside, into the clear, cloudless night dotted with myriads of stars. "Look at the heavens and see if you can count the stars. That's how numerous you descendants will be," He said. Once again, Abram believed God, and because he did so God was pleased with him. In fact, Abram would become known as the "father of all who believe" (Rom. 4:11) because he believed that God would honor His promises even when the situation was impossible. God also repeated his promise about the gift of the land of Canaan.

"O Sovereign Lord," Abram replied, "how can I be sure of that?" The Lord responded by telling Abram to slaughter a heifer, a goat, a ram, a dove and a pigeon and cut their carcasses into half. That was the customary way of cementing a vow in those days: walking between the split carcasses indicated that a similar fate would befall any party who broke the agreement.

As the sun set, tired old Abram fell into a deep sleep during which he had a nightmare about a dreadful darkness. Then he then heard the Lord speaking to him again: "Your descendants will be strangers in a strange country. For 400 years they will be enslaved and mistreated. However, I will punish the nation they serve as slaves, and they will leave that place with great possessions and return to possess this land. For now, however, the sins of the local inhabitants have not yet reached their full measure. When it does your descendants will displace them. You, however, will die in peace at a good old age." Then Abram saw a smoking firepot and a blazing torch passing between the carcasses. The fire symbolized God's presence and assured Abram that the divine promise would, in time, become a reality.

▪ 11 ▪   The Birth of Ishmael and the Confirmation of the Covenant

Genesis 16-17   *Date: circa 2000 B.C.*

ONE DAY Sarai came to Abram with a plan that she thought would solve their problem of childlessness, an idea that would "help" God realize his plan for them. She suggested he sleep with her Egyptian servant-girl Hagar. If Hagar conceived and gave birth to a son then she, Sarai, would adopt the child and build her own family through him.

This was an acceptable practice at that time. One of the main purposes of marriage was to have children who would carry on the family name, and if the wife couldn't produce a son herself it was up to her to make an alternative arrangement. This she would usually do by procuring a slave girl to serve as her surrogate. Abram agreed to the proposal—something he would come to rue bitterly.

When Hagar became pregnant she began to look down on her sterile mistress. Sarai soon grew tired of Hagar's insolence and complained to Abram, who told her to deal with her slave as she saw fit. Sarai then began to mistreat the girl so badly that she ran away towards her homeland. Partway there, while she was resting by a desert spring, the angel of the Lord spoke to her. "Hagar, servant of Sarai, where are you going?" the angel asked.

"I'm running away from my mistress Sarai," Hagar answered.

"Go back and submit to her," the angel of the Lord told her. "You will have a son. You are to name him Ishmael, for the Lord has heard your misery" (Ishmael means "the Lord hears"). "He is going to be a wild donkey of a man. Everyone will find him difficult to get along with him," the angel of the Lord continued, and then added, "I will give you so many descendants that they too will be too numerous to count."

Hagar returned to Abram and Sarai and gave birth to Ishmael. Ishmael is commonly thought to be the father of the Arabs.

With each passing year, however, God's promise of a son through Sarai seemed increasingly impossible. However, the issue didn't seem so urgent any more. After all, Abram had Ishmael, a son whom he loved dearly.

Thirteen years after the birth of Ishmael, when Abram was about 99 years old, the Lord appeared to him yet again. "I am God Almighty," He said. "I am going to confirm my covenant with you. You are going to have many, many children." Abram fell on his face as God repeated the fact that he would become the father of kings and of many nations, and that his descendants would one day possess the whole land of Canaan. God even told him to change his name from Abram to Abraham. Abraham means "father of many". God then ordered that he and his household be circumcised. From that time on circumcision became a sign of God's special relationship with Abraham and his descendants, a physical mark indicating that Abraham and his descendants were different from everyone else. They were special because they had come into being as a result of God's special promise to a man who could not, humanly speaking, have children. They were also special because God promised to bless all the other people of the world through them. Even today Jews continue to circumcise their boys.

God also gave Sarai a new name: Sarah, which means princess. "She is going to be the mother of nations," God said. "Kings will come from her."

The thought that a 99-year-old man would father a son through his 90-year-old wife struck Abraham as so unlikely, so ludicrous, that he began to laugh. He turned to God and said, "Lord, let your blessing fall on Ishmael..." Instead, God once again repeated his promise of a son through Sarah. He even told Abraham to name the boy Isaac, the Hebrew word for "laughter".

God assured Abraham that a great nation would also come from Ishmael, but that his covenant promise of a Saviour would be fulfilled through Isaac, the son yet to be born to Sarah, the descendant of Shem. The Savior would not come through Hagar the descendant of Ham. As a sign that he accepted the imposition of God's gracious covenant, Abraham had Ishmael and all his servants and slaves circumcised.

▪ 12 ▪ The Lord Visits Abraham

Genesis 18   *Date: circa 2000 B.C.*

ABRAHAM WAS sitting at the entrance of his tent one hot afternoon when he saw three men approaching. He got to his feet, hurried to meet them and invited them over for refreshments. Once his guests were comfortably seated he separated a choice calf from his flock. While his servants slaughtered and cooked the animal Sarah quickly baked some fresh bread. As the meal was being prepared he served his guests cheese and milk. In the Middle East hospitality was a very important social virtue.

At some point Abraham realized that one of the guests was the Lord Himself appearing in the form of a man, and that his two companions were angels, also disguised as men. Abraham continued to wait on his guests, standing politely under a nearby tree as they ate.

After the meal the Lord turned to Abraham. "Where is your wife Sarah?" he asked.

"In the tent," Abraham replied.

"When I return to you about this time next year she will have a son," the Lord said. When Sarah, who'd been eavesdropping from inside the tent, heard this ridiculous prophecy she laughed to herself. They had heard that promise before—her husband had staked his life on it—yet nothing had come of it. They were now far past childbearing age; the idea was preposterous.

"Why did Sarah laugh? Is anything too hard for the Lord?" the Lord asked. Sarah was afraid and possibly ashamed when she realized she'd been caught eavesdropping.

"No, I didn't laugh," she lied.

"Yes, you did," the Lord corrected her gently.

After the meal the guests departed for Sodom, with Abraham accompanying them a little way to see them off. As they walked together the Lord said, almost as if to Himself, "Will I conceal from Abraham what I am about to do? He will become a mighty nation through which the other nations of the world will be blessed. I chose him because he will teach his children to follow the ways of the Lord God so that the Lord will realize His promises through him." Then he turned to Abraham. "I am going to Sodom and Gomorrah to see if their sins are really as great as the reports which have reached me indicate," the Lord confided.

Abraham immediately understood the implications of what the Lord said: these cities were about to be punished for the evil they indulged in. He thought of his nephew Lot and realized that he and his family risked being destroyed along with the rest of the city. "Lord," Abraham said, "will you destroy the righteous along with the wicked? Surely not! The Judge of all the earth will do the right thing! What if there are fifty righteous people in Sodom? Will you spare the city for the sake of those fifty righteous people?"

"If I find fifty righteous people I will spare the city for their sake," the Lord assured him.

"Now that I am bold enough to speak to the Lord, even though I am nothing but dust and ashes, what if there are forty-five people? Will you destroy the city because it is five people short?" Abraham asked. His sense of urgency caused him to be bold in God's presence.

"I will not destroy it if I find forty-five righteous people there," the Lord said.

"What if there are only forty?" Abraham asked.

"If there are forty, I won't do it," the Lord answered.

"Please, don't be angry with me Lord, but what if you only find thirty righteous people there?" Abraham pleaded.

"If there are thirty, I will not do it," the Lord replied.

Abraham pressed on, almost recklessly now. "Lord, now that I've been so bold as to speak to you—what if you only find twenty?"

"I will not destroy it for the sake of the twenty," the Lord answered.

Abraham mustered the courage to approach the Lord one last time. "Please don't be angry with me," he said, "but let me speak just once more time. What if there are only ten righteous people there?"

"I will not destroy the place for the sake of ten righteous people," the Lord assured him. After that they parted. Abraham returned to his tent wondering what the dawn would bring.

▪ 13 ▪ The Destruction of Sodom and Gomorrah

Genesis 19   *Date: circa 2000 B.C.*

AFTER HIS rescue from the king of Elam, Lot had moved back to the Canaanite city of Sodom. Although he had foolishly chosen to live and work in that evil place, its sexual deviancy and perversity greatly distressed him (2 Peter 2:7-8). One day when he was sitting by the city gates he noticed two men approaching, and he invited the strangers to spend the night at his house. Although the men initially demurred—as was culturally expected—Lot insisted.

Inns appear later in Middle Eastern history, so ancient customs pertaining to hospitality demanded that people offer food and lodging to strangers. In fact people were usually keen to have travelers spend a night with them so they could be brought up-to-date with what was happening elsewhere. The men of Sodom, however, had different ideas. Before Lot's guests retired for the night a crowd of them surrounded the house.

"Where are the men who came to you tonight?" they shouted at Lot. "Bring them out so we can have sex with them." They undoubtedly thought that Lot-the-outsider had invited the men home for just such a purpose. Lot stepped outside courageously, shut the door behind him, and faced the crowd.

"My friends, don't do this wicked thing," he shouted. "Look, I have two daughters, both virgins. Let me give them to you. You can do whatever you like to them. But don't harm these men for they are under the protection of my roof!" In that old Bedouin culture a host would go to any length to protect his guests while mere women were regarded as personal property that the head of the household could dispose of as he saw fit. Even so, living in that degenerate society had obviously warped Lot's moral sensibilities.

The men of Sodom would have none of it. "Get out of the way," they shouted. "You're nothing but a foreigner yourself! Do you think you can tell us what to do? We'll do worse to you than to your guests!" The Sodomites then surged forward to grab him. Suddenly the door behind Lot opened. His guests pulled him to safety inside and then miraculously struck the crowd with blindness. While the crowd outside milled around in confusion the guests asked Lot if he had any other relatives in town. "Get them out of here," they warned. "This place is so evil the Lord has sent us to destroy it."

Lot slipped through the blinded, panicky crowd and warned the two young men who were engaged to marry his daughters. Sadly, they thought he was joking and did not take him seriously. Just before dawn the angels urged Lot to take his wife and daughters and run from Sodom as fast as their legs would take them. When Lot still dithered the angels grabbed him and forced him and his family from the city.

"Run for your lives! Don't look back and don't stop until you get to the mountains or you will be swept away."

"Please sirs," Lot begged. "I can't run all the way to the mountains. I'll never make it. Allow me to flee to the little hamlet of Zoar over there."

"Very well," they replied. "Now run quickly!" Lot and his two daughters reached Zoar just as the sun rose over the land. His wife did not make it. She disobeyed the angel's command not to look back; when she did, she turned into a pillar of salt.

Just as Lot and his daughters stumbled into Zoar the Lord began raining burning sulfur on Sodom and Gomorrah. The two cities were completely devastated. Every living thing in them perished.

Even though Sodom didn't have 10 righteous people God took care to save the one marginally righteous man and his family. Fearing retribution

42

from the surrounding Canaanites, Lot and his daughters fled from Zoar as well. The three of them lived as impoverished outcasts in a cave in the mountains.

That morning Abraham walked to where he had interceded on behalf of the cities. He looked down onto the plain and saw dense pillars of smoke rising heavenward. That plain, once the most fertile part of Canaan, became an inland lake known today as the Dead Sea. Neither plants nor fish can live in its briny water. There comes a point when the "cup of iniquity" of particular societies is full. The total destruction of Sodom and Gomorrah was a foretaste of what the rest of Canaanite society would experience some 500 years later in fulfillment of Noah's curse.

One day Lot's daughters, knowing that no one from the area would marry them, hatched a plan to allow the family line to live on. They got their father into a drunken stupor and made themselves pregnant by him. Both women gave birth to a son. The older daughter named her son Moab, which sounds like the Hebrew for "from father" and the younger daughter named her son Ben Ammi, which means "son of my people". Their descendants, the Moabites and the Ammonites, would later cause the Hebrew people much grief.

▪ 14 ▪ Abraham and Abimelech, Isaac and Ishmael
Genesis 20, 21, 25:12-18   *Date: circa 2000 B.C.*

AFTER THE destruction of Sodom and Gomorrah Abraham moved to the region of the Negev, near the city of Gerar. Sarah, despite her great age, was still a very striking woman, and once again Abraham's fearful nature got the best of him. Afraid that someone might kill him to get her, he told her to again resort to the ruse they'd used earlier in Egypt: they would introduce her as his sister, not his wife.

The ruler of Gerar, Abimelech, did notice Sarah and, like Pharaoh before him, took her into his harem. Once again the Lord intervened by taking away from Abimelech and his family the ability to conceive children. Then He spoke to the king in a dream: "You are as good as dead because the woman you took is already married."

"Lord," Abimelech responded, "I acted with a clear conscience. The man said she was his sister. I have not done anything wrong. I did not know that she was married. Will you destroy our nation because I acted in ignorance?"

"I know that you acted with a clear conscience," the Lord said. "That is why I kept you from sinning with her. Return her to her husband. He is a prophet and will pray for you. If you don't, you and your people will die."

Early the next morning Abimelech summoned his officials and told them about his encounter with God. They then summoned Abraham and questioned him, and gave Sarah back to him along with a thousand shekels, sheep, cattle and slaves. They also assured him he could live wherever he liked in their territory without fear of being molested. Abimelech's generosity stood in stark contrast to Abraham's fear and duplicity.

When Abraham prayed for Abimelech and his people God removed the affliction that had struck them. The two men then agreed not to ever harm each other. After this event Abraham rededicated himself to the Lord.

· · · · ·

More than 25 years after God first promised a son to Abraham the long-awaited event finally took place: Sarah gave birth! In spite of Abraham's fears and doubts, in spite of his efforts to take matters into his own hands, God was true to His word. They named the boy Isaac, the Hebrew word for laughter, just as the Lord had commanded. They had laughed in disbelief, now they were laughing with joy!

Hagar and Ishmael, on the other hand, were not laughing. It must have been a terrible shock to Hagar when old Sarah actually gave birth: now Isaac, not her Ishmael, would inherit Abraham's position and wealth.

As the boys grew up, Ishmael teased and mocked his little half-brother so much that eventually Sarah told Abraham to get rid of him and his mother Hagar. This idea greatly distressed Abraham for Ishmael was, after all, his oldest son. Nevertheless God affirmed that he should do as Sarah suggested, comforting him with the promise that He would also make a great nation of Ishmael's descendants. Early the next morning Abraham gave some food and a skin of water to Hagar and ordered them to leave.

Hagar and Ishmael wandered deeper and deeper into the desert until they ran out of water. Despairing, Hagar placed her parched son in the shade of a bush and, sobbing, left him there. She could not bear to watch him die of thirst. Suddenly she heard the voice of the angel of the Lord.

"What is the matter, Hagar? Don't fear. God has heard the boy crying. Take him by the hand. God will make him into a great nation." God then opened her eyes to a nearby well. She staggered to it, filled the water-skin and slaked Ishmael's thirst.

Ismael grew up to be a man of the desert and an expert archer. His mother procured a wife for him from Egypt, and in time he had 12 sons. Their tribe became known as the Ishmaelites, whom many Arabs would later claim as their ancestor. Ishmael himself eventually died when he was 137 years old.

· 15 · Abraham Tested

Genesis 22, 23　　　　　　　　　　　　　　　　　　　　　　　*Date: Circa 2000 B.C.*

ABRAHAM's joy at seeing Isaac grow into a strong, healthy lad dulled the pain of losing Ishmael. His sometimes wavering faith in God had not been misplaced. He now knew that nothing was impossible with God, and was more determined than ever to obey Him meticulously. The greatest test of his obedience came when Isaac was a teenager.

"Abraham!" God called out one day.

"Here I am," Abraham replied.

"Take your beloved son Isaac to the area of Moriah. I want you to sacrifice him on a mountain there," God said. Abraham must have wondered if he'd heard right. Human sacrifice? Did God possess the same vindictive nature as the Canaanite idols? Abraham came to the conclusion that God did order him to carry out the horrible command, but that He would bring his son back to life (Heb. 11:17-19). And so he got up early the next morning, cut firewood, saddled his donkey and set off, taking Isaac and two servants with him.

During the three days it took them to reach the foot of the mountain God had appointed Abraham kept the real reason for their journey from his son. Upon arrival he told his servants to stay with the donkey while he and Isaac went up the mountain. "We will worship and we will come back," he told them, affirmed in his faith that God would give him back his son after he'd carried out the awful command. He laid the firewood on Isaac's shoulders, took the fire and the knife himself, and set off.

Something bothered Isaac as he climbed the mountain with his father. "Father?" he asked.

"Yes, my son."

"We have fire and wood, but where is the lamb for the burnt offering?"

"God himself will provide a lamb, my son," Abraham responded.

When they reached the summit they built an altar of stones and arranged the wood on it.

Then Abraham took his son, tied him up, and laid him on the wood. He raised the knife over his head and was about to slay his Isaac when a voice rang out: "Abraham! Abraham!" It was the angel of the Lord.

"Here I am," Abraham said.

"Don't harm the boy," the angel of the Lord said. "Now I know that you fear God for you did not withhold your only beloved son from me." Abraham then saw a ram with its horns caught in a nearby thicket. He cut the ropes with which he'd tied his son and they sacrificed the ram instead. Abraham named that place "The Lord Will Provide", because God had provided a sacrifice in place of his son there.

Again the angel of the Lord addressed Abraham. "Because you did not withhold your only son from me I will bless you and give you as many descendants as the sand on the seashore and the stars in the sky. They will conquer their enemies. Because you obeyed me all the nations of the earth will be blessed through them."

God would keep this promise, first through the Jewish people and then in a special way through Abraham's descendant Jesus Christ. In fact the offering of Isaac was a "type", a prefiguring of certain aspects of the life and ministry of Jesus Christ. Just as Isaac carried the wood on which he was nearly sacrificed, so Christ would, one day, carry the wooden cross on which he would be sacrificed near that same site. And just as God provided a ram to die in place of Isaac so, nearly 2000 years later, he would provide Jesus Christ to die in place of sinful people.

· · · · ·

Sarah lived to be 127 years old. When she passed away Abraham and Isaac mourned for her. Although God had promised Abraham that his descendants would possess all of Canaan, he didn't actually own any of it yet—not even a little burial plot! He asked the local community if they would sell him the cave of Machpelah in which to bury Sarah. The deal was sealed in the presence of witnesses and the title deed handed to Abraham. At long last he was the legal owner of a piece of the land God had promised him: a little graveyard.

▪ 16 ▪ Isaac Marries

Genesis 24   *Date: circa 1950 B.C.*

"I AM GOING to send you on an important errand," Abraham told his chief steward Eleazar one day. "You are to go to my relatives in Haran and get a wife for Isaac. I don't want him to marry a Canaanite woman." He then had the steward place his hand on the inside of his leg and swear in the name of the Lord, the God of heaven and earth, that he would carry out this responsibility. Placing one's hand in such an intimate place was a way of underscoring the importance and sensitivity of the matter.

"What if I cannot find a woman willing to go to Canaan," the servant asked. "Should I take Isaac back to Haran?"

"No, not under any circumstance," Abraham replied. "God, who had me leave my native land, promised that He would give this land of Canaan to my descendants, so don't take my son back there. If you cannot find a suitable woman you are released from this oath."

The servant loaded 10 camels with provisions and gifts and headed for Northwest Mesopotamia. Weeks later he arrived. The midday heat had passed; it was the time when local women headed for the well to fill their clay jars to get water for cooking and for evening ablutions.

"Oh Lord, God of my master Abraham, please make me successful today and show kindness to my master Abraham," the servant prayed. "Look, the town's young women are coming to draw water. I'm going to ask some of them to give me a drink. Let the one who says, 'Here, sir, drink. And let me water your camels as well' be the wife for Isaac.'" He had not even finished praying when a very beautiful young woman carrying a jar on her shoulder showed up.

"Would you be so kind as to give me a little water?" Abraham's servant asked her.

"Of course, sir," she said and poured him a drink. "Let me draw some water for your camels as well," she continued, and emptied the rest of the water in her jar into the trough and proceeded to draw enough to satisfy all 10 camels! As she was working the servant watched her closely.

"Tell me, whose daughter are you?" he asked when she had finished. "Would it be possible for us to lodge with your father?"

"My name is Rebekah. I am the daughter of Bethuel, Nahor's son," she replied. "We have plenty of room as well as extra straw and fodder," she continued. "I'm sure you can spend the night with us." When Eleazar heard that Rebekah was the granddaughter of his master Abraham's brother Nahor he bowed his head and worshipped the Lord. He knew that the Lord has answered his prayer and would bless this journey. He reached into a saddlebag, pulled out a gold nose ring and two gold bracelets and gave them to helpful girl. At this she ran home to tell her family about the encounter.

When her older brother Laban saw the golden nose ring and bracelets and heard her story he hurried to the well. That evening, just before supper, Abraham's servant said, "Before we eat, I need to tell you something." He then related the sequence of events that had brought him to Haran, his prayer at the well, and how he perceived Rebekah to be the answer to that prayer. "Now tell me," he concluded, "if you will be kind to my master Abraham and give your daughter as a bride to his son."

Both Rebekah's father Bethuel and her brother Laban said they felt the matter was from the Lord. Then Abraham's servant bowed down to the ground and worshipped. After that he produced a large dowry of gold, silver jewelry and clothing. Dowries compensated a clan for the loss of a member and any children she might bear. Soon afterwards Rebekah and some servant girls packed their bags, mounted the camels and began the long journey back to Canaan with Abraham's servant.

One day when Isaac was in the desert meditating he saw a caravan approaching. He recognized that it belonged to his father and went out to meet it. When Rebekah saw a man striding across the desert towards them she asked the servant who the person might be.

"That is my master," the faithful man replied. Rebekah then covered her face with a veil as a sign of modesty. When they arrived at Abraham's encampment the servant reported all that had transpired. Isaac and Rebekah married soon afterwards. He soon grew to love his bride.

▪ 17 ▪ Isaac's Children

Genesis 25   *Date: circa 1900 B.C.*

AFTER THE DEATH of Sarah, Abraham decided to marry again. His second wife, Keturah, bore him 6 sons, all of whom had children. Although Isaac inherited everything he owned, he gave gifts to his other children and sent them eastward. Various Arab tribes would later trace their ancestry to these descendants of Abraham from Keturah.

Abraham lived to be 175 years old. When he died his sons Isaac and Ishmael buried him in the cave of Machpelah, the little graveyard he'd bought for Sarah many years earlier.

Isaac's wife Rebekah also struggled to bear children. After nearly 20 years, however, God intervened and she became pregnant with twins! She could feel them jostling in her womb and, worried, asked the Lord what this might mean. He told her that the two boys would each become a nation, but that the descendants of the older child would serve those of the younger. This was contrary to traditions of birthright, which stated that the oldest son would receive the greater blessing as well as the bulk of his parents' inheritance.

The first child turned out to be a ruddy, hairy little fellow. His parents called him Esau, which probably meant "Hairy". His twin was born immediately after him—so close, in fact, that he emerged grasping his brother's heel. They called him Jacob, which means, "He grasps the heel". "Grabbing someone by the heel" was also an idiom meaning "to deceive someone". That turned out to be a very appropriate name for the child.

As the twins grew up Esau became a skilled hunter, a real outdoorsman. His father Isaac loved him because he regularly brought home wild game. Jacob, on the other hand, preferred to stay close to home. His mother Rebekah loved the lad who kept her company.

One day Jacob was cooking some delicious smelling lentil stew when Esau returned from one of his hunting expeditions. "Quick, give me some of that red stew," he said. "I'm famished."

"I'll give you the stew for your birthright," his younger brother said quickly.

"What good is a birthright when you're dying of hunger," Esau responded impulsively. "Just give me the stew!"

"Swear that you'll give me your birthright and I'll give you the stew," Jacob insisted. Esau rashly swore on oath that his birthright belonged to Jacob. He then ate his fill and left without thinking about the enormous consequences of what he had done. The incident later earned him the nickname Edom, meaning "Red", after the color of this bowl of lentils.

▪ 18 ▪ God Confirms His Covenant with Isaac

Genesis 26   *Date: circa 1900 B.C.*

Once again famine plagued the land of Canaan. Like his father Abraham, Isaac was tempted to flee to Egypt, but the Lord appeared to him and told him not to do so.

"Stay in the land and I will bless you. I will confirm the promise I made to your father Abraham because he obeyed me and kept my commandments," the Lord said. "Not only will your descendants inherit this land, I will make them as numerous as the stars in the sky. All the nations of the world will be blessed through them." Resisting the urge to take refuge in Egypt, Isaac went to Gerar, where his father's old ally Abimelech was still king.

Rebekah caught the eye of one of the men of Gerar, and he asked Isaac about her. Just like his father, Isaac feared for his life when people noticed his wife. Resorting to his father's ruse, he told the man she was his sister. Sometime afterwards king Abimelech looked down from his palace window and noticed Isaac caressing Rebekah. A cold chill must have gripped him as he remembered what had happened to his household when he had mistakenly taken Sarah into his harem. He quickly summoned Isaac and reprimanded him for lying about his wife and ordered his people not to molest Isaac's family on pain of death. In spite of Isaac's cowardice, God again ensured that the bloodlines leading from Abraham to the promised Messiah remained unsullied.

The Lord blessed Isaac richly during his years in Gerar. He harvested bountiful crops and his herds and flocks grew so large that the locals began to envy him. They started filling in wells dug in the past by Abraham's servants. Eventually King Abimelech himself asked Isaac to leave the area. Isaac's tribe had grown so powerful he feared it would destabilize his little city-state.

Isaac moved some distance away and dug fresh wells, but once again Gerar's herdsmen quarreled over water rights. Isaac moved again and dug fresh wells but, once again, the men of Gerar harassed him. Isaac, ever keen to avoid direct confrontation, moved yet further away. This time he was far enough from Gerar to avoid harassment. He named his new encampment Rehoboth, meaning "spacious". "The Lord has given us space. We will flourish here," he said.

Then the Lord appeared to him one night to once again reconfirm the covenant He'd made with his father Abraham. "I am the God of your father Abraham. Don't be afraid, Isaac. I am with you," the Lord told him. "For Abraham's sake I will bless you and give you a great number of descendants."

Isaac responded to this affirmation by building an altar and worshiping the Lord God. He even moved his entire household to that special place. Once again his servants had to dig new wells. While they were still digging for water, King Abimelech, along with his personal advisor and army commander came to see him.

"The Lord is clearly with you," they said. "We'd like to make a treaty with you. Just as we always treated you well and sent you away in peace, we'd like you to swear on oath not to harm us." Although their memory was more selective than Isaac's, Isaac agreed. He put on a big feast and early the next morning the two parties swore on oath not to molest each other in the future. That same day Isaac's well diggers informed him they'd struck water. Isaac called the well "Shiba", which mean "oath". The town that grew up around the well came to be known as Beersheba, which means "Oath Well".

AS ISAAC GREW OLD his eyes failed and he became blind. Thinking he might soon die he decided to settle his affairs. He called his son Esau, told him to hunt for some fresh game and promised he'd bless him after the celebratory meal.

A father's blessing was very meaningful for it meant becoming the head of the clan as well as receiving the bulk of the inheritance. Rebekah overheard what Isaac told Esau and didn't like it! She wanted her favorite son Jacob to receive the blessing, as the Lord had promised her when the twins were still in her womb, instead of the wild, impulsive Esau. As soon as Esau had left on his hunting expedition she called Jacob.

"Go fetch a couple of young goats and I'll cook them the way your father likes," she commanded. "Then you must pretend to be Esau and give your father the food. That way you'll receive the blessings instead of him."

"How is that going to work?" Jacob asked. "My brother is hairy and I'm smooth-skinned. What if father touches me? He'll realize I'm trying to trick him and curse me instead!"

"Let his curse fall on me," Rebekah responded. "Just do as you're told..." She quickly prepared Isaac's favorite food, covered Jacob's hands and neck with goatskin and dressed him in some of Esau's clothes. Then she handed him the food and sent him into Isaac's presence.

"Father," he said.

"Who is it?"

"It's me, your first born son Esau," Jacob lied. "I did as you told. Please sit up and eat some of the game I caught. Then you can give me your blessing."

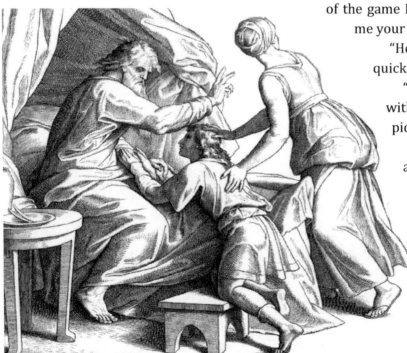

"How did you manage that so quickly?" Isaac asked surprised.

"The Lord your God was with me," Jacob answered piously.

"Come near me, my son, and let me touch you. I want to know if you are really Esau." Isaac was suspicious. He reached out and touched Jacob. "The voice belongs to Jacob, but the hands belong to Esau... Are you really Esau?"

"I am," Jacob lied again.

"Then bring me some of your game." Jacob gave his father the food along with some wine. "Come, kiss me my son," Isaac said after he'd eaten. When he caught the strong odour of Esau's clothes he was convinced that he was dealing with his oldest son.

"My son smells like a field the Lord has blessed. May God bless you with the earth's riches. May other nations serve and bow down to you. Be the lord over your brothers. Let those who curse you be cursed and let those who bless you be blessed." The beautiful words rolled from the blind patriarch's lips.

Jacob had no sooner received his stolen blessing and left his father's presence when Esau appeared. He too prepared a meal and brought it to Isaac. "Sit up father," he said. "Eat, so that you can give me your blessing." At this Isaac became very agitated.

"Who are you?" he cried out.

"Why, I'm your firstborn son Esau," Esau replied puzzled.

"Who offered me a meal ahead of you?" Trembling violently Isaac continued, "I have just finished blessing him. He will be the blessed one!"

When he heard this Esau cried out, "Bless me too, father!"

"Your brother has deceived you. He stole your blessing," Isaac replied.

"That is the second time he has deceived me," Esau cried. "First he took my birthright, and now he has stolen my blessing! He lives up to his name, Jacob, the heel-grabber, the deceiver! Father, surely you must have a blessing for me too!"

"I've made Jacob lord over his brothers and blessed the fruit of his labor. There is not much left, my son."

"There must be something…" Esau began weeping loudly.

Then Isaac spoke again. "Although you are not blessed with the richness of the land, and although you are subservient to your brother, you will be a man of war. One day you will grow restless and free yourself from your brother's bondage."

After these events the vengeful Esau planned to kill his brother as soon as their father had died. When Rebekah got wind of Esau's plans she called Jacob and told him that for his own safety he had better go away for a while. Quickly hatching another plan, she told the naïve Isaac that Esau's Canaanite wives were spoiling their lives. She didn't think Jacob should marry one as well, and suggested Isaac send him to her family to find a wife for himself. Isaac dutifully agreed. He called Jacob, commanded him to find a wife from his mother's family, and sent him on his way.

▪ 20 ▪ Jacob's Ladder, Jacob's Marriage

Genesis 28:10-22; 29, 30   *Date: circa 1900 B.C.*

AFTER HIS hasty departure from Canaan Jacob headed north for Haran to his uncle Laban. One evening when it was too dark to travel any further he put his tired head on a stone in a field and fell into a deep sleep. That night he had an amazing dream. Angels made their way up and down a stairway that reached to heaven. The Lord stood at the top of the stairway.

"I am the Lord, the God of Abraham and Isaac," The Lord declared. Jacob then received the same promise God had given to his grandfather and to his father: "I will give you and your descendants the land on which you are lying. You will have so many descendants they will fill it from one end to the other. Through them all the people of earth will be blessed. I am with you and I will watch over you wherever you go. One day I will bring you back to this land. I will not forsake you but will carry out my promises to you".

Jacob woke up in fear. "This is an awesome place," he said. "The Lord is here and I didn't know it. This place is the gateway to heaven! It is the house of God!" At dawn he set the stone he had laid his head on up on end and poured some oil on it. He called that place Bethel, Hebrew for "House of God", and made a vow saying, "If the Lord watches over me and provides all I need on this journey and I can return home safely, then the Lord Jehovah will be my God. I will give back to him a tenth of all that He gives me".

Jacob continued his journey. One day he met some shepherds gathered around a well, and asked them where they were from. "Haran," they replied.

"Do you happen to know my relative Laban?" Jacob asked.

"Yes, we do. Look, that is his daughter Rachel coming with their flocks," one of them responded, pointing to a lovely girl approaching the well. When Rachel and her flock arrived Jacob heaved the heavy stone lid off the well's mouth and, much to the girl's surprise, began watering her sheep for her. He then greeted her and, sobbing with emotion, told her he was her cousin. When her father Laban heard a nephew from Canaan had arrived he hurried to welcome him.

Jacob, an accomplished sheepherd himself, started working for his uncle. After a month Laban suggested he pay Jacob for his labour.

"I'll work for you for seven years if you give me Rachel in marriage," Jacob said.

"It's a deal," Laban said. So, for the next seven years Jacob worked for Laban. He was so in love, however, that the years seemed like days to him. At the end of the period everyone in the area was invited to the week-long wedding party of song and dance. After the festivities Jacob and his veiled bride retreated to the bridal chamber. When he woke up the next morning, however, Jacob discovered to his consternation that he had spent the night with Rachel's older sister Leah, and not with Rachel! Peeved, he confronted his uncle.

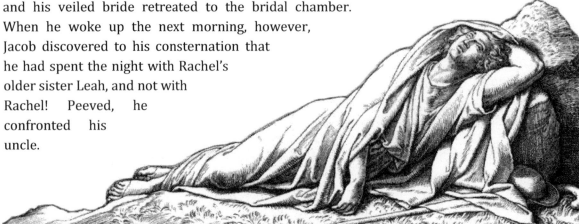

"In our culture we never give the younger daughter in marriage before the older one," Laban said. "I'll give you Rachel as well if you work for me for another seven years." Jacob had no choice but to agree. After the celebrations were over Laban gave him Rachel as well; Jacob, who'd duped his brother out of his birthright and his father's blessing, had found his match! However, he kept his word and labored another seven years for his uncle. Laban gave each of his daughters a slave girl as a wedding present. Leah's was called Zilpah, and Rachel's was called Bilhah.

▪ 21 ▪ Jacob's Children, Jacob's Departure

Genesis 29:31-ch. 31   *Date: circa 1900 B.C.*

WHEN THE LORD saw that Jacob loved Rachel but not Leah He comforted the older sister by enabling her to bear children. She gave birth to four sons, Reuben, Simeon, Levi and Judah. Rachel became very jealous, and resorted to old Sarah's strategy: she gave Jacob her slave girl Bilhah to bear children on her behalf. Bilhah gave birth to Dan and Naphtali.

When Leah saw that she was not getting pregnant any longer, she too gave her slave girl to Jacob. Zilpah gave birth to Gad and Asher. Then Leah herself started getting pregnant again and gave birth to Issachar, Zebulun and after that to a girl, Dinah. Then, at long last, the Lord responded to Rachel's prayers for a son of her own and she gave birth to Joseph. Much later Rachel gave Jacob his twelfth son, Benjamin.

After Jacob had completed his second seven-year stint of service he told his uncle Laban that he'd met his contractual obligations and was ready to return to Canaan. However Laban was loath to see his hard-working nephew go. "I am aware that the Lord has blessed me because of you. Please stay. Name your wages!" he said.

"When I first came your flocks did not amount to much," Jacob responded. "Let me go through the herd and pick out the spotted sheep and goats for myself while you keep the pure white ones. That way we can easily distinguish your herd from mine. For that price I will keep tending your sheep for the foreseeable future." Laban agreed, and while Jacob's sons tended his herd Jacob himself took care of Laban's flock. Under the Lord's blessing and careful management Jacob's herd grew very large. He became a wealthy man in his own right, owning slaves, flocks, camels and donkeys. He grew so rich, in fact, that his uncle Laban grew jealous. Although Laban changed the terms of the contract ten different times, each time Jacob came out ahead. Laban and Laban's sons' attitude toward Jacob changed ominously.

As the mood darkened the Lord reminded Jacob of the stairway dream back at Bethel, and told him it was time to head back to his father Isaac in Canaan. Rachel and Leah heartily agreed; they too were tired of their father's schemes. While Laban was out in the fields shearing sheep they loaded their belongings onto their camels and, driving their flocks ahead of them, headed for Canaan. The superstitious Rachel took advantage of her father's absence to steal the family's idols.

It took Laban three days to discover his nephew had deserted him. By that time Jacob's caravan had crossed the mighty Euphrates River and was heading south. Still Laban set off in hot pursuit. However the Lord warned him in a dream not to harm Jacob.

"What's this you've done," he complained when he finally caught up with Jacob. "You should have let me know that you wanted to leave and we would have sent you off in style. You didn't even give me a chance to say farewell to my children and grandchildren. You've done a foolish thing. I could have harmed you but the Lord told me in a dream not to do so. And why did you steal our family's idols?"

"I was afraid you'd take your daughters away from me if you knew I was leaving," Jacob said. "As for your idols, I don't know anything about them. If you find your idols here, we shall put the thief to death. Go ahead, look through all our stuff and see if there is anything among it that belongs to you." Laban searched through all of Jacob's possessions. When he came to Rachel's tent she apologized for not standing but, she explained, it was the wrong time of the month for her. She was, in fact, sitting on the stolen idols!

When Laban came up with nothing Jacob, tired of his uncle's antics, angrily confronted him with his grievances. Seeking to prevent a family feud from erupting, Laban suggested they make a covenant of peace. They gathered a pile of stones to serve as a boundary marker, which they called Mizpah, meaning "watchtower". Then they shared a meal and pledged not to harm each other in the future. The next morning Laban said goodbye and returned home.

▪ 22 ▪   Jacob Wrestles with God and Meets Esau

Genesis 32, 33   *Date: circa 1900 B.C.*

AS THEY GOT closer to home Jacob decided to send messengers to Esau to inform his brother of his return. He well remembered how he had schemed to steal his brother's blessing and birthright, and worried that the volatile Esau still nurtured his grudge. The messengers made their way to Mount Seir, Esau's lair in Edom, the craggy terrain south of the Dead Sea. When they returned, Jacob's men reported breathlessly that Esau was on his way with 400 men. In great fear Jacob divided his caravan into two groups and sent them in different directions, hoping that at least one group would escape the assault he assumed his brother was about to launch against them. Then, in desperation, he prayed to the God of his grandfather Abraham and his father Isaac. He acknowledged that he was unworthy of the blessings with which God had blessed him, then reminded God of His covenant promises to his ancestors, and prayed for deliverance from his brother.

 In the morning he went through his flocks, picked out a large number of animals, divided them into groups and sent them, one after the other, ahead of him, hoping the gifts would appease Esau. That night Jacob sent his family across the nearby Jabok River while he remained behind, alone. He had done what he could to try to ensure the safety of his family. There was nothing else to do but wait...

Suddenly a man approached him in the dark, grabbed hold of him and began to fight with him. Quietly but furiously Jacob and the stranger wrestled throughout the night. Day broke and still the stranger had not overpowered Jacob. The man then touched Jacob's hip, and it popped out of its joint. Still Jacob still would not give up the fight.

"Day is dawning. Let me go," the stranger said.

"Not unless you bless me," Jacob said, panting.

"What is your name?"

"Jacob"

"From now on you will be called Israel. You have struggled with God and have overcome," the stranger said.[5] Israel means, "He struggles with God".

"Please, tell me your name," Jacob insisted.

"Why ask for my name? Let me bless you." The stranger then blessed Jacob and disappeared just as the sun broke over the horizon.

"I was face to face with God and yet my life was spared," Jacob said to himself in awe as he limped off. Catering to his penchant for naming places, Jacob called that spot Peniel. Peniel means "Face of God".

As he reached his camp Jacob saw Esau and his men approaching. Walking ahead of his family he approached his brother with trepidation, bowing seven times in abasement. Unexpectedly, the mercurial Esau ran to meet him and embraced his brother. They wept together and Esau asked to be introduced to the rest of the clan.

"What was the point of all those droves of cattle?" Esau inquired.

"They are a gift to win your favor," Jacob said. He insisted his brother accept the lavish gifts and gently but firmly refused his offer of protection. Later that day Esau and his band returned to Seir while Jacob's caravan plodded slowly onwards towards Shechem. Upon arrival he bought a plot of land and built an altar he called El Elohe Israel, meaning "God, the God of Israel". God had brought him back to Canaan, as He had promised.

▪ 23 ▪ The Rape of Dinah

Genesis 34 & 35   *Date: circa 1900 B.C.*

ONE DAY Jacob's daughter Dinah went to visit some local Canaanite women in nearby Shechem. A man named Hamor ruled Shechem. While Dinah was there Hamor's son, also called

---

[5] There were occasions in the Old Testament when God granted people tangible manifestations of Himself. Theologians called these divine manifestations "theophanies". These theophanies were usually but not always in human form, and could be occasions of either blessing or judgment. Major theophanies include the Lord appearing to Abraham upon his arrival in the Promised Land, reaffirming His covenant with him, and setting out to destroy Sodom (Gen. 12:7-9; 17:1; 18:1); God appearing to Moses on Mount Sinai; and later to Moses, Aaron, his sons and the seventy elders of Israel (Ex. 19:20; 33:18-34:8; 24:9-11).

Shechem, seduced and raped her. He then told his father he liked Dinah and asked him to approach Jacob and settle on a bride price.

When Jacob's sons heard what had happened to their sister they were furious, although they controlled themselves when Hamor and his son Shechem came to ask for Dinah's hand. "Please let my son marry Dinah," Hamor asked. "In fact, I propose that we become allies. Then you are free to intermarry with us, and we with you. You will be able to settle among us, buy property and trade among us. We'd become one people! We'll all be better off." His son Shechem pitched in as well. "Just name your bride price," he said, "and we'll pay it."

Not only had Dinah's shrewd brothers no desire to integrate with these Canaanites, they were after revenge. They devised a plan on the basis of the sign of the Abrahamic covenant, circumcision. "Our religion does not allow us to intermarry with those who are uncircumcised," they said piously. "If your people were circumcised, however, we would be free to intermarry and become one people with you."

That seemed reasonable to Hamor and his son. They returned to Shechem to sell the idea of circumcision to the townsfolk. "If our men are circumcised then that wealthy clan of Jacob is prepared to integrate with us. Think of it! In time all their livestock and property will become ours!" The rest of the tribe also thought this was a great idea and so the men allowed themselves to be circumcised.

Three days later, when they were still in pain from the operation, Jacob's sons Simeon and Levi grabbed their swords, headed for Shechem, brutally killed all its defenseless males and looted the town. This scared Jacob. "What have you done?" he complained. "If the other Canaanites join forces against us we are done for!"

"He should not have treated our sister like a prostitute," they responded curtly. Although a brutish event, the story of Dinah's rape is important because it pertained to God keeping his covenant promise to Abraham. Through Dinah's rape Satan once again sought to assimilate Jacob's clan into Canaanite society. However, the descendants of Abraham had to remain ethnically pure and distinct from the surrounding people and nations so that there would be no doubt that the promised Saviour, when he eventually came, was a descendent of Abraham and his wife Sarah.

The Lord led Jacob to Bethel where, years earlier, he had dreamt about the stairway to heaven. He ordered his household to get rid of their idols and to purify themselves in preparation of the sacrifice he wanted to make there. As they traveled the Lord created great fear of Jacob's clan in the hearts of the local Canaanites. No one dared seek revenge for the massacre at Shechem. At Bethel, God renewed the Abrahamic covenant with Jacob. He reiterated the promise that he would be the father of kings, indeed of a whole nation, and that one day they would take over the lands of the Canaanites. Jacob then moved south to Bethlehem. Sadly, on the way there Rachel died giving birth to her second son, Benjamin.

Sometime later Reuben, Jacob's oldest son, slept with his father's concubine Bilhah. Now Jacob's three oldest sons, Reuben, Simeon and Levi, were all out of favor with their father, something which would have repercussions when, on his deathbed, he gathered his sons around him to bless them.

From Bethel Jacob's little tribe wended its way slowly to Mamre, the burial ground which Abraham had bought from the locals, and where his father Isaac was still living. At long last father and son were reunited—but not for long. Isaac died soon afterwards, at the ripe old age of 180. Jacob and Esau buried him in the family sepulcher.

▪ 24 ▪ Joseph Sold Into Slavery

Genesis 37, 39   *Date: circa 1850 B.C.*

JACOB LOVED Joseph, the first son of his favorite wife Rachel, more than any of his other children and treated the handsome lad with such partiality that his brothers began to hate him. Nor did the fact that Joseph reported his siblings' misdemeanors to their father, who then rewarded him with a beautiful ornamental robe, help his relationship with his brothers.

One night Joseph dreamt that he and his brothers were binding sheaves of grain in the fields. Suddenly his sheaf stood upright while his brothers' sheaves bowed down to it. When he shared the details of his dream his brothers took great offense at the suggestion that one day they would be subservient to him. When, in a second dream, Joseph saw the sun, the moon and eleven stars all bowing down before him even his father Jacob was taken aback.

"You don't really think your mother, your brothers and I will one day bow before you, do you?" he asked. But he could not forget his son's dreams either...

Once when Joseph's brothers had taken their father's flocks to graze near Shechem Jacob told Joseph to go see how they were doing. His brothers saw him coming in the distance. "Look," they said, "the dreamer is on his way. Let's kill him, get rid of his body and tell father that a wild animal got him. That'll be the end of his dreams!"

Reuben, the oldest, protested. "No," he said, "don't kill him. He is our brother after all." Hoping to rescue Joseph later, he suggested they throw him into a dry well. Then they grabbed Joseph, stripped him of his fancy robe and threw him into the pit. Deaf to their brother's muffled cries they sat down to eat while Reuben went to look after the flock.

While they were enjoying their meal a trading caravan appeared over a hilltop. Suddenly Judah had an idea. "Let's sell our brother to those Ishmaelites," he suggested. "That way his blood won't be on our hands."

The others liked this suggestion. They pulled Joseph out of the well and sold him as a slave to the Ishmaelites, who hauled him down to Egypt and sold him to someone named Potiphar, the captain of Pharaoh's guard.

When Reuben came back and learned that his brothers had sold Joseph into slavery he tore his clothes in misery—but by then it was too late to rectify the situation. They dipped Joseph's ornamental robe into a basin of goat's blood and took it back to their father Jacob. "Look what we found in the field," they said. "Do you recognize it?"

Jacob, once so skilled at deceiving others, fell for his sons' ruse. "My son's robe!" he cried. "A wild animal has devoured him..." He tore his clothes with grief, put on sackcloth and refused to be comforted.

·····

Although he was now a slave, Joseph threw himself wholeheartedly into his work—so much so that the Lord blessed his master's household because of him. He learned the Egyptian language and earned his master Potiphar's trust and, in time, became his general manager.

Potiphar's wife could not help but notice her husband's handsome young aide. She began to pester him to go to bed with her but Joseph politely yet firmly refused. "My master trusts me. How can I do such a wicked thing and sin against God?" he told her. After that he tried never to be alone with her.

One day when there were no other servants present, the woman seized Joseph by his cloak and tried to seduce him. Joseph turned and fled, leaving her with nothing but the cloak in her hands. Shamed, she cried for help and accused him of trying to take advantage of her. Later she repeated her story to Potiphar. Angry and disappointed, he sent Joseph to the royal prison.

Although things in his life had gone from bad to worse, Joseph again gave himself wholeheartedly to the prison duties he was allocated. Once again the Lord blessed him for his faithfulness and, in time, the warden grew to trust him so much he basically had Joseph manage the prison for him.

Seeking to serve faithfully irrespective of his circumstances enabled Joseph to develop management skills that would one day stand him in good stead.

▪ 25 ▪ Judah and Tamar

Genesis 38   *Date: circa 1850 B.C.*

WHILE JOSEPH was a slave in Egypt his brother Judah married a Canaanite woman named Shua. They had three sons, Er, Onan and Shelah. Er, the firstborn, eventually married a woman name Tamar. Because Er was a wicked man, God took away his life before he had children of his own, leaving Tamar a widow.

Judah then told his second son Onan to lie with his sister-in-law Tamar so that she would bear a child who would carry on Er's family line; allowing one's family line to die out was unthinkable. Onan, however, refused to get his sister-in-law pregnant because he knew that the child she might conceive would be considered his deceased brothers' offspring, not his own. This act of selfishness displeased the Lord, so He took Onan's life as well. Fearing his only surviving son Shelah would die if he slept with Tamar as well, the superstitious Judah sent her back to her parents.

Some time later Judah's Canaanite wife died. After the period of mourning he decided to go to the town of Timnah, where his herdsmen were shearing sheep. Somehow Tamar learned where he was going, disguised herself with a veil and sat by the roadside pretending to be a prostitute. Judah approached her and told her he'd give her a young goat for her services. When she wanted a pledge he gave her his personal seal and staff.

When Judah later sent one of his workmen to reclaim his seal and staff, they couldn't find the supposed prostitute anywhere. Tamar had quickly changed back into her widow's outfit and returned to her parents.

Some three months later Judah was told that his estranged daughter-in-law must have slept with someone, for she was pregnant. The only way to remove the shame Tamar had brought to the family was by honor killing. Not realizing he was the child's father, Judah ordered her to be burned to death.

When Tamar was brought before her accusers she produced Judah's personal seal and staff as proof that he was to blame. Judah had to admit that he had wrongfully withheld his third son Shelah from her and that she had been right to try and keep her husband's name alive. Tamar eventually gave birth to twins, Perez and Zerah.

The fulfillment of the promised Saviour would be through Judah—even though at this stage Judah himself showed little concern for the things of God or the preservation of his lineage. His first wife Shua was explicitly described as a Canaanite; children of that union would have led to his clan's integration into Canaanite society, something which his great-grandfather Abraham and grandfather Isaac feared greatly (Gen. 24:3; 28:1). Tamar, on the other hand, was nowhere described as a Canaanite. Her clever plan insured the continuation of the line of Judah as a separate cultural entity. Two thousand years later the apostle Matthew would give her an honorable mention in Jesus' genealogy (Mat. 1:3).

▪ 26 ▪   Joseph Becomes Viceroy of Egypt

Genesis 40, 41   *Date: circa 1850 B.C.*

ONE DAY two notable inmates arrived at the prison where the innocent Joseph was serving time. For some reason Pharaoh had fallen foul of both his cupbearer and his chief baker and had them incarcerated. The prison warden assigned Joseph to look after them.

One morning when Joseph was doing his rounds he noticed both men looking glum, so he inquired if everything was all right. They shared that they had each had a disturbing dream. They sensed their dreams were meaningful, but could not make any sense of them.

"The interpretation of dreams belongs to God," Joseph said. "Tell me what you saw."

"I saw a vine with three branches," the cupbearer began. "It blossomed and produced clusters of grapes. I squeezed the grapes into Pharaoh's cup and placed it into his hand."

"The dream means that in three days Pharaoh will restore you to your former position," Joseph explained. "When he does, please mention my plight to him because I have been imprisoned unjustly," he added.

When the chief baker heard that positive interpretation, he was keen to share his dream as well. "There were three baskets on my head with all kinds of delicacies for Pharaoh in the top one. However, birds got at them and ate them," he said hopefully.

"In three days Pharaoh is going to execute you and hang your corpse from a tree. The birds will eat your flesh," Joseph predicted somberly. Three days later Pharaoh celebrated his birthday. As part of the festivities he restored his cupbearer and executed the baker—just as Joseph had foreseen.

For the next couple of years the happy cupbearer forgot all about the unfortunate Joseph still in prison. Then, one night, Pharaoh had a dream that he sensed was significant. He called his wise men and magicians and told them about it. "I was standing by the Nile," he began, "when seven healthy, fat cows emerged from the water and started grazing among the reeds. Then seven scrawny cows emerged and devoured the seven fat cows. After that I awoke, only to fall asleep again. This time I dreamt about seven full, healthy heads of grain on a single stalk of wheat. Then seven poor, scorched heads of grain sprouted and devoured the seven healthy heads. When I woke up again the dreams wouldn't leave my mind..."

The wise men were stumped; they didn't know what to make of the dreams. Then, suddenly, Pharaoh's cupbearer remembered how, while he was in prison, Joseph had correctly interpreted his and the baker's dreams. He stepped forward and shared the incident with his master.

Pharaoh quickly dispatched a detail of soldiers to the prison. They took Joseph from his dungeon, had him take a bath and shave his beard, gave him a fresh set of clothes and ushered him into the throne room. "I hear you are able to interpret dreams," Pharaoh said. "I have had a dream which no one is able to interpret."

"No one but God can interpret dreams, my Lord," Joseph replied. "Tell me the dream and God will give Pharaoh its meaning."

"The two dreams refer to the same thing," Joseph responded after Pharaoh had reitterated them to him. "God is communicating to Pharaoh what is about to happen. The seven healthy cows and the seven full heads of grain refer to seven years of plenty. For the next seven years Egypt will have bumper crops. The seven scrawny cows and the seven poor heads of grain refer to seven years of famine that will follow the seven years of bounty. During the years of famine the good years will be forgotten. The land will be ravaged. God has revealed the matter to you. There is no escaping it.

"Let Pharaoh choose a wise man to manage the collection of the extra grain during the years of plenty," Joseph continued. "Have this man supervise the building of silos in which to store that grain. Then, when the famine hits, the country will not be ruined."

Joseph's interpretation rang true with Pharaoh and his wise men. Not only did he and his officials approve of Joseph's plan, Pharaoh was so impressed that he appointed Joseph to the rank of viceroy and commissioned him to prepare the country for the coming famine.

Joseph was 17 when his brothers sold him into slavery and 30 when he became viceroy of Egypt. For 13 terrible years he had been a slave or a prisoner. Then, overnight, he became one of the highest authorities in the land with all the privileges that came with the job. He was given an Egyptian name and eventually married Asenath, the daughter of an Egyptian priest. She bore him two sons, Manasseh and Ephraim. Manasseh sounds like the Hebrew word "to forget". At long last he could forget the years of slavery and imprisonment.

During the seven years of plenty the land was so fruitful that Joseph and his commissioners could not keep track of all the grain pouring into the numerous silos they built. Then the good times came to an end and the land was devastated. The people headed for the royal palace and demanded that Pharaoh provide for them. "Go to Joseph," he told them. "He will take care of you."

Joseph put the management skills he'd learned as Potiphar's slave to good use. He opened the royal granaries and started selling the vast quantities of grain he and his men had collected. His government profited and the people received what they wanted.

Genesis 42-43:1-14   *Date: circa 1850 B.C.*

THE FAMINE HIT the surrounding countries, including Canaan, so hard that even the wealthy Jacob and his clan faced starvation. When Jacob heard that there was grain for sale in Egypt he told his sons to go and buy some. They took their pack-animals and made their way across the Negev desert to Egypt. Jacob was so afraid that something untoward might happen to Benjamin, the son of his deceased beloved Rachel and full brother of his favorite, but lost, son Joseph, that he refused to let him go on the journey.

The other ten made it safely to Egypt and headed for the nearest grain distribution point. Joseph, supervising proceedings there, recognized them immediately, though they did not recognize him; over the course of twenty years the Hebrew shepherd boy had become a distinguished, smooth-shaven, well-dressed Egyptian statesman. His brothers bowed low before him. As they did so Joseph could not help but remember the dreams of his youth…

"Who are you and where have you come from?" he demanded harshly, choosing to speak to them through an interpreter.

"We're from the Canaan," they answered. "We have come to buy grain…"

"You are lying. You are spies. You have come to see where our land is weak!"

"Oh no, my Lord. We are brothers. There were twelve of us, but one is gone and the youngest is at home with his father. We are honest men, not spies. We simply came to buy grain!" they protested.

"I don't believe a word you are saying. As surely as Pharoah lives, you will be thrown into prison. One of you will return home and fetch that supposed younger brother. Produce him, then I might believe your story!" Joseph then had his brothers thrown into prison.

Three days later Joseph summoned them. "I fear God," he said. "I will release all but one of you. Get that youngest brother and I will believe you."

The brothers were terrified of this august, all-powerful ruler who could dispose of them as he saw fit. "Didn't I tell you not to kill our brother Joseph," Reuben inveighed against his brothers, not realizing that Joseph understood everything he said. "You ignored his distress and his pleas for his life. Now we are being punished for what we did to him…"

Joseph was so touched by these words that he turned away and wept. When he had regained control of his emotions he had his brother Simeon bound before their eyes and thrown into prison. He then received their payment for the grain, had their bags filled, and quietly instructed his servants to place each man's pouch of silver in the bags as well.

That night when the brothers were setting up camp one of them opened a sack of grain to feed a donkey and discovered his silver. Fear gripped them; was God playing some kind of cruel game with them? When they got back to Canaan each one discovered their silver in their bags. With sinking hearts they told their father all that had taken place and the demands the ruler of Egypt had made on them.

When he heard their story Jacob despaired. "Joseph is gone, now Simeon is gone and you want to take Benjamin as well! You are depriving me of my children... Everything goes against me!" he cried. Reuben tried to assure him that Benjamin would be safe, even offering the life of his own sons in lieu of him. But Jacob refused to countenance the risk of Benjamin facing that terrifying Egyptian ruler.

There was, however, no let-up in the famine. The food the brothers had brought from Egypt was consumed all too soon and, once again, the family faced starvation. Jacob told them to go back to Egypt to get more grain.

"Egypt's ruler warned us not to return without our brother," Judah reminded him. "When the man interrogated us we had no idea where his questions would lead. We could not know that he would demand to see Benjamin. As it is, we must take him if we are to have any hope of success. I will forever take the blame if something happens to him."

"What must be must be," Jacob said resignedly. "Take the best products of our land and offer it to the man: some balm, honey, spice, myrrh, almonds... And take double the silver so you can return that which you found in your sacks. Now go, take your brother, and may the Lord God give you grace in the man's eyes."

▪ 28 ▪ Joseph Reveals His Identity

Genesis 43:15-45   *Date: circa 1850 B.C.*

THE BROTHERS hurried down to Egypt to present themselves to its stern ruler. To their surprise they found him in a jovial mood. They were even invited to a banquet at his house, though this did not sit well with them at first. They were afraid he was luring them into a trap. They approached a steward and tried to return the silver.

"Don't worry," the man said. "I received the silver. The God of your father must have placed it in your sacks." He then had Simeon released from prison and, upon arrival at Joseph's house, gave them fodder for their animals and allowed them to freshen up.

When Joseph made his entry they again bowed low before him and offered him the presents they had brought from Canaan. Speaking through a translator Joseph asked how they were doing and inquired about their aged father. He then turned to Benjamin and asked if this was the young man they had told him about. He barely managed to bless his younger brother before his emotions overcame him. He hurried from the banquet hall, gained control of himself, washed his face and re-entered. Sitting by himself at the head table he ordered that the meal be served.

To the brothers' astonishment the stewards seated them in the order of age, from the oldest to the youngest. And when the food was served they served five times as much to Benjamin as to the rest of them. As the meal progressed the brothers began to relax and enjoy this feast in time of famine. In the meantime Joseph told his steward to fill his brothers' sacks with grain. He also ordered him to hide his elaborate silver chalice inside Benjamin's sack.

The next morning the brothers headed home with bags full of grain. Before they had traveled very far, however, Joseph ordered his steward to chase them down and confront them with the supposed theft of his silver cup. When the soldiers caught up with them, the brothers vehemently denied any wrongdoing. They were so certain of themselves that they told them that if the cup was found on any of them, that individual ought to die and the rest of them would become slaves.

"Very well," the man responded. "Whoever has the chalice will be enslaved. The rest of you will be free from blame." They lowered their bags and, beginning with the oldest, had their bags searched. To their great consternation it turned up in Benjamin's bag! In great distress they tore their clothes and trudged despondently back to the city where, once again, they threw themselves face-down before the imposing Egyptian viceroy.

"What have you done," the man scowled. "Men like me find out the truth by divination!"

"We don't know what to say, my Lord," Judah spoke up. "We do not know how to prove our innocence. God is punishing us for our past sins and now we are your slaves..."

"No," Joseph said. "Only the one on whom the cup was found will become my slave. The rest of you may return to your father in peace." Joseph had planned the entire charade to lead to this point. How his brothers responded now would determine if they had changed over the years or if they were still the same cruel bunch. Would they leave Benjamin enslaved in Egypt and run for safety, or would they stick up for him?

Judah stepped forward. "Please, my Lord, allow me to explain. Do not be angry with me, even though you are like Pharaoh himself..." Then, in very moving terms, he told the story from their perspective: how they had gone in good faith to Egypt to buy grain, how they had had to produce Benjamin on the second trip and the pain that had caused their father, who had already lost Benjamin's older brother. He explained how he had promised to guarantee Benjamin's safety, and would bear the blame all his life if he didn't keep that promise. "Please, my Lord," he concluded, "Let the boy go free and let me stay as your slave instead. I cannot bear to witness my father's misery should he not return."

After Judah's moving speech Joseph could not contain his emotions any longer. He ordered his Egyptian attendants and the translator to leave and then he broke down, weeping so loudly they could hear him outside the room. "I am Joseph!" he cried out in Hebrew through his tears. "Is my father still alive?" His brothers were stunned, dumbfounded, and unable to speak for fear. "Come near," Joseph said to them. "I am your brother Joseph whom you sold as a slave to Egypt. Don't fear, don't worry, and don't be angry with yourselves. God sent me ahead of you in order to save many lives. There have been two years of famine already and there will be five more years before it lets up. However God sent me ahead of you to save your lives. It was not you who sent me here, it was God himself! Now hurry back to Canaan and tell father that his son Joseph is telling him to come to Egypt so you may live near me and so that I can provide for you and your flocks."

After the tearful reunion the brothers spent time catching up with each other. When Pharaoh heard that Joseph had been reunited with his family he was delighted for him, and directed him to send some Egyptian carts to Canaan to make the move easier. Before they headed home Joseph gave them all abundant provisions for the journey along with new sets of clothes. His gave his brother Benjamin five sets of clothes and a pile of silver.

▪ 29 ▪   Jacob's Last Days
Genesis 45:25-50   *Date: circa 1850 B.C.*

JACOB WAS STUNNED when he learned that his beloved son Joseph was alive and well—was, in fact, Egypt's fearsome ruler! Not until his sons had explained everything and he saw the Egyptian carts sent to carry him to the land of the Nile was he convinced.

Although Jacob eventually ordered his clan of some seventy people southwards, he did so with trepidation; when his father Isaac and grandfather Abraham had run to Egypt to escape difficulties they'd encountered nothing but trouble. So, when his convoy got to Beersheeba, Canaan's last town before the desert separating them from Egypt, Jacob stopped to offer sacrifices to the God of his fathers. That night the Lord appeared to him in a vision. "Jacob, Jacob!" He called.

"Here I am, Lord," Jacob replied.

"I am the Lord, the God of your fathers. Don't be afraid to go down to Egypt. I will accompany you, make you into a great nation and one day bring you back again. Your son Joseph will be at your death-bed." Encouraged by these affirming promises Jacob gave the order to cross the Negev desert and head for Egypt. Judah, emerging as the clan's next leader, led the way.

When Joseph heard that his family had crossed the border he mounted his chariot to meet them. He threw his arms around his father and wept for a long time. Later he introduced them all to Pharaoh, who seemed intrigued by their ancient patriarch.

"How old are you," he asked Jacob.

"My pilgrimage has lasted 130 years. It has been short and difficult. It does not compare to that of my fathers," Jacob responded. "Let me to bless you," he added, and then proceeded to bless the ruler of the greatest power on earth.

When Pharaoh learned that Joseph's family were shepherds he granted them the land of Goshen near the city of Ramses. He also asked that Joseph's capable brothers be put in charge of his own flocks. Little did the small group of economic migrants realize that for the next 400 years they would be living in Egypt. Under Joseph's protection they acquired property. They also started to increase rapidly in numbers.

In the meantime Egypt continued to suffer from the calamitous famine. Year after year the people came back to Joseph to buy grain. When they ran out of money he accepted their cattle in exchange for grain. When they had nothing left to offer but their labour and their land, he bought all their real estate, with the exception of the land belonging to Egypt's religious elite, and turned Egypt into a vassalage in which the landholders had to give one fifth of their crop to the state. This arrangement stayed in force for centuries afterwards.

Jacob lived the last 17 years of his life in Egypt. Prior to his death Joseph brought his two sons to him to have him bless them. He wanted to be sure that they would have the same recognition as the rest of Jacob's offspring.

"I never expected to see you again, yet the Lord has let me see your children as well!" Jacob said. When the boys knelt before him he crossed his arms so that his right hand fell on the younger Ephraim and his left hand on the older Manasseh's head. This annoyed Joseph for it meant the younger son would receive the greater blessing. Thinking the nearly blind Jacob had it wrong he tried to move his father's hands.

"I know what I'm doing, my son," old Jacob said. "The older boy will also become a great people, but the younger will be greater than he. His descendants will become a group of nations." He then blessed the boys saying that the same God who had shepherded their forefathers Abraham and Isaac would bless them too and make them a byword of blessing in Israel. He then invited his own sons to receive his final blessing as well.

Jacob reprimanded Reuben, Simeon and Levi for the evil they had committed: Reuben for sleeping with his father's concubine, Simeon and Levi for the massacre of Shechem. The others each received a blessing according to their character, with the primary blessing falling on his fourth son, Judah. He would become the ruler among his brothers and his scepter would, one day, be handed to "the one to whom it belongs" and to whom the nations would be obedient. This was a prophecy that the Savior promised to Adam and Eve, the coming Messiah, the ultimate ruler to whom all the nations will bow one day, would be a descendant of Judah. Jacob then instructed his family to bury him in the cave near Mamre where Abraham, Sarah, Isaac and Rebekah lay. Then he lay down on his bed and died.

Joseph grieved deeply over the loss of his father. He ordered Egypt's doctors to embalm him and obtained permission from Pharaoh to bury his father in Canaan. Joseph, his brothers and Egypt's leading dignitaries travelled to Mamre to attend the funeral. The local Canaanites were so impressed by the solemn ceremony that they called the place Abel Mazraim, which means "the mourning of the Egyptians".

With their father now dead and buried the brothers feared that Joseph would exact revenge for the way they had treated him. Once again they cast themselves before him and offered themselves as slaves.

"Don't fear," Joseph assured them kindly. You meant to harm me but God turned it into good. As a result of what happened many lives were saved. I will provide for you and your children." He lived to be a great-grandfather. Just before he died at the age of 110 he called the ever-increasing descendants of Jacob around him.

"I will die soon," he told them. "One day, however, the Lord will lead you back to Canaan, the land He promised on oath to our forefathers Abraham, Isaac and Jacob. Swear to me that when he does, you will take my bones with you!"

Job 1, 2   *Date: era of the patriarchs*

JACOB'S TWELVE sons would later become known as the patriarch (Acts 7:8). Sometime during this era of the patriarchs a terrible drama unfolded elsewhere in the life of a man called Job.

Job lived in Uz, a place somewhere east of Canaan, probably in Edom. Like Melchizedek, he had a sufficiently wide knowledge of the most-high God, the unseen creator of the heavens and the earth, to serve as the basis for a life-changing relationship with Him. This important, God-fearing man shunned evil and tried to lead a blameless life. God blessed Job with seven sons and three daughters as well as with enormous herds. In fact, he was considered the greatest man among all the peoples of the East.

One day, however, a messenger rushed into Job's presence. "The Sabeans attacked! They carried off your oxen and donkeys and killed the servants!" the man bawled. "I'm the only one who managed to escape!" He was still speaking when another servant came running. "Lightening from heaven struck your sheep and shepherds! All perished and I am the only one to escape!" Then another man came running. "Chaldean raiders carried off your camels and killed the servants! I'm the only one who escaped!" he shouted. While he was still speaking a fourth servant came running and gasped, "Your sons and daughters were at a banquet when a mighty wind swept in from the desert and struck the house. It collapsed and killed them all! I'm the only one to get out alive!"

At this deluge of calamitous news Job tore his robe and shaved his head in sorrow. Then he fell to the ground and worshiped God! "I came naked from my mother's womb, and I will depart naked from this world," he said. "The Lord has given and the Lord has taken — may His name be praised." In spite of the overwhelming catastrophes, he refused to blame God.

But Job's troubles were not over. Some time later huge, painful boils broke out over his body. They became so itchy that he found a shard of pottery and, sitting on an ash heap, scraped himself to get some relief. He was ruined, his health broken. At this disgusting sight his wife turned on him. "Are you still maintaining your integrity?" she lashed out. "Curse God and perish!"

"You are a foolish woman," Job remonstrated. "Shall we accept the good from God but not the bad?"

• • • • •

What Job did not know was that he was the focus of a spiritual drama. God had summoned the angels and Satan into His presence, and demanded from the latter where he had been.

"I have roamed back and forth across the earth," Satan, who had usurped Adam's place as ruler of the world, replied (1 John 5:19).

"Did you notice my servant Job?" God asked. "He is blameless, unique among men in terms of his uprightness. He fears me and shuns evil."

"Little wonder," the accuser of God's people (Rev. 12:20) retorted. "You have put a hedge around him so that no evil can get through to him or his household. You bless everything he puts his hands to. You have made him wealthy and famous. But if you take away the things you've given him he will curse you to your face!"

"Go ahead! Do what you want with everything Job possesses," God responded. "Do not, however, touch the man himself." At this Satan left the presence of God and orchestrated the loss of Job's herds and children. What appeared like natural calamities from a human perspective was, in fact, Satan at work.

Sometime later the angels, including Satan, presented themselves once again to God.

"Where have you come from?" God asked Satan.

"I have roamed back and forth across the earth," Satan responded.

"Have you noticed how Job has maintained his integrity in spite of the fact that you incited me to permit you to ruin him without reason?" God said.

"Skin for skin," Satan replied. "A man will give all he has to preserve his life. Strike his skin and bones and he'll curse you to your face."

"He is in your hands," God said. "But you must spare his life." At this Satan left God's presence and caused Job to be afflicted by disgusting, itchy boils.

• 31 • **Job Argues With His "Comforters"**

Job 2:11-ch. 25   *Date: era of the patriarchs*

WHEN SOME of Job's friends learned of the calamities which had overwhelmed Job they decided to visit him. Deeply shocked at the sight of their bankrupt friend sitting on an ash heap scraping his awful boils with a broken piece of pottery, they wept for him. They tore their robes, put dust on their heads as a sign of their deep sorrow and sat in silence for a whole week, sharing their friend's deep misery and waiting for him to address them first.

When the calamities first hit, Job had shown great faith but the trials had taken their toll. "May the day I was born be cursed," he said when he eventually opened his mouth. "Would that I had been stillborn and not seen the light of day. Why is life given to those who long for death? My worst fears, all that I dreaded, have happened to me. I have no peace, no quietness, no rest; all I experience is turmoil!"

Then one of the friends, Eliphaz, spoke up. He reminded Job of his former glorious state, but noted that God does not punish the innocent. All Job needed to do was accept the Lord's disipline and his fortunes would surely change.

Job accepted Eliphaz's contention that his misfortunes stemmed from God, but resented the suggestion that God was disciplining him for some sin. "Show me what I have done wrong," he said, and I will be quiet!" Then he turned to God and burst out: "If I have sinned, what have I done wrong, O watcher of men? Why have you targetted me? In what way have I become a burden to you?"

Job's imperious challenge to God was too much for Bildad, the second of Job's friends. Eliphaz had spoken gently, but Bildad reacted heatedly at Job's outburst. "How can you say such things?" he demanded. "You are nothing but a blustery wind..." Bildad went on to argue

that because God is just He will not pervert justice, so the calamities which had befallen Job were proof of his sinfulness. He had deserved what he'd received from the hand of God and the best he could do was plead for mercy. If he did God would restore his fortunes. Bildad failed to see that pleading for mercy implied asking for forgiveness... and Job was convinced he had not done anything wrong to deserve all this.

"I know that what you are saying is true," Job acknowledged. He knew that God was righteous and just. He also knew that God was awesome, all-powerful and all-knowing. Job, however, was deeply frustrated. Was God a neutral, mysterious type of sovereign not accountable for his actions? If so any attempt on his part to vindicate himself would lead nowhere: he doubted God would give him a hearing, and even if He did he ran the risk of being overwhelmed by a God who "mocked the despair of the innocent" and failed to administer justice. He questioned why he should maintain his integrity, since God had already treated him as if he were guilty. "If only there were someone who could mediate between God and us," he complained, "then I would be able to defend myself... You know I am not guilty!" he cried out to God, "but no one can rescue me from your hand..." He then expressed his desire to die and be done with it all.

Job's third friend was a hard, pitiless man name Zophar. Ignoring the possibility that Job might actually be innocent, he mocked his desire to know the real reason for his sufferings. He called Job "witless", incapable of growing in wisdom, and urged him to "put away the sin that is in your hand".

At this Job's patience ran out. "Wisdom will die out with you," he said acidly. "I've become a laughingstock to my friends, even though I am blameless. Those at ease are contemptuous of those less fortunate." He then launched into a diatribe about the way God does whatever He pleases, irrespective of the good or bad consquences of His actions on people. "As for your maxims," he said to his friends, "they are made of ash and your arguments of clay! Don't interrupt me, let me finish speaking! I will not give up my hope in God—even if He slays me! I'm happy to present myself before Him, if I could, because I know I would be vindicated!" Then he addressed God directly again. "Just tell me what I've done wrong, God! Stop hiding your face from me. Call me and I will step forward and give an account of myself. Stop eroding my hope the way a torrent sweeps away the soil..."

This seemingly insolent response angered Eliphaz. "No wise man fills his belly with the hot east wind," he stated; to him Job's venting was nothing but hot air. He then made the point that men are essentially corrupt in God's eyes, and that all of Job's irreverent talk not only proved he was culpable but that he had become a bad example to others. He berated Job for his arrogance and repeated the traditional maxim that God punishes people because they shake their fist at Him. He then described the fate of the wicked in poetic terms, being careful to include all the calamities which had befallen Job: lightening, marauders, being stripped of one's possessions, houses turned to rubble...

"You are all miserable comforters," Job responded. "I've heard all those platitudes before. It's easy for you to make long-winded speeches—I could do the same if I were in your place." Then, once again, he turned to God, whom he perceived as his real enemy, as a merciless, pitiless tyrant. He was not God's enemy, but God had become his enemy and apparently for no good reason! As for his friends, he considered them devoid of wisdom. Their worthless advice only made a bad situation worse, worse than death itself!

Bildad resented Job's demeaning, belittling attitude to them. He curtly expressed his wish that Job stop placing himself at the center of things and start speaking some sense. Then, in heavily metaphorical and poetic terms, he expressed the opinion that Job had failed to come to grips with the doctrine that God punishes the wicked in this life.

"How much longer are you going to torment me?" Job cried in response. "All you do is reproach me and attack my integrity! God has wronged me, not I Him! But though I cry 'I've been wronged' He doesn't respond to me! I've been reduced to a stinking bag of bones. Have some pity, friends, for God has struck me." In spite of his mental turmoil Job suddenly cried out in faith. "I know that my Redeemer lives and that he will, one day, stand over my grave. Even though I die I will see God in the flesh, with my own eyes—how I yearn for that day! Don't tell me that the root of my troubles lies with me; in doing so you bring judgement on yourselves".

Zophar, the most emotional of the friends, was deeply offended—dishonored, in his own words—by Job's final remarks. He launched into an eloquent poem about the fact that the universe was moral; in the end, justice would prevail and those who do evil will lose out. The presumption, of course, was that things would go well with those who are righteous—as he considered himself to be. While Zophar insisted on a simplistic correlation between spiritual and physical wellbeing, Job was wrestling with his relationship with God irrespective of what was happening to him physically or materially.

Job was astonished by his friends' lack of sensitivity. They appeared deaf to what he was trying to say and bereft of compassion. He drove home the point that wicked people often lived happy and prosperous lives to the day they died! The implications of this terrified him so much that his body was seized with trembling, but the evidence was everywhere to be seen. "So stop trying to console me with your nonsense," he concluded. "Your answers are nothing but falsehoods".

"Is it for your piety that God is rebuking you?" Eliphaz responded sarcastically. "Your wickedness is great!" Then he launched into a volley of speculations on Job's sins and concluded with a moving call to repentance. "Submit to God and be at peace with him... Return to the Almighty and you will be restored... Pray to him and he will hear you... He will deliver even one who is not innocent..." Sincere as his words were, Eliphaz too failed to understand that Job's primary desire was not to return to health and wealth but to an understanding of God's mysterious, seemingly arbitrary, providential ways.

Job reacted to Zophar and Eliphaz's accusations by boldly reasserting once again that he was blameless. He again expressed his desire for a fair hearing with God, convinced that the encounter would vindicate him—terrifying though it would be. He expressed his deep frustration that although God knew exactly where he, Job, was, God would not let Himself be found. Using detailed observations about the nature of things he bolstered his contention that God does not, in fact, punish the wicked. In the end the wicked just die and are forgotten. "God does not charge anyone with wrongdoing... If this is not so, prove me false and reduce my words to nothing," he concluded.

Bildad then summed up his and his friends' contentions. "God is so awesome and pure that even the moon and the stars are impure in his eyes. That being so, who does man, who is but a maggot, think he is?"

Job dismissed with curt sarcasm Bildad's inane and hurtful contention that he was nothing but a hopeless, sinful worm. "What advice you offer, what wisdom you display! Who helped you utter these words, whose spirit spoke from your mouth?" he asked acidly. After poetically describing the power of God in nature he concluded that "these are only the fringe of his works." God's ways were, indeed, mysterious and incomprehensible but that did not mean that man was a worthless worm. For Job, acknowledging mystery was more honest than holding to a tidy set of teachings which twisted the facts to fit the system. "I will never admit you are right; I will not deny my integrity until I die!" he asserted. His parting shot to his "friends" was a reminder of their theology—that God punishes the wicked—and applied it to them!

▪ 32 ▪ Elihu's Speech

Job 26-37   *Date: era of the patriarchs*

JOB'S INTERACTION with his friends had come to an impasse. He refused to accept their simplistic theology, which could only be maintained by making him out to be an evil person, and they refused to accept that he did not deserve what he got.

None of these three friends were Israelites. Eliphaz was a descendant of Esau, the father of the Edomites (Gen. 36:12). He lived in Teman, an Edomite town known for its worldly wisdom (Oba. 1:9; Jer. 49:7). Bildad was a descendent of Shuah, a son of Keturah, Abraham's second wife whose offspring settled in the Arabian peninsula (Gen. 25:1-2). Zophar came from the Naama tribe which was not listed among the clans of Israel. Job's three friends could only offer the best of the traditional "worldly" wisdom of the era.

In Job's final defense he recalled his glory days as a wealthy, respected community leader whose opinion mattered, to whom people turned for advice, and who had expected to live to a ripe old age. He then bemoaned the depths to which he had been reduced: disreputable youngsters mocked him and he had lost his dignity. Worst of all, God had afflicted him, but instead of giving him a reason for the affliction He had merely afflicted him even more! He concluded by proving his integrity and innocence by reciting all the things he had not done: he had not lusted after other women, had not lied, had not denied justice to anyone, had not withheld good things from the poor, nor had he trusted in the material things with which he was blessed. He had not rejoiced in his enemy's misfortunes, nor witheld hospitality from anyone, nor treated his tenants unfairly, and he had not harboured any secret sin in his heart. Job had grown so confident of his own innocence and integrity that he boldy signed off on them: "I now sign my defence. Let the Almighty answer me... If I could I would give account to him of my every step, I would approach him boldly, like a prince!"

Suddenly a new character, "Elihu the son of Barakel", stepped onto the stage. Elihu meant "God is Jehovah" and Barakel meant "God blesses". He was a Jew and represented the wisdom of Israel.

Elihu was incensed at both Job's self-righteousness and at the others' inability to refute him. Unlike them, however, he did not falsely accuse Job of guilt or blame him for imaginary things. He had listened carefuly to all that Job had said and—unlike the others—quoted him frequently. Although he was wordy and pompous, he was an eloquent, intelligent man not affected by the others' rancourous attitudes. He had also picked up on an inconsistency in Job's argument. Job had questioned God's justice yet, if given the chance to present his case, he was convinced he would be vindicated because of it! Elihu responded that if God was capricious, what was the point of arguing one's case before him? He then went on to present a more balanced theology.

Elihu did not claim to understand what was taking place from God's perspective, but sought to assure Job that God's sovereign power and wisdom would, in the end, be redemptive. God, after all, was a gracious teacher who used suffering for various purposes, sometimes punitive, sometimes educative and sometimes disciplinary. He rejected Job's contention that God did not communicate with men, affirming that He did so through visions and dreams, as well as through pain and suffering. Elihu strongly and repeatedly affirmed that God only did what was right, and that He would punish evildoers. He also repeatedly pointed out that Job's contention that God treated the good and evil equally was both arrogant and wrong, as that would make God the author of evil. He then asserted that Job had kept company with evildoers, a roundabout critique of his non-Jewish "friends".

Elihu concluded his dialogue with a poem about the grandeur of God as seen in the thunderous power of the autumn rains and the winter storms. If man could not understand the recurring mysteries of nature, how could he possibly understand the mystery of divine providence? Just as no one could look at the sun after it had swept the skies clean, so also God's awesome majesty was beyond the reach of mere men. Questioning God's way was folly; man could only humbly revere Him.

▪ 33 ▪ God's Response to Job

Job 38-42   *Date: era of the Patriarchs*

AT LONG LAST God Himself responded to Job. Instead of giving him a straight answer, however, He picked up where Elihu had left off: He revealed His character by taking him on a journey through the wonders of nature. He also reprimanded him for some of the things he had said and the extreme language he had used during his ordeal. "Who is this who darkens my counsel with words without knowledge?" was the first in a long series of rhetorical questions in which God established His power and wisdom, and showed the severe limitations of human knowledge.

"Brace yourself like a man," God continued. He then plied Job with straigthforward questions about the natural world, none of which he could answer. He had dared to question God's management of the created order; now God revealed just how little Job knew about it. "Will the one contending with the Almighty correct him?" God challenged. "Let God's accuser answer him!"

Humbled, Job acknowledged that he had no answer to God's questions. "I am not worthy; how can I reply? I will put my hand over my mouth and speak no more..." Gone was the attitude that if given the chance he would approach God like a prince! Gone was his self-assuredness. Although still afflicted with suffering, God's tour-de-force had chastened and humbled him.

However, he also came to realize that God was not his enemy! God had put him in his place, yet He had not accused him of any supposed sins committed prior to this period of severe trial!

But God was not yet finished. In a second series of rhetorical questions God established His power to punish the wicked and humble the proud. He rebuked Job for questioning His justice by giving vivid descriptions of two uncontrolable and probably mythical animals, behemoth and leviathan, to remind Job that He, the creator and sustainer of the natural order, was also Lord of the moral order. Wild beasts like "leviathan" symbolized evil world powers beyond the control of God's people who would one day be judged and brought low (Psalm 74:12-14; Isa 26:21-27:1; Rev. 12:9).

Job got the message and confessed, repenting of his arrogance, "You can do all things, and your purposes cannot be thwarted. I spoke of things too wonderful for me, of things I did not undertand. I had heard about you before, but now I have seen you. I despise myself and repent in dust and ashes". God had so overwhelmed him with mysteries he could not explain that Job began to question his doubts. In so doing he came to accept that God knew what He was about. Without having his personal questions answered Job had become a true man of faith. The reassertion of God's sovereign power, combined with the assurance that God was not, as he had come to think, his enemy but his friend, was enough to see Job through. God had not abandoned him in a capricious moment. Job's soul was satisfied.

God then addressed Eliphaz, Bildad, and Zophar, the three gentile "friends" who had insisted they spoke on His behalf. "I am angry with you because you did not speak right of me, as Job has." God told them. Job had spoken with deep emotion and got some facts wrong, but he had sought to maintain his intellectual and moral integrity as he presented his case with brutal honestly before God. They, on the other hand, had parroted beautiful sentiments about God, misunderstood what was actually going on, and slandered their friend mercilessly. God ordered them to go to Job with seven bulls and seven rams, offer sin offerings, and ask Job to intercede on their behalf. Job readily agreed to do so.

After Job had prayed for them his brothers, sisters and other friends and acquaintences came to visit him. They had kept their distance during his trials, but now came with a gift of a piece of silver and a gold ring. Fellowship was restored, and the Lord blessed the latter part of Job's life more than the first. His flocks doubled to what they had been before, he had another seven sons and three beautiful daughters, and he lived to be "old and full of years".

Job, the greatest man of the East, was not part of the covenant community of Israel and had not received the revelations of the patriarchs. He had no idea that he had played a role in an invisible spiritual contest. Yet his faith, though shaken, was vindicated. Although God had not fully explained the reason for his mysterious suffering he, like Abraham, Isaac and Jacob, had discovered that persevering faith pleases God.

BACK IN EGYPT Jacob and his family had settled in the land of the Pharaohs. Since Joseph was viceroy his relatives had been warmly welcomed and given the land of Goshen, some of the best grazing land in the country.

In Egypt it hardly ever rained. Far to the south, however, rains in the tropical regions of sub-Saharan Africa caused the river Nile to swell every spring. When those surging waters reached the flat Egyptian desert to the north the river would overflow its shallow banks and leave a layer of fresh, fertile mud along the strip of land bordering the river, making it suitable for agriculture. The Egyptians were utterly dependent on the great river—so much so that they worshiped it. They also developed a remarkable civilization on their long strip of fertile land hemmed in by the desert on either side, but it was a civilization preoccupied with death. Their main literary work, "The Book of the Dead", consisted of incantations and instructions thought to help one overcome difficulties and obstacles in the afterlife. Important people had themselves embalmed and mummified after death and buried in elaborate tombs, the most famous of which were the pyramids.

God had promised Jacob that He would make his family into a great nation during their sojourn in this strange, exotic land, and that is exactly what happened. The Israelites multiplied rapidly. Then, after about thirty years, Joseph died. A new Pharaoh, to whom Joseph meant nothing, became concerned that the large and growing number of non-Egyptian Israelites could threaten the state if they opted to side with an enemy in time of war. He responded to this perceived threat by enslaving the entire Hebrew nation. Egyptian slave masters started working them ruthlessly. The more they afflicted them, however, the more numerous the Israelites became!

Year after year, decade after decade, generation after generation the people of Israel served Egypt as forced laborers building massive construction projects. All the while they continued to increase in number, just as God had promised Abraham centuries earlier.[6] At one point Pharaoh became so concerned about the burgeoning Hebrew population that he ordered their midwives to surreptitiously kill the Hebrew baby boys as they were born. These brave women refused to carry out the dreadful order. When Pharaoh called them to account they lied, saying that Hebrew women were tough; they could give birth without the help of a midwife. Pharaoh, desperate to curtail the growth of the Israelites, then ordered his soldiers to drown newborn Jewish baby boys by throwing them into the Nile. Only the girls could live.

Pharaoh may have been driven by his own political agenda, but there was another force at play behind the scenes. If Satan could wipe out the Jewish nation or so dilute them as a people, then God's promise to Abraham that the world would be blessed through his descendants

---

[6] Ex. 12:40 states that the Israelites lived in Egypt for 430 years and Gen. 15:13 and Acts 7:5 that they were mistreated for 400 years.

would be annulled. The channel through which the Savior would come would be destroyed, God's promise of salvation would be void, and Satan would be the victor!

▪ 35 ▪ Moses' Early Years

Exodus 2:1-10   *Date: circa 1570-1530 B.C.*

MOSES WAS BORN in Egypt after Pharaoh had given the order to drown Jewish baby boys in the Nile. His parents, Amram and Jochebed from the tribe of Levi, recognized that there was something unique about their newborn son, and hid him for the first three months of his life. As the baby grew and became more vocal, however, they realized it would soon be impossible to continue hiding him in their simple hut. Then they carried out a carefully thought-through plan of action: Jochebed made a papyrus basket, coated it with tar to make it waterproof and walked upriver from their slum in Goshen to the place where members of the royal family came to bathe and relax. There she placed Moses in the basket and released it to the river Nile. She told her daughter Miriam to hide nearby to see what would become of her baby brother.

Moses' little ark floated down the river until it got stuck among the reeds close to where Pharaoh's daughter was bathing. When the princess heard a crying baby she sent of one of her slave girls to investigate the matter—and when she laid eyes on the beautiful, helpless baby boy she was moved with compassion. She realized that it was a Hebrew child who should have been killed under her father's edict, but instead of casting the baby back into the river she decided to adopt him. At that moment the quick-thinking Miriam stepped into the open and inquired if her royal highness needed the services of a wet nurse. When the princess said yes, Miriam hurriedly fetched her mother.

"Take this baby and nurse him on my behalf," the princess told Jochebed. "I'll pay you for your services." In this wonderful way Moses was able to live in safety with his parents until he was fully weaned. He then moved into the royal palace where he lived as Pharaoh's daughter's adopted son. She gave him the name Moses, which means "drawn out", for she had drawn him out of the water.

Moses received the best education available in his day, mastering the wisdom of the Egyptians and grew powerful in word and deed (Acts 7:22). However, he never forgot his roots. His early years with his enslaved blood parents had made a deep impression on him. As he grew up in the palace his affinity for the oppressed people of Israel grew deeper than for the oppressors who had adopted him.

▪ 36 ▪ Moses Kills an Egyptian

Exodus 2:11-25   *Date: circa 1530 B.C.*

OVER THE generations the Hebrews had, by and large, deserted the worship of the God of Abraham, Isaac and Jacob. Moses' parents Amram and Jochebed, however, still believed in Him (Heb. 11:23) and must have taught Moses about the nature of the one true, creator God and His covenant promises to their forefathers. Their teaching was not in vain. Although awesome power, honor and wealth were available to Moses he chose instead to throw in his lot with his own hard-pressed people. In faith he turned his back on a life of ease and pleasure (Heb. 11:24-26).

Sometime after Moses made his history-changing decision to identify himself with the despised Hebrews he decided to see their situation first-hand. While wandering around he saw an Egyptian beating a Hebrew and, after checking to make sure no one was looking, killed the

man and buried the body in the desert sand. The next day he saw two Hebrew men fighting and challenged the one in the wrong.

"Who appointed you as a ruler and judge over us?" the man retorted. "Are you going to kill me like you did the Egyptian?" Moses' heart skipped a beat. Someone had witnessed the murder! Word would soon get back to Pharaoh, who would have him arrested. Fearing for his life he fled into the desert.

Moses had rushed ahead in his own strength and

according to his own agenda, mistakenly supposing that his fellow Hebrews would understand that he was God's instrument for their deliverance (Acts 7:25). He ended up with murder on his conscience, hiding in the desert fearing for his life. He fled eastward to the land of Midian on the far side of the Sinai Peninsula.

He was sitting near a well when some local girls came to draw water for their herd. As he watched them work some other shepherds arrived, pushed the girls aside and started to water their own sheep. Moses' sense of justice flared up again. He stood up to the bullies, then he helped the girls water their sheep. When they returned home earlier than normal they told their father about the Egyptian stranger who had helped them.

"Where is he?" their father asked them. "Why did you leave him at the well? Go and invite him over for a meal."

Moses accepted the invitation—and ended up staying with the family. The father turned out to be a Midianite priest named Ruel (also known as Jethro). In time Moses married one of the daughters, Zipporah. They had two sons. Moses named the first Gershom, which sounds like the Hebrew word for "stranger"; he had become a stranger in a foreign land. He called his second son Eliezer, which means, "God is my helper", because God had helped him escape from Pharaoh (Ex. 18:2).

Totally unaware that the sovereign Lord was preparing him for his life's work, Moses roamed the solitary desert with his father-in-law's sheep. He was in the prime of life—yet his life had come to a dead-end. All his hopes and aspirations for himself and his people had come to naught while his fellow Hebrews back in Egypt groaned under the cruel whip of their slave masters.

▪ 37 ▪ The Burning Bush: God Calls Moses

Exodus 2: 23-ch. 4   *Date: circa 1450 B.C.*

FOR FORTY years Moses roamed the lonely wastes of the Sinai desert. He who had been groomed to become a ruler in Egypt was now a mere shepherd, an occupation loathed by Egyptians. This was a far cry from the hustle and bustle of the great cities of Memphis, Rameses and Thebes with their enormous pyramids. It was a far cry from the thronging masses clamoring in markets, the regal priests occupied with mysterious tasks in awe-inspiring temples overlooking the mighty Nile, the scribes who had mastered the mystery of writing, the engineers focusing on Pharaoh's next construction project, the harried bureaucrats and civil servants entering and leaving the royal palaces and other centers of power.

Although Moses had received the best education the ancient world could to offer, it was not sufficient to prepare him for the ministry God had planned for him. It took forty long, weary years in the desert to wean him from the ambitions and worldly impulses which once drove him.

Then one day when he was tending the flock near Mount Horeb in the southern part of the Sinai Peninsula, Moses saw a burning bush. As he watched this flaming bush he noticed that although it was on fire, it did not burn up—it just kept on burning and burning without turning to ashes. As he drew near the curious sight he heard a voice calling him from within the bush.

"Moses, Moses!"

"Here I am," Moses replied.

"Don't come any closer," the voice warned him. "Take your sandals off. The ground you are standing on is holy." After Moses had slipped off his sandals the voice said, "I am the God of your ancestors Abraham, Isaac and Jacob." At this Moses hid his face because he was afraid to look at God.

"I have seen my people's affliction. I have heard their cries, I know their sorrow and I have remembered my covenant with Abraham, Isaac and Jacob," God said. "The time has come to rescue them from bondage and take them back to Canaan. Moses, I am going to use you to bring my people out of Egypt." God was about to fulfil the promise made to Abraham some five centuries earlier that after 400 years of bondage in a strange country He would deliver His people and settle them back in Canaan. It had taken this length of time for the Amorites living in Canaan to reach such depths of evil that they were ripe for judgment (Gen. 15:12-21). At long last, that time was at hand.

Moses did not like what he heard. For the past 40 years he had lived a quiet life and now, at the ripe old age of 80, he was not interested in picking up the ambitions of his youth. His former self-confidence, hopes and aspirations had died long ago. He had given it his best shot once and had failed. "Who am I, God, that I should go to Pharaoh and deliver the people of Israel from Egypt?" he asked.

"I will accompany you," the Lord responded. "When you have brought the people of Israel out of Egypt you will worship me here by this mountain. That will be a sign for you."

"Suppose I go to the Israelites and tell them that the God of their fathers has sent me to deliver them, and they ask me who this God is, what can I tell them?" Moses asked. In the course of 400 years as Egyptian slaves most of the Hebrews had forsaken the worship of the true God and embraced the idols of Egypt. For Moses to declare that he represented the God of their ancestors would not impress them. They would want to know more about this God. What was He like? Could He be trusted to carry out promises made ages earlier?

"Tell the people that my name is 'I am that I am'. Tell them 'I am' is the one who sent you." In this strange-sounding answer to Moses' query God revealed His covenant name Yahweh (or Jehovah) for the first time. The word Yahweh is related to the verb "to be"; God communicated that He is the self-existent one, unchanging from everlasting to everlasting. God also told Moses to remind Israel that He had revealed Himself to their forefathers Abraham, Isaac and Jacob and had pledged the land of Canaan to them.

"So go," God urged Moses, "tell the elders of Israel that I appeared to you. Assure them that I have seen what the Egyptians have done to them and that I promise to deliver them from their misery and lead them back to Canaan. They will listen to you. Then you are to go to

Pharaoh and ask him for permission to take a three-day journey into the desert to offer sacrifices to me. Pharaoh will not grant permission until forced to do so. Not until I strike the Egyptians with great wonders will he let you go. When he does, the Egyptians will be so favorably disposed towards you that they will give you whatever you ask of them."

God told Moses exactly how the events would unfold. He had determined in advance how He would carry out the next stage in the history of His covenant people.

▪ 38 ▪ Moses' Commission

Exodus 4   *Date: circa 1450 B.C.*

IN SPITE OF God's assurances, Moses did not rise to the occasion. Forty years of exile had so disheartened him that he found it hard to believe the Lord's promises. "What if the people won't listen to me? What if they don't believe that you appeared to me?" he said.

"What are you holding in your hand?" God asked him.

"A staff," Moses replied.

"Throw it onto the ground," God ordered. Moses did so and instantly his shepherd's staff turned into a snake. He ran from it, but God commanded him to grab it by the tail. Overcoming his fear, Moses did so and the snake became a shepherd's staff again.

"Now put your hand inside you cloak," God instructed. When Moses pulled his hand back out of his cloak he saw to his horror that it was badly infected with leprosy.

"Put your hand back into you cloak," God said. Moses did so and his hand was restored to full health. "If the people won't believe you show them these miracles," God continued. "If they still won't believe you then take some water from the Nile and pour it on the ground. It will turn into blood when it hits the earth."

In spite of these miraculous signs Moses still resisted. "Oh Lord, I have never been a good public speaker. I am slow of speech and tongue." For the past forty years he had spoken the Midianite language. It was related to Hebrew, but over 400 years of separate development had become significantly different. Furthermore, he had been raised as an Egyptian prince and was fluent in Egyptian. His knowledge of Hebrew, learned as a young child, was poor. However, God reminded him that He had created his mouth and would help him speak.

Moses continued to resist God's appointment. "Oh Lord," he begged, "Please appoint someone else." The disappointing failure of his life had made the once impetuous, ambitious young man fearful, hesitant and unbelieving in his old age. God told him that those who had wanted to kill him back in Egypt had died, and that his brother Aaron, an eloquent speaker, had set out to find him and would act as his spokesman. Eventually, after more reassuring, Moses submitted.

Moses made his way home but did not tell his family about the burning bush and his encounter with God. Instead, he told his father-in-law that he wanted to go back to Egypt to see if any members of his family were still alive. He took his wife Zipporah, his sons Gershom and

Eliezer and, with his shepherd's staff in hand, set off on the long journey back across the desert. On the way Zipporah had their two sons circumcised. As a family they were identifying once more with the people of God: circumcision was a sign of His covenant with them.

God also led Moses' brother Aaron to meet them in the desert. The two brothers were reunited at Mount Horeb, where Moses told Aaron all that God had said and the miracles He had performed. Then the brothers made their way together back to Egypt.

▪ 39 ▪   God Encourages Moses But Hardens Pharaoh's Heart

Exodus 5, 6   *Date: circa 1450 B.C.*

ONCE THEY arrived in Egypt, Moses and Aaron met with the elders of the Israelites. Aaron related everything the Lord had told Moses, and Moses performed the miracles before them to prove the story's veracity. When the elders heard about the Lord's concern for them their hopes rose and they bowed before Him in worship.

Next Moses and Aaron headed for the royal palace and, as representatives of Egypt's great labor force, were ushered into the throne room. They did not demand the complete liberation of their people. Instead they asked for a three-day holiday to go and offer sacrifices to their God. Pharaoh haughtily dismissed the request out of hand. "Who is this Lord of yours? I don't know him. I will not obey him. I will not let you go," he responded. Then he ordered the Egyptian task masters to cease providing the Hebrew slaves with straw, which was used as a binding agent in the baked mud bricks used for his grand construction projects. They would have to go and get their own straw, yet Pharaoh still insisted that they produce the same number of bricks.

The distressed Jews simply could not meet Pharaoh's demand. Although their leaders appealed to him, their heart-rending requests fell on deaf ears. The pitiless ruler accused them of laziness and insisted they produce their full quota of bricks. In despair they turned on Moses. "May the Lord judge you for what you have done to us!" they shouted. "You have turned Pharaoh against us with your demands. You will be the cause of our death!"

God had told Moses in advance that He would harden Pharaoh's heart—he was prepared for that, but not for negative response of the people whom he was trying to help. Yet the Jewish elders were right; Moses' actions had made things worse instead of better. "Lord, what are you doing? Why did you send me to Pharaoh? Instead of saving your people things have only got worse for them!" he lamented.

God gently reminded Moses who He was: the God of their forefathers who had not only revealed Himself to them but who had tied Himself to them with a series of covenants. He again pointed out that He was not indifferent to His people's plight, and that His purpose was immutable, unchangeable. His mighty hand would cause such a change in the hard-hearted Pharaoh that he would actually drive the people out of his country. "Go and tell the Israelites that I will deliver them," God said. "I will take them as my own people and I will be their God. I

will be known among them as the one who delivered them from slavery and brought them to the land I promised to your fore-fathers." Encouraged, Moses shared these things with the leaders of Israel, but they were so disheartened they had no ears for him.

"Lord, if my own people won't listen to me, why would Pharaoh listen to me?" Moses asked.

"I have made you like a god in Pharaoh's eyes," the Lord said, "and Aaron like your prophet. Go to Pharaoh and declare to him everything I command you. I will harden his heart, and even though I will cause miracles and wonders he will resist all you say. Then I will accomplish such a wonder that he will let you go. Eventually the Egyptians will recognize that I am the Lord. Now go back to Pharaoh. When he asks you for a miracle throw your staff to the ground and it will turn into a snake once again."

Eventually the proud king would be forced to acknowledge that God is omnipotent and that nothing and no one can prevent Him from delivering His people. Their salvation from bondage would be such a hugely significant, miraculous event in the life of Israel that it would be etched forever on their national consciousness. If ever they doubted that they were God's special people, they only needed to look back for confirmation to this period in their history.

• 40 • The First Four Plagues

Exodus 7-8   *Date: circa 1450 B.C.*

FORTIFIED BY God's promises, Moses and Aaron returned to the royal palace to repeat their request. When Pharaoh asked them to perform a miracle to prove that their Hebrew God had really sent them, Moses had Aaron throw his staff to the ground and, as in the desert, it turned into a snake. Pharaoh called upon his magicians to do the same thing and, remarkably, they managed to duplicate the miracle! Their magic wands also turned into snakes when cast to the ground!

Pharaoh was acting as Satan's representative, so it was the power of Satan that enabled Egypt's sorcerers to perform their feat. To demonstrate that God was more powerful than Satan, however, Moses' snake went after the evil magicians' snakes and swallowed them up! Moses then grabbed his snake by the tail and it promptly turned back into a shepherd's staff, leaving Pharaoh's sorcerers without the symbols of their authority.

Ancient Egyptians worshipped the serpent. This miracle was like a warning shot: their gods would not be able to save them; they would be completely overwhelmed by Jehovah, the God of the Israelites. Nevertheless Pharaoh hardened his heart and would not let the people go. As a result a horrific succession of ten plagues was about to strike Egypt.

First the Lord directed Moses to intercept Pharaoh on the banks of the Nile. There Aaron struck the Nile with Moses' staff—and the river turned into blood. Egypt was utterly dependent on the Nile; it was their source of life. Suddenly their life-giving river turned into a reeking cesspool of death. Blood, a symbol of death, was another warning of the fate of those who resist God. Once again Pharaoh's sorcerers were able to duplicate the miracle, making an already

desperate situation worse. To survive the people had to dig wells until the blood had washed out of the Nile. Still, Pharaoh refused to budge.

A week later the Lord told Moses to inform Pharaoh that because of his stubbornness the land would swarm with frogs. Aaron then swung his staff in every direction and millions of frogs rose out of the streams and canals. They covered everything and everyone and were everywhere, even in Pharaoh's bed! Again his sorcerers could produce yet more frogs but could not provide relief. Pharaoh was forced to summon Moses and Aaron and beg them to pray to the Lord to take away the frogs, promising to let the people go to offer their sacrifices.

"I give you the honor of choosing the time when you would like to be rid of the frogs," Moses said cheekily.

"Let it be tomorrow," Pharaoh said.

"It will happen as you wish so that you may know that there is no one like the Lord our God," Moses replied. "The only frogs left will be those remaining in the Nile." He cried out to the Lord in prayer and the next day the droves of frogs died. The people swept the little carcasses into huge heaps, the stench of which filled the land. However, when Pharaoh saw that this second plague had passed, he hardened his heart once again.

The Lord then told Aaron to strike the dust of the ground with Moses' staff. When he did so Egypt's dust turned into gnats. The Egyptians were famous for their personal hygiene, especially their pagan priests. These men were so meticulous that they would shave their heads and bodies every three days to ensure that they harbored no vermin. Being covered with gnats caused them to feel disgusting and disqualified them from carrying out their religious duties. This was also the first one which Egypt's sorcerers were not able to reproduce. "This is the finger of God," they told Pharaoh, forced to acknowledge the Lord's sovereignty. Nevertheless Pharaoh continued to harden his heart.

The first three plagues had not only afflicted the Egyptians but had also struck the Jews in Goshen. That was about to change. Henceforth the Lord would distinguish between His people and their oppressors.

The fourth plague consisted of dense swarms of flies invading everything from the royal palace to the humblest hut. They ruined everything in Egypt with which they came into contact—while the land of Goshen was spared. At the prospect of total ruination Pharaoh began to waver. He called for Moses and Aaron and told them that they could have their religious holiday, but they were not to go out into the desert. He still wanted to maintain some control over those he considered his slaves.

Moses refused to bargain. The Lord had told them to take a three-day journey into the desert and they had to obey him. Pharaoh relented, but warned them not to stray too far away. Moses, in turn, warned Pharaoh not to turn back on his word. He prayed for relief, and not a fly remained in the land. Once again Pharaoh refused to let the people go.

Exodus 9-10   *Date: circa 1450 B.C.*

THE LORD instructed Moses to tell Pharaoh that if he continued to resist He would strike the Egyptians' livestock with a plague that would kill their livestock but leave that of the Israelites untouched. That is exactly what happened. Pharaoh's investigators reported that while their own livestock was dying off in droves not one animal belonging to the Israelites had died. Pharaoh still refused to relent...

The sixth plague, like the third, struck Egypt without warning. God instructed Moses to throw handfuls of ash from a furnace into the air in Pharaoh's presence. As the dust settled, the Egyptians and their remaining cattle broke out in festering sores and boils. Nevertheless Egypt's arrogant dictator still refused to give in.

The Lord then told Moses to warn Pharaoh that if He did not let the Jewish people go He would unleash a storm of unequaled ferocity. He was also to point out that Jehovah God could easily have wiped them out by now but had kept them alive to show His power, so that His name might be held in awe throughout the earth. Then, while the land of Goshen enjoyed a lovely, balmy day, the rest of Egypt experienced a storm unlike any in its entire history. It lacerated the land. Wild thunderclaps accompanied huge hailstones and lightning. The seventh plague destroyed everything exposed in the fields—people, animals and crops.

Pharaoh quickly summoned Moses. "This time I have sinned. The Lord is right and I and my people are in the wrong," he said, and he asked Moses to plead with God for the hail to stop. God answered, but Pharaoh's seemingly contrite heart hardened yet again, and he would not let the people go.

Moses informed Pharaoh that because of his stubbornness, swarms of locusts—so dense that they would cover the earth—would devour what was left of the food supply. When his advisers begged him to let the Israelites go because the land already lay in ruins, Pharaoh summoned Moses and Aaron and asked them whom they were planning to take into the desert for worship.

"All of us will go," Moses replied. "Our wives, our children, our cattle—every single one of us will celebrate this festival to the Lord." Pharaoh didn't like that. He feared his slaves would make a break for freedom if he let them all go. If he kept their women and children behind, then he could ensure that the men would return home after their festival. Angrily he drove Moses and Aaron from his presence.

Moses stretched out his staff. Suddenly an east wind carrying swarms of locusts began to blow over the land. The thick carpet of insects devoured what little had not been destroyed by the hail. No greenery was left in the land.

Pharaoh again seemed quite contrite. "I have sinned against you and your Jehovah God," he acknowledged. "Now forgive me and pray that this deadly plague would be taken away." When Moses prayed the wind changed direction, picked up speed, and carried the hordes of locusts into the sea. However, Pharaoh still would not let the people go.

The ninth plague also struck without warning. God told Moses to stretch his hand heavenwards, and when he did the land was plunged into utter darkness. The blackness was so dense that no one could move. This was a direct assault on one of the Egypt's chief gods, the sun god Ra, a god considered so important that his name was incorporated into the word pha*ra*oh itself. Every one of the immobilized and terror-stricken Egyptians would have realized their god was impotent before Jehovah, the God of the Hebrews, who continued to grant the light of day to His people in Goshen.

After three terrible days of pitch darkness Pharaoh summoned Moses once again. "Go serve the Lord, you and all you people. Just leave your flock and herds behind!" Moses knew that if the people's livestock remained in Egypt they would come back for them, so he flatly refused Pharaoh's offer. "We will not leave behind a single animal," he said. "We will use some of our animals as sacrifices to our God and until we know what He wants of us we are not leaving a single hoof."

Pharaoh lost his temper. He ordered Moses out of his sight, threatening to take his life if he ever saw him again. Before leaving Moses told him there would be one last plague, an event of such severity that he, Pharaoh, would actually drive the Israelites out of the country. "The Lord will pass through the land and slay every first-born son, from your own son down to that of the lowliest slave girl. Even the first-born among your remaining cattle will perish. The wailing throughout Egypt will be like nothing ever heard here before. Among the Israelites, however, all will be quiet—you won't even hear a dog barking there. Then you will know that the Lord distinguishes between the Egyptians and the Israelites. The officials standing here will come and bow before me and beg us to leave," he said. Then he turned on his heel and left the royal palace.

▪ 42 ▪ The Final Plague and the Passover

Exodus 12   *Date: 1447 B.C.*

THE TENTH plague would be such a momentous event that it was in a category by itself. Moses explained to his people what was about to happen: On the tenth day of the month the head of each household was to take an unblemished, year old male lamb or kid goat and personally look after it for four days. Then they were to slaughter those lambs at dusk without breaking any of its bones, and smear some of its blood onto the sides and tops of the doorframes of their huts. They were to roast the animal's meat and eat it with bitter herbs and unleavened bread. They were to do so quickly, dressed as though ready to travel at a moment's notice: cloaks tucked into their belts, staffs in hand, and wearing their sandals. Future generations would commemorate this as the Feast of Unleavened Bread.

Under no circumstance were they to go outside after dark, for that night the Lord's Angel of Death would pass through Egypt and kill every first-born, whether man or animal. However, any house that had blood smeared on the top and sides of its doorframes would be spared. And that is what happened. At midnight the Angel of the Death struck all the firstborn males in the land of Egypt, from the crown prince down to the prisoner in his cell and the beast in its stable. The heart-rending weeping and wailing could be heard across the land as one Egyptian family after another discovered its dead.

God instructed Moses to ensure that this dreadful event would be remembered in the future by means of a special sacrifice and celebration. When, eventually, they settled in Canaan and their children asked them about its meaning they were to explain that they were remembering the "Passover sacrifice": because a lamb had died in their place the angel of death had "passed over" them when he struck down the Egyptians.

▪ 43 ▪ The Exodus

Exodus 12 *Date: circa 1447 B.C.*

PHARAOH'S stubborn defiance of God was the immediate reason for the plagues, but the rest of the Egyptians were also affected because they shared in the guilt of their rulers. They had carried out their leader's awful commands and for years had kept the Israelites in terrible and ruthless bondage.

Pharaoh called Moses and Aaron again and this time his will appeared to be broken. "I have sinned against the Lord your God and against you," he said. "Go, take your possessions and worship the Lord just as you please. And… please bless me," he implored. He had lost his foolish contest with Jehovah. Now he wanted to get rid of the people whose omnipotent deity had created such havoc. The rest of the Egyptians also feared for their lives and urged the Israelites to leave at once.

Moses instructed Israel to ask the Egyptians for gold, silver and clothing, which they did not hesitate to give. God fulfilled the promises made centuries earlier that when they left Egypt they would not do so empty-handed (Gen. 15:14; Ex. 3:21). The Egyptians proved the truth of the latter half of that age-old promise: that God would curse those who cursed Abraham's descendants.

Most of Israel had turned to idol worship during their long stay in Egypt (Josh. 24:14; Ezek. 20:6-9), so there was nothing about them which merited God's favor. His affection for them was based solely on the covenant He had made with Abraham and, as such, was an act of unmerited grace. Not even their faithlessness could thwart God's purposes or keep Him from fulfilling His promises. However, the plagues had renewed

Israel's faith in Jehovah God. After witnessing such mighty acts on their behalf there could be no reason for them to return to their idols. In the course of their history their prophets would refer again and again to these mighty acts of God leading up to their deliverance from Egypt as proof that they were, indeed, God's special covenant people.

The nation gathered together at Rameses, one of the cities they had been forced to build, and under Moses' supervision they were organized into army-like divisions and set out for a place called Succoth. Among the ranks and files marching towards the desert a small group of men carried an ancient coffin containing Joseph's mummified body. He had insisted some 400 years earlier that when they eventually returned to the land God had promised their forefathers they were to take his remains and re-bury them there. Joseph had never doubted that the people would one day return to Canaan.

Many Egyptians joined the Israelites in their exodus. There had been some intermarriage (Lev. 24:10) and some Jews bought Egyptian slaves prior to their departure (Ex. 9:44) while others, including court officials, had grown to fear the word of God. Through the rite of circumcision these people could become full participants in the Jewish community.

The Israelites did not need to wonder which direction they should go because the Lord created a special cloud, visible to all, which led them forward. It also served as a shield, sheltering the people from the baking desert sun (Ps. 105:39), and at night it turned into fire and illuminated the area below. No matter how often Israel rebelled, strayed or murmured during their desert wanderings God never took the cloud away from them (Neh. 9:19).

The shortest way to Canaan was northwards along the coast road, but that route would take them through Philistine territory, and the Philistines were renowned warriors. The Israelites were but recently emancipated slaves. Not only were they untrained for war, the abject humiliation to which they had been subjected for centuries had left its mark: they were not yet capable of taking decisive action when facing great odds, and their faith was still so feeble it could not bear much opposition. There was much that God needed to teach them before they were ready for active service.

God led the people southwards, away from Canaan, for He had told Moses that He would take Israel to worship Him at Mount Horeb in the Sinai Desert (Ex. 3:12). Although the route they were taking was in the right direction it was blocked by the Red Sea. It appeared as if the pillar of cloud had led them into a dead end, with the sea on one side and the desert on the other. Any military force coming up behind them would be able to mow them down.

• 44 • Crossing the Red Sea

Exodus 14-15   *Date: circa 1447 B.C.*

PHAROAH'S SPIES informed him that the former slaves had worked themselves into a cul-de-sac between the sea and the desert. He and his officials—the very ones who had begged him to let the Israelites go—thought that they had been given a golden opportunity to recapture their former work force. Pharaoh quickly mobilized his army and, leading from the front with his elite battalion of 600 chariots, set off to recapture the cornered Israelites. The plagues had devastated the land of Egypt, but Pharaoh's army, one of the greatest military forces of the ancient Near East, had survived the debacle. That would change in the coming showdown.

When the Israelites saw the Egyptian army closing in on them they were terrified. "Were there not enough graves in Egypt that you led us into this wilderness to be killed?" they cried to Moses and the Lord. "Didn't we ask you to leave us alone? It would have been better for us to serve the Egyptians than to die here!" How quickly they forgot God's displays of power on their behalf before they left Egypt. Although it appeared to them as if the Lord had deserted them, He was merely setting the stage for their enemies' destruction.

"Fear not," Moses told the people. "Just stand still and wait. The Egyptians you see today you will never see again. The Lord will fight for you." In an impossible situation not of their own making there was nothing to do but to wait in silent expectancy for the Lord to work out His salvation on their behalf (Isa. 26:3). Suddenly the command of the Lord came to Moses: "Stop crying out to me and move forward! Lift your rod, stretch it over the sea and divide it. Then walk through the dry land which will appear!"

Then the Angel of the Lord[7] who had been travelling in front of the Israelite divisions together with the cloud moved between them and the Egyptians. Throughout the night the

---

[7] Many theologians believe that most references to the Angel of the Lord in the Old Testament refer to appearances of the pre-incarnate Christ, the second person of the Trinity. The Angel of the Lord sometimes appeared in human

cloud plunged the Egyptian side into darkness but gave light to the Israelite side. And when Moses stretched his rod over the sea the Lord caused a strong east wind to blow all night so that the waters divided. The next morning they were able to walk across the dry seabed to the other side. When everyone had crossed safely the cloud moved again, enabling the Egyptians to pick up their pursuit. Rashly Pharaoh gave the order to follow Israel across the sea bottom. The Lord then caused their chariot wheels to jam, throwing them into confusion and panic.

"Stretch your hand over the sea," the Lord directed Moses. When he did the waters flooded back and the Egyptian army was drowned. Soon the soldiers' corpses covered the shoreline. When the people of Israel saw the Lord's tremendous power at work against Egypt on their behalf they feared Him and put their trust in Him and in His servant Moses.

The crossing of the Red Sea became one of the great defining moments in the history of ancient Israel. Not only did the event make a huge impression on their enemies at the time (Josh. 2:10-11), the Old Testament prophets referred to it afterwards as irrefutable proof of Jehovah God's remarkable working on behalf of His people (Neh. 9:9; Ps. 106:7-8; Isa. 51:15; Nah. 1:3-4, etc.).

●●●●●

The enemy was no more. The Egyptian slave masters were dead. At long last the Israelites were free from oppression, free to become what Jehovah God intended them to be. Moses and the people's first response was a great redemption hymn, the Bible's first song, while Miriam, Aaron and Moses' sister, led the women in a special worship service of their own. Indeed, God's people had much to sing and celebrate: His redemptive power and grace had turned their groaning, sighing and crying into praise and worship. They sang about His triumphs, His glory, His faithfulness and His mercy to them, and how He had thrown the enemy's horses and riders into the sea and dashed them to pieces. The Lord God had become their redeemer, their salvation, their strength and their song. No one had ever thought of God in those terms until that time.

The Israelites recognized that God had come to view Pharaoh and his army as His enemy because of their treatment of them, the people on whom He had set His love. They marveled at the effortless ease of God's glorious victory over their oppressors and His amazing, loving kindness towards them. "Who is like You, O Lord, among the gods?" they asked rhetorically. "Who is like you in holiness, fearful in praise and doing wonders?"

Israel's song of deliverance reflected a confidence they did not have when they were serving the enemy as defeated slaves. When the surrounding nations—the Edomites, the

---

form (Hos. 12:3-4), and sometimes as fire (Ex. 3:2; 14:19). He would speak in the first person as the Lord Himself (Gen. 22:15-18; Ex. 3:2) or was associated directly with God: "*Pay attention to him and listen to him: he will not forgive your rebellion, since my Name is in him. If you listen carefully to what He says and do all that I say...*" (Ex. 23:19; (Gen. 48:15-16). The presence of the Angel of the Lord was as good as the presence of the Lord Himself (Ex. 23:20, 23).

Moabites and the Canaanites—heard about these events, they would tremble in fear of Jehovah, who had proven Himself mighty to save those upon whom He had set His affections. Nothing could resist the power of almighty Jehovah God. He would, beyond any shadow of doubt, complete the undertaking that He had begun on their behalf: "in your unfailing love you will lead the people you have redeemed... to your holy dwelling".

The people's confidence was not misplaced. Even though they would face numerous adventures and enemies in the centuries ahead, the conclusion of the divine enterprise was never in doubt. Their song on the shore of the Red Sea ended with the glorious truth that "the Lord shall reign forever and ever".

· 45 ·   Food and Drink

Exodus 15:22-27   *Date: circa 1447 B.C.*

AT LONG LAST Israel could travel unhindered to their rendezvous with God at Mount Horeb, deep in the southern part of the Sinai Peninsula. They turned their backs on the Red Sea and headed into an inhospitable wasteland that would test the most intrepid travelers. Just as they had been utterly dependent on God for their salvation from slavery so they had to learn utter dependence on God's grace for daily sustenance.

After three day's journey through the hot, dusty desert they reached the first oasis, a place called Marah. There they discovered, to their consternation, that the water was so bitter it was not fit to drink. They had started their journey with a song on their lips and a light heart. Now, just three days later, they were grumbling and complaining about water. Reality was setting in. It was becoming clear that walking with God was not going to be easy. There would be disappointments and discouragements.

Although it was God's cloud that had led them to these bitter waters, they complained to Moses, and he cried out to the Lord on their behalf. The Lord commanded Moses to throw a piece of wood lying nearby into the water. When he did the water turned sweet.

After the people of Israel had quenched their thirst God addressed them again. He told them that if they listened to and obeyed His commandments He would not afflict them with any of the diseases that had afflicted the Egyptians. Their obedience or lack thereof had played no role in their salvation, but now that they were redeemed people God laid claim to their obedience, not as a harsh slave-master as the Egyptians had been, but as their Redeemer-Lord.

From the bitter waters of Marah, the cloud led the Israelites to a substantial oasis called Elim. It consisted of twelve springs and a large copse of palm trees. After a period of refreshment there God led the people even deeper into the desert.

Moses knew the inhospitable terrain well from the days—not long ago—when he was herding sheep in that region. Keeping a flock of sheep alive in such an environment was a challenge; keeping thousands of people alive in such a wasteland required ongoing miracles. When the food ran low the people again complained against Moses. "If only the Lord had taken our lives back in Egypt, where we had meat and bread to eat" they muttered. "You've led us into this wilderness to let us die of hunger!" God had promised to meet with them at Mount Horeb, yet they questioned whether He would provide for them on the way (Ps. 78:19).

The Lord responded to their ingratitude by giving them meat. That evening an immense migration of quails, not uncommon in the Middle East, settled on the camp. The people caught as many of the exhausted birds as they wanted, and plucked and cooked them for supper. The next morning the Lord showered the people with a white, coriander-like substance. When the people woke up and saw the small, round, white foodstuff all around them they had no idea what it was. They named it "manna", which means, "What is this?" Every morning, before the sun grew warm and melted it, they were to gather just enough to see them through the day. Any leftovers would be infested with maggots by the following day. Only on the sixth day of the week could they collect double because the seventh day was to be their day of rest. One small pot of manna would be stored in a golden pot and kept as a memento of God's goodness to them. It would resist spoiling for centuries (Heb. 9:4). For 40 years the Israelites would collect manna every morning, grind it into flour and bake it into bread-like loaves (Num. 11:8). Without fail God supplied them with as much of this "angel food" (Psalm 78:25) as they needed for as long as they needed it.

Although the food issue was resolved, the water issue was not. The community traveled through the desert to a place called Rephidim, where their water supply again ran out. Once again they had the opportunity to present their needs to God in prayer and trust him for a solution, and once again they failed the test of faith. Once again they condemned Moses for their problem and demanded from him that which only the Lord could provide. "Your quarrel is not with me," Moses told them. "Why are you putting the Lord to the test?" Then he turned to the Lord. "Lord, these people are almost ready to stone me," he cried out. "What will you have me to do?"

"Take some of the elders of Israel and walk into the desert to the big rock of Horeb. Strike it with the rod you struck the water of the Nile with, and I will cause water to flow from the rock." When Moses did as he was told copious amounts of fresh water burst from the rock, enough to satisfy all their needs. Moses renamed the place "Massah and Meribah", which means "Testing and Quarreling". The word "rock" would become a title for Jehovah God. He would become known as their Rock of Salvation (Deut. 32:15).

• 46 • The Amalekites Attack and Moses' Father-in-law Pays a Visit

Exodus 17:8-18:27   *Date: circa 1446 B.C.*

THE TRIALS the Israelites had faced in the wilderness so far pertained to the provision of their daily needs. One day, out of the blue, they faced a different kind of trial.

In deserts wells and oases were highly prized and often fought over by competing tribes (Gen. 21:25; 26:19, 20; Ex. 2:17; Num. 20:19; Jud. 5:11). News that water had become available from the Rock near Rephidim must have spread fast in that parched land. The Amalekites, a tribe of desert dwellers descended from one of Esau grandsons (Gen. 36:12), evidently decided that they wanted control of the new oasis and attacked Israel to gain possession of it. This was the first time that Israel was called upon to do some fighting. As slaves God had not called on them to fight. Now that they were a free people, however, they were expected to fight for their God-given privileges. Moses appointed a trusted man named Joshua to lead Israel against the Amalekites, while he promised to intercede to God on their behalf.

The battle commenced when the Amalekites attacked Israel from the rear, where the weakest stragglers were trailing (Deut. 25:17-18). Joshua quickly moved his untrained slaves into position against the hardened Amalekite warriors; humanly speaking they didn't stand a chance.

Moses, Aaron and a trusted companion named Hur climbed to the top of a hill from where they could watch the battle and pray. As long as Moses held up his hands in prayer Israel prevailed, but when his arms got tired and dropped the Amalekites prevailed. The battle see-sawed back and forth, in time with Moses' arms. Finally Aaron and Hur found a big rock for Moses to sit on and held his arms aloft for the rest of the day. In response to Moses' ongoing intercession God turned the tide, and Joshua and his band defeated the Amalekite marauders.

After the Amalekites were routed the Lord told Moses to write the event into a memorial book. He also promised that one day the Amalekites would be completely annihilated. Moses responded by building an altar and calling it "Jehovah-Nisse", which means "the Lord our Banner".

∙∙∙∙∙

News travels fast in the desert. When Moses' father-in-law heard about all that God had done through Moses for the people of Israel he decided to pay them a visit. Moses' wife Zipporah and their two sons Gershom and Eliezer, whom Moses had sent back home during his conflict with Pharaoh, came with him. They caught up with Israel at Rephidim.

After showing them around the camp, Moses told them all about their miraculous deliverance from Egypt, the trials they had experienced in the desert, God's gracious provision of food and water, and their recent victory over Amalek. When his father-in-law heard everything that God had done for His people he acknowleged that Jehovah had proven Himself to be greater than all other gods. After offering a burnt offering and sacrifices, Moses, Aaron and the elders of Israel held a banquet in his honor.

Keeping a vast people in line was no small task, and Moses' father-in-law could not help but notice Moses' tremendous workload, particularly with respect to settling disputes between people. One day he took his son-in-law aside. "Listen, my son, the work is too heavy for you. Select some capable men to help you govern this nation," he advised.

Moses took the matter to the Lord, who affirmed the rightness of that suggestion (Num. 11:14). He then chose trustworthy, god-fearing men and created a military style hierarchical leadership system. Only those at the top of the pyramid, the leaders of a thousand families, would report to Moses, leaving him with a more manageable workload.

▪ 47 ▪ Israel at Mount Horeb: The Sinaitic Covenant

Exodus 19-20:21   *Date: circa 1446 B.C.*

FOR THREE months the people of Israel traveled southward through the desert to Mount Horeb, also known as Mount Sinai. Then, one day, the mountain appeared on the horizon! They had arrived at the place where God had promised to meet with them. They would spend the next eleven months here, during which time God would inaugurate a new era for this redeemed people. The grounds of His relationship with them would change. Till now He had dealt with them on the basis of the covenant he had made with their patriarch Abraham. Now, at Mount Horeb, He would spell out the conditions for His ongoing relationship with them as His chosen, redeemed people. It would become known as the Sinaitic Covenant.

The Abrahamic covenant was unconditional; it depended solely on God remaining faithful to His age-old promise to Abraham. It was based on unmerited grace—and it had come true. They had become a large nation[8], and after 400 years of oppression He had redeemed them

---

[8] Bible scholars have questioned whether some of the inexplicably large numbers are historically credible. Did Israel really consist of 600,000 males (i.e. more than 2 million people) when it left Egypt? The Bible itself suggests that the number may not have been that large. There were only two midwives attending the entire nation (Ex.1: 15) and the discouraging report of the 12 spies reported that the people of Canaan "are stronger than we are", not something they would have said if Israel's army was overwhelmingly larger than that of the enemy (Num. 13:31). When Moses addressed the people 38 years later he reminded them that when the Lord redeemed them from Egypt He did not do so because they were a great and powerful nation, but that they were, in fact, "the fewest of all peoples" (Deut. 7:7) and that the indigenous Canaanites were "greater and stronger" than they themselves were (Deut. 9:1). One explanation is that the census lists were multiplied by a factor of ten as an expression of faith in God's promise that they would, one day, be virtually innumerable, "like the stars of the sky or the sand on the seashore" (Gen. 22:17). Read publicly on various ceremonial occasions the carefully collated numbers were an affirmation and prophecy that God would bless His already blessed people multiple times, even ten times over! If read as such the book of

from Egypt and was taking them back to the land He had promised (Ex. 2:24; Ps. 105:41-42). He had, as it were, "carried them on eagle's wings" (Ex. 19:4).

The Sinaitic covenant, on the other hand, would be conditional. If they kept its terms God would count them as His treasured possession and turn them into a holy people. The terms would be spelled out in a set of laws and regulations that would set them apart from all the nations of the earth. The new relationship didn't abrogate the Abrahamic covenant—it remained in force. However, it added a new dimension to their relationship with God as a redeemed nation: they were to recognize His supreme authority over them in every area of their lives. He now had a double claim on them. He was both their creator and their redeemer. As such He now intended to exercise His right to rule them, to be their King and lawgiver. Henceforth they were called to fear, serve and obey only Him.

▪ 48 ▪ The Ten Commandments: The First Stone Tablet

Exodus 20:1-12   *Date: circa 1446 B.C.*

THE HEART OF the Sinaitic covenant was the law, the moral essence of which was summed up in the Ten Commandments. The giving of the Ten Commandments was an awe-inspiring event. First the people had to go through a two-day period of ceremonial cleansing, for God could only be approached with the greatest reverence. After that period of preparation God addressed them from the mountain in a voice so loud it could be heard by all. His voice was accompanied by the sound of trumpets, loud thunder and lightning. Awe and terror gripped the people's hearts. If the giving of the law was accompanied by such frightening displays, how much more frightening would violating it be!

First God revealed Himself as the Lord, their God who had brought them out of slavery in Egypt, and then He proclaimed to them the following:

1. *"You shall have no other gods before me".*

Jehovah God was to be the people's sole and supreme object of worship; He was their creator, redeemer and ruler and would not abide rivals.

2. *"You shall not make for yourselves any carved image or any likeness of anything that is in heaven above or on the earth beneath or in the water upon the earth. You shall not bow down to them, nor serve them for I the Lord your God am a jealous God who visits the sins of the fathers upon the children to the third and fourth generation of those who hate Me, but who shows mercy to thousands of those who love Me and keep My commandments".*

Numbers is a celebration of what God had already done for his people as well as an expression of the expectation of yet greater blessing. An example of the ancient Hebrews utilizing this 10-fold poetic licence is when they sang, "Saul has slain his thousands, and David his tens of thousands" (I Sam. 18:7).

This commandment forbade visible representations of God. He, a spiritual being, was not to be worshipped through man-made images but in spirit and in truth. The people were not to contribute anything that appealed to their physical senses in their worship of an invisible God. God described Himself as "a jealous God" who would not tolerate rivals for the affections of His people. The consequences of breaking this commandment would be felt by subsequent generations who were likely to follow the wrong practises of their parents. But to the thousands of people who would lovingly obey the commandment God promised to pour out His mercy.

3. *"You shall not use the name of the Lord your God in vain for the Lord will not hold him guiltless who uses His name in vain".*

The "Name of the Lord" referred to everything Jehovah God had revealed about Himself: His being, His attributes, His word, His titles, and His works (Psalm 20:1; 135:3; John 1:12). This command forbade speaking contemptuously or irreverently about anything that had to do with Him. His people were to fear His glorious name, to hold it in the highest esteem, and to speak of it with awe and sobriety (Deut. 28:58).

4. *"Remember the Sabbath day to keep it holy. Six days you shall labor and do all your work, but the seventh day is the Sabbath of the Lord your God. In it you shall not do any work... for in six days the Lord made the heavens and earth, the sea, and all that is in them, and rested the seventh day. Therefore the Lord blessed the Sabbath day and hallowed it".*

The people were to work for six days and then rest from their labor on the seventh day. That day was to be kept holy, or set apart, as a special day for the Lord.

5. *"Honor your father and your mother so that your days may be long in the land which the Lord your God gives you."*

This commandment was concerned with the preservation of society's basic social order. It enjoined children to esteem, obey and be subject to their parents. They were to refrain from anything that grieved or offended them, seeking instead to imitate all that was good in them (Prov. 6:20; Col. 3:20). The overall principle was that this would result in a healthy life-style, a basic ingredient for a long life.

• 49 • The Ten Commandments: The Second Stone Tablet

Exodus 20:13-17   *Date: circa 1446 B.C.*

THE FIRST FOUR commandments spelled out the people's basic obligations towards God and defined their relationship with Him. The fifth commandment, which showed that parents were to hold authority over their children in the same way as God does over His people, was a bridge to the last five commandments, which pertained to people's relationship with their fellow men.

6. *"You shall not kill."*

The sixth commandment forbade murder and with it all such evil passions as envy, vicious anger, hatred, and desire for revenge (Mat. 5:1,22). God wanted His people to know that He considered human life to be sacred, and that He reserved the right to determine when it would end.

7. *"You shall not commit adultery."*

The seventh command affirmed that the marriage relationship, established in the garden of Eden before Adam and Eve's fall into sin, was the highest, most important, most sacred of all human relationships. God commanded His people to be faithful to their marriage partner for life. The sanctity of marriage was considered foundational for the maintenance of social order.

8. *"You shall not steal."*

In the eighth commandment God established the security and protection of one's personal possessions. His people were not to take that which rightfully belonged to someone else. The command also precluded withholding from God or another person that which was rightfully theirs. (Prov. 21:7; Jer. 17:11)

9. *"You shall not bear false witness against your neighbor."*

The ninth commandment prohibited the sins of slander, flattery and the crime of perjury—any unjust communication that might negatively affect another person's reputation. It sought to inculcate in God's people the habit of speaking truthfully and honestly. Maligning someone's character was a serious offence in God's eyes (Prov. 12:22; Is. 63:8; Zech. 8:16; Rev. 21:8).

10. *"You shall not covet your neighbor's house, or your neighbor's wife, or his manservant, or his maidservant, or his ox, or his donkey, or any thing that belongs to your neighbor."*

The tenth commandment forbade the unlawful desiring of that which belonged to someone else. The first nine commandments condemned overt acts but the final one pertained to the inner life of God's people. The command not to covet, more than any of the other commandments, would reveal the depth of mankind's sinful nature. God knew the secret recesses of His people's hearts. He also knew that wrong desires were the first step towards active, willful sin, and that all sin proceeded from evil thoughts secretly entertained in the heart (Mat. 15:9). He would not be content with mere external obedience or outward religiosity, but required inner sincerity and purity.

This last commandment would be the most difficult, indeed, impossible commandment to keep. It would reveal to the people how utterly hopeless their plight would be if their standing with God depended solely on keeping His law. The law would be God's wonderful guide for their lives, but it was humanly impossible to fulfill it completely. Something more than the law was needed...

• 50 • The Altar

Exodus 20, 24; Deut. 5   *Date: circa 1446 B.C.*

GOD'S SELF-REVELATION as the Holy God on Mount Sinai during the declaration of the Ten Commandments had been accompanied by billowing smoke, violent shaking, lightning, fearful thunder and loud trumpet blasts. The fear of God overwhelmed the people as they instinctively recognized that they were sinners, unable to meet the demands of a holy God.

"Speak to us yourself, but do not have God speak to us or we will die!" they begged Moses. Perceiving that they could not deal with God directly, they feared for their lives and begged Moses to mediate with Him on their behalf.

God was pleased with the people's recognition that they needed a mediator. He later promised that one day He would raise up a prophet from among them into whose mouth he would put His words, just as He had done with Moses (Deut. 18:17-18). That promise was ultimately realized in Jesus Christ.

Moses reassured the people that God's purpose was to test them and instill in them such a reverential fear and awe of Him that they would not dream of violating His commands. He then ascended the mountain into the thick darkness where God was. There God reiterated to him that under no circumstance were they to build idols for themselves. His chosen people were not to worship anyone or anything but Him.

On the day on which the law was given God also provided for the failure to keep it. He instructed Moses to build a simple altar of uncut stones at the foot of the mount. When they failed they were to sacrifice a sheep or goat in recognition of the fact that only if God's righteous judgement of them was deflected onto a substitute was there any hope for them. Although an animal sacrifice could not, in and of itself, meet the judicial requirement of God, it looked forward to the day when God Himself would provide a sacrifice of such merit that it could cover the penalty of all infractions mankind had ever committed.

After Moses had communicated God's words and law the people responded unanimously, "Everything the Lord said we will do!" Early the next day Moses gathered 12 stones representing the 12 tribes, and built another altar at the foot of the mountain upon which he sacrificed offerings to the Lord. After this ratification of the covenant Israel's 70 leading elders—all the representatives of the nation—ascended partway up the mountain and saw the manifestation of God's personal presence. The sight of Him was so amazing that afterwards

Moses struggled to describe it; merely noting that under His feet was something that looked like sapphire, as clear as heaven.

As recently as the day before, anyone but Moses who had dared to approach the mountain would have been killed. Now, however, God invited these same people's representatives to eat and drink in His presence without doing them any harm—such was the power of blood sacrifice, and what it looked forward to and symbolized: the eventual efficacy of the death of Jesus Christ.

After this unique meeting God asked Moses to remain behind in order to receive further instructions and commands, along with a gift of stone tables inscribed with the Ten Commandments. Moses would spend the next 40 days and nights on that mountaintop.

· 51 · The Tabernacle

Exodus 25-27; 30; 36-38   *Date: circa 1446 B.C.*

UP ON THE MOUNTAIN God gave Moses instructions to build a sanctuary in which He promised to dwell among them. This structure, to be built of gold, silver, bronze, valuable fabrics, animal skins, and precious gems, would become known as the "tabernacle". The tabernacle and the rules governing its ceremonies symbolically express the various aspects of God's redemption of His people. It would also keep alive the hope of the fulfillment of God's promises to Adam and the Patriarchs.

The tabernacle complex measured 150 x 75 feet (45 x 23 meters) and was enclosed by a wall of fine, white linen curtains. White symbolized purity; the sinner was, first of all, reminded of the gulf that separated him from God. Right inside the entrance into the outer courtyard stood a bronze altar where animals were sacrificed. No one could approach the actual tabernacle tent without passing by that large, ever-smoking, bloodstained altar, the fire of which was never allowed to go out (Lev. 6:13). It was the place where sin was judged. It communicated the fact that although the punishment for sin was death, a substitutionary sacrifice could atone for sin and restore one's relationship with God.

The second item in the outer courtyard was a bronze, washing basin. It stood between the altar of burnt offering and the entrance into the tabernacle tent. This laver was polished to such a hue that it served as a mirror. It was filled with water and was where the priests cleaned themselves after they had administered the sacrifices on behalf of the people. Sacrificing animals was a messy business, and contact with death caused the priests to be unclean. Nothing unclean could abide in God's presence (Rev. 21:27). In short, purification of sin was symbolized by blood and water.

The tabernacle tent itself was constructed of wooden frames overlaid with gold and set in silver bases. Hanging from these frames were fine linen curtains made of red, blue and purple yarn, elaborately embroidered with cherubim and held together by golden clasps. Three protective layers of durable leathers covered the outside.

The tabernacle consisted of two rooms. A magnificent heavy curtain separated the larger one, known as the Holy Place, from the smaller one, known as the Most Holy Place. It was decorated with images of cherubim, the same angelic beings that had kept sinful man from re-entering the Garden of Eden after the fall. They re-enforced the lesson that sinful man could not freely approach the holy God.

The Holy Place, where priests ministered daily, contained three things: a table overlaid with gold, a golden lamp, and a golden altar of incense. Once a week the priests placed twelve freshly baked loaves of bread on the table along with some pure incense (Lev. 24:5-9). The bread was called the Bread of the Presence as it symbolized the ongoing communion that God made available to the twelve tribes of Israel on the basis of the atoning sacrifices.

The golden lamp was called the menorah (Lev. 24:2,4). It had a central stem with six branches and was adorned with almond-like flower buds and blossoms. The lamp was the source of light in the Holy Place, for the tabernacle had no windows. It was also a symbol of new life, the almond tree being the first tree in the Middle East to bud in the spring. The menorah was kept burning day and night.

The golden altar stood in front of the heavy curtain that veiled the Most Holy Place. It was decorated with horns, the symbol of power and strength. Like most of the furniture in the tabernacle, it had golden rings with gold covered poles running through it so that it could be carried without being touched. This golden altar was known as the altar of incense. Fire taken from the bronze altar of sacrifice in the courtyard would be used to light the incense on this altar (Lev. 16:9, 12-13; Num. 16:46). Incense was a symbol of grace. Those who had been brought into a right relationship with God were free to approach him for worship and intercession.

Only the priests were permitted to enter the Holy Place, and only the High Priest could enter the Most Holy Place. This he did once a year on the Day of Atonement to carry out his duties as the people's representative. The only furniture in this small room was the Ark of the Covenant. It was a chest just over 4 feet long (1.22 meters) and 2 feet wide and high (61 cm) made of acacia wood and overlaid both inside and out with gold. Inside the ark were the stone tablets containing the Ten Commandments and a golden pot of manna. Aaron's rod would be added to the ark at a later date (Heb. 9:4). The tablets of stone were a reminder of God's moral nature and legal demands; the manna of God's sustaining grace, and the rod of God's judgement.

The ark's lid was made of solid gold, with cherubim at each end with their wings spread upwards. This cover was called the "mercy seat" because, on the annual Day of Atonement, the High Priest would slaughter a bullock, enter the Most Holy Place and sprinkle the "blood of propitiation" on it. To propitiate was to placate or appease the wrath of God (Lev. 16).

The space above the ark and between the golden cherubim's wings was where the Shekinah Glory resided. This was the expression used by later Jews to refer to God's divine presence in the form of a cloud, apparently radiant, over the mercy seat (Lev. 16:2). The outer courtyard was lit by natural daylight, the Holy Place by a golden lamp stand, and the Most Holy Place by radiation from the Shekinah Glory.

Whenever the nation travelled the priests carried the ark at the head of the column using two gold-covered acacia poles. Touching the ark was prohibited and punishable by death. The ark itself remained invisible, hidden under a blue leather blanket.

God repeatedly told Moses to ensure that His instructions with respect to the building of the Tabernacle were to be followed exactly. It also came to be known as the "Tent of Meeting" and the "Tent of the Testimony", for there God would meet with His covenant people on the basis of the sacrificial system and rituals which would, one day, be fulfilled in Christ (2 Chron. 6; Ps 24:3; Jer. 17:12; Ezek. 1). It was to be placed in the middle of the Israelite encampment with the tribe Levi—soon to be appointed as the priestly tribe—living in its immediate vicinity (Num. 1:50; 2:17).

▪ 52 ▪ Israel's Priesthood

Exodus 28-29; Leviticus 21-22

GOD HAD redeemed the people of Israel from slavery in Egypt, had established Himself as their God and had condescended to live among them. They remained, however, a sinful people. To prevent His wrath from breaking out against them God ordained a priesthood. Only the priests were permitted to enter into the Holy Place and approach God on the people's behalf, and only their leader, the High Priest, could enter the Most Holy Place once a year. Moses' brother Aaron and his sons were the first to be appointed priests.

God's instructions pertaining to the priests were as detailed and precise as they were with respect to the tabernacle. Their clothing was symbolic in nature and bestowed dignity and honour. These garments were comprised of an ephod or outer robe, a breastplate, a turban and a sash. The garments of the priests, including the undergarments, sashes and turbans, were to be made of fine white, woven linen, which symbolized purity. The high priest was to be provided with two sets of official clothing. One set, worn only when he entered the Most Holy Place on the Day of Atonement, was to be of spotlessly white pure linen (Lev. 16), symbolizing that only the righteous and holy could enter into God's presence. As soon as he emerged from the Most Holy Place on the Day of Atonement he was to remove this garment and put on his "regular" garment, the ephod, breastplate, and turban.

The ephod, or outer robe, was of finely woven linen with blue, purple and scarlet yarns and gold filament. Attached to the shoulders were two onyx stones on which the names of the 12 tribes were engraved. Fastened to the front with gold chains was a breastplate with twelve different precious stones mounted on it. Each stone was engraved with the name of one of Jacob's sons, now the names of Israel's tribes. Thus whenever the High Priest entered the Holy Place it was as though he carried the names of God's people on his heart.

The breastplate also held an object called the "urim and thummin" which were probably two precious stones used by Israel's leaders to ascertain the mind of the Lord (Num. 27:21; 1 Sam. 28:6). Urim meant "curses" or sometimes "fire", while thummim meant "perfections". "Consulting the ephod" became a euphemism for finding out what the appropriate course of action should be (1 Sam. 23:6, 10; 30:7-8).

Underneath the ephod the High Priest wore a loose garment made out of a single cut of blue cloth. Its hem was embroidered with pomegranates. Small gold bells at the bottom could be heard as he moved about the Holy Place. He also wore a turban of fine linen with a plate of pure gold inscribed with the words "Holy to the Lord".

▪ 53 ▪ The Golden Calf

Exodus 32; Deuteronomy 9:7-29   *Date: circa 1446 B.C.*

MOSES REMAINED on the mountain for forty days receiving instructions about the tabernacle and the priesthood. Then God gave him the two stone tablets upon which He had inscribed the Ten Commandments.

As the days, then weeks, went by without a sign of Moses, the people ran out of patience and turned to Aaron. "We don't know what became of this Moses, who brought us out of Egypt" they complained. "You make us a god to go before us," they demanded. Israel had been an idol-worshipping nation prior to their deliverance from

Egypt (Joshua 24:14), and they quickly reverted to their default position.

Aaron caved in to their demands. He asked them to donate their golden earrings, which he forged into a golden calf. It resembled one of Egypt's main idols, Apis. He then introduced it to the people as the god that had led them out of Egypt. He then built an altar and declared the next day to be a special religious holiday. That morning they all rose up early and after fulfilling such religious duties as they saw fit, threw a party.

At this point the Lord told Moses to go down the mountain saying, "The people *you* led out of Egypt have corrupted themselves". By worshiping a golden calf Israel had broken their newly forged covenant with God and God responded by repudiating them. "They have quickly turned from my commands," God explained to Moses, "and made a molten calf before which they are worshipping and which they claim brought them out of Egypt. I have seen this people and they are a stiff-necked people. Leave me alone so that my anger may burn against them and destroy them." If at this critical moment Moses had relinquished his role as mediator, God's judgment would have fallen on them. Once again, however, Moses resorted to intercession on behalf of the Lord's covenant people.

"Lord, why should your anger burn against these people whom *you* brought of out Egypt with *your* mighty hand?" he prayed. He would not let God walk away from His covenant people, even though they had broken their half of the covenant, thus rendering it null and void. In his prayer he appealed to three characteristics of God: His grace, His glory and His faithfulness. He did not deny that the Israelites were a stiff-necked people. He knew that there was nothing in them that God should esteem them, that their only hope lay in God's grace, the same grace that had caused Him to redeem them from Egypt in the first place. He reminded the Lord that even though they were a stubborn people they were, nevertheless, His people. He had purchased them and they were His property!

Moses also reminded God of His glory. How could God be glorified in the eyes of the surrounding heathen nations if He destroyed the very people whom He had previously redeemed? His name would become a reproach among them! The third basis on which Moses interceded was an appeal to God's faithfulness. God had made specific, unconditional promises to the patriarchs in the Abrahamic covenant—how could God go back on those oaths now? God heard Moses' prayer and answered it. The Bible states that the Lord "repented of the evil which He thought to do to His people". He again began to refer to the people as *His* people. Now it was time for Moses to confront the nation.

• 54 • Fellowship Restored

Exodus 32-33   *Date: circa 1446 B.C.*

MOSES MADE HIS way down the mountain carrying the two stone slabs upon which God had written the Ten Commandments. Half way down he met his servant Joshua. This faithful man had waited patiently for the entire period Moses had spent alone with God on the summit.

"There is the noise of war coming up from the camp," Joshua said.

"No," Moses replied, "that is not the sound of war but of merriment."

They descended further. Suddenly the scene below came into view: people were dancing obscenely around the image of a golden calf. In a fit of anger and indignation Moses hurled the stone tablets against the ground and broke them. Then he approached the camp and demanded to know from Aaron what had happened that he had allowed such sin to happen. Aaron was quick to shift the blame.

"The people told me to make them a god because they had no idea what had become of you. When I cast their gold into the fire, this calf came out!" Uncaring about the crowd's response Moses marched through the revelling mass, took hold of the calf, cast it into the fire, ground the molten mass to dust, and threw it into a brook that flowed from the mountain. Then he made the people drink from it (Deut. 9:21).

"Who is on the Lord's side? Let him come to me!" he shouted. The entire tribe of Levi stepped forward. Every one of them had resisted the awful abomination and remained faithful to Jehovah. "Thus says the Lord, the God of Israel, take your sword," Moses called out, "and go from one end of the camp to the other and slay these people." He demanded quick action so that the survivors might come to their senses and not provoke further divine wrath. The Levites responded quickly, killing about 3000 of their fellow Israelites that day. The day ended in shock and dread as people sobered up, realized what they had done and feared that the worst of God's wrath was yet to come. The Levites would later be rewarded for their faithfulness by being put in charge of Israel's religious life (Deut. 33:8-11).

The next morning Moses reminded the people that they had sinned grievously, but he was met with stony silence. There was no evidence of true remorse and genuine repentance. Moses again fell on his face before God. Again he interceded on behalf of this disobedient, unrepentant people. "Oh Lord," he cried out, "These people have sinned greatly. Nevertheless, God, forgive them—even if that means blotting out my name from your book." Moses loved these people with a sacrificial love. For forty days and nights he lay prostrate before the Lord confessing their sin and interceding for them (Deut. 9:18-20). He pleaded with God not to destroy His own people whom He had redeemed; to remember His promises and to be true to His name.

"I will only blot out those who sinned against me," God answered. God's all-consuming holy wrath had been averted. He would not totally destroy the people. He would, however, still punish those who had sinned and remained hard-hearted. Suddenly He struck His unrepentant people with a plague.

▪ 55 ▪ "A Nation Set Apart"
Exodus 34

AFTER THE plague had abated God repeated the promises He had made to Abraham, Isaac and Jacob: He would eventually lead the people away from Mount Sinai and to the fertile, beautiful land that "flowed with milk and honey". He promised to drive out the current inhabitants of the land but added, "I will not personally go with you. If I did, I might destroy you on the way, for you are a stiff-necked people." The people had broken their covenant with Him and forfeited their privileged relationship. On hearing God's threat to withdraw His presence the people, at long last, began to show genuine remorse. As an outward sign of their repentance they removed their jewelry. They now repudiated the golden calf and once again placed Jehovah God at the center of their worship.

Moses again interceded for the now penitent people. "If your presence does not go with us, do not send us from here. It is only your personal presence among us that assures us that you are pleased with us. Without that, what sets us apart from any of the other nations of the world?" God responded by assuring Moses that because he was pleased with him He would, once again, go with them and give them rest. This emboldened Moses to request something he had long wanted to experience.

"Now show me your glory," he asked.

At this God told Moses to hew two new tablets of stone like the ones he had shattered, and ascend Mount Sinai once again. "I will write the words that were on the tablets which you broke," God promised.

When Moses reached the summit the Lord descended in a cloud and revealed His glory to Moses, though He did not reveal His face. At this Moses bowed his head and worshipped. "If I have found grace in your sight, O Lord," he prayed, "then even though this is a stiff-necked people, I pray that you will forgive us, go with us and accept us as your inheritance".

God promised to renew his covenant and do unprecedented miracles on the people's behalf. If they continued to obey His statutes He would lead them into the promised land of Canaan. They were not, however, to enter into any alliances with the Canaanites. Israel was called to be a separate, distinct people.

Moses spent 40 days—his second such stint—with God on the mountain. This time he wrote down all the specific cultural and ceremonial details that God gave him. These were designed to set the nation apart from the surrounding nations and allow them to be completely consecrated to and submitted to Jehovah. The Lord also re-wrote the Ten Commandments on the blank tablets Moses had prepared. "If Israel obeys me fully and keeps my covenant," God said, "then out of all the people on earth you will be my treasured possession. You will be a kingdom of priests and a holy nation" (Ex. 19:5-6).

When Moses eventually came down from Mount Sinai his face radiated brightly from having been in God's presence. When Aaron and the other people saw how the skin on his face shone they were afraid to approach him. The feelings of guilt after their terrible failing prevented them from enjoying the presence of God, even if only reflected through His servant. Moses gave them God's laws and then covered his face with a veil.

Whenever Moses wanted to discern the mind of the Lord prior to the construction of the tabernacle he would withdraw to a tent outside the camp, which he called "the tent of meeting". When he entered it the pillar of cloud descended on the tent. On seeing this, every man would stand at the entrance to this tent and worship. Moses would remove the veil and the Lord would speak to him face to face, as a man would speak to a friend.

▪ 56 ▪ Regulations for Life, Offerings and Feasts
Exodus 21-23; *Leviticus 1-7; 11-19*

GOD SPELLED out very precise regulations designed to set the Israelites apart as a distinct people. These instructions, or "Levitical rules", pertained to everyday living, "kosher" food practises, sacrifices and offerings acceptable to God, and were designed to foster communal solidarity, encourage spiritual growth and give specific content to the way the people were to worship and submit to God.

The rules for everyday living related to such issues as the treatment of slaves, social responsibility, the protection of property and the resolution of personal injuries. They also included detailed procedures concerning defiling skin diseases, unlawful sexual relationships and purification after childbirth. Certain animals, such as pigs, were considered unclean and were not to be eaten. There were strange-sounding prohibitions such as not cooking a kid goat in its mother's milk (Ex. 23:19; 34:26; Deut. 14:21), a common Canaanite practice. These dietary laws made it more difficult for the people to associate with the religious practices of the surrounding nations, who freely ate the forbidden foods in their religious celebrations. The Lord summed it all up by saying, "Be holy because I, the Lord your God, am holy". To be holy was to be set apart for God and distinct from the rest of the world.

In addition to the regulations for everyday living God also gave detailed instructions about the sacrificial system. He outlined at least five different kinds of offerings that the people could bring to the priests to sacrifice on their behalf.

The burnt offering consisted of completely burning a sheep, goat or, for the poor, two birds. The person offering the sacrifice would place their hands on the sacrificial animal's head to identify with it. The priest would then kill the animal, throw its blood against the altar, wash the entrails and legs and burn the carcass in its entirety. God declared that the life of the animal was in the blood, and it was the blood that atoned for sin.

The sin, or purification, offering atoned for a specific but unintentional sin. The fatty portions of the animal were burned while the priests and Levites could eat the remainder as an expression of communion between God, His people and His mediators.

The guilt, or trespass, offering atoned for sins that violated the rights of another and required specific restitution. It was much like the sin offering.

Grain offerings consisted of fine flour or loaves mixed with olive oil, which did not contain leaven or honey. Their purpose was to secure God's good will. A handful of the offered food would be burned with incense giving a pleasant aroma while the rest was given to the priests.

Fellowship or peace offerings were rendered in praise to God. Like the sin and guilt offerings, people were to bring animals that were without defect. The fellowship offering was an expression of thankfulness when the people sensed God's blessing, or in response to the fulfilment of a particular vow.

The sacrificial system communicated the fact that Jehovah God recognized that His people's sins had caused them to be alienated from Him and from each other, but also pointed to the fact that God's wrath could be appeased by a substitutionary sacrifice. However, the endless, ongoing need for animal sacrifices indicated that in and of themselves they were insufficient. They looked forward to some kind of ultimate fulfilment.

The third set of regulations pertained to a cycle of feasts and sacred days. God repeatedly stated that the seventh day of the week, the Sabbath, was to be a day of rest. Once they got to Canaan they were to let the land lie fallow every seventh year. It was to be a year of rest; God promised to bless them sufficiently during the other years to see them through the year of rest. Every fiftieth year was to be a "Year of Jubilee" when debts were cancelled, slaves set free, and land returned to its original owners.

Every spring three feasts were celebrated right after each other. Passover, which celebrated the nation's deliverance from Egypt, took place on the fourteenth day of the month of Abib (March/April). Families would get together, slay a lamb and cook it with bitter herbs. They would remember how God had slain the firstborn sons of the Egyptians but had passed over their homes and spared their sons.

The following week they would celebrate the feast of Unleavened Bread, in which they remembered the Exodus, their rapid departure from Egypt. On the second day of this feast they also celebrated the Feast of First Fruits. In it they celebrated the Lord's provision by presenting the first sheaves of grain along with a burnt offering.

On the sixteenth day of the month of Sivan (May/June) they celebrated the Feast of Weeks. It would later become known as Pentecost, or Harvest Thanksgiving. During it they offered new grain in their thankfulness to God for the harvest.

Four feasts were celebrated during the fall month of Tishri (Sept./Oct). During the Feast of Trumpets (also known as Rosh Hashanah), which fell on the first day of that month, the people were to assemble at the sound of trumpets and present themselves by means of sacrifices to the Lord.

Yom Kippur, the Day of Atonement, fell on the tenth day of that month. It was a day of fasting and prayer, the most solemn day of the year. On that day the High Priest entered the Most Holy Place in the tabernacle to make atonement for sin. Before he entered he first offered a ram and a bull to atone for his own sins. Then he laid his hands on one of two goats and confessed the people's sins, thus symbolically transferring their guilt to the animal. This scapegoat was then released into the desert, indicating the removal of their sin far from them. The other goat was sacrificed as a sin offering. The High Priest then took a censer of burning coals from the altar, onto which he put two handfuls of fragrant incense and, dressed not in his normal, elaborate garments, but in his simple linen clothes, entered the Most Holy Place. He also carried a bowl with bull's blood in it and one with goat's blood, which he sprinkled onto the mercy seat of the Ark of the Covenant. On this solemn day the sins of the people were atoned for.

The feast of Tabernacles, or "Booths", was celebrated from the 15th to the 21st of the month of Tishri. Once settled in Canaan, the people were to make little outdoor shelters of branches in which they would live for the week, relive their journey through the wilderness, and thank God for the bounty of the land. It culminated on the 22nd of the month with the Sacred Assembly during which offerings were offered.

God established the annual cycle of feasts to ensure that the people would never forget how He had redeemed them from slavery and had made a wonderful provision for both their material and spiritual needs. They were to be His very own, truly distinctive and beloved people.

▪ 57 ▪ The Inauguration of the Tabernacle and the Ordination of the Priests

Exodus 39 – 40; Leviticus 9-10; Numbers 1-4　　　　　　　　　*Date: circa 1446 B.C.*

THE COVENANT relationship between God and His people had been restored. Moses had returned after his second forty-day stint on the mountain, had assembled the people and given them the details of their new civic and religious life. He then encouraged them to donate the necessary gold, silver, precious stones, yarns, leathers, woods, and other materials necessary for the construction of the tabernacle. Given this opportunity to show their gratitude the people responded with such overwhelming generosity that Moses had to ask them to stop giving!

The next weeks and months were a blur of activity. Under the supervision of two craftsmen whom God had given special skills and abilities, the tabernacle and its accoutrements began to take shape. It took about six months to complete the project. Moses made sure everything was exactly as the Lord had stipulated; every object was placed in the right location, including the stone tablets of the Ten Commandments into the ark, which in turn was placed in the Most Holy Place.

The tabernacle was placed in the center of the Israelite camp, with the various tribes encamped around it in a systematic arrangement. The Levites, charged with serving in the tabernacle, were separated from the rest of the people and allotted specific areas immediately surrounding the tabernacle's vicinity. Step by step the rabble of redeemed slaves was introduced to a new God-centered sense of order, community and culture.

The leaders of Israel then presented special gifts to the Lord: 6 covered wagons and 12 oxen with which to transport the tabernacle and those of its furnishings that did not need to be hand-carried. These were handed over to the Levites. Next the representatives of the twelve tribes came forward, one per day. Each tribe offered to the Lord exactly the same set of gifts: a silver platter and bowl containing flour mixed with oil for use as a grain offering, a golden ladle filled with incense and a number of animals for burnt offering and fellowship offerings.

Then Aaron and his sons were called to the tabernacle entrance where they were washed, dressed in their ceremonial robes, and consecrated for service. Aaron, the new high priest, was anointed with a special oil (the word "messiah", comes from the Hebrew word for "anointing"). After the anointing, the blood of sacrificed beasts was applied to their right ear lobes, right thumbs and right big toes as a symbol of total obedience. They ate the meat of the sacrificial ram at the tabernacle's door as a sign of communion with God and spent the next week in prayer and worship in the tabernacle.

After the ordination week they celebrated Passover. When all was done Aaron lifted his hands and blessed the people in words taught by God Himself: "May the LORD bless you and keep you. May the LORD make his face to shine on you and be gracious to you. May the LORD lift up his countenance upon you and give you peace." Then he and Moses went into the tabernacle. When they re-emerged God indicated His acceptance of them by revealing His glory with a bolt of fire that consumed the sacrificed animals on the altar. That sacred fire was not allowed to go out.

The people shouted for joy at the fact that God was with them, and then they fell facedown in awe before this supernatural display of His holy presence. The glorious cloud which had led them out of Egypt and which had settled on the peak of Mount Sinai moved over the tent and settled on it. God's glory filled the tabernacle; He, their King and leader, was now living in their midst.

▪ 58 ▪ The Priests Disciplined and the Census
Leviticus 10, 21-22; Numbers 1, 3-4

GOD HAD given Moses detailed instructions concerning the need for personal and ceremonial purity among the priests. They were to treat with respect the sacred offerings which the people brought and perform their duties exactly as proscribed. God emphasized again and again that He was a holy God and His holy name was not to be profaned.

No sooner had the tabernacle and the priesthood been established, however, when Aaron's sons Nadab and Abihu showed contempt for the sacred system. The two brothers, newly consecrated as priests, attempted to light their censers with "strange fire", and offer it to the Lord. It seems that they lit their censers not with fire taken from the brazen altar but with fire that they themselves had kindled, thus effectively presuming that there could be another basis for acceptance with God than substitutionary sacrifice. Fire immediately shot from the presence of the Lord and slew them both.

Moses warned Aaron and the remaining brothers not to display grief over the righteous judgement that had befallen their family members. He and the other priests had to realize that serving God was for real—they were not playing at being priests but were serving a holy God who Himself dictated how He was to be appeased and approached.

The Lord then instructed Moses to take a census of the Israelite community in which every person was to pay half a shekel of silver (about 6 grams). The census, an indication of ownership, was God's way of communicating that He had laid claim to each and every one of them. The amount people were to pay was the same for rich and poor. To the rich it was a very small amount; while no one was so poor that they could not afford it. The money collected was to be used in the service of the tabernacle.

All in all the people spent nearly a year at the foot of the mountain. During that time they had been moulded into a nation with its own unique cultural and religious patterns revealed to them by God. At long last they were ready to move on...

· 59 · The Journey Is Resumed

Numbers 9-12   *Date: circa 1445 B.C.*

THE LORD instructed Moses to make two silver trumpets for Aaron's remaining sons. Different trumpet blasts signified different things: one summoned Israel's leaders, another called the people to fall into marching order, another rallied the people to battle, and yet others were used during worship.

One day the cloud lifted from the tabernacle where it had hovered since the inauguration ceremony. The time had come to resume the journey to the promised land of Canaan. The people packed their belongings, took down their tents and, upon hearing the appropriate trumpet blast, fell into line and followed the cloud northward. The ark, carried by Levites, led the convoy. They were followed by the tribe of Judah and then, in stately order, by the other tribes. The tribe of Dan made up the rear guard. They had arrived at Mountain Sinai as an unruly rabble; they departed as an orderly army with its own unique national identity.

Whenever the cloud set out, Moses prayed, "Arise, O Lord! May your enemies be scattered and flee before you!" and whenever the cloud came to rest he said, "Return to the countless thousands of your people Israel, O Lord!"

Sometimes the cloud lingered only a day or two, sometimes it hung in one place for a month or even a year. At night the cloud looked like fire. When the cloud lifted they moved, and when it hovered over the tabernacle they stayed—there was no predicting the matter; their sovereign Lord led them as He saw fit. The people merely had to watch the cloud to know what to do.

They set out in good spirits—but that soon faltered. A bare three days into their journey they complained about their hardships. God's response to this petty ingratitude was a burst of purging fire that consumed a number of the people on the outskirts of the camp. The people cried out to Moses, and when he interceded for them the fire died down. They called that place Taberah, the Hebrew word for "burning".

Their journey through the wilderness would be marked with repeated acts of ingratitude and rebellion, illustrating not so much the profound impact their new monotheism had on them as the fact that they were prone to rebellion, ingratitude and apostasy. God responded to each provocation with both judgement and mercy.

Not long after the events at Taberah people started complaining about the monotonous manna. The first to complain were not Jews but the non-Israelites who had joined them when they left Egypt. Spurning the Lord's daily provision, they hankered for the meat, fish, fruits and vegetables they had enjoyed back home. Their complaining soon spread through the camp. Once again the people forgot that back in Egypt they had been slaves eking out a marginal existence. Their false, nostalgic ideas about the past led them to despise God's plentiful and nutritious—even if boring—provision for the present. They basically said that being an Egyptian slave was preferable to walking with the Lord towards the Promised Land while enjoying His provision on the way!

Moses was taken aback by their demand. The people were clamouring for the impossible: meat in a place where it simply could not be had. He cried out to God with a very moving lament stating that the burden of caring for these people was simply too great for him. The Lord's response was two-fold. He endowed 70 of Israel's elders with the same spirit He'd granted Moses so that they could help him carry the burden of leadership. The Lord then told them that because the people had clamoured for meat he would judge them by giving so much of it that it would make them sick. Even Moses found that almost impossible to believe, and reminded God of the numbers of people involved. The previous provision of quail had been close to the shores of the Red Sea, where large flocks of exhausted migrating birds would settle after making the crossing. Here, in the middle of the desert, there was no natural supply of meat.

"Is the arm of the Lord too short?" God responded. Suddenly a hard wind blowing in from the distant sea carried huge flocks of quails inland, all the way to the Israelite camp. The meat-crazed people grabbed the dazed, flapping birds, killed them and stuffed some into their mouths and others into baskets. They collected up to 60 bushels per person! When the meat was still in their mouths, however, the Lord struck many of them with a plague. They named that place Kibroth Hattaavah, or "Graves of Craving", after those whom they had to bury as a result of their unseemly craving.

No sooner had Moses recovered from the depressing quail saga when, at the very next stop, his brother Aaron and his sister Miriam started gossiping about his Cushite wife. Zipporah had died and Moses had remarried a Cushite woman. Cushites came from the south of Egypt, in what is Sudan today. Miriam seemed to have resented this woman, possibly because she was black and represented the ruling Egyptian class to which they had once been enslaved.

Miriam had been an amazing woman. When Moses was a baby she had helped save his life and reunited him with his mother. Upon the people's successful crossing of the Red Sea she had led the people in worship. Now, however, she turned against her brother, and infected the malleable Aaron with her venom. Soon the real reason for their underhanded attack became apparent. "Does the Lord only speak through Moses?" they asked rhetorically. "Hasn't He spoken through us as well?" They were jealous of the fact that Moses, their younger brother, was God's chosen mediator.

Moses did not try to defend himself. The Lord then summoned the three siblings to stand before him. Aaron and Miriam were ordered to step forward. "When I reveal myself to my prophets I do so through visions and dreams," the Lord told them. "But that is not the case with my faithful servant Moses. I speak clearly to him, not in riddles but face to face. Why were you not afraid of speaking against him?"

When the cloud lifted the principal instigator, Miriam, had turned white with leprosy. According to the recently received Levitical law people with this infectious disease were to be excluded from the community. She had become an outcast, a pariah. Shocked, Aaron begged forgiveness from Moses and pled on his sister's behalf. Instantly Moses turned to the Lord, "O God, heal her. Please!" God did so but insisted on having her confined outside of the camp for a week to shame her.

"If her father had spit in her face," God said, referring to a cultural practice parents used to shame disobedient children, "would she not have suffered disgrace for a week?" The people stayed where they were until she was allowed back.

· 60 ·   Exploring Canaan and the Rebellion at Kadesh Barnea

Numbers 13-15; Deuteronomy 1   *Date: circa 1445 B.C.*

THE CLOUD lifted and the nation followed it northward to Kadesh Barnea, the last stop before Canaan. The long-awaited conquest was about to be launched. The time to eradicate the idolatrous and irredeemably perverse Canaanites and to claim their inheritance was at hand.

Prior to the offensive the people asked that a band of spies be sent to explore the best approaches and lines of attack. When God ratified this request Moses chose respected men, one from each tribe, and sent them on the mission. "Go up," he instructed them, "and see what the place is like. Find out what the people are like, if their cities are walled, if the land is fertile, where it is forested. Bring back some of the fruits of the land..."

The twelve set off full of hope and with a sense of adventure. For forty days they crisscrossed the land and when they eventually returned they brought back such a huge cluster of grapes that it took two of them to carry it on a pole between them. With bated breath the people gathered to listen to their scouts.

"The land is extremely fertile, flowing with milk and honey," they reported. "But," ten of the scouts continued, "the inhabitants—the Amalekites, Hittites, Jebusites and others—are not just very powerful, they live in strongly fortified, impregnable cities! It is impossible for us to take these cities!" Their report frightened the people.

Two of the spies, Caleb and Moses' aid Joshua, disagreed. "We can do it!" Caleb stated confidently, convinced that God would enable them to overcome all hurdles. "We should go up and take possession of it right away!" He saw the long list of different Canaanite peoples and their fortified cities as a long string of God-glorifying victories, not as impossibilities! But he and Joshua were wasting their breath. "Those people are much bigger and stronger than we are! They are huge! There are even Nephilim among them! We cannot do it. We look like grasshoppers to them!" the others insisted.

The fear-induced distortions and exaggerations of the ten spread like wildfire. Wailing and raging, the people first turned against Moses and Aaron, then against God Himself. Forgotten was the fact that God had devastated Egypt—the most powerful nation the world had seen to date—on their behalf, and that He would surely do the same thing to Canaan's small city-states. Forgotten was the delivery through the Red Sea, the fire and voice at Mount Sinai, the miracles in the desert, the daily provision of food and drink and God's gracious promises. Instead, they abandoned themselves to a frenzied outburst of unreasonable anger and grief. "If only we'd died in Egypt or in the desert," they cried. "The Lord brought us here so these giants can kill us and take our wives and children. Let's choose another leader and return to Egypt!" Once again, slavery in Egypt seemed a better prospect than the adventure of walking with God.

This time both Moses and Aaron fell on their faces before the people and interceded for them. Caleb and Joshua tore their clothes as a sign of their grief, mourning the loss of faith even as they tried to turn the tide of public opinion. "It is a wonderful land," they cried out. "Don't be afraid—just don't rebel against the Lord! If He is pleased with us we will overcome the enemy! The protection over the people of the land is gone!" Deaf to the truths of Caleb and Joshua's fervent pleas and the prayers of the prostrate Moses and Aaron, the people talked of stoning them instead.

Suddenly a frightening display of the glory of the Lord, visible to the whole raging crowd, appeared at the tabernacle. "How long will these people disregard me?" God asked Moses rhetorically. "I will strike them down with a plague and make you into a greater and stronger nation," he said.

"Oh Lord," Moses cried out, "if you destroy the people then the Egyptians will hear about it and your reputation will be ruined. They will suggest that you slaughtered your people in the desert because you were incapable of carrying out your plan. Oh Lord, for your own name's sake, forgive these people, just as you have been doing all along!" The surrounding nations were watching to see how this divine venture would end, and Moses was aghast at the thought that God would allow it all to culminate in disaster, word of which would get back to Egypt. If that happened, Jehovah God would become an object of derision!

The Lord responded by pardoning them once again—but added solemnly, "Not one of you who treated me with contempt will see the land which I promised your forefathers. Only Caleb and Joshua, who had stood alone against the nation, will enter it."

Judgement fell immediately on the ten unbelieving scouts, and all those over the age of twenty were condemned to spend the rest of their lives wandering aimlessly in the desert. Not until every adult lay buried in the sand would their children, the ones they claimed God was out to destroy, take the land.

The people mourned bitterly when Moses reported God's judgment. The next morning they told him that they would, after all, enter the promised land. But it was too late. Moses warned them that the Lord would not accompany them. Any advance would be in their own strength and would be met with defeat. In spite of Moses' protestations some of them rashly formed an army and headed out. They were routed in short order.

• 61 • The Rebellion of Korah

Numbers 16-17   *Date: circa 1445 B.C.*

THE NATION turned its back on Canaan and followed the cloud back into the Sinai desert. It wasn't long before Moses faced another rebellion against his and Aaron's leadership.

Korah was a member of the Kohathite clan of the tribe of Levi that had been commissioned to serve the Lord in the tabernacle (Num. 4:1-20). Korah, however, wanted to be a priest, a position set aside for the sons of Aaron. One day he, along with some Reubenites called Dathan and Abiram and 250 other community leaders, confronted Moses and Aaron. They accused them of failing to make good on the promise to lead them to the promised land, denounced their supposed dictatorial tendencies, and claimed that, in God's eyes, all people were priests. "The whole community is holy and the Lord is with every one of us," they said. "Who are you to set yourselves above us?" However the system of government, which God had established with Israel at Sinai, was not a democracy but a theocracy: God ruling directly through servants He had appointed. For these men to rebel against these servants was an attack on God's rule.

Moses responded by falling on his face before God. When he eventually rose to His feet he announced that there would be a showdown the next day in which the Lord would reveal who was right. Holding censers full of burning incense they were all to appear before the tabernacle and let the Lord choose between them.

The next morning all 250 leaders stood with Moses and Aaron before the tabernacle holding their burning censers. Then the glory of the Lord appeared. "Move away from the tents of Korah, Dathan and Abiram," the Lord warned. Moses quickly shooed the people back from the rebels' tents, leaving them and their wives and children isolated.

"If these men die a natural death," Moses said, "then I am not the Lord's servant. But if the earth swallows them alive then you will know that they were in rebellion against the Lord." He had no sooner finished speaking when the earth ripped open beneath the three ringleaders' feet and swallowed them, their families and everything they owned. While the people scattered, fearing that the earth would swallow them as well, fire from the Lord slew the 250 rebellious leaders still standing with their censers before the tabernacle.

Aaron's son Eleazar was told to collect the scattered censers, hammer them into sheets of bronze and use them to overlay the altar to remind the people that only God's appointed priests, Aaron's descendants, could approach it. God would not abide usurpers.

The next day the people woke up morose, blaming Moses for the events of the previous day. As they crowded angrily around Moses and the tabernacle, God threatened once again to put an end to all of them. Moses and Aaron again fell on their faces to intercede for them. Suddenly Moses rose to his feet and ordered Aaron to do his priestly work. He was to quickly light the incense in his censer with fire from the altar and stand among the people. The plague had already broken out. Aaron stood between the living and the dying in his role as mediator until the plague receded—but not until it had killed 14,700 people.

To settle, once and for all, the question of Moses and Aaron's leadership, the Lord ordered Moses to gather twelve staffs, one from each of the leaders of the twelve tribes. Each staff had its owner's name carved into it, with Aaron's name on the staff representing the tribe of Levi. The Lord then told the people that the staff that sprouted would be the one belonging to the man of His choosing.

The staffs were placed in the Most Holy Place. When Moses collected them the next day Aaron's staff had not only sprouted leaves as though it were still part of a tree, but had budded, blossomed and produced almonds! God established once and for that Israel's priesthood belonged to Aaron and his descendants, and not to anyone else. Aaron's budding rod was subsequently placed in the Ark of the Covenant.

▪ 62 ▪ 38 Years of Wandering in the Desert

Numbers 20   *Date: circa 1445-1405 B.C.*

THE PEOPLE OF ISRAEL wandered aimlessly in the desert for about 38 years. One after another the adults of the generation which had left Egypt died off. Miriam, Moses' sister, also died and was buried in the desert.

The people complained yet again to Moses: "Why did you bring us out of Egypt to this terrible place. There is no water here!" Once again Moses and Aaron fell on their faces before the Tabernacle and again the glory of the Lord appeared to them. The Lord then told Moses to take his staff, go to a nearby rock, and speak to it. Then water would come gushing out. Moses rose from the ground and, staff in hand, walked to the rock. Then, suddenly, years of frustration burst from him. After all these years this stubborn people, for whom he had stood in the breech time and again, still complained, still failed to trust the Lord to meet their basic needs. Nothing seemed to have changed...

"Listen, you rebels!" he shouted. "Do you want us to provide you with water from this rock?" Then he struck the rock twice with his rod. Water did, indeed, flow from it, but the Lord was not happy with Moses' violation of His command to speak to the rock, not to strike it. Because of this act of disobedience Moses too would be denied entry into the Promised Land. He named that place Meribah, which means, "quarrelling".

After this sad event the people were, at long last, ready to advance against Canaan. They planned to move up the "King's Highway", the north-south road which ran along the eastern side of the Dead Sea, and launch an attack from the east. That meant passing through the land of the Edomites. The Lord had forbidden Israel from going to war against Edom (Deut. 2:4-6). They were the descendants of Esau, Jacob's twin, and thus descendants of Abraham, to whom God had promised many nations (Gen. 17:4). Twice Moses sent messengers to the king of Edom requesting permission to pass through his territory. Even though he offered to pay for any food and water they might consume en route, their request was rebuffed both times. The Edomites even mobilized their army to keep the Israelites out; there was no alternative but to walk around the territory of Edom.

When they came to Mount Hor, near the border of Edom in what is southern Jordan today, the Lord told Aaron to appoint Eleazar as his successor, for he too would soon die. In a somber ceremony Moses removed the high-priestly garments from his brother and enrobed Eleazar. Afterwards the three of them climbed to the summit of Mount Hor, where Aaron died. Moses and Eleazar buried him there. The people of Israel mourned him for thirty days.

▪ 63 ▪ The Bronze Serpent

Numbers 21:1-9   *Date: circa 1405 B.C.*

ISRAEL'S FIRST military confrontation with the Canaanites after the debacle at Kadesh Barnea 38 years earlier was a resounding victory. While they were still close to Mount Hor the Canaanite king of Arad launched a raid against Israel and took a number of captives. Israel vowed to the Lord that they would totally destroy the city of Arad if He granted them victory. The Lord heard their request and Israel kept its vow. They named the place "Hormah", which means "devoted to destruction".

However defeat easily follows victory. Flush with excitement from their first engagement they set off from Mount Hor. Due to Edomite intransigence they had to hike along a long, circuitous route south and eastwards, away from Canaan. They had been so close, had even received their first taste of victory… and now they were back to wandering in the wilderness. Somewhere along that long detour their patience ran out.

Although Moses was the immediate object of their venom, their real target, once again, was the Lord. "Why did you bring us out of Egypt to die in this desert," they complained as their parents had done. "There is no water, there is no bread and we despise this miserable manna!" Their contemptuous attitude towards God's faithful provision of the supernatural "angel's bread" (Ps. 78:25) was a rejection of His sustaining grace, and He responded by sending venomous snakes whose bite led to an agonizing death. Instead of being sustained with manna from heaven they were suddenly killed by virulent creatures slithering along the earth. Helpless in the face of this onslaught they turned, repentant, to Moses.

"Pray for us! We sinned when we complained against you and the Lord! Pray that God will take these snakes away!"

As he had done so often, Moses turned to the Lord to intercede on behalf of His people. God did not get rid of the vipers immediately. He instructed Moses to make a snake out of bronze. The snake is a symbol of the devil, for it was in the form of a snake that Satan first appeared to Eve in the Garden of Eden. Moses swiftly did as he was told, put the bronze snake on a pole, held it aloft and urged all who had been bitten to look upon the detestable creature. Only by gazing at it could people who had dismissed God's gracious provision prevent the venom from surging through their bodies and killing them.

Their parents had died because of disobedience. Now this generation faced a choice: live life as God's redeemed people in the Promised Land or also die in the desert. The difference between blessing and curse, life and death, lay in looking purposefully and obediently at a symbol of sin. Over a millennium later the Lord Jesus Christ referred back to this cursed snake

on a pole to explain his mission: just as Moses had lifted up the snake in the desert, he too would be lifted up, and everyone who looked to him, who believed in him, would receive eternal life (John 3:14; 6:48-51). The curse He bore when hanging on the cross to become sin on behalf of sinners would be the basis of salvation for all who would avail themselves of it. Moses' bronze snake was a "type" which received its fulfilment in Christ.[9]

---

[9] A "type" is a historical event, which foreshadows certain defining characteristics of later salvation history. Types can be Old Testament people (like Melchizedek), rituals (like the sacrificial system), institutions (like the priesthood), events (like the flood) or feasts (like the Passover) which became a pattern for something which would take place in the future. The "antitype" is the later event that the earlier "type" helps us understand. Types usually point to Christ and are used to explain different aspects of His life and ministry. The difference between a type and an analogy is that both the type and its antitype were events that actually took place in history.

Numbers 21-24   *Date: circa 1405 B.C.*

ONCE AGAIN the Israelites were on the move. They skirted Edom on their way to the Arnon Gorge, a vast wadi flowing into the Dead Sea. The Amorites controlled the territory from the Arnon Gorge to the Jabbok River. When Israel requested the right of passage across the Amorite's land, Sihon, their king, mustered his army and marched against them. Unlike the Edomites, however, the Amorites were not descendants of Abraham. Israel routed the Amorites in the ensuing battle.

North of the Jabbok was the land of Moab. The Moabites were terrified of the Israelites. God's humbling of Egypt on their behalf had provoked great fear of them in the surrounding nations (Deut. 2:25). Furthermore, the Moabites themselves had been at war with the Amorites and had lost; they knew that they did not have a chance against Israel. A pastoral people, they described Israel as a "horde that licks up everything around it, like an ox licks up a pasture". The ox symbolized strength and power.

Unaware of the fact that God had forbidden Israel from attacking them because they were the descendants of Lot (Deut. 2:9), and knowing he could not defeat them in a conventional battle, Balak, their king, decided that their only hope lay in fighting them at a spiritual level. He decided to call on the services of a famous soothsayer living in a town on the Euphrates River, a man with an international reputation who was thought capable of manipulating the will of the gods. Moses later dubbed the man "Balaam", a derogatory term meaning "people eater".

In the ancient world it was thought that the power of ritual curses, when uttered by powerful soothsayers, would be fulfilled unless cancelled by an opposing force. In this way Balak hoped to get the upper hand in the battle he foresaw. He did not know that centuries earlier, in His covenant with Abraham, God had promised that whoever cursed His people would himself be cursed (Gen. 12:3).

When Balak's emissaries arrived Balaam invited them to spend the night, during which time he would seek God's mind on the matter. That night God told him he must not go with the Moabite delegation to curse Israel, for Israel was under His blessing. Balaam was sensitive enough to realize that this deity, Jehovah God of Israel, was an altogether different kind of god from those he had hitherto invoked and sought to control. He wisely refused king Balak's blandishments.

When his emissaries returned to Moab empty-handed Balak sent a second, larger delegation, and authorized them to offer Balaam a great reward for his services. Balaam again reminded them that God had told him not to go. Once again, however, he invited them to spend the night so that, once again, he might ascertain God's mind on the matter. This greatly displeased God, for it presumed He was a fickle being. God would teach Balaam that once uttered, God's words were not open to change. He told Balaam he was free to go to Moab, so long as he did exactly as told.

The next morning Balaam saddled his donkey and set off with the Moabite emissaries. Suddenly Balaam's donkey saw an angel of the Lord, sword drawn, standing in the middle of the road. The beast immediately veered into a field. Balaam, who saw nothing unusual, beat his animal to bring her back onto the road. The angel then appeared in a narrow path between two vineyards with stonewalls on either side. To avoid the celestial being only the donkey could see, it squeezed close to one of the walls, pinching Balaam's leg. Once again Balaam beat the poor creature to get it back on track.

The angel then moved to a place so narrow there was no way the donkey could move around it, whereupon the beast lay down in the middle of the path. Humiliated and furious Balaam began beating it with his staff. At this the Lord opened the animal's mouth, enabling it to say rather plaintively, "What have I done to deserve these three beatings?"

The enraged Balaam didn't even stop to wonder at the voice coming from the beast! "You made me look like a fool! If there was a sword handy I'd kill you right now," he shouted. The animal had, indeed, made Balaam look ridiculous — much more so than he'd imagined. A donkey, an animal better known for stupidity and stubbornness than spiritual insight, saw unseen realities, which the internationally renowned soothsayer could not.

"Don't you know me," the animal replied aggrieved. "Have I ever done this to you before?" Grudgingly Balaam conceded that it had not. Then the Lord opened Balaam's eyes so that he too could see the angel with its drawn sword standing before him. Fearing for his life, he dropped to the ground.

"Why did you beat your donkey?" the angel asked. "If it had not been for her I would have killed you..." With one eye on the angel's sword Balaam confessed that he had sinned. "I didn't know you were blocking the road," he added. "If you want me to I'll go back home..."

"Go with these men," the angel said, "but make sure you only say what I tell you."

When the impatient king Balak heard that Balaam was finally on his way he went to the border to welcome him. "Why did you delay?" he scolded him. "Did you not think I would reward you enough?"

"I am here now," Balaam replied irritated. "Remember, I cannot say whatever I want. I can only speak what God tells me to!"

In a manner typical of ancient diviners he began his rituals by offering sacrifices. Then Balak escorted him to a lookout point from which they could see the Israelite camp in the distance. The next day Balaam instructed king Balak to build seven altars and sacrifice a bull and a ram on each of them. While the king and his advisers stayed with the sacrifices he climbed a nearby knoll where God met with him and ordered him what to say.

He returned to those who hoped his curses would render the Israelites ineffective in battle, and spoke his first divinely inspired oracle. He stated poetically that He could not curse Israel because she was immune from curses. She was blessed by God and unique among the nations, and he desired that his end be like that of the people of Israel. Understandably, King Balak was upset. The man he'd hired to curse his enemies blessed them instead!

"What can I do?" Balaam replied curtly. "I can only speak that which the Lord puts in my mouth..." Balak then took him to a different vantage point and forced him to try again. Once again seven oxen were slaughtered on seven altars while Balaam went off by himself to get a word from the Lord. The result was no different. Balaam's second oracle was an expansion of the first: Israel was unique in physical and spiritual strength because Jehovah God, their king, was with them, and He would not act contrary to His word.

"If you cannot curse," Balak burst out, "don't say anything at all!"

"I must say whatever God tells me," Balaam responded.

"Let's try from somewhere else," Balak said, still hoping that a change of perspective would lead to a change in fortunes. Another seven oxen were sacrificed. This time the Spirit of the Lord came directly on Balaam. He fell face first before God and uttered his third oracle. He foresaw God's tremendous blessings on the people currently living in the orderly arrangement of tents spread out before him. Their land would be wonderfully productive, their kings exalted, and their enemies defeated. He even repeated God's promise to Abraham, that those who bless Israel would be blessed and those who cursed her be cursed.

Angry and frustrated, Balak tried to dismiss him but God's Spirit impelled Balaam to utter a fourth oracle, a warning to Balak, in which he foresaw a ruler coming out of Israel in the distant future—a clear reference to Christ—who would lead Israel to final victory over all its enemies.

Balaam's next three utterances seemed to pour from him almost against his will. Each was a "curse oracle" which foresaw one nation after another rising up and taking arms against each other. Balaam, the man hired to curse Israel, became God's instrument to reaffirm Jehovah's blessings to a generation which was about to accomplish that which their fathers had failed to do 38 years earlier: the conquest and subjugation of Canaan. In spite of their numerous shortcomings, sins and rebellions, God once again reaffirmed his desire to richly bless Israel.

OUTSIDE FORCES like those of Balak or Balaam could not invoke God's wrath against His people. Only if they themselves compromised their commitment to His covenant would He turn against them.

Blithely unaware of God's intervention on their behalf in the Balaam affair, Israel was gearing up for a new stage in their national existence: the conquest of Canaan. The dry, dusty desert years were drawing to an end. Across the Jordan River a city culture beckoned the simple desert men who had known nothing but the rigors of the wilderness.

One day beautiful Moabite and Midianite women entered their camp and offered to introduce them to the sensual worship of Baal at the nearby shrine of Beth Peor. Many of the Israelite men, including some of its leaders, succumbed to these temple prostitutes' licentious advances.

This was Israel's first encounter with the sexually focused worship of the Canaanite fertility god Baal. God's wrath, which should have been directed at the Baal worshiping Canaanite nations, was now directed at Israel instead. He ordered Moses to execute those Israelite leaders who had engaged in this depraved and idolatrous behavior, and to put their bodies on display. When God made His covenant with Abraham at the beginning of the nation's history He had passed between the dismembered animal carcasses, as if to say: may this happen to the party that breaks its part of the covenant. That is exactly what God now demanded of those who had broken covenant with Him. Responding quickly, Moses called on Israel's judges to carry out the divine command. Even while the ringleaders were being executed, a plague broke out among the rest of the Israelites.

The action of a man called Zimri, a Simeonite clan leader, was particularly shocking. He brought a Midianite woman right before Moses in front of the tabernacle. Aaron's grandson Phinehas grabbed a spear, followed the couple into a tent, and with a single, violent strike, thrust it though the both of them. His decisive action led God to call a halt to the plague, which by then had killed some 24,000 people.

Later God told Israel to wage a war of annihilation against Midian because of the leading role it had played in the seduction of Israel. A special force of 12,000 men, 1000 warriors from each tribe, along with the zealous Phinehas, who symbolized the religious dimension of the conflict, went to war against Midian. In the ensuing conflict the Israeli army razed all Midianite settlements and killed every man, including the five kings who made up the Midianite coalition. Balaam too was found among the dead. However, instead of annihilating them totally as they had been ordered to do, the Israelite army kept the plunder along with the captured women, children, flocks and herds. In the ancient world women and children were considered chattel that could be disposed of at will.

Moses was angry with the victorious soldiers for keeping the women—they were the cause of the problem in the first place! In the end he decreed that only virgins, those sure not to have engaged in the seduction at Beth Peor, were to be spared. The enemy thought it could defeat Israel by having their women seduce them; in the end their daughters were added to the covenant people.

After a 7-day period of ritual purification the spoils of war were divided among the soldiers, the community at large, and the priesthood. The officers of the special force of 12,000 men presented Moses with many articles of gold to express their gratitude to the Lord that not a single one of their soldiers was lost in battle. These were placed in the tabernacle as a memorial.

• 66 • The Second Census and the Appointment of a Successor
Numbers 26-27; 32-36   *Date: circa 1405 B.C.*

ONE MAJOR logistical matter needed to be attended to before the people could advance: a new census. There had been no census for a generation, not since Sinai. To properly plan their conquest and the division of the land Israel's leaders needed accurate information on the state of the nation. The people were counted tribe by tribe, and the size of each would determine the size of their allotment in the Promised Land. The results were remarkable. In spite of the harsh desert environment, the plagues and other setbacks, their overall number was virtually the same as it had been 38 years earlier. In spite of everything, God had not failed them.

The tribes of Reuben and Gad, as well as half the tribe of Manasseh possessed large herds and flocks. After the census they approached Moses and asked if they could stay in the newly conquered lands east of the Jordan River. It was ideal for their needs as pastoral people. To Moses their proposal seemed seditious: were they turning their backs on the good land God had promised them and would their defection not leave the rest of the people to face the Canaanites alone?

The tribal leaders quickly made it clear that they were not rebelling but merely suggesting an alternative plan. They had no intention of leaving the rest of the people to cross the Jordan and fight the Canaanites alone. They would, in fact, be prepared to lead the conquest! They had actually come to Moses to discuss the matter before God.

Moses relented, striking a bargain with them: if they led the conquest of the land he would grant them the newly conquered lands. The Gadites, Reubenites and the half tribe of Mannaseh then set about building settlements for their wives and children and pens for their animals. They would cross over the river and fight alongside their fellow Israelites before returning to settle with their families and livestock east of the Jordan.

The Lord then explained to Moses what regions were included in the Promised Land, just like one would on a title deed. The western boundary was the Mediterranean Sea, the southern border ran eastwards as far as Edom, the eastern border curved northwards from Edom to the Sea of Galilee, and the northern border ran past Mount Hermon back to the Mediterranean. The land was to be allocated by tribe according to its size. The priestly tribe, the Levites, were not counted in the census. Their inheritance would consist of 48 cities and surrounding pasture scattered throughout the land. Six of these cities were to be designated cities of refuge for those who had accidently killed someone.

It must have been difficult for Moses to make provision for the entry of other people into the land while he himself would not be allowed to set foot in it. His moment of sin when he struck the waters of Meribah must always have been before him. Although he pleaded to be allowed to enter Canaan, the Lord told him not to speak of the matter anymore (Deut. 3:25-27). Instead He told him to go up a mountain from where he could enjoy a wide view of the Promised Land, after which he would die. On hearing this, faithful Moses, who always had the best interests of God's people at heart, prayed that the Lord would choose and equip a suitable successor to shepherd the community through the next phase of its national life.

God revealed that His chosen successor was Joshua. Moses took his faithful aide-de-camp before Eleazar the high priest and commissioned him in front of all the people.

• 67 • Moses' Farewell Speech

Deuteronomy   *Date: circa 1405 B.C.*

ALL WAS NOW in place; the only thing that remained was for Moses to bid farewell to his rebellious but beloved people. He began by reminding them how God had delivered them from Egypt, had formed them into a distinct nation at Sinai, and was about to bless them with their own homeland. He then reviewed their experiences since Mount Sinai and how God had not forsaken them in spite of all their ups and downs. He reiterated the Ten Commandments along with a succinct synopsis of the law: they were to love the Lord their God with all their hearts, all their souls and all their minds. The people's ongoing relationship with God would not only be determined by dutiful obedience, but also by heartfelt love. Parents were to teach the law to their children at every opportunity.

He reminded them that God had set His affection on them because He loved them as well as because of the covenant He had made with their ancestors. He then gave a further exposition of the law and of various rules and regulations designed to prosper them and set them apart as a holy nation. They were to completely destroy the existing inhabitants of Canaan and remove every aspect of their idol worship lest they be corrupted by them.

He called on them to renew their commitment to their covenant with God. He reminded them of the blessings of obedience and, if they failed to do so, of the curses they had placed themselves under. Their obedience or disobedience would decide how their history would unfold. There, on the plains of Moab, Moses set before the people the offer of life and death: "I present to you today the choice between life and prosperity, or death and destruction! I urge you to love the Lord your God, to walk in His way and to abide by His commands. If you do you will live and increase, and the Lord will bless you in the land you are about to possess. But if you turn away from the Lord and are disobedient to Him, if you turn to other gods to worship them, then I declare to you today that you will be destroyed! You will be expelled from the land! Choose life so that you will live and so that your children will love and obey Jehovah God, for He is your life!"

He told the people that upon entry into the Promised Land they were to re-dedicate themselves to the Lord and ratify their covenant with Him by reading aloud the blessings and curses at a special ceremony to be held at Mounts Ebal and Gerizim. He also taught them a poem, the "Song of Moses", as an easy-to-remember format of impressing on them God's covenant ways. This poem would be passed on from one generation to the next. Parts of it are quoted verbatim in numerous psalms, most of which were written hundreds of years later. It began with a proclamation of God's greatness and His perfect ways, followed by an acknowledgement that the people strayed from those ways. Next came a recital of the Lord's goodness to them. In spite of His blessing and goodness, however, they would reject their Lord and Saviour for idols and demons. They would anger God to such an extent that He would punish and eventually reject them. The poem concluded by stating that when their strength was gone the Lord would once again have compassion on them. He would take vengeance on their adversaries and make atonement for His people.

Moses encouraged the people not to fear. "I am now an old man, no longer able to lead you," he said. "The Lord told me that I would not cross the Jordan River with you. However, God Himself will cross the river ahead of you and deliver the nations living there into your hands. You must do to them all that the Lord commands you. Be strong! Be courageous! Do not fear because Jehovah God is with you and will not forsake you!"

The Lord then called Moses and Joshua to present themselves at the tabernacle for Joshua's final commissioning. During the ceremony the Lord appeared in a cloud and again spelled out in general terms the future history of Israel. He then commanded Joshua to be strong and courageous as he shouldered the task of leading the people into the land, for He, Jehovah God, promised to be with him.

Lastly, much as the patriarchs gathered their children around them and blessed them prior to their death, Moses gathered the people of Israel around him and blessed each tribe individually. This must have been a very moving event. Moses was the only leader they had ever known, and he was about to depart from them.

The Lord then instructed his faithful old servant to ascend Mount Nebo, from where He showed him the length and breadth of the Promised Land. The old man's heart must have been filled with both satisfaction and pain. No one knows how he died on that mountain, who buried him, or where he was buried. For thirty days the people grieved the loss of their leader, the man who had spoken with God face to face as with a friend.

Joshua 1   *Date: circa 1400 B.C.*

JOSHUA HAD been groomed to take command of Israel for many years. He had served as Moses' aid since he was a young man, and Moses had chosen him to lead Israel in its first military encounter. That battle must have deeply impressed him with the fact that victory comes from the Lord, for his troops had had the upper hand only as long as Moses' arms were raised in intercession.

Moses had chosen Joshua to accompany him on Mount Sinai. This must have been another formative experience in the young man's life. Along with Israel's other leaders he had seen the Lord and had fellowshiped with Him (Ex 24:9-11). He had been one of the 12 spies sent into Canaan, and upon their return only he and Caleb had believed that Jehovah God would enable them to overcome the challenges ahead. He had learned that the majority is not always right, and that disobedience and unbelief have fatal consequences.

Yet in spite of all his training Joshua was deeply aware of his inadequacies. During his commissioning God told him repeatedly not to be afraid but to be strong and courageous. "As I was with Moses, so I will be with you," God promised him. More importantly, God stressed to Joshua that he was not to depart from the terms of God's covenant with Israel, the details of which were written down in a series of scrolls he had received from Moses, scrolls which later formed the Bible's first five books, the Torah (or Pentateuch).

Joshua received those scrolls as a special, normative and authoritative revelation from God, who told him to meditate on them day and night, to read them, to study them, to let their teachings shape his thinking, and to be careful to obey them. That, God told him, would be his formula for success. Joshua was a great leader and military commander, but the key to his success was his careful attention to the word of God. In his final address to Israel at the end of his life Joshua would urge them to "be careful to obey all that is written in the book of the Law of Moses, without turning to the right or to the left" (Joshua 23:6).

Joshua's was the first generation expected to live by a divinely inspired written code. That was a major religious transition. Up until that time God had made His will known directly to select people such as the patriarchs and Moses. Although God personally confronted Joshua a few times, and occasionally gave him instructions through the priests, his generation as well as subsequent ones were to be guided by and live in obedience to the Torah, the written record of the covenant God had made with Israel.

Only Joshua and Caleb knew the nature of the land they were about to invade. They knew that, humanly speaking, the obstacles ahead were overwhelming. Israel was no match for those fortified cities and giants that he and Caleb had seen, the mere report of which had terrified the previous generation. However, he believed God's promise to never leave him nor forsake him (Jos. 1:5).

The years of formation and training in Egypt, at Sinai, and in the desert were over. The people were about to live as a nation in the land God had promised them. All that remained was to conquer it from its irredeemably evil inhabitants. For the next seven years he, Joshua, would lead this conquest, walking according to the spirit and injunctions of the Torah.

· 69 · Rahab and the Spies

Joshua 2   *Date: circa 1400 B.C.*

GOD HAD TOLD Abraham about half a millennium earlier that it would take 400 years for the sin of the inhabitants of Canaan to reach such proportions that they were ripe for judgement (Gen. 15:16). Now that time was at hand, and Israel was to be God's means of judgement.

Israel's conquest of Canaan would be a brutal, bloody story, but it began with the salvation of an Amorite prostitute who switched allegiance.

Joshua selected two men to enter the land ahead of the main army to gather useful information for the upcoming assault. The scouts decided to visit a prostitute in the city of Jericho whose house was perched on the city wall. What better person than a prostitute from whom to get the pulse of the land? Having strangers visit her would not seem abnormal, she would know what a wide range of people were thinking, and could be interrogated without being asked awkward questions from bystanders.

Over the years Rahab had heard—probably from gossiping customers—about Israel's amazing God. She shared with Joshua's spies that she was aware that their God had rescued them from Egypt and had caused the Red Sea to dry up on their behalf. She informed them that their recent defeat Moab and Midian had terrified the people of Canaan, and that she was convinced that Jehovah, their God, was the God of heaven above and the earth below. In her heart she had identified herself with Israel's God; now she was prepared to identify herself with His people. If found out this would be considered treason and lead to torture and execution. However, Jericho's king did not suspect her loyalty when he learned that the two Jewish spies who had infiltrated his city were at her house. He quickly dispatched some soldiers to arrest them.

When Rahab saw the soldiers approaching she pushed the spies through a ceiling hatch onto the roof and hid them under stalks of flax drying there. She then told the soldiers that the men they were looking for had indeed visited her, but had hastened off at dusk, just before the gates closed for the night. The king's men, not wanting to return empty handed, rushed towards the fords of the Jordan River hoping to catch up with the Hebrew spies.

After sending the soldiers on their wild-goose chase Rahab called the spies back down. "I have shown kindness to you," she said. "Now you must show kindness to me and my family. What sign will you give me that you will spare my life and that of my family when you take the city?"

"Our lives for yours," the men responded. "We will treat you well if you don't tell anyone about this. When we come to take the city hang a red rope from your window. Anyone who is in the house during the assault will be spared. If anyone is outside the house his blood will be on his own head."

"Agreed," Rahab replied. She then let the men down through the window, telling them to head towards the hills and hide there for three days, by which time the pursuit would have been called off. The men did as she suggested. They eventually returned to Joshua and reported that the Lord was with them. They had nothing to fear; the people of the land were melting in fear because of the Israelites and their God.

The Amorites were the most corrupt of the various peoples that occupied Canaan, and Rahab was a prostitute. Yet in spite of her birth and occupation she became an object of God's

grace and was eventually accepted as a full-fledged member of the people of Israel. She married someone from the tribe of Judah and they had a son name Boaz, who married a Moabite convert to the worship of Jehovah named Ruth. Their son, in turn, would be king David's forefather. In time, the Lord Jesus Christ would be born from David's descendants. Centuries later two New Testament writers would describe her as a model of faith (Heb. 11:31; Jam. 2:25).

• 70 • Across the Jordan!

Joshua 3-5   *Date: circa 1400 B.C.*

"CONSECRATE YOURSELVES!" Joshua told the people, "Tomorrow the Lord will do amazing things on your behalf." He then explained how the next day would unfold: priests would carry the Ark of the Covenant to the edge of the Jordan River. As soon as they set foot in the river the flow would be cut off and they would cross on the dry land to the other side.

Even though the river was at full flood, events unfolded exactly as predicted. The priests carrying the ark stood in the middle of the dry riverbed until the nation had crossed to the other side. No sooner had they stepped onto the bank than the river started running at flood speed again, just as it had before. Joshua had ordered twelve men, one from each tribe, to pick up a boulder from the riverbed where the Ark was and pile them on the west bank. That cairn would serve as a reminder to future generations that Israel had crossed the Jordan on dry ground and help them remember that Israel's God acts powerfully on behalf of His people, and encourage them to continue to fear and serve Him. As a result of this miraculous crossing God also exalted Joshua in the eyes of the people. They now stood in awe of him as they had of Moses. They had every confidence that He would be a great military leader.

When the indigenous people of the land heard how the Israelites had crossed the river en-masse they were terror-stricken. They undoubtedly expected Israel to launch its assault immediately, but instead of pressing their temporary advantage God called on them to celebrate two sacraments of consecration, one of which, circumcision, would completely incapacitate the army. Circumcision was the mark of the covenant that God established with Abraham and his descendants, the sign that one was a member of God's chosen people. During Israel's wanderings in the desert this rite had lapsed, and before they could proceed God demanded that the uncircumcised generation born in the desert bear this mark of His special relationship with them. When this ceremony of re-consecration had been concluded God assured the people that he had "rolled away the reproach of Egypt from them". In other words, the shame of slavery and homelessness was, at long last, gone. They were a free, covenant people, laying claim to their divinely promised inheritance. The place on the west bank of the Jordan River where this took place became known as Gilgal, which sounds like the Hebrew word for "roll".

While camped at Gilgal the people also celebrated the Passover, the meal that recalled their divine deliverance from Egypt. It was during this Passover meal that the people ate some of the produce of the land for the first time. The next day the manna, which had sustained them all those forty years on their journey ceased to fall from heaven. The bounty of the Promised Land was now sufficient.

As Joshua explored the vicinity of Jericho a mysterious person with a drawn sword suddenly appeared before him. Joshua boldly approached the individual and asked him if he was on their side or on that of their enemies.

"Neither," the person replied. "I have come as commander of the army of the Lord." Joshua fell face down to the ground in reverence.

"What message does my Lord have for his servant?" he asked, recognizing that the person before him was Jehovah God manifesting Himself in human form.

"Take off your sandals for the place where you are standing is holy ground," was the response. Once their relationship had been defined God gave Joshua detailed directions with respect to the upcoming battle with Jericho.

Joshua 6   *Date: circa 1400 B.C.*

JOSHUA'S OVERALL strategy consisted of dividing Canaan in two by striking westward through the middle of the country, thus preventing the Canaanites from forming a single front. Once Canaan had been successfully bisected he planned to take the southern sector first, and then the north. Standing in the way, however, was the well-fortified fortress of Jericho. It had to be taken. They could not afford to have this enemy stronghold at their rear.

God, their commander-in-chief, had given Joshua a most unorthodox set of instructions: for six days the army was to march once around the city in silence behind seven trumpet-blowing priests and the Ark of the Covenant. On the seventh day they were to repeat this exercise seven times! Then, on the seventh circumambulation, the priests were to blow a long blast on their horns and the soldiers were to give a loud shout—and then the walls would collapse!

Jericho, Israel's first conquest was to be completely destroyed. Any gold, silver and other metal objects, which could not be burned, were to be donated to the tabernacle treasury. Joshua warned that if the men did not adhere to these instructions they were liable to bring disaster on themselves.

Events unfolded just as the Lord had predicted. Every day the long column of silent soldiers marched to the sound of the trumpet around the city. Ancient Jericho occupied about six acres (abt. 2.5 hectares), so the head of Israel's army column would be heading back to base while the tail was still approaching the city. Although nothing happened the army faithfully repeated

this seemingly futile exercise every day of that week. Every day they fell into formation, marched towards the city, circled it, and headed back to their encampment. The people of Jericho watching from the top of the walls started taunting them but, undaunted, Israel carried out the ridiculous exercise just as God had told their commander Joshua.

On day seven they set off at daybreak. Seven times they marched around the city, probably several columns deep to accommodate all the soldiers. Then the priests gave a long blast on their ram's horns and the soldiers gave a mighty shout. Suddenly those walls crowded with jeering people collapsed. Israel's army charged into the defenceless city and put every man, woman and child to the sword while the two former spies made straight for Rahab's house and brought her and her family to safety.

Joshua wanted Jericho's charred ruins to remain as a memorial of God's victory in their first battle in the Promised Land so he pronounced a curse on anyone who rebuilt it. Although the site itself was soon resettled, the curse was fulfilled centuries later when a man named Hiel rebuilt the city's walls (1 Kings 16:34).

▪ 72 ▪ Ai

Joshua 7-8	*Date: circa 1400 B.C.*

ISRAEL'S SPECTACULAR triumph over Jericho was followed almost immediately by an unexpected and hugely demoralizing defeat—the only one in Joshua's campaign against Canaan and the only record of any Israelites slain in combat.

Joshua's scouts informed him that the next obstacle in the westward push to divide Canaan was a little town in the hills nearby called Ai. Flush after the resounding victory against Jericho and acting on the advice of his vanguard, Joshua hastily dispatched an expeditionary force of 3000 men to take it. What he did not know was that one of his men, a certain Achan, had broken God's command, thus causing God to remove His favour from them. During the sack of Jericho, Achan had stolen several kilograms worth of silver, about half a kilogram of gold and a beautiful robe of intricately worked Babylonian cloth. Although he knew God's instructions that Jericho's silver and gold were to be turned over to the Levites and all other plunder destroyed, he wanted a share of the goods and buried the haul in his tent.

The men of Ai launched a bold attack and routed the Israelites, killing 36 of them. The post-victory glow of Jericho suddenly turned to panic: "the hearts of the people melted and became like water". Joshua and the elders of Israel tore their clothes, put dust on their heads and lay facedown before the ark until evening. "Lord," Joshua cried out, "why did you let us cross the Jordan if your plan was to destroy us at the hands of the Amorites? The people of the land will learn of this defeat and be emboldened. They will surround and defeat us—and how will you be glorified in that?"

"Why are you lying on your face?" the Lord rebuked him. "The reason I am not with you is because Israel has violated the covenant! It has stolen that which was devoted to me. Until you destroy that which was devoted to destruction I will not be with you anymore. Now get up and consecrate yourselves. Tomorrow I will reveal the guilty party."

The next morning they ferreted out the guilty party, probably by casting the Urim and Thummim (1 Sam. 14:36-43). Throughout the long process Achan remained silent. Right to the end he hoped that he would not be found out. Inevitably, however, he was identified.

"My son," Joshua said to Achan, "Give glory to God. What have you done?" When he saw that it was useless to hide the matter any longer Achan came clean: "I coveted, I took, I hid..."

The loot was quickly recovered and put on display. Subsequent punishment was swift and severe. Achan, along with his sons and daughters, his livestock and all his possessions, including the stolen goods, were taken out to a nearby valley. There they were stoned to death. A pile of rocks was heaped over the remains. In a play on Achan's name that valley came to be known as "Achor", meaning, "trouble".

Achan's sin had dire consequences for others as well as for himself, but when the people responded to judgment by excising sin their fellowship with God was restored. God encouraged the demoralized Joshua, and assured him of victory in the second battle against Ai. Years later the prophet Hosea would write a poem in which he described the Valley of Achor, the Valley of Trouble, as a door of hope (Hos. 2:14-15).

This time Joshua mustered the entire military. Under cover of darkness he sent part of his army to lie in ambush behind Ai. In the morning the rest of his forces launched a frontal attack.

The army of Ai again counter-attacked. When Joshua's men pretended to fall back the men of Ai fell for the ruse and chased headlong after the retreating Israelites, leaving their city defenceless. Suddenly Joshua raised his javelin over his head. At this signal the men waiting in ambush came out of hiding, quickly captured the defenceless city, and set it on fire. The army of Ai, suddenly caught between two Israelite armies, didn't have a chance. Just as Moses had kept his arm aloft during Israel's first battle years earlier, so Joshua too kept the arm holding his javelin aloft for the duration of the battle, indicating that God was directing them.

The population of Ai was put to the sword and their king captured. Joshua had him hung on a tree until evening, then ordered the body be buried under a pile of rocks by the city's main gate. Unlike Jericho, the people were free to keep the plunder and the livestock. Since the flow of manna had stopped, their means of support for the duration of the campaign would consist of the produce of the land and plunder from the defeated Canaanites.

The defeats of Jericho and Ai had shown the Israelites that the capture of Canaan would involve miraculous interventions together with common sense, strategic thinking and hard fighting. God had promised them the land, but gaining possession of it would happen through strict obedience and hard work over the long haul.

▪ 73 ▪ Recommitment to the Covenant at Mounts Ebal and Gerizim

Joshua 8, Deuternonomy 27-28   *Date: circa 1400 B.C.*

IN HIS FAREWELL address Moses had instructed Israel that upon entry into Canaan they were to assemble on the slopes of Mounts Ebal and Gerizim and ratify their covenant commitment to God.

Mount Ebal was a barren, rocky mound of about 3000 feet about 1/3 of a mile distant from the slightly lower but lush Mount Gerizim. The valley between them formed a basin of remarkable acoustic quality, while the ledges of limestone strata around it were like a series of stone benches. It was to this natural amphitheatre that Joshua led the people.

Following Moses' instructions Joshua built an altar of uncut stones on Mount Ebal (Deut. 27:4) on which he offered burnt and fellowship offerings. Then he had the law copied on special plaster-covered stones. After that he had the tribes of Simeon, Levi, Judah, Issachar, Joseph and Benjamin climb the slope of Mount Gerizim, while the other six tribes of Reuben, Gad, Asher, Zebulun, Dan and Naphtali positioned themselves on Mount Ebal (Deut. 27:4-13). The Ark of the Covenant and a copy of the law were placed in the middle of the assembly. Then Joshua solemnly read the curses just as Moses had recorded them. After each curse the tribes on the barren Mount Ebal responded by saying "Amen!", meaning "let it be so"...

"Cursed is the man who makes an image or idol!"	AMEN
"Cursed is the man who dishonours his father or mother!"	AMEN
"Cursed is the man who withholds justice!"	AMEN
"Cursed is the man who commits sexually immoral acts!"	AMEN
"Cursed is the murderer!"	AMEN
"Cursed is the man who does not uphold the words of this law!"	AMEN

Once all the curses had been read and ratified Joshua read the blessings, to which the tribes on the fertile Mount Gerizim responded with loud "amens".

"If you fully obey the Lord your God and carefully follow His commands He will exalt you in the earth and accompany you!"	AMEN
"The Lord will bless you in the city and in the country!"	AMEN
"The Lord will bless you with children, and crops and livestock!"	AMEN
"The Lord will defeat the enemies that rise up against you!"	AMEN
"The Lord will establish you as His holy people!"	AMEN

In an impressive, interactive way the people were reminded again of the basic principle on which God would deal with them. He would bless obedience and curse disobedience in His people, something the recent debacle at Ai had graphically demonstrated.

God knew that the people would break the law, so He had also instituted the sacrificial system as the means of restoring fellowship. Prior to this covenant ratification ceremony an altar on Mount Ebal, the mount of cursing, was made of uncut stones to show the people that they had nothing in-and-of themselves to contribute to their redemption.

Centuries later Jesus Christ passed through that area. The people had built an altar on Mount Gerizim, the mount of blessing, seeking to placate God by offering Him the best they had to offer. While there Jesus struck up a conversation with a local woman, who asked him if Mount Gerizim was the right place from which to approach God. Jesus directed her away from the mountain and the self-righteousness associated with it and towards Himself. He was the long-awaited Messiah (John 4:1-26) who would perfectly fulfill the demands of God's law and become the perfect sacrifice that would atone for sin once and for all.

Joshua 9-10   *Date: circa 1400 B.C.*

AFTER THE FALL OF Ai the formidable city of Gibeon and its dependencies were next in line. The Gibeonites realized, however, that they did not stand a chance against a people for whom the Jordan River ceased to flow, for whom the walls of Jericho collapsed, and who had razed Ai to the ground. In a desperate attempt to save their lives they resorted to a ruse. A delegation loaded stale, mouldy supplies of food and old, cracked wineskins on pack-donkeys, dressed in worn-out clothes, and went to the Israelite camp. "We have come from a distant country to make a treaty with you," they said upon arrival.

"How can we know that you don't come from nearby?" the men of Israel asked suspiciously as they ushered the foreigners to Joshua.

"Who are you and where have you come from?" Joshua asked them.

"We have come from a distant country because of the fame of the Lord your God. We have received word of all He has done for you: how He rescued you from Egypt and enabled you to deal with the two Amorite kings east of the Jordan," they said, being careful to omit more recent events like the miraculous crossing of the river and the conquests of Jericho and Ai, news which would not yet have reached their supposed "distant country".

"The leaders and people of our country urged us to offer you our services, and make a treaty with you. Look, our provisions were fresh and our clothes new when we set out on our journey."

The Israelites were keen to carry out the Lord's command to remove the inhabitants of Canaan, so they inspected the delegation's clothes and sampled their provisions—but they failed to take the matter to the Lord. They were satisfied that what they saw corroborated the story. Even Joshua, who could have used the Urim and Thummim to inquire of the Lord (Num. 27:18-21), was taken in by the Gibeonite's ruse. He and the nation's leaders made a peace treaty with them to let them live, which they ratified by an oath.

It took three days for the Israelites to discover that they had been hoodwinked. The people grumbled against their leadership for their rash decision, but the leaders recognized that oaths made in the name of God could not be rescinded. As a result of this treaty Israel was bound to protect the Gibeonites. They were not wiped out but ordered to serve the Israelite nation in the menial capacity of woodcutters and water carriers.

Canaan consisted of independent, mutually hostile city-states that had set aside their differences to face the common Israelite enemy. Gibeon's defection was a significant blow to this Canaanite coalition for it was an important city with a large, well-trained army. When Adoni Zedek, the king of Jerusalem, heard what had happened to Jericho, Ai and Gibeon he was greatly alarmed. He urged his coalition with four other Amorite kings to punish Gibeon and forestall further defections.

On the basis of their treaty with Israel the Gibeonites turned to Joshua for help. This time Joshua enquired of the Lord, and when the Lord responded favorably he moved quickly. Under cover of darkness his army quick-marched the twenty miles from their base camp at Gilgal to Gibeon and took the unsuspecting besiegers completely by surprise. As their enemy fled in disarray southward towards their fortified cities God Himself intervened, hurling huge hailstones on them. The hail killed more people than had fallen in battle. The victory would be the Lord's, not Israel's.

Joshua realized that this was a unique, divinely granted opportunity to eliminate the southern confederacy in a single blow. However, the sun was about to set and under cover of darkness the enemy's surviving units would be able to regroup in their fortified cities to fight another day. Joshua turned to the Lord and asked for a miracle of stupendous proportions: he prayed that the day be prolonged so they could finish the job. "O sun stand still over Gibeon"— and it did! The sun stopped in the middle of the sky and delayed setting for about a full day until the Israelites had destroyed the enemy army. There was never a day like that before or since, when the Lord so listened to a man! The animistic Canaanites would have concluded that their gods of nature had turned against them.

The five captured coalition kings were brought to Joshua. To further bolster his troops' morale he had his officers place their feet on the necks of these supposedly powerful kings. "Don't be afraid or discouraged," he told them. "This is what the Lord will do to all the enemies you will fight." The kings were then put to death.

Joshua followed up this victory with a quick series of sharp attacks and mopping up operations against the rest of the now largely defenceless southern cities. One exception was the city of Jerusalem. Although Adoni-Zedek, their king, was one of the five killed, the city itself was not taken until after Joshua's death (Judg. 1:8). After their rapid subjugation of southern Canaan the Israelite army returned to their families and livestock in their base camp at Gilgal.

▪ 75 ▪ The Conquest of Northern Canaan

Joshua 11   *Date: circa 1400 B.C.*

JABIN, THE KING of Hazor, took the lead in forming a very large coalition of northern city-states to repel the Israelite invaders. Unlike the five-city southern coalition, this massive army included large numbers of horses and chariots. The massive forces arrayed against him may have intimidated Joshua, but the Lord told him not to fear them. He promised to hand them over to him the next day.

Once again Joshua resorted to a surprise attack and, once again, the enemy was caught off guard. Joshua's army drove the Canaanites into the mountains, where chariots were of little use. After the battle Joshua had the enemy chariots burned and the Achilles tendons of the horses' hind legs cut, thus making them unfit for warfare. Israel's confidence was to be in the Lord, not in that era's latest military hardware.

After defeating the northern coalition's main army the Israelites began taking the region's fortified cities. In total they defeated 31 kings one after the other, destroying their major cities and carrying off the plunder. Within a few months they had conquered the hill country running like a spine up-and-down Canaan, the dry Negev in the south, the undulating foothills in the west sloping toward the Mediterranean, and the fertile lands on both banks of the Jordan River.

As for the Gibeonites, their commitment to Israel never faltered. They never defected back to the Canaanites. Once the land was conquered and divided among the tribes of Israel, their city of Gibeah became part of the inheritance of the line of Aaron: it became a priestly city. 400 years later David had the tabernacle and altar placed there. Later, when newly installed as king, Solomon would go there to burn offerings to the Lord. The genealogies of those who returned from the Babylonian exile centuries later included Gibeonites. Even though they were originally subject to the same divine judgment as the other people of the land, and even though they were liars and deceivers, they had sought refuge with the people of God and so became participants of grace.

• 76 • The Division of the Land

Joshua 13-21   *Date: circa 1400 B.C.*

CANAANITE MILITARY might was broken in a number of epic battles. Most of their armies had been defeated and its great fortresses (with the exception of Jerusalem) taken. There were, however, still many smaller towns and enclaves as well as the territory of the Philistines that needed to be subjugated. That task became the responsibility of the individual tribes.

First, however, they had to divide the land according to the principles laid down by Moses (Num. 26:52-56). Jacob had twelve sons and the land was to be given to their twelve tribes. Joseph's portion was split between his two sons, Ephraim and Manassah. The tribe that did not receive a large allotment of contiguous land was Levi. God's instruction to Moses was that He himself would be their inheritance. They were to minister to the spiritual needs of the nation (Josh. 13:33; 18:7).

The land east of the Jordan River had already been given to the tribes of Reuben, Gad and the half tribe of Manasseh. The large and increasingly important tribe of Judah was given the southern region.

Caleb now approached Joshua. He had served God whole-heartedly ever since they had both returned with a good report from the initial spying expedition. He was an old man now, well into his mid-eighties. Throughout the conquest he had fought bravely. He approached his old friend Joshua and reminded him of a promise Moses had made to him over 45 years earlier, that he would receive the land on which his feet had trod. "I am still as strong and vigorous as I was on the day Moses sent us out to spy out the land. Now give me this hill country so that I can clear it of the Anakites."

Joshua blessed him, and then gave him Hebron and the surrounding area within Judah's portion. Hebron was the place where Abraham and Sarah, Isaac and Rebekah and then Jacob—the fathers of the faith—were buried. Through decades of faithful service he'd kept alive that vision of liberating the nearest thing to a Jewish sacred site from the pagan Canaanites. The old man promptly took Hebron, driving out the descendants of Anak, and offering his daughter Acsah in marriage to the man who took the neighbouring town of Debir. That individual turned out to be his nephew Othniel, who later became one of Israel's judges.

The powerful tribes of Ephraim and the second half of Manassah were assigned the northern frontiers. The tabernacle and the Ark of the Covenant were moved to a central location called Shiloh within the territory of Ephraim.

For some reason the remaining tribes did not take full possession of the regions they were assigned. Perhaps they were too content with their traditional nomadic way of life to put forth the effort to fully subjugate and develop their assigned territories. Joshua called for a national assembly at Shiloh, the new center of their national life, to address this issue.

After berating the remaining tribes Joshua suggested they each send three men to survey their respective areas. The land would then be divided into plots to be divided among the clans by lot. After that the responsibility of claiming full possession of the territory assigned to them was up to the individual clans.

The small tribe of Benjamin received a tract of land between Judah and Ephraim. Although not large, it included the important cities of Jericho, Bethel, and Gibeon.

The Simeonites were not given a totally separate area but an enclave within the vast territory of Judah. Jacob had prophesied centuries earlier that the descendants of Simeon would be scattered among the tribes of Israel because of their wanton slaughter of the people of Shechem.

Zebulun, Issachar, Asher and Naphtali were given land grants in the far north. Dan was given Philistine land between Jerusalem and the Mediterranean Sea. Because it failed to dispossess the Philistines living there this warlike people would plague Israel for years afterwards.

The tribe of Levi was granted forty-eight special priestly cities with surrounding pastures throughout the land. Six Levite cities, three on the eastern side of the Jordan River, and three on its western side, were designated as "cities of refuge". They were to be places of protection for those who had accidentally killed someone. If the city elders determined the fugitive was innocent of malice they were to let him live in safety in their city until the death of the serving high priest. After that he was free to return home without fear of revenge. The tie with the high priest reminded Israel that its civic laws flowed from its relationship with God.

When all the land had been allotted the aging Joshua requested and received the town of Timnath Serah, in the hill country of Ephraim.

The Lord gave the Israelites all the land He had sworn to their ancestors. Caleb's bold action against the residual Canaanites living on the territory he'd inherited stood in stark contrast to the insipid response of most of the rest of the nation. The enemy's military might was broken, yet Israel fell short of taking full possession of the land. Perhaps they were tired of fighting and wanted peace and quiet to enjoy the spoils of war. They were conquerors, the ruling elite, and satisfied with the status quo. The nation would come to rue its indolence.

Joshua 22 *Date: circa 1400 B.C.*

ONLY SOLDIERS can appreciate the bonds that form during military campaigns, so it must have been an emotional parting when the army was disbanded. The men had fought side by side and won resounding victories against overwhelming odds. They had marvelled at God's amazing miracles on their behalf. They had subdued the land, and now the time had come for everyone to disperse to their respective allotments.

The tribes of Reuben, Gad and the half tribe of Manasseh had kept their promise to help the rest of the nation conquer the land. They were keen to be reunited with their families and start a new life in their own land east of the Jordan River. Before their departure, however, Joshua summoned them to a farewell exhortation. He praised them for not deserting their brothers. Fearing that those tribes' relative isolation would cause them to turn away from the Lord he reminded them of God's faithfulness and urged them to stay true to the commands and laws He had given to Moses. "You are to love the Lord your God, to walk in His ways, to obey His commands, to hold fast to Him and to serve Him with all your heart and all your soul," he enjoined them. The last farewells were said, and the two and a half tribes were on their way to the east of Jordan.

Soon terrible news reached the main Israelite camp! The recently departed eastern tribes had built an imposing altar on the banks of the Jordan! That could only mean one thing: apostasy! Constructing any altar besides the one in the tabernacle at Shiloh meant breaking with the worship of Jehovah God. When the sickening report reached the rest of Israel they re-gathered at Shiloh to go to war against their countrymen. Apostasy had to be rooted out if they were not to fall under the wrath of God! Tired as they were of fighting, and much as they loved their comrades-in-arms across the river, they were not about to compromise God's truth and honour. Civil war seemed inevitable...

Before declaring war, however, Israel's leadership dispatched a delegation led by Phinehas, the priest who had distinguished himself as a defender of righteousness when Israel had succumbed to immorality and idolatry at Peor (Num. 25:6-18). The delegates confronted the eastern tribes and underscored the fact that the entire nation would suffer as a result of their disobedience and faithlessness. Had they forgotten the consequences of Achan's sin? The delegation graciously offered the tribes sections of their own land on the west side of the river, closer to Shiloh "where the Lord's tabernacle stands", if for some reason they felt that their own land was outside the blessing of the Lord.

When the Easterners heard their compatriots' concerns they agreed that if their friends' interpretation of events was right then they deserved to be punished. "If this has been in rebellion or disobedience to the Lord do not spare us this day. If we have built this altar to turn away from the Lord and offer our own sacrifices on it, may the Lord Himself call us to account". They then explained that they had, indeed, built an altar, but had no intention of ever sacrificing anything on it! The structure was not a sign of their turning away but was designed to be a memorial to their unity! Joshua had feared that the eastern tribes would secede because of their relative isolation. They themselves were afraid that their isolation might one day lead the rest of the nation to reject them because they didn't live in the "real" Promised Land. So they had built a memorial they named "A Witness Between Us That Jehovah is God" to remind their fellow Israelites that they too were full-fledged members of the covenant community.

When the western delegation realized that the altar was just a memorial and that their fears were unfounded Phinehas and the other representatives of Israel were delighted, and the nation praised God. There was no more talk about going to war with their brothers across the Jordan.

▪ 78▪   Israel Reconfirms Its Covenant With God

Joshua 23-24   *Date: circa 1380 B.C.*

AT LONG LAST the people had rest. The major battles were over, and even though the Canaanites had not all been driven out, the nation was at peace. Each family took possession of its homestead and settled into the routine of daily life. Farmers tended their fields, harvested their crops, reared their livestock, and raised families. They sold their surpluses in local market towns where craftsmen practised their skills and traders attended to their business. Three times a year those who could do so traveled to the tabernacle at Shiloh to celebrate the great pilgrim feasts.

Twenty or more years passed in relative quiet. Then, one day, Israel's community leaders, elders, judges and officials, received a summons from Joshua. He was now a very old man and knew he would soon pass from the scene.

When they had all arrived Joshua reminded them of the great things God had done on their behalf. He called on them to remember God's past acts of covenant grace: He had kept every one of His promises as He led them to victory, gave them the land, and enabled them to settle in it. God, however, would also be faithful to His words of warning. They had to continue to walk in obedience if they wanted to enjoy His ongoing blessings.

Joshua reminded the leaders that there were still Canaanite enclaves and admonished them not to associate with or intermarry with these pagan people lest they become ensnared in their ways. The problem was not that the people could not marry non-Jews. After all, Moses had married a Cushite and Salmon had married Rahab. However, these spouses had rejected their pagan heritage and embraced the God of Israel.

Joshua went on to assure Israel's leaders that the Lord would help them finish the task if they but set themselves to it. If they loved the Lord they would be invincible. Then he warned them that if they ever broke covenant with the Lord His anger would burn against them and they would be removed from the land He had given them.

Joshua's second address was during a convocation at Shechem where, once again, he challenged the people to remain faithful to the Lord their God. He reviewed their history, starting with Abraham's pagan background right through the stories of Isaac and Jacob, to their present blessed condition. Just as God had promised, they had received land they had not toiled for, vineyards and olive groves they had not planted, and cities they had not built (Deut. 6:10-11). He urged the people to give their undivided loyalty to the Lord, not because of their illustrious heritage but because of what God, in His sovereign, electing grace, had done for them. He challenged the people to choose whom they would devote themselves to: the pagan gods Abraham had turned his back on, the idols of Egypt, the terrible gods of Canaan which demanded human sacrifice, or the Lord God who had delivered them from slavery and given them the good land He had promised.

"Far be it from us to forsake the Lord and serve other gods," they assured him.

"You are unable to serve the Lord your God. He is a holy God who will not forgive you if you rebel against Him," he responded.

"No," the people assured him. "We will serve the Lord!"

"Then throw away your idols and devote yourself solely to the Lord God," Joshua pleaded. Already the fertility gods of the remaining Canaanites were leading some of them astray.

"We will," they promised.

There was nothing left to say. Joshua penned a fresh copy of the law in their presence and gave it to the people. He then erected a large stone to preserve the memory of the day they renewed their commitment to the Lord. He had done what he could. He had sought to impress on Israel in every way he knew the importance of walking in faithfulness and obedience to the word of God. He had preached it to them, he had handed them a written copy of the law, and he had erected a memorial. It was up to them now...

Joshua died soon afterwards at the ripe old age of 110 and was buried on his inherited land. No one was appointed to take his place.

• 79 • Spiritual Declension

Judges 1-3   *Date: circa 1380-1300 B.C.*

AFTER THE DEATH of Joshua the people of Israel asked the Lord who should take the initiative against the remaining Canaanites. The answer was the tribe of Judah. It invited the small tribe of Simeon, whose territory they surrounded, to join them. They attacked and routed a 10,000 man Canaanite army at a place called Bezek and captured its king. They cut off his thumbs and big toes, incapacitating him as a soldier.

The army of Judah then attacked the Jebusite city of Jerusalem, on the border of their territory and the territory belonging to the tribe of Benjamin. Although they set the city on fire, they were unable to capture the inner fortress. Later the Benjamites also attempted to take the city, but they also failed to do so. The fortress would hold out for centuries.

The Judah-Simeon coalition carried out various other campaigns; they even razed the Philistine coastal cities of Gaza, Ashkelon and Ekron, though these were soon retaken and repopulated by the ongoing Philistine migration from Crete. The other tribes also fought battles but although they succeeded in exploiting the indigenous Canaanites as cheap labor they never managed to drive them out completely. They were also unable to take such cities as Tyre and Sidon on the northern Mediterranean coast, a region that became known as Phoenicia. Canaanite culture and religious practices in Phoenicia would flourish and deeply influence Israel's later history.

At this time the "Angel of the Lord" appeared with a message of judgement. Not only had the Israelites failed to eradicate the morally abhorrent Canaanites and destroyed their places of worship, they had started intermarrying with those pagans. They had broken the covenant with God and as a result He had withdrawn His hand of blessing from them. He would no longer drive out the Canaanites.

When the people received this message they wept—but they were crocodile tears. The generation after Joshua did not have the spiritual vitality of their parents. The pressure of the pagan culture surrounding them would continue to test the genuineness of their relationship with God and their attitude toward the covenant He had made with their forefathers.

▪ 80 ▪   Othniel, Ehud, Shamgar, and Deborah

Judges 3-5   *Date: circa 1380-1250 B.C.*

THE FIRST DESPOT to overrun Israel as a result of its spiritual declension was the king of Aram Naharaim, an area in northern Mesopotamia. After 8 years of subjection to this distant oppressor the people cried out to the Lord. In response God's Spirit came upon Caleb's nephew Othniel, who went on to win a great victory against the invaders. After Othniel's triumph the nation enjoyed 40 years of peace.

After that Israel again broke covenant, as a result of which God allowed a coalition of Moabites, Ammonites and Amalekites to attack and defeat them. For 18 years Eglon, the obese king of Moab, dominated the region from his encampment near the ruins of Jericho.

Once again the people of Israel cried out to the Lord. This time He raised up Ehud, a left-handed Benjamite. Ehud made a short sword that he strapped to his right thigh under his clothes. He then traveled to Eglon to pay the annual tribute. After sending his men home Ehud headed back to king Eglon and obtained a private audience by suggesting that he had a secret message meant only for the king's ears. Ehud then surreptitiously reached for his sword and thrust it deep into the corpulent king, killing him instantly. Ehud carefully locked the door into the throne room from the inside and slipped away through a window. The officials' slow response enabled him to escape to the hill country of one of Israel's most powerful tribes, Ephraim. Blowing the war-trumpet he urged Israel to strike while the enemy camp was leaderless and in confusion. His brave, bold leadership rallied the people and they routed the Moabite invaders by cutting off their escape across the Jordan. Suddenly the tables were turned; Moab was now subject to Israel. For the next 80 years they enjoyed peace.

The Israelites again began to neglect God's law and turned to idolatry. A man called Shamgar came after Ehud. This hero delivered Israel from the Philistines by slaying 600 of them using an ox-goad, a bronze-tipped pole used to goad cattle.

After Shamgar a remarkable woman named Deborah became Israel's leading judge and prophetess. Because of the evil Israel did in the Lord's eyes He handed them over to Jabin, a Canaanite king. His army commander Sisera terrorized the northern tribes for 20 years with a substantial force of 900 iron chariots. Eventually Israel cried out to the Lord. He instructed Deborah to call on a man named Barak to lead a campaign of deliverance. She told him that the Lord would lure the Canaanites into the Kishon River valley, where they would fall into his hands. When Barak was reluctant to go alone, Deborah acquiesced to accompany him, but told him that due to his lack of faith the glory of killing Sisera would go to a woman.

When king Jabin heard that the Israelites were mustering by the Kishon River he dispatched his army, including his chariot battalion. Humanly speaking Barak's smaller and lightly armed forces did not have a chance. At the critical moment, however, a sudden cloudburst caused the Kishon to burst its banks. Sisera's chariots bogged down in the muddy mess, and his army was thrown into confusion. Barak's forces quickly went on the attack and defeated the demoralized enemy.

Sisera himself ditched his useless chariot and fled northwards on foot to an encampment of Bedouin Kenites whom he knew to have friendly relations with his king. He did not know, however, that the Kenites were descendants of Moses' father-in-law and were thus sympathetic to Israel as well. A woman named Jael welcomed the exhausted army commander into the safety of her tent. After refreshments Sisera soon fell into a deep sleep. Then Jael picked up a wooden mallet and forcefully drove a tent peg through his temple. Barak, who had been tracking Sisera, arrived soon afterwards.

"Come," Jael said, "and I will show you the man you are pursuing." The honor of killing the general did, indeed, go to a woman!

Deborah and Barak celebrated their divinely orchestrated victory in an epic poem, a masterpiece of ancient literature known as the Song of Deborah. In powerful language it described the terrible conditions during the years of oppression. The roads were unsafe, commerce was at a standstill, the cities were pillaged, the people disarmed. But when Israel remembered and recounted the righteous acts of the Lord, defeat turned to triumph and freedom. The poem described the battle vividly, including the Lord's divine intervention at the Kishon, and mentioned the heroic participation of certain tribes and the defeatism of others. It gave a special blessing to Jael for boldly dispatching Sisera and poignantly recalled Sisera's mother waiting anxiously for word about her son's fate. The poem concluded with a plea that all the Lord's enemies would perish but that the righteous would grow in strength like the rising sun. After this astonishing victory Israel enjoyed another 40 years of peace.

IN ANCIENT times the belief that particular gods were associated with particular regions was very common so, to "hedge their bets", the people of Israel began to combine the worship of Jehovah with that of local Amorite deities. God condemned this kind of syncretism in the strongest terms. He demanded His people's exclusive loyalty. Since the nation had broken covenant they once again found themselves at the mercies of an invading army.

The Midianites, descendants of Abraham and his second wife Keturah, were bedouins living in the Arabian Desert to the south. Israel had defeated them years earlier when this people had sought to prevent Israel's progress towards Canaan (Num 22:7). Now, however, Israel watched helplessly while year after year—for seven years in row—the camel-riding Midianite throngs swarmed the land at harvest time and helped themselves to Israel's crops and livestock. Fearing for their lives the impoverished Israelites would flee to caves and strongholds in the hills, terrain not suitable for the camel-riding desert-dwellers.

Once again the people cried out to the Lord for mercy. This time He sent a prophet who pointed out their failure to worship God exclusively in spite of His goodness to them. The Lord also sent an angel in the form of a human being to a young man from the tribe of Manasseh.

Gideon was busy threshing wheat when the angel appeared to him. Threshing involved beating grain with a flail to separate the heavier kernel from the chaff, a chore normally done in the open so the wind could blow the chaff away. Gideon, however, was busy threshing inside a winepress, a type of stone pit in which farmers would trample grapes to squeeze out the juice. He hoped the Midianites wouldn't notice his activity down there.

"The Lord is with you, mighty warrior," the angel greeted him. The angel must have had a droll sense of humor because Gideon, sweating and choking in a winepress in fear of the Midianites did not look or act heroic. He also failed to recognize the individual speaking to him as an angel.

"If the Lord is with us, sir, then why has this happened to us? Whatever happened to all those miracles God did in the past, which our fathers told us about?" he complained.

"Go in such strength as you have and save Israel from the Midianite oppression. Am I not sending you?" the angel said. But Gideon would have none of it. "Who am I to save Israel? My clan is the weakest in Manasseh and I am the youngest in my family...".

"I will be with you, and you will strike down the Midianites," the angel responded. At this Gideon, with a typical display of lavish Middle Eastern hospitality, slaughtered and cooked a kid goat, baked some unleavened bread and offered it to his guest. The angel instructed him to take the meat and the bread to a rock and to pour out the broth. When the angel touched the food with his staff, fire flared from the rock and consumed the food. Gideon cried out in fright as he recognized it was an angel before him, but the angel assured him he had nothing to fear. Grateful, Gideon built an altar and called it "The Lord is Peace".

That night the Lord asked him to purify his own family of idols. His father Joash, a leading person in the community, had erected an altar to Baal as well as an Asherah pole (Asherah, considered Baal's wife, was symbolized by a carved pole beside Baal's altars). Gideon was to tear these down, take one of his father's bulls and sacrifice it as a burnt offering. He obeyed, but under the cover of darkness.

When the townspeople woke up to find their Baal altar and Asherah pole destroyed, it did not take them long to identify the culprit. The angry mob made its way to Joash's house and demanded that he hand over his son so that they could kill him.

After the years of Midianite oppression, Joash himself harboured doubts about Baal's efficacy. "If Baal is really a god, let Baal himself deal with him," he told the crowd, and refused to hand his son over to them. From that day Gideon received the nickname "Jerub-Baal", meaning "let Baal deal with him".

In spite of his initial obedience, Gideon's confidence in God was shaky. "If you really plan to save Israel by my hand as you promised," he prayed, "then let me place a wool fleece on the threshing floor. If in the morning the fleece is wet with dew and the ground around it is dry I will know that you plan to save Israel through me." That is exactly what happened. Still doubtful, Gideon asked the Lord to reverse the miracle. This would be a greater miracle than the first, as the fleece would absorb water more easily than the hard threshing floor. Instead of berating and punishing Gideon for his unbelief, God dealt gently him. The next morning Gideon found the ground to be covered with dew and the fleece dry as cork. After these assurances Gideon was ready to obey the Lord's commands.

▪ 82 ▪ "For the Lord and for Gideon!"

Judges 7 – 8   *Date: circa 1280-1200 B.C.*

GIDEON WENT and mustered an army. Some 32,000 men rallied to the cause, a paltry number compared to the overwhelming Midianite horde. Then, to Gideon's surprise, the Lord told him he had too many men! There was to be no ground for boasting. He, the Lord, was to receive the credit for the upcoming victory.

In accordance with Israelite rules for war Gideon gave all those who were afraid the chance to return home (Deut. 20:8). 22,000 men availed themselves of this opportunity, leaving Gideon with 10,000 stouthearted fellows. But in the Lord's scheme of things they were still too many. He instructed Gideon to take the men to a nearby spring for a drink. There he was to separate out those who cupped up the water in their hands from those who got down to drink. Only 300 of the men proved to be constantly alert soldiers. Gideon sent all the others home.

That night Gideon's puny force of top-notch men moved into position on the hilltops overlooking the Midianite camp. There Gideon's faith wavered once again when he looked down on the vast encampment spread out in the valley below. The Lord then encouraged him to sneak into the enemy camp and eavesdrop. He and his servant crept down and overheard two men talking. "I just dreamed about a round loaf of barley bread which tumbled into our camp and struck the tent with such force it collapsed," one man said to another. People in the ancient world held that the gods communicated important information by means of dreams.

The man's friend immediately made the connection between barley bread, the staple food of the oppressed people, and Gideon. "Your dream refers to the sword of Gideon," he responded gloomily. "God has handed the entire Midianite camp into his hand..." Gideon realized that what he'd overheard was no coincidence. Reassured and ready to fight, he worshipped God and returned to his men.

"Get up! The Lord has handed the Midianites into your hands," he called out. He divided his soldiers into three groups of 100 men, gave them each a ram's horn as a trumpet and had them hide their torches inside their clay supply jars. "Do exactly what I do," he instructed them.

They approached the enemy camp from three sides and, following Gideon, blew their trumpets, smashed their jars so the torches inside flared up, and bellowed their war cry, "For the Lord and for Gideon!" When they heard the smashing sounds, the shrieking war cries and the deafening trumpet blasts at close range the Midianites panicked. The hundreds of torches gave the impression of a large army. In confusion and disarray the Midianites started fighting among themselves and fled pell-mell towards the Jordan in hope of reaching the safety of the desert beyond.

Gideon quickly called for reinforcements to help with the mopping-up operation. The powerful tribe of Ephraim cut the Midianites' escape route at the Jordan. They felt insulted, however, that Gideon had not called on them earlier. Gideon carefully diffused this tribal jealousy. He also severely punished two Israelite towns that refused to provide his exhausted army with provisions.

After Gideon's great victory over the Midianites the people of Israel invited him to be their ruler. Gideon refused, stressing that theocracy, or direct rule by God, was the chosen form of government for Israel. During this period of the judges the priesthood had fallen into disrepute (Jud. 17:8-13). Although Gideon turned down the position of ruler, he decided to assume the role of priest instead. He asked each person to give him a single gold earring from the plunder from which he manufactured an ephod, a replica of the one worn by the high priest.

The land had peace for 40 years but the Israelites came to worship at the ephod that Gideon placed on display in his home. Sadly, Gideon, who had led his family's break with Baal worship, now led them into idolatry of his own making. He became very wealthy and fathered a total of 70 sons with his many wives. He died at a ripe old age.

▪ 83 ▪ Abimelech

Judges 9   *Date: circa 1820-1200 B.C.*

IN ADDITION to his 70 sons Gideon also had a son named Abimelech with a concubine from the town of Shechem. After his father's death Abimelech asked the citizens of his home town whom they would rather have rule over them: those 70 sons who were outsiders, or himself who, as one of their own, would have their best interests at heart. They chose him and gave him money from the local Baal temple with which to get started. He used these funds to hire a company of mercenaries with whom he murdered all his brothers; only Jotham, the youngest, escaped. His fellow Shechemites then crowned him as Israel's pseudo-king.

When Jotham heard this he climbed Mount Gerizim, which overlooked the town. Shouting down from there, he employed a clever allegory about various trees to illustrate his point: his father Gideon and his 70 true sons were like the good trees while Abimelech resembled a worthless thorn bush. He then cursed the people of Shechem saying, "If you have acted in good faith towards my father and his family may Abimelech be your joy and you his! But if you have not, let the wild fire of Abimelech consume you along with himself." He then fled to safety. His curse, however, lingered...

Three years later the relationship between Abimelech and the citizens of Shechem soured so he decided to reside elsewhere. The Shechemites started to disrupt the trade into and out of their city, thus preventing Abimelech from collecting revenue. As the situation deteriorated the vindictive Abimelech decided to turn Shechem into an object lesson for anyone contemplating disloyalty: he wiped it out and scattered salt over it. The earth was no longer fertile and the city was left in ruins for almost 200 years (I Ki. 12:25).

Abimelech then headed for the town of Thebez, which had apparently also shown signs of displeasure with his rule. Its citizens locked themselves in the fortified tower. As he approached its entrance to set it on fire a woman on the roof dropped a millstone on his head, cracking his skull. Being killed by a woman was considered dishonourable, so he begged his armor bearer to finish him off. On seeing that their paymaster had died his mercenaries went home. Jotham's curse had come true

After Abimelech's brief, brutal rule a judge called Tola from the tribe of Issachar led Israel for 23 years. Jair of Gilead, who judged Israel for 22 years, followed him.

• 84 • Jephthah

Judges 10-12   *Date: circa 1096-1080 B.C.*

ONCE AGAIN Israel succumbed to idolatry. They worshipped the Baals and Ashtoreths, the most common idols of the region, as well as more local deities such as Chemosh and Milcom of the Moabites and Ammonites, and Dagon of the Philistines. As a result of Israel's obeisance to those local gods, God allowed the Ammonites and the Philistines to oppress Israel for 18 years.

Eventually the people of Israel confessed their sin and cried out to the Lord for help. However, the Lord was not there just to be called on in an emergency. He had repeatedly delivered them just to see them sink back into idolatry. This time He withheld His help. "Go and cry out to the gods you are worshiping and let them save you," He told them. At this unexpected response Israel repented with more than mere words: they actually got rid of their idols! When they had returned to God on His terms, God's heart went out to them. He could not bear their suffering any longer...

One of the regions most oppressed was Gilead, on the east side of the Jordan River. The elders of Gilead approached a guerilla leader called Jephthah and offered him the position of commander-in-chief if he would lead the campaign against the Ammonites. Years earlier Jephthah had been disowned by his family, and had fled to a desolate region where he had turned a bunch of renegades and brigands into an effective fighting force.

Jephthah first tried to negotiate peace with the enemy. The Ammonite king responded by requesting that the Israelites give back the trans-Jordan territory taken from him during Israel's journey up from Egypt. Jephthah's detailed response revealed his in-depth knowledge of Israel's history. The Ammonite king did not respond, however, and war was imminent. At that critical moment the Spirit of the Lord empowered Jephthah. He mustered an army and made a vow to the Lord: in the event of a victory he would sacrifice as a burnt offering whatever came to meet him out of the door of his house upon his return home.

In the subsequent battle the Lord granted the Israelites an overwhelming victory. However, national jubilation turned to personal tragedy. Upon returning home Jephthah's only child came out to meet him happily dancing and celebrating her father's victory. In bitter anguish of spirit Jephthah tore his clothes. "Oh, my daughter," he cried. "You've made me a miserable man, for I made a vow to the Lord that I cannot break!" Jephthah's daughter, realizing her father's rash vow meant death for her, begged him for two month's reprieve. She spent that time in the hills with her friends to prepare for the ordeal and mourn the fact that she would never marry. Their family line died out the day Jephthah carried out his awful vow.[10]

The story of Jephthah had another tragic epilogue that further highlighted the fact that without a strong centralized leadership Israel steadily declined. After Jephthah's victory the large and powerful tribe of Ephraim denounced him—just as they had Gideon—for not inviting them to join in his campaign. The proud Ephraimites launched a civil war—which they promptly lost. Jephthah then deployed his troops along the fords at the Jordan River. Whenever an Ephraimite survivor came to the crossing Jephthah's Gileadites asked him if he was an Ephraimite. If the fugitive said "no", they made them say the word "Shibboleth", which means "an ear of grain", and which was pronounced "Sibboleth" in the Ephraimite dialect. Anyone whose accent gave him away was killed. With a loss of 42,000 men Ephraim was finished as an effective fighting force.

---

[10] Should God's people carry out their vows, no matter how ill conceived? Jephthah, desperate for success, was evidently prepared to do whatever he thought it took, even if it meant sacrificing his only daughter (in desperate situations Israel's pagan neighbors considered child sacrifice the ultimate bargaining plea with the gods. 2 Kings 3:27). Because breaking one's vow was a sin according to the Mosaic Law (Num. 30:2) Jephthah clearly believed he had to go through with it. He was wrong. The Mosaic Law strictly forbade human sacrifice (Lev. 18:21; Deut. 12:31). The Bible also teaches that "an undeserved curse does not come to rest" (Prov. 26:2). God would not have punished Jephthah for not carrying through with this particular, pagan-inspired vow.

Jephthah led Israel for 6 years. After him three minor judges, Ibzan, Elon, and Abdon each led Israel with a rule of between 7 to 10 years. The spiritual, moral and social decline of Israel continued.

· 85 · Samson's Birth and Marriage

Judges 13-15   *Date: circa 1100-1055 B.C.*

THE PHILISTINES, a warlike people, originally came from Crete. They had been colonizing Canaan's Mediterranean coast since Israel was in Egypt and had successfully established five cities there. When Israel once again broke the covenant, the Lord allowed them to terrorize the nation for over 40 years, the longest period of oppression during the times of the judges.

During that difficult period there was a man from the tribe of Dan named Manoah, whose wife was unable to bear children. One day the Angel of the Lord in the form of a human being appeared to her and said, "Although you are sterile and childless, you are going to have a son". He instructed her to refrain from drinking anything fermented or from eating anything unclean, and not to shave the child's head, because he would be a Nazirite, someone set apart for God (Num. 6:1-12). "He has been set apart to God from birth for the purpose of beginning Israel's delivery from the oppression of the Philistines," the stranger informed her. Later the angel appeared to Manoah as well, and repeated the instructions he'd given. When Manoah inquired after the stranger's name he would not identify himself. He simply replied, "my name is beyond understanding." When Manoah sacrificed a goat, the stranger ascended heavenward in the rising flames, and the couple realized that they had been in the presence of God.

Manoah's wife soon became pregnant and gave birth to a son. They named him Samson. The boy grew and experienced God's blessing and the stirring of the Spirit as a young man. Then Samson became infatuated with a Philistine woman. In spite of the fact that the Mosaic Covenant forbade intermarriage with the idolatrous inhabitants (Deut. 7:1-3) he stubbornly insisted that his parents get her for him. During the period of the judges "everyone did as he saw fit", and Samson reflected the spirit of the age.

Samson and his parents set off to ask for the girl's hand in marriage. On the way he separated a little way from his parents when, suddenly, out of nowhere, a young lion pounced on him. Then the Spirit of the Lord came on him in a rush of power and he tore the beast apart with his bare hands. He continued on his way without telling anyone about his feat; touching a dead carcass was a violation of his Nazirite vow (Num. 6:6, 9). Sometime later Samson, when he and his parents made the trip again, this time for the wedding, he turned aside to look at the carcass of the lion he had killed. He noticed that a swarm of bees had nested inside it. The unusual location of the honey gave him the idea for a riddle.

Wedding celebrations lasted seven days, and because Samson didn't bring his own "best men" the Philistines provided him with 30 fellows to keep him company. He challenged them to figure out his riddle. As a reward he would give them each a new set of clothes.

"Let's hear it," they said.

"Out of the eater, something to eat; out of the strong, something sweet," Samson replied.

Thirty Philistines racked their brains trying to come up with the answer but to no avail. Finally they turned to Samson's bride and threatened to burn her and her family to death if she didn't wheedle the answer from him before the end of the wedding festivities.

For the rest of the week Samson's bride pled, wept and nagged. "You don't really love me!" she sobbed. "You tell my people a riddle but won't share the answer with me!" She wore him down with her constant cajoling and, on the last day, Samson caved in. She promptly told her townsmen and, triumphant, they told Samson the answer: "What is sweeter than honey? What is stronger than a lion?"

Samson was furious that they had not played by the rules and walked out of his own wedding party. Then the Spirit of the Lord descended on him once again. He hiked the twenty miles to the Philistine city of Ashkelon, struck down thirty well-dressed gentlemen, stripped them of their clothes, hiked back to Timnah and paid off his debt. Angrily he moved back in with his parents.

Eventually, however, his anger subsided and he decided to reclaim his bride—only to learn that she had been married off to someone else! This time Samson was really incensed. Holding every Philistine in the region responsible for the affront, he determined to get even. He went and caught 300 foxes, tied them in pairs by their tails, wedged a burning torch between their tails and let the animals loose in the Philistines' grain fields. Running crazily to escape the fire they were dragging behind them, the animals also torched the vineyards and olive-groves. When the Philistines discovered the reason for this outrage they went and burned Samson's bride and her father to death.

Now there was no restraining the feud between Samson and the Philistines. Enraged he went and slaughtered many of them, then took refuge in an inaccessible cave. The Philistines assembled an army and marched against Judah. Upon learning that the only thing the invaders wanted was Samson, the men of Judah went to his cave to hand him over to the enemy. "What are you doing to us?" they cried abjectly.

"I'm only doing to them what they did to me," Samson replied. "Swear to me that you yourselves won't kill me." When they agreed he allowed them to tie him up and give him to the enemy. Sensing victory, the Philistines shouted with glee as they swarmed him.

Suddenly the Spirit of the Lord again came on Samson in power. He snapped the ropes binding him, grabbed a donkey's jawbone lying nearby and struck down a thousand Philistines. Then he celebrated his victory by naming that place Ramath Lehi, which means "Jawbone Hill".

Suddenly, however, he felt completely drained and parched with thirst. "Lord, you have given your servant a great victory," he cried out. "Must I now die of thirst and fall into their idolatrous hands?" In response the Lord opened up a spring of water for him to drink.

After Samson's victory at Jawbone Hill the people of Israel began to look to him for leadership and, for the next twenty years, he governed them to the best of his ability.

▪ 86 ▪ Samson's End

Judges 16   *Date: circa 1075-1055 B.C.*

ONCE AGAIN Samson's weakness for Philistine women got him into trouble. One day he wandered down to Gaza, the southern-most town of the five Philistine cities, and decided to spend the night with a local prostitute. Word soon got out that he was in town, and the men of Gaza planned to kill him on his departure from the city in the morning. He left the house at midnight, however, tore the locked gates out of the city walls and dumped them on a hilltop some 40 miles (abt. 64 km.) distance.

After that Samson fell in love with Delilah, another Philistine woman. When the Philistine rulers got wind of the relationship they promised her a large amount of silver if she could pry the secret of his great strength from him. Thus bribed Delilah set to work. "What is the secret of your great strength?" she asked Samson one day. "How can you be subdued?"

"Tie me with fresh bowstrings," he said, "and I will become as weak as other men." One day after he had dozed off, she tied him up. However, when the Philistines came out of their hiding place to arrest him Samson easily snapped the bowstrings.

Delilah continued to pester him. "Tie me with fresh ropes and I'll become as weak as other men," he said. Once again she tied him up when he was asleep. Once again he snapped the ropes as if they were threads when the Philistines were about to arrest him.

"You're making a fool of me," Delilah wailed. "Tell me! How can you be tied?" This time Samson skirted dangerously close to the truth. "Weave my locks of hair into a loom and I'll be as weak as other men," he told her. Once again, however, he shook himself free.

"Three times you've made a fool of me," Delilah cried. "How can you say that you love me if you won't confide in me?" She kept nagging him until, one day, he caved in. "I was set apart to

God from birth as a Nazirite," he told her somberly. "As a sign of that vow my hair must never be cut. If I were to shave my head my strength would leave me..."

This time, Delilah informed her countrymen, she had gotten to the truth of the matter. She lulled Samson to sleep and had someone cut off his long braids. When the Philistines rushed him again he was easily overcome. They gouged out his eyes, bound him in shackles and took him to Gaza. There he was set to work grinding grain, a job reserved for women and donkeys.

The Philistines attributed the victory to their god Dagon, not to the fact that Jehovah God had deserted Samson. Later they organized a great celebration. At the height of the festivities the revellers called to have blind Samson brought into the hall to entertain them.

From the noise around him Samson knew he was near the center of Dagon's temple. "Put me where I can feel the supporting pillars so I can lean against them," he begged the servant. Then he prayed: "O Sovereign Lord, remember me! Give me back my strength one last time so I can get revenge on the Philistines for gouging out my eyes..." He braced himself between the

pillars and pushed with all his might. "Let me die with the Philistines," he cried as the pillars shifted from their bases.

The rulers and all the people died with Samson when the roof crashed down. His family came to collect his body and gave him an honourable burial. Samson was later listed as as one of the heroes of faith (Heb. 11:32). In spite of his obvious weaknesses, God used him during his 20 years as judge to mitigate the Philistine domination of Israel.

Judges 17-21   *Date: era of the judges*

TWO EVENTS from the period of the Judges illustrate how Israel slid ever deeper into a moral and religious morass and graphically illustrate the book's contention that without central leadership "everyone did as seemed right in their own eyes" (17:6; 18:1; 19:1; 21:25).

In the first event a man named Micah confessed to his mother that he had stolen a large amount of silver from her. On returning it she used some of it to make a household idol. Micah then dressed one of his sons in an ephod and ordained him to look after the family shrine.

Later Micah, caring little that only a direct descendant of Aaron could be legitimately ordained as priest, invited a passing Levite, a grandson of Moses (Jud. 18:30), to stay and officiate at his homemade shrine.

In the meantime, the tribe of Dan, caught between the Amorites and Philistines, found it difficult to take possession of the region allotted them (Jud. 1:34-35) and appointed five scouts to find a new location. While travelling these men came to Micah's house where they met his pseudo-priest, who assured them they would succeed in their venture. The men continued northward and discovered a defenceless town in a lush, well-watered valley near the foot of Mount Hermon. It was ideal for their purposes. They quickly headed home and convinced their tribesmen of the place's virtues. Before long 600 armed Danites set out for their new "promised land". When they got to Micah's house they decided to steal Micah's idols and convince the renegade "priest" to join them.

The Danites then continued northward to attack and burn the town to the ground and killing all its inhabitants. They then rebuilt the place and named it "Dan". It became Israel's northern-most frontier post. The shrine they built for their stolen idol and their fraudulent priest continued as the focal point of their religious life.

▪ ▪ ▪ ▪ ▪

The second event not only reflected the deplorable state into which the priesthood had fallen but also the low moral ebb of the average Israelite.

A Levite from a remote area in Ephraim took a concubine from Bethlehem. This woman was unfaithful to him, after which she returned to her parental home. About four months later the Levite decided to go and persuade her to come back to him.

The woman's father welcomed him heartily, but after four days the Levite set off for home with his concubine. By evening they had traveled as far as the Benjamite city of Gibeah. The laws of hospitality required people to look after visitors, and eventually an old man invited them to stay at his house. However, while they were enjoying a meal together a band of bisexual Gibeahite louts surrounded the house and, pounding on the door, demanded that the old man hand over his guest for their enjoyment. The host was outraged, but the Levite callously pushed his concubine out the door. The mob gang-raped and abused her all night.

Towards dawn the poor woman managed to crawl back to the old man's house, only to die at his doorstep.

When the Levite found her there the next morning he carried her body home, where he dismembered it into twelve parts, sending one part to each of Israel's tribes. Shocked by the lewd behaviour and brutal murder, the nation was moved to action. They rallied at Mizpah—all, that is, with the exception of the Benjamites who, in solidarity with their Gibeahite clansmen, boycotted the assembly. The nation affirmed that such evil could not go unpunished and mustered a huge army for a punitive expedition. When the Benjamites refused to hand over the rapists the rest of the nation felt it had no choice but to go to war against it.

The Benjamites were renowned as fierce warriors, just as the patriarch Jacob had predicted long ago (Gen. 49:27). In the first two battles they inflicted heavy defeats on Israel's much larger army. Stung by this unexpected turn of events Israel wept, fasted, and inquired of the Lord as to whether they should give up the fight or not. "Go," the Lord assured them. "Tomorrow I will give them into your hands." Thus assured the Israelites went to battle a third time. This time they struck down the Benjamite army and then systematically destroyed every Benjamite town and put everyone to the sword.

The punishment was extremely harsh, on the same level as that meted out to the original Canaanites. The Mosaic Law, however, stipulated that any Israelite city that harboured "wicked men who lead others astray" should be exterminated (Deut. 13:12-18). As the tribe of Benjamin harboured such an abomination it had become just like the Canaanites they had displaced. A mere 600 men managed to escape.

Instead of celebrating their bloody victory, the people of Israel re-gathered at Bethel to mourn the virtual elimination of one of the 12 tribes. Furthermore the men of Israel had vowed not to give their daughters in marriage to the Benjamites. They wept before the Lord saying, "Why should Israel today be missing one tribe?"

They resolved the dilemma by enquiring if any of Israel's towns had failed to respond to the national call to arms. Jabesh Gilead was found guilty and its inhabitants, with the exception of its 400 virgins, were put to the sword. These were given to the 600 surviving Benjamites. A further 200 girls were kidnapped during the annual festival at Shiloh, after which the Benjamites and their brides set to rebuilding their tribe.

Spiritual and moral decline led to social and political anarchy. There was no strong, central leadership and "every man did what was right in his own eyes".

• 88 • Ruth

Ruth	*Date: era of the judges*

SOMETIME DURING the period of the judges famine ravaged the land. Circumstances for a man from Bethlehem became so dire that he, his wife Naomi, and their two sons took the drastic step of moving to the neighbouring land of Moab. The man died there and the two boys, who had married local Moabite girls, also passed away.

When Naomi heard that the famine in Judah had ended she decided to return home. Her two daughters-in-law pledged to stick with her. As the three of them headed towards Israel, however, Naomi began to feel badly about putting her own welfare ahead of theirs. No self-respecting Jewish man would marry a foreign widow, especially a loathed Moabite, and she herself was too old to have children. "Return home. May the Lord grant you both rest as you become the wives of men," she encouraged the weeping girls. "As for me, my life is bitter for the hand of the Lord has gone out against me." Persuaded, one of them kissed her mother-in-law goodbye and returned to her parental home in Moab.

"Look, your sister-in-law is going back to her people and her gods," Naomi urged Ruth, the second girl. "Return with her!"

Ruth would not hear of it. The example of Naomi's life, faith and hope in Jehovah had made a deep impact on her. "Don't make me leave you," she begged, clinging to the old woman. "I will go where you go and stay where you stay. Your people will be my people and your God my God. I will die and be buried where you die and are buried. May the Lord deal severely with me should I leave you." Ruth knew that serving Naomi's God meant identifying herself completely with His covenant people.

When the two entered Bethlehem tongues started wagging. "Is this the same Naomi?" people asked. "Don't call me Naomi anymore. Call me Mara." Naomi means pleasant, mara means bitter. "The Lord has brought misfortune upon me and made my life bitter," she explained. "I left here full, I have returned empty." She acknowledged that her afflictions were not mere bad luck but were orchestrated by the sovereign God.

After settling somewhere, Ruth asked Naomi for permission to go gleaning. Gleaning, an activity warranted under Mosaic Law (Lev. 19:9-10; 23:22; Deut. 24:19-21), allowed poor people to collect stray ears of grain left behind by the harvesters. As it happened, Ruth found herself working in a field belonging to a wealthy bachelor named Boaz.

One day Boaz swung by his fields to see how his labourers were getting on. "The Lord bless you," he called out to his workers. Suddenly Ruth caught his eye. "Who is that young woman?" he asked his foreman.

"She is the Moabitess who returned with Naomi," the man replied. "She asked if she could glean after the workers and has been working tirelessly since morning."

Boaz approached the girl. "Listen my daughter," he said, "don't go elsewhere to glean. Stay close to the servant girls, pay attention to where the men are working and follow after them. I've told them not to touch you. And whenever you are thirsty, help yourself to some of the water in the jars the men have filled for themselves."

Surprised at this unexpected attention, Ruth bowed to the ground before her benefactor. "Why should I, a foreigner, find favour in your eyes, my Lord?" she asked.

"I have heard how you have cared for your mother-in-law, and how you chose to leave your homeland to live among us," he replied. "May the Lord, the God of Israel, under whose wings you have sought refuge, reward you richly." Boaz instructed his men to leave extra grain behind for Ruth to glean. That evening Ruth shared the day's events with her mother-in-law.

"I know Boaz," Naomi explained. "He is not just a very kind man, he is also a close relative of ours. He is, in fact, one of our kinsman-redeemers. Don't go to anyone else's field, or you might be harmed." Kinsman-redeemers were responsible for looking after needy family members, redeeming them if they had been sold into slavery, buying back family land, and marrying childless widows of deceased brothers. This latter responsibility, called levirate marriage, assured that the brother's name would live on (Deut. 25:5-10).

As time went on Naomi wondered how to gently persuade Boaz, who was clearly fond of Ruth, into a levirate marriage. She devised a plan, which Ruth carried out to the letter. One night after Boaz had finished eating and drinking he lay down at the far end of the threshing floor and promptly fell asleep. Ruth approached him quietly, uncovered his feet and lay down. In the middle of the night Boaz awoke and was astonished to find a woman lying at his feet. "Who are you?" he demanded.

"I am your servant Ruth. Since you are a kinsman-redeemer, please spread the corner of your garment over me." Ruth answered. By using this metaphor Ruth was asking him to take her under his wing. It was a bold request for marriage.

Boaz didn't hesitate. "I will," he said. "Everyone in town knows what a noble woman you are. However, there is another man who is a closer relative than I am. He has first claim on you. I will sort the matter out."

Very early in the morning Boaz sent Ruth home with a large gift of grain and a warning not to tell anyone about their encounter. He then made his way to the city gate, a public place where business was transacted and legal matters resolved. When the other kinsman-redeemer showed up Boaz rounded up 10 elders to serve as witnesses. "Naomi wants to sell a piece of the land that belonged to her husband," he informed the other man. "Since you are the closest relative, you have first right to it. Do you want it?"

The man jumped at the chance. "I'll take it," he said.

"If you do, you will also have to marry Ruth the Moabitess," Boaz responded. At that the man backed off. Not only would he have to marry a foreigner but also the land would legally pass to the first son of their union. "In that case, you buy it," the man responded. According to the custom of the times he took off his sandal and gave it to Boaz to symbolize the transfer of property: henceforth Boaz could walk freely on the land.

"You are all witnesses to the fact that today I have bought this property along with Ruth the Moabitess to maintain the family's name so that it will not disappear from the town records," he declared.

"We are witnesses," the elders affirmed. "And may she give you as many sons as Rachel and Leah gave Jacob," they intoned.

Boaz took Ruth as his wife. She bore him a son, whom they named Obed. The neighbour-hood women, who had earlier lamented Naomi's misfortune, now gathered to share in her happiness as she helped care for her grandson. In time, Obed became the father of Jesse, who was the father of king David. Ruth, like Rahab the Canaanite (her husband Boaz's grandmother) would later be included in the genealogy of Jesus Christ (Mat. 1:5). Although appalling spiritual, moral and social decline marked the days of the judges, there remained a remnant of true believers like Naomi, Ruth and Boaz who remained faithful to the covenant.

▪ 89 ▪ Samuel's Childhood

I Samuel 1-3   *Date: circa 1080 B.C.*

IN THE FINAL years of the judges there was a Levite named Elkanah who had two wives, Hannah and Peninnah. Hannah was barren. Peninnah, on the other hand, could bear children and took every opportunity to deride Hannah for her inability to do so.

Every year Elkanah and his wives made the pilgrimage to the tabernacle at Shiloh. On one such trip Hannah could not bear her grief any longer. She went to the tabernacle precinct and poured out her heart to the Lord. "Oh Lord Almighty," she whispered, "if you give me a son I will dedicate him to you for the rest of his life."

Eli, the high priest, was sitting nearby when he saw a strange woman mumbling incoherently. He thought she was drunk and rebuked her.

"No, my Lord, I am not drunk," Hannah responded sadly. "Your servant is in anguish and I am pouring out my heart to the Lord..."

"In that case, go in peace," Eli said. "And may the God of Israel grant whatever it was you asked of him," he added.

The Lord remembered Hannah's prayer and she gave birth to a son whom she named "Samuel", which means "God hears". She also kept her vow. When Samuel was about three years old she took him to Shiloh and presented him to Eli to serve in the tabernacle.

"I now give this child back to the Lord," she concluded. "His whole life will be in His service." Then her heart welled up with joy and she broke into a song of vindication and thanksgiving to the Lord for his past, present and future blessings. Centuries later that song would inspire Mary, the mother of Jesus, to compose a similar hymn when she learned that she too was to give birth miraculously.

Little Samuel was left in the old priest's care and soon made himself useful doing odd jobs around the tabernacle. Every year his mother would lovingly make him a new linen robe, which she would give him on those joyous, long anticipated, reunions during their annual pilgrimage to Shiloh. After that the Lord blessed Hannah with three more sons and two daughters.

Eli, the high priest, was a likeable man but he failed to discipline his own sons Hophni and Phinehas for their outrageous behaviour. They treated people's offerings with contempt and, in ways reminiscent of the ritual prostitution common among Israel's Canaanite neighbours, slept with the women who served at the tabernacle.

In that dark era of the judges the Lord rarely spoke to His people. One day, however, a man of God appeared at the tabernacle and confronted Eli. "Although you are a priest in the line of Aaron," the man declared, "you will be punished for dishonoring the Lord. No descendant of yours will live to an old age. Your sons Hophni and Phinehas will die on the same day and I will raise up a priest in their place who will serve the Lord faithfully".

One night Eli and Samuel were asleep in the tabernacle compound. Suddenly Samuel woke up to hear a voice calling him by name. He got up and ran over to Eli. "Here I am," he said. "You called me..."

"No, I didn't call you," Eli replied drowsily. "Go back to sleep."

No sooner had Samuel crawled back into bed than he heard his name called a second time. He got up again and went to Eli. "Here I am," he said. "You called me..."

"No, my son," Eli said. "I didn't call you."

When Samuel returned for the third time Eli realized that the Lord was calling the boy. "Go back to bed and lie down," he said. "If you hear the voice calling you again, say 'speak Lord, your servant is listening'".

Then the Lord came and stood before Samuel saying, "I am about to do something which will make people's ears tingle. Because Hophni and Phinehas have treated the priesthood with contempt, and because Eli failed to discipline them, I am going to carry out all the judgement which was prophesied against this family."

In the morning Eli pressured young Samuel to tell him what God had said, and Samuel related what had happened. "He is the Lord," Eli responded sadly. "Let Him do what is best in His eyes..."

As Samuel grew up all Israel began to recognize that he was a prophet attested by God. While Eli grew increasingly blind with age, Samuel saw things with increasing clearness. He became known as "The Seer".

1 Samuel 4-7   *Date: circa 1075 B.C.*

DURING THE late period of the judges the Philistines were Israel's chief enemies. On one occasion one particular military engagement with this warlike people led to the death of about 4000 Israelites soldiers. Recognizing that the Lord was not with them, Israel's leaders decided to fetch the Ark of the Covenant from Shiloh. They remembered how it had been at the head of Israel's armies during the campaign against Jericho and mistakenly thought that they could guarantee the Lord's presence by repeating that strategy.

When the delegation returned with the ark Israel's army greeted it with such a great shout that the noise carried all the way to the Philistine lines. "Why all this shouting in the Hebrew camp?" the Philistines asked themselves.

When they discovered that the ark had arrived, the doughty but superstitious Philistines trembled with fear. "Woe to us!" they cried. "This is the god that struck down the Egyptians with all kinds of plagues! Men of Philistine, we must fight like we've never fought before! Be brave or we'll be subjected to those Hebrews!" The Philistines then fought with furious determination. They went on to slaughter some 30,000 Israelites and captured the Ark of the Covenant. Both Hophni and Phinehas were killed, just as the Lord had predicted to young Samuel years earlier.

Soon the news reached Eli. By now he was old, obese and blind. The shock of hearing that the Ark, the symbol of God's presence with His people, had fallen into enemy hands sent such a strong a convulsion through the old priest's body that he fell off his chair, broke his neck and died.

The series of tragedies was not over yet. When Eli's daughter-in-law heard the awful news she went into premature labour, living just long enough to name her newborn son "Ichabod", which means "the glory has departed". Years earlier, when the tabernacle was consecrated, God's glory had filled it. Now all evidence of God's presence was gone: the Glory of Israel had departed. In the aftermath Shiloh, and possibly the tabernacle itself, was destroyed (Ps. 78:60-61; Jer. 7:12, 14; 28:9).

In high spirits the Philistines took the ark to the city of Ashdod and placed it in the temple of their idol Dagon. The next morning, however, Dagon's priests were shocked to find Dagon facedown on the ground before the ark. They picked him up and put him back on his pedestal, but the morning after the idol had again toppled off it. This time his head and hands had broken off and were lying on the threshold. In those days severed heads and hands were battlefield trophies (Jud. 8:6; 1 Sam. 17:51; 29:4; 1 Chron. 10:10). The message was clear: Jehovah, the God of Israel, had defeated Dagon in his own temple. Meanwhile a plague of tumors broke out among the citizens of Ashdod. They moved the ark to Gath, but as soon as it arrived the plague broke out there too. They shipped the ark to the Philistine city of Ekron, but once again people started dying the moment it arrived.

After seven months of devastation the Philistines decided to return the ark to Israel, together with a valuable gift, which they hoped would atone for their guilt. They placed the ark on a cart and hitched it to two cows that had recently calved. The newborn calves were then separated from their mothers. "If the cows return to their calves then we know that the events of the last months just happened by chance, but if the cows pull the cart of their own accord to Israel this will be a supernatural sign that the God of Israel, the ark's rightful owner, was behind our great disaster," they argued.

The lumbering beasts, lowing all the way, dragged the cart the nine miles from Ekron to the border town of Beth Shemesh. The people there were out harvesting when the ark appeared. They lifted it onto a large rock, chopped the cart into firewood and, right there on the spot, slaughtered the cows as burnt offerings. Unable to contain their curiosity some in the crowd lifted the ark's lid, the mercy seat, and peeked inside to stare directly at the tablets of the law. This was a capital offence (Num. 4:5; 20) and God promptly struck 70 of them dead. Suddenly aware of the unapproachable holiness of Jehovah God, the Jewish villagers, like the Philistines, now wanted to get rid of the ark. Shiloh had been razed in the recent war, but some men from Kiriath Jearim, a village up the road, carried the ark to the house of one of their elders, Abinadab. They commissioned his son Eleazar to guard it. It would remain there for the next 40 to 50 years.

Eli and his sons were dead, the tabernacle was destroyed and Israel had lost the recent war with the Philistines. It was at this low point in Israel's history that Samuel succeeded to the nation's religious leadership. The tragic events of the recent past had softened people's hearts, and he urged them to full repentance. They needed to get rid of the Baals and Ashtoreths and recommit themselves to serve God exclusively. Samuel called the people to assemble at Mizpah for a period of fasting and national repentance.

When news of the Israelite convocation reached the Philistines they quickly mustered their army and seized the opportunity to attack them. Terrified, the Israelites urged Samuel to intercede with God on their behalf. While Samuel was sacrificing a burnt offering the Lord hurled down such loud peals of thunder that the Philistine soldiers fled in disarray. Emboldened, the Israelites rallied together to destroy many of their enemies.

After the battle Samuel erected a commemorative stone that he named "Ebenezer", meaning "The Stone of (divine) Help". During the rest of Samuel's long leadership the Philistines were contained in the territory along the south coast.

1 Samuel 8-10   *Date: 1052 B.C.*

LIKE HIS predecessor Eli, Samuel too grieved over the behaviour of his two sons. When he was old the elders of Israel confronted him, "You are old and your sons are not following the Lord. We want you to appoint a king like the other nations have, someone to lead us into battle." Samuel was unhappy with their request, but he took the matter to the Lord. "It is not you, they are rejecting, but me," the Lord said. "Warn them how human kings exploit their subjects, then give them what they want..."

God's promise to Abraham had, in fact, envisioned a monarchy (Gen. 17:6, 16), as had Jacob's blessing to Judah (Gen. 49:10) and Balaam's God-inspired oracle (Num. 24:17-19). Much later Moses had spelled out the parameters within which any potential monarch was to operate (Deut. 17:14-20). Kings in the ancient world claimed to be "sons of the gods" (Is. 14:13-14; Ezek. 28:2, 9), a claim on which they based their sovereignty. Israel's kings, on the other hand, were to recognize that they were vassals under the authority and judgement of Israel's real king, Jehovah (Ex. 15:6, 18; Num. 23:21; Deut. 33:5; Judg. 5:3-5; 8:22-23). Their great temptation would be to act unilaterally, usurping authority that was not theirs. Although it was God's will that Israel have a king, wanting a king "such as the other nations have" was wrong, and for this the people were culpable.

Samuel warned them of the long-term consequences of kingship: the man would draft the best of their young men and women into his service, tax them heavily, expropriate the best of their land and create a parasitical retinue. In time they would become his slaves... No matter how negatively Samuel described the sought-after institution, the people refused to change their minds. Soon afterwards the Lord revealed to him that he would meet a Benjamite whom he was to anoint as king.

God used the occasion of some stray donkeys to bring Samuel into contact with a young man named Saul. When Saul had been searching in vain for their lost animals his servant suggested they consult a local "seer", or prophet, he'd heard about. "The man you are looking for is Samuel," some local girls said. "He just came to town today to bless the sacrifice." As Saul and his servant entered the town they met an old man.

"Excuse me," they asked him, "Could you tell us where the seer's house is?" Samuel looked at the tall, handsome young man asking for directions and the Lord said to him, "This is the man I told you about." God had chosen someone who closely matched the people's wishes: a regal-looking man who had the makings of a good warrior.

"I am the person you are looking for," Samuel said. "Walk on ahead of me to the high place. You will eat with me this evening." Then he added cryptically: "All of Israel's desire is turned towards you and your family."

Saul understood the import of Samuel's words. "Why me, someone from the smallest clan of Israel's smallest tribe?" he asked. That evening Samuel ushered Saul into a meeting hall, seated him at the head table and honoured him by serving him the choicest of the food.

Early the next morning Samuel took a flask of oil and poured it on Saul's head. "The Lord has anointed you to lead His inheritance," he said. "On your way home you will meet two men near Rachel's tomb who will tell you that your lost donkeys have been found. When you get to the great tree of Tabor you will meet three men going to worship God at Bethel. Accept the two loaves of bread they will offer you. When you get to Gibeah you will meet a procession of prophets coming down from the high place prophesying and accompanied by people playing various musical instruments. There the Spirit of the Lord will come on you with great power. You too will prophesy and be changed into a different person. Once all these things have occurred, go and do whatever you need to do, for God will be with you."

On the way home events played out exactly as Samuel had predicted; in fact the people at Gibeah couldn't believe their eyes when they saw Saul prophesying! Saul kept the matter of the private anointing to the kingship to himself.

▪ 92 ▪ Samuel and Saul

1 Samuel 10-12   *Date: 1052 B.C.*

SAMUEL AGAIN summoned the people of Israel to Mizpah, the place where he had begun his own career as judge (1 Sam. 7:5). He reminded them of his misgivings about their decision to elect a hereditary monarchy. Then he divided them by tribes and clans. Lots were cast until Saul was chosen.

When the choice was announced, however, Saul was nowhere to be found—he was hiding among the piles of baggage! After the Lord revealed Saul's whereabouts Samuel introduced the shy giant to the people: "Here is the man God has chosen! There is no one like him among the people!"

"Long live the king! Long live the king!" they shouted. Then Samuel explained the regulations, rights and duties of kingship to the people. The scroll containing this social contract was deposited "before the Lord", probably in the tabernacle, which had been rebuilt after its destruction by the Philistines. Most of the people were impressed by God's choice, but a group of skeptical troublemakers refused to honour him. Saul did not respond to their baiting.

Not long afterwards the Ammonites besieged Jabesh Gilead, the trans-Jordanian town that, years earlier, had provided wives for Saul's tribe of Benjamin. The town offered to negotiate surrender but pled for a week's grace when the Ammonites demanded that they gouge out the right eye of every single citizen. The men from Jabesh Gilead quickly sent a delegation to Saul's hometown of Gibeah.

When Saul heard about the dire situation in Jabesh Gilead the Spirit of God came upon him powerfully. With burning indignation he slaughtered a pair of oxen and had messengers carry the pieces throughout the land with the threat that he would slaughter the oxen of anyone who failed to answer the call to arms. The fear of the Lord fell on Israel. Recognizing Jehovah's hand in Saul's forceful response the people responded en masse. Saul and his huge army immediately launched a surprise attack on the Ammonite invaders and totally defeated them. Not only had Saul confirmed himself as an effective king, he had, in one fell swoop, gained the loyalty of Israel's trans-Jordan region.

After this victory Saul's soldiers wanted to execute those who had not supported him when he was chosen to be king but, statesmanlike, Saul demurred. "No one will be put to death," he said, "for it was the Lord who rescued Israel today."

Samuel then invited all the people to go to Gilgal where they gladly reaffirmed Saul as their king. At this meeting the political leadership of Israel was officially transferred from Samuel to Saul. In a moving farewell speech Samuel challenged the people to find any fault in his dealings with them. He then summarized God's faithful leadership of them throughout their history. God was the one who had miraculously and powerfully delivered them time and again in spite of their repeated violation of covenant commitments. Nevertheless they had demanded a human king and once again God had given them the desire of their hearts. Samuel's point was clear: if they were to flourish, both they and their newly appointed king had to recognize that God was their real sovereign. If they rebelled against His commandments, He would turn against them.

Although it was the dry season in Israel, God underscored his authority with a frightening display of thunder and rain. Terrified, the people asked Samuel to intercede on their behalf: "We have added to our sins by asking for a king," they acknowledged.

"Don't be afraid," Samuel comforted them. "Although you have done wrong, henceforth serve the Lord with all your hearts. Don't turn to useless idols." He assured them that God would never completely reject them. He had chosen them and for the sake of His own name He would not fail to keep the covenant he had made with their forefathers. "As for me," he added, "I will not fail to pray for you, nor will I fail to teach you the ways of the Lord."

▪ 93 ▪ Saul's Disobedience

1 Samuel 13-14   *Date: Saul's reign, 1052-1010 B.C.*

THE PEOPLE HAD chosen Saul to lead them into battle, and he obliged them. He established a standing army of 3000 soldiers, 2000 of whom were stationed at Micmash under his command and 1000 of whom were in his hometown of Gibeah under his son Jonathan's command.

One day Jonathan unilaterally attacked a Philistine outpost. The Philistines responded by mobilizing their army. Saul then mobilized the nation to attack the enraged Philistines, but his army was far smaller and poorly equipped. The Philistines commanded the blacksmith trade, and had forged ahead into the Iron Age with their chariots and superior weaponry. Israel's army possessed only two iron swords, those belonging to Saul and Jonathan. When Saul's tiny army saw the enemy's vast superiority they began defecting in droves.

Samuel had warned Saul not to engage the enemy before he had come to offer burnt and fellowship offerings on behalf of Israel, which he had promised to do within a week. When

Samuel did not show up by day seven Saul, assuming the role of a priest, offered the burnt offerings himself. He had no sooner done so than Samuel appeared. "What have you done?" the prophet asked angrily.

"You didn't come and the army was disintegrating," Saul complained. "I felt compelled to offer the burnt offering to seek the Lord's favor before the Philistines launched their attack".

"You foolishly failed to obey the command of the Lord your God. If you had, he would have established your kingship over Israel for all time, but now it will not endure. God has sought out a man after his own heart whom he will appoint in your place." With those words Samuel turned on his heel and left.

Meanwhile Jonathan noticed an outpost of Philistines. "Let's reveal our position," he said to his armour-bearer. "If those uncircumcised fellows challenge us to a fight, we'll take it as a sign from the Lord that He has given them into our hands. If the Lord is on our side He can save by few as well as by many." When the Philistine soldiers baited them Jonathan and his armour bearer killed twenty of them. After that, events unfolded much as they had with Gideon: God caused the enemy to panic so that they ran in all directions slaying each other in the confusion.

When Saul heard the tumult in the Philistine camp he mustered what was left of his forces and attacked the confused enemy. It could have been a decisive victory but Saul had foolishly bound his soldiers with an oath: anyone who ate anything before evening would be accursed. Tired and hungry, Jonathan, in hot pursuit of some Philistines and unaware of his father's injunction, saw a honeybee nest in a hollow tree and ate some of the wild honey. Strengthened, he continued the fight. That night Saul suggested they resume their pursuit of the Philistines. Ahijah the priest, perhaps sensing that something was wrong, suggested they first enquire of the Lord. When the Lord failed to respond Saul announced that the person who had caused the Lord to withdraw His presence would die. They cast lots to find the culprit, and it fell on Jonathan. "Tell me what you have done," he demanded of his son.

"I tasted a bit of honey," Jonathan responded.

"May God deal severely with me if you do not die," Saul said sternly. His men, however, rebelled at this gross injustice. "Should Jonathan, the Lord's means of securing this great victory, die? Never!" Saul was forced to rescind the order and his army disbanded.

• 94 • Saul Rejected

1 Sam. 15   *Date: 1052-1010 B.C.*

SAUL REIGNED for 40 years. Much of what he accomplished in that period would, in human terms, be considered noteworthy. He fought successfully against virtually all the enemy nations surrounding Israel: the Moabites, Ammonites, Edomites and the Philistines.

The Lord had told Saul through Samuel that he was to declare war on the Amalekites. The instructions were crystal clear: they were not to spare a single Amalekite nor take any plunder. The spiritually hardened and rebellious nation, which had attacked Israel on their way up from Egypt, was to be completely obliterated, as had been predicted long ago (Ex. 17:14; Num.

24:20; Deut. 25:19). Saul defeated the Amalekites in short order but failed to carry out the command to annihilate them. He captured their king Agag alive and allowed his troops to take the best of the livestock.

After the battle Samuel learned that Saul had gone to Carmel, where he had set up a monument in his own honour, and then moved on to Gilgal. When Samuel caught up with him there Saul welcomed him effusively. "The Lord bless you! I've done exactly what the Lord told me to do!" he said.

"Then what is all this lowing and bleating I hear?" Samuel demanded.

"I obeyed," Saul insisted. "We wanted to sacrifice the best animals to God!"

"The Lord delights much more in obedience than sacrifice," Samuel responded. "Because you spurned the word of the Lord he has spurned you as king of Israel." As Samuel turned to go, Saul grabbed him by the hem of his robe so that it tore. "In the same way the Lord has torn the kingdom from you and given it to a better man," Samuel said

"I have sinned," Saul lamented. Hoping to salvage his credibility he begged Samuel to honour him before the people. Reluctantly Samuel agreed. Samuel mourned over Saul after-wards but never went to see him again.

· 95 · David Anointed King

1 Samuel 16   *Date: circa 1020 B.C.*

NOT LONG after rejecting Saul the Lord told Samuel to stop mourning. "Fill your horn with oil. I'm sending you to Bethlehem to anoint one of Jesse's sons as king to replace Saul". Samuel duly made his way to Bethlehem and invited Jesse and his sons to a sacrifice. When he saw the oldest son, Eliab, he felt sure this must be the Lord's choice.

"Do not look at outward appearances," the Lord told him. "I judge a person according to the state of his heart." One by one Jesse's seven sons stepped forward, but God's choice was not among them. Puzzled, Samuel asked if anyone was missing. Jesse's youngest son, a lad about 15 years old whom he'd thought too unimportant to be considered, was taking care of the family's sheep. Samuel quickly dispatched someone to fetch him.

"Anoint this man," the Lord told Samuel when David finally appeared. "He is the one!" Samuel poured the oil over David's head and declared him to be the next king of Israel. The Spirit of the Lord came in power upon David from that day onward. At the same time the Spirit of the Lord departed from Saul and was replaced by an evil spirit that often troubled his soul. Saul's servants suggested they find a skilled musician to play soothing music whenever this evil spirit tormented him. One of them remembered that a certain David, a son of Jesse from Bethlehem, was a skilled harpist.

Saul drafted David into his service, little knowing that God would give the kingdom to this unsophisticated, musically gifted and spiritually sensitive shepherd-boy. And so, without any scheming on his part, David found himself at the royal court, observing its ways and intrigues and becoming acquainted with the nation's leaders. Saul was pleased with David, whose playing calmed his troubled spirit, and soon promoted him to be his armour bearer. On completion of his term of duty at the royal court David returned home to resume his humble occupation as shepherd over his father's sheep.

Although David knew he would be the next king, he was content to let God work things out on his behalf. Little did he realize that he would have to go through many years of difficult preparation and be tested severely before taking up the task for which he had been anointed. He would be hated, outlawed, persecuted, and "hunted like a mountain partridge" (1 Sam. 26:20). Eventually, however, he could testify, "I waited patiently for the Lord and he heard my cry" (Psalm 40:1). David never forgot that he had been but a humble shepherd when the Lord chose him to be king over Israel; he likened his own relationship with the Lord to that of a dumb sheep living its life in utter dependence upon its shepherd (Ps. 23). "Commit your way to the Lord. Trust in Him, and He shall bring it to pass," David later testified. "Rest in the Lord, and wait patiently for Him" (Ps. 37:5-7).

▪ 96 ▪ David and Goliath

1 Samuel 17   *Date: circa 1019 B.C.*

ONCE AGAIN war broke out with the Philistines. This time Saul and his forces were arrayed on one side of a valley and the Philistines on the opposite side. Every morning and evening the Philistines sent a heavily armored giant named Goliath into no-man's land to taunt the Jewish army. Goliath was probably one of the last remaining "sons of Anak" of whom most were killed during the conquest at the time of Joshua. Day after day the fearsome giant challenged Israel to send a soldier to engage him in one-to-one combat on behalf of their respective armies. "If he defeats me we will become your slaves, but if I prevail you will become our slaves," Goliath shouted.

Scared and humiliated, the once brave Saul didn't know how to respond. The empowering Spirit had left him and now he was helpless. For forty long, frustrating days the Israelites gazed impotently at the menacing hulk taunting them from the valley floor.

Back in the solitary fields surrounding Bethlehem young David was looking after the family's sheep. One day his father Jesse told him to take fresh provisions to his older brothers serving on the front lines. Just as David arrived there Goliath stepped forward to thunder his verbal abuse against Saul and his men. When David heard the giant railing he turned to those near him and asked, "Who does this uncircumcised Philistine think he is to defy the army of the living God?" Word of his contemptuous appraisal of Goliath reached Saul, who sent for him.

"Let no one be afraid of this man," David told the king. "I'll go and fight him!"

David's bravado seemed ludicrous to Saul. "You're but a boy and this man has been a fighter from his youth."

"Sir, your servant has been keeping his father's sheep," David responded. "When a lion or a bear seizes a sheep I chase after it and kill it. The Lord who delivered me from the maw of the bear will deliver me from the hand of this uncircumcised Philistine as well."

Deciding it was worth the risk, Saul responded, "Go, and may the Lord be with you." He offered David his coat of armour, helmet and sword, but David rejected the cumbersome gear. Instead he grabbed his staff, sling and shepherd's pouch, chose five smooth stones from a nearby stream, and headed for the battlefield.

When Goliath caught sight of an unarmed youth approaching him he launched into a tirade. "Get over here and I'll feed your carcass to the vultures and wild beasts!"

"You come against me with sword, spear and javelin, but I come against you in the name of the Lord Jehovah, the God of Israel's army whom you have defied!" David shouted back. "Today the Lord will hand you over to me! Then the whole world will know that there is a God in Israel and that it is He, not swords or spears, who is the source of victory!" Then he reached into his bag, picked out a stone and, running towards Goliath, placed it into his sling, whirled and released it. The missile struck the giant below the ridge of his helmet and sank into his forehead. The man tottered and then fell face down. David ran to the prostrate brute, grabbed his sword and cut off his head. This sudden, shocking turn of

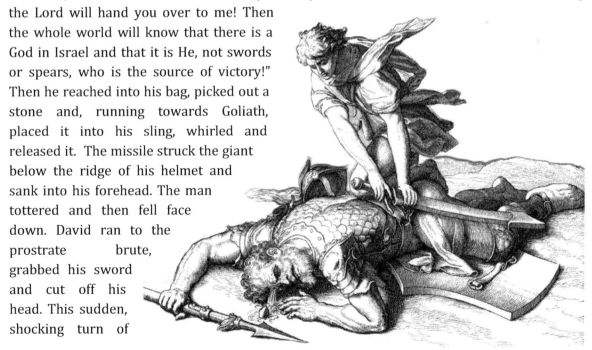

events produced panic in the Philistine ranks. They turned and ran. With a shout Israel's army surged forward. They slaughtered many and plundered the enemy camp.

"Find out for me who that young man is," Saul ordered his chief general Abner. David was still holding Goliath's head when Abner invited him to officially introduce himself to the king. Afterwards David carried the severed head to Jerusalem, a city not yet under Israel's control, where he posted it as an advance notice of what was to come.

• 97 • Saul Tries to Kill David

1 Samuel 18-20   *Date: circa 1015 B.C.*

AFTER DAVID'S remarkable confrontation with Goliath Saul made him a permanent member of his staff. David and Saul's son Jonathan, the heir to the throne, became close friends. Jonathan cared so much for David that he gave him his own armour, belt, sword and bow. Now properly outfitted, David carried out his military assignments so successfully that Saul promoted this young, winsome warrior to a high rank. Before long he was the most popular soldier in the land. After battle Israel's women would sing and dance in the streets, "Saul has slain his thousands, but David his ten thousands!" Such accolades rankled the insecure Saul who became increasingly jealous of his young underling.

Once when an evil spirit again troubled Saul, David was summoned to play the harp. Suddenly the king, consumed with envy, grabbed his spear and hurled it at David. He missed, but tried again another time. Both times David managed to elude him. When killing David directly did not work Saul sent him to the front lines in the hope that he would be slain in battle. That strategy also backfired. David's remarkable successes as a military commander made him more popular than ever. Saul grew increasingly afraid as he recognized that the Lord who had departed from him was now with David.

One day the obsessed Saul devised another plan to get rid of David. He offered his daughter Merab in marriage for the bride price of leading a campaign against the Philistines. "Be valiant for me and fight the Lord's battles," the hypocritical Saul said.

"Who am I or my father's family that I should be the king's son-in-law?" David responded meekly. Saul gave his daughter to someone else instead. Later David would write about "him whose words were smoother than butter, but had war in his heart; whose words were softer than oil, yet were drawn swords" (Psalm 55:21).

When Saul learned that his younger daughter Michal was in love with David he decided to repeat his ruse. He summoned David and told him he could have another shot at becoming the king's son-in-law. When David protested that he was too poor to afford a bride price Saul said that all he wanted was 100 Philistine foreskins! Circumcision was the symbol of the Israelites' dedication to their God; Saul calculated that having David cut off the foreskins of their slain soldiers would so infuriate the Philistines that they would hunt him down and kill him. Much to his chagrin David presented the king with double the number of the grisly trophies. Saul had no option but to give David his daughter Michal in marriage.

Although he stood to lose the throne Jonathan did not share his father's malice towards David and defended him before his father. Saul listened and swore on oath that he would not slay David. His assurances were short-lived. When David returned successfully from another altercation with the Philistines the evil spirit again got the better of him. He summoned David to play the harp and again hurled his spear at David. Once again David ducked in time. Determined to finish the job, Saul now sent a platoon of soldiers to stake out David's house and kill him when he stepped outside in the morning.

Michal, David's wife, learned of her father's plan and enabled her husband to escape under cover of darkness. David later wrote a psalm about this critical event: "Deliver me from my enemies, O my God," he prayed. "Defend me from those that rise up against me. Deliver me from evil and bloody men who lie in wait for my soul, who are gathered against me though I had not committed any sin or transgression." He celebrated his safe escape the next morning by singing, "I will sing of your power, of your mercy in the morning!" (Psalm 59:1-3; 16).

"Why did you deceive me and help my enemy escape?" Saul demanded shrilly of his daughter.

"He threatened to kill me if I didn't go along with this ruse," the quick-witted girl responded.

David made his way to Ramah, where Samuel was living. There he poured out his heart to the trusted old man of God. Saul and his soldiers tried to capture him but God once again intervened and delivered the future king out of their hands.

Later David sneaked back home to touch base with his friend Jonathan. "What have I done, that your father is after my life?" he complained.

"No," Jonathan countered, "I would know if my father wanted to kill you."

"He knows about our friendship and does not want to grieve you so he is keeping you in the dark," David insisted. "I tell you, there is but a step between me and death."

"What would you like me to do?" Jonathan asked.

"Tomorrow is the New Moon festival when I'm supposed to be at the state dinner with the king. Instead, I'm going to hide somewhere. If your father asks about me, tell him you gave me permission to go to my hometown to attend our clan's annual sacrifice. If your father loses his temper then you can be sure that he is determined to put an end to my life. And if I am guilty of anything, then kill me yourself!"

"Never," Jonathan responded. The two friends reaffirmed their bond of friendship, promising never to harm each other or anyone of the other's family. Then Jonathan outlined his plan. "On the evening of the day after tomorrow hide in the vicinity of the large stone at Ezel. I will shoot at it, as if I were target shooting. If I tell the boy with me that the arrows are on this side you are safe but if I tell him they are farther away your life is, indeed, in danger and you must flee."

At the state dinner the next day Saul asked Jonathan why David was absent. When Jonathan responded that he had given David permission to go to his family, Saul's anger flared up and he cursed his son. "As long as David is alive you will never have the kingdom," he yelled. Then, losing all control, he hurled his spear at his own son, just missing him. Angry and grieved, Jonathan stormed from the room.

The next day was his appointment with David out in the field. Jonathan shot his arrow and then shouted to the boy with him that it had landed beyond him. After he dismissed the boy David emerged from his hiding place. Weeping, the two friends reaffirmed their friendship and guardianship over each other's families. There was no option but to go their separate ways.

▪ 98 ▪ David the Fugitive

1 Samuel 20-23   *Date: circa 1012 B.C.*

DAVID WAS NOW an outcast running for his life. He first went to Nob, where the tabernacle now stood. David had always had a great love for the tabernacle, the tent that symbolized God's presence with His people. He wrote and sang, "How lovely is your dwelling place, O Lord of hosts! My soul longs for the courts of the Lord... a day in your house is better that a thousand elsewhere" (Ps. 84:1, 2). It was almost as if he wanted to see it one last time.

David lied to Ahimelech, the high priest, about why he was traveling alone. Then he asked the priest to enquire of the Lord on his behalf, and then obtained from him some basic provisions together with the sword of Goliath, which had been stored there.

Unknown to him an Edomite name Doeg, Saul's chief herdsman, was in Nob and noticed David at the temple talking with the high priest. When he informed Saul that he had seen Ahimelech give David food and weapons, Saul had Ahimelech brought in for questioning. He refused to believe Ahimelech's genuine lack of knowledge that David was on the run. The paranoid king accused him of treason and ordered the reprehensible Edomite to put every living creature in the town of Nod to the sword. Only Abiathar, the son of Ahimelech, escaped. He fled to join David, taking with him the ephod from the tabernacle.

David was remorseful that his lying to Ahimelech had ended in disaster not just for that man but also for many others. He decided to leave Israel altogether and seek asylum among the Philistines—with Goliath's sword hanging from his hip! The servants of Achish, king of Gath, soon identified him. David was arrested and brought before the king for interrogation.

Terrified, David decided that the only way to save himself was by pretending to be insane. He let his spittle run into his beard and started scratching the doorway. David, the Lord's annointed, could hardly have degraded himself lower. "What's this," the Philistine monarch complained. "Don't I have enough madmen to contend with that you have to bring in this specimen as well? Look at him! He's insane! Get him out of here!"

David crossed the border back into Judea, where he hid in the region around the cave of Adullam. There he regained his spiritual bearings. Repentant and chastened he penned the 34th Psalm, "When this poor man cried the Lord heard him and saved... Blessed is the man who takes refuge in the Him... The righteous may have many troubles, but the Lord delivers them from all of them... The Lord saves those who are crushed in spirit."

Saul and his men continued to search for David in order to kill him. Time and again David would cry to God for protection and sing His praises upon deliverance. "God most high vindicates me and rebukes those who hotly pursue me. He has sent me His love and His faithfulness" (Ps. 57:2-3). The intensity and emotion of David's life on the run from Saul were reflected in several other psalms.

David's family also feared for their lives and joined him in the hideouts at Adullam. Later he secured asylum for them in Moab, the land of Ruth, his great-grandmother. In time other fugitives and disaffected people joined David until he was leading a militia of some 600 men who were deeply devoted to him. One time, when the Philistines army was encamped in the vicinity of Bethlehem, David was reminiscing about the good old days back home. Without thinking, he let out that he longed for some fresh water from the village well. Three of his companions, who later became known as "The Three Mighty Men", promptly took off for Bethlehem. They broke through the Philistine lines, drew water from the village well, carried it back through the enemy lines, and gave it to David to drink. David was so moved by their devotion that he refused to drink it. Instead he poured the precious liquid onto the ground as a drink offering to the Lord.

In spite of his own troubles David still had a heart of compassion for his fellow Israelites. When he learned that the Philistines had laid siege to the nearby, fortified town of Keilah, he asked the Lord if he should move against the invaders. When God gave the go-ahead David and his men not only routed the enemy, but also captured substantial flocks of sheep to replenish their provisions. Word soon reached Saul, who set out immediately, confident that David was inside the fortified city.

Hearing that Saul was on his way, David once again requested Abiathar the priest, to inquire of the Lord. He learned that the town of Keilah would turn against their erstwhile saviour and hand him over to Saul. Deflated, David and his men retreated to the caves in the desert of Ziph, where Saul pursued him relentlessly in his jealousy-fuelled quest for David's life. David wrote, "I cried out to the Lord for mercy! I poured out my complaint to him and told him my troubles. My Spirit grew faint in me and men had hidden snares in the paths I took. No one cared. I had no place to turn to for refuge. Then I cried to the Lord, 'You are my refuge!' Listen to my cry, for I am in desperate need. Rescue me from those pursuing me, for they are much too strong for me..." (Psalm 142).

No matter how Saul hounded and provoked him, David dealt with him honorably and with self-restraint. Instead of luring Saul into a trap David waited, biding the Lord's time. The king's mad obsession led to a long cat-and-mouse game between them during which Jonathan courageously defied his father and met up with his friend David. Strengthening him in the Lord, Jonathan acknowledged that David would one day be king over Israel. The two friends renewed their covenant before the Lord, after which Jonathan returned home. Neither realized that that would be their last meeting.

When the nearby Ziphites—David's fellow tribesmen—learned of his whereabouts they too sent word to Saul, who asked them to trace David's movements. Being betrayed by his fellow tribesmen was deeply painful, something David expressed in the 54th Psalm: "Save me, O God, vindicate me... Ruthless men seek my life, men who do not regard God... Let evil recoil on those slanderers." After escaping to the wilderness of Maon David sang out, "O Lord, you have delivered me from all my troubles and have let me look in triumph on my foes." Whether the occasion was painful or joyous David continued to express his devotion to God, as well as his wide range of emotions, in psalms and poetry.

Saul pursued David to the desert of Maon. David hurried his men along one side of a mountain while Saul moved in for the kill along the other side. At the critical moment, however, a messenger reached Saul to inform him that the Philistines had launched a major invasion, forcing him to abandon the hunt. The Lord ensured that David was saved from seemingly certain destruction without him having to strike a single blow against the man who was still Israel's legitimate king. He and his men fled yet again, this time to the rocky crags of En Gedi on the shores of the Dead Sea.

▪ 99 ▪ David Spares Saul's Life

1 Samuel 24-26   *Date: circa 1012-1004 B.C.*

AFTER SUCCESSFULLY repelling the invading Philistines, Saul learned that David and his men had taken refuge in the wilderness of En Gedi. With 3000 elite soldiers he renewed his efforts to catch his elusive nemesis. David and some of his men had hidden themselves in a large cave when suddenly they saw the profile of a familiar figure outlined against the light of the entrance. Saul had entered the cave to relieve himself. A single sword-stroke stood between David and the throne.

"He is in your hands!" his men mouthed in his ear. "This is the day of which the Lord said, 'I'll hand over your enemy to you!' He's at your mercy!" David quietly crept up behind the unsuspecting king, silently cut a corner off his robe and retreated back into the cave. No sooner had he done so than his conscience smote him. Although he had not injured the king, he regretted harming the dignity of the monarchial office to which God had appointed Saul. He realized that how things are done was more important than any good that might result by taking matters into his own hands. As he wrote later, "Commit your ways to the Lord, trust in Him, and let Him bring it to pass... Be still before Him, wait patiently on Him, and do not fret when wicked men seem to succeed in their ways." (Psalm 37:5, 7)

Completely unaware of how close he had been to death, Saul left the cave with David following. "Why do you believe those who say that I am determined to harm you?" he shouted after Saul. "The Lord placed you in my hands today. My men urged me to kill you; I had to restrain them! But I will not lay hands on the Lord's anointed one!"

Surprised, Saul turned to see his son-in-law prostrate before him. "Look, my father, here is the corner of your robe which I cut off while you were in the cave. I am not guilty of wrongdoing or rebellion that you should hunt me down!"

"Is that you, my son?" Saul responded subdued, deeply shaken and moved to tears with emotion. "You are a better man than I am. No one else would let his enemy get away like that. You have rewarded my evil with good," he continued. "I know that you will become king after me. Promise to me on oath that when you come to the throne you will not kill my posterity," he pled. After receiving David's assurances he went home.

While David withdrew even further south, to the border region between Judah and the Negev desert, Samuel, the last of Israel's judges, died. All of Israel gathered at Ramah, his hometown, to mourn and lament the passing of the faithful prophet.

David and his men were always very careful not to interfere with the life of the local farmers in the areas where they took refuge. They paid for any supplies and defended the locals from wandering bands of cross-border raiders. One day David sent some of his men to request some provisions from a very wealthy local rancher named Nabal, a descendant of Caleb and a member of his own tribe of Judah. It was sheep-shearing season, a time of celebration, feasting and goodwill when one could expect people to be generous (2 Sam. 13:23). David's envoys, however, were turned away insolently. "Who is this David, this son of Jesse?" Nabal taunted contemptuously. "He's nothing but another servant that has run away from his master. Why should I give him food earmarked for my servants?"

David, taken off guard by the disdainful farmer's humiliating rebuff, lost his cool. "I have protected that man's flocks in vain! May God deal with me severely if I leave a single male of his family alive by morning!" He ordered his men to gird their swords and avenge the insult.

One of Nabal's servants had overheard the exchange between Nabal and David's men and rushed home to warn Nabal's beautiful wife Abigail. She moved fast, getting her servants to amass a generous gift and take it to David. She herself followed and on meeting David fell on her face before him. She acknowledged her husband's boorish behaviour, saying he was aptly named 'Nabal', which means 'fool', and asserted her confidence that he, David, would become king of Israel. "The Lord will certainly make you into a lasting dynasty. When that day comes you will not want the unbearable burden on your conscience of having shed innocent blood," she said. Her wise words melted David's vindictive heart. Without trying to minimize the evil he was about to perpetrate, he praised God for intervening by means of this intelligent, fast-acting woman.

When Nabal came out of his stupor the next morning his wife told him how she had averted David's vengeance. On hearing this, the man had a heart attack and died ten days later. David received the news of Nabal's death and blessed the Lord who had restrained him from committing evil while at the same time punished the wicked. Later he sent messengers to Abigail to ask for her hand in marriage. She accepted his proposal.

David did not trust Saul's empty assurances of safety so he and his men stayed among the rocks and caves of the wilderness. Once again the Ziphites informed Saul of his whereabouts. The news again inflamed the king's malice and he resumed his pursuit.

After David's scouts had determined the location of Saul's army he suggested a perilous mission: to sneak into the enemy camp that night, right into Saul's tent! Abishai, his nephew (1 Chron. 2:15, 16), agreed to accompany him. Silent as mice they slipped into the camp, past Saul's generals and into the royal tent. The Lord had put them all into a deep sleep so no one raised the alarm. "The Lord has delivered your enemy into your hand," Abishai whispered. "I can pin him to the ground with a single spear thrust."

David shook his head. "No," he said. "No one who harms the Lord's anointed will be counted guiltless. The Lord Himself will strike him down or he will die naturally or in battle, but I will not touch him. Now grab his spear and water jug and let's get out of here." They slipped out of the encampment, crossed a gorge and climbed to the top of a nearby hill. From there David shouted to Saul's chief general, "Hey Abner! You're going to have to give an account of yourself! Why did you not guard the king, the Lord's anointed? Someone came in the night to take his life! Have a look around: where are the king's spear and water jug?"

Saul immediately recognized the voice denouncing his general. "Is that you, my son David?" he called out.

"It is, my Lord," David responded. "Why are you pursuing your servant? What have I done to deserve this? Listen to me, my Lord! If the Lord is using you to punish me for any sin I have done, I will accept it. But if others are inciting you against me, may they be cursed!"

"I have sinned," Saul responded. "Come back, my son. You have spared my life and I will not try to harm you again. I have been greatly mistaken and acted foolishly."

"Here are your spear and water jug, my Lord. Please send one of your men to pick them up for you. The Lord delivered you into my hands but I refused to lay hands on you. May the Lord value my life as much as I value yours, and deliver me from all my troubles," David responded.

Saul was humbled, at least temporarily, and realized that one day the kingdom would, indeed, belong to David. "May God bless you, my son David," he responded. "You are destined to be a great man who will surely prevail." Then he returned home.

David returned to the caves, unable to trust the empty promises of a fickle king. Their paths never crossed again.

• 100 • The Ziklag Affair

1 Samuel 27, 29-30   *Date: 1010 B.C.*

SOMEWHERE ALONG the line David's focus once again shifted from God's unfailing protection to a black assessment of their current position. Although he used to sing about the Lord delivering him from all tribulation: "Though an army besiege me, my heart will not fear" (Ps. 27:3), now he became despondent and fearful.

There is no evidence that David inquired of the Lord when he decided that the safest place was to seek asylum among Israel's archenemy, the ruler of the Philistine city of Gad, king Achish. Word of David's feud with Saul had long since reached the Philistine king. He welcomed David, thinking he could put him to good use against his northern rival.

Even though David and his band of some 600 men were persecuted outcasts they had, nevertheless, married and started families. King Achish allowed them to live in the town of Ziklag, a town originally given to Judah (Josh. 15:31) but which they had failed to take. It was located on the edge of the Negev desert, near the Judean/Amalekite border. For the next 16 months David and his men used Ziklag as a jumping off point for raids against Israel's other enemies, notably the Amalekites. All the while David told king Achish that they were raiding Israel. David could be a first-rate liar. Later he would plead with God to save him from this besetting sin: "Keep me from deceitful ways" and advised others to "keep their tongues from evil and their lips from speaking lies" (Ps. 119:29; 34:13). King Achish came to believe that David had become so obnoxious among the people of Israel that henceforth he would serve the Philistines.

News of Samuel's death soon reached the Philistines. Emboldened by the fact that the Israelites had lost their great spiritual leader, they declared war. King Achish ordered David to join the general mobilization. "I look forward to showing you what we can do," David said evasively yet with seeming bravado. He had refused to harm the king of Israel, yet now he found himself drafted to fight against him and his own people.

Although David had strayed in terms of wholeheartedly trusting the Lord, the Lord providentially intervened to extricate him from this dilemma. The other Philistine military leaders were not convinced that, in the heat of battle, David and his men would not turn and align themselves with Saul. "Isn't this the same David about whom they sang, 'Saul slew his thousands, but David his ten thousands?" they insisted. They then ordered Achish to dismiss his division of potential Jewish fifth columnists.

"What have I done to deserve this?" David complained; the master prevaricator kept up the charade.

The next morning the Philistines headed north to Jezreel for the showdown with Saul while a relieved David and his company retraced the three-day journey back to Ziklag. After the long march the men finally crested the last hill—only to find a deserted, smouldering mass of ruins. The Amalekites had plundered and torched the city and captured its entire population, including their wives and families. David and his exhausted men were overwhelmed with grief. Suddenly it seemed as if God, who had always protected and dealt kindly with David, had turned against him. To make matters worse his men mutinied. For years these faithful followers had trusted his judgement—and now he had led them to utter disaster.

Feeling utterly abandoned David stood alone and helpless before his enraged men. It was a turning point for David. Looking death in the eye he turned his face heavenward and found strength in the Lord. His hope and confidence renewed, he turned to Abiathar the priest and ordered him to bring the ephod containing the urim and thummum. For the first time in a long while, he sought the Lord's counsel about how to proceed.

"Go after them," the Lord responded. "You will overtake them and recover everything!" Tired as they were, the men again rallied behind their leader. They found the Amalekites partying wildly on account of the great amount of spoil they had taken. David's vengeful men fell on them like hungry wolves. All that night and the next day they put the Amalekite raiders to the sword. And, joy of joys, they found their families unharmed and all their possessions intact. They also took large amounts of spoils that the raiders had collected on earlier campaigns.

The baser elements of David's band refused to share the spoil with the exhausted soldiers who had not joined in the fight, but David would have none of it. "These gifts from the Lord will be shared equally," he insisted. David was back in fellowship with God and aware of his own indebtedness to Him. When they got back to Ziklag, David sent some of the spoil as a gift to various cities in Judah, so ingratiating himself to them.

The Ziklag affair awakened in him a deep sense of ongoing dependency on the Lord. As Jehovah's vassal, he was, at long last, fit to become king of Israel. "Preserve me, O God, for in you I put my trust," he sang later, no doubt recalling his forlorn yet hopeful prayer before the ruins of Ziklag. "Cast your burden on the Lord and He will sustain you." (Ps. 55:22).

▪ 101 ▪ Saul Removed

1 Samuel 28-31; 2 Samuel 1   *Date: 1010 B.C.*

WHEN SAUL saw the enormous Philistine army facing Israel on the battlefield he was struck with terror and foreboding. He tried to inquire of the Lord but the Lord had long ago stopped communicating with him.

Earlier in his career Saul had sought to eliminate mediums from the land; now, desperate for guidance, he was reduced to consulting one. In disguise and under cover of darkness he asked a spiritist to call up Samuel from Sheol, the place of departed spirits. To the medium's own great consternation she saw an apparition of Samuel appearing out of the ground. Mediums communicate with evil spirits who pose as people who have died, a practice that God had forbidden (Deut. 18:9-22).

"I am greatly troubled," Saul told the apparition. "The Philistines have invaded the land and the Lord has departed from me. Because he refuses to answer me I have called you up to tell me what to do..."

"Why turn to me when the Lord Himself has become your enemy?" the spirit replied. "Because of your disobedience the Lord has torn the kingdom away from you and given it to David. You will lose the battle against the Philistines. Tomorrow you and your sons will also be in Sheol."

At this the terror-struck Saul fell to the ground. The medium saw that Saul was deeply shaken and offered him some food. She slaughtered a calf, baked some pita bread and served it to Saul and his men. It was to be their last meal, eaten in dreadful anticipation of the coming dawn. Late that night, hoping against hope that there was still a chance of success, Saul returned to the battlefield, to die during the tragic battle between Philistine and Israel that David so narrowly avoided.

The pathetic mismatch took place on Mount Gilboa. The Philistines mowed down Saul's forces and closed in on Saul himself, killing his sons including the faithful Jonathan. Then an archer wounded Saul; now he could neither fight nor flee. Fearing he would fall into the enemy's hands he asked his armour bearer to slay him. When the terrified man refused Saul committed suicide by falling on his own sword, and the armour bearer, in a mad expression of loyalty, followed his example. The remnants of the army scattered and fled.

When the Philistines scoured the battlefield the next day they found the bodies of Saul and his three sons. They cut off Saul's head and hung his body and that of his sons from the wall of the nearby town. They then placed his armour in their pagan temple and sent messengers throughout the land proclaiming their victory. That night some courageous men from Jabesh Gilead, the city which Saul had liberated when newly established as king, stole the bodies under cover of darkness and gave them a proper burial.

Many years later, when Israel was once again rebellious, God reminded them of the fate of king Saul: "I gave them a king in my anger, and removed him in my wrath" (Hos. 13:11). God was faithful to His covenant and this was a reminder that it cut both ways. He would punish those who broke it as well as reward those who kept it.

Meanwhile, back at Ziklag, David and his men were waiting to hear what had happened. When the news came he and his men rent their clothes in sorrow. They wept and fasted for the king of Israel and his son Jonathan, and for the state into which the nation had fallen. Always wont to express his emotional and spiritual state in poetry and song, David wrote a moving tribute celebrating his late arch-enemy's bravery and virtues with the repeated refrain, "How the mighty have fallen!" He also expressed his grief over the demise of his best friend Jonathan: "My brother, your love for me was wonderful".

Now that Saul and Jonathan were dead the way to the throne was open.

2 Samuel 2 - 5   *Date: 1010-1003 B.C.*

DAVID DID not rush into the vacuum created by Saul's demise. He sought the mind of the Lord, who directed him, his men and their families to cross back into Israel and settle in Hebron. David was determined to let the Lord unfold His plan gradually rather than force himself on the entire nation. Not long afterwards the leading men of Judah came to anoint him as king of that large and strong tribe.

In the meantime Abner, the commander-in-chief of Saul's army, took his late master's surviving son Ishbosheth to Mahanaim, across the Jordan, far from both the Philistines and David, and crowned him as a puppet king over Israel's eleven other tribes. Abner then marshalled an army against David near the pool of Gibeon. David's chief general Joab moved his men into position on the far side of the pool. An initial engagement between twelve men from each side was short-lived and inconclusive but in the subsequent battle Abner's force was routed. Asahel, a fleet-footed brother of David's general Joab, chased after the enemy general. Just as he was closing in on him, Abner stopped in his tracks and thrust the butt end of his spear backwards—straight through the fast-running Asahel. Then he shouted down to Joab from a nearby hilltop, "How much longer are you going to let your men kill their fellow Israelites? Don't you realize this will end in bitterness?"

"As surely as God lives," Joab shouted back, "If you had not spoken I would have continued the pursuit." He then called his men to a halt and each side retreated to their respective headquarters. Skirmishes lingered on for another five years between the tribe of Judah in the south and the eleven tribes of Israel in the north. David's side grew steadily stronger and Isbosheth's side steadily weaker.

One day Abner flew into a rage when his puppet king Ishbosheth accused him of having slept with one of his late father's concubines, behaviour interpreted as assuming royal prerogatives. Abner retaliated by terrifying Ishbosheth with a threat to transfer his allegiance to David and see him established as the rightful king over both Judah and Israel. He then led a diplomatic delegation to Hebron to finalize the details with respect to the transfer of allegiance. David's first stipulation was that his first wife, Michal, who had been given to another man, be restored to him (1 Sam. 25:44). Abner pressured Ishbosheth to concede and David regained his position as Saul's son-in-law. Abner then tried to persuade the various leaders of Israel to switch allegiances to David.

David's general Joab was furious at David for honoring Abner. Pretending he wanted to speak to Abner in private, he pulled him aside and stabbed the unsuspecting rival general in the stomach. Joab's revenge killing appalled David. Cursing Joab, he made his whole royal retinue dress in mourning and pay their respects at Abner's funeral. David himself walked behind the bier and composed a lament in Abner's honor. This public display of grief helped convince the people that he had no part in the murder.

Soon afterwards two of Ishbosheth's underlings killed their master while he was taking a siesta. Hoping to curry favour with David they brought him the decapitated head. Instead of honoring them David punished them for their treacherous deed.

Left leaderless the elders of the eleven tribes made their way to Hebron. Recognizing David as the Lord's choice, they stated, "When Saul was king you were our real military commander. The Lord had said you were the one who would shepherd and rule His people". Then they anointed him king over all of Israel. David was 30 years old when he began to reign over Judah and 37 when he began his reign over all of Israel. At long last God's promise to him had been realized.

· 103 · Jerusalem Becomes the City of David

2 Samuel 5-6; 1 Chronicles 11-16   *Date: 1003-995 B.C.*

THE HOMELESS WANDERER ascended the throne promised him many years earlier. He had waited patiently for God to work things out, and now his rivals were dead and buried. Because he had let the Lord work out His purposes in His own way the patriarch Jacob's prophecy concerning the tribe of Judah was, at long last, fulfilled: "your father's children shall bow down before you" (Gen. 49:8).

One of David's first military campaigns as king of all of Israel was against the seemingly impregnable fortress of Jerusalem in the middle of the country. It did not belong to any tribe, but was held by the Jebusites, a Canaanite people. Jerusalem was a natural fortress sitting on two hills, Mount Moriah, where centuries earlier Abraham had once offered Isaac, and Mount Zion where in time the temple would be built. David promised that the man who led the attack would become his commander-in-chief. His general Joab rose to the challenge and entered the city via the water shaft. After capturing the city David enlarged it, fortified its walls, and made it his capital city. King Hiram of the city-state of Tyre in Phoenicia (Lebanon today), famous for its large cedar trees, sent him carpenters and stonemasons to build a royal palace. The city soon came to be known as "The City of David".

When the ever-menacing Philistines learned that Israel had united under David they assembled a great army to fight against him. Before all three battles David humbly sought the Lord and obediently carried out His instructions no matter how strange they first appeared. Each time the Philistines were defeated, unaware that Jehovah God was with David in a way He had not been with Saul for a long time.

Even before David was crowned king of all Israel God had ensured that he would have the necessary help to carry out the task. During the difficult waning years of the house of Saul more and more internally displaced persons—even those from Saul's own tribe of Benjamin—had joined David's forces until he commanded a great army (1 Chron. 12:8; 12:22). A series of victories against the surrounding nations so enhanced his international reputation that these too were afraid of attacking him (1 Chron. 14:17).

177

No sooner had David established his kingdom than he resolved to place the ark, the symbol of God's presence with his people, at the center of his administration in Jerusalem. The ark had languished, forgotten and neglected, in the house of Abinadab. Not once had it been consulted during the forty years of Saul's reign (1 Chron. 13:3). For David, however, the ark was deeply meaningful. Now, with his kingdom secure, he decided to restore it to its rightful place of prominence in Israel's religious life. "I will allow no sleep to my eyes and no slumber to my eyelids," he sang, "until I find a place for the Lord... a resting place for the ark" (Psalm 132:4, 8).

David led a procession of 30,000 delegates from all over Israel to the house of Abinadab, placed the ark on a new ox cart and headed back towards Jerusalem. The whole procession celebrated joyfully, singing, and making music on their harps, lyres, tambourines and cymbals. Suddenly one of the oxen stumbled and a priest named Uzzah reached out to steady it. Instantly he fell down dead. God had given very specific instructions concerning the transportation of the ark which had been ignored: priests were to run long poles through special rings on the side of the ark and then heft it up on their shoulders. No one was to touch the ark under any condition (Ex. 25:12-15; Num. 7:9). God was a holy God who demanded unquestioning, explicit obedience, and who had promised to discipline those who deviated from the terms of the covenant. David, angry, afraid and humiliated, abandoned the ark in the house of a Philistine living nearby and slunk off to Jerusalem.

Obed-Edom was from the same clan as Goliath had been (1 Chr. 20:5) but was probably a convert to Judaism. For the three months that he hosted the awesome symbol of God's presence, the Lord blessed him and his household. When David learned of this his fears subsided and he decided to have another go at transporting the ark to Jerusalem. This time he carefully followed the Torah's instructions, and this time there were no tragic mishaps.

When he sensed that all was well David's heart welled up with praise and joy—so much so that he took off his long, cumbersome royal robe and, wearing nothing but the plain white garb of the worshipper, danced, sang, and praised God with all his might as the Levites carried the ark through the city gates. "Lift up your heads, O you gates, be lifted up, you ancient doors, that the King of Glory may go in," he sang. "Who is the King of Glory? The Lord strong and mighty, the Lord mighty in battle..." (Ps. 24). They carried the ark through the streets of Jerusalem to a tent that David had pitched for it in the city. There they offered burnt and peace offerings to the Lord. David then blessed the people, and distributed gifts of food to everyone.

Michal, David's first wife, was looking down on the events from a window in the royal palace. Possessing as little spiritual insight as her father Saul, she could not grasp why the occasion was so joyful. When she saw her husband dancing with ordinary people she despised him and when David eventually came home to bless his own household she mocked him for his public display of exuberance.

"I danced before the Lord, who chose me over your father to rule over His people Israel. Of course I will dance with joy before Him!" David protested. God was grieved and Michal bore no child until the day she died.

David assigned the Levites, with Asaph as their head, to lead the Israelites in perpetual worship. He himself composed a beautiful psalm extolling the Lord for his greatness and faithfulness to His covenant purposes (1 Chron. 16). Daily worship and offerings were resumed at last.

• 104 • The Davidic Covenant
2 Samuel 7; 1 Chronicles 17 *Date: circa 1000 B.C.*

DAVID WAS settled in Jerusalem and, at long last, the nation was at peace. Then David summoned his friend Nathan the prophet to discuss what was on his mind. "Here I am, living in a house of cedar, while the ark of God remains in a tent. I would like to build a suitable temple for the Lord."

That night the word of the Lord came to Nathan. "Go and tell David that he is not the one to build me a temple. Remind David that I was the one who took him from the pasture and made him ruler over my people Israel. I have been with him and have enabled him to overcome his enemies." The Lord followed this up with an unconditional promise. "Tell David that I will make his name great, and that I will establish a "house" for him. His successor will be the one to build a temple for me. I will be like a father to him; when he does wrong I will punish him, but I will never take away my love from him as I did from Saul. David's dynasty will last forever. His throne will be established for all time!"

When Nathan conveyed the Lord's message to David, he bowed his head and worshipped God. "Who am I, Lord God, and what is my house that you have blessed me so much?" Instead of David building a house for God, God had promised him an eternally enduring house and throne. An unending succession of kings occupying David's throne also meant that the promise of the Abrahamic covenant—that Israel would become a source of blessing to all the nations— would be fulfilled through one of his royal descendants.

David continued worshipping as God's promise sunk in: "You speak of your future plans for the house of your servant... this is not the normal way the Sovereign Lord deals with man... What more can I say? It is for the sake of Your word and in accordance with Your will that You will do these things. No God compares to You, no people on earth have been so blessed as Your people Israel. You have confirmed that You will be Israel's God forever and You, Lord, will glorify Yourself by keeping Your promises."

"Lord, do as You have promised!" would be the repeated cry of David's heart and the expectation of his faith. What he could not foresee, however, was that the ultimate fulfilment of this covenant would take place through the atoning life and work of his greatest descendant, Jesus Christ.

Sam. 8-10; 1 Chron. 18-19   *Date: circa 1003-995 B.C.*

WITH THE promise that his house would always exist before God David once more rose to subjugate Israel's enemies. He broke the power of the Philistines, taking Gath, their main stronghold, and also defeated and subjected the neighbouring Moabites in trans-Jordan. His victories over Moab and Philistine fulfilled promises hundreds of years old, promises made in the time of Abraham and Moses (Gen. 15:18; Num. 24:17).

Next David turned his attention northward to defeat a large coalition of Syrians and Arameans, and built garrisons in their cities to control them. Wherever David went the Lord— the secret of his success—granted him victory. The defeated nations became his subjects and brought tribute. David dedicated vast quantities of silver and gold to the Lord.

One day David was thinking about his late friend Jonathan and inquired if anyone was left alive from the house of Saul to whom he might show kindness. Years earlier he had made a solemn promise that when he ascended to the throne he would deal gently with Jonathan's descendents (1 Sam. 20:16-17; 42).

They located a former servant of Saul named Ziba who informed David that Jonathan had one surviving son. Five years old when his father was slain in battle his terrified nanny had grabbed him and fled for their lives. In her haste, however, the poor woman had dropped the boy causing him to be crippled (2 Sam. 4:4). Even his name, Mephibosheth, meaning "shameful thing", spoke of his unfortunate condition.

When ushered into David's presence Mephibosheth fell on his face before the man whom his grandfather had hounded mercilessly. "Mephibosheth," David said gently. "I want to show you kindness for the sake of your father Jonathan." David restored Saul's property to Mephibosheth and arranged for Ziba to serve him and farm the land. As for Mephibosheth himself, he was invited to feast at the king's table from then on, as though he were a member of the royal family.

Some time later Nahash, the Ammonite king, died and was succeeded by his son Hanun. The old king had once shown kindness to David, so David sent a diplomatic mission to express his sympathy. The suspicious Hanun, however, took them to be spies and greatly humiliated them. Such a response in those days was nothing less than a declaration of war, and David was forced to act. In the ensuing battle the Ammonites were defeated and they too became vassals subject to Israel. David had reached the pinnacle of his reign.

• 106 • **David and Bathsheba**

2 Samuel 11-12   *Date: circa 980 B.C.*

IT WAS LATE spring when David sent his army under Joab's command to resume military activities against the Ammonite capital Rabbah. He himself decided to remain in Jerusalem and relax. One evening he rose from his bed to stroll around the roof of his splendid new palace.

From that vantage point he caught sight of a beautiful woman bathing in a neighbouring villa. Determined to satisfy his suddenly inflamed passion he inquired about her, and was informed that she was Bathsheba, the wife of Uriah, a Hittite army officer out on the battlefront with Joab. David had her summoned to the palace — and committed adultery with her.

Some weeks later David received a message from Bathsheba saying that she was pregnant. David, knowing that his reputation would suffer irreparable damage if word got out that he was the child's father, resorted to extreme measures. He sent a message to Joab ordering Bathsheba's husband Uriah to report to the palace under the pretense of giving a military report. After listening to his faithful officer, David sent him home with a royal gift in the hope that the man would sleep with his wife and then be led to believe that Bathsheba's child was his own. The next day David learned that his scheme had failed. Uriah protested that while the Ark of the Covenant was housed in a tent and the king's armies were enduring hardships on the battlefield he could not indulge himself at home.

David then invited Uriah to dine with him—and made him drunk. But even in his intoxicated state Uriah refused to sleep anywhere but with the king's servants. Callously the increasingly desparate David planned his next move. In cold blood he wrote a letter to Joab ordering him to place Uriah in the most exposed position on the battlefield and then withdraw, leaving the man behind to be killed by the enemy. David's devilish plan succeeded, and Uriah was buried with full honours. As soon as the official period of mourning was over David brought Bathsheba into his harem as his wife. The plan appeared to have succeeded, but it was abundantly clear that the things David had done displeased the Lord. His fearful fall into sin would have profound consequences.

David's once sensitive conscience had hardened and there was no sign of remorse. Yet the Lord granted him no inner peace either. Later he testified; "When I kept silent my bones wasted away through my groaning all day long, for day and night your hand was heavy on me and my strength was sapped as in the summer heat" (Psalm 32:3). This state of depression dragged on for many months.

Sometime after Bathsheba's baby was born the Lord sent the prophet Nathan to visit David. It was not easy to confront and rebuke a monarch, so Nathan began by telling a story. "Once upon a time there were two men in the same town, one rich and the other poor," he began. "The rich man possessed large flocks while the poor man had nothing except one little ewe lamb which had grown up with his children, and which they loved dearly. One day the rich man, instead of slaughtering one of his own sheep, took the poor man's ewe and prepared it for a guest." David burned with indignation at the rich man's heartless, inexcusable cruelty and contemptuous selfishness. "As the Lord lives, the man who did this thing shall surely die!" he exploded.

"You are that man," Nathan declared boldly, pointing his finger at the king. Then, speaking as the representative of the Lord God of Israel, he reminded David of the Lord's past blessings to him: how the Lord had delivered him from the hand of Saul and made him king over all Israel and how He had given him everything he had desired, right down to Saul's own daughter. Yet he had despised the Lord's commands and had committed evil in His sight. Nathan then pronounced God's judgment. "As a result the Lord is going to bring calamity on your household. Someone close to you is going to lie with your wives—only what you did in secret will be done to you in broad daylight in the sight of all Israel."

Faced with the grievous truth about himself David suddenly crumbled. God's arrow had pierced his defences and his eyes were opened to the magnitude of his awful actions. He cried with the anguish of genuine repentance, "I have sinned against the Lord!" The extent of his sorrow is revealed in Psalm 51, "Have mercy on me O God, cleanse me from my sin according to your unfailing love and compassion... I have done evil in your sight... Do not cast me away... Restore to me the joy of my salvation" (Psalm 51:1-4, 11-12). Even though David's sin was very great, he was restored to fellowship with God when he repented. Against the backdrop of the blackest sin, God's grace appeared even more beautiful.

There was no sacrifice under the Mosaic covenant that could purchase atonement for sins of so grievous a nature. However the atonement which Jesus Christ, the perfect fulfillment of all the promises, would later accomplish was effective for repentant people in every time period. Although the Lord assured David through the prophet that He had pardoned him, He also informed him that the baby born to Bathsheba would die. God's moral laws could not be broken without consequences.

No sooner had Nathan left than Bathsheba's baby became sick. David fasted and pled with God for the life of his little child but it was all to no avail. After seven days the child died. Then David got up from the ground, washed himself, put on fresh clothes, went to the tabernacle to worship God, and returned home to eat. The period of pleading for his baby son was over and David quietly accepted the reality saying, "I will go to him, but he will not return to me." Not long afterwards Bathsheba became pregnant again. When the baby was born they named him Solomon, which means "peace". Then the Lord sent Nathan to tell David to call the child Jedidiah, which means, "loved of the Lord". God was gracious and David's fellowship with Him was restored.

During all this family drama Joab had continued the siege of Rabbah, the capital of the Ammonites. David now mustered a great army and this time accompanied them to the front. The Lord was with him again and gave him victory.

▪ 107 ▪ Incest and Fratricide in David's Family

2 Samuel 13, 14   *Date: circa 978-969 B.C.*

DAVID'S LIFE after his personal and moral failure was never quite the same. He had brought the name of the Lord into disrepute and now, just as Nathan had predicted, divine judgment would consist of trouble within his own family.

David's eldest son Amnon, the crown prince, became infatuated with his half-sister Tamar. He pretended to be sick and had Tamar make special bread for him. When she entered his bedroom to give it to him he raped her. When he had finished with her his love turned to hate and he sent her away. At this the distraught girl moved in with her brother Absalom, David's third son. David was furious when he heard what had happened; and yet, although the law was clear with respect to such cases (Lev. 20:17), he did not punish Amnon. Perhaps his own conscience still bothered him.

Absalom, with unusually thick hair, was known as the most handsome man in Israel. His mother was a Gentile idolatress, the daughter of the king of Geshur, a city in Syria (2 Sam. 3:3). By marrying her David had disobeyed the Lord's command to not enter into marriage relationships with the idolaters of the land (Deut. 7:3). For two years this handsome prince nursed an implacable desire to wreak revenge on what had happened to his sister.

One day he invited his father, the king, to the annual sheep-shearing celebration. As he'd expected, David declined, but agreed to send Amnon, the crown prince, in his place. Absolom's other brothers and half-brothers also joined the group. Absalom ordered his servants to wait until the party was in full swing and Amnon was drunk—and then strike him dead. They did exactly as told. The other princes fled in a panic. David wept bitterly when he heard that his oldest son was dead.

No city of refuge in Israel would shelter someone who had committed first degree murder so Absalom sought asylum with his mother's family in Geshur. Three years passed, and David's fatherly, sentimental heart began to pine after his proud, handsome son.

Joab, David's chief general, hoping to curry favor with both the king and a popular prince, planned to effect reconciliation. He hired a "wise woman" to go to David and claim to be a widow whose two sons had got into a fight, during which the one had slain the other. Her clan demanded that she hand over her one remaining son for capital punishment, leaving her with no one to carry on the family line. When David assured her that he would guarantee the safety of her last son, the woman, like Nathan before her, applied the story to the king's own situation, arguing that he should spare the life of his son Absalom. Although David discerned Joab's hand in the matter, he still allowed himself to be convinced. He ordered his general to bring Absalom back to Jerusalem, though with the strange proviso that his son should not appear in person before him.

For two years Absalom did not see his father. He knew, however, that they would have to be reconciled if he was to have any hope of acceding to the throne. He sent for Joab and demanded that he challenge David on his behalf to either restore him fully or have him executed. At this David accepted him back into the royal palace.

Amnon had raped his half-sister and Absalom, the brother, had killed him in revenge. And just like Eli and Samuel before him, David had failed to discipline his sons. Even worse, he had failed in his former habit of always enquiring of the Lord before he took action.

▪ 108 ▪ Absalom Rebels and David Flees

2 Samuel 15-17   *Date: circa 978-969 B.C.*

NOW THAT HE had regained access to the palace Absalom plotted his next move. He procured a chariot and an impressive personal retinue to create an impression of power. He also made a point of rising early and intercepting common people at the city gate who were on their way to the royal palace looking for justice. He would listen carefully, commiserate, and ingratiate himself to them while spreading insinuations about the weakness of his father's administration. He assured them that things would be different if he were in control. Gradually Absalom stole the hearts of the common people. David could not have been ignorant of his son's schemes to seize the kingdom, but he appeared unusually apathetic during this period of his life.

One day, four years later, Absalom decided to strike. He made his way to Hebron, the place where David had been crowned king of Judah, and where he himself had been born. 200 dignitaries accompanied him from Jerusalem. He also invited someone named Ahithophel, one of David's closest advisors to join his rebellion. Ahithophel was also the grandfather of Bathsheba, whose husband David had murdered (2 Sam. 23:23, 34, 39; 11:3). Absalom correctly calculated that Ahithophel would want to avenge the dishonor David had brought on his family.

When Absalom's network of men around the country responded to the signal "Absalom reigns!" they swept up the people with them and hailed him as their new king. A messenger informed David, now about 60 years of age and in poor health, of the turn of events: his favorite son was threatening to take his life and his throne! David's response to the crisis was, once again, strangely passive. Perhaps he thought that the blows falling on him were divine punishment that he ought not resist. Leaving ten of his concubines to look after the palace, the once brave warrior ran for his life.

Although Absalom had stolen the hearts of many of the people, those nearest to David remained loyal and joined him in flight. His palace servants and his old contingent of 600 warriors stuck with him. So did several clans, including a company of Gittites, who were not even Jews. The Levites also remained loyal, and followed David carrying the Ark of the Covenant, the symbol of the Lord's presence. Possibly fearing that the ark would fall into the wrong hands, David sent it back to the city. He recognized that his own restoration would depend on God's undeserved favour and not on His symbolic presence.

Meanwhile Absalom lost no time in getting to Jerusalem. Unknown to him David had arranged for two priests to remain in the city and secretly keep him up-to-date with the events as they unfolded.

David and his companions continued to flee, their heads covered, their feet bare, and their hearts weeping. When David was told that his old confidante and advisor Ahithophel had joined the conspirators he was deeply hurt: "My own friend, whom I trusted, with whom I ate bread, has lifted his heel against me" (Psalm 41:9). When they arrived at the top of the Mount of Olives another of his former advisors, Hushai, met them, his robe torn and his head covered in dust as a sign of mourning. David urged this faithful man to return to the city and make himself available to Absalom so as to frustrate Ahithophel's advice.

Ziba, the former servant of Saul and now the steward of Saul's crippled grandson Mephibosheth also met the fleeing king. Feigning kindness and loyalty he presented the king with a convoy of saddled donkeys and generous provisions of food.

"Where is your master Mephibosheth?" David inquired. Ziba claimed that Mephibosheth had decided to remain in Jerusalem in the hope that the nation would turn back to the house of Saul and make him king. Taking the man's words at face value David granted him everything that belonged to Mephibosheth.

As David and his followers hastened toward the Jordan River a Benjamite from Saul's clan named Shimei appeared on a high ridge. He hurled down rocks at the fleeing party and rained curses on David. The king endured the man's insulting behaviour in silence. He knew he had sinned grievously and wondered if the Lord had sanctioned Shimei's behaviour.

Traveling eastward the fugitives crossed the Jordan and arrived totally exhausted in the town of Mahanaim. There they pitched camp, rested and regrouped, uncertain of God's will for their future.

• 109 • Absalom Defeated

2 Samuel 17-18   *Date: circa 975-969 B.C.*

AS SOON AS Absalom installed himself in the royal palace he turned to Ahithophel for advice. Ahithophel told him to commit so offensive an act that any hope of reconciliation with his father would be impossible, making his troops even more emboldened to fight. Absalom then pitched an open tent on the palace's flat roof and there, in public, raped his father's concubines—unwittingly carrying out part of the punishment God had foretold via the prophet Nathan (2 Sam. 12:11).

Recognizing that any delay now would be fatal, Ahithopel next advised Absalom to take a small army and strike David's camp while they were tired and demoralized. "Kill only the king himself. Once he is gone his supporters will capitulate and accept you as king—and peace will return to the land." Although Absalom liked what he heard he called Hushai for a second opinion.

The clever Hushai knew he had to convince Absalom to postpone an immediate assault in order to give David's men time to regroup. "Ahithopel's advice is not good this time," he stated boldly. "You yourself know that your father and his men are experienced fighters, and right now they are as angry as a bear robbed of its cubs. Furthermore, your father is too good a strategist to spend the night with his troops." Hushai went on to advise that Absalom mobilize the entire nation and personally lead them into a battle. The plan appealed to both Absalom and his men as a sure way to guarantee success. When Ahithophel saw that his advice was not followed he saddled his donkey, went home, put his household in order, and hanged himself.

Having won some breathing space for David, Hushai informed the two priests who then sent couriers to inform David of events. While Absalom mustered his nation-wide army David also prepared for the coming showdown. Thousands of men picked up their weapons and made their way to Mahanaim to help their beleaguered monarch. Support came from totally unexpected quarters, and with renewed confidence in God David organized his men into three battalions, each one under the leadership of his most experienced commanders: Joab, Joab's brother Abishai, and Ittai the Gittite. As they marched out to battle David pleaded with his commanders to be gentle with his son Absalom.

The two armies met in the Forest of Ephraim. The battle was bloody, though brief. David's men slew 20,000 rebels and Absalom's army scattered in confusion. Absalom himself tried to escape on a mule. As he raced under a large oak tree his famously thick trusses of freely flowing hair got caught in its low-lying branches. The mule galloped on, leaving him hanging in mid-air. Incapable of extricating himself, he hung there deserted and terrified, awaiting his fate. One of David's soldiers saw him there and reported it to Joab. Leaving the soldier, the ruthless general found the hapless prince and, defying David's express orders, thrust three javelins into his heart. He then had his soldiers take down the body and throw it into a pit. The battle was over.

Waiting at the city gate of Mahanaim David did not doubt that his forces would win the battle. His greatest fear was for the welfare of his rebellious but beloved son. The first runner waffled, evidently not wanting to hurt the king's feelings. Just then the second courier arrived. "Greetings my Lord," he said. "The Lord has avenged you this day against those who rebelled against you."

"What about Absalom?" David asked, "Is he safe?"

"May all those who seek to do you harm be as that young man is," the man replied.

David, overwhelmed with sorrow, withdrew to the chamber above the gate. "O my son, my son Absalom, would that I had died in your place," he wept. The victorious army returning to Mahanaim expected a royal welcome for putting their lives on the line to keep David on the throne. Instead they found that their king, paralyzed by grief, had withdrawn into his own private world. What should have been a victory celebration became a day of mourning instead.

"Shame on you!" the straight-talking Joab berated David. "It seems that if we had all died and Absalom lived today you would have been well pleased!" Stirred into action, David quickly took his place at the city gate to congratulate and thank his troops, while the remnants of Absalom's army fled to their homes.

2 Samuel 19-10   *Date: circa 975-969 B.C.*

ISRAEL WAS in turmoil. David had turned the tables on the usurper whom most of the country had supported. But with Absalom dead most people realized that David still had the strongest claim to the throne. David sent word to the elders of Judah, his own tribesmen, many of whom had sided with Absalom and therefore feared his wrath, and asked them why they were so slow to invite him back. He told them that he was ready to pardon the rebels, and even offered Joab's position as chief general to Absalom's renegade general Amasa. At this the leaders of Judah met him at the Jordan River to welcome him back.

Shimei, the man who had cursed David when he was on the run, fell before the king begging mercy, and David magnanimously granted the man his life. Next to meet him was the crippled Mephibosheth. He was unshaved and unwashed since the day David was forced to flee Jerusalem, as a sign of his grief. "Why did you not join me?" David interrogated him.

"My Lord, I am lame. I tried to saddle my donkey and join you with provisions, but my servant Ziba betrayed and slandered me. I know that my grandfather's descendants deserve nothing but death—do what is right; I have no ground for appeal."

"You and Ziba divide the land among you," David responded.

"He can have it all," Mephibosheth responded meekly. "It is enough for me to know that the king is at peace in his own house."

David had won back the support of the men of Judah who accompanied him back to Jerusalem. The leaders of the northern tribes now complained that they had been slighted. The old jealousy between Judah and the rest of Israel reared its ugly head again. Sheba, an influential Benjamite, repudiated his allegiance to David and united the other tribes behind him against David. Once again the unity of the kingdom was threatened. David hurried to Jerusalem, determined to deal with Sheba's rebellion in short order. He told his new commander Amasa to assemble the men of Judah. David was worried that Sheba's rebellion would do more harm than Absalom's. When Amasa delayed, Joab's men marched out instead. Suddenly Amasa showed up. The defiant Joab pretended to greet him, then he stabbed him to death.

Sheba had holed up in a fortified town called Abel. Surrounding the town, Joab's men built a siege ramp and started battering it. Suddenly an old woman shouted down at Joab. "We are a peace-loving, faithful town known for our wisdom. Why would you want to destroy a city that is a part of the Lord's inheritance?" she berated him.

"I'm not interested in destroying your town. Hand over the king's enemy Sheba and we'll leave you in peace," Joab responded.

"That man's head will soon be thrown to you off the wall." She then convinced her fellow townspeople to decapitate Sheba, and when the man's head fell at Joab's feet he called off the siege. Joab returned to Jerusalem where David reinstated him as commander-in-chief. His throne was secure.

2 Samuel 21; 24; 1 Chronicles 21   *Date: circa 968-964 B.C.*

DAVID WAS back on the throne but his troubles were not over. Famine broke out and lasted three years. When David inquired of the Lord he learned that it was divine retribution for the fact that years earlier Saul had put many Gibeonites to death.

Back in the days of Joshua the Gibeonites had managed to delude Joshua into making a peace treaty with them. At some stage during his reign Saul broke that ancient treaty and sought to annihilate the unarmed and docile Gibeonites. That sin had been left unpunished. David immediately recognized the state's obligation to reaffirm the treaty. He invited the leaders of the Gibeonite community to the palace and asked what he could do to rectify the wrong.

"We are not interested in Saul's silver or gold, nor do we ask for the life of any man in Israel," they replied. "Give us seven surviving descendants of the house of Saul and we will hang them in Gibeah, Saul's hometown." Their deaths would be sufficient to atone for the injustice they had suffered. David acquiesced, giving them permission to execute seven males from Saul's bloodstained household. He did not, however, allow them to take lame Mephibosheth, the son of his old friend Jonathan.

The war had ended and the Gibeonites were avenged, but battles against the Philistines continued. During these altercations David acknowledged the greatness of his mighty warriors, while penning psalms of gratitude to God for every victory won.

One day, however, David decided to count the number of fighting men at his disposal. His advisors, including Joab, warned him against this plan but he insisted. His head was turned by success that, in a moment of spiritual folly, he attributed to his own acumen. Counting presumes ownership. Instead of recognizing that Israel was the Lord's possession, David came to regard it as his own, a nation which he had led to its present state of power and stability.

Reluctantly Joab and his officers took on the task, taking over nine months to travel through the land and compile a register. Eventually they reported that Judah had 500,000 and the rest of Israel had 800,000 valiant men capable of military service[11].

No sooner had the report been given than David's conscience was stricken over what he had done. "I have sinned greatly and acted foolishly," he confessed. "O Lord, please take away my sin..."

Early the next morning the Lord ordered the prophet Gad to confront David with a choice from three alternative punishments: seven years of famine, three months of civil war, or three days of the plague. David was deeply distressed, knowing that it was his folly that caused such

---

[11] The account in 1 Chronicles 21:5 states that in total Israel boasted 1,100,000, of whom 470,000 were from the tribe of Judah. The lesser number, specifically described in 2 Samuel as "valiant", refers to seasoned soldiers, while the larger number refers to all men of arm-bearing age. The difference in the figures for Judah is a case of rounding up.

awful consequences. He chose the plague, hoping that God would be merciful. It raged across the land and claimed 70,000 victims. The Lord then commissioned the "destroying angel" to strike Jerusalem. David could actually see the Angel of Death with its sword unsheathed, hovering over the city just outside the walls on Mount Moria by the threshing floor of one Araunah the Jebusite. He and the elders of Israel, dressed in the penitent's sackcloth, fell on their faces before the Lord.

"Lord, why punish your people, those innocent sheep? I am the one who sinned. I am the one who ordered the census. Punish me and my household instead..." David prayed. He then went to Araunah and insisted on buying the threshing floor, even though Araunah would have given it to him. "No, I want to pay the full price," David countered. "I will not offer the Lord that which cost me nothing". He then built an altar and sacrificed burnt offerings that atoned for sin, together with peace offerings, which spoke of renewed fellowship and communion with the Lord. In the covenant God had made with Israel at Sinai he had promised that if the people humbled themselves and confessed their sin He would restore them to fellowship with himself (Lev. 26:40-42). Faithful to His covenant and His justice appeased, God stopped the plague.

Perhaps it was then that the idea of building the temple on that particular spot entered David's mind (1 Chron. 22:1). After all, this was also the place where God had provided a sacrifice for Abraham to keep him from slaying his son (Gen. 22:14). The place became a symbol of God's grace, and so was emminently suitable for the temple.

• 112 • Adonijah's Revolt and Solomon Crowned

1 Kings 1   *Date: circa 962 B.C.*

MOST OF David's life had been turbulent, and his last days would be no different. Now close to seventy years old, he could not keep warm no matter how many blankets were piled on him. His attendants chose a beautiful Shunammite girl named Abishag to wait on him and keep him warm by lying beside him.

Adonijah, David's oldest living son, thought he could take advantage of the king's weakened hold on affairs of state by making a bid for the throne. Once again, a handsome son whom David had failed to discipline threatened the stability of the kingdom. Adonijah arranged to have a personal bodyguard of fifty men run before his chariot and managed to win the support of Joab and of Abiathar the high priest. The conspirators then arranged a banquet just outside Jerusalem's city walls, to which they invited various royal officials and Adonijah's brothers, though not Solomon or the prophet Nathan.

Nathan got wind of the events and urged Solomon's mother Bathsheba to go to David and remind him that he had sworn that her son Solomon would be his successor. While Bathsheba was still speaking with the king Nathan arrived and confirmed the fact that Adonijah was attempting to seize the throne. "Is this your will, my lord?" he asked. "Is this something you, my lord, sanctioned without telling your servants?"

On hearing this David was stirred to action, for before Solomon was born God had revealed that he was to be his successor (1 Chron. 22:9-10). "As the Lord, who has redeemed my soul from all distress, lives," he said to Bathsheba, "your son Solomon will reign after me as I promised you." After that events moved quickly. Solomon was placed on the royal mule, brought to the appointed place and anointed king. Immediately trumpets blew across the city and the shout went up, "Long live king Solomon!"

When the people heard that Solomon had taken his place on the royal throne, there were such shouts and acclamations of joy that the ground seemed to shake from the noise. The roar was so loud that those attending Adonijah's banquet outside the city walls could hear it. When news reached them that the king had anointed Solomon as his successor Adonijah's guests were thrown into a panic. Unceremoniously each one fled to his own home. Fearing for his life Adonijah ran to the tabernacle and grabbed the horns of the altar, thus claiming asylum. Solomon refrained from executing him but sternly warned his older half-brother that further protection was conditional upon his good behaviour. Adonijah's brief, unsuccessful revolt was the last hiccup of David's reign.

▪ 113 ▪ David's Last Years

2 Samuel 23; 1 Kings 2; 1 Chron. 22-29   *Date: circa 962-960 B.C.*

DAVID SPENT his remaining years encouraging, instructing and supporting Solomon, the new king. He also got to work on a project that had been on his heart for a long time, namely the building of a temple for the Lord in Jerusalem. This wish was not granted to him personally, but the Lord had assured him that the task would be accomplished by his successor. Now that he was relieved of the burden of the monarchy he spent his retirement years making extensive preparations for this centralized place of worship. He donated vast quantities of gold, silver, bronze, iron, wood, marble and precious stones and the people also gave wholeheartedly. He also secured stonecutters, masons, carpenters and other skilled craftsmen.

The Lord had inspired David to draw up very specific plans for the temple and the materials to be used in its construction. From among the Levites he appointed 24,000 men to be in charge of construction. He had a palatial structure in mind. The Lord's house was to be "of great magnificence and fame and splendor in the sight of all the nations".

Just before he died David summoned all of Israel's leaders: the tribal heads, the entire officer corps of his army, the bureaucracy, everyone of note. Rising to his feet to deliver his final charge, the old warrior-king reminded them how the Lord had first chosen him, then Solomon to sit on the throne of Israel. He explained how he had wanted to build a temple, a permanent resting-place for the Ark of the Covenant, but that God had denied him that honour because he had been a man of war. Solomon would be a man of peace, and was the one chosen to build the temple. He then handed Solomon the architectural drawing of the temple and turned over to him the vast treasures he had amassed for its building. "Be strong and courageous, my son, and do the work," he enjoined him. "Do not be afraid and do not be discouraged, for the Lord will enable you to accomplish the task ahead of you." He charged him to follow Jehovah God wholeheartedly all the days of his life. "If you seek Him you will find Him, but if you reject Him He will reject you forever," he warned.

Turning to the rest of the assembly, David warned them that Solomon was an inexperienced young man who would need their help to realize out the ambitious construction plans he placed before them. The nation's leaders offered their allegiance to Solomon. In the presence of the whole assembly David was moved to praise God for His greatness and goodness. He acknowledged that God was the source of all the abundant provision for the temple. He prayed that the God of their forefathers Abraham, Isaac and Jacob would keep these people's hearts loyal to him.

The speeches and prayers over, the people enjoyed a great banquet together. Throwing that huge feast would be David's last public act. Surrounded by his subjects, enjoying the presence of the Lord, it was a fitting end to a remarkable career.

Just before he died David called his son Solomon and sought privately to pass on to him the lessons he had learned in the course of his tumultuous life. He impressed on his young successor that if he was to be successful and guarantee an unbroken succession he had to obey the Law of Moses carefully in all areas of life. He also advised Solomon regarding certain men: Joab, whom David had allowed to live for his faithful service, was to be executed for the murders he'd committed (2 Sam. 3:22-30; 20:8-10). If Shimei the Benjamite showed signs of disloyalty he too was to be executed.

Then David died "full of days, riches and honor, and his son Solomon reigned in his stead" (1 Chron. 29:28). He had prepared for his departure as best he could and now he was "going the way of all the earth" in peace. David was convinced about two things: the Lord would not abandon him to the grave (Psalm 16:9-10) and when he rose from the dead he would be face to face with the Lord whom, through all the vagaries of life, he had sought to love and serve. He had been anointed by God, and had ruled Israel for 40 years. God had made an everlasting covenant with him to establish his throne. One day from one of his descendants, an even greater David, would rule with righteousness forever...

▪ 114 ▪ Solomon's Wisdom

1 Kings 2-3; 2 Chronicles 1   *Date: 971-970 B.C.*

UNDER SOLOMON Israel evolved from the tribal confederacy it had been under David into a centralized state under an absolute ruler. The young king began well, dealing wisely with the remaining enemies of David's line and so securing the throne. The first person he had to deal with was his older brother. Adonijah had professed allegiance, but then asked permission to marry Abishag, the girl who had tended David in his latter years. She had been part of David's harem—and taking ownership over a deceased king's harem was tantamount to claiming succession to the throne. Solomon correctly perceived Adonijah's request as an act of treason and had him put to death. He knew himself to be God's anointed, and viewed sedition as an act of rebellion against God. He then removed Abiathar the high priest from office and replaced him with Zadok. Abiathar was exiled to a little town called Anathoth because of his participation in Adonijah's rebellion—and God's prophecy that Eli's family would be cut off from the priesthood was fullfilled (1 Sam. 2:27-36). Centuries later the prophet Jeremiah would be born into this family of exiled priests in Anathoth.

David's old general Joab knew he was next. He sought refuge by fleeing to the altar of the Lord. He had not only participated in Adonijah's rebellion, but had also committed cold-blooded murder by killing two rival army commanders. Solomon had his new commanding general Benaiah execute him. The Law of Moses stipulated that manslayers could find sanctuary at the altar, but not murderers (Exod. 21:14).

Shimei, the troublemaker from the house of Saul, was another person David had warned Solomon about. The new king ordered him not to leave Jerusalem. For three years Shimei stayed within the city walls, but then ventured outside. When Solomon heard this he had him executed. By consistently applying the full measure of the law to all who disregarded the will of "the Lord's anointed" Solomon established himself as a firm but just ruler.

Although David had moved the Ark of the Covenant to Jerusalem years earlier, the tabernacle with the bronze altar still stood at Gibeon. There Zadok and his fellow priests continued to offer sacrifices to the Lord every morning and evening as prescribed in the Law of Moses (1 Chron. 16:39-40). Early in his reign Solomon and his entourage travelled to Gibeon to offer a massive sacrifice of 1000 animals as an expression of his devotion to Jehovah God. That night God appeared to him in a dream and offered to give him anything he asked for.

"You were very kind to your servant, my father David, because he was faithful and righteous, and now you continue to show kindness to me," Solomon responded. "You have made me my father's heir even though I am but a youth. Give me, therefore, a wise and discerning heart so that I can govern this great people of yours justly." Solomon humbly acknowledged his dependence on God if he were to carry out the task assigned to him.

Solomon even composed a psalm that asked that he be endowed with justice and righteousness (Psalm 72). In another psalm he acknowledged that unless the Lord builds the house, the worker labors in vain (Psalm 127). Pleased that Solomon chose the affairs of His people over personal gain, God granted him unequalled practical wisdom and discernment. He added wealth and honour and the promise of long life if he continued to walk in obedience to the Mosaic Law. Upon his return to Jerusalem Solomon stood before the Ark of the Covenant while the priests offered more sacrifices as an expression of his gratitude and dedication to Jehovah.

A seemingly intractable judicial incident illustrated the new king's great wisdom and insight. Two prostitutes sharing a house both gave birth to baby boys within days of each other. One morning the first mother woke up to find a dead baby in bed with her—but, according to her, that child was not hers: she accused the other mother of exchanging babies in the middle of the night. As the women stood before the king vehemently accusing each other, Solomon asked for a sword, then ordered his aid to cut the living baby in half and divide it between the two fighting women. "Please, my Lord, don't kill the baby," the real mother burst out. "Give her the child, if you have to!" The other woman, however, concurred with the king's idea. "Yes, my Lord, cut the child in two," she said. "Then neither she nor I will have it."

"Don't kill the child," Solomon ordered. "Give it to the first woman. She is its mother." When Israel heard how Solomon had handled the matter they held him in high respect.

Solomon's life testified to unequalled practical, administrative and judicial prudence. His reputation for "hokmah", or practical wisdom, was unsurpassed and far ranging, and including such subjects as botany and zoology. He became one of the great sages of his time. He was also a prolific writer, composing some 3000 proverbs and 1005 songs. Of his writings Ecclesiastes, Song of Solomon, and the core of the book of Proverbs, along with two Psalms, are recorded in the Bible. Proverbs is thought to be a "court manual" he collated to teach wisdom, integrity, justice and righteousness to his court officials in a pithy, easy-to-remember manner.

▪ 115 ▪ Solomon Builds the Temple

1 Kings 5-7; 2 Chronicles 2-5   *Date: 968-960 B.C.*

SOME TIME AFTER the conquest of Canaan under Joshua the people of Israel began converting existing Canaanite open-air, hilltop sanctuaries into places of worship for Jehovah. Prior to the Mosaic Law worshipping on "high places" was not considered wrong (Gen. 12:7-8; 22:2-4; 31:54) but the Mosaic Law forbade the practice. People were only allowed to present their sacrifices and offerings at the bronze altar in the tabernacle (Deut. 12:1-21)—yet Solomon continued to allow the practice. In spite of this early failing, however, Solomon demonstrated his love and commitment to the ways of his father David. And for that God blessed him.

The peoples of the ancient Near East, including the Israelites, generally regarded their king as the son, vice-regent, or representative of their chief god. Temples were viewed as the god's temporal palaces that reflected the greatness and power of the people's deity. Solomon (and his father David before him) wanted to build a structure of such magnificence that it would communicate to all the peoples of the east that Jehovah was the greatest and most glorious of all deities, and that Israel was a kingdom of priests and a holy nation, "a light for the Gentiles" (Ex. 19:6; Is. 42:6-7). The time had come for Solomon to turn his attention to the massive project of building a temple "for the name of the Lord".

The construction of the temple began in the fourth year of Solomon's reign and would take 7 years to complete (I Kings 6:1). He re-established the friendly relationship his father had enjoyed with Hiram, king of Phoenicia, in what is now Lebanon, and purchased huge amounts of cedar wood from him. He conscripted 30,000 men to work on a rotational basis in the Phoenician forests cutting timber and floating it down the Mediterranean coast to Israel. At the same time 70,000 carriers and 80,000 stonecutters were employed in cutting and carrying massive limestone blocks from the hills north of Jerusalem. Skilled Israelite and Phoenician craftsmen cut and prepared the timber and stone off-site. To preserve the temple area's sanctity actual construction was done as silently as possible; no hammers, chisels or other iron tools were used on site.

The structure's basic layout was similar to the pattern God gave Moses for the tabernacle, but at 90 feet long, 30 feet wide and 45 feet high, it was about twice as large. Its courtyard, however, was much larger, and the temple furnishings were on a much grander scale, though each kept the same spiritual significance as in the tabernacle. Solomon hired a skilled metallurgist name Hiram to cast two elaborate bronze pillars over 27 feet high and 8 feet in diameter with capitals in the shape of lilies, which were erected at the portico of the Temple. The southern pillar was dubbed Jakin, meaning, "He shall establish", and the northern one Boaz, meaning, "in Him is strength", evidently references to the upholding power of the Lord. Hiram also cast a huge circular metal bowl measuring about 15 feet across and decorated with gourds below the rim. This "Sea of Bronze" was the new laver. It could hold up to 17,500 gallons of water (2 Chron. 4:5) and was used by the priests to wash their hands and feet (Ex. 30:17 -21; 40:30-32). This "sea" sat on four groups of 3 life-size bronze bulls, each one of which faced one of the 4 points of the compass. The 12 bulls apparently represented the 12 tribes.

The other objects in the temple courtyard were also made of large quantities of burnished bronze or pure gold. The altar, the tables, the lampstands, the vessels inside, and even the doors, were either gold-plated or pure gold. The inside of the Most Holy Place was overlaid with fine gold as were the sculptured cherubim that would overshadow the Ark of the Covenant. The heavy curtain was magnificently embroidered in blue, purple and crimson yarn.

Rising above its stepped inner and outer courtyards (2 Chron. 4:9; Jer. 36:10) the temple's outside walls were clad in white limestone and gold so that the beautiful, scintillating structure was visible from all directions. Most heathen temples were located in the middle of the capital city. Mount Moriah on which the temple stood (also known as Mount Zion) was just outside the old city, symbolizing the "otherness" of Israel's God.

▪ 116 ▪ The Temple Dedication

1 Kings 8; 2 Chronicles 6-7   *Date: 960 B.C.*

THE BUILDING of the temple was completed. All that remained was to bring in the Ark of the Covenant, the symbol of God's presence. By this time it only contained the stone tablets on which the Ten Commandments were inscribed. This law underscored the fact that Israel had submitted to the Sinaitic Covenant, adherence to which would assure them of God's blessing. The pot of manna and Aaron's budding rod appear to have been lost in the tumultuous intervening period.

Referred to as God's throne, the lid, or the mercy seat of the Ark of the Covenant, was where God received the blood shed during the annual sacrifice on the Day of Atonement. Ever since David had it brought up from Obed-Edom's house it had remained in the tent he had provided for it. The transfer of the Ark to its new abode took place during the Feast of Tabernacles, which commemorated God's faithfulness to Israel during their desert years. It was one of the feasts all Israelite men were expected to attend.

The installation of the ark in the temple was, in effect, a symbolic re-enactment of the enthronement of Jehovah God as king over Israel. Once the priests had placed it under the cherubim in the Most Holy Place the Shekinah glory, a cloud of light, filled the temple, just as it had filled the tabernacle centuries earlier. Before this overwhelming visible manifestation of God's presence the priests, unable to perform their duties, withdrew, and King Solomon was overawed at God's faithfulness to his father David and at the inestimable privilege he had had of building a temple for the Lord and securing a place for the Ark of the Covenant. Accompanied by trumpets, cymbals, harps, and lyres the song rang out: "The Lord is good; His love endures forever!"

Then Solomon knelt in public before the altar in the posture of a vassal king and spread his hands towards heaven. Referring to himself repeatedly as "God's servant", he led the people in a moving prayer of dedication. The king praised God and asked Him to keep His promise to his father David that one of his successors would always sit on the throne if they walked faithfully before God. He recognized that the heavens could not contain such a great God, never mind the temple he had built. Yet he pleaded at length that God would always hear the prayers of His people when they turned towards the temple. With amazing insight he envisaged various scenarios that would, indeed, play out in Israel's history. "When the people sin and then turn back to you, praying in this temple, then hear, forgive, restore…" He acknowledged that God's real dwelling place was in heaven, recognizing that the symbol of God's presence was different from God's actual presence. He went on to ask that God would hear His people's prayers and show them mercy in judgement when they violated the terms of the Mosaic covenant, and he pleaded God's grace on God-fearing foreigners. He concluded by reminding God of His sovereign, electing grace that had made Israel His own inheritance.

After the inauguration ceremony Solomon blessed the people, again expressing God's covenant faithfulness. He prayed that Israel would remain obedient to their covenant obligations, and live up to their calling to be a testimony to the nations. The ceremony, originally planned to last a week, was extended to two weeks, and ended with a massive number of sacrifices. Not since the days of Joshua had the nation celebrated such a major renewal of its covenant with Jehovah God. Now, as never before, Israel was in a position to fulfill her calling to be a kingdom of priests and a holy nation (Ex. 19:5-6). The vast assembly that had gathered for the occasion returned home joyful. Not one word of all the promises God had given to Moses had failed.

1 Kings 4, 9-10; 2 Chronicles 7-9   *Date: circa 966-960 B.C.*

GOD GRANTED Solomon enormous wealth; it was said that in Jerusalem silver and gold were as common as stones. Its population increased and the people "ate, drank, and were happy". Solomon ruled from the Mediterranean Sea in the west to the Euphrates River in the east, and from the Phoenician border in the north to Egypt in the south. He also controlled the trade routes between Egypt, Anatolia and Mesopotamia.

Usually when a sovereign died subject nations rebelled or withheld taxes, thus forcing the newly enthroned king to re-establish his authority over them. Psalm 2 was probably a "coronation poem" composed when Solomon ascended the throne of Israel. It was, essentially, a warning to Israel's vassals not to rebel against the "Lord's anointed", the king of Israel. In Solomon's case the subject nations heeded the warning. In contrast to David's reign there was peace with the surrounding nations. "Every man lived in safety under their own vine and fig tree". It was a golden age indeed!

Solomon's judicious administration, his ability to create an effective bureaucracy overseeing the national and international affairs of the state, his conscription of non-Israelite work corvées drawn from the adjacent regions of Ammon, Moab and Edom (cf. 5:13-14; 9:15; 2 Chron. 2:2; 8:8), and his creation of a large standing army which, for the first time, included horses and chariots, were major changes in policy. They moved Israel away from a tribal confederacy toward a centralized state run from Jerusalem. As a result of this nation-building Solomon increased taxes, though not, apparently, on his own tribe of Judah; it is not mentioned in the tax lists.

After completing the temple Solomon built a large, impressive palace complex near the temple to underscore the idea that Israel's king was God's vice-regent. In the ancient world the king's palace symbolized both his own greatness as well as that of his god. The audience hall alone (known as the Palace of the Forest of Lebanon) was bigger than the temple building, and was the palace where Solomon displayed some of his fabled wealth, including hundreds of golden shields just for display (gold is too soft for military purposes), a throne inlaid with ivory and overlaid with gold situated on a dais reached by six steps decorated with lions on each step. All articles in the palace were made of gold. In many ways, Solomon's prestige was rooted in the fact that he had attained the apex of ancient worldly aspirations.

Subsequent to Solomon and Israel's renewal of the ancient covenant the Lord appeared to Solomon a second time to bless him. As before, the blessing was on condition that he continued to walk with God with integrity and uphold the conditions of the Mosaic covenant. Faithfulness and obedience would result in a continuous line of descendants on the throne while disobedience and turning away from God would result in judgement, exile, the destruction of the temple, and ridicule from the surrounding nations.

It took Solomon some 20 years, or about half his reign, to complete his major building projects in Jerusalem. He went on to build an ostentatious palace for his Egyptian wife. He also built terraces connecting the temple and palace complexes to the rest of Jerusalem, and enlarged the city walls to encompass both building complexes. He then rebuilt and fortified numerous towns and cities as far away as Tadmor in the Syrian desert (2 Chron. 8:2-6).

The Jews were not, by nature, a sea-going people, yet Solomon built a port at Ezion Geber (near modern Elath) and a merchant navy manned mostly by King Hiram's Phoenician sailors. His ships plied the Arabian coast as far as Yemen and Ophir (probably modern day Oman and the United Arab Emirates) for gold and rare woods. He grew to enjoy tremendous international prestige and influence. Distant rulers travelled to Israel to meet with him and view his great splendor. One of the foreign dignitaries was the queen of Sheba.

Sheba was located in present day Yemen or southern Oman, and dominated the regional spice and incense trade. The queen had heard of Solomon's ability to exploit his nation's strategic location and may have hoped to establish a trade alliance with him. She arrived with a large caravan loaded with exotic spices, gold and precious stones. However, her impressive retinue paled beside the magnificence of Solomon's palace, his court, and the ceremonies taking place in the new temple. She plied him with difficult questions, probably in the realms of theology, ethics and diplomacy, and was deeply impressed with his insight and wisdom: "Not even half of what I was told about you in my own country was told to me," she exclaimed, and then praised Jehovah, Solomon's God, who had blessed him so abundantly. Israel had great potential in fulfilling its God-given purpose of being a light to the nations.

• 118 • Solomon's Decline

1 Kings 11; Ecclesiastes   *Dates: circa 950-932 B.C.*

GOD HAD greatly blessed Solomon with overwhelming abundance, but with that came many temptations. The Lord wanted His people to look to Him for protection, and had specifically forbidden Israel's kings from acquiring horses and building chariots (the tanks of the ancient world). David had been so sensitive to this command that he'd hamstrung captured horses (2 Sam. 8:4). As Solomon leaned increasingly on his own understanding and wealth, however, he drifted away from the simple, trusting faith of his father.

Solomon's preoccupation with building extensive defense systems and monumental buildings eventually drained the nation's resources and turned the population against him (1 Kings 12:4), and the appearance of grandeur and power they projected proved to be ephemeral, little more than a façade of strength and greatness. His system of forced labour became a major source of resentment against his rule, and his conniving wheeling and dealing soured his relationship with King Hiram of Phoenicia (1 Kings 12:4; 2 Chron. 8:2). His greatest downfall, however, was his love of women. The Mosaic Law specifically forbade intermarriage with non-Jews (Deut. 7:3-4), the establishment of harems by kings (Deut. 17:17), the accumulation of large amounts of wealth by kings (Deut. 17:17) or entering into any kind of covenant with any other god (Ex. 23:31-33). Solomon was guilty on all counts.

Early in his reign Solomon made an alliance with Pharaoh, the king of Egypt, known to us from secular sources as Pharaoh Siamunas [978-959 B.C.], and married his daughter—even though he was already married to an Ammonite woman named Naamah. In fact his penchant for foreign wives would greatly undermine his moral authority. He built up an enormous harem of 700 wives and 300 concubines. Although many of these women were the result of political alliances with surrounding states that were sealed by marriage, the love he had for Jehovah at the beginning of his reign had turned into a love for women by the end of it. His wives turned his heart from the exclusive worship of Jehovah to the acceptance of and participation in their cult practises—some of which were horrific. The ancients might worship the gods of nations more powerful than their own, but Solomon ended up worshipping the gods of peoples he controlled. He who had once declared that the fear of Jehovah is the beginning of wisdom (Prov. 1:7), ignored his own advice—and became a fool.

God, who does not bear fools easily, raised up adversaries against Solomon. A certain Hadad, an Edomite prince who had managed to escape to Egypt from one of David's successful campaigns against his country, returned home and started an insurrection. This affected Solomon's southern trade route. Meanwhile someone called Rezon (also known as Hezion) led a guerilla band in the northeast, so that Solomon lost control of Damascus, the gateway to the north. Rezon established the rival kingdom of Aram (Syria) around Damascus which would, in years to come, become one of Israel's great adversaries.

Another challenge came from Jeroboam, a hard-working, ambitious individual from Ephraim, the largest tribe in the north, whom Solomon had recruited to supervise the work-corvées from that part of his kingdom. Solomon had heard that the prophet Ahijah had foretold that Jeroboam would one-day rule in Israel, and tried to have him assassinated. Jeroboam managed to escape to Egypt, where he sought asylum with the new Pharoah Shishak.

God was angry with Solomon because he no longer walked with Him. Unlike his father David who, through all the vicissitudes of his life had remained devoted to Jehovah, Solomon completely broke covenant with the God of Israel. God, who had warned him twice of the consequences of disobedience, now spelled them out again. He would tear the kingdom away from his son and give it to one of his subordinates though, for David's sake, one tribe would remain loyal.

Sometime before he died Solomon, old and jaded, took stock of his life and apparently turned back to worshipping Jehovah God. He wrote down his reflections in a book known as Ecclesiastes that, in time, became part of Israel's wisdom literature and, as such, entered the biblical canon. In it he bitterly described the limits of human endeavor. He recognized that all his accomplishments were little more than empty vanity, an evanescent vapour, and that self-indulgence was self-destructive. He concluded that the only thing that would have given him meaning and joy would be to have always lived a God-centered life.

Like Saul and David before him, Solomon reigned for 40 years. The wisest man of his age, the man most endowed to live a successful life, in the end failed to live up to his potential. He left behind him a kingdom in spiritual and political decline. He was buried in Jerusalem and succeeded to the throne by his son Rehoboam.

• 119 • The Kingdom Divides Under Rehoboam

1 Kings 12, 14; 2 Chronicles 11-12   *Date: reigned 930-913 B.C.*

SOLOMON'S SON Rehoboam succeeded him. Although the expected place for the coronation was Jerusalem, the northern tribes invited him to a coronation ceremony in Shechem, in the north of the country. They also summoned Jeroboam back from Egypt to be their representative.

The work-corvées and heavy taxation had created great dissatisfaction towards the end of Solomon's reign. Upon Rehoboam's arrival the people pleaded with him to now lighten the tax load. Rehoboam first consulted the elders who had served under his father, but rejected their advice to respond favourably to the people and so win their support and loyalty. Instead he foolishly followed the advice of his peers, telling the people, "my father scourged you with whips, but I will do so with scorpions!" He perceived himself as the ultimate authority and not merely as God's vassal. The northern tribes, thoroughly fed up with the rule of David's house, then seceded and turned to their spokesman Jeroboam for leadership. Thus God's prophecy through the prophet Ahijah was fulfilled.

Rehoboam dispatched someone called Adoram to redeem the situation—another unfortunate choice, for this hated man had been in charge of forced labor; the people stoned him to death. Rehoboam's coronation had turned into a lynching party that led to the enthronement of Jeroboam instead. He managed to escape to Jerusalem, where only the southern tribe of Judah and the smaller tribe of Benjamin remained loyal to him.

His pride wounded, Rehoboam mustered an army and planned his revenge. This time, however, he submitted when a man of God warned him against going to war against his fellow Israelites, because the events which had taken place were of God's doing. He proceeded to reign over the Southern Kingdom from Jerusalem. His kingdom was strengthened by the influx of a large number of godly people, particularly Levites, from the newly established Northern Kingdom of Israel, so they would not be cut off from worshipping Jehovah God at the temple in Jerusalem. However, Rehoboam allowed the people of Judah to establish various shrines to foreign idols. Soon all kinds of detestable and abhorrent practices—including shrines that offered the services of male prostitutes—were operating openly. Before long there was no difference between the religious practices in Judah and those of the nations they had displaced. The fact that Rehoboam's mother was an Ammonite may have affected his religious orientation.

In the fifth year of his reign Shishak (Shoshenq I of secular history [r. 945-924 B.C]), the Pharaoh of the newly resurgent Egypt who had granted asylum to Jeroboam, attacked and conquered Jerusalem. It was the first major invasion of Judah by a foreign power since the days of Saul.

The prophet Shemaiah confronted the king and the leaders of Judah, telling them that just as they had abandoned the Lord, so He would abandon them to Shishak. When Judah's leaders humbled themselves however He had mercy on them. Shishak entered and pillaged Jerusalem but did not destroy it. Rehoboam was now reduced to being an Egyptian vassal, and many of the treasures his father had amassed in both the temple and the palace were gone.

Throughout his reign Rehoboam had to deal with ongoing skirmishes with Jeroboam's Northern Kingdom. Obedience would have brought peace but disobedience to the Mosaic covenant, as so clearly foretold centuries earlier, brought war. He died in 913 B.C. after reigning for 17 years.

▪ 120 ▪ Jeroboam I Sets the Pattern for the Northern Kingdom
1 Kings 12—14   *Date: reigned 931-910 B.C.*

MEANWHILE, IN THE Northern Kingdom of Israel Jeroboam's immediate fear was that in time the ten tribes, over which he ruled, would re-affirm their allegiance to the house of David, especially if they continued to travel south to Jerusalem for worship during the great annual religious feasts. To combat this he decided to create an alternative religious system. He placed two golden calves at religious shrines at opposite ends of his kingdom in the towns of Bethel and Dan, and claimed that these represented the gods that had delivered the people from Egypt. Essentially he sought to create a synthesis between religious concepts common to the surrounding nations with components taken from Israel's history. Although he himself may have thought of his golden calves as symbols standing for Jehovah, they soon became idols to his people. Jeroboam's brazen attack on the Mosaic Covenant had far-reaching consequences and he became the model of an apostate, morally depraved king.

One day Jeroboam went to the shrine at Bethel to offer a sacrifice. He had no sooner done so when a young man, a prophet from Judah, stepped out of the crowd and boldly addressed the altar itself. "Altar, oh altar!" he cried. "A son named Josiah will be born to the house of David who will burn the bones of the priests who are sacrificing here. As a sign that the Lord will do this this altar will split apart and the ashes on it spill to the ground."

Livid with rage, Jeroboam stretched out his hand. "Seize that man!" he ordered. Immediately his outstretched hand shriveled and he could not pull it back. A king's hand symbolized his power, and by paralyzing it God demonstrated whose authority would prevail. At the same time the altar split apart and the ashes spilt out. Suddenly fearful, Jeroboam pleaded with the man to intercede on his behalf. God was merciful and restored his hand. Chastened, the king sought to invite the prophet home for a meal, an invitation the man firmly declined. He declared that God had told him not to consume anything during his assignment and to return home by a different route from the one by which he had come.

Several men in the crowd, the sons of an old prophet who at some stage had compromised and fallen from God's grace, witnessed the confrontation and told their father about it. The old man quickly got on his donkey and caught up with the prophet. He too invited the man to his house, and again the young man firmly declined.

"I too am a prophet. An angel of the Lord told me to find you and offer you refreshments," the old man lied. The young prophet, tired from the day's events, caved in and followed the old renegade home. While they were sitting around the table the word of the Lord came to the old man who cried out, "Because you disobeyed the Lord and came with me to eat and drink when you should not have, you will not be buried with your fathers!"

After the meal the young man saddled his donkey and resumed his journey, but before he could cross the border into Judah he was attacked and killed by a lion. This was God's judgement on his disobedience and a solemn warning to Jeroboam. In spite of this the king did not abolish the eclectic religious system he had devised which was so at odds with the terms of the Mosaic Covenant.

Sometime later Jeroboam's son fell ill. Finally, in desperation, he urged his wife to travel incognito to the prophet Ahijah who, years earlier, had predicted that he would become king of Israel. Ahijah was now old and blind, but still in fellowship with the Lord, who communicated to him that Jeroboam's wife was on her way. When he heard her footsteps at the door he greeted her, "Come in, wife of Jeroboam. Why the pretense? I have bad news for you. Go tell your husband that Jehovah, the God of Israel, says: 'I tore the kingdom from the house of David and raised you up as king over my people instead. But, unlike David, who wholeheartedly sought to do what is right in my eyes, you have provoked me to anger by ignoring me and making for yourself other gods. Because of this I will bring disaster and shame on your family—your male descendants will be devoured by wild animals.'

"As for you, return home," the blind seer continued, "as soon as you enter your city your son will die. He will be your only child to be buried with honour. The Lord will raise up a king over Israel who has no connection with the house of Jeroboam. The Lord will uproot Israel from this good land that He gave them and scatter them beyond the Euphrates River because the people have angered Him by worshiping idols and because they have embraced the sin into which your husband led them."

Jeroboam reigned for 22 years. The spiritual decline he initiated led to a long, political decline and he lost control of Damascus, which became the independent state of Syria (or Aram). Even though Jeroboam had turned his back on God, God continued to abide by the covenant agreement of judgment in response to compromise.

• 121 • Abijah and Asa: Kings in Judah

1 Kings 15; 2 Chron. 13-17   *Dates: reigned 913-911; 911 – 870 B.C.*

BACK IN THE Southern Kingdom Rehoboam was succeeded by his son Abijah (also known as Abijam), whose mother was a granddaughter of Absalom. His short reign of three years was marked by ongoing warfare with the Northern Kingdom. One major conflict took place in the

18th year of Jeroboam's reign. Abijah mustered an army of some 400,000 men and went on the offensive, even though Jeroboam's army was twice as large. The two armies squared off near the border, in the hill country of Ephraim. Abijah climbed a hill from which he could address the enemy army, whom he charged with rebellion against Jehovah. "We have not forsaken the Lord our God like you have. Do not fight against us since you will not succeed," he enjoined them. Though outnumbered two to one, and caught in a smart ambush, God enabled Abijah to win a resounding victory. This display of faith was, however, uncharacteristic. His son Asa succeeded him in Jeroboam's 20th year as monarch of the Northern Kingdom.

Asa must have been quite young when he ascended the throne in Judah for he reigned for 41 years. He began well, putting the Mosaic Covenant back at the center of Israel's national life. He removed the pagan shrines, incense altars and most of the high places that had flourished under his father Abijah and his grandfather Rehoboam. He even demoted his grandmother because of her idolatrous behaviour. He also built a string of forts along his northern border, and the land enjoyed peace and prosperity—until Zerah the Cushite led an army equipped with a division of 300 chariots against him.

Asa cried out to the Lord: "Lord, there is no one like you to strengthen the powerless against the powerful. Help us, Jehovah our God, for we depend on you!" The army of Judah went on to win a decisive victory against the invaders and captured large amounts of booty.

After this the Spirit of God came on a prophet named Azariah with a message assuring the king that the Lord would be with him for as long as he sought after the Lord. If he remained strong and faithful then God would reverse the distress and trauma that He had inflicted on the nation when it had departed from the terms of the covenant under Asa's predecessors. Greatly encouraged, Asa redoubled his efforts to clean the land of idols, even getting rid of those that he had captured in battle. The people swore whole-heartedly to seek the Lord afresh, and the Lord gave them many years of peace. At the same time more and more people started migrating to Judah from the Northern Kingdom.

During the 36th year of Asa's reign, Baasha, who by then had seized the throne in Israel, fortified the border town of Rama in an attempt to stop the flow of migration southward. Asa responded by stripping the temple of its silver and gold and sending it with a delegation to Damascus. He encouraged Ben-Hadad, the king of Syria, to break his treaty with Israel and make a peace treaty with him instead. Ben-Hadad agreed and attacked Israel, conquering large tracts of its territory. Asa's strategy was successful from a human perspective, but God sent a prophet to rebuke him. "Did the Lord not deliver you from the Cushites and your other enemies when you relied on Him? You have acted foolishly in relying on the king of Syria and not on the Lord. From now on your kingdom will be at war. The eyes of the Lord search continually over the earth looking to strengthen the hearts of those people whose hearts are fully committed to him," the man declared.

Instead of repenting Asa lost his temper. He had the prophet imprisoned, and began to brutally oppress some of his own subjects. In the 39th year of his reign he was afflicted with a disease that crippled him, but instead of turning to the Lord he placed his faith in his physicians. Two years later he died. Asa, who had begun so well and been used of God for many years to bring spiritual renewal to Judah, ended his long reign badly.

· 122 · Rapid Decline: A String of Evil Northern kings

1 Kings 15-16   *Date: 910 – 853 B.C.*

AFTER JEROBOAM I the politics of the Northern Kingdom became extremely unstable and troubled as the curses of the Mosaic Covenant played out. One king after another did evil in the sight of the Lord by continuing to walk in the ways of Jeroboam I, the model of evil. Jeroboam's son Nadab, a man as evil as his father had been, reigned for a mere two years (910-909 B.C.). Baasha, one of his own men, assassinated him during a battle against the Philistines. This brute then killed all of Jeroboam's remaining male relatives, thus fulfilling the prophet Ahijah's words to Jeroboam's wife (1 Kings 14:14).

Baasha managed to hang on to the throne for 24 years (909-886 B.C.), the 3rd longest reign in the history of the kingdom. Through the prophet Jehu, God declared that the same fate that had befallen the house of Jeroboam, would overtake Baasha's family as well.

Baasha's son Elah succeeded him. He was assassinated after a mere two years in office (886-885) while in a drunken stupor by one of his officers, Zimri, who went on to kill every member of Baasha's family. History—including the fulfilment of the prophetic word—had repeated itself.

Zimri's reign lasted for a mere week (in 885 B.C.), the shortest in Israel's history. When the army heard that Zimri had murdered Elah they proclaimed Omri, a more senior army commander, as king instead. Omri attacked Israel's capital Tirzah where Zimri was holed up. When Zimri saw that he had lost support he set the citadel on fire and died in the conflagration. Six years of civil war (885-880 B.C.) followed. Some supported a man called Tibni while others stood behind Omri. Omri emerged as the victor and for the next 12 years (880-874 B.C.) became one of the Northern Kingdom's most powerful and internationally significant monarchs. Secular history reports that he defeated the Moabites, while Assyrian records of that period call Israel "The Land of Omri", and that he made a peace treaty with the king of Phoenicia which was sealed with the marriage of his son Ahab to their king's daughter Jezebel. The Biblical report, however, ignores all these accomplishments, merely mentioning that he purchased a centrally located and easily defendable hilltop on which he built a new capital city, called Samaria. Omri himself is summed up as one "who sinned more than all the kings who had preceded him".

Although Omri was the worst king of Israel to date, his son Ahab's 22-year reign was even worse. He and his wife, the Phoenician princess whom the Jews derisively called "Jezebel" (meaning "chaste virgin" in Phoenician but "dunghill" in Hebrew) would become the most notorious married couple of Jewish history. Ahab not only promoted the cult instituted by Jeroboam I, he also institutionalized the worship of Baal, to which his wife was devoted. He built a temple and altar to this awful deity (2 Kings 16:3) in Samaria and allowed the Baal priests to take charge of Israel's religious life. The worship of Jehovah had been replaced with that of the old Canaanite deities.

· 123 · Elijah Bursts Onto the Scene

1 Kings 16   *Date: ministered circa 870-850 B.C.*

THE GREAT PROPHET Elijah strode dramatically out of obscurity onto the Northern Kingdom's national stage and singlehandedly faced down its idolatrous royal family and religious elite.

The Northern Kingdom had reached the nadir of idolatry and sin when Elijah burst onto the scene. During the 58 years since its secession from the South, seven kings had come and gone, each of them more wicked than his predecessor.

The Mosaic Covenant meant nothing to King Ahab. Nevertheless, God did not leave His people without a witness: one of the Old Testament's greatest prophets ministered during the reign of one of Israel's most evil kings at a time when almost all other voices speaking on behalf of Jehovah had been silenced.

Little is known about Elijah's background. We don't know anything about his parents, whether he ever married or had children, at what age he began his ministry, or what religious education he had received. We do know that he was thoroughly familiar with the Pentateuch—the books of Moses—and all that God had done for Israel, that his name means "Jehovah is my God", and that he came from a wild, hilly place in Gilead called Tishbe, on the east side of the Jordan river. Word of the apostasy of the royal palace in Samaria reached this rugged, solitary man, "zealous for Jehovah, God Almighty" (1 Kings 19:10) and, deeply grieved and disturbed, he began interceding on behalf of the nation for he was a powerful man of prayer. As he did so the Lord must have directed his attention to a particular passage of the Pentateuch: "Be careful that you are not enticed to turn away from Jehovah and follow after and bow down to other gods, for Jehovah's anger will burn against you and He will shut the heavens so that it will not rain and the land will yield no produce and you will perish from the good land which the Lord has given you" (Deut. 11:16-17). The passage accurately described Israel's sin: if Jehovah God was indeed the one whom the books of Moses claimed He was then, according to the terms of the covenant, He could be expected to punish the nation by means of a drought. Laying hold of God's word, Elijah started praying earnestly that it might be so (Jam. 5:17) in order that the worship of Jehovah God might be restored. As he prayed he received the assurance that God had granted his request, and that he should go to Samaria to inform the king.

It required courage for a rustic backwoodsman to appear uninvited before a despot and pronounce a message of judgement. The chance of escaping with one's life were slim for the king's heathen wife had already had numerous others put to death for their devotion to Jehovah. Undaunted, however, Elijah set off, a lone figure on a dangerous mission to the nation's new capital city. Unannounced he appeared before the apostate monarch, and with great assurance and confidence proclaimed Jehovah's message of judgement: "As surely as the Lord, the God of Israel whom I serve, lives, for the next few years it will not rain nor will there be any dew on the land except I say so!"

God had been patient. He had even blessed the nation with a period of stability and economic growth under Ahab's father Omri; yet the royal family, those responsible for the welfare of the covenant people, had persisted in defying Him by breaking the terms of the covenant. Now the day of wrath had come. Drought would turn the land of milk and honey into a desiccated, parched wasteland. A protracted famine, untold suffering and slow death would stalk the nation—and the dead, impotent idols they worshiped would be helpless to do anything about it. Much as it pained Elijah to see his fellow Jews suffer, his overriding concern was that the apostate nation's covenant relationship with Jehovah be restored and God's name honored and glorified among His people—whatever the cost.

· 124 · Elijah Disappears From the Scene

1 Kings 17   *Date: ministered circa 870-850 B.C.*

NO SOONER HAD Elijah completed his mission when the Lord spoke to him again: "Leave this place. Go east and hide in the Cherith Ravine on the east side of the Jordan. You will be able to drink water from the brook and I have ordered ravens to supply you with food." He had boldly confronted King Ahab and now God removed him from the scene. The drought symbolized the removal of God's blessing from his people—and that included the removal of His spokesperson. The greatest sign of covenant blessing is when God's "teachings fall like rain, his words descend like dew, like showers on new grass" (Deut. 32:2). Nor was there a greater sign of divine displeasure than when God ceased to speak (Amos 8:11-12).

Without hesitating Elijah obeyed. Deep in the wilderness, cut off from the company of others near the headwaters of the bubbling brook Cherith, he waited while every morning and every evening, without fail, a pack of unclean ravens brought him his daily bread and meat. As God's decree to punish the nation by means of a drought was being fulfilled he watched the stream reduce to a trickle and then stop flowing altogether. When there was no more water the word of the Lord came to him: "Go to the Sidonian village of Zarephath and stay there. I have commanded a widow there to supply you with food". Sidon was gentile territory, the heartland of Baal worship and the place from which Ahab's evil consort Jezebel hailed (1 Kings 16:31). When he eventually arrived there he saw a woman gathering firewood. "Would you bring me a little water to drink?" he asked. Without question the kind-hearted woman went to fetch some of the precious liquid for the stranger. "And please, also bring me a piece of bread," he called after her.

At this the woman turned around. "As the Lord your God lives, I have no bread," she replied. "I only have a handful of flour and a little jug of oil left. I'm collecting these few sticks to make a meal for my son and myself—and after that we will die," she explained with quiet, hopeless despair.

"Do not fear," Elijah said gently. "Go home, make me a small cake of bread from your remaining flour and oil and bring it to me. Then make some for yourself, for the Lord God of Israel says that the jar of flour and the jug of oil will not run dry until such a time as He sends rain to the land." Something about the confidence with which the prophet uttered his words convinced the widow to trust the promise made in the name of the God of Israel. She obeyed— and discovered that there was always enough flour in the sack and just enough oil in the jug for the next meal.

If, however, the widow of Zarephath had hoped that her troubles were over because she was sheltering a prophet she was wrong. In spite of the daily miracle of food, her son fell sick, grew worse and then died. The one person on whom her love and care was focused, the one who could take care of her in her old age was gone.

"What do you have against me, oh man of God?" she burst out. "Did you come to remind me of my sin and kill my son?" Elijah must have shared the fact that the drought was in response to his prayers because Israel had deserted Jehovah for Baal. Perhaps she wondered if this calamity was a result of the fact that she too was a Baal worshiper…

In spite of her bitter sorrow, she consented to let Elijah carry her son's body to his room. The prophet laid the lad's lifeless body on his bed. He too was deeply upset by the turn of events, and perplexed as to the meaning of this tragedy. Surely this was not the way God rewards those who seek to serve Him? He closed the door to his room and cried out to the One

who had promised to defend the cause of the widows (Deut. 10:18). "Oh Lord my God, you are the one who has allowed this tragedy to befall the widow with whom I am staying." Then he stretched himself out on the boy and pleaded, "Lord God, let this boy return to life!"

Nothing happened. He stretched himself on the boy a second time and again cried to the Lord. Again nothing happened. He refused to give up. He lay on the boy a third time—and this time the Lord responded: life surged through the corpse! Flushed with joy he picked up the child, carried him down the stairs and handed him back to his mother: "Look, your son is alive!" What happiness filled that house as the two of them watched the child scampering around. The woman looked at him. "I now know that you truly are a man of God, and that the words of the Lord you speak are truth," she said. As for Elijah, this divine ratification of his ministry must have greatly emboldened him before he set out to confront the priests of Baal.

• 125 • Elijah Confronts Ahab Again

1 Kings 18   *Date: circa 870-850 B.C.*

SOME THREE years after Elijah had gone into hiding the word of the Lord came to him again: "Go, present yourself to Ahab and I will send rain on the earth!"

It is not difficult to imagine the bitter anger Ahab and Jezebel nursed against the man they held responsible for the terrible drought. While Jezebel sought to kill all the prophets of Jehovah she could lay her hands on, Ahab had searched everywhere for Elijah. He had even required assurances on oath from the rulers of the surrounding nations that they would not provide asylum for the Hebrew prophet. Confronting this pair required great courage but without hesitation Elijah left the safety of Zarephath, crossed the border back into Israel, and headed for Samaria.

The drought had been severe and the land was desiccated. Ahab had ordered his palace administrator Obadiah to help him explore every spring in every valley in the hope of finding a patch of grass to keep their horses and mules alive. While the king had headed in one direction, Obadiah had headed in the other. Suddenly Obadiah ran into Elijah! He recognized him instantly and bowed before him. "Is this really you, my lord Elijah?" He could hardly believe his eyes. The most wanted man in the land was striding calmly towards Samaria.

"Yes, it is I," Elijah replied. "Go and tell your master that I am here."

"What have I done to offend the Lord to deserve this?" Obadiah asked. "You are handing me over to the king to be put to death. He has searched everywhere for you. If I go and tell him that you are here, and you disappear before he gets here, he will have my life. I have worshiped Jehovah since my youth and am hiding a hundred of God's prophets from the murderous Jezebel. And now you tell me to go to Ahab and tell him you are here? He will surely kill me."

"As the Lord Almighty whom I serve lives, I will present myself to Ahab today," Elijah assured him. Although kings are not accustomed to be summoned, Ahab must have galloped to his rendezvous with the bold and uncompromising prophet with trepidation. He knew he could not kill the prophet as he needed him to "say the word" for the drought to end (1 Kings 17:1). "Is that you, you troubler of Israel?" he greeted Elijah bitterly. If he thought he could intimidate the prophet he was badly mistaken.

"I am not responsible for the trouble afflicting Israel. You and your father's house are because you have forsaken the Lord's commands and have bowed the knee to Baal instead," Elijah responded unflinchingly. "I want you to summon the nation for a meeting with me on Mount Carmel. The 450 prophets of Baal and the 400 prophets of Asherah whom Jezebel provides for are to be there as well," he summarily ordered. Ahab must have grasped that the stage was being set for a showdown. Desperate, he did as he was told.

▪ 126 ▪ Jehovah or Baal?

1 Kings 18   *Date: circa 870-850 B.C.*

FROM ALL the corners of the Northern Kingdom the people made their way to Mount Carmel. Suddenly the attention of the restless crowd was drawn to the 450 fierce Baal prophets wearing their special vestments and religious headgear as they took up their positions. Then the king, surrounded by his bodyguard and his chief counsellors, arrived with great pomp and ceremony.

After that Elijah stepped forward. A hush must have fallen over the crowd as all eyes turned towards the strange, lone man at whose command the heavens refused to send rain. The king and his priests' fear and hatred of the man they held responsible for the calamity must have been palpable—yet they dare not touch him.

Ignoring the Baal prophets Elijah faced the common people. "How much longer will you vacillate between two opinions? If Jehovah is God, follow him; if Baal is god follow him," he challenged them. Unlike their spiritual and temporal leaders, the people had not yet fully embraced Baalism. They had not wanted to abandon the worship of Jehovah altogether, yet they did not want to fall out of favor with their rulers either. Elijah challenged them to stop vacillating. Would they or would they not wholeheartedly worship and surrender themselves to the living God who had revealed himself to Abraham, Isaac and Jacob, and who had led them from Egypt, made a covenant with them and had given them the land? There could be no compromise, no middle way, for Jehovah had revealed Himself to be a jealous God who would not tolerate a competitor for His people's affections (Ex. 20:4).

The people remained silent as Elijah's voice rang out. "I am the only one of Jehovah's prophets left, while Baal has 450 prophets to serve him," he cried. Although he had recently learned from Obadiah that there were some 100 prophets in hiding, they were too afraid to step into the open. There was no evidence of them on Mount Carmel.

"Get two bulls. Let the Baal priests choose one, cut it up and place the pieces on wood on an altar but not set fire to it. I will do the same," Elijah shouted. "Then have them ask their god to set fire to the offering. Afterwards I will call on Jehovah God to do the same. The god who answers with fire, He is God!" A stir, followed by a murmur of affirmation rippled through the crowd. This was a reasonable proposal. It would, once and for all, settle the question of whom they should worship and serve.

God had used supernatural displays of fire as a symbol of Himself on various occasions in Israel's past. He had spoken to Moses out of a burning bush (Ex. 3:2-5); He led his people through the wilderness at night by means of a fiery cloud (Ex. 13:21); He spoke to them at Mount Sinai from fire (Ex. 19:18); He had lit the offerings of His people (Lev. 9:24) and that of great king David (1 Chron. 21:26). Fire symbolized the presence of a holy, enlightening, purifying and punishing God. It would be a clear proof to the people that the God of Elijah was indeed the very Jehovah God of their forefathers, as well as indicate that God had accepted Elijah's sacrifice on behalf of the sins of the people. God needed to be appeased before His blessings would be unleashed and the rain would come.

The Baal prophets chose their calf and sacrificed it. Then they started calling out to Baal: "Oh Baal, hear us! Oh Baal, answer us." Hour after hour passed while the Baal prophets worked themselves into a frenzy, leaping and dancing frenetically round and round the altar and keeping up their chant: "Baal, hear us! Baal, answer us! Baal, respond to us!" But there was no response. No fire came.

Around noon Elijah began to ridicule them. "You should cry louder! Isn't Baal a god? Maybe he is deep in thought. Or maybe he is busy with something, or away on a journey. Or he may be sleeping and you need to wake him up!" The Baal prophets redoubled their efforts. They shouted even louder, and began to lacerate themselves with swords and spears so that their blood gushed out—but all to no avail. For all their enthusiasm, for all their fervour and zeal, there was no divine response.

Sometime that afternoon Elijah invited the people to come close to where he was so that they could see clearly what he was about to do. There was an old, broken-down altar to the Lord on the slope of Mount Carmel. As specified by the Mosaic Law (Ex. 20:25-26), Elijah carefully restacked the twelve uncut stones scattered on the ground, each of which represented one Israel's 12 tribes, into a rough altar. Although the nation had been divided, Elijah saw them as they were in God's eyes: one covenant people. Then he dug a shallow trench around the altar, stacked some wood on it, slaughtered the calf, cut it up, and laid the pieces on the altar, just as prescribed in the Torah (Lev. 1:6-8). When everything was ready he ordered some bystanders to fill four jugs of water from the brook Kishon still trickling in the valley nearby and pour the water over the altar on the offering and on the wood. He had them do this three times until the offering and wood were soaking wet and the dripping water filled the trench. Then, before the sun set, when the evening sacrifice would be sacrificed in the temple in the Southern Kingdom's capital Jerusalem, Elijah stepped forward and began to pray. "O Lord, the God of Abraham, Isaac and Israel, let it be known today that you are the God in Israel and that I am your servant and have done all these things according to your command. Hear me and answer me, O Lord," he cried fervently, "so that the people will know that you Jehovah are God, and that you are turning their hearts back again to yourself!" That is what this showdown was all about.

For a brief moment all was still... and then, suddenly, a bolt of fire fell from the cloudless sky and burned up the sacrifice, the wood, the water in the trench, the soil—even the 12 stones were reduced to dust. Nothing could resist it and through it Jehovah affirmed that He was, indeed, the one living, covenant-keeping God to whom Elijah had born effective witness. When the people saw what had happened they fell on their faces. "Jehovah, He is God, He is the Lord!" they cried, all doubt removed.

"Seize the Baal prophets! Don't let a single one escape," Elijah ordered. The atoning sacrifice was of no avail to the Baal prophets for they were not the Lord's people. Elijah had them taken down to the Kishon valley where he slew them as stipulated in the Mosaic Covenant (Deut. 13:1-5; 18:20-22). King Ahab was too stunned to protest the wholesale purging of the evil which had brought judgement on the nation, and too afraid to interfere with this popular outburst of religious fervor.

After disposing of the Baal prophets Elijah suggested the king get a bite to eat; he looked like he needed sustenance. "I hear the sound of heavy rain," Elijah continued. There was not a cloud in the sky but the prophet could see by faith that which was invisible to others (Heb. 11:1, 13, 27). They could expect a torrential downpour. He left the monarch and climbed to the top of Mount Carmel where, far from the crowd, he sat down, his face hanging between his knees, and began to pray fervently for rain (James 5:17-18). After a while he lifted his head and told his servant to go and look over the sea. The man reported that nothing had changed. Again Elijah prayed, again he sent the man to look over the sea, and again the man reported that nothing had changed. The scene repeated itself six times. On his seventh trip the servant reported seeing a tiny cloud, no bigger than a man's hand, rising from the sea.

"Go tell Ahab to hitch up his chariot and head home before the rain prevents him from doing so," Elijah ordered the servant. The king again did as he was told and headed home to Jezreel, where his impatient wife was waiting in suspense.

Suddenly the wind picked up, whipping thick, black clouds through the darkening sky. Thunder clapped and the rain began to pour down. Through flashes of lightening the king caught glimpses of an amazing spectacle: the Lord's prophet, cloak tucked into his belt, was running ahead of him with supernatural strength all the way to Jezreel, where the queen was waiting.

• 127 • Post-Carmel Depression and Restoration

1 Kings 19   *Date: circa 870-850 B.C.*

WHEN HE ARRIVED home, Ahab told Jezebel all that had taken place, though he refused to recognize the hand of God in the events of the day. Elijah was to blame! The prophet had mocked and scorned and belittled and, through some feat of sorcery, had brought fire from heaven! Her pride wounded, the enraged Jezebel dispatched a messenger to Elijah with an ominous message: "may the gods judge me severely if by this time tomorrow you have not joined those you have slaughtered".

All of a sudden fear's cold tentacles gripped the prophet's heart. His focus shifted and he lost sight of the God who had worked so miraculously on his behalf. All he could see was a vengeful woman vowing to kill him and, in a panic, he ran for his life. He headed south, deserting the nation he had been called to serve. He crossed the border into Judah but even there he didn't feel safe, for at that time there was a rapprochement between the two kingdoms; there was no guarantee that Judah would not extradite him back to Israel. He left his servant in the southern town of Beersheba and headed into the Sinai wilderness. For hours he plodded seemingly aimlessly in the desert before collapsing in the shade of a juniper tree. "Lord, I have had enough. Take my life. I'm no better than my ancestors..." he prayed. From the mountaintop to the wilderness, from facing down the king and his evil prophets to fleeing in a panic from a woman, from seeking God's glory to begging God to take his life... Elijah was depressed, tired of the loneliness and the grind of constant opposition. Deeply discouraged, he became convinced that his life and ministry had been a failure. Ahab had not had a change of heart after the victory at Carmel, the nation had not re-embraced the worship of Jehovah, and the queen was after his life. There was no joy in service anymore, and he was ready to give up.

Exhausted, he fell into a deep, refreshing sleep. Suddenly he felt someone nudging him. An angel, one of God's ministering spirits (Heb. 1:14), woke him and urged him to eat. Elijah looked around and saw a jug of water together with a loaf of fresh bread baking over some hot coals. He ate and drank and fell asleep again. Sometime later the angel woke him again. "Get up and eat some more. You will be going on a long, arduous journey." Elijah did so, and strengthened by the food traveled the next 40 days and nights through the wilderness until he reached Mount Sinai where, centuries earlier, God had spelled out the great covenant that was to govern Israel.

Elijah spent the night in a cave. The next morning the Lord spoke to him. "Elijah, what are you doing here?" It was as if the Lord wanted his servant to take stock of his situation.

"Oh Lord, I have been very zealous for you. The people of Israel have rejected Your covenant, broken down Your altars and killed Your prophets," Elijah blurted out. This much was true... "I am the only one left," he complained. This was not true. "And they are also trying to kill me," he concluded rightly. His focus had shifted from God to himself and his circumstances.

"Leave the cave and stand on the mountain in my presence," the Lord instructed him. "I am going to pass before you." When Elijah stepped out of the cave he was forcefully reminded of God's great power: a tremendous gust of wind came from nowhere and tore great chunks of rock from the mountain. But the Lord did not appear to Elijah in the wind. An earthquake followed the wind, but the Lord did not appear to him in the earthquake either. A fire followed it, but the Lord did not appear in the fire either. A storm, an earthquake, fire, those were the signs that had accompanied the giving of the law on that mountain centuries earlier (Ex. 19:16-18; Heb. 12:18). Before those fierce reminders of the law Elijah retreated back into the cave. Then, suddenly, he heard a still, small whisper, and he knew that Jehovah himself was there. Reverently Elijah pulled his cloak over his face and moved towards the mouth of the cave.

"Elijah, what are you doing here?" the whisper inquired again, and the prophet repeated his sad complaint. "Oh Lord, I have been very zealous for you, Jehovah God Almighty. The people of Israel have rejected Your covenant, broken down Your altars and killed Your prophets. I am the only one left and they are also trying to kill me."

"Head back the way you came," the Lord instructed him. "Make your way to Damascus and crown Hazael king over Syria. Then anoint Jehu the son of Nimshi as king over the Northern Kingdom of Israel. Jehu will kill those who escape Hazael's sword, and Hazael will put to death those who escape the sword of Jehu. Also anoint Elisha from Abel Meholah to succeed you as prophet... and there are 7000 people in Israel who have not bowed down and worshiped Baal!"

Instead of leaving his servant brooding in a cave the Lord put him back to work. He encouraged him with the fact that even in the most terrible of times He had a remnant of those who remained faithful. Evil would not triumph and the prophetic ministry would continue after him. Instead of a natural calamity the sovereign Lord would now use the machinations of evil rulers to purge His people.

Comforted, Elijah retraced his steps. His first stop was Abel Meholah, some 160 miles away. There he found Elisha plowing his father's field. He went up to the young farmer, cast his mantle over his shoulders, and turned around to go.

"Let me say farewell to my parents," Elisha said running after him, "and I will follow you." Becoming a disciple of a hunted man like Elijah took courage and devotion, yet Elisha responded without hesitating. He slaughtered his yoke of oxen, set his wooden plow on fire, and held a farewell feast for his friends and relatives. He knew he would follow Elijah and never again return to his old life as a farmer.

• 128 • Ahab's Refusal To Accept That Jehovah Is Lord

1 Kings 20   *Date: circa 870-850 B.C.*

A COALITION of some 32 kings (the word "king" in those days was used by both rulers of empires as well as rulers of independent city-states), under the overall leadership of Ben-Hadad, king of Syria (Aram), declared war on Ahab's Israel. They broke through the Northern Kingdom's defences and besieged the capital city Samaria. Confident he would win, Ben-Hadad peremptorily demanded that Ahab hand over all his silver and gold along with his wives and children. When Ahab communicated that he was prepared to meet those demands Ben-Hadad upped the ante, stating that his men would also come and ransack the palace and the houses of all of Ahab's officials. Ahab refused this outrageous request. Piqued at this unexpected rebuff, the Syrian monarch threatened to reduce Samaria to dust.

"Let not the one who puts his armor on boast like the one who takes it off," Ahab responded drily. Now thoroughly enraged, Ben-Hadad ordered his men to prepare to attack the city. Just then a prophet arrived at Ahab's court in Samaria and announced, "Thus says the Lord! I will give the vast army before you into your hands, so that you will know that Jehovah is the Lord."

"Who will make this happen?" Ahab asked. "And who will launch the first attack?"

"The young officers from the provinces," the prophet stated. "And you will start the battle." On the basis of that advice Ahab summoned the 232 officers serving under his provincial commanders, assembled the rest of his small army of 7000 behind them and launched a noontime attack, just when Ben-Hadad and his allies were in their tents getting drunk. The bold sortie led to a stunning, altogether unexpected victory. The invaders were routed, though Ben-Hadad himself managed to escape on horseback.

"Fortify the city and make all necessary preparations because the king of Syria will attack again next spring," the prophet advised.

Back in Damascus Ben-Hadad's advisors told him the reason he had lost was because the gods of Israel were gods of the hills. If they rebuilt their army and fought the Jews on the plains they would win. Following this dubious advice Ben-Hadad mustered another huge army and marched against Israel the following spring. Israel's army looked "like two small flocks of goats while the Syrians covered the countryside".

Once again the prophet approached King Ahab saying, "Thus says the Lord! I will deliver this great army into your hand. Then you will know that I am the Lord." The result was exactly as predicted. Israel inflicted huge casualties, and the remnants of the Syrian army fled to a nearby city. When its wall collapsed another large number of enemy combatants were killed. Upon learning that Ben-Hadad was still alive Ahab welcomed him like a brother and signed a peace treaty with him.

When word of the treaty got out another one of the prophets asked a colleague to strike him with a sword. Wounded and in disguise, the prophet stood by the side of the road. When the king passed he called out, "Your servant was fighting in the thick of the battle when another soldier ordered me to guard a captive at the cost of my life. When I was busy doing something else the enemy soldier escaped."

"Then that is your sentence," the king responded. "You have pronounced it yourself." At this the prophet removed his disguise and declared, "This is the word of the Lord! You freed a man I had determined should die. Your life will be in place of his, your people in place of his people." Upon hearing this the king headed morosely for his palace in Samaria.

▪ 129 ▪ The Naboth Affair

1 Kings 21   *Date: circa 870-850 B.C.*

ONE DAY QUEEN Jezebel found Ahab sulking in bed because a certain Naboth, owner of a vineyard adjoining his palace, refused to sell him his land at any price. The brave Naboth recognized an authority higher than the king and honored the Mosaic Law that forbade the sale of inherited land (Lev. 25:23; Num. 36:7). "Is this how you behave as king of Israel?" Jezebel ridiculed her husband. "Cheer up, I'll get you Naboth's vineyard!" She wrote letters in Ahab's name to the city elders ordering them to proclaim a fast as if they had uncovered a great misdeed, and to find some scoundrels who would falsely accuse Naboth of cursing both God and the king. The callow city elders obeyed and had both Naboth and his sons stoned to death so that there would be no one left to inherit the land (2 Kings 9:26). Jezebel then urged the king to get up and take possession of this illgotten property.

While the king had been distracted with the Syrian invasions Elijah and his new helper Elisha seemed to have been busy training young men for ministry in "schools of the prophets" in Bethel and Jericho (2 Kings 2:3, 5). No sooner had the atrocity been committed, however, when a word of the Lord came to Elijah. Once again the prophet made the trek to Samaria to deliver God's message of condemnation to the contemptible monarch.

"So you have found me, my enemy!" Ahab greeted him with foreboding.

"I have found you," Elijah answered, "because you have sold yourself to work evil in the Lord's sight. You have murdered and seized property. This is what the Lord says, 'In the place where dogs licked the blood of Naboth dogs will lick your blood, and they will eat Jezebel by the wall of Jezreel. Every single one of your male descendants will be exterminated. Those killed in the city will be eaten by dogs and those killed in the countryside devoured by vultures.'" When he heard the awful judgement the king was deeply shaken. He tore his clothes, put on sackcloth, fasted, and abased himself. However, he did not seek to reintroduce the worship of Jehovah in his kingdom and did not seek to restore Naboth's vineyard to his next of kin. In spite of Ahab's period of superficial, personal reform God did not repeal His judgement. However He honored Ahab's public display of humility by delaying the extermination of his family until after his death.

▪ 130 ▪ King Jehoshaphat of Judah

1 Kings 22; 2 Chronicles 17-20   *Date: r. 872-847 B.C.*

DURING THE fourth year of Ahab's reign in the Northern Kingdom of Israel, Jehoshaphat succeeded his father Asa in the Southern Kingdom of Judah. He was thirty-five years old when he ascended the throne in Jerusalem. For most of his life he walked in the ways of the Lord and sought to live according to the demands of the Mosaic Covenant, as a result of which the Lord blessed him. The surrounding nations feared him, and the tribute they brought enabled him to fortify his cities, build storage depots and keep a standing army.

Jehoshaphat's relationship with Ahab was amicable. He married his son Jehoram to Ahab's daughter Athaliah to cement an alliance that was probably meant to serve as a bulwark against the growing threat of Assyria. Its brutal ruler Ashurnasirpal II (884-859) pushed into Phoenicea in the north, and his successor Shalmaneser III defeated the Syrians in the battle of Qarqar near Damascus in 853. In spite of the apparent logic of Jehoshaphat's alliance with the evil Ahab the Lord condemned it. It would have awful consequences.

During a summit meeting between the two kings Ahab asked Jehoshaphat to help him recover the border town of Ramoth-Gilead which the now weakened Syrians had taken earlier.

Jehoshaphat acquiesced, but stipulated that he first wanted to seek the mind of the Lord. At this Ahab invited four hundred court prophets to the palace. Professing to speak on behalf of Jehovah these paid sycophants assured the two kings that their mission would end in success.

Jehoshaphat had little confidence in these yes-men. "Is there not a real prophet of Jehovah here whom we can consult?" he asked Ahab.

"There is one, but I hate him. He never prophesies anything good about me. His name is Micaiah," Ahab responded.

"I'd like to hear what he has to say," Jehoshaphat said. At this Ahab sent a messenger to fetch Micaiah. "Micaiah, should we or should we not go to war against Ramoth-Gilead?" Ahab asked him.

"Attack and win the victory! They will be handed over to you," Micaiah said facetiously, mimicking the false prophets. When Ahab insisted that he tell the truth Micaiah did so. "I saw the people of Israel scattered like sheep without a shepherd on the hilltops. The Lord said to them: 'these people have no master. Let them go home in peace...'" the prophet replied, predicting Ahab's death in the upcoming battle. But Micaiah was not finished yet. "The Lord of heaven showed me that he has put a lying spirit in the mouth of these prophets of yours. He has decreed disaster for you," he concluded.

"Imprison Micaiah. Put him on bread and water until I return safely," the incensed king ordered.

"If you return safely then I am not a prophet of the Lord. Mark my words, people!" the brave man of God declared as he was led to prison. In spite of the dire warning Ahab and Jehoshaphat went ahead as planned. Ahab even convinced Jehoshaphat to go into battle wearing his royal robes while he himself went disguised as an ordinary soldier.

The Syrian king had ordered his thirty-two charioteers to make straight for Ahab and kill him. When these soldiers saw someone in royal robes they presumed he was Ahab and moved in for the kill. Jehoshaphat saw the danger coming and cried out to the Lord. Suddenly the enemy charioteers chasing him realized he was not, in fact, the king of Israel and dropped their pursuit. Elsewhere a Syrian footman randomly drew his bow. The arrow soared across the battlefield and struck Ahab between the sections of his armour.

"Turn around and get me out of here," Ahab ordered his driver. "I've been hit." While the battle raged around him Ahab, bleeding copiously, sat propped up in his chariot. He died at sunset. His body was taken to Israel's capital city Samaria where he was buried. Afterwards, when the blood was washed from his chariot at a pool used for bathing by prostitutes some dogs lapped it up, just as the prophet had predicted.

Jehoshaphat returned safely home to Judah's capital Jerusalem, where a prophet named Jehu, the son of the prophet Hanani who had confronted Jehoshaphat's father Asa years earlier, rebuked him for his unholy alliance with Ahab. Jehoshaphat responded positively to the Hanani's rebuke, and initiated a second period of reform. He destroyed the pagan places dedicated to the worship of Baal and Asherah and rid the land of the male shrine prostitutes associated with them. He also sent a delegation of royal officials, Levites and priests throughout the land to teach people the Book of the Law of Moses, and appointed judges to newly fortified cities, instructing them to judge justly according to the law and in fear of God. He did not, however, remove the popular high places where people continued to make sacrifices to Jehovah, in contradiction to God's clear command that that was only to take place in the temple in Jerusalem.

Some time after this a vast coalition of Moabites and Ammonites declared war on Judah. The aggressors crossed south of the Dead Sea and headed towards Jerusalem. Alarmed, Jehoshaphat proclaimed a fast, and called people from all over Judah to come together to seek the Lord's help. Then Jehoshaphat stood up in the courtyard of the temple and prayed in the hearing of all the people. He affirmed God's omnipotence and sovereignty over the nations, and reminded God of His faithfulness in driving out the godless inhabitants of the land and giving it to Israel. He also pointed out that God had forbidden the Israelites from attacking Ammon when they came up from Egypt, yet now these same Ammonites were threatening their existence. "Oh God, will you not judge them? We are powerless against them. We don't know what to do, but our eyes are fixed on you!" he cried.

Then the Spirit of the Lord came on Jahaziel, a Levite of the clan of Asaph. "Listen, King Jehoshaphat and people of Judah. This is the word of the Lord: Do not be afraid of this vast army moving against you. The battle is not yours, but the Lords! You will march against them tomorrow. Take up your positions, stand firm and watch how the Lord will deliver you from their hands!" The people were greatly encouraged by these words.

Early the next morning Jehoshaphat encouraged his people to have faith in God. He appointed a choir to sing the praises, splendor and holiness of the Lord at the head of his army. As their song went heavenward, chaos broke out among the invading coalition and the various parties started decimating each other. When Jehoshaphat's army approached and looked into the valley below, they saw dead bodies scattered everywhere. The alliance had self-destructed; leaving behind so much loot it took Jehoshaphat's army three days to collect it. They renamed that place the Valley of Beracah, which means the Valley of Praise.

Upon their return to Jerusalem the people entered the Lord's temple with more praise and worship. This crushing defeat of Israel's enemies put the fear of God into the other nations, and the kingdom of Judah remained at peace for the rest of Jehoshaphat's reign.

Although his previous alliance with the Northern Kingdom proved to be a fiasco, Jehoshaphat tried another joint venture with Ahab's successor, his son the wicked Ahaziah. They constructed a fleet of trading ships. No sooner were these ships built, however, than a prophet predicted that the enterprise would end in failure; the ships wrecked before they set sail on their first voyage.

After reigning for twenty-five years Jehoshaphat died and was buried with his forefathers in Jerusalem, the city of David. On the whole he had been a good and godly king... but he had failed to remove the high places where God's people continued to worship. His son Jehoram succeeded him to the throne.

1 Kings 22; 2 Kings 1   *Date: 853-852 B.C.*

MEANWHILE, BACK in the Northern Kingdom, no sooner had Ahab died when Elijah's prophecy concerning his family went into effect. His oldest son, Ahaziah, as evil as his father had been, reigned for only two years during which time Moab, which had been a tribute-paying nation since David's time, revolted. Before he could deal with this crisis, however, he was badly injured when he fell through a latticed window in an upper room in his palace. In blatant defiance of the Mosaic Law (Lev. 20:6, 27; Deut. 18:10) he sent messengers all the way down to the Philistine city of Ekron to inquire from the soothsayers associated with the idol Baal-Zebub if he would recover from his injuries. At that time Philistine fortune-tellers were held in high repute when it came to predicting future events (Isa. 2:6). By inquiring of them the Israelite king publicly rejected the God of His own people. Centuries later Jesus Christ would refer to Baal-Zebub (meaning "Lord of the Flies") as the prince of demons.

The angel of the Lord directed Elijah to intercept king Ahaziah's ambassadors. "Return to the palace," he ordered them, "and tell the king: 'Is there no God in Israel that you send men to consult the Philistine idol? The Lord has declared that you will not rise from your bed. You will certainly die." Ahaziah's men, impressed by the authoritative stranger who knew all about their secret mission, abandoned their journey, returned to the palace and relayed their run-in with the mysterious prophet and his galling message of judgement.

"Describe this man," the king demanded.

"He wore cloak of hair and a leather belt."

"That was Elijah the Tishbite!" Ahaziah concluded angrily. He then dispatched a captain with fifty soldiers to arrest the prophet. They found him sitting serenely on a hilltop. "In the name of the king you are to come down, man of God," the captain ordered, using the term "man of God" sneeringly.

"If I am a man of God, may fire from heaven consume you and your fifty men," Elijah replied. The prophet's responsibility was to declare how God had determined to punish those who persecuted and mocked his faithful spokesmen. Judgement was instantaneous: a flash of lightening killed the entire squad.

Ahaziah dispatched a second platoon, the captain of which was as insolent as his predecessor. He and his men received a similar fate: a fireball from heaven consumed them as well. Obstinately Ahaziah sent a third platoon, but their captain fell humbly and respectfully on his knees before Elijah. He pleaded for his life and that of his soldiers—and found mercy. Assured by the Lord that it was safe to go with this man Elijah accompanied the officer to the royal palace where, word for word, he repeated the Lord's dreadful message of doom. No sooner had he discharged his duty than the king died of his wounds. He had no son to succeed him to the throne.

AFTER THE revival at Mount Carmel, "schools of the prophets" emerged in the Northern Kingdom to train young men for the ministry. Much of Elisha's ministry was devoted to them. He would become their "master" (2 Ki. 2:3, 5, 17; 4:1-7; 4:38-41; 6:1, 4-7).

For thousands of years the divine curse of death, "dust you are, and to dust you will return" (Gen. 3:19) had played itself out in history. Only the godly Enoch had been exempted. Now, centuries later, God chose to honor faithful Elijah in similar fashion. In spite of his human failures Elijah had walked in fellowship and with wholehearted faith in the omnipotent, covenant keeping God of Israel. He had spoken boldly on God's behalf and had been an instrument of revival and judgment. Now his ministry was coming to an end.

After the Lord revealed to Elijah that he would be taken from this earth he urged Elisha to part company with him, possibly to spare his faithful companion the grief of witnessing his departure, or possibly to test his loyalty and resolution to follow to the end. Elisha refused to leave his side. The two made their way to Bethel, where a "school" or company of prophets met them. They asked Elisha if he knew his master would be taken from him that day. "I know, but don't speak of it to me," was the sad reply. The scene was repeated three times at three different schools. Each time Elisha resolutely refused to part from Elijah.

The two men made their way to the Jordan River. While a group of the prophets watched from a distance Elijah took off his distinctive cloak, rolled it up and used it to strike the water. Suddenly the river divided, just as it had when Israel crossed into the Promised Land for the first time. The two men crossed from the idolatrous Northern Kingdom into the trans-Jordan wilderness. There Elijah turned to Elisha.

"Is there one last thing I can do for you before I am taken away?" he asked.

"Let me receive a double portion of your spirit," Elisha requested.

"You have asked for something difficult," Elijah responded. "But if you see me when I am taken from you it will be as you asked." Only if he kept his eye on his master to the end would Elisha receive what he so desperately needed to be effective in ministry. They continued to walk and talk together when, suddenly, a chariot of fire pulled by horses of fire appeared between them. Elijah stepped aboard and, in a whirlwind, rode triumphantly to heaven. His old leather cloak fell back to earth.

"My father, my father, the chariot and horsemen of Israel!" Elisha cried out in grief as he watched his master depart. In a burst of deep emotion, he took his own robe and tore it in half. Elijah was gone but he would be remembered as a great man of God. The Old Testament scriptures closes with a reference to him and Moses (Mal. 4:4-5), and centuries later he would appear with Moses and Jesus on the Mount of Transfiguration (Mat. 17:3-4).

After Elijah's departure Elisha picked up his master's robe and returned to the river Jordan. Copying his master he struck the flowing waters with the robe, and the river parted for him too. The young prophets on the far side of the river saw this and recognized that the spirit that had empowered Elijah now rested on his humble servant Elisha.

As Elisha walked to Bethel a gang of young louts began to mock and jeer him. Bethel was where Jeroboam had set up his golden calves. "Go up, baldy! Go up, baldy!" they shouted at him. Word of Elijah's supernatural departure had spread rapidly and been received with ridicule by the people of this apostate city. Reflecting their parents scoffing attitude, the towns' youths wanted nothing to do with God's prophets. They wanted rid of him just as they were now rid of his master.

Insulting God's ambassadors is an insult against God Himself, and liable to severe judgment (Psalm 105:15; Mat. 10:40). When Elisha cursed the young men in the name of the Lord two

bears rushed out of the surrounding woods and mauled 42 of them. Their mangled bodies were a terrible reminder to their parents that their sins would have dire consequences in the lives of their children, just as the Mosaic covenant had stated.

Elisha left Bethel behind and traveled to Mount Carmel, the place where Elijah had had his showdown with Baal. Then he made his way to the Samaria, the nation's capital.

▪ 133 ▪ The Miracle of the Pools of Water

2 Kings 3   *Date: circa 852-841 B.C.*

AFTER THE DEATH of Ahaziah, Joram, another son of Ahab, became king of Israel (he was also called Jehoram at times, the same name as Jehoshaphat's son and successor in Judah). Joram reigned for 12 years. He was an evil man, though not as bad as his father and brother had been. He maintained the shrines at Dan and Bethel but removed the Baal idols. The latter was probably a political move designed to win favor with Jehoshaphat, the god-fearing king of Judah whose favor he was currying.

After the division of the land the Moabites became vassals of Northern Israel, and the Edomites became vassals of Judah. For some 150 years the Moabites had paid a hefty annual tribute to Israel. When Ahab died, however, their king Mesha saw his chance to escape from under Israel's yoke, and revolted. King Joram responded by mobilizing his army and inviting Jehoshaphat, the king of Judah, to join him in this expedition against a common enemy. Jehoshaphat was keen to mend relationships with his northern neighbour.

The two kings decided to attack from the south, and enlisted the help of the king of Edom whose territory they had to cross. They marched down around the south of the Dead Sea, then up the ancient "King's Highway" along its eastern shore. After a week on the road, however, they ran out of water and faced disaster before they even got to the battlefield! "What now?" Joram panicked. "Does the Lord want to hand us over to the Moabites?"

"Is there not a prophet of the Lord here?" Jehoshaphat inquired. To his pleasant surprise he learned that Elisha was with the troops.

"Why should I have anything to do with you? Why don't you go to your father and mother's prophets, and inquire of them? Were it not for the presence of Jehoshaphat, the king of Judah whom I respect, I would have nothing to do with you," Elisha rebuked the king of Israel, and then asked for someone to play the harp. The gentle music calmed his mind and helped him focus. Then he heard the Lord speaking to him, and he relayed the message to the kings. "It will not rain, but the Lord will fill this valley with water so you, your men and your beasts can drink. This is easy for him. He will also enable you to defeat the Moabites!" The next morning, just when the daily sacrifice was being offered in the temple in Jerusalem, water miraculously streamed in from the desert of Edom.

In the early morning light the pools of water looked like pools of blood to the Moabite army in the distance. Thinking that the invaders had turned on each other, they seized the moment and attacked—only to be slaughtered by the Israelites. Their land despoiled, surrounded and facing certain defeat, the frantic Moabite king fled to a nearby fortress, and hoping to pacify his gods sacrificed his first-born son on the city wall in view of the enemy. Sickened at the spectacle of human sacrifice the invaders returned to their own countries. They had met their objectives: Moab's military power was broken and it was again reduced to being a vassal of Israel.

▪ 134 ▪ The Shunamite Woman

2 Kings 4, 8   *Date: circa 852-841 B.C.*

ONE DAY when Elisha was passing through the town of Shunem on the road to Samaria from Mount Carmel a wealthy woman invited him for dinner. He began to stop by there often, and eventually this hospitable family built a guest room on the flat roof of their house where Elisha and his servant Gehazi could spend the night whenever they passed through the area.

One day Elisha told Gehazi to invite the woman up. "You have gone to all this trouble on our behalf," he said. "Is there anything I can do for you in return?" After his role in defeating the Moabites Elisha had ready access to the highest offices of the land and could secure favours from them.

"I am satisfied with my lot in life, here among my own people" the woman replied, and left. Perplexed, Elisha turned to his servant for inspiration. He pointed out that she had no child, and that the chance of her conceiving was very low since her husband was an old man.

"Call the woman back," Elijah said. "Around this time next year you will have a child," he told her when she re-appeared.

"Please, my lord, you are a man of God. Do not lie to your servant," she responded sadly. The following year, however, she gave birth to a son, just as Elisha had promised. No doubt he was more welcome than ever in that happy little household.

Some years went by. One morning the boy was with his father in the harvest fields. Suddenly the lad cried out in pain: "My head, my head!" The father, not suspecting anything serious, told one of his workmen to carry him home to his mother. She held him in her lap as his condition worsened. Around noon he died. Stunned, she carried the little corpse to the room she had prepared for Elisha and laid him on the bed. Then, in an act of faith, she saddled a

donkey and hurried off to Mount Carmel to find the prophet. There, clasping his feet, she blurted out in bitter distress, "My Lord, I did not ask you for a son, and when you promised one I asked you not to raise my hopes." Immediately Elisha understood what had happened. He instructed Gehazi to take his staff, run to the house, and to lay it on the boy's face. He evidently hoped that this act would restore the boy to life.

"I will not leave you," the woman responded with stubborn faith, so Elisha got up and went home with her. On the way they met Gehazi, whose mission had failed. The woman had sensed correctly that prophetic anointing was not something that could be delegated to others. When they reached the house Elisha found the dead child laying on his bed, a direct challenge to his faith. Asking the others to leave the room, he shut the door and prayed to the Lord. Then he got on the bed and stretched himself on the cold little body, mouth-to-mouth, eyes to eyes and hands to hands. His every action replicated those of his great predecessor Elijah, when he had raised the son of the widow of Zarephath. But the boy remained dead. Elisha got up and walked to and fro across the room, possibly at wit's end.

He stretched himself a second time on the dead child and then, suddenly the child beneath him went into a sneezing fit, and opened his eyes. Perhaps the dust from Elijah's robe had tickled his nose. What joy filled Elisha's heart as he told Gehazi to fetch the mother. She fell at his feet in silent gratitude, then took her son and went out.

Many years later, probably after her husband had died, Elisha informed the Shunammite woman that a famine lasting seven years was coming, and advised her to go away for that period of time. Leaving her home and property demanded confidence in the trustworthiness of God's messenger, but the woman did not hesitate. She took her son and left for Philistine where they lived for the next seven years.

Once the famine was over she returned home to Shunem—only to find that someone else had taken possession of her property. Once again she refused to submit to fate and went to king Joram's court to appeal. At that very time the king was questioning Gehazi, Elisha's servant, regarding the "great things" his master had done. Just as the Shunammite woman appeared Gehazi was relating how Elisha had raised her son from the dead. The king confirmed with her that the story was true, and then assigned an official to ensure that she received back all her rightful possessions, together with the income from the land during the whole period of her absence.

Once again God had worked providentially on behalf of the Shunammite woman who loved Him and who had opened her home to the prophet.

• 135 • Food in a Time of Famine

2 Kings 4   *Date: circa 852-841 B.C.*

ONE DAY A destitute widow of one of the prophets came to Elisha and shared her heart-breaking story. Her late husband had run up debts that she was unable to pay, and now the merciless creditor was seeking to enslave her two sons.

"What do you have in your house?" Elijah asked.

"Nothing but a little bit of olive oil," the woman answered hopelessly.

"Go and borrow from your neighbours as many empty pots and jars as you can," Elisha said. "Lock the door behind you. Then you and you sons start pouring oil. As you fill one jar put it aside and fill the others until all are full". The woman promptly followed Elisha's instructions, gathering as many pots as her faith could conceive. The oil kept pouring until the very last jar was full. With a bounce in her step she told Elisha what had happened. "Go sell the oil and pay off your debts," he instructed her. "You and your sons can live on what is left over".

• • •

During the famine he'd mentioned in advance to the Shunamite woman, Elisha went to teach at one of the schools of the prophets in Gilgal. While there he asked his servant to prepare a pot of stew for the men. A well-meaning prophet went to gather some herbs, found a wild vine with innocent-looking gourds, brought some home, and threw them into the pot. As soon as they tasted the mixture, however, the hungry men discovered that the gourds in it were poisonous! "Agh, there is death in the pot," they cried disappointed. Elisha called for some flour and added it to the poisonous brew.

"You can serve it now," he said. "It is ready to eat." Gingerly at first, then with gusto, the men consumed the now wholesome stew.

• • •

Another time a man brought twenty loaves of barley bread to Elisha and his understudies. This was a significant gift in a time of poor harvests. He was from Baal Shalishah, a town so identified with Baal worship that it was reflected in its name. Yet even in that idolatrous town there was someone who sought to obey the Mosaic covenant by giving the first fruits of the land to the Lord in recognition of His goodness, and for the maintenance of the temple priesthood (Ex. 23:19; 34:26; Deut. 26:1-11; Num. 18:13; Ez. 44:30).

"Distribute the food to the people, so they may eat," Elisha said.

"What?" the servant replied incredulously, "Do you expect to feed a hundred men with these few loaves?"

"Go and distribute the food," Elisha repeated unperturbed. "The Lord says that the people will be satisfied and that there will be food left over." They distributed the food, everyone had had their fill and there was some left over for another day. This event foreshadowed the miraculous feeding of even larger crowds in the ministry of the Lord Jesus Christ.

• 136 • Naaman the Leper

2 Kings 5   *Date: circa 852-841 B.C.*

THE KING OF Syria, Ben-Hadad, had a commander-in-chief whom he greatly respected and valued, but who suffered from leprosy. Although Naaman was a great man at the top of his profession he lived under the sentence of death. There was no cure for the repulsive, incurable and infectious disease of leprosy.

On one of their raids the Syrians captured a young Israelite girl who ended up as a servant to Naaman's wife. "If only my lord could visit the prophet in Samaria. He would cure him of his leprosy," the girl said to her mistress one day. Her confidence and earnestness impressed Naaman's wife, who passed the information on to her husband. He, in turn, told the king.

"Go to Samaria," the king told his faithful commander. "I'll write a letter of introduction to the king of Israel for you." The pagan king could only imagine that such an amazing wonderworker would be serving at the royal court, and before long Naaman was on his way to Samaria carrying a small fortune with him as payment for his healing.

When Joram, the king of Israel, read the letter from the king of Syria he tore his clothes in despair. "Does the man think I am God, that I am expected to heal someone with leprosy? The man is just trying to pick a quarrel with me..."

When Elisha heard about the drama taking place at the palace he sent a message to the king. "Why have you torn your clothes? Send the man to me. He will learn that there is a prophet in Israel." Joram dispatched Naaman to Elisha.

When the heavy-laden, pompous entourage pulled up in front of the prophet's house the door opened and a servant appeared briefly. "Elisha says that if you want to get well, go and wash seven times in the Jordan River." Elisha realized that Naaman's hopes lay in him as a prophet, not in Israel's God. His clear, unequivocal injunction to wash in the Jordan was designed to get Naaman to submit humbly to God's demands.

Wash seven times in the Jordan? Climb down from his chariot and reveal the full state of his abject condition before his entire retinue? Abase himself seven times at the command of a man who had treated him as if he were a servant? Enraged the great warrior whipped his chariot around and thundered off. "I thought he would stand before me, call on the name of Jehovah his God, move his hand over the leprous spots, and I would be healed," he fumed. "Anyway, why couldn't I wash in our rivers back in Damascus? They are better than any river in Israel!"

Gingerly, with real concern for their master, some of Naaman's servants approached him. "My father, if the prophet had asked you to do some difficult feat, would you not have done it?" they remonstrated gently. "Why not heed his advice when all he tells you to do is to wash and be clean?" Naaman weighed up his servants' arguments. Everything boiled down to one thing: would he submit or not? He changed direction and headed for the Jordan. There he stripped off his armour and meekly descended into the muddy water. The entire company must have held their breath as their master stuck his head underwater once, twice, three... seven times in total, just as the prophet had commanded. After the seventh time he looked at his body—and his skin had become as clean and wholesome as that of a little child!

When Naaman stepped out of the Jordan River he was a transformed man in both body and soul. His heart welled up with thanksgiving—and so it should! There were many lepers in Israel at that time (Luke 4:27) yet God passed them by to show His grace on an undeserving, idol-worshipping gentile. He headed straight back to Elisha's house. This time the prophet met him in person.

"Now I know that there is no God in all of the earth but in Israel," the general said with humble thanksgiving. Please, accept a gift from your servant."

"As the Lord lives," Elisha responded, "I will not accept anything." And although Naaman tried to persuade him, Elisha resolutely resisted the temptation. The gentile general had to realize that God's grace had no strings attached. He was to return to his own country and testify that silver or gold were of no use when dealing with the God of Israel.

Naaman then affirmed "I will never again offer any sacrifice except to Jehovah God. But may the Lord forgive me this one thing," he continued. "My master the king leans on my arm when he enters the temple of Rimmon to worship his god there, and I have to bow down with him."

"Go in peace", Elisha responded. He perceived that Naaman was uncomfortable with this compromise to his newfound faith, but chose to leave it to the ongoing work of God's Spirit to strengthen the man's faith and testimony.

Watching Naaman return to Syria with all that gold and silver and those beautiful clothes that could have been theirs was, however, too much for Elisha's avaricious servant Gehazi. Concocting a plausible story supposedly from his master, he hurried after Naaman and secured two talents of silver and two sets of clothes for himself. The he returned home and resumed his role as Elisha's solicitous servant.

"Where were you Gehazi?" Elisha asked, giving his servant the opportunity to confess his sin.

"I haven't been anywhere," the man lied glibly.

"My spirit was with you when Naaman got down from his chariot to meet you," Elisha responded. "Because you have compromised God's offer of free grace Naaman's leprosy will cling to you and your descendents forever." Stunned, Gehazi staggered from Elisha's presence. His skin had already turned leprous.

• 137 • A Servant's Eyes are Opened and an Army is Blinded

2 Kings 6   *Date: circa 852-841 B.C.*

ELISHA DEVOTED much of his time and energy into training young men in the schools of the prophets. In spite of Israel's spiritual declension some of those schools flourished. At one such place they needed more accommodation and, together with Elisha, they headed for a copse of trees near the banks of the Jordan River to cut some timber.

While one of the young men was swinging his ax the axe-head suddenly flew off its handle, sailed through the air, landed in the river and sank to the bottom. "Oh, my master," the man cried out crestfallen. "That wasn't my axe. I borrowed it from someone..."

"Where did it fall," Elisha asked. He then cut a stick and threw it where the man pointed. All of a sudden the iron axe-head floated to the surface of the water.

"Go get it," Elisha said.

Elisha would inform King Joram about various ambushes and traps Ben-Hadad the king of Syria laid for him. Furious at seeing his carefully laid plans thwarted time and again the Syrian monarch began to suspect that a spy in his inner circle was passing information to the other side.

"No, my lord, there is no spy," one of his advisors informed him. "The Israelite seer Elisha has the ability to tell the king of Israel whatever you say, even in your bedroom."

"Find out where he is. I want that man captured," Ben-Hadad ordered. After learning that the prophet was living in the city of Dothan the king dispatched a formidable army that encircled the city under the cover of night. Early in the next morning when Elisha's new servant rose to attend to his chores he saw that enemy horses and chariots surrounded the city.

He rushed back to Elisha. "Oh, no, master! What are we going to do!" he panicked.

"Don't be afraid. Those who are on our side are more numerous than those in the enemy army," Elisha responded calmly, aware of the great angelic hosts protecting them. He turned his face heavenwards and prayed, "Lord, open his eyes that he may see..." Suddenly the servant could also see the invisible: the slopes surrounding Dothan were full of celestial horses; he and Elisha were safe in a protective ring of fiery chariots.

When the army descended towards him Elisha prayed again, "Lord, smite these people with blindness". God did just as he asked. Elisha then strolled towards them. "You are looking in the wrong place," he told them. "Follow me and I'll lead you to the man you are looking for." Meekly the men followed Elisha—right into the heart of Samaria, Israel's capital city, and to the man they were ultimately seeking, the king of Israel.

Once inside the city Elisha prayed again: "Lord, open their eyes so they can see." Suddenly they saw that with eyes wide open they had walked right into a trap!

"What shall I do," the king of Israel asked excitedly. "Will I order my men to kill them?"

"No, treat them as prisoners of war. Feed them, then allow them to return home," Elisha instructed. Following Elisha's advice the king magnanimously fed the enemy soldiers and sent them home.

• 138 • The Siege of Samaria

2 Kings 6:7   *Date: circa 845 B.C.*

THE SYRIANS LEFT Israel in peace for a lengthy period of time, but then, one day, their king Ben-Hadad suddenly launched a surprise attack. Although the God of Israel had healed his commander-in-chief and foiled his attempt to capture Elisha, he continued to defy Jehovah, who continued to use him to chastise Israel for its unfaithfulness. This time the entire Syrian army surrounded Samaria to starve it into submission through a protracted siege.

The food situation inside the city became so desperate that even carrion and refuse sold for exhorbitant prices. As King Joram was walking along the city wall a desperate woman cried out for help. "If the Lord won't help you, where am I going to find the help you need," the king responded bitterly. "What is your problem?"

"A woman and I agreed that we would kill my son and eat him and then do the same later to her son. So we cooked my son and ate him, but then she hid her son and refused to give him up." The Lord had warned Israel centuries earlier that if they broke their covenant with Him He would raise up enemies who would besiege and force them to resort to cannibalism (Lev. 26:27-29; Deut. 28:49-53). Israel had broken the covenant—and God's word, as always, did not fail.

When the king heard the woman's horrendous story he rent his clothes in sorrow. However, just like his father Ahab, he refused to recognize that the crisis was divine judgment on his own idolatrous behaviour. Remembering that the prophet Elijah had been instrumental in the catastrophic drought of his father's reign, the embittered, apostate Joram concluded that Elisha must now be responsible for the current crisis. Like mother like son: just as Jezebel had sworn that she would kill Elijah, her son Joram now swore that he would decapitate Elisha. He promptly dispatched a man to carry out the deed.

Aware of the king's plan Elisha instructed his companions to prevent the officer from entering the house. Eventually the king himself showed up. "Listen to the word of the Lord," Elisha faced the king. "At about this time tomorrow there will be plenty of food to go around". The prophet knew that Jehovah God was compassionate. He brought judgment but, for the sake of His own name, He would yet show mercy to idolatrous Israel.

"Even if God were to open floodgates from heaven this cannot happen," one of the king's officers sneered.

"You will witness what I've just said with your own eyes but you will not eat any of it," Elisha responded to the skeptical officer.

Outside the city gate, caught between the enemy army and the city walls, were four lepers, pariahs who were barred from mixing with ordinary people by the Levitical law (Lev. 13:46). "Why should we sit here until we die," they said to each other. "We can't go into the city where, in any case, there is famine. Let's surrender to the Syrians. If they spare us we live, if not we die." And so, at dusk, they set out towards the Syrian encampment—and discovered that there was no-one there! It was completely deserted! Earlier the Lord had made the Syrian soldiers hear the noise of a great army approaching—the clanging of chariots, the snorting of horses— making them think that Joram had hired a coalition of Hittites and Egyptians to come to his rescue. Believing they were about to be attacked by this overwhelming force the panic-stricken Syrians had fled helter-skelter, leaving everything behind.

The lepers entered the first well-provisioned tent and ate and drank their fill, took as much silver, gold and clothing as they could carry, hid it, then returned and helped themselves to more booty. Although they had no sense of divine intervention in the unexpected turn of events, they suddenly realized that they were enriching themselves while the people back in the city were starving. "This is a day of good news! We've got to let the king and the people know that the enemy has retreated," they agreed. "If we wait any longer and they find out that we did not let them know what has happened, we will be punished!" They headed for the city gate and called out to the gatekeeper, "Hey! We went to the Syrian camp, and found it deserted! There is no one there; they left everything behind!"

By now it was the middle of the night, but their report was immediately forwarded to the king. He got up and met with his high officials. "The Syrians know we are starving. This is a trap," he concluded. "They have simply pulled back in order to draw us out of the city so they can attack us with full force."

"Let's send some scouts to get to the bottom of this," one of the king's men advised. "If we lose them, well, we're lost anyway." The king acquiesced and the scouts set out. To their amazement the evidence of an army retreating in utter disarray lay strewn along the road all the way to the Jordan River. They reported their findings to the king, and when word of the Syrian retreat became public the gates were thrown open and the entire population swarmed through the narrow opening to reach the plentiful food and plunder in the deserted enemy camp. The stampede became so unruly that the king told the skeptical officer to restore order, and he was run down and trampled to death in the melee. The word of the prophet was fulfilled down to its smallest detail.

▪ 139 ▪ Elisha and the Regional Powers

2 Kings 8-9   *Date: circa 841 B.C.*

ELISHA WENT to Damascus, the capital of Syria where Ben-Hadad, the enemy, was still on the throne. By now Ben-Hadad was very sick man. He told Hazael, one of his underlings, to take the prophet a gift and have him consult the Lord as to whether he would recover or not. He had apparently lost confidence in the power of his own idols.

Hazael prepared forty camel-loads of the finest things found in Damascus and went to Elisha. We don't know whether Elisha accepted or rejected the lavish present; he may have passed it on to the schools of the prophets back in Israel. "Tell the king that he will recover, although the Lord has shown me that he will die," Elisha responded enigmatically. Elisha foresaw that the disease itself would not kill the king, yet his death was imminent. He then fixed his gazed so steadfastly on Hazael that the man became uncomfortable. Suddenly, he burst into tears.

"Why are you weeping?" Hazael asked perplexed.

"Because of the terrible harm you will do to Israel," Elisha responded somberly. "You will burn its fortified places, put its young men to the sword, dash its little children to the ground and rip open its pregnant women". In an instant the Lord revealed the future of Israel to the prophet. Although he knew that the nation deserved its fate, which was nothing more than had been promised in the Sinaitic covenant, he was deeply moved by the impending terrible afflictions that his people would undergo.

"Who am I that I should do such things," Hazael countered. He didn't want to be perceived for the brute he was.

"The Lord has shown me that you will be king over Syria," Elisha responded.

Hazael turned on his heel, went back to his master the king and reported that he would get better. The next day, however, he held a thick wet cloth over his enfeebled master's mouth and nose and suffocated him to death. Ben-Hadad had lived a violent life and now met a violent end. Hazael usurped the throne and became the next king of Syria.

...

In the southern kingdom of Judah, Jehoram succeeded his father Jehoshaphat. He married Athaliah, daughter of Ahab, the evil king who ruled over the Northern Kingdom.

Although Jehoram was also an evil man the Lord refrained from destroying Judah because of His covenant promise to preserve a dynasty for David. Nevertheless things did not go smoothly. Edom, which had been under Judah's control since the time of David, rebelled. Jehoram tried to crush the rebellion but failed, barely escaping with his own life. He reigned for eight years and then died at the age of forty. His 22-year-old son Ahaziah succeeded him as king over Judah. Like his father Jehoram and his mother Athaliah, he too was an evil man.

Now that the royal houses of Judah and Israel were related by marriage they sought to patch up their former differences and form an alliance again. Together they went to battle against Hazael, the new king of Syria. Joram, the king of Israel, was wounded and retreated to the city of Jezreel to convalesce. His nephew Ahaziah, the king of Judah, came to visit him. At the same time Elisha summoned a younger prophet. "Take this flask of oil, head straight for Ramoth-Gilead and find Jehu, one of Israel's army commanders. Separate him from his mates and anoint him in private as the next king of Israel. Then head for the door and run," he instructed him. Years earlier the Lord had revealed to the prophet Elijah that Hazael would be king over Syria and Jehu king over Israel and would be the Lord's instrument of vengeance on the evil dynasty of Ahab (1 Kings 19:15-17; 21:21-24).

The young prophet found Jehu sitting with his fellow officers, exactly as Elisha had foretold. "I need to see you alone, captain. I have a personal message for you," he said. Jehu followed his visitor out of the room, and when they were alone the prophet anointed him and commanded him to destroy the whole house of Ahab. Then he opened the door and fled.

When Jehu reappeared his fellow officers pressed him to tell them what that was all about. "The man said, 'This is what the Lord says, I anoint you king over Israel,'" Jehu finally admitted. At this they spread their cloaks before him as a sign of honour. Then they blew the trumpet and shouted, "Jehu is the new king of Israel!"

The freshly anointed Jehu immediately headed for Jezreel, where Joram, the reigning king of Israel was recovering from his battle wounds and where Ahaziah, the king of Judah, was visiting him. As he and his troops came within sight of Jezreel, the lookout on the tower sent word to Joram. "Send out a horseman to find out if they come in peace," the king ordered. When neither this messenger nor the next returned the lookout reported, "their leader is driving like a madman—it must be Jehu, the son of Nimshi!"

"Hitch up my chariot," the king ordered, and he and king Ahaziah rode out together to meet Jehu. The two parties met at the plot of ground which had once belonged to Naboth and which Ahab, Joram's father, had stolen. "Jehu, have you come in peace?" Joram asked.

"How can there be peace when the land abounds in the idolatry and witchcraft which your mother Jezebel introduced?" Jehu responded roughly.

Joram turned his steed and tried to escape shouting, "Ahaziah! Treachery!" Jehu calmly drew his bow, released the arrow and shot the king through the back, piercing his heart. "Throw his body in the field that belonged to Naboth," Jehu orderer. This was exactly what Elijah had prophesied to Ahab: dogs would lick his family's blood in the place where they had murdered Naoth. In the meantime Ahaziah also tried to escape, but was eventually fatally wounded. His body was taken back to Jerusalem for burial in the royal tomb.

As word of these events got back to Jezreel, Jezebel, Ahab's widow and Joram's mother must have realized that she was next. She prepared herself for the inevitable and installed herself at a window near the city gate to await her fate. When Jehu arrived and saw the queen mother he called to her eunuchs: "Throw her out the window!" They threw her down; on impact her blood splattered over the wall. Jehu's cavalry trampled her underfoot.

Later Jehu decided that Jezebel should be given a proper burial. She was, after all, the daughter of a Phoenician king. But it was too late. Hungry dogs had devoured her body, leaving nothing but her skull, feet and hands. Then Jehu remembered Elijah's terrible prophecy concerning her: "thus says the Lord, dogs will devour Jezebel by the wall of Jezreel" (1 Kings 21:23).

· 140 · Jehu Establishes Israel's Fourth Dynasty

2 Kings 10:1-36   *Date: circa. 840 B.C.*

KINGSHIP NORMALLY passed from father to son, with new dynasties forming when the royal line was broken. Within less than 90 years of its establishment, Jehu ushered the Northern Kingdom into its fourth dynasty. The first had consisted of Jeroboam I and his son Nadab, and lasted about 22 years. Baasha and his son Elah formed the second dynasty, which lasted about 24 years, and was followed by Zimri, who only lasted one week. The third dynasty, established by Omri lasted over 40 years. His son Ahab, who reigned for 21 years, was followed by his son Ahaziah (not king Ahaziah of Judea). Now Jehu had killed Joram, Ahab's other son, around the year 840 B.C. There was not a good king among them. They all supported the alternative religion instituted by Jeroboam I, while Ahab's marriage to the Phoenician princess Jezebel had led to the instatement of the worship of the fertility cult of Baal.

Jehu's first acts were the elimination of all possible contenders to the throne and the eradication of Baal worship. He moved with singular ruthlessness on both fronts.

Firstly he orchestrated the decapitation of the 70 remaining members of Ahab's dynasty by the officials in Samaria. Their heads were put in baskets and sent to Jehu's headquarters in Jezreel, where he had them stacked in two piles at the city gate. The next morning he told the crowd that while he was the one who had conspired against king Joram and had killed him; it was their own leaders who had killed the 70 royal princes. He then told them that they had been the Lord's instruments carrying out the prophecy against the house of Ahab as spoken by the prophet Elijah.

Jehu then ordered the execution of anyone else in the whole country who was left alive of the house of Ahab. He also purged the royal court of the late king Joram's officials and close friends and advisors, including the state priest. Once all possible sources of opposition had been crushed he headed for the capital city. En route his entourage intercepted a group of relatives from king Ahaziah of Judah. Jehu had them seized and killed as well. Inasmuch as the two royal families were related, he wanted to ensure that no possible claimant to the throne of Israel was left alive.

After these bloody encounters Jehu's party met a certain Jehonadab, the leader of an ascetic group of conservative patriots called the Recabites. They were nomadic desert bedouins who eschewed wine and trusted the Lord for the needs of daily life (Jer. 35). Jehu invited the man into his chariot so that the leader of the puritanical sect would personally witness his zeal for the Lord.

Upon their arrival in the capital city Samaria, Jehu, pretending to be a devotee of Baal, organized a great feast in the idol's honour, which all its priests were obligated to attend. Once they were all crowded into the Baal temple Jehu's officials distributed brand new robes for them to wear. The ceremony began with Jehu himself overseeing the appropriate sacrifices. Then he and Jehonadab stepped outside the room—whereupon he promptly ordered his soldiers to go in and kill every Baal priest present. Easily identified in the ensuing melee by their new robes, not one escaped. The soldiers then broke into the inner shrine, destroyed the so-called "sacred stone" of Baal and demolished the rest of the temple. To show his contempt for Baal, Jehu had the site converted into a public latrine.

God commended Jehu for his zealousness in removing the house of Ahab and in seeking to exterminate Baal worship from Israel. As a reward God promised him that his dynasty would last for four generations.

Sadly Jehu, who started with such explosive energy, proved to be a disappointment. He did not seek to eradicate the state religion, namely the worship of the golden calves as instituted by Jeroboam I at Dan and Bethel, as a result of which Israel's steady moral decline continued and the nation suffered politically. Bit by bit, it lost its trans-Jordan territories in the ongoing conflict with king Hazael of Syria.

Jehu reigned over the Northern Kingdom for 28 years. Upon his death, his son Jehoahaz succeeded him.

• 141 • Athaliah Tries To Exterminate Judah's Royal family

2 Kings 11:1-16; 2 Chron. 22:10-23:11　　　　　　　　　　*Date: r. 841-835 B.C.*

IN THE SOUTHERN kingdom of Judah the House of David was also nearly exterminated by Athaliah, mother of the recently murdered king Ahaziah and granddaughter of Omri (2 Kings 8:26). She was the malevolent power behind the throne during her late son's reign. She now seized the opportunity to take over the reigns of power herself by having all heirs to the throne killed, i.e., her own grandchildren! However, Ahaziah's sister, princess Jehosheba managed to hide one of the royal princes, a baby called Joash, in a bedchamber. The child was later smuggled from the palace to the temple where she and her husband, the high priest Jehoiada, hid him for the next six years. No one, no matter how evil, would be able to thwart God's plan of salvation through the lineage of the great king David.

When little Joash reached the age of seven, Jehoiada the High Priest secretly secured the allegiance of the military heads, the temple personnel and clan heads of Judah. He confided to them the existence of the prince: "The king's son shall sit on the throne," he declared, "for the Lord promised David that his descendants would reign." He then laid out the details of a plan to seize back the throne: two companies of soldiers would protect the young king while the rest were assigned to critical points in the city, including the temple and the royal palace. When everyone was in place Jehoiada and his sons would bring the young king into the open, crown him, present him with a copy of the Mosaic covenant, and anoint him.

The plan went off without a hitch and, before long, the people of Jerusalem were cheering the new monarch: "Long live the king! Long live the king!" When Athaliah heard the commotion she raced to the temple. On entering the precinct she saw the young boy-king with a crown on his head surrounded by officers, Levites, priests, trumpeters and a jubilant crowd. "Treason, treason!" she shouted, and tore her robes. Jehoiada ordered the army commander to seize her, remove her from the temple grounds, and execute her along with anyone who followed her. The reign of the only woman who ever ruled Israel had come to its bloody end.

The young king was taken to the palace. Together with Jehoiada, he and the people covenanted together that henceforth they would serve only Jehovah God. The remnants of Baal worship were removed and the covenantal system of worship was re-instituted in the land.

• 142 • King Joash: Began Well, Ended Badly

2 Kings 11-12; 2 Chron. 24　　　　　　　　　　　　*Date: r. 835-795 B.C.*

THE YOUNG KING, under the nurture of Jehoiada the high priest, did what was right in the sight of God. Early in his reign Joash ordered the priests to collect all the money brought as various offerings and use it to repair the temple. After the years of neglect under Athaliah and Ahaziah it had fallen into disrepair.

Years later the priests were still collecting money but work on the temple had not yet started. Finally, when he turned 30, Joash ordered the priests to account for themselves. They refused to give up the money they had collected, feeling it was rightly theirs. Then a chest with a hole in its lid was placed at the temple door and the people invited to contribute towards the renovations of the temple. The response was so enthusiastic that before long enough money had been collected to begin restoring the great edifice. Carpenters and masons were hired and the necessary building materials purchased. Work progressed rapidly, and when all was done there was enough money left to purchase the gold and silver dishes and other articles needed for use in the service of the Lord.

Some time after the temple renovations Jehoiada the high priest died at a ripe old age of 130 years. He was buried with full honours in the royal mausoleum because of his contribution to the preservation of the royal family and the good work he had done for the city of David.

After Jehoiada's death king Josiah recruited new advisers, a group of fawning toadies who led him astray. The religious reforms he had launched under Jehoiada's tutelage were abandoned and the idols were dusted off. As a result God's anger flared up against Judah. He sent various prophets to warn the king and his people about the catastrophic course they were taking, but they would not listen.

One day the Spirit of the Lord came on Zechariah, the son of the late high priest Jehoiada. He stood before the people and boldly declared, "Because you have forsaken the Lord, He has also forsaken you." On the king's orders the son of the man to whom he owed his life was stoned to death in the temple courtyard. "May the Lord see what you have done and call you to account," Zechariah cried as he lay dying.

The Lord's judgement was not long in coming. Hazael of Syria marched against Judah with a puny force, yet was able to rout Judah's numerically superior army and severely wound the king in the process. Joash had to buy the Syrians off by stripping the temple of the very golden objects he himself had once dedicated to the service of the Lord.

Joash had been severely wounded and, while he was recovering in his bed, some of his officials killed him. They wanted to avenge his wanton murder of Zechariah. The king was buried in Jerusalem but not in the royal mausoleum. He had reigned over the Southern Kingdom for 40 years, and was succeeded by his son Amaziah.

· 143 · Jehoahaz, Jehoash, and Jeroboam II of Israel

2 Kings 13, 14   *Date: 814-753 B.C.*

JUST OVER HALFWAY through Joash's reign over Judah, Jehu's son Jehoahaz ascended the throne of the Northern Kingdom. He was an evil man who maintained the state religion as instituted by Jeroboam I. God judged his ongoing rejection of the Sinaitic covenant by letting

Hazael, the king of Syria win one battle after another against Israel. Israel's army was reduced to a shadow of what it had been in the days of King Ahab. Under these pitiable circumstances Jehoahaz finally turned to Jehovah God for help. Then God, according to His covenant faithfulness, changed the international dynamic and Israel was not plagued by Syrian incursions during the closing years of Jehoahaz's 17-year reign.

Jehoahaz's son Jehoash (also known as Joash), succeeded his father to Israel's throne. He again did evil in the sight of the Lord by not eliminating Jeroboam I's system of worship. Though not a god fearing man, he recognized the prophet Elisha's long service to the nation and sought to honour him by visiting the elderly prophet when he was on his deathbed. The Syrians had, once again, been getting the upper hand over Israel, but were never quite able to inflict a decisive defeat. The king recognized that Elisha's ministry and intercession had been largely responsible for Israel's relative prosperity.

"Get a bow and some arrows," Elisha instructed the king from his bed. Then, in a gesture of intimacy, Elisha took the kings hands in his own and said, "Open the east window and shoot an arrow from it". Eastward lay the land Israel had lost to Syria (2 Kings 10:33).

The king obeyed. "That was the Lord's arrow of victory over Syria," Elisha said. "You will defeat the Syrians at Aphek. Now take the arrows and strike the ground." The king bent down, struck the earth three times, and then straightened up. "Why did you stop?" Elisha asked angrily. "If you had struck the ground repeatedly you would have utterly destroyed the Syrians. Now you will only defeat them in battle three times."

Not long after the royal visit Elisha died and was buried. Later, at another funeral, the people suddenly saw a band of Moabite raiders heading their way. They tossed the corpse into Elisha's sepulcher and ran for their lives. When the dead man touched the bones of Elisha, however, life surged through him and he rose to his feet. The efficacy of the prophet's service and intercession on behalf of the nation would live on after him.

King Jehoash went to war against Hazael of Syria and, as the prophet Elisha had predicted, defeated him three times in succession. After 16 years on the throne he died and was succeeded by his son Jeroboam II.

With its capital Damascus, Syria lay to the northeast of Israel. To the northeast of Syria was the rising power of Assyria, with its capital in Nineveh. It was beginning to put pressure on Syria as it thrust westwards to gain access to the Mediterranean Sea. The Assyrians managed to capture Damascus sometime around 802. The Syrian King Hazael died or was killed and was succeeded by his son Ben-Hadad III. Because of Assyrian pressure from the north, Syria was in no position to threaten Israel. This enabled Israel to flower for one last period under the lengthy 41-year reign of Jeroboam II. In fact both the Northern and Southern Kingdoms experienced a period of economic and military prosperity at this time, not seen since the days of Solomon. Both kingdoms managed to expand their territory, recovering virtually everything that had been lost to the Syrians and other enemies since the days of the united monarchy.

Jeroboam II was a capable administrator and military leader and under his long, effective reign the Northern Kingdom achieved the summit of its military power and commercial development. He had no interest, however, in the things of Jehovah God, nor did the new leash of economic and political life result in spiritual renewal. Like his father, grandfather, and great-grandfather Jehu, he continued the state religion of the golden calves at Dan and Bethel. There was no recognition that the nation's blessings flowed from the hands of a merciful and generous God. Such spiritual life as there had been in the north degenerated into blatant sin while that of the southern kingdom solidified into empty formalism.

When Jeroboam II died in 752 B.C. he left behind a kingdom which looked strong, wealthy and stable but which was spiritually rotten. The prophets Hosea and Amos warned the nation of the dire consequences of their apostasy, but it was to no avail.

▪ 144 ▪ King Amaziah and King Uzziah of Judah

2 Kings 14-15; 2 Chron. 25-26   *Date: 796-739 B.C.*

THE NORTHERN Kingdom enjoyed a period of unprecedented peace and prosperity in the breathing space created by Assyrian pressure on Israel's arch-enemy Syria. Meanwhile Amaziah ruled over the Southern Kingdom of Judah. He reigned for 29 years and did what was right in the Lord's eyes, though not with the wholehearted zeal of King David. He did not, for instance, remove the high places, the local shrines where people offered sacrifices instead of at the one sanctioned place, the temple in Jerusalem.

Once he had established his authority he had the murderers of his father Joash executed. In accordance with the Law of Moses, however, he did not punish their families. Then he carefully rebuilt Judah's army—though a prophet of the Lord told him to dismiss the 100,000 mercenaries he had hired from the tribe of Ephraim, of the Northern Kingdom. These men, furious that they were not allowed to participate in the planned war against the Edomites (and so profit from the booty), wreaked havoc in Judah on their way home. Amaziah went on to defeat the Edomites, executed a large number of their soldiers and took one of their cities. Then, astoundingly, he had the captured Edomite idols carried to Jerusalem where he bowed down and offered sacrifices before them.

In anger the Lord sent a prophet to challenge the king: "Why are you worshipping gods who could not save their own people from your hand?"

"Did I ask you to be my advisor?" the king said dismissively. "Stop it, or I'll have you killed."

"Because you have done this I know that God has determined to destroy you," the prophet said before turning and leaving.

Amaziah then challenged king Jehoash of the Northern Kingdom to war. He was angry over the conduct of the Israelite mercenaries, and his victory over Edom had gone to his head. "Glory in your victory over Edom but don't mess with me," Jehoash responded. "It will lead to your downfall and that of Judah." But Amaziah would not listen. In the subsequent battle his army was routed. Jehoash headed unhindered for Jerusalem, breached a huge hole in its wall and absconded with many temple and palace treasures. He also took many hostages, including Amaziah himself, who was apparently held captive in the North for a decade (791-782 B.C.).

In the meantime the people of Judah placed his 16-year-old son Uzziah (also known as Azariah) on the throne. Later, the northern king Jeroboam II released Amaziah and father and son reigned together in Judah for many years.

The return of the apostate older king did not sit well with a group of Judean patriots who began conspiring against him. When king Amaziah learned of their plot he fled, but they caught up with him and killed him. His trust in the foreign gods of Edom had failed him.

His son Uzziah now ruled in his own right in Jerusalem. He rebuilt Judah's army into a well-equipped and innovative military machine. Since his northern border with Israel was secure his forces concentrated on the south, successfully defeating the resurgent Philistines and the Arabs, forcing the Ammonites to pay tribute, and rebuilding the port of Elath. He then embarked on an ambitious building program in Jerusalem and elsewhere. Uzziah loved the soil, and gave a great deal of attention to developing Israel's agricultural potential.

Zacheriah the High Priest taught the king to fear the Lord and as long as he did so God granted him success. Although Uzziah sought to walk according to God's covenant, he too continued the policy of "non-interference" with respect to the removal of the high places where people sacrificed ostensibly to Jehovah God but in contravention of the Mosaic Law. Spiritual life in Judah and Israel during those good economic times was shallow. The prophet Joel (770-765 B.C.) and Hosea (775-725 B.C.), sought to address this.

Unfortunately, success seemed to have gone to Uzziah's head just as it had with his father Amaziah. Sometime around the year 750 B.C., after the death of the High Priest, he tried to expand his power further. He attempted to combine in himself the offices of priest and king, something common in the surrounding pagan nations' kings. Azariah the new chief priest along with 80 other priests warned their monarch against this usurping of power. In a fit of anger Uzziah raged against the courageous priests. While he was standing at the altar about to burn incense, God suddenly inflicted the king with leprosy. Driven post-haste from the temple complex he was forced to live in a separate house away from the palace for the rest of his 52-year reign. His son Jotham became his co-ruler and intermediary with the public, though Uzziah probably remained the power behind the throne.

• 145 • Joel: The Day of the Lord

Joel   *Date: circa 780-760 B.C.*

THE PROPHET JOEL prophesied during the "good times" Judah experienced under king Uzziah. He was a far-seeing prophet who saw right through to the end of history. His first message, however, was of impending judgement. To help people grasp the impact of what would happen to the nation he linked its fate to a great horde of locusts that had recently swept through the land. The horrible, destructive infestation of locusts had destroyed every bit of vegetation in their path, left farmers in despair and taken away the people's joy. God had worked in judgement through the laws of nature, and Joel explained that the great army of locusts, which had invaded the land, foreshadowed a much greater catastrophe, a cataclysmic military defeat that would engulf the nation. God would raise up a foreign, unstoppable, disciplined army larger than any they had ever seen before. The earth and people's hearts would tremble at its advance as it swept everything before it. Joel referred to this impending judgement on Judah as the "day of the Lord".

There was nothing new about this aspect of Joel's prophecy, for the Mosaic covenant stated clearly that this was exactly what would happen if Israel broke its terms (Deut. 27-28). The covenant also stipulated that the only way to avoid this terrible fate was through repentance and the restoration of fellowship with Jehovah God. "Repent and turn wholeheartedly back to God and you will be spared the horror of the coming day of the Lord," Joel cried out to the people of Judah. He explained the nature of genuine repentance: "Even now turn to the Lord with all your heart, with fasting, weeping, and mourning; rend your hearts and not your garments. Return to Jehovah your God for He is gracious and merciful, slow to anger, and abounding in steadfast love, and repents of evil. Who knows whether He will not turn and repent, and bless instead!"

The prophet urged the people to prepare for war by turning the technology of peace into instruments of war. "Beat your plowshares into swords and your pruning hooks into spears." The era of warfare would last until the final day of judgement. As Joel looked to that final day he saw it as a day of great decision. Some would face due punishment for their sin but the Lord would continue to be a refuge for His people. Their future would be glorious. "In that day the mountains will drip sweet wine and the hills will flow with milk." The Lord "will restore to you the years which the swarming locusts have eaten... you will have plenty to eat and be satisfied, and praise the name of your God..." The later prophets Isaiah and Micah (Is. 2:4; Micah 3) also foresaw the day when the process of militarization Joel had advocated would be reversed: one day the nations will beat their swords into plowshares and their spears into pruning hooks as they submit to the Messiah's reign.

In Joel's mind the "day of the Lord" was more than one single, coming judgement. It was any event in history in which God would move in judgement. All of these would one day culminate in the "great and terrible day of the Lord"; at the end of history the Messiah would come to judge the nations. Although he clearly saw the imminent invasion of Judah and the final judgement on that "great and terrible day", he also caught a glimpse of something marvelous in between: "It shall come to pass that I will pour out my Spirit on all mankind; your sons and your daughters will prophesy, your old men will dream dreams, and your young men will see visions. Even upon the menservants and maidservants in those days, will I pour out my Spirit." He saw what was for him a mysterious era beyond the confines of the Mosaic covenant when the Spirit of God would be poured out on all kinds of people, Jew and Gentile, and all classes or ranks of people.

Centuries later the apostle Peter would quote the prophet Joel on that dramatic day of Pentecost when the Holy Spirit was poured out on the people of God to usher in a new era. That era would last until the "great and terrible" final Day of Judgment, when Christ will return.

• 146 • Jonah Runs From God

Jonah 1-2   *Date: circa 745 B.C.*

GOD`S MESSAGE through Joel in Judah was similar to that which the prophet Jonah of the Northern Kingdom of Israel was commissioned to preach to the newly assertive Assyrians. Their capital Nineveh, one of the greatest cities of the ancient world, was founded by the mysterious Nimrod at the dawn of civilization (Gen. 10:11). Located on the eastern shore of the Tigris River on the famous trading route between the Levant and India, it became the greatest city of the ancient Middle East under a huge building campaign begun by its king Shalmaneser III (859 – 824 B.C.) which his successors continued.

Years later the pressure that Shalmaneser III's grandson had put on Syria provided welcome relief for Israel. After his death in 782 B.C., however, a coalition of northern mountain tribes invaded Assyria. For several decades—until the redoubtable Tiglath-pileser III seized the throne in 745 B.C.—Assyria was engaged in a war that threatened its very existence. It was during this period that God called Jonah to declare His message of judgement to Nineveh.

Though a prophet, Jonah was also a strong Jewish patriot. He had had the joy of telling his king Jeroboam II early in his reign that he would be a success on the battlefield (2 Kings 14:25). Jonah was well informed about international affairs and realized that it was only a matter of time before Assyria would reassert its power. When that happened, the severely weakened buffer state of Syria would collapse—and Israel would be left facing the Assyrian juggernaut directly. And that, he realized, would spell the end of Israel's revival. More than anything Jonah wanted Assyria to collapse as well. He feared however, that should Assyria repent, his merciful God might just relent! He found his assignment so disagreeable that he headed in the opposite direction, to the port of Joppa. There he found a boat going to Tarshish, a Phoenician mining town on the far side of the Mediterranean Sea, about as far from Nineveh as Jews of that era could conceive. He paid his fare and the boat set sail.

They had not been long at sea when the Lord sent such a violent storm that the boat threatened to break up. While the hardy pagan sailors feared for their lives Jonah, emotionally drained by his willful disobedience, had gone below deck and was fast asleep. Eventually the captain went below and shook him awake. "How can you sleep? Get up and call on your god. Maybe he'll take pity on us so that we will not perish!" Jonah stumbled onto the deck after the captain.

Meanwhile the other sailors said to each other, "Let's cast lots to see who is responsible for this disaster." The lot fell on Jonah. "Who are you? What is your nationality? What have you done to make all this trouble?" the pagan mariners interrogated him.

"I am a Hebrew. I worship Jehovah, the God of heaven who made the land and the sea," Jonah shouted above the din. His words terrified the superstitious men. "What should we do to you that your God would calm the sea for us?" they shouted at him.

"I am indeed the reason for this storm," Jonah replied. "If you throw me overboard the sea will become calm." The men, a decent lot, were hesitant so they renewed their efforts at the oars. However, their gallant attempt was of no avail. The sea grew ever more violent, so finally they gave in. "O Jehovah Lord," they cried to Jonah's God. "Don't hold us responsible for killing an innocent man!" Then they took hold of the prophet and threw him overboard. Instantly the tumultuous sea grew calm. Thinking their action had appeased Jonah's angry God, an awesome fear gripped the mariners' hearts, and they made sacrifices and vows to Jehovah.

As the tossing waves dragged Jonah downwards he too cried to the Lord. Just as he felt his life ebbing away the Lord directed a great fish to swallow him whole. When he regained consciousness Jonah realized that he was not in "sheol", the land of the dead, but inside a great, moving leviathan. With seaweed wrapped around his head and almost suffocating as the great fish dove "to the roots of the mountains" Jonah knew his only hope was mercy from the Lord, and he vowed to "make good" whatever the Lord asked of him. At this the Lord directed the dyspeptic fish to vomit out Jonah somewhere on the coast of Palestine. God still had work for the prophet to do.

· 147 · Jonah preaches to Ninevites

Jonah 3-4   *Date: circa 745 B.C.*

THE LORD SPOKE to Jonah a second time, and in unequivocal terms: "Go to the great city of Nineveh and proclaim to it my message!" Jonah had learned the hard way that there was no escaping the presence of the sovereign Lord so, dutifully, if unhappily, he set off for Nineveh. The sheer size of the bustling pagan, militaristic capital of Assyria must have exacerbated his fears. Nevertheless, upon arrival he began declaring his message of judgement: "Forty more days and Nineveh will be destroyed! Forty more days and Nineveh will be destroyed!"

Other prophets had spoken similar messages of doom without getting much of a hearing but, in Jonah's case, something remarkable happened: his message spread like wildfire! The people of Nineveh believed him! They even declared a fast and put on sackcloth as evidence of their sincerity. When news of the Hebrew prophet's message reached the king he too put on sackcloth, sat in the dust and issued a decree stating that every man, woman and animal was to refrain from eating and drinking. He urged everyone to turn from his or her evil ways, and pleaded with Jehovah God to have compassion and relent from the coming judgement.

There must have been something about the prophetic urgency with which Jonah spoke, as well as his demeanor and looks (the fish's gastric fluids must have done terrible things to his body) which caused people to take him seriously. Furthermore, his message of imminent destruction was plausible because at that time Assyria was dealing with a major invasion by a coalition of mountain tribes from the north, which at one point, came within 100 kilometers of Nineveh. The destruction of Nineveh was a real possibility.

When God saw the people's repentant response, He relented of His fierce anger and spared the city. The greatest city of the world at that time had been humbled and lay repentant before Jehovah, the God of Israel. Jonah should have been delighted. Instead he was angry and vented to God. "I knew this would happen when I was still back at home! That's why I tried to run away! I knew you are a gracious and compassionate God who is slow to anger and who abounds in love!" He knew from both the Mosaic covenant and from Israel's history that divine punishment could be averted by sincere contrition. He knew that even if the Assyrians did not fully grasp all the right doctrines concerning God, approaching Him with heartfelt sorrow and repentance would draw out His mercy and grace. "Take away my life. I prefer to be dead than live with this," Jonah told God. After all, on the basis of the Mosaic Law he would be perceived as a false prophet! (Deut. 18:21-22) His words had not come true! How could he go home and face his fellow Jews?

"Do you have any right to be angry?" God asked him. Jonah didn't even bother to respond. He went to a hilltop east of the city, made himself a little shelter, sat down and waited to see what would happen. He must have hoped that Nineveh's repentance was superficial, and that the judgement he had threatened would still take place.

God continued to deal gently with Jonah, and caused a leafy vine to grow up and provide extra shade. This greatly pleased the cantankerous prophet. However, the next morning the Lord caused a worm to attack the vine so that it withered and died. He also sent a scorching wind to blow in from the eastern desert. Jonah nearly fainted from heat stroke in that shimmering heat. "I wish I were dead," he moaned.

Once again the Lord addressed him. "Jonah, what right do you have to be angry about the vine?"

"I'm angry enough to die," Jonah responded. Not only did his work as a prophet seem like a failure, his one bit of physical comfort, a bit of greenery and shade, was gone.

The Lord responded with great pathos. "You are concerned about a plant which you did nothing to deserve, and which came and went in a day. Should I not be concerned about a great city of over a hundred and twenty thousand people who live in ignorance?"

Centuries later the Lord Jesus would refer to this story. "As Jonah was in the belly of the whale for three days and three nights, so the Son of Man will be three days and three nights in the heart of the earth" (Mat. 12:40). The story of Jonah typified how Jesus was destined to die on behalf of a sinful, ignorant world, to descend into hell and to rise again on the third day to accomplish the salvation of people, whoever they were, if they sincerely repented and turned to Him.

Amos   *Date: cira 765-753 B.C.*

AMOS WAS another prophet to emerge in the "good times" of the Northern Kingdom during the second half of the reign of Jeroboam II. Like Jonah, he too declared the impartiality of God, who dealt equitably with one and all in accordance with His covenant promises. Those who fulfilled its conditions would be blessed, no matter who they were, while those who failed to meet its conditions would be judged. To those who regarded themselves as better than others, as privileged in the sight of God—as Israel did during those good times—Amos' message came as a brutal corrective.

Amos first delivered a series of warnings against the countries surrounding Israel: Syria, the Philistines, Tyre, Edom, Ammon and Moab were all going to be destroyed because of their cruelty. Even his home country of Judah did not escape the prophet's denouncement. It would be set ablaze because it had failed to keep the Mosaic Law and followed after false gods. Then Amos started launching one volley after another against the crimes, injustices and debauchery of the Northern Kingdom.

He began by reminding the people of the special relationship Israel once had with Jehovah. He had chosen them from among all the peoples of the earth and delivered them from the bondage of slavery in Egypt. They had walked with God and He had given them prophets to reveal His secrets to them. Now, however, they would be treated no differently than the surrounding nations because they had proved to be just as ungodly as they were. Like them they had erected idols, notably the golden calves at the shrines in Dan and Bethel representing fertility and wellbeing. As a result "an enemy will overrun the land", Israel would be destroyed, and the people exiled.

Amos communicated his message in graphic terms, drawing from his experience as a shepherd: "as a shepherd saves from the lion's mouth only two leg bones or a piece of an ear, so will the Israelites be saved". He reminded the people of all the times God had tried to awaken them, to stop them in their tracks, and to prevent their downward trend. God had sent famine, drought, blight, pestilence, and war—but it was all in vain: the wealthy and powerful continued to exploit the poor and take bribes in their quest for ever larger homes and vineyards. There was no justice in the land.

Amos not only thundered against the numerous social injustices of the era of Jeroboam II, he also called people back to a proper relationship with Jehovah God: "Thus says the Lord to Israel: 'Seek me and live!' He called on them to repent of their ways, to call upon the God of their salvation, the one who loved them, and the one who patiently tried to awaken them spiritually and draw them back into a proper, covenant relationship with Himself. He also addressed the superficially religious people who attended all the rituals and ceremonies while at the same time complaining about the mess in their society, and that they could not wait for God to come and straighten matters out. Amos told them that when "the day of the Lord" came it would be a day of darkness, not of light. God was not on their side. He despised their hypocritical religious activities, their burnt offerings, and the noise of their songs and the melody of their harps.

Others were complacent, enjoying the good things in life while poor people were being exploited and judgement in the courts was being perverted. To them Amos declared, "woe to those who are at ease in Zion. Woe to those who lie on ivory beds or on their couches eating lamb or beef and who sing idle songs to the sound of the harp". The prophet urged them to "let justice roll like waters, and righteousness like an ever flowing stream!"

Neither the people nor Amaziah, the high priest of the false shrine at Bethel, took kindly to Amos' message. Amaziah complained to king Jeroboam II, "Amos is conspiring against you. He is declaring that you will die by the sword, and that Israel will be exiled from the land". He also told Amos to leave Israel, that if he insisted on prophesying he should do so back in his home country of Judah: "Don't ever prophesy at Bethel again, because it is the king's sanctuary and a temple of the kingdom".

Amos responded bluntly, stressing that he was a mere herdsman and farmer, but that the Lord had taken him from his flock and told him to prophesy to the people of Israel. He then predicted a terrible judgement against Amaziah: his wife would be violated, his children would be killed, the nation exiled, and he himself would die in a pagan country.

God had in mind to bring immediate judgement in the form of locusts and fire, but because of Amos' intercession on behalf of Israel He relented. Then the Lord showed him a vision of a plumb line that symbolized the Mosaic covenant, the standard by which the people would be judged. The repressive social injustice of their society went against the standard of holiness to which they were called (Ex. 19:6), and consequently both the shrines at Dan and Bethel and the dynasty of Jeroboam II would be destroyed. Judgement had been delayed, but the end was at hand. The nation would be plucked off like fruit ready for the harvest. God would spare His people no longer. They would cry out in desperation for a word from the Lord but He would be silent then. It would be too late. God would regard the Israelites who had prided themselves as being "God's chosen people" as no different from the pagan nations around them.

Yet in the gloom Amos also saw a glimmer of hope. Israel would be destroyed—but not totally. A tiny remnant would remain. Although most would perish, the purging of the coming judgement would produce a remnant faithful to the Lord. From those few the Lord would restore the house of David. And although the imminent future of the Northern Kingdom was bleak, Amos could also see beyond judgement and exile to a future period of glorious restoration and prosperity for the faithful remnant.

Later the prophets Isaiah, Jeremiah and Micah would pick up this theme of the remnant (Isa. 9:6-7; Jer. 33:15, 17; Mic. 5:2). They too would affirm that God's covenant with David would not be abrogated, even in times of divine judgement. One day David's "greater son", the Lord Jesus, would sit on the throne and not only Israel, but also all the nations of the world would be blessed through him. Centuries later, at the first council of the church, the apostle James reminded the delegates of Amos' prophecy that all the nations, even the gentiles, would bear the name of the Lord (Acts 15:17).

THE PROPHET Hosea, like Amos, also ministered to the Northern Kingdom, which he often referred to as Ephraim, its biggest tribe. Hosea's life became a tragic drama illustrating God's love for His people, the deceitful attractiveness of the world, and the faithlessness of the human heart.

While still a bachelor Hosea started warning the nation of God's impending judgment for breaking the terms of the Mosaic covenant. He told them that God would raise up the scourge of the Assyrians to sweep across the land. But the people paid him no heed. His message of impending judgement did not accord with their experience of the good times they were enjoying under Jeroboam II. As for the king, he tried to form a political alliance with Assyria, the very nation Hosea was decrying.

When no one paid attention to him the Lord told Hosea to marry a girl named Gomer, and told him up front how Gomer would become unfaithful to him, just as Israel had become unfaithful to Jehovah God. In fact, she would become a street prostitute... just like Israel had prostituted itself to various idols. God also told Hosea that they would have three children whom He would name for him. The prophet understood that instead of merely preaching the word of the Lord his sad marriage would be a living parable, an object lesson that reflected God's experience with Israel. So he courted Gomer and she eventually agreed to marry him. Hosea grew to love Gomer and before long they were expecting their first child. When the boy was born the Lord told him to call him Jezreel, which means "cast-off". The boy's off-putting name was a warning: the Lord would cast off Israel if it did not turn from its wicked ways.

Later Gomer gave birth to a baby girl. They were to call her Loruhamah, which means, "Not pitied" because God would cease to pity His people. He would hand them over to the cruel Assyrians if they did not turn from their rebellious ways. After Loruhamah, Gomer gave birth to another baby boy. He was to be called Loammi, which means, "Not my people". God was saying, "I will not be your God, and you will not be My people anymore."

Then Gomer started to fulfil the Lord's somber prediction: she became unfaithful. Hosea arrived home one day to discover that she had left him and their children for another man. That man, however, soon tired of her and passed her on to someone else. Hosea was heartbroken and shamed by his wife's behaviour.

Gomer's situation went from bad to worse until she was completely destitute and sold herself into slavery. When word of his wife's situation got back to Hosea the Lord told him to go and buy her back: "Love her as the Lord loves Israel." So Hosea found her owner, paid him off, and led his wife home. "If you refuse to be intimate with another man I will live with you and take care of you," he promised, once again pledging his love to her.

In the end Gomer became a faithful, caring wife and mother. Although her willful evil desires had taken her to the depths of shame and disgrace, Hosea's love and faithfulness eventually broke through to her.

While all this was taking place Hosea continued with deep emotion and tears to warn the people of Israel that God was about to judge them by means of the Assyrians. He knew that God had experienced the same range of emotions for Israel that he had felt for Gomer. "How can I give you up?" he records God asking with heartbreaking sadness. Those He loved deeply had spurned Him. "Like Adam, they have broken the covenant," the Lord complained through his prophet. He would go so far as to "block her path and wall her in" to keep Israel from chasing after idols the way Gomer chased after her lovers. In spite of the fact that the Lord had nurtured Israel from her earliest days as a nation, even though He had drawn her with cords of kindness, Israel had cruelly spurned Him. Its love and devotion to Him, said the Lord, was like the morning mist that soon disappears.

Hosea also used the metaphor of a half-baked pancake to describe Israel. On the outside their religious rituals looked good, but close inspection showed that her priests rejected the knowledge of God and that the people's hearts were bound to their idols. Instead of hypocritical lip service and sacrifices the Lord wanted mercy and righteousness. Israel had "sown the wind" by looking to Assyria as a possible powerful ally instead of looking towards Him and as a result they would "reap the whirlwind"; Assyria would sweep over them, swallow them up, and take them all away. Their capital city Samaria would be laid waste, their high places destroyed, and they would become wanderers among the nations.

Yet in spite of all the sorrow God experienced in His relationship with Israel He refused to let go of them altogether. He was still wooing them, inviting them to reject the overtures of Assyria: "Return, O Israel, to the Lord your God, for you have stumbled because of your iniquity. Return to the Lord and say to him, 'Assyria will not save us... say, 'our God' no more to your idols".

Hosea's message to Israel contained an amazing prediction about a time when Israel would be without a king and without the sacrificial system in the temple. He then anticipated a day towards the end of history when Israel would, at long last, turn back to God, her true husband, and seek His blessing. Like Gomer, Israel would come back home trembling. God's response to such heart-felt repentance would be wonderful: "I will heal their faithlessness; I will love them freely, for my anger has turned from them... Israel will blossom, will be beautiful and will flourish like a garden!" In fact, one day the names of Hosea and Gomer's children will be reversed. He will say to those named "Not My People", "You Are My People" and they would whole-heartedly respond, "You are My God". Just like Hosea had ransomed his wife, the Lord would ransom Israel from the power of the grave: "Where, O death, are your plagues? Where, O grave is your destruction?" Hosea records the Lord shouting victoriously at this prospect. Centuries later, the apostle Paul would quote this verse as he described the Christian believer's resurrection from the dead (1 Cor. 15:55).

2 Kings 15-17   *Date: circa 752-722 B.C.*

WHEN JEROBOAM II of Israel died in 752 B.C. his son Zechariah inherited a kingdom that had the appearance of strength and stability but was, in fact, rotten to the core. Zechariah was as evil as his father had been and was assassinated by a man named Shallum six months after taking office. This fulfilled the Lord's prophecy to Jehu that his descendants would sit on the throne for 4 generations (2 Kings 10:30), together with Amos' prophecy that the house of Jeroboam II would be killed by the sword (Amos 7:9). Shallum reigned for only one month before he too was assassinated. The first thing his assassin Menahem did upon assuming the throne was to attack the city of Tipshah because it refused to recognize his legitimacy. Menahem's brutality even extended to ripping open the city's pregnant women.

During Menahem's ten-year reign (752-742) the Assyrians reasserted themselves under Tiglath-Pileser III, also known as Pul. Menahem bought them off with the tremendous sum of thousand talents of silver that he extracted from the population (a talent was about 75 pounds). Menahem's son Pekahiah succeeded him but after 2 years was killed in another coup-d'etat by Pekah, one of his chief officers. The palace intrigues in Israel's capital Samaria were apparently between pro-Assyrian and anti-Assyrian factions.

The anti-Assyrian Pekah managed to reign for 20 years, during which time Assyria under Tiglath-Pileser III grew from strength to strength. Pekah's attempt to forge an alliance with Syria failed. Damascus, the Syrian capital, fell to the Assyrians, along with most of the Northern Kingdom of Israel. The Assyrians marched most of the population into exile. Although the capital Samaria was still standing it was clear that the Kingdom's days were numbered.

Hoshea, a leader of Israel's pro-Assyrian faction, assassinated Pekah and succeeded him as king. He placated Tiglath-Pileser III and became his vassal. When the Assyrian despot died in 727 B.C. his son Shalmaneser V succeeded him. Hoshea thought this was an auspicious time to throw off the Assyrian yoke by forging a secret alliance with an apparently resurgent Egypt. Seeking support from the Pharaoh was Hoshea's undoing. When Shalmaneser learned that Hoshea had stopped paying tribute and was scheming against him with the Egyptians he ordered the invasion of the Northern Kingdom. Samaria withstood the siege for just over two years. When it fell in 722 B.C. the surviving remnant was hauled into exile and Hoshea imprisoned in Nineveh. Later the king of Assyria repopulated Samaria with pagan immigrants who went on to practice a syncretistic religion that included elements of Israelite worship. The mixed race became known as the Samaritans.

Israel had reaped the curses of the Mosaic covenant. Despite repeated pleadings through the prophets to repent they had persisted in their rebellion against the Jehovah God. Just as surely as obedience would have resulted in blessing, so sin resulted in judgment. They had rejected God's decrees, and in following the worthless idols and practices of the nations around them they "themselves became worthless". In His anger the righteous God "thrust them from

His presence" and removed them from their homeland into exile in Assyria. The Northern Kingdom of Israel ceased to exist.

▪ 151 ▪ Isaiah's Vision[12]

Isaiah 6   *Date: 740/739 B.C.*

WHILE THE Northern Kingdom went into terminal decline the little kingdom of Judah struggled on. It had prospered economically and militarily under King Uzziah's long 52-year reign. Like the North, however, Judah also forsook its covenant commitments to God and wandered blindly, irrationally towards national calamity.

God, in His mercy, still spoke to His people through prophets. A young man called Isaiah, who would appear before four successive kings of Judah in over sixty years of ministry, emerged on the scene. He would become the most majestic and lyrical of Israel's prophets. In one of the striking analogies for which he became famous Isaiah cried, "The ox knows its owner and the donkey its master's feeding trough, but Israel does not know to whom it belongs". As God's spokesman he offered the nation pardon and forgiveness if it turned from its ways: "Come now, let us reason together... though your sins are as scarlet, they shall be white as snow, though they are red as crimson, they shall become like wool!"

---

[12] The book of Isaiah is one of the grandest pieces of prophetic writing of all time. Not only is this beautiful literature composed in grand, rolling cadences, its revelation of Christ and His coming kingdom is so complete that the book is sometimes called "the Gospel according to Isaiah". When one considers that Isaiah lived some seven centuries prior to Christ all these Messianic prophecies constitute a powerful argument for the book's divine inspiration.

Many contemporary scholars deny that the prophet, whose name it bears, wrote the whole book. If one denies *a priori* the possibility that the prophets received supernatural communication that included predictive prophecy from a sovereign God who is working out His plan of salvation in history, then one is forced to take this position. For those who accept that premise, however, there are good reasons for holding to a single authorship.

Firstly, until the rise of form criticism the only name which had ever been associated with the book is that of Isaiah, the son of Amoz. The Jews of ancient times fully accepted the unity of the book, as is evident from the Qumran Scrolls and book of Ecclesiasticus, which is dated from 2nd century B.C.

Secondly, chapters 40-55 of Isaiah are some of the grandest pages of ancient sacred literature. If, as postulated, a post-exilic "second Isaiah" wrote them, why is there no mention of this towering prophetic giant so late in ancient Israel's history either in the book itself or in any other historical record?

Thirdly, the New Testament quotes numerous times from different sections of the book of Isaiah, and specifically ascribes each quote to Isaiah (Mat. 3:3 > Isa. 40:3; 8:17 > 53:4; 12:17-21 > 42:1-4; 13:14 > 6:9-10; 15:7,8 > 29:13; Mark 1:2 > Isa. 40:3; 7:6,7 > 29:13; Luke 3:4-6 > Isa. 40:3-5; 4:17 > 61:1-2; John 1:23 > Isa. 40:3; 12:38 > 53:1; 12:39-41 > 6:10; Acts 8:28-33 > Isa. 53:7-8; 28:25-27 > 6:9-10; Rom. 9:27-29 > Isa. 29:16; 45:9; Rom. 10:15-21 > Isa. 52:77; 53:1; 65:1, 2.)

Fourthly, the book has common themes and turns of phrase. For instance, both parts of the book include oracles against Babylon (13-14:23; 46-47), both refer in numerous places to both the coming Messiah, and the term "the Holy One of Israel" occurs twelve times in chapters 1-39 and thirteen times in chapters 40-66—yet only five times elsewhere in the rest of the Old Testament.

In the year 739 B.C. the long-reigning King Uzziah died. During that period of political uncertainty the young Isaiah had a vision of God sitting in purity, holiness and power on His throne. The experience was life transforming: "I saw the Lord sitting upon His throne, high and lifted up. The train of his robe filled the temple. Above Him stood seraphim, glorious types of angels, with six wings. With two they covered their faces, with two they covered their feet, and with two they flew. They called to each other saying, 'Holy, holy, holy is the Lord Almighty! The whole earth is full of His glory!'"

"Woe is me," Isaiah cried as he fell on his face before the sovereign Lord. "I am ruined, for I am unclean and live among an unclean people—yet my eyes have seen the King, the Lord of Hosts!" Then God ordered one of His seraphs to touch the prophet's mouth with a live coal taken from the altar. This symbolized the answer to sinful man's problem: there was a sacrifice that would atone for sin and take man's guilt away. Then Isaiah heard the voice of God saying, "Who will I send? Who will go and speak for us?"

"Here I am! Send me!" the young prophet responded immediately. At this the Lord told Isaiah to go tell the people of Judah that even though they would hear and see, they would be kept from understanding and perceiving. Their hearts would become so calloused and their spiritual sensitivity so dulled that they would not turn to God and receive healing.

"For how long must I preach this message, O Lord?" Isaiah asked. The Lord told him to persist until the cities were deserted and in ruin, its people exiled and forsaken.

As with many of the other prophets, God also gave Isaiah a message of hope. In judgement God would remember mercy. He would save and preserve a remnant of true, faithful believers for Himself: "But just like a shoot that springs from the stump of a tree that is cut down, a holy seed will remain to live again," the Lord promised.

• 152 • Kings Jotham and Ahaz of Judah and the Vision of Immanuel

2 Kings 15-16; 2 Chr. 27- 28; Is. 7-8   *Date: c. 740 B.C.-728 B.C.*

IN THE SOUTHERN Kingdom of Judah, Uzziah's son Jotham became the next king. Like his father, Jotham sought to do what was right in the eyes of the Lord, though he too compromised with respect to removing the popular local shrines where people persisted in their non-sanctioned forms of worship. Nevertheless the period of national prosperity begun under his father continued during his 16-year reign. He continued his father's building program, fortified the nation and once again defeated the Ammonites.

Jotham's successor Ahaz was a wicked man. He was twenty years old when he ascended to the throne in 743 B.C. and reigned in Jerusalem for 16 years. Ahaz not only compromised regarding Jehovah-worship at local shrines, but also actively participated in the idolatrous practices of the surrounding nations. He made idols for the worship of the pagan Baal deities and even sacrificed his children in the fire. The names of the places where these horrific practices took place, the Hinnom and Kidron valleys, would become bywords of wickedness and a symbol for the day of judgment (2 Kings 23:10; Is. 30:31; Jer. 7: 30-34).

Ahaz reigned in Judah during the final decline of the Northern Kingdom. Pekah the king of Israel, and Rezin, the king of Syria, had joined forces and marched against Jerusalem in an attempt to remove Ahaz, install a puppet king and force Judah to join their coalition against Assyria. The Syro-Israelite alliance ravaged the northern part of Judah, killing or capturing thousands of people. The Edomites moved into Elath, Judah's seaport on the Red Sea and the Philistines captured various cities in the south. Surrounded by hostile enemies, the situation was so dire that "the hearts of Ahaz and his people were shaken as the trees of the forest are shaken by the wind".

At this critical moment the Lord confronted the king through the prophet Isaiah. Ahaz was to stand firm and not lose heart because of those "two smouldering stubs of firewood" the kings of Syria and Israel. Their plotting to tear Judah apart would not happen. Soon the Northern Kingdom of Israel would be "too shattered to be a people". God then invited Ahaz to ask for a sign of his choosing to strengthen his faith. However, the young king was determined to do things his own way; he wanted to cut a deal directly with the Assyrian monarch Tiglath-Pileser. In a hypocritical show of piety he brushed off the prophet, telling him he would not put the Lord to the test.

"You've tested men's patience; will you also test the patience of God?" Isaiah responded heatedly. "The Lord will give you a sign: the virgin will be with child and give birth to a son, whom she will call Immanuel. Before he is old enough to choose right from wrong the land of the two kings you dread, Israel and Syria, will be laid waste. As for your kingdom and your household: the Lord will call the Assyrians, upon whom you have placed your hope, to shame you, and ravage the land."

In its immediate context this prophecy referred to a virgin in the royal household who would soon marry and give birth to a son who would be named Immanuel. This is exactly what happened. Before the child was weaned the Assyrians attacked and despoiled both Israel and Syria. Centuries later, however, the gospel writer Matthew recognized that when detached from its immediate historical context Isaiah's words had a fuller meaning. The prophecy of a virgin giving birth to a boy who would be named Immanuel (which means "God with us") would be fulfilled in the most literal sense in the virgin birth of Jesus Christ.

Isaiah himself later elaborated on the nature of this true messianic child in the most exalted terms: "The people walking in darkness have seen a great light, a light has dawned on the people living in the shadow of death. For to us a child is born, a son is given, and the government will be on shoulders. He will be called Wonderful Counselor, Mighty God, Everlasting Father, Prince of Peace. The increase of his government and peace will be without end. He will reign on David's throne and establish His kingdom with righteousness and justice forever!"

King Ahaz rejoiced in the news of the impending downfall of both Israel and Syria. The Lord, however, also communicated through Isaiah that the Assyrian army would one day ravage Judah as well. The single comfort would be that the devastation would only "reach up to the neck". Judah's capital, Jerusalem, would be spared.

The Assyrian ruler Tiglath-Pileser III summoned his new vassals to Damascus to pay tribute to him. While there Ahaz was very impressed with a pagan altar he saw and sent instructions back to Jerusalem to make a copy of it. Since the Assyrian gods had enabled that nation to be victorious, he reasoned, they must be superior to Jehovah, the God of Israel. When he got back to Jerusalem he systematically dismantled all the furnishings in the temple associated with the worship of Jehovah. When he died in 728 B.C. he was nothing but a fawning Assyrian toady, one of the weakest and most reprobate of Judah's 20 monarchs. The people refused to bury him in the royal tomb of the kings.

• 153 • King Hezekiah of Judah

2 Kings 18:1-12; 2 Chr. 29-31   *Date: r. 726-697 B.C.*

TWENTY-FIVE YEAR old Hezekiah succeeded his father Ahaz. Unlike his father, however, Hezekiah immediately began a life-long battle to return the nation back to its covenant commitments as spelled out in the Torah. His first official act consisted of assembling the priests and Levites and calling on them to consecrate themselves and clean and re-dedicate the temple to the service of Jehovah God. "Our fathers were unfaithful to the Lord. They did evil in His eyes and forsook his ways. That is why the Lord's anger has fallen on us so that we have become an object of horror and scorn," the king said. "I want to renew the covenant," he continued, "so that the Lord's wrath will turn away from us."

Encouraged, the priests and the Levites started the big clean-up with diligence. All the accoutrements that had been used in idol worship and all other rubbish were thrown into the Kidron Valley outside Jerusalem, where his father Ahaz had built altars to Baal. It now became a garbage dump. Once the purification was complete Hezekiah, the city's leading officials and the people of Jerusalem went to the temple where the priests offered sacrifices to atone for the sins of Israel. While the priests were busy with the sacrifices a choir of Levites and a band of trumpeters and other musicians sang the psalms of David and Asaph in praise to God. All those assembled knelt in worship before Jehovah God.

After the official sacrifices had been made Hezekiah invited the people to offer their own sacrifices and thank offerings. The response was so great that the Levites had to help with skinning all the animals. Six hundred bulls and three thousands sheep and goats were sacrificed, and there was great rejoicing at this rapid and exuberant re-establishment of temple worship. Not long afterwards Hezekiah sent emissaries to invite all the people to celebrate Passover in Jerusalem. He even invited those who had not yet been sent into exile from the Northern Kingdom. Although most of the latter mocked Hezekiah's emissaries, a contingent from the tribes of Asher, Manasseh and Zebulun did show up and were warmly welcomed.

250

The great assembly first celebrated the Feast of Unleavened Bread in remembrance of their hasty departure from Egypt and the need to keep themselves pure from the leavening effects of sin. Then they slaughtered the Passover lamb in memory of Israel's deliverance from the Angel of Death in Egypt and God's claim over them by virtue of His being their redeemer (Ex. 12:27; 13:15).

The people's enthusiasm was infectious at this first celebration of the Passover in a long, long time. There was such great rejoicing that they decided to extend the feast for a second week, with the king providing thousands of bulls, sheep and goats to feed the people. This was the first time the Passover had been celebrated jointly by people from the north and the south since the days of King Solomon.

After the feast the northern contingent, full of newfound zeal for Jehovah, destroyed whatever high places, Asherah poles and other idols it found on its way home. Because Hezekiah wholeheartedly followed the Lord by submitting to the Mosaic Law the Lord blessed him in all he did, so that he prospered greatly.

• 154 • Sennacherib of Assyria Invades Judah

2 Kings 18-19; 2 Chron. 32; Isaiah 30, 31; 36-37   *Date: 701 B.C.*

AN ASSYRIAN INVASION had been looming for years. Hezekiah's father Ahaz had turned himself into an Assyrian vassal in 734 B.C. In 722 B.C. the Assyrians had invaded the Northern Kingdom and ruthlessly exiled the bulk of its population, and by 711 B.C. they had crushed a Philistine revolt that had been supported by Egypt.

The prophet Isaiah had warned Hezekiah against forming a coalition with Egypt as Philistia had done. Egypt, the prophet stated in no uncertain terms, would lose the conflict against Assyria. Thus warned, Hezekiah did not try to resist Assyrian hegemony. However, when the Assyrian king Sargon II died and his son Sennacherib took his place in 705 B.C. Hezekiah changed his mind.

Once again Isaiah tried to warn Hezekiah against forging an alliance with the Egyptians. "Woe to the obstinate nation, to those who carry out plans which are not mine, says the Lord, who form an alliance, but not with my Spirit, who look for help from Egypt and not from me. Your alliance with Egypt will bring nothing but shame and disgrace... Woe to those who go down to Egypt for help, who trust in horses and multitudes of chariots but do not look to the Holy One of Israel for help... The Egyptians are men, not God; their horses are flesh, not spirit. When God stretches out his arm they will stumble, fall and perish".

Nevertheless Hezekiah stubbornly persisted in his plan. First he defeated the Philistines, who were loath to join another anti-Assyrian coalition. He then prepared Jerusalem for the inevitable Assyrian siege by blocking all water supplies located outside the city walls and building a tunnel from inside the city to supply it with water. He re-enforced the city's inner walls, building an outer wall with defensive towers, and storing large amounts of weaponry. He did what he could to prepare his capital for the coming showdown.

The prophet Isaiah pleaded, "In repentance and rest are your salvation, calmness and trust will be your strength... The Lord longs to be gracious to you and to have pity on you. How happy are all who wait for him!" But the prophet's words fell on deaf ears.

The Assyrians were not long in responding to Hezekiah's rebellion. In 701 B.C. they swept through Judah, taking all of its cities with the exception of Jerusalem. In his annals Sennacherib noted that he "shut the king (of Judah) like a caged bird inside Jerusalem." Hezekiah tried to buy him off by stripping the treasury, the royal palace and the temple of all its gold and silver. Sennacherib took the gold but was not appeased. "Your country is desolate, your cities are burned with fire," Isaiah lamented. "Strangers have stripped your land, they have laid it to waste. The Daughter of Zion (i.e. Jerusalem) is left like a workers' hut abandoned in a harvested field of melons. If the Lord Almighty had not left a remnant, we would have been wiped out like Sodom and Gomorrah."

The prophet then began to plead with the people. "Stop doing wrong, do what is right! Seek justice, defend the cause of the oppressed, fatherless and widows" he cried. It was not yet too late! "Come, let us reason together, says the Lord. Though your sins are as crimson they will be white as snow..."

Sennacherib sent a delegation to Jerusalem to try and browbeat the city into submission. The Assyrian field commander shouted so loudly that the people on the walls of Jerusalem could hear what he was saying. "Your confidence in the ability of your God to save you from the might of the Assyria army is utterly misplaced. Your so-called strategies and military prowess are nothing but empty words! And don't expect your God to help you! No god has succeeded in saving the peoples of the nations we have conquered! Or are you trusting in that broken reed, Egypt, which, when you lean on it, will pierce your hand? I have come to attack and destroy this land because your God Jehovah told me to do so!" He then raised his voice even more and faced the people on the wall. "Listen to what the king of Assyria has to say! Make your peace with me and I will be easy on you. I will take you to a good land where you will be well treated! Don't let Hezekiah talk you into trusting Jehovah God! No country's god has been able to save his land from me—and neither can yours!"

When Hezekiah's delegation reported back to him, he and his officials and the leading priests tore their clothes, put on sackcloth and went to the temple. Hezekiah also sent someone to the prophet Isaiah. "Tell Isaiah that this is a day of distress, rebuke and disgrace. May Jehovah your God rebuke the Assyrian commander for ridiculing Him. Pray that the Lord will let a remnant of the people survive." He had finally come to realize that only God's intervening grace could save them from calamity.

"Tell the king not to be afraid of these blaspheming Assyrians. They will return to their own country where their king will be killed," Isaiah assured the king.

Sennacherib suddenly received a report saying that the king of Cush and his army were marching out to fight him. A sense of urgency gripped the Assyrians. Even though they were numerically superior they did not want to be caught between this advancing army on one side and the fortress of Jerusalem on the other. Sennacherib wrote a brief, threatening note and had it delivered to Hezekiah: "Don't be deceived by the God you depend on," it said. "You have heard how we have completely destroyed all other countries that resisted us!"

King Hezekiah received the note, went to the temple, laid it before the Lord, and prayed. "O Lord of Hosts, God of Israel, the one who sits enthroned between the cherubim. Only you are God over all the nations of the earth. Now, Lord, listen to the way Sennacherib insults You! True, the Assyrians have laid waste all the other nations and burned their gods in the fire. But those gods were nothing but wood and stone made by human hands! Now, Jehovah God, deliver us so that all these nations will know that You alone are Lord and God!"

Then the prophet Isaiah sent Hezekiah a message from the Lord. Sennacherib, the king of Assyria who had ridiculed and blasphemed "the Holy One of Israel" would return home by the same way he came. He would not enter the city, nor even fire a single arrow against it. "I the Lord will defend and save it for my own sake and for the sake of my servant David."

That night the angel of the Lord swept through the Assyrian camp and killed 185,000 soldiers. The next morning Sennacherib broke camp and retreated in disgrace to his capital city Nineveh while Jerusalem stood firm on Mount Zion.

One day when Sennacherib was worshipping in the temple of his idol, his sons assassinated him. His youngest son, Esarhaddon, succeeded him as king of Assyria.

Isaiah's predictions to both Ahaz and Hezekiah that Mount Zion, a synonym for Jerusalem, would not fall into enemy hands led to a "Mount Zion theology" among Judah's nationalists. Surely, they insisted, Jehovah would *never* let Jerusalem fall into enemy hands. It was, after all, the center for the worship of the one true God.

· 155 · Hezekiah's Illness

2 Kings 20; 2 Chron. 32; Isa. 38-39

YEARS LATER KING Hezekiah fell ill. Isaiah told the king to put his household in order for the Lord had revealed to him that his sickness would end in death. This bitter news hit Hezekiah hard. He turned towards the wall and wept disconsolately. "Remember Lord my faithful, wholehearted devotion and obedience," he pleaded. "Oh Lord, must I die while in the prime of life? My life is like a weaver's cloth torn from the loom!" There was so much unfinished business that Hezekiah still wanted to do. He moaned to the Lord "like a mourning dove" but grew weaker and weaker.

However, the Lord responded favorably to Hezekiah's prayer. He told Isaiah to tell the king that He would add fifteen years to his life, and to assure him that Jerusalem would not fall into the hands of the Assyrians. "How will I know this to be true?" Hezekiah asked puzzled. As a sign that the Lord would do what He had promised Isaiah told the king to look out of the window at the palace staircase built by his father Ahaz. The Lord then caused the shadow cast by the sun to creep backwards ten steps when it should be moving forwards. Hezekiah was convinced. Once healed he exulted, "The Lord has spoken to me, and I will walk humbly all my years. The Lord restored me to health and forgave my sins! Surely every living thing praises you, as I do today!" The Lord graciously gave Hezekiah an extra 15 years of life.

News spread of Hezekiah's fatal illness and subsequent healing accompanied by the miraculous event in the heavens. It even reached faraway Babylon, a society in which astrology played an important role. Located south of Assyria on the banks of the Tigris River it had once been a great empire but, like every other nation in the Middle East at that time, it was now eclipsed by the Assyrian super-power. Their king Marduk-Baladan (probably Marduk-aplu-idinna of secular history) decided to send a delegation to Jerusalem to learn about the strange event and possibly to see if he could forge an alliance against their common enemy, Assyria.

Sadly, Hezekiah failed this "test" of success. He had become proud of his great wealth and of the honor that came with being an impressive regional power, and showed the Babylonian delegation all the gold, silver, weaponry and other treasures he had amassed.

After the Babylonians had left, Isaiah made his way to the royal palace. "Who were those men and where did they come from?" he asked as if he didn't know.

"They came all the way from Babylon," Hezekiah replied.

"What did you show them?"

"Everything. I showed them all my treasures."

"Hear the word of the Lord Almighty," Isaiah said sternly. "There will come a time when everything in your palace will be hauled off to Babylon. Nothing will be left. Some of your descendants will be taken away and made eunuchs in the palace of the king of Babylon."

"The word of the Lord which you have communicated is good," Hezekiah responded, selfishly pleased that there would be peace and security in his own lifetime.

When Hezekiah finally died he was buried with honor in the tomb of David's descendants. He had reigned in Jerusalem for twenty-five years and, in spite of his failures, had been an outstanding king of Judah who had sought to do what was right in the eyes of the Lord. Manasseh, his son, succeeded him.

• 156 • Isaiah Continues to Prophecy

Isaiah 40-66   *Date: 715-700 B.C.*

ISAIAH CONTINUED to prophesy right down to the reign of Manasseh. His initial vision of God had a lasting impact on him and he repeatedly referred to God as "the Holy One of Israel". The bedrock which underlay his theology was the fact that the exalted, eternal, omnipotent, transcendent, majestic, moral, holy Jehovah, who was sovereign over the affairs of the nations, had a special relationship with Israel by virtue of the covenant He had made with them at Sinai.

From beginning to end Isaiah described Jehovah as being intolerant of sin, particularly of pride, unbelief, injustice and idolatry. Sin was rebellion against God, but if Israel's leaders heeded the prophetic word they would enjoy righteousness and peace. Resistance, however, would lead to greater hardness of heart and affect the whole nation, which God would judge according to the stipulations of the Mosaic covenant. Even so, God would always preserve a remnant of the righteous through which to carry out his covenant promises.

Isaiah affirmed God as the only one who knows the future. He made exceptional supernatural predictions ranging from the destruction of an empire yet to come (13:19-22; 21:9) to the reassembling of the nation and the rebuilding of the city. He predicted time periods and even named a particular foreign monarch centuries before the man was born (10:21-22; 11:12; 44:24-45:13). Later Isaiah's focus shifted to events far remote from the era in which he himself lived. In fact he himself could not fully grasp the nature and interrelation of the series of historical events and personalities he so sublimely prophesied.

After discharging his prophecy about Judah's inevitable downfall and exile, Isaiah sought to provide hope and comfort. God would never totally abandon them: "Be comforted, be comforted my people, says your Lord. Speak comforting words to Jerusalem. Proclaim to her that the days of her hard service are completed, that her sin has been paid for. A voice of one calling in the desert cries out, prepare the way for the Lord, make a straight path in the wilderness." He reminded the people that God's covenant with them would not be broken. One day He would re-gather them like a shepherd gathers his flock and, carry them close to His heart, and lead them gently back across the desert to the city of Zion.

Isaiah also reminded the people that their incomparable, sovereign Jehovah God was more than capable of carrying out his purposes for He is the one who sits enthroned above the circle of the earth, who reduces princes to nothing and who consults no one but Himself. There was no need for Israel to fear that God would ultimately forget them. The time would come when they would again place their hope in Him, and He would renew their strength so that they would soar on eagle's wings, run and not grow weary, walk and not faint.

Over time Isaiah came to realize that the spiritual renewal that he foresaw would be affected by a shadowy figure who was yet to come, someone he referred to as the "servant of the Lord". Then, one day, he grasped the full import of God's intentions. This promised One, this coming Messiah, whom the other prophets had also anticipated, would not, in the first instance, be a great ruler restoring the fortunes of Israel. Instead He would be a man of sorrow and suffering, who would bear in His own body the sins of his people. Like a lamb led to the slaughter, He would willingly die for their transgressions. It would not be power, but suffering love to which the human heart would respond in faith. Isaiah described the Messiah's substitutionary, atoning sacrifice as the answer to mankind's spiritual dilemma some seven centuries before Jesus Christ stepped into history to accomplish exactly that. As God told Isaiah after revealing this marvelous plan of salvation to him, "My thoughts are not your thoughts, nor are My ways your ways. As the heavens are higher than the earth so are My ways higher than your ways and My thoughts than your thoughts" (55:8-9).

Like the rest of the Old Testament prophets Isaiah foresaw the coming of the Messiah, but did not grasp the fact that this Messiah would, in fact, come twice: first as a suffering saviour and then, at the end of history, as a victorious ruler and judge. Thus his uncannily accurate predictions of these two separate events often ran together.

• 157 • Micah: God Builds His Case

Micah — right — *Date: circa 735-725 B.C.*

THE PROPHET Micah was a contemporary of the great Isaiah, and part of his message was the same. In identical terms they anticipated an era when the nations would stream to Jerusalem, from where the Lord would rule the nations, settling any disputes between them: "He will judge among the nations far and near, and they shall forge their swords into plowshares and their spears into pruning hooks. Nation will not take up arms against nation nor will they prepare for war anymore. Instead, every man will sit under his own vine and under his own fig tree, and no one will make them afraid" (Isaiah 2:4; Micah 4:3).

Isaiah ministered to the nation's elite in the capital city Jerusalem while Micah was a countryman ministering in the poor, hilly region. Both prophets addressed the same situation, but to different audiences. God wanted everyone in Judah to hear this message of judgement and hope. Micah often played on his name, which means, "Who is like Jehovah?" He asked, for example, "Who is a God like you, who pardons sin and forgives the iniquity of the remnant of Israel? You do no stay angry forever but rejoice in showing mercy."

Micah began his message by drawing a beautifully poetic picture of the sovereign Jehovah God coming in person from heaven to judge the cities of Samaria and Jerusalem, Israel's two capital cities, for their ungodliness: "The Lord is coming forth from His dwelling place. The mountains melt like wax beneath Him; the valleys are cleft in two because of Israel's transgression. Samaria will become a pile of rubble, her idols shattered, her temple burned..." This, of course, is exactly what happened when the Assyrians swept across the region, destroying everything in their wake. Then, using a series of ominous puns, Micah described the enemy's advance, town by town, towards Jerusalem. As each town fell Judah's collapse and the dissolution of the Davidic monarchy came closer.

Micah then looked across the centuries to the end of history and, in an exalted Messianic vision, saw what Isaiah had also seen: the Messiah coming to establish his kingdom. He foretold exactly where this God-like ruler would be born: "But you, O Bethlehem Ephrathah, who are little among the clans of Judah, from you shall come forth one who will be a ruler in Israel, whose origin is from of old, from eternity". Centuries later the Jewish religious leaders knew to search for the child in the town of Bethlehem (Mat. 2:1-6).

Next Micah painted the picture of a courtroom to eloquently present God's case against his people, a rhetorical device that later prophets would also use. The Lord was the plaintiff lodging a complaint against His people, the prophet was God's lawyer, and Israel's mountains and hills were the jury. God presented His case saying that He had sought the people's wellbeing. The evidence was His deliverance of them from slavery in Egypt, the establishment of His covenant with them and His bringing them into the promised land of Canaan. In spite of this they had turned their backs on Him. The Mosaic covenant demanded that His people show social concern and justice for the poor (Ex. 22:26; 23:4-9), but the nation's affluent civil and spiritual leaders had become utterly corrupt: "the rulers give judgement for a bribe, the priests teach for hire, and prophets divine for money..." Their oppression, bribery, and injustice deserved judgement.

The people responded by asking God what he wanted from them. If he wanted more sacrifices, they'd be happy to oblige: "with what shall I come before the Lord, and bow myself before God on high? Shall I come before Him with burnt offerings, with calves a year old? Will the Lord be pleased with thousands of rams, with ten thousands of rivers of oil?" Micah made it clear that the Lord was not interested in their sacrifices but in heart-felt obedience: "He has showed you, O man, what is good. What does the Lord require of you but to do justice, to love mercy, and to walk humbly with your God". But because the people failed to heed the warning they would be "swept from the land".

Like Isaiah, Micah then looked beyond judgement to the day when God would forgive the surviving remnant of people. God's character does not change. "He does not remain angry for ever because He delights in steadfast love. He will again have compassion on us and will tread our iniquities under foot. He will cast all our sins into the depths of the sea and show His faithfulness to us as in the days of old."

▪ 158 ▪ Nahum: The Fall of Nineveh

Nahum   *Date: 660-655 B.C.*

NΛHUM MINISTERED about 150 years after Jonah's reluctant mission to Nineveh. By then circumstances had changed dramatically. The Assyrians had reasserted themselves, had deported the population of the Northern Kingdom and had overrun Judah. Although they lost 185,000 men in their ill-fated siege of Jerusalem in 701 B.C., they continued their seemingly irresistible expansion, pushing into Egypt and razing its capital city Thebes. It was left to Nahum to announce that Assyria, the era's great super-power, would collapse and that nothing would remain of its proud capital Nineveh.

Nahum's message seemed unbelievable at the time because it was delivered when Assyria was at the apex of its power and Nineveh, on the Tigris River, was the world's largest city. Its double walls boasted 1200 towers and 14 gates; were eight miles in circumference, a hundred feet high and so wide that three chariots could race side by side around them. King Sennacherib's huge palace, where its great hall measured 6000 square feet, was guarded by bronze lions and white marble bulls. The king's armory contained countless chariots and other military equipment. Nineveh was a magnificent, hugely imposing, and apparently impregnable fortress. Assyria had also become a byword for unmatched rapacity and cruelty. Various monuments and records from the reigns of it's kings boast of the hitherto unmatched violence, cruelty and horror which these rulers meted out to the people they subjugated.

While the Assyrian hordes were burning, pillaging, raping and killing, God declared that their days were numbered, and that the city which had existed almost from the beginning of human civilization would be overthrown, never to rise again. "Where is the lions' den?" Nahum mocked in reference to the winged lion, the symbol of the Assyrians. He then reminded Nineveh of what they had done to the Egyptian city of Thebes which, like Nineveh, was located on a great river: "Are you better than Thebes on the Nile, protected with water around her, seemingly impregnable? Yet she too was carried away into captivity, her little ones dashed to death at the heads of the streets, lots cast for her chief men, all her great men bound in chains and carried away".

Both Jonah and Nahum described God as being slow to anger. However in the 150 years between the two prophets God's patience with Nineveh had finally run out. Assyria had become the object of God's wrath. Even though it had served as God's rod of discipline against Israel it would be judged for its relentless cruelty. Its capital Nineveh would come to an end "with an overwhelming flood".

Nahum proclaimed the fall of Nineveh in minute detail. He described soldiers, clad in red, advancing with red shields against the city, how the city tried to prepare itself for the attack, how the enemy chariots raced through the suburbs outside the city walls, and how the defenders retreated to the walls to defend the heart of the city. Part of the Tigris River served as the moat around the place where the palace and city walls merged. Nahum describes how "the river gates were opened and the palace melted away". All of this is exactly what happened. In the spring of 612 B.C., when a coalition of Babylonians and Scythians advanced against the city, heavy rains undermined a section of the wall. When it collapsed it was as if the river opened the gates and caused the palace to melt away, letting the invaders into the city through the breech. The slaughter was so great that the Tigris ran red with blood. Everything was pillaged, just as Nahum predicted: "Nineveh is like a pool, and its water is draining away... She is pillaged, plundered, stripped." Less than 90 years after Sennacherib's invasion of Judah, Nineveh was wiped off the map, lost to history under the desert's shifting sands. It wasn't until 1820 that the English archeologist Austen Henry Layard discovered its buried ruins in the desert of northern Iraq. Just like the later prophet Zephaniah had predicted, it had become a "lair for wild beasts" (Zeph. 3:3).

The message of Nahum's great, divinely inspired prophecy is that God controls the destinies of the nations. Ultimately, He is in charge of history. He raises up kings and kingdoms, allows them to exist, then lets them collapse. No amount of wealth or military might could save a nation from His judgement once His patience with them runs out.

Nahum's prophecy against Assyria was primarily meant for Israel, where it was received as a message of comfort and hope: Nahum's name means "consolation". Using the words of the prophet Isaiah (Is. 52:7), Nahum described the great joy and relief with which Israel would receive the good news of Nineveh's destruction: "Behold on the mountains the feet of him who delivers this good news, who proclaims that henceforth there will be peace!" The apostle Paul later used this verse to describe the immense joy people would experience when they hear and received the good news of God's grace in Jesus Christ (Rom. 10:15).

▪ 159 ▪ The Evil Kings Manasseh and Amon

2 Kings 21; 2 Chron. 33   *Dates: 698-640 B.C.*

MANASSEH WAS ONLY twelve years old when his father Hezekiah died, but he reigned for fifty-five years—longer than any other king in Judah's history. Right from the beginning young Manasseh spurned the ways of Jehovah God. He became an out-and-out pagan even thought he knew about the miracles God had accomplished on Israel's behalf during his godly father's reign. He restored the worship of Baal and Asherah and rebuilt the idols and pagan altars in the Lord's temple. Inside the temple courts he erected altars to the "starry hosts": it seems that he had embraced the religion of the Assyrio-Babylonians, which was deeply rooted in astrology. He sacrificed his sons to idols and practised sorcery and witchcraft and shed the blood of many innocent people. This repugnant man's influence was so malignant that under his reign the people of Judah and Jerusalem became more evil than the nations Israel had displaced when they first entered the land under Joshua. God sent messengers to warn Manasseh of the consequences of his actions but he paid them no heed; in fact tradition states that he had the prophet Isaiah sawn in two.

In response to these outrages the Lord unleashed the Assyrians against him. They captured Mannaseh and led him by a hook through his nose to Nineveh. In deep distress in his dungeon he finally humbled himself before Jehovah God. The Lord, moved by his prayers, heard his plea and graciously had him released from prison and returned to Jerusalem. Manasseh then tried to initiate a religious reform but, sadly, his personal reformation took place too late in his reign. Although the idols were removed from the temple the people continued to worship at high places outside Jerusalem.

After Mannaseh was buried in his palace garden his evil son, the twenty-two year old Amon succeeded him. Whatever changes for good his father had tried to implement toward the end of his reign were quickly undone. His own officials assassinated Amon after reigning for just two years. The people of the land then lynched the assassins and, in 640 B.C., installed Amon's eight-year-old son Josiah to be the next king of Judah.

▪ 160 ▪ King Josiah Renews the Covenant

2 Kings 22-23; 2 Chron. 34-35   *Date: 640-606 B.C.*

YOUNG JOSIAH proved to be a good king, following the ways of his great forefather David and obeying the Lord God with his whole heart. At the age of 20 he started a vigorous campaign to purge the land of idol worship. In his zeal he had the idols and their altars smashed and crushed to powder. He did away with the idolatrous priests and had their graves burned. He also got rid of mediums and sorcerers as well as those who worshipped the sun, moon and stars. His iconoclastic purge even extended to the regions of the former Northern Kingdom of Israel, including the North's old shrine at Bethel. He personally oversaw its demolition and had the bones of the priests who had served there defiled, thus fulfilling the prophecy of the nameless prophet who had confronted Jeroboam I centuries earlier (1 Kings 13:3).

In the 18th year of his reign (622 B.C.), Judah was sufficiently stable and the temple treasury sufficiently full for Josiah to embark on a new project. He was determined to have the temple restored and sent instructions to that end to Hilkiah the high priest. Soon a lively buzz filled the temple complex as carpenters and masons set about their task. During the clean-up Hilkiah found a scroll containing the book of the Law of Moses that must have been misplaced during the reign of Josiah's apostate father or grandfather. The king was told about it and had it read to him. Josiah was so deeply disturbed by what he heard that he tore his robes in distress and repentance. "The Lord's anger burns against us for our fathers have not obeyed the words in this book," he cried to his attendants and to Hilkiah the priest. "Go and inquire of the Lord on our behalf."

They went to a prophetess called Huldah, who responded, "Tell the king that all the disasters and curses spelled out in the book of the covenant will take place because this people has forsaken the Lord, and provoked Him to anger by worshipping other gods. However," she continued, "also tell the king that because he was responsive to the word of the Lord and humbled himself with tears, that these disasters will not take place during his reign. He will be buried in peace in the royal tomb."

When King Josiah heard this word of prophecy he summoned all the elders of Judah and Jerusalem to the temple. There, in the presence of the priests, Levites, and common people he read aloud the words of the Book that had been found. Afterwards both the king and his people renewed their commitment to adhere to the covenant, which the nation had made with God back at Mount Sinai. Josiah then re-instituted the feasts of Passover and Unleavened Bread. He and his officials provided tens of thousands of sacrificial animals to make it a true national celebration. King Hezekiah had once ordered a Passover feast but the Israelites had not celebrated it on such a grand scale since the days of the prophet Samuel!

This was a time of political turmoil in the surrounding nations. The power of Assyria's hegemony had been broken and the Babylonians had captured Nineveh. The surviving Assyrian remnant fled to the city of Haran on the northern Mesopotamian plateau. Pharaoh Neco of Egypt then mobilized his army to support the enfeebled Assyrians against the Babylonians. In 609 B.C. he marched his army across Judah to get to Carchemish, near Haran in the north of Syria, to fight Nebuchadnezzar, the newly installed expansionist king of Babylonia. Josiah, doubting the motives of the Egyptians, threatened to attack them. Pharaoh Neco tried to dissuade Josiah from doing anything rash. "I have no quarrel with you, king of Judah. I am at war with Babylonia, and am hurrying to meet him. Stop opposing me or God will destroy you." Pharaoh's warning to Josiah was, indeed, in harmony with God's will. God had consistently urged Israel to refrain from involvement in the international politics of the day. He had promised to be their protector in spite of all the intrigues of the great powers swirling around them. But Josiah, who was generally so careful to obey the Lord, failed to follow the simple way of faith. He had his army attack the Egyptians on the plains of Megiddo. Although disguised as an ordinary soldier, an Egyptian archer shot him. His officers drove him to Jerusalem where he died.

All of Judah mourned the death of their nation's godly king. The prophet Jeremiah, who had held Josiah in high regard, (Jer. 22:15-16) composed a special lament in his honour. As the prophetess Huldah had predicted, he was buried in the royal tomb. His early death kept him from witnessing the demise of his nation.

• 161 • Zephaniah Restates His Predecessors' Messages

Zephaniah   *Dates: circa 639-629 B.C.*

THE PROPHET Zephaniah was a great-great-grandson of good king Hezekiah and was probably born during the long reign of the evil Mannaseh. His ministry came after an extended period of prophetic silence in the wake of Mannaseh's elimination of anyone who spoke on Jehovah's behalf. He would have lived through the evil Amon's brief reign and into the reign of the godly Josiah. In fact, his ministry may have been the stimulus that prompted the young, reforming king to zealously embrace the ways of Jehovah God.

Zephaniah's prophecy was a repeat of his predecessors' messages in terms of both content and style. The people of Judah, standing on the cusp of divine judgement, would have one more opportunity to take God's warnings to heart. The prophet began with a sweeping statement about the upcoming destruction, a warning reminiscent of God's warning to Noah prior to the great flood: "I will sweep everything from the face of the earth, both men and animals... The wicked will have only piles of rubble left when I cut man from the face of the earth". He then spoke much about the "day of the Lord", an expression he picked up from his predecessor Joel. Joel had used the phrase to refer to the imminent day of destruction facing Judah, to all God's acts of judgement, and to the series of events with which history will draw to a close, when God will judge the nations and reward the righteous. Zephaniah used the term to describe all occasions when God punishes wickedness, rights wrongs, and vindicates the righteous. He described the day of the Lord as a time when God's simmering anger would boil over: "Be silent before the Sovereign Lord, because the day of the Lord is near," he urged the kingdom of Judah. The day of the Lord would be the day when God would stretch out his hand against the nation to punish its idolatrous priests, its princes, its business community, and its complacent and wealthy citizens.

Like Amos, Zephaniah described this day of wrath and anguish as a day of darkness and gloom. Although divine punishment was now unavoidable, he, again like Amos, urged the humble of the land to seek righteousness and humility, and to be obedient so that they would be sheltered on the day of the Lord's fierce anger.

Zephaniah then uttered a brief series of prophecies against Philistia, Moab, Ammon, and Cush—the various nations that had threatened Judah in the past. His denunciation of these foreign nations reminded the people of Judah that all people must one day render account to Jehovah God. After proclaiming judgement on the nations Zephaniah focused on the city of Jerusalem, denouncing its oppressive rulers, false prophets and law-breaking priests. In poignant language he quoted God as lamenting, "Surely Jerusalem will fear me and accept correction!" But their persistent unrepentance led to their deserved fate: "the whole world will be consumed by the fire of the Lord's jealous anger."

But that was not the end. The prophet's final word was one of restoration after the immediate judgement of Judah by the Babylonians. He foresaw the day when Jerusalem would be glad and free of all fear. The Lord, Israel's King, would again take great delight in his people, would quiet them with his love and would rejoice over them with singing. The Lord's closing encouragements to his people through the prophet were, "I will judge all those who oppressed you. I will rescue the lame and gather those of you who were scattered and bring you home. I will restore your fortunes before your eyes and bestow honor and praise on you in the presence of the people of the earth."

• 162 • Habakkuk Questions God

Habakkuk   *Date: circa 612-587 B.C.*

HABAKKUK MINISTERED about 20 years after Zephaniah, sometime after the fall of Nineveh to the Babylonians in 612 B.C. He would have rejoiced at the demise of the dreaded Assyrians and hoped that the removal of that cruel power would usher in another period of peace and prosperity for the land of Judah.

The other prophets addressed the people with messages of judgement and comfort from the Lord, but Habakkuk addressed God directly. The little book he left behind is a record of the dialogue he had with God about the profound questions and conundrums that perplexed and bewildered him. He had been praying for righteousness to be restored in the land but it seemed that God was silent and his prayers left unanswered. "Lord," he cried in anguish, "how long before you listen to me? How long must I cry 'violence!' before you incline your ear?" He was distressed by the injustice and the spiritual and moral decay into which Judah had again fallen after the death of King Josiah.

"Look at the nations and see what I am doing," the Lord responded. "Be amazed and astounded, because I am in the process of doing something you won't believe if I told you!" If Habakkuk expected God to respond with revival blessing he was to be deeply disappointed. "I am raising up the Babylonians—that feared, ruthless, impetuous, guilty people whose strength is their god, who are a law unto themselves, who are fiercer than wolves and whose horses are swifter than leopards—to sweep across the earth like a desert wind and to devour all before it like vultures," God explained. God had toppled the Assyrian empire but would now raise up another imperialist power, the Babylonians, to serve as His rod of judgement.

That was not the answer Habakkuk had hoped for! "Are you not from everlasting, Oh Lord, my God, my Holy One?" Habakkuk cried out, humbly acknowledging that Jehovah transcends time and is the unchanging sovereign over human activity. God had appointed the Babylonians to judge and discipline the people of God, and while it was not what he had hoped for, he would submit. He, however, was troubled by one aspect of God's revelation: How could Jehovah God, whose eyes are too pure to look on evil and who cannot tolerate sin, utilize a godless and wicked nation to punish his own people? "We may be in a deplorable state," Habakkuk admitted, "but we are nothing compared to those godless Babylonians!"

In his confusion over God's ways Habakkuk reviewed what he knew to be sure about the character of God and then made a decision. "I will station myself on the watchtower and will look to see how God will respond to me". He would leave the problem with God but wait expectantly—and probably nervously as well—for God to respond.

God's answer was not long in coming, and He urged Habakkuk to write it down. "Write the vision plainly on tablets so that a herald can run with it and spread the news. What I am about to reveal to you may seem like it is a long way off but rest assured that it will take place. If it seems slow, wait for it. It will come, inexorably, without delay." God then uttered a principle of faith that would be picked up centuries later by the New Testament writers: "He who is not upright will fall, but the righteous will live by faith". The apostle Paul used it to show that people's standing with God was based on a persevering, responsive life of faith in the person of the Lord Jesus Christ. For Habakkuk it meant that those of God's people, who remained faithful to God irrespective of the circumstances around them, would surely live.

The Lord then uttered a series of taunts, woes and

evils for which the Babylonians would be judged. God was perfectly aware of their evil acts, immoral behavior and astral spiritism and assured the questioning prophet that they would receive their just reward in due time.

Habakkuk had received his answer: the sovereign Lord had everything under control and was working out His plans for all the nations. "The Lord is in His holy temple; let all the earth keep silent before him," was his response. He then prayed one of the great prayers of Scriptures. "Lord, I have heard about you and stand in awe of your works. Repeat them in our day, but in wrath remember mercy." He recognized that God was no different from who He had been in the past, when He had acted in supernatural judgement against Egypt, when He led his people through the sea, and when He granted Joshua's request that the sun and the moon stand still. The prophet was left reeling in awe as he recalled God's past greatness: "I hear, and my body trembles, my lips quiver," he cried. At the same time he affirmed his faith in God's promised vengeance on the Babylonians: "I will wait quietly for the day of trouble to come upon the people who invade us."

Habakkuk not only resigned to God's unalterable will, but also determined not to let circumstances, no matter how unfavorable, shake his faith in God anymore: "Though the fig tree does not blossom, though there is no fruit on the vines, though the olive crop fail and the fields yield no fruit, though the flocks are gone and no herds remain in the stalls, yet I will rejoice in the Lord, I will rejoice in God my Saviour!" he affirmed. Habakkuk had come to accept that the relative difference of good and evil between people was utterly insignificant before the blazing holiness of God. His faith was strengthened, his joy returned and he could once again worship Jehovah God in awe and wonder.

• 163 • Warnings Through the Prophet Jeremiah

Jeremiah 1-27   *Date: 627 – circa 582 B.C.*

THE PROPHET JEREMIAH began his long ministry during the reign of Josiah and continued on through a succession of kings right to the reign of Judah's final king. His early ministry overlapped partly with that of Habakkuk and Zephaniah, and his later years with the early ministries of Ezekiel and Daniel.

Jeremiah's response to God's call to be a prophet was almost visceral. "Ahhhh! Lord, God! Not that!! I don't know how to speak and I'm only a youth," he cried out. The idea of becoming a prophet terrified him for he was a deeply emotional and shy person. Sometimes all he wanted to do was to quit, but the divine fire burning in his heart would not let him: "The word of the Lord has brought me nothing but insults and reproach all day long. But if I say to myself that I'm not going to talk about the Lord or mention His name any more, then His word burns like a fire in my bones! I cannot hold it in, cannot keep from speaking it!"

This sensitive man loved nature, especially birds, to which he referred repeatedly: "There were no people, and every bird has flown away"; "The wicked are like those who snare birds";

"Even the stork in the sky knows her appointed seasons, and the dove, the swift and the thrush observe the time of their migration. But my people do not know the requirements of the Lord"; "My inheritance is like a speckled bird which the other birds of prey surround and attack", etc. Through him, God warned the people of Judah repeatedly of the dire consequences of continuing down the path of sinful rebellion, but they rejected both the message and the prophet himself. Not once in the course of his long ministry did they responding positively to him—and yet no king had the power and authority he exercised. Whatever he said as God's spokesman about the nations took place exactly as he predicted.

Again and again he reminded the people of God's covenant love and longing for them: "I, God, remember the devotion of your youth, how as a bride you loved Me..." "What fault did your fathers find in Me that they strayed so far..."; "My people have exchanged their glorious God for worthless idols...". They knew how the Northern Kingdom had strayed and been wiped out but still paid no heed to the warning: "Faithless Israel is more righteous than unfaithful Judah". Realizing that the covenant curses of Deuteronomy were now unavoidable he urged Judah's kings to accept the inevitable. Disaster in the form of the Babylonians would pour over them like a boiling pot tilting from the north, he said.

He had scathing denunciations for those who claimed that no harm would come to Jerusalem because, as in the days of Isaiah, Jehovah would not allow the city to fall: "Those prophets and priests who say 'peace, peace' when there is no peace dress the wound of the people as though it were not serious! They will fall among the fallen, they will be brought down," he cried.

Judah's kings viewed him as a traitor, and there were repeated attempts on his life, even from his own family! He was pilloried, kept in a dungeon, and thrown into a cistern where he sank into slime reaching up to his neck until rescued by a foreigner. Once while under house arrest he had his scribe Baruch go to the temple and read out loud from a scroll in which he had recorded the Lord's warnings. Some of the king's officials were moved by these words. They told Baruch to go into hiding while they took Jeremiah's scroll to king Jehoiakim. The king had someone read it to him and whenever the man finished reading three of four columns he would cut them off the end of the scroll and throw them contemptuously into a fire pot burning nearby.

Jeremiah also resorted to visual aids to communicate his message. Even his life as a bachelor became an object lesson: God told him he was not to marry or have children because the children born in his lifetime would die by the sword and lie unmourned like refuse in the field until they were devoured by the birds of the air and the beasts of the field. Almost a century earlier God had told the prophet Hosea to marry a woman whom God had predicted would become unfaithful to him. Hosea was told to woo her back as an object lesson of God wooing unfaithful Israel. By Jeremiah's time, however, the time of divine wooing was over and the day of judgement was at hand.

Once he was told to wear a linen belt without ever washing it. When it was really dirty he was told to bury it. Then, sometime later, he was told to dig it up. He did so, but the belt was now useless, rotten through and through. In the same way, God said, he'd carried Israel for many years, but now he was casting the unclean nation off because it was rotten to the core.

In order to communicate that Judah should not rely on Egypt the prophet once buried a rock under a particular spot in the Egyptian capital to indicate the exact place where Nebuchadnezzar would set his throne after he'd defeated that country. Another time, when the surrounding nations of Edom, Moab, Ammon, Tyre and Sidon had all sent envoys to Jerusalem to try and forge a common alliance against Babylon, he walked the city's streets wearing a yoke, trying to convince these nations of the futility of their endeavour. Instead of trying to form an alliance against Babylon it would be much better for them to bow their necks under Babylon's yoke. Only the Edomites followed his advice; they realigned themselves with Babylon and took part in the plunder of Jerusalem (Ps. 137:7; Ez. 35:1-6).

As often happened to the prophets, Jeremiah's gaze could suddenly lift past the immediate future and foresee events that would take place centuries later. While the Babylonian armies were outside the walls of Jerusalem the Lord gave him a wonderful vision of the future restoration of Israel based on the Davidic covenant. Although the old conditional covenant God had made with Israel at Mount Sinai was in shambles, His unconditional covenant promises to Adam, the patriarchs, and King David remained in force, and became the basis for a new hope for the people of Israel. God promised to make a new covenant with them: "This is the covenant I will make with them," the Lord declared through Jeremiah, "I will put my law in their minds and write it on their hearts and they will be my people and I their God. I will make a righteous branch sprout from David's line who will bring justice and righteousness in the land. Judah will be saved and Jerusalem will live in safety. It will be called 'The Lord Our Righteousness'. This will be come about as certain as sun follows night," the Lord stated, "because I have loved Israel with an everlasting love".

Because Jeremiah knew that the temple would be destroyed and the people exiled, he tried to instill in them a sense that the important thing, in God's eyes, was the issue of the heart. They would be able to survive as Jehovah's people in a strange land if their hearts were in right relationship with God. He predicted that God's new covenant with them would not be a collective one like the Sinaitic covenant had been, but a personal one in which individual people would receive "hearts of flesh". Because the new covenant was made on a personal, individual level, judgement would also be personal: "In those day people will no longer say that the children's teeth are set on edge because of the sour grapes their fathers have eaten".

Centuries later the New Testament writers would apply this new covenant promise to the new birth which people experience when they turn to Christ in genuine repentance and obedient faith (Heb. 8:8-13).

2 Kings 23-25; 2 Chronicles 36   *Date: 606-586 B.C.*

THE GODLY KING Josiah was succeeded as king of Judah, by his son, Jehoahaz. This evil man reigned only 3 months. Pharaoh Neco imprisoned him in Syria and then carried him off to Egypt where he died, just as the prophet Jeremiah had predicted.

The Pharaoh then placed Jehoahaz's brother, Jehoiakim, on the throne in Jerusalem. He managed to reign 11 years but he too did evil in the Lord's eyes; he was the one who threw Jeremiah's message into the fire as it was read to him. During his reign king Nebuchadnezzar of Babylon invaded Judah. He took Jehoiakim prisoner together with articles from the temple, which he placed in his own temple in Babylon.

The next king, Jehoiachin, was also evil and only survived 3 months on the throne. Nebuchadnezzar attacked again and laid siege to Jerusalem. He deported the king, the royal family, the whole army, all the skilled workers and prominent people of Judah. Only the very poor were left. More of the temple and palace treasures also made their way to Babylon.

Jehoiachin's uncle, Zekekiah, was next on the throne. During his 11-year reign the desperate situation in Judah only got worse. He was a proud, hard-hearted man who adamantly refused to humble himself when warned by the prophet Jeremiah. The people became increasingly unfaithful, bowed to their neighbour's idols and defiled the temple.

Nebuchadnezzar once again marched against Jerusalem. After a prolonged siege Zedekiah was captured, his sons killed before his eyes and he himself blinded and carried off to Babylon. The magnificent temple which Solomon had built, together with the palace, were burnt and the city itself left in ruins. Almost everyone who had remained was sent into exile.

Jehovah God had sent messages via His prophets again and again because "He had pity on His people and on the place where He dwelt". But they refused repeatedly to listen and scoffed at the warnings. Eventually the Lord's anger was aroused to the point of no return and, in the end, "He thrust them from His presence". The year was 586 B.C. The ancient curses of the Sinaitic covenant had been fulfilled to the letter (Deut. 28:53-55).

Lamentations   *Date: 586 B.C.*

JEREMIAH WAS broken-hearted. Every one of the dreadful words about uprooting, tearing down, destruction and overthrowing, which God had told him when he was first called to be a prophet, had come true. A note in the Septuagint, the Greek translation of the Old Testament, says that he went up a hillside that overlooked the devastated city and its razed temple. There he sobbed his heart out and wrote a remarkable series of beautiful acrostic poems, known today as the Book of Lamentations.

In the first poem Jeremiah described the state of the city and its survivors, and poured out the depths of his sorrow, loneliness, and sense of abandonment. "How deserted lies the city once full of people... all her splendor is gone... she has become unclean. Bitterly she weeps at night; there is none to comfort her... her few remaining people scavenge for bread. I weep about these things and my eyes overflow with tears. Comfort is far from me. The enemy has prevailed. See my distress, O Lord, for I am tormented and disturbed. There is no-one to comfort me. My heart faints..." The prophet recognized nevertheless that in the midst of all of this "the Lord is righteous".

In his second acrostic Jeremiah described the totality of the calamity which had swept over Jerusalem. He did not attribute it to Nebuchadnezzar but to the terrible judgement of God. What had taken place was in fulfillment of the ancient Mosaic covenant: "The Lord has fulfilled His word, the things He decreed long ago." In His wrath against Judah the Lord withdrew his protecting hand and allowed the nation to be hurled down, to be swallowed up without pity, to be consumed by the enemy. In His fierce anger He spurned Israel's kings and priests and turned His back on the temple and the altar, the symbols of His presence with His people. He had allowed the city's walls to be razed and its king and princes to be exiled. Jeremiah accused the nation's false prophets of being primarily responsible for bringing on God's wrath: "your prophets' visions were false, were worthless. They did not expose your sin. Their oracles were misleading." He never questioned God's righteous judgement, seeing that everything God did was consistent with His character and His covenant commitments.

In the third poem Jeremiah described his personal suffering: "I am the man who has seen affliction, who has experience God's wrath. He has driven me into darkness; there is no light. I am wasted away, an old, broken man before my time because God filled me with bitterness and tribulation, forced me down a twisted path from which I could not escape... My life is filled with affliction, bitterness, gall, wandering. My soul is downcast."

Then, suddenly, in the middle of this poem his heart cries out in hope springing from his abiding faith. "Yet I remember this and thus have hope: the Lord's great love will not cease and his mercies do not end here. His faithfulness is new every morning. It is good to wait quietly for the Lord's salvation. He will not cast us off forever. Even though He causes us grief now, he will have compassion on us according to His abundant and steadfast love. He does not willingly afflict people..." Jeremiah recognized that God destroyed Jerusalem not to cast it off forever but to restore it to something akin to His original purposes.

After this burst of hope, Jeremiah pointed the way forward for his afflicted people: "Why should the survivors complain about the punishment of their sins? They should examine their ways and return to the Lord. They should lift up their hearts and hands to God in heaven and confess that they have transgressed and rebelled against him!"

In his fourth acrostic poem Jeremiah seemed to have left his vantage point overlooking the city to wander through its rubble, composing snap-shots of the things he saw. Once compassionate mothers have ceased caring about their children who are dying of thirst and crying out in vain for food; the mothers are cannibalizing them instead. Once wealthy people are unrecognizable skeletons, blacker than soot, perishing in the streets or lying on ash heaps. People are defiled and wandering blindly through the streets. Those who died by the sword were better off than the survivors.

In his concluding lamentation Jeremiah voiced his deep sense of shame at the situation the nation found itself it. "Remember what has happened to us Lord, and look upon our disgrace. Our land has been turned over to strangers, we are aliens given no rest in our own land. We are ruled by slaves and are feverish from hunger. Our women have been raped, our princes hung up by their hands and our elders shown no respect. Our young men and boys stagger under

great weights. The joy has disappeared from our hearts."

Again the prophet acknowledged that the people deserved what they received. "Woe to us because we have sinned, and for this we are heartsick!" And, once again, he lifted his head and cried out in faith and hope: "You, Lord, reign forever! Surely you will not forget us? Restore us to yourself, O Lord, so that we may be restored! Renew our days as in the past! Surely you are not so angry with us that you have utterly rejected us?"

Years later, in the week prior to his crucifixion, Jesus would also sit on the Mount of Olives overlooking the city of Jerusalem and weep over it. Jeremiah the heartbroken but ever faithful prophet would be overshadowed by the Lord Jesus

Christ. Isaiah had prophesied that he would be "a man of sorrows and acquainted with grief" (Is. 53:3).

Jeremiah also wrote a letter to the exiles in Babylon. He advised them to settle down and make a life for themselves in Babylon. They were to "seek the peace and prosperity of Babylon" because as it prospered so would they. He also informed them that the period of their exile would last seventy years. After the seventy years they would be restored to the Promised Land (Jer. 25:11-14; 29:10).

• 166 • Obadiah's Condemnation of Edom

Obadiah   *Date: uncertain, possibly circa 585 B.C.*

NOT MUCH is known about the prophet Obadiah; scholars even debate the timing of his sharp, prophetic sermon, the shortest of the Old Testament prophetic oracles. Like Jeremiah and Ezekiel, he most probably survived Babylon's destruction of Jerusalem and witnessed the Edomites' opportunistic exploitation of Judah's calamity.

The Edomites were the descendants of Jacob's twin brother Esau: Israel and Edom were as closely related as two nations could be, though their relationship was awkward and at times broke into open warfare. When the Babylonians were advancing southwards the Edomites had been part of an alliance, with Judah and the region's other nations, against the invaders. However it quickly surrendered, as Jeremiah had urged all the region's nations to do. Then, when the Babylonians took Jerusalem, it joined in the plundering and sacking.

The main thrust of Obadiah's message focused on Edom's exploitation of Israel during its time of trouble. Israel grew to accept the fact that God's judgement of them at the hands of the Babylonians was just. However, the fact that the Edomites joined the enemy in ravaging them left deep wounds. The prophets Jeremiah and Ezekiel denounced them for this low act, as did one of the psalmists (Jer. 49; Lam. 4:21-22; Ez. 25:12; 35:15; Psalm 137).

According to Obadiah, however, Edom would be judged primarily because of its haughtiness and pride. The Edomites were a proud people. They were proud of their geographical location in an almost impregnable natural fortress in the craggy mountains located in the southern desert from which they controlled the key trading routes between Egypt and the various other nations of the Middle East. Edom's most famous city, Petra, was a natural fortress accessible only through a long, narrow crevasse, a mere 4 or 5 meters wide that a handful of soldiers could defend. Obadiah described them as living like eagles on the heights, in the clefts of the rocks. Because it controlled major trade routes, little Edom grew wealthy, and to secure its position, it had made many alliances with the great powers of the day (vs 9). Edom was also proud of its reputation for worldly wisdom (vs 8, Jer. 49:7). In fact, two of Job's friends came from the Edomite cities of Teman and Shuh.

Obadiah traced the development of Edom's increasingly despicable behaviour towards Judah. Initially they stood from afar to see how things would develop. Psalm 137 states that they encouraged the Babylonians to "tear Jerusalem down to its foundations". When the city eventually fell they rejoiced over the awful calamity, and as soon as the opportunity arose they joined in the plunder and made off with whatever the Babylonians had left behind. Not content with that, they then laid ambushes at key junctions to kill Jewish fugitives or hand them to the Babylonians. When the opportunity offered itself Edom's national pride, self-sufficiency, and so-called wisdom quickly turned to rapaciousness and inhumane cruelty.

Even if Edom paid no attention to the prophet's message the Jewish survivors heard and treasured it. They believed him, and during their Babylonian exile added his sermon to their canon of prophetic writings. It has been part of God's word to every generation ever since.

The lasting truth of Obadiah's message is that God will judge the nations. "The day of the Lord is at hand for all nations. It will be done to you as you have done to others; your deeds will return to haunt you! The descendants of Edom will disappear completely from the face of the earth, but the Lord will deliver and bless His people after He has disciplined them!" the prophet predicted. "They will return to Mount Zion and, one day, when the Lord establishes His kingdom, they will rule with Him over those who were once their enemies."

It took 600 years but Obadiah words came true. The Edomites were completely wiped off the face of the earth. The Nabatean Arabs captured their supposedly impregnable capital Petra in 312 B.C., after which the region came to be known as Idumea. Herod the Great, the king of Israel who tried to kill Jesus Christ, hailed from there, but his line died out when his great-grandson Agrippa died childless around 100 A.D. Their magnificent city of Petra was lost to history until rediscovered by an explorer in 1812. Today it is a tourist attraction.

• 167 • Ezekiel: Prophet of the Exile

Ezekiel   *Date: oracles given between 593-571 B.C.*

King Nebuchadnezzar invaded Judah and captured people to take back to Babylon on three occasions. Each deportation, in 605, 598 and 586 B.C. respectively, was of increasingly larger numbers until only the poorest of the poor were left in the land. Ezekiel, a priest, was deported to Babylon during the second deportation.

Ezekiel was a contemporary of Jeremiah, though about 20 years younger in age. Like Jeremiah he too spoke against the false prophets who had preached peace when there was no peace. He too insisted that the future of Israel lay with the exiled community, not with those left behind in Jerusalem. He too rejected the idea that what happened to the nations was a result of blind fate. He too emphasized the fact that people are personally responsible for their actions, rejecting the popular wisdom encapsulated in a proverb about fathers eating sour grapes and the children's teeth being set on edge. He too condemned Israel's leaders for failing to take care of the flock, the Lord's people. Like Jeremiah, he too foresaw that although the exile would be lengthy, it would end in restoration. He too foresaw that the Lord would establish a new covenant with Israel that would have a deep inward dimension and would be appropriated individually. Unlike Jeremiah, however, Ezekiel does not often share his personal struggles.

Ezekiel and most of his fellow captives were deported to a place called Tel Abib, in Babylon. While Jeremiah continued to minister to the dwindling remnant of God's people in Jerusalem, Ezekiel ministered "in the midst of" the exiled community. He loved the phrase "in the midst of". He himself lived "in the midst of" his people; Israel lived "in the midst of" the nations"; Egypt would be scattered "in the midst of" the nations; one day a Davidic king would again live "in the midst of" God's people; the Lord would one day again make Himself known "in the midst of" them; a day would come when Israel would no longer suffer disgrace "in the midst of" the nations because the Lord's sanctuary would be "in the midst of them". One day the Lord would display His glory "in the midst of" all the nations of the world.

In accordance with Jeremiah's instructions, the exiles started to build new lives for themselves. The people were free to organize their communal life, establish businesses and move into their own homes. Ezekiel grew to be held in high esteem by the exiled community. Its elders would gather at his house to consult him, and it was from there that he gave some of his prophecies. In fact it was from house groups like these, in which the Jewish community would study the Torah and the prophets, probing the reasons for the calamities that had befallen them, that, in time, the more formal structure of the synagogue (which simply means "assembly") emerged. As the Jews of the exile assembled for worship and religious instruction in synagogues they rediscovered their faith. With the temple and the sacrificial system gone they became a people of The Book. Their adherence to the Torah and their attention to the words of the prophets enabled them to maintain and nurture their identity as Jehovah's people in a foreign land.

Ezekiel received his first vision in 593 B.C. when he was thirty years old. He saw God surrounded by heavenly beings and sitting on a throne with intersecting wheels: God revealed Himself as One who could move rapidly and instantly in any and all directions. His presence was not limited to the temple in Jerusalem, but He was also present with the exiles in Babylon.

Ezekiel was overwhelmed when he saw the wheeled throne of God departing from the temple altogether, but the affirmation now of God's omnipresence must have been a source of great comfort. Although God's presence had departed the temple and the building itself was reduced to rubble, He still reigned on the exalted throne in heaven. Ezekiel also heard a voice speaking: "Son of man, I am sending you to the stubborn, obstinate and rebellious people of Israel to speak my words to them. Do not fear them or feel threatened by them but speak my words faithfully, whether they want to hear it or not." The Lord then gave him a scroll to eat, an act that symbolized his assimilation of the word of God. He did so, and it tasted as sweet as honey. Sweet though it was to the taste, its application would prove to be a different matter. "Although some of your countrymen will reject my message I will make you as hard as the hardest stone so that you can persevere in your proclamation, no matter how the people respond," God told him. This call to the ministry so disturbed Ezekiel that for seven days he sat overwhelmed in bitterness and anguish of spirit.

Then the word of the Lord came to him again. "Son of man, I have made you a watchman for Israel. Hear the words and warnings I am giving you for them. I will hold you accountable for the blood of the wicked if you do not warn them to turn from their evil ways." Then the Lord again revealed His glory so that he again fell on his face before God.

Ezekiel, more than any other prophet, used symbols and allegories and a wide range of literary genres to communicate God's messages. His preaching included proverbs, parables, dirges, illustrations, and apocalyptic dream-like visions. He described Judah as a wild, worthless vine, as well as a baby girl who had been cast away, then rescued to become a queen who later turned to prostitution. Samaria and Judah were like sisters who became prostitutes. Pharaoh and Nebuchadnezzar are both described as eagles. He also made use of drama when predicting Jerusalem's upcoming, final, calamitous destruction. He dramatized the final siege of Jerusalem by making a model of the city, erecting toy siege works against it and lying bound with ropes beside it for a total of 430 days. This represented the number of years in which the nation had sinned against God. He then went on a starvation diet and cooked his meager rations over dung to illustrate the desperate state of affairs in Jerusalem during the siege. He shaved his head and beard and separated the hair into three piles: the first pile he burned, illustrating what would happen to Jerusalem after the siege, the second pile he cut with a sword to illustrate the subsequent slaughter, and the last pile he threw into the air to illustrate the exile.

At one stage the Lord told Ezekiel that his wife would die. "The word of the Lord came to me saying, 'with one blow I'm going to take away your wife, the delight of your eyes. I don't want you to grieve over her or shed any tears. Mourn quietly in your heart.'" Although his wife died that very day Ezekiel went about his business as normal. When people asked him why he was acting so callously he told them that they would be so worn out with weeping and mourning for their own sins that they wouldn't have any emotional strength left to grieve at the news of Jerusalem's final collapse.

Many of Ezekiel's later prophecies were against other nations. In them he answered a question that must have been uppermost in the minds of the Jews of the exile: if this is how God deals with his special covenant people, what will he do to the nations who did this to us? In one prophecy after another he announced God's judgement against the surrounding nations. The king of Tyre, the center of Baal worship and Egypt's Pharaoh, to whom Israel traditionally looked for help, were castigated in particular. Without them Israel would not have fallen as far as it did.

• 168 • Ezekiel's Remaining Years

Ezekiel   *Date: oracles given between 593-571 B.C.*

THERE ARE a number of themes to which Ezekiel returned time and again in the course of his ministry to the exiles in Babylon. Like that of the prophets who preceded him, he drove home the fact that God's punishment of Israel — their decimation, deprivation, exile and the loss of the promised land — was not a sudden, rash, impulsive decision nor the result of the blind forces of history. No, it was the culmination of a long-term, steady pattern of their disobedience to the Mosaic covenant. All that had happened to them, and all the things he predicted would still happen, was a holy God's punishment and disciplining of his wayward people. In defiantly breaking the covenant again and again the nation had removed itself from God's blessings and exposed itself instead to God's severity and judgement.

Unlike Isaiah, who depicted God as the sovereign of the universe, Ezekiel's focus was on Jehovah as the covenant-keeping God of Israel prior to and during the exile and, in fact, until the end of time. He described Israel's restoration as taking place in two phases: the first, when Cyrus allowed the people to return to their homeland, was but a type, a foreshadowing, of the total restoration that would take place at the end of the age.

The nation as a whole had sinned, but Ezekiel also stressed that each individual was personally responsible for his own actions and would be judged accordingly. There was no room for fatalism or determinism, or for blame shifting: "The person who sins, he will die. The son will not suffer for his father's evil, or the father for the son's evil." Yet the Lord derived no pleasure from the death of the wicked. "So repent and turn from your evil ways lest your iniquity result in your ruin. Put away your sins and get a new heart and a new spirit! Why die, O people of Israel? 'I have no pleasure in anyone's death, says the Lord God, so turn to me and live!'"

Although the people were personally responsible for what they did, Ezekiel also had stinging rebukes for Israel's leaders, "the shepherds of Israel" who should have taken care of the Lord's flock, but who looked after their own interests instead: "Oh shepherds of Israel who feed yourselves, should you not have fed the sheep? You eat their fat, clothe yourselves with their wool, and slaughter the fatlings without taking care of the flock. You have ruled them harshly and with force, and because you did not shepherd them they ended up scattered all over the earth."

After that Ezekiel offered a series of hopeful yet challenging messages on what God had in store for the future for Israel. The dead nation would be

274

brought back to life. The Lord would regather his scattered people. "The Lord will gather them from faraway countries and bring them back to the fountains, pastures and heights of Israel, where they shall lie down in peace. He will bring back the strays, bind up the crippled, strengthen the weak and watch over the fat and strong and nourish them in justice." One day they would be re-established under a king, a descendant of David. At that time God would make a new covenant of peace with them: He would establish them and increase their numbers. He would become their God once again and they would remain His people forever! He foresaw that this messianic prince would restore the holy city and its temple and bring order, peace and blessing. His description of the future was reminiscent of Isaiah's portrayal of the millennial kingdom.

Right from his first vision of God as an indescribably splendid, mysterious, all-seeing, mobile being, one of Ezekiel's themes was the glory and transcendence of God. It was this that determined Jehovah's conduct and set the course of history, and it was this that He wanted the people to grasp. 74 times Ezekiel stated God's reason for acting as He had "so that they would know that I (Jehovah) am the Lord".

Even if God had abandoned the temple and temporarily turned His back on His people, He remained the great, glorious, omnipresent and omnipotent sovereign of Israel seated on His glorious throne.

• 169 • Daniel's Training and Nebuchadnezzar's Dream

Daniel 1-2   *Date: circa 605-602 B.C.*

DANIEL WAS born into Judah's ruling elite and, as a teenager, was taken into captivity during Nebuchadnezzar's first deportation in 605 B.C. Upon arrival in Babylon he and his three friends, Hananiah, Mishael and Azariah, were selected to enter a three year training program to prepare them for service at the royal court. To encourage these bright, young Jewish deportees to change their identity they were given new names, each of which referred to one of Babylon's gods: Belteshazzar, Shadrach, Meshach and Abednego. However, the young men resolved to quietly resist, determining to remain ceremonially pure by not violating the Torah's dietary laws. This simple, brave act enabled them to maintain their Jewish identity in the face of a foreign environment that sought to mould them into its own image.

When Daniel asked for permission to follow a vegetarian diet the chief official had his doubts: "If you young men look worse than your peers, the king will have my head!"

"Why don't you test us for ten days," Daniel suggested diplomatically, "then compare our appearance with that of the other young men." The official agreed—and after ten days the four young Jews looked better nourished than the others!

The four excelled in their studies, and when king Nebuchadnezzar interviewed them upon graduation he found them superior in every matter. They entered into the king's service, with Daniel becoming a junior advisor and administrator in the royal palace.

One night the king had a vivid and disturbing dream. Such dreams were regarded in the ancient world as portents of things to come, so the king called on his wise men for an interpretation. "Tell us the dream and we will interpret it for you," they said.

Nebuchadnezzar, however, insisted that they tell him what he'd dreamed about in the first place! He wanted to test the validity of their claim to supernatural guidance. If they succeeded he would honour them; if they failed he threatened to dismember them.

"There is not a person on the face of the earth who can do what the king requests," the sages objected strenuously. "No one can reveal the matter except the immortal gods, and they do not live among men," they said, inadvertently revealing that Babylon's magicians and astrologers were, in fact, incapable of obtaining access to things supernatural. Nebuchadnezzar flew into a rage and ordered all these charlatans executed. The edict included Daniel and his friends even though, as junior members of the king's group of counselors, they had not been consulted.

When Daniel learned of the matter he went home and explained the situation to his three friends, urging them to plead to God for mercy. That night he had a vision of the king's dream along with its interpretation. He got up and praised "the God of his fathers" for His wisdom and power in revealing the matter to him.

"Don't execute the wise men," he told the commander. "Take me to the king."

"Are you able to tell me what I saw in my dream?" the king asked him.

"No diviner or magician can explain the mystery the king has asked," Daniel replied. "But there is a God in heaven who can reveal mysteries. He has shown the king what will take place in times to come. As you were laying on your bed," Daniel continued, "you saw an enormous, dazzling statue. Its head was of pure gold, its chest and arms of silver, its abdomen and thighs of bronze, its legs of iron, and its feet of iron and baked clay. While you were watching a rock not cut by human hands struck the statue's feet and smashed them to pieces. The statue disintegrated and was swept away by the wind without leaving a trace, while the rock became a mountain that filled the earth. That was your dream, O king. Now we will interpret it.

"You, O king, are the head of gold. The God of heaven has made you the absolute ruler over all, whether man or beast." Indeed, Nebuchadnezzar was the supreme authority in the Middle East, the world that affected Israel. "After you another kingdom will rise. Symbolized by silver, it will be inferior to yours," Daniel continued. This took place when the Neo-Babylonian Empire fell to the Medo-Persians in 539 B.C., a mere 22 years after Nebuchadnezzar's 45 year reign. The two arms represented the coalition of the two nations. Although it covered more territory and lasted over 200 years, the power of the Medo-Persian kings was limited: they could not annul a law once it had gone into effect.

"Next a third kingdom, one of bronze, will arise to rule over the earth," Daniel said. The Greeks, under the leadership of Alexander the Great (Dan. 8:20:21) defeated the Medo-Persian Empire in 331 B.C. and established an even larger empire.

Daniel then gave an extended explanation of the fourth kingdom. "Finally, the statue's legs represent a fourth kingdom. It will be as strong as iron and will smash everything into pieces.

Just as you saw that its feet and toes were a mixture of iron and clay, it will become a divided kingdom, having some of the strength of iron yet brittle because of the clay." This fourth kingdom became a reality when Rome defeated the last remnant of Greek political independence in 31 B.C. It would rule for hundreds of years with great strength and brutality from the Atlantic to the Indian Oceans. Furthermore, it would divide into two halves, its capital cities becoming Rome and Constantinople. The Roman Empire was indeed powerful but its rulers became increasingly constrained by the pressure exerted by the masses of ordinary people. The iron represented the legal and cultural heritage of Rome and the clay the inherent weakness of populism. In its final form this kingdom was so diverse that, as in the King's dream, "the people were a mixture and would not remain united any more than iron unites with clay".

The final part of Daniel's interpretation of the dream pertained to the rock that would strike the statue. "The rock means that during the time of those kings the God of heaven will establish His kingdom," Daniel said. "It will destroy those other kingdoms but will itself never be destroyed; it will last forever." The rock, which brought the whole structure down and went on to fill the earth and last forever, symbolized the spiritual kingdom that Christ inaugurated. It is growing and will, when Christ comes again, fill the earth. "The great God has shown the king what will take place. The dream is true and its interpretation trustworthy," Daniel concluded.

When Daniel finished speaking the king fell on his face before the man who had done the humanly impossible. "Your God is the God of gods, the Lord of kings, and the revealer of mysteries!" he cried out. Not only had Daniel told him his dream, the interpretation made perfect sense.

The king then promoted Daniel to rule over the whole province of Babylon, and put him in charge of the wise men. Daniel's three friends were also promoted. This was also God's way of preparing Babylon for the arrival of the tens of thousands of displaced Israelites who would follow during the subsequent exiles of 597 and 586 B.C.

· 170 · Nebuchadnezzar's Statue

Daniel 3   *Date: circa 600 B.C.*

APPARENTLY INSPIRED by his dream, Nebuchadnezzar decided to build a statue of his own. His 90-foot (abt. 27.5 meters) high gold statue was erected on a plain just outside the city of Babylon. He then summoned the empire's administrative officials to participate in a dedication ceremony intended to exact an oath of loyalty from them. Anyone who refused to bow to the statue when the music started would be thrown into a blazing furnace, probably one of the huge kilns used to supply bricks for Nebuchadnezzar's vast building projects.

When the music started everyone fell prostrate before the statue—all that is, except for Daniel's friends Shadrach, Meshach and Abednego. Nebuchadnezzar was quickly informed that, "some Jews whom you placed over the affairs of the province of Babylon, who pay no attention to you, do not serve your gods nor worship the image of gold you have set up". The king was furious at this public display of disobedience, but the stouthearted Jews stood their ground.

"If as a result of this act we are thrown into this blazing furnace, our God can save us from it. And even if he does not, we will not serve your gods nor worship the image you have set up." The people of Israel had learned to eschew idolatry while in Babylon. It was that, after all, which had led to their exile in the first place.

At this refusal to recognize him as the ultimate authority Nebuchadnezzar lost his temper. He had the oven heated to seven times its normal temperature and ordered the three men to be thrown into it. Soon, however, he leaped to his feet in amazement! The blazing heat had overcome the soldiers who had thrown the men into the overheated oven but the three Jews inside it were alive and well! Only the ropes which bound them were gone. In fact, the king saw four men, not just three, walking unharmed in the flames! "Didn't we throw three men into the fire?" he asked bewildered. "I see four men in there, one of whom looks like a son of the gods!" The king approached the blazing furnace and called to the men inside. "Shadrach, Meshach and Abednego, you servants of the Most High God, come out of there!"

As the men stepped into the open the angelic being God had sent to protect them disappeared. The crowd of dignitaries crowding around them saw that the fire had not so much as singed one of their hairs. Their robes were not scorched and there was no smell of fire on them.

Acknowledging Jehovah's superiority over all other gods, Nebuchadnezzar issued a decree stating that anyone who maligned the God of Shadrach, Meshach and Abednego would be cut into pieces and their house turned into a pile of rubble "for no other god can save in this way". The exiled community of Jews must have been greatly encouraged.

▪ 171 ▪ Nebuchadnezzar Loses His Mind

Daniel 4   *Date: circa 582-575 B.C.*

IN THE LATTER part of Nebuchadnezzar's 43-year reign, while he was enjoying life in his palace, he had a terrifying dream. He called again on his astrologers and magicians, but even though he related the dream to them this time, they could make no sense of it. Finally he summoned Daniel, in whom, he admitted, "the spirit of the holy gods lives and for whom no mystery is too difficult to interpret."

"Before me stood an enormous tree which was visible from all over the earth," the king began. "Its leaves were beautiful and its fruit abundant. The beasts of the field sheltered under it, the birds of the air lived in it, and every creature fed from it. Then a holy messenger came down from heaven and ordered it be cut down, its branches removed, its leaves and fruit stripped, and the animals taking refuge in it were scattered. Only its stump, bound with iron and bronze, was to remain in the ground. It would be drenched with the dew of heaven and given the mind of an animal for seven years. The holy messenger then announced that the purpose of all this was 'so that the living would know that the Most High is sovereign over the nations, which He gives to whomever he wishes, even to the lowliest of men.'"

When Daniel heard the dream he immediately understood its dreadful impact; to someone steeped in Israel's prophets the dream's interpretation was easy. The prophets often used trees to describe the rulers of nations (Isa 2:12-13; 10:33-34; Ezek. 31:3-17). Ezekiel had used the image of the beasts of the field and the birds of the air to represent different ethnic groups that profit from a king's reign (Ezek. 31:6). New life growing from a sawed-off tree-stump was an image familiar from Job and Isaiah (Job 14:7-9; Isa. 11:1). The tree stump would be given the "mind of an animal", suggesting a type of derangement from which the king would suffer.

Daniel was reluctant to share the interpretation, not out of fear but out of deep concern for the monarch. Finally he took a deep breath. "My lord, I would that this dream applied to your enemies," he began. "You are that tree, oh king. Your greatness has grown so that it reaches the sky and your dominion stretches to the distant parts of the earth. The announcement of the holy messenger means that the Most High has decreed that you will lose your mind and be driven from your palace. You will behave like an animal for seven years. Only then will you acknowledge that the Most High rules over the kingdoms of the world. The command to leave the stump means that your kingdom will be restored to you when you acknowledge His sovereignty. O king, please accept my advice," Daniel pleaded boldly. "Renounce your sins and act righteously." Like all of Israel's prophets, he knew that judgement could be averted by genuine repentance.

A year later Nebuchadnezzar was strolling on the roof of his royal palace and looking down on the magnificent citadels, hanging gardens, terraces, ziggurats, the extravagant temple to Marduk, the shrines to various other gods, the city's 27 kilometers of double walls, and the great processional avenue leading from the famously decorated Gate of Ishtar to his palace. "Behold the great city of Babylon which I have built as my royal residence by my own mighty power and for the glory of my own majesty!" he began pompously. Suddenly his boasting was interrupted by a voice from heaven.

"This is what has been decreed for you, King Nebuchadnezzar. Your authority is taken away from you. You will be driven from people and live like an animal. Seven years will pass before you acknowledge that the Most High is sovereign over the nations of the world and gives them to whomever He wishes." Then, all of a sudden, something snapped in the king's mind, and he started acting like an animal. He neglected taking care of himself and ate grass like an ox. For seven years he was hidden from public view.

At the end of this period the humbled king lifted his eyes towards heaven and his sanity was restored. He wrote a decree to all his people and surrounding nations in which he explained his dream and its outworking. The pride and boasting were gone. Instead he praised, honored and glorified Jehovah, "the Most High God who lives and reigns forever. Before Him all the people of the earth are as nothing. He does as He pleases in heaven and on earth, and no one can hold him to account."

When the king's sanity was restored, his honor and splendor were returned to him and he became even greater than he had been before. Now, however, he walked in humility before the King of Heaven "who does all things right, whose ways are just, and who humbles those who walk in pride."

The Jews of the exile had seen that even apparently absolute dictators were under Jehovah's sovereign control. He was ultimately in charge and had not abandoned them!

▪ 172 ▪ Daniel's Vision of Four Beasts

Daniel 7   *Date: 553 B.C.*

NEBUCHADNEZZAR died in 562 B.C. and was succeeded by a series of family members. The next noteworthy monarch was Belshazzar, who ruled as coregent with his father Nabonidus from 553 to 539 B.C.

During the first year of Belshazzar's co-regency, Daniel received a most remarkably detailed vision of the future[13]. It was reminiscent of Nebuchadnezzar's dream of the statue some fifty years earlier. In that vision the four empires to come were presented in terms of their political structure, but now Daniel caught a glimpse of these empires' moral and spiritual characteristics. He saw the four winds (or spirits) of heaven stirring up the Great Sea and four great beasts rising out of it. The "sea" for prophets represented the gentile nations while the "wind" referred to God's sovereign power over events. The first beast was a winged lion, the symbol of Babylon. Larger than life statues and reliefs of this mythological creature decorated the city gates or guarded its royal palaces. Daniel saw someone tear off the creature's wings and then lift it up and give it the heart of a man. This probably referred to king Nebuchadnezzar who became more humane after God had humbled him.

The second beast looked like a bear, and symbolized the Medo-Persian Empire. One side was larger than the other, reflecting the fact that the Persian element of the coalition was stronger than the Median one. The three ribs in the beast's mouth symbolized the three major nations it conquered: Babylon, Egypt, and the Anatolian kingdom of Lydia. A voice urged it to devour much meat, suggesting it would wage war on a large scale.

---

[13] Daniels visions are described in a literary genre called "apocalyptic literature". This is a type of symbolic, visionary, prophetic literature that tended to be composed during times of oppression. It used what seems to modern readers bizarre images of a dream-like nature, was mediated and explained to the prophet by an angel, tended to have an eschatological focus (i.e. with respect to the restoration of things at the end of time), consisted of polarities such as the wicked versus the righteous, heaven and earth, the present age and the age to come, sought to encourage repentance, and promised restoration and blessing. Whereas normal prophetic literature looked forward to an eschatological kingdom arising in history through a son of David, apocalyptic literature saw it breaking into history in a transcendent manner. Instead of referring to the expected Messiah who would usher in this new era as a "son of David", as normal prophecy does, the apocalyptic writers referred to Him as a "son of man who will come riding on the clouds". Jesus Christ identified Himself with both concepts. Ezekiel, Daniel and Zechariah all made use of the styles, as did John in the book of Revelation.

The third animal in Daniel's vision was a leopard with four wings. The leopard aptly symbolized Alexander the Great's rapid conquest of Anatolia, Egypt, Babylon, and Persia, all the way to the Indian Ocean (334-331 B.C.). The leopard had four heads, each of which was given authority to rule. After Alexander's premature death the territory he had conquered was divided into four separate kingdoms located in Greece, Western Asia, Egypt, and Persia respectively.

The fourth, ten-horned beast was unlike any known animal. It was particularly powerful and terrifying with claws of bronze. This frightful beast represented bloodthirsty, imperial Rome that stamped underfoot and enslaved countless peoples from the British Isles to Persia. The ten horns represented the same set of rulers, previously depicted as the ten toes on Nebuchadnezzar's statue, who will one day arise.

While Daniel was staring at the beast's horns he saw another horn, a little one, emerge. It had human-like eyes, symbolizing intelligence, and a mouth that spoke boastfully. It grew to be a large, imposing horn that waged war against the saints. It seems to refer to an individual called the Antichrist elsewhere in Scripture who will arise in the last days and persecute the saints. God will allow this ruler to have his way for a set period of time.

Next Daniel saw movement in the courts of heaven. Thrones were set in place and the "Ancient of Days", a title which stressed God's eternal being, took His place on a flaming, wheeled throne (Ezek. 1:13-21). His hair was white as wool and his clothes as white as snow, symbolizing the maturity of His judgement and His holiness. A river of fire, symbolizing purity and judgment (Deut. 4:24), flowed from before him, and many thousands of individuals, probably angels (Deut. 33:2), stood before him. When the court was seated the books were opened. The stage was set for the rulers and nations of the earth to be judged.

Next Daniel described someone "like a Son of Man" coming with the clouds of heaven. He approached the "Ancient of Days", was ushered into His presence, and was granted authority, glory and sovereign power. The court then passed judgement on the Antichrist being, after which all the people and nations of the world fell down in worship before this Son of Man. He then established His own kingdom, one that would never pass away and never be destroyed. Many years later Jesus Christ would take the title "Son of Man" for himself (Mark 8:31; John 1:51, etc). He would also proclaim that He would return one day at the end of time "on the clouds" (e.g. Mat. 24:30; 26:64; Mark 13:26), just as Daniel had seen in his vision.

The vision so troubled Daniel that he turned pale and could not share it with anyone until much later.

· 173 · Daniel's Vision of the Ram and the Goat

Daniel 8   *Date: 551 B.C.*

TWO YEARS after his vision of the four beasts Daniel received another vision which revealed more details about the second (Persian) and third (Greek) kingdoms. In it Daniel saw himself transported to the citadel of Susa, a city about 200 miles east of Babylon. There he saw a ram with two horns of unequal size. It represented the two members of the Medo-Persian alliance; their kings carried a heraldic banner of a ram's head into battle. Daniel watched as the ram charged unopposed towards the west, north and south, areas that would be conquered by the Medo-Persian Empire.

Next Daniel saw a male goat with a single, prominent horn charging at the ram in a great rage, breaking off its two horns and trampling it into the ground. The goat aptly symbolized Greece and its single, great horn stood for Alexander the Great. His final defeat of Persia came in 331 B.C. The goat became very great but, at the height of its power, its large horn was broken off and replaced by four smaller horns. After Alexander's untimely death in 323 B.C. at the age of 33 his great empire was divided into four parts.

After that Daniel saw a small horn grown out of the four horns. It continued to grow southwards and eastwards towards the "Beautiful Land", namely Israel (Dan. 11:16; 41, 45; Jer. 3:19; Ezek. 20:6; 15). The person in history who matches the little horn was Antiochus Epiphanes IV, who ruled from 175-164 B.C. "Epiphanes" was a title meaning "divine manifestation" which Antiochus claimed for himself; the Jews called him "Epimanes", which means "madman". He ruled from 175-164 B.C. Antiochos' persecution of the Jews in 168 B.C. was very brutal and very bloody. He killed many of their leaders, including the high priest. Daniel saw the "little horn" then set itself up as prince of the hosts, i.e., as leader of the Jews, who would abolish the daily sacrifice in the temple for a period of three years. Antiochus Epiphanes IV did indeed forbid the keeping of Jewish religious traditions from 167-164 B.C, terminated the morning and evening sacrifices, and desecrated the temple by placing an altar of Zeus in it. It came to be known among the Jews as "the abomination of desolation" (11:31). However, the angel also told Daniel that the vision "concerned the end of time". Although in terms of its immediate context it pertained to the period of terrible persecution the Jews endured under Antiochus Epiphanes IV, he would serve as a proto-type of the Antichrist who will emerge in the future, just prior to Christ's second coming. Jesus Christ would refer to this much later when He spoke about the end of the age (Mat. 24:15).

Daniel was appalled at the vision. The knowledge that his people would, once again, undergo severe persecution greatly distressed him. For several days he lay exhausted, unable to attend to his duties at Belshazzar's court.

▪ 174 ▪ The Fall of Babylon

Daniel 5   *Date: the night of October 11/12, 539 B.C.*

DURING THE night of October 11, 539 B.C., while the Medo-Persian army was laying siege to the city of Babylon, King Belshazzar hosted a great banquet to which he invited the city's leading nobles along with their wives and concubines. During the drunken orgy Belshazzar, in an act of nationalistic revelry, called for the gold and silver goblets that Nebuchadnezzar had brought from the temple in Jerusalem. These objects were now used to toast the superiority of the man-made gods of Babylon.

Suddenly a human hand appeared on the wall and slowly, deliberately, began writing something on the white plaster. As the king watched his face turned white with fear, his knees knocked together and his legs buckled under him. He cried out for the nation's astrologers and diviners to decipher the message, promising great rewards—but no one was able to interpret the cryptic message.

When the queen heard what had happened she made her way to the banquet hall. "Oh King, live forever! Don't be alarmed and don't look so pale! There is a man in your kingdom in whom the spirit of the holy gods lives. He has the insight, intelligence and wisdom of the gods. This man, Daniel, has the ability to interpret dreams."

Belshazzar quickly summoned Daniel. "If you can tell me the meaning of this writing you will be clothed in purple, receive a gold chain, and be promoted to third highest ruler in the kingdom."

"You may keep your gifts and give your rewards to someone else," Daniel responded coldly, and then proceeded to rebuke the king. He reminded Belshazzar of the way Jehovah God had

humbled Nebuchadnezzar until he was forced to acknowledge that the Most High God was the ultimate sovereign over kingdoms and their rulers. "Even though you knew this, O Belshazzar," Daniel went on sharply, "you did not humble yourself. Instead you set yourself up against the Lord of Heaven by drinking from the goblets of His temple. Instead of honoring the God who holds your life in His hand, you praise gods of silver, which cannot see, hear or understand."

After this stinging rebuke Daniel turned to the writing on the wall. "This is what is written: MENE, MENE, TEKEL U-PARSIN." The first words were monetary units and alluded to the concepts of "numbered" and "weighed". U meant "and" and PARSIN could mean both "broken in two" and "Persian". Daniel grasped that the first word, MENE, meant that the time God had allotted to the Babylonian Empire was numbered. Its repetition stressed the certainty and imminence of the matter. TEKEL referred to the fact that God had "weighed", or evaluated, Belshazzar and found him deficient. The double meaning of PARSIN meant that the invading Persians would break his kingdom apart.

In spite of the awfulness of the message Belshazzer kept his promise. Daniel was dressed in purple and elevated to third highest ruler in the kingdom. The last official act of the empire that had razed Jerusalem, taken its people captive and destroyed their temple was to honor the captive who predicted its downfall.

That night the combined armies of the Medes and the Persians poured into the city. Babylon fell and before morning Belshazzar was dead. Daniel survived and became a trusted advisor to the new monarch, Darius the Mede, also known as Cyrus[14].

• 175 • Daniel in the Lion's Den

Daniel 6   *Date: 538 B.C.*

UPON THEIR defeat of the Babylonians, the Medo-Persian alliance had to incorporate large amounts of new territory and numerous different ethnic groups into their empire. To facilitate management of this vast terrain king Darius divided his realm into 120 provinces whose governors were to report to three royal commissioners. Having heard of Daniel's integrity and competence he appointed him as one of those commissioners.

Daniel so distinguished himself in this role that the king planned to promote him to prime minister, even though he was well into his eighties by now. This rankled with Daniel's corrupt colleagues, so they plotted to get rid of him. Daniel's integrity was blameless so they knew the only way would be to force him to choose between his God and his king. They proposed a law in which people were to offer their prayers solely to the king, as the representative of deity on earth, for a period of forty days. Those who refused to do so would be thrown to the lions. Darius liked the idea. It catered to his vanity, and he probably regarded the act as a pledge of loyalty.

As his colleagues had surmised, Daniel refused to let the edict deter his time-honoured routine of getting on his knees three times daily to pray to Jehovah God. His enemies quickly

---

[14] The word "darius" is a derivative of "dara", which means "king" in Avestan, the language in which the scriptures of Zoroastrianism, ancient Persia's state religion, was written. In other words, "Darius" was an honorific like the Egyptian title "Pharaoh" or the Roman title "Caesar".

There are differences of opinion among scholars who the "Darius" in the book of Daniel refers to. It probably refers to Cyrus, the ruler of the Medo-Persian empire from 559-530 B.C., something which the alternative reading of Daniel 6:28 seems to support: "*Daniel prospered during the reign of Darius, that is, the reign of Cyrus*" (see footnote, NIV). The other alternative is that Darius was a man named Gubaru whom Cyrus appointed as his official vice-regent over his Babylonian domain. In any case the Darius the Mede in Daniel is not the same person as Darius the Great (Darius I) who ruled Persia from 521-486 B.C., nor was he Darius II, who ruled from 423-404 B.C.

informed the king that his newly appointed prime minister, whom they described disparagingly as "one of the exiles from Judah", had violated the decree and deserved to be executed.

King Darius was deeply distressed at this unexpected turn of events. However, with his corrupt officials reminding him of the legal constraint he was under, there was nothing he could do. Under Persian law once the king had issued an edict he himself was legally bound to keep it.

The king gave the orders. "May your God, whom you serve continually, deliver you," he said somberly to Daniel, expressing a faint hope in the power of Daniel's God. Daniel was lowered into the large pit of lions and the stone over its entry hole sealed to prevent his escape. The king was so anxious about Daniel's fate that he lost his appetite, cancelled all entertainment and could not sleep. At the first blush of dawn he hurried to find out what had happened to Daniel. He had the stone removed and in an anguished voice called into the dark hole: "Oh Daniel, has the God whom you serve continually been able to rescue you from the lions?"

Daniel voice rose cheerful but courteous from the bottom of the murky pit. "O king, live forever! My God sent his angel to shut the mouths of the lions so they would not hurt me because He found me innocent!"

Marvelling and overjoyed, the king had Daniel lifted out of the lion's den. He then commanded those who had hatched the plot, along with their families, to be thrown into the pit instead. Before they hit bottom the hungry lions overpowered and crushed them.

Like Nebuchadnezzar and Belshazzar this heathen king was also caused to praise and glorify Jehovah God. In fact, Darius issue a decree ordering his subjects to fear and reverence the God of Daniel. This must have greatly encouraged the Jewish exiles to continue to trust Jehovah and His plans for them.

Daniel 9   *Date: 538 B.C.*

IN DARIUS' FIRST full year as king of the new Medo-Persian Empire, Daniel was reading a copy of the book of Jeremiah. He took the numbers pertaining to prophetic fulfillment in Scriptures literally and realized that the 70 years of exile which the weeping prophet had predicted should end soon (Jer. 25:11-12; 29:10-14). Daniel was undoubtedly also aware of Isaiah's prophecy about a king named Cyrus who would order the rebuilding of Jerusalem and the temple to Jehovah God (Isa. 44:28; cf. 45:1-2, 4, 13).

The Babylonian's first deportation of Jews from Jerusalem, of which Daniel himself was a victim, had taken place in 605 B.C. In the way time was measured back then part of a year was calculated as a whole year, so now in 538 B.C., 69 years had already past. Although God had clearly spelled out the direction of history with respect to His people through the prophets, Daniel turned to God with earnest pleading for the actualization of God's plan.

In his prayer Daniel voiced deep contrition for the things that had led to the exile in the first place. Although he had personally remained faithful to God he identified himself with his covenant-breaking people. He confessed their rebelliousness and refusal to listen to the prophets whom God had sent to warn them: "We are covered with shame... but You are righteous..." They had deserved all the punishment they had received from Jehovah's hand. Daniel then reminded God how He had glorified His name by delivering the people from Egyptian bondage centuries earlier. He pleaded that God would turn away from His wrath and restore the desolate city of Jerusalem and its ruined temple. "We do not make this request based on our righteousness," he concluded, "but because of your great mercy. O Lord, listen! O Lord, forgive! O Lord, hear and act! O Lord, do not delay, because your city and your people bear your name!"

While Daniel was still praying in this manner the angel Gabriel appeared to him in human form and outlined what would happen to the people of Israel from the time Jerusalem and the temple were rebuilt until the establishment of God's kingdom on earth. They would suffer at the hands of the Gentiles, but by the end of that period God would have accomplished five things: transgression and rebellion against Him would have come to an end, sin would have been atoned for, everlasting righteousness would have been instituted, and the words of the prophets would have been realized. The angel used multiplications of the number seven to carefully date his chronology of future events. The end of the period would be seventy times seven, which is 490 years later. Using the calendar of that era this corresponds with the rejection of Jesus Christ by Israel and His subsequent crucifixion and resurrection.

Soon after Daniel's prayer that Israel be restored, Cyrus issued his famous decree allowing the Jews the return home. Daniel retired from public service not long after that (Dan. 1:21).

Ezra 1-4   *Date: 537 B.C.*

AS THE PROPHET Isaiah had predicted nearly two centuries earlier, a certain king Cyrus would arise and issue an edict allowing the Jewish exiles to return to their land (Isa. 44:28; 45:1). This monarch was Cyrus, king of Persia, who strode onto the stage of history and issued his famous decree in 538 B.C.: "Anyone who wishes may go up to Judah and build a temple to the God of Israel who is in Jerusalem".

Not all the Jews took advantage of Cyrus' offer. Many had no desire to leave the lives and businesses they had established, to go back to a pile of ruins. However, a year later, in 537 B.C., nearly 50,000 of them did return to Jerusalem under the leadership of a man called Sheshbazzar.

Victorious armies often made off with the idols of their defeated foes. Since the Jews had no image of their god, Nebuchadnezzar had taken the temple utensils instead. Cyrus gave these back to the returnees, a gesture meant to encourage them to resume the full-orbed worship of Jehovah. This, he hoped, would make them loyal citizens, who would pray on his behalf,

Although the first group of returnees was led by Shesbazzar, grandson of King Jehoiachin, a man named Zerubbabel assumed leadership once the group reached Judah, and Joshua, a descendant of Aaron, was appointed as high priest (1 Chron. 3:17-19; 3:8-11; Zech. 3:1). Upon arrival they rebuilt the altar and, for the first time in over 70 years, morning and evening sacrifices were again offered to Jehovah. Then they celebrated the Feast of Tabernacles.

The Jews, who had flourished in Babylon, now contributed tons of gold and silver towards the rebuilding of the temple. By the next year, in 536 B.C., they celebrated the completion of its foundations with joy and tears. Joy because the Lord was re-establishing them according to His covenant promises, and tears because the old people wept as they remembered the magnificence of Solomon's first temple. No sooner had the foundations been laid, however, than the project stalled in the face of local opposition.

While the Jews were in exile people from elsewhere had moved into Canaan. These people had added the worship of Jehovah, who they regarded as the god of the land, to their own pantheon of deities (2 Kings 17:30-33). They had also intermarried with the few Jews who had been allowed to remain. In time the descendants of this racially and religiously mixed people came to be known as the Samaritans. When these people, called the "people of the land" at this stage, proposed to help with the rebuilding, Zerubbabel rejected their offer. Even though they worshipped Jehovah, they did not do so with the exclusivity demanded by the Torah (Exod. 20:3). Zerubbabel realized that giving "outsiders" a role in financing and rebuilding the temple would give them a share in controlling it, something which would inevitably lead to conflict and syncretism. The "people of the land" then resisted the community's attempt to rebuild the temple by bribing officials to work against them. They managed to frustrate any attempt at reconstruction for the next 15 years, to the great discouragement of the newly-returned exiles.

Many years later a priest named Ezra, a prolific writer, wrote a history of this era. One of his purposes was to answer the doubts many post-exilic Jews had about genuine political and religious restoration. He sought to assure the community of returnees that God had a future for them, but that they had to rebuild the temple and re-establish the priesthood. He also underscored their identity as the continuation of Jehovah's unique covenant people by listing their genealogies back into the pre-exilic era.

▪ 178 ▪ Daniel's Final Vision

Daniel 10-12   *Date: 536 B.C.*

THREE YEARS after Cyrus became king of Persia and a year after the first wave of Jewish returnees had returned to their homeland, Daniel had a vision in Babylon. He was now close to 90 years old and retired from public service. As he was praying by the banks of the Tigris River he saw an imposing individual, dressed in the whitest linen, wearing a belt of fine gold. His body had the appearance of chrysolite, his face looked like lightening, and his arms and legs were like polished bronze. Daniel's companions fled in terror and he was left alone gazing at this awe-inspiring person. He felt weak and fell to the ground.

"Daniel, you are highly esteemed," a voice said. "Stand up and listen carefully." Trembling, Daniel got on his feet. "Do not fear. From the day you humbled yourself before God and sought understanding your petition was heard. I was resisted for a period but have now come to explain what will happen to your people in the future."

"I am overcome with anguish, my Lord," old Daniel stammered. "My strength is gone and I can hardly breathe..." The heavenly being touched him and spoke of a successful warfare in the angelic world to encourage Daniel, in light of the disturbing things he was about to learn about the future of his fellow Jews.

The vision covered two phases: the period of time prior to the Messiah's first coming (11:2-35) and the period of time prior to His second coming (11:36-12:4). The angel told Daniel that three more Persian kings would follow after Cyrus and then a fourth king, far wealthier than his predecessors, would "stir up everyone against the kingdom of Greece". This proved to be Ahasuerus, called Xerxes I by the Greeks, who marshalled an enormous military might against Greece but was defeated at the naval battle of Salamis in 480 B.C.

Next the angel spoke about a mighty Greek king whose empire would be broken into four and parcelled out among those not of his own descendants. This, of course, was Alexander the Great, who finally overthrew the Persian Empire. When Alexander died prematurely in 323 B.C. his empire was divided among his four chief generals (see also Daniel 7:6; 8:8, 22).

The angel then focused at length on two of these generals because their kingdoms, Syria and Egypt, bordered Israel to the north and south. Secular history saw the exact outworking of all the details of what the angel told Daniel in the reigns of Seleucus I Nicator (312-281 B.C.) and Ptolemy I Soter (324-285) and their heirs. In sharing all these details the angel was painting the background to the main thrust of his message, namely the devastation to which the Jewish people would be subjected under Antiochus Epiphanes (r. 175-164 B.C.).

This loathsome individual was, from a secular perspective, a minor player but the angel gave more information about him than he did about all of the previous rulers combined. He was the "little horn" in one of Daniel's earlier visions (ch. 8) and became a "type", or model, of the Antichrist described in the book of Revelation. He initiated a terrible persecution of the Jewish people. Determined to extirpate Judaism and Hellenize the Jews, he plundered the temple in Jerusalem, forbade the Jews from "keeping the holy covenant" (i.e. the Law of Moses), burned copies of the Torah, abolished the festivals, the sacrificial system and circumcision, ordered an attack on the religious element of the population on the Sabbath day and enslaved many people (1 Macc. 1:44-54). He even installed an image of the Greek idol Zeus in the temple and on December 16, 168 B.C., had a pig—an unclean animal—offered on the altar. The Jews called this outrage "the abomination that causes desolation".

The prophecies contained in Daniel's final vision were fulfilled with such startling exactness (there are about 135 prophecies in Daniel 11, all of which were fulfilled) that many liberal scholars believe that the book must have been written after the events they describe. However, Jesus Christ stated explicitly that Daniel was, indeed, the author of these verses (Matt. 24:15; Mark 13:14).

Half-way through Daniel's final vision the events described jumped from the time of Antiochus Epiphanes to a description of the Antichrist who will arise towards the end of history: "There will be a time of much distress such as has not taken place since the formation of nations". Centuries later the Lord Jesus Christ would call this period "the Great Tribulation" (Mat. 24:21). This Antichrist will "do as he pleases" and "exalt himself above every other god". The situation for the Jewish community will be desperate but there is hope for the true believers. The angel told Daniel, "Your people—everyone whose name is written in the book of life—will be delivered." The angel spoke of a physical resurrection when those who believe and seek to live according to God's will in this life will receive their eternal reward, while those who do not will be judged, shamed and suffer eternal loss.

After this Daniel was instructed to "close up and seal" the words of this revelation until the time of the end. Before doing so however, another heavenly being appeared asking the question, "How long will it be before these amazing things are fulfilled?" Times were given in cryptic fashion, but just as surely as the first half of the vision has been fulfilled in astonishing detail so will the second half. The mystery of the dates would be revealed when the events actually come to pass.

Finally the heavenly messenger dismissed old Daniel with the promise that although he would die, he would be raised from the dead at the end of time and be richly rewarded by the Lord for his faithful service.

MEANWHILE, IN JERUSALEM the remnant community of returned exiles continued to face opposition from the surrounding people with respect to rebuilding the temple. The foundations had been laid back in 536 B.C. but later the people became discouraged and apathetic with respect to the project. Then, 15 years later, a new king, Darius I, ascended the throne of Persia. The following year the Lord raised up two new prophets, Haggai and Zechariah, to challenge the people to resume work on the temple.

Haggai delivered several short, sharply focussed messages over a period of about four months to the Jewish governor Zerubbabel, to Joshua the high priest, and to the people as a whole. He confronted them with the fact that their priorities were wrong: they were busy aggrandizing their own houses while failing to complete the temple of God. The latter was needed to enable them to return to the system of Levitical worship. He pointed out that the reason they were barely meeting their basic needs although they worked hard was because the Lord had withdrawn His blessing from them. "Carefully consider your ways," Haggai challenged them. "Go fetch timber from the mountains and build the temple so that the Lord will be honored and take pleasure in you!" The people feared the words of the prophet and were stirred to action.

About a month after the work had recommenced, Haggai delivered a word of encouragement from the Lord. "Does this building not seem like nothing compared to Solomon's glorious structure?" the Lord asked rhetorically. "But be strong, Zerubbabel, Joshua and all of you. Work for I am with you!" God reminded them of His covenant with them after they came out of Egypt, and then made a most remarkable prediction: "The Lord will once again shake the heavens and the earth. The desired of all nations will come and fill this temple with a glory even greater than that of Solomon's temple! In this place God will grant peace!" This prophecy was partly fulfilled when the promised Messiah, Jesus Christ, ministered in the place they were building, and will be fully evident when He returns in all His glory for a second time. This oracle must have greatly encouraged the people: although their resources were limited God was pleased with their efforts and would bless them in ways they could not begin to imagine.

Two months later Haggai received another message from the Lord. Because their priorities had been wrong everything else they tried to accomplish had gone wrong as well. Their harvests were only a fraction of what they had been because God had sent heat, drought, mildew and hail to keep them impoverished. However, now that they had restarted work on the temple they would immediately see the Lord's blessing on their lives again.

On the day he received this message of blessing, Haggai also received an oracle specifically for their governor Zerubbabel. In this remarkable prophecy the Lord said that He would shake the heavens and the earth, and would overthrow the rulers of the nations. Zerubbabel would become the Lord's chosen servant and He would make him like His divine signet ring. Decades earlier God had told Jeremiah that he had taken His signet ring, a symbol of ownership and authority, from Zerubbabel's grandfather king Jehoiachin and given it to Nebuchadnezzar (Jer. 22:24-25). Now, however, the grandson is given the promise that the curse would be undone: the status that God had awarded to the line of David was returned to it. God assured the struggling remnant community of returnees that He had great plans for them, for the temple they were building, and for the Davidic dynasty. He had not written them off and His covenant was still in force.

▪ 180 ▪ Zechariah Has Eight Visions In One Night

Zechariah chapter 1-6   *Date: 24th day of the 11th month of 520 B.C.*

TWO MONTHS after Haggai commenced his ministry God also called the returned Jewish community to repentance through the words of the young prophet Zechariah: "Return to me and I will return to you! Don't be like your forefathers who ignored the prophets' call to repentance. Look at what happened to them! Everything I decreed about them has come to pass!" In response to this message the people underwent a heart-felt repentance in which they recognized that they had indeed deserved God's punishment. When the people heeded the call to repentance Zechariah's message changed. He began to encourage them with prophecies about the promised Messiah who would overthrow the forces of ungodliness to establish His kingdom.

On the night of the 24th of the 11th month of the year 520 B.C. Zechariah received from the Lord a series of eight visions. In his first vision Zechariah saw a man riding a red horse in a ravine of myrtle trees. Myrtle trees were symbols of God's blessing (Isa. 55:13). Other riders who were investigating the state of the earth followed the horseman. These heavenly scouts reported that the world was at rest. The Persian Empire under Darius I was indeed at peace at this time. When an angel asked how much longer He would withhold His mercy from Judah, the Lord responded with kind, comforting words. "I am very jealous for Jerusalem but very angry with the nations that feel secure." These Gentile nations had added to the calamity that had befallen Israel. The restoration community, however, would successfully rebuild the temple, and the Lord would comfort and bless Judah's towns.

In the second vision the prophet saw four horns representing the gentile powers that had caused Israel to be scattered. Then he saw four smiths who would exact retribution from the nations that had caused Israel's suffering. This was in accordance with the Abrahamic covenant (Gen. 12:3).

In his third vision Zechariah saw a man with a measuring line measuring the width and length of Jerusalem. Another angel predicted that one day Jerusalem would be a vast metropolis without walls because of the great number of its residents, and that the Lord Himself would be its protection and glory. Rebuilt Jerusalem in Zechariah's day would be but a pale indication of what the city will be like when the Messiah eventually takes up residence there (Isa. 60; Ezek. 48:35). In response to this vision the prophet called on the Jews still in Babylon to escape from it and help with the rebuilding of Israel. The Lord Almighty would punish Babylon because of what it had done to Israel, "the apple of God's eye" (Deut. 32:10). This came to pass in 275 B.C. when the last of Babylon's inhabitants was exiled and its once famed ruins succumbed to the desert sands.

Then Zechariah encouraged the community in Jerusalem to rejoice at the prospect of the Lord coming to live among them. When He does "many nations will be joined with the Lord and become His people." Isaiah, Joel and Amos had made similar prophecies.

In the fourth vision Zechariah saw the high priest, Joshua, dressed in filthy clothes, representing Israel's unclean state. The clothes were removed, and when Joshua was dressed in rich, clean garments a voice proclaimed, "See, I have taken away your sin". Joshua was also given a turban, so completing the full vestments of the high priest. In God's sight Israel was now restored as a priestly nation (Ex. 19:6; Isa. 61:6). Then an angel declared, "I will bring my servant the Branch", referring again to the long-promised Messiah. "He will remove the sin of this land in a single day." Zechariah prophesied, "At that time each of you will invite your neighbour to sit under your vine and fig tree." This will happen when Jesus Christ comes again in power and glory to judge the nations and bring righteousness to the land. At that time Israel will invite its neighbours (i.e. the gentiles) to enjoy with them the peace and prosperity which the Messiah will bring. The curse of sin will be fully undone and the Messiah will win back the paradise that Adam lost.

In the fifth vision Zechariah saw a solid gold, menorah-like lampstand fed by seven pipes channeling oil to it directly from two olive trees. The covenant community, created to be a light to the nations, would be sustained not by human effort but by the supernatural provision of God's Spirit flowing through the human channels of Zerubbabel and Joshua. The work of the Lord, including the rebuilding of the temple, would be done "not by might, nor by power but by the Spirit of the Lord". The Lord promised that just as Zerubbabel had laid the temple's foundation stone, so he would also lay its capstone to shouts of "God bless it, God bless it!" The great mountain of rubble and other obstacles would be cleared, and though their temple might seem small and insignificant compared to its predecessor, they were "not to despise the day of small things".

Zechariah's sixth vision was of an unrolled scroll about 30 feet long and 15 feet wide flying through the air. On it were written some of curses from the Torah. Although the banner focused on the consequences of stealing and bearing false witness, it represented the entirety of the law. Its underlying message was that the Mosaic Covenant was still in effect—even in the privacy of the people's own homes! Just as obedience would be rewarded, disobedience would be punished.

In vision number seven Zechariah saw a measuring basket with a heavy lid of lead. Inside was a woman who symbolized Israel's sin. Two other women with the wings of a stork picked it up and, assisted by the wind, carried it away to Babylon. In other words, one day faithful or kind servants of the Lord, assisted by His Spirit, would purge Israel of Babylonian-like idolatry and wickedness.

Zechariah's last vision, like the first, concerned horses. Pairs of red, black, white, and dappled steeds were eagerly pulling four chariots from between two bronze mountains. The horses' colours represented different types of judgement (Rev. 6:1-8; 19:11, 14). The horses themselves symbolized the four winds (or spirits) of heaven going out in all directions to execute the will of the Lord. The northbound horses had given the Spirit rest in the land of the North. Israel, bounded in the east and south by desert and on the west by the Mediterranean Sea, was almost invariably attacked from the north. The vision communicated that one day Israel would no longer be under threat. This too was a prophecy that will be fulfilled when the Messiah, Jesus Christ, comes again.

· · · · ·

After that memorable night Zechariah was told to receive silver and gold from some recently returned exiles from Babylon, make a crown and place it on Joshua's head. This coronation of Israel's high priest symbolized the eventual sovereignty of Israel's Messiah, Jesus Christ. The name "Jesus" is the Greek version of "Joshua". He will rule as both king and priest (see Isa. 2:2-4; 56:6-7; Ezek. 40—43; Mic. 4:1-7; Hag. 2:6-9).

Zechariah then declared that henceforth Joshua would be known as "the Branch". The metaphor of the "branch" was a known prophetic designation for the expected Messiah as a son of David. (Isa. 53:2; Mic. 5:2). The prospect of a son of David ruling as priest and king in a rebuilt temple in Jerusalem and inaugurating an era of peace and tranquillity was the consummation of all Old Testament prophetic utterances. After this symbolic coronation ceremony, the crown was to be kept in the temple upon its completion, as a memorial of God's promises to the remnant community.

▪ 181 ▪ Zechariah's Four Oracles About Ritualism

Zechariah chapters 7 & 8   *Date: 518 B.C.*

Two years after his night of visions the word of the Lord came again to Zechariah. Representatives had come to Jerusalem from the town of Bethel, once a center of apostate worship in the Northern Kingdom. For the duration of the exile the people of this town had mourned and fasted every fifth and seventh month. Now they wondered if they should continue this tradition.

Although this seemed like a perfectly reasonable question it appears that the Bethelites were using this tradition to establish their spiritual credentials. So, instead of answering their question directly, the prophet used the occasion to probe the essence of the nation's spiritual life. The Lord, through His prophet, responded with a question. "During those seventy years were they actually fasting for Him or for themselves?" If rituals were not accompanied with a repentant heart, confession and obedience, they were nothing but lifeless, useless activities. Then the Lord reminded Zechariah of His words to earlier prophets when pre-exilic Jerusalem was prosperous. He had warned them to administer justice and show mercy, particularly to the weak, the aliens, and the poor. But Israel had stubbornly paid them no heed. "When I called them they refused to listen, so when they called on me I refused to listen." He had ended up scattering them among the nations as if a whirlwind had blown them in all directions and left the "pleasant land" desolate.

Then the Lord reminded Zechariah again that He was "burning with jealousy" for His people. He promised to return and live with them in Jerusalem. He would bring His people back to the Promised Land from the four corners of the earth and the land would enjoy a glorious era of security and prosperity. One day the cycle of apostasy and punishment would come to an end.

Hard as it might be for the remnant community to imagine this wonderful prospect, its realization was but a small thing for the Lord. The Lord told the people to draw strength from the words of previous prophets, such as Haggai, who had encouraged them to rebuild the temple. "So let your hands be strong!" the Lord exhorted them. "Just as I purposed to bring disaster on your forefathers for their disobedience I am now determined to do good to you."

He then reminded them of four things He hated: lying, injustice in the courts, planning evil against one another, and committing perjury. Just as surely as covenant disobedience had brought covenant curses now renewed obedience would lead to divine blessing.

Then the Lord Almighty spoke through Zechariah again on the subject of fasting. One day celebration and festivals would replace fasting, He promised. In fact, Jerusalem would become the center of divine blessing for the whole earth! The inhabitants of the world's great cities would travel to it with eagerness to entreat the Lord residing there, and Jewish guides would lead groups of gentiles into the presence of the Lord. God's ancient promise to Abraham that all peoples of the earth would be blessed through his descendants (Gen. 12:3) would be fully realized. This will happen when Christ inaugurates his kingdom.

▪ 182 ▪ The Second Temple Completed

Ezra 5   *Date: circa 520-515 B.C.*

THE COMMUNITY of returnees had responded positively to the ministry of the prophets Haggai and Zechariah and resumed rebuilding the temple. No sooner had they set to work, however, when Tattenai, the provincial governor, asked to see their building permit. In the fifth century B.C. a number of rebellions convulsed the Persian Empire, and Zechariah's messianic prophecy about a descendant of David who would sit on the throne of Israel may have led him to believe that the Jews were planning to crown Zerubbabel king (Zech. 3:8; 6:9-15). While allowing work on the temple to continue, he inquired from king Darius if the late king Cyrus really had issued an edict granting permission to the Jews to rebuild their temple. A search of the archives revealed that the project had, indeed been approved, and Darius instructed Tattenai not to interfere with the project but to facilitate it. The remaining work as well as the subsequent ongoing costs of the sacrifices would be paid in full out of the provincial treasury. The king even threatened to impale those who resisted the project. A polytheist, the king wanted to be in good standing with every god worshipped in his empire.

With this kind of royal backing the temple was completed in 515 B.C, about 21 years after its foundations were laid. The dedication ceremony was a joyful occasion with extensive offerings, including twelve rams, one for each of the tribes of Israel. Priests were installed and duties allocated to the Levites, all in accordance with the original instructions given to Moses many centuries before. Five weeks after the dedication ceremony the community joyfully celebrated Passover and the Feast of Unleavened Bread. Temple worship in Jerusalem had been restored and the people of Israel had renewed their identity as God's chosen people.

▪ 183 ▪ Esther Crowned Queen of Persia

Esther 1-3   *Date: 482-473 B.C.*

KING DARIUS was succeeded by the Persian king Ahasuerus, also called Xerxes. His royal throne was in the citadel of Susa. Round about 482 B.C. he organized an important and lenghty conference for all his nobles, officials and military leaders. It ended with a weeklong banquet in which wine was served in abundance in the royal palace's elaborately decorated garden. At the same time Queen Vashti organized her own banquet for the women of the royal palace.

On the last day the king, drunk, ordered his eunuchs to fetch Vashti and parade her before the people so all could admire her beauty. Vashti flatly refused to degrade herself. Snubbed and furious, king Xerxes called in his advisors. They suggested he make an object lesson of her in order that her "insolence", instead of emboldening women, would remind them of their place in society. A royal decree deposing Vashti was promptly issued.

Even if the king regretted deposing Vashti when he was sober, reinstating her was out of the question: the decrees of the Medo-Persians could not be repealed. The king's attendants persuaded him to commission an empire-wide search for beautiful young virgins, one of whom he could select to be his next wife.

One of these girls was a lovely Jewish orphan called Hadassah. Her Persian name was Esther, meaning, "star". Her older cousin Mordecai, whose ancestors had been taken to Babylon by Nebuchadnezzar, had raised Esther. When the first group of exiles had returned to Jerusalem Mordecai's family had chosen to stay where they were. Many Jewish exiles had established prosperous businesses and lived comfortably as a distinct, cohesive community centered on the synagogue.

Before Esther moved into the royal harem, Mordecai cautioned her not to reveal her nationality or family background. He himself "sat at the king's gate", possible in some employment at the royal court. Esther's natural beauty and charm soon won over the eunuch in charge of the harem, who gave her preferential treatment. After the preparatory year of beauty treatments she was presented to the king, who was immediately smitten and chose her above the other contestants. Esther was crowned queen in place of Vashti with great pomp and ceremony. All the while Mordecai continued advising Esther, though he was careful to keep his connection with the queen from becoming public knowledge.

One day Mordecai overheard two disgruntled army officers plotting to assassinate the king. He quickly informed Esther, who told her husband. The culprits were apprehended and subsequently impaled, ancient Persia's normal punishment for heinous crimes. The event, including the detail that Mordecai had uncovered the plot, was duly recorded in the royal archives.

About four years after Esther's coronation a loathsome individual named Haman managed to ingratiate himself with the king. Haman was an Agagite; Agag was the Amalekite king whom Samuel had killed centuries earlier (1 Sam. 15:32-33). Haman was promoted to the highest honor and the king ordered the royal officials to bow to him whenever he passed by. Mordecai, however, could not bring himself to bow to a man who represented a people with whom God was at war (Ex. 17:14-16; Deut. 25:19).

Word of the stubborn Jew soon reached the vain Haman. Scorning the idea of merely taking revenge on Mordecai alone, he devised a diabolical plan to exterminate all Jews throughout the empire. First of all he cast lots to determine the most propitious day for the genocide. The lot fell on the 13th day of the last month of the year. That was 11 months hence. Next Haman informed the king that there was a people scattered across the empire whose customs differed from all others and who refused to obey the law. "It is not in the king's best interests to tolerate them," he advised. He did not identify the Jews by name for he must have known that previous Persian monarchs had issued decrees in their favour (Ezra 1:1-4; 6:3-5, 8-12). Giving his signet ring to Haman, Xerxes told him to write the necessary legislation and seal it on his behalf. Decrees were quickly dispatched to the far reaches of the empire with the order to annihilate every single Jew, young or old, on the selected day. While the king and Haman sat down for a drink, the city of Susa was reeling in shock and consternation.

▪ 184 ▪ The Tables are Turned

Esther 4-10   *Date: 482-473 B.C.*

THE JEWISH community was stunned by the utterly unexpected calamity that had struck them. Mordechai tore his clothes, put on sackcloth and ashes and wept and wailed as he headed for the king's gate. When Esther heard that Mordecai was sitting outside in great distress she ordered a trusted eunuch to find out what the problem was. Mordecai explained exactly what had happened, gave the man a copy of the edict, and told him to urge Esther to appeal to the king on behalf of her people.

Esther told the eunuch to remind Mordecai that anyone who walked into the king's presence uninvited risked instant death unless the monarch extended his scepter towards him or her—and he had not invited her in for a month.

"Do not think, Esther, that you personally will survive because you are in the royal palace," Mordecai responded. "If you do nothing now deliverance will come from elsewhere while you and your family perish." He was convinced that divine providence would prevail on behalf of God's covenant people. "Who knows," he challenged the girl he had raised, "but that it is for such a time as this that you were lifted to your royal position!"

"Gather all the Jews in Susa and fast for me for three days and nights," Esther replied. "My maids and I will do the same. After that I will enter the king's presence, even though that is against the law. If I perish, I perish…"

On the third day Esther donned her royal robes and dared to enter the king's throne room. When the king saw her he was pleased to see her and extended his scepter. "What can I do for you, Queen Esther?" Xerxes asked. "Ask of me anything you want. I will give you up to half my kingdom," he added in typical Middle Eastern hyperbole. He quickly granted her simple request that he and Haman come that day to her banquet. As they were drinking wine after the meal Esther extended the same invitation for the next day.

After the banquet Haman went home in high spirits, boasting to his family and friends about his vast wealth, his many sons, and his exalted status in the royal palace. "Furthermore, I'm the only person queen Esther invited to a banquet she gave in honor of the king, and I'm invited again tomorrow. But," he raged, "none of this gives me any pleasure as long as that Jew Mordecai is sitting at the King's Gate!" Mordecai had consistently refused to bow when Haman passed by.

"Build a 75 foot stake," Haman's wife and friends suggested, "and obtain permission to impale Mordecai on it first thing in the morning. Then go and enjoy your dinner engagement." The plan delighted Haman and he had the stake erected right away.

That night the king, suffering from insomnia, ordered someone to read to him from the latest volume of the royal archives. Towards morning they reached the entry about Mordecai exposing the conspiracy to assassinate him, but there was no record of him having been rewarded. Just then Haman arrived, and the king asked him, "What should be done to the man whom the king wants to honor?"

Convinced that king had him in mind, Haman let his imagination run wild. "Let him be dressed in one of the king's robes, seated on one of the king's horses, and lead through the streets by one of the king's princes declaring, 'This is what is done to the man whom the king seeks to honor.'" Haman was already relishing the glory.

"Go immediately and do exactly what you recommend to Mordecai the Jew," the king ordered. Haman was shocked and mortified, but had no choice but to obey. Deeply humiliated he paraded the honored Mordecai through the city streets. Then he rushed home in shame.

"Mordecai is a Jew. You cannot stand against him and you will certainly come to ruin," his friends asserted somberly, discerning rightly that an invisible force stood with the Jewish people. Just then the king's eunuchs arrived to whisk the wretched Haman off to the queen's second banquet.

Once again the king asked Esther to voice her request. "If I have found favor with you, my lord," Esther responded, "I ask that you spare my life and that of my people, for we are destined to be slaughtered."

The king was astounded. "Who would dare do such a thing?" he demanded.

"The enemy is this vile Haman," Esther answered, pointing to the man. Enraged, the king got up and stepped into the palace garden, leaving the terrified Haman to plead for his life. He fell on the couch on which Esther was reclining just as the king abruptly re-entered the room.

"Will this man even molest the queen in my own house?" he roared. The words were no sooner uttered than one the king's attendants pulled a bag over Haman's head, indicating he was condemned. A eunuch spoke up, "Haman had a 75 foot stake erected at his house on which he'd planned to impale Mordecai."

"Impale him on it instead," the king ordered. The deed was done, and fortunes were reversed. King Xerxes promoted Mordecai to the position of Haman, the great hater of the Jews. Although Haman was gone the Jews were not yet secure because the terrible edict still stood. And so, once again, Esther entered the throne room uninvited to intercede on behalf of her people.

The king could not repeal the original decree. Instead he authorized Mordecai to draw up new legislation and seal it with the royal signet ring that was reclaimed from Haman. Couriers rode quickly throughout the empire authorizing the Jews to assemble and defend themselves against anyone who dared to attack them on the prescribed day.

When news of the new decree broke, there was celebration and feasting among the Jewish community. Many people of other nationalities even became Jews, identifying themselves with Israel's God. Because Mordecai was now second in rank to King Xerxes local officials did what they could to help the Jews prepare for the possible onslaught eight months hence. On that fateful day the Jews quickly got the upper hand over those who sought to exploit the previous decree. There were not many. Some 800 men were killed in Susa and about 75,000 across the rest of the empire. Haman's 10 sons were publicly impaled to dissuade anyone else from messing with God's covenant people. The Jews renounced their right to plunder, a fact that did not go unnoticed in a culture where the spoils went to the victor.

Some time later the Jews established the annual feast of Purim, named after the Persian word "pur", referring to the lot that Haman had cast to determine the day on which they were to be annihilated. That day when sorrow was turned into joy was to be remembered forever.

Zechariah 9-14

THE PROPHET ZECHARIAH'S final set of oracles were not tied to any event in his own life, and appear to have been uttered long after the temple in Jerusalem had been completed. Like the pieces of a jigsaw puzzle, the seemingly disparate prophecies only make sense when matched with the big picture—the person of Jesus Christ. Almost all of them were fulfilled either at Christ's first coming or will take place when He comes again.

The first of these oracles was a message of judgment against the major cities of Israel's historic enemies. Zechariah then uttered one of the great messianic visions of the Old Testament: "Behold your king coming to you riding on a donkey, O daughter of Jerusalem. He is gentle, righteous, and brings salvation to all." All four of the gospel writers later attested that this prophecy was fulfilled during Christ's triumphal entry into Jerusalem (Matt. 25:5; Mark 11:1-10; Luke 29:28-38; John 12:12-15). Zechariah saw both aspects of the coming Messiah: the lowly humility of Christ's first coming, when He brought salvation to mankind and, later, the ultimate victory of His second coming when He will restore His people and defeat all who refuse to bow the knee to Him. Like the other prophets he could not separate the events of the two comings, failing to grasp that there would be an era for the gentiles between the two appearances.

The next part of Zechariah's oracle was about the Lord's care for Israel. The Lord would punish the "shepherds" (Israel's leaders) who had led the people astray, and would personally take over the nation's leadership. In a sweeping messianic prophecy he described Israel's coming Redeemer-King as "the cornerstone", "a tent peg" who holds everything in place, and as "a battle bow". Because the Lord will be with Israel the nation will overcome all who resist it. Even though they would once again be scattered among the peoples of the earth, they would remember Him in their exile, after which they would again be restored to the Promised Land.

Next Zechariah's focus shifted to Israel's great future sin and its subsequent punishment. They would so detest the good shepherd whom the Lord would provide for them that they would pay thirty pieces of silver to be rid of him. This money would be thrown to the potter in the house of the Lord. At this the good shepherd would revoke his covenant of graciousness and union with them and leave them at the mercy of oppressors. This prophecy was fulfilled when the Jewish leaders paid thirty pieces of silver to Judas Iscariot to betray Jesus Christ. Judas returned the money, "throwing it into the house of the Lord", and the Jewish leaders used it to buy "the potter's field". After Israel rejected its Messiah, God did indeed let foreign nations punish them. The Romans destroyed Jerusalem in 70 A.D. and scattered its people.

Next Zechariah acted the part of a useless shepherd exploiting sheep that had rejected the good shepherd. The ultimate fulfillment of this prophetic enactment will be the Antichrist making a covenant with Israel during the Great Tribulation, then breaking it and persecuting them instead (Dan. 9:27).

Zechariah's last set of oracles described several events pertaining to the period of the Great Tribulation just prior to Christ's second coming, notably the final siege of Jerusalem, Israel's conversion, and the establishment of the Messiah's kingdom. Using very striking language he described how "all the nations of the earth" will gather against Jerusalem but not prevail against her. He then described Israel's future national repentance and spiritual renewal. One day the Lord would pour out His Spirit of grace and supplication on them, and "they will look on the one they have pierced and mourn for him as one would grieve for an only child". The apostle John, referencing this passage, stated that the Jews would mourn about the crucified Christ at His second coming (Rev. 1:7). Through Zechariah God promised to respond to Israel's national repentance by opening up a fountain that would purify them of all vestiges of idolatry, false prophecy and unclean spirits. The fount, which cleans sinners of all their sins, is the atoning blood of Christ (1 John 1:7).

Zechariah followed this up with a short poem in which he described how the Lord's shepherd would be struck and the sheep scattered. Centuries later the Lord Jesus, claiming to be Zechariah's good shepherd, quoted this passage when he told his disciples they would be scattered after his death (Matt. 26:31, 56; Mark 14:27, 50).

In his final oracle Zechariah again described how all nations would gather against Jerusalem and capture, plunder and rape it. When all seems lost, however, Jehovah will intervene and fight on behalf of his people. Cosmic phenomena will attend this Day of the Lord and a sudden plague and great panic will devastate the armies that will wage war against Jerusalem.

The prophet then saw the water of life flowing from the city of Jerusalem and the people living in security. During that wonderful Messianic era the distinction between secular and sacred would cease to exist as even the most common objects will be dedicated to God's glory and honor. The Canaanites, the people who symbolized moral and spiritual abasement more than any other, would be no more; everyone in the land would worship and serve Israel's Messiah King!

▪ 186 ▪ The Second Return Under Ezra

Ezra 7-10   *Date: 458 B.C.*

THE GREAT PERSIAN King Darius had reorganized his domain into 20 provinces and led the empire to the height of its glory. In 486 B.C. he was succeeded by his son Ahasuerus (Xerxes), who married Esther. He is best known for losing the naval Battle of Salamis to the Greeks. After his assassination in 464 B.C. his younger son Artaxerxes I ascended to the throne. Under him the empire continued to decline. Restive indigenous peoples sought to shake the Persian yoke; the Greeks took Cyprus, the Babylonians and Egyptians rebelled, and parts of Asia Minor broke away altogether. The restoration community in Jerusalem, however, remained faithful to the central government.

Almost 60 years had passed since the inauguration of the temple. Although the people eschewed idol worship and attended the temple, formalism had made inroads. The teaching of the law was neglected and the people's zeal for God had begun to wane.

During the 7th year of reign of Artaxerxes I, Ezra, a highly respected, well-educated teacher from a priestly family convinced the king to issue another decree allowing a second cohort of Jews to return to Judah. Persia had just lost Memphis to the Greeks, leaving the eastern Mediterranean seaboard exposed to Greek raiders. Artaxerxes, keen to strengthen the pro-Persian presence in the region, authorized Ezra to re-establish religious, judicial and educational facilities in Judah. He even contributed a large amount of silver and gold to the cause. Though fully aware of the international developments motivating the king, Ezra recognized that behind the scenes Jehovah God was at work on behalf of His people. "Praise be to the Lord, the God of our fathers," he worshiped, "who has put it into the king's heart to honor the house of the Lord in Jerusalem..."

In the spring of 458 B.C. those interested in returning "home", numbering between four and five thousand people, assembled on the banks of the Ahava canal in Babylon. Under Ezra's leadership the group humbled itself before Jehovah and implored Him for help and protection for the long and dangerous journey ahead of them. They carried some 22 tons of silver and 3.4 tons of gold bullion among them, much of it donated by wealthy Jews living in Babylon. Ezra had it carefully weighed and distributed among trustworthy men, but was ashamed to ask the king for an armed escort because he had told the king, "the gracious hand of our God is on all who look to Him, but His anger is against all who forsake Him." Ezra's trust in God was not misplaced. After a journey of over 700 miles lasting nearly four months the caravan arrived safe and sound in Jerusalem.

There must have been joyous reunions of long-separated family members and friends. Sin offerings were burnt and the king's orders were handed over to the local governors, who promised their assistance to the community and the temple.

Not long after Ezra and his cohort of new immigrants had arrived, however, they were confronted with the reality of the earlier returnees' religious formalism. Some of them had even intermarried with women of the surrounding peoples, a serious compromise forbidden by the Law of Moses. This, after all, was one of the very things that had led Israel into idol worship and subsequent exile in the first place! (Ex. 34:11-16; Deut. 7:1-5) Ezra was appalled. He tore his clothes, pulled out his hair and sat in moral indignation until the evening sacrifice. Then he fell on his knees, lifted his hands up to Jehovah God, and prayed. Though personally innocent he chose to identify with the people: "Our sins have reached higher than our heads and our guilt reaches up to heaven", he confessed. "Our nation deserved all the misfortunes which befell it. But you, Lord, showed us grace for a moment. You left us a remnant and gave us a temple that lights up our eyes and gives relief to our bondage. You have not deserted us. You have shown us kindness and granted us favour in the sight of the king of Persia. But what can we say now? Once again we are polluting ourselves with the corruption of the original inhabitants by intermarrying with them, disregarding the commands you gave to us through the prophets. If we again break your commands would you not be fully justified in destroying what remains of us? Here we stand before you in our guilt... None of us can stand in your presence..."

While Ezra wept and prostrated himself in front of the temple, a large crowd of people gathered around him. They too began to weep bitterly as they started to realize the seriousness of their sin. Then a man stepped forward and suggested to Ezra that the community make a vow to send back to their homelands the foreign, idolatrous wives and any children of these unions. Such drastic measures were the only way in which the community could maintain its distinct identity as Jehovah's covenant people. God had made his covenants with their ancestors and called them to be separate from the surrounding polytheistic world. How could He achieve his salvific purposes for the world through His people if they were assimilated into it? Ezra rose from the ground and made the community promise on oath that they would carry through with this proposal. He then issued a solemn proclamation summoning the entire community to assemble in Jerusalem in three days' time.

On the day of the assembly that winter of 458 B.C. it poured with rain. With the water coursing down from heaven Ezra climbed the podium and berated the people for their unfaithfulness and urged them to separate themselves from their foreign wives. It took about three months to finalize the settlements for the 113 men who had married foreign women. The Israelites were once again a holy people, separated unto their God.

▪ 187 ▪ Nehemiah and the City Walls
Nehemiah 1-12   *Dates: 444 B.C.*

THE PERSIAN KING Artaxerxes I had backed Ezra and given the restoration community in Judah legal autonomy under the trusted teacher's leadership. Thirteen years later he supported another trustworthy Jew in his service named Nehemiah. He was the palace cupbearer who not only ensured the health of the king's wines but also wielded great influence due to his close access to the monarch.

Some men from Judah came to Susa for a visit. They reported to Nehemiah that while the temple had been rebuilt, Jerusalem's walls remained in ruins and its gates burned. This spelled trouble for a small community living on the fraying edge of an empire they had loyally backed. Political storm clouds were gathering and the city was left defenceless.

Nehemiah wept when he heard the news. Then he prayed and fasted, confessing Israel's disobedience to the Mosaic Law, but reminding the Lord of His covenant commitment to bring them back to the place He had chosen as a dwelling place for His name (Deut. 30:1-5). "We are your people whom you redeemed... Now grant me favour in king's eyes," he prayed as he asked God to bless his plan to petition the king about the matter. In the world's eyes Artaxerxes might be viewed as the highest authority on earth, but Nehemiah knew Jehovah God was the true sovereign and Lord of history.

One day Artaxerxes noticed that his cupbearer was uncharacteristically sad and asked what was bothering him. "May the king live forever," Nehemiah responded politely. "Why should I not be sad when the city where my forefathers lie buried is in ruins and its gates burned?"

"What would you like?" the king asked his faithful servant. Nehemiah sent a quick, silent prayer heavenward and then continued courageously, "If it please the king and if I have found favour in your sight then send me to Jerusalem to rebuild it." Nehemiah was asking for big things, for his was a big God.

Artaxerxes knew the merits of a strong fortress of loyal Jews in the increasingly unstable region. Sensing the king's approval, Nehemiah was emboldened and dared to ask for letters of safe conduct, permission to use timber from the royal forest, and a royal escort for the journey. The king agreed and not long afterwards Nehemiah was leading a delegation to Jerusalem charged with rebuilding the city's defences.

Soon after their arrival Nehemiah embarked on a secret, nighttime inspection of the city's perimeter to get an idea of the scale of the problem and formulate a strategy. Then he gathered the community's leaders and shared the reason for his return. The community responded enthusiastically and each family group set to work repairing their adjoining section of walls and gates.

When the surrounding peoples heard that Jerusalem's tiny population was once again trying to rebuild the city's walls they ridiculed and mocked their efforts. Nehemiah asked God to turn their enemy's insults back on their own heads, while also posting guards day and night to deal with any menace. The people, meanwhile, pulled out all stops and built the wall halfway up in record time. However, the population of Jerusalem became bone weary from the relentless work and the strain of constant threat. In spite of Nehemiah's inspirational leadership, their courage waned and their energy flagged. Nehemiah reassured them that their mighty God was with them. He also divided his work force into two groups. One fully armed group stood guard while the other continued building "with one hand, while they held a weapon in the other".

Then, as if he didn't have enough to worry about, Nehemiah encountered opposition within the community that threatened their unity. Wealthy Jews had loaned money to poor Jews whose fields, vineyards and homes they used as collateral. When these poorer Jews could not make the payments—partly as a result of heavy Persian taxation—they stood to lose their possessions. In some cases the wealthy even enslaved the children of destitute Jews in lieu of payment. Things had become so ugly that the surrounding people reproached their rapaciousness. When Nehemiah heard this he was outraged. He made the rich promise to return the poor people's possessions and cease charging interest on loans. He himself set the example by not claiming the taxes due to him as governor. Instead he personally provided for some 150 men who were working on the wall.

Once the internal dissent had been resolved the community again focused on the wall. Before long the gaps between the gates were filled in, though the gates had not yet been hung.

Then opposition resumed from the surrounding nations under the leadership of Sanballat, Geshem and Tobiah. The latter had marital ties within the restoration community but was a deceiver who kept sending intimidating letters to Nehemiah. Next Sanballat sent an open letter accusing Nehemiah of planning a revolt and having himself crowned king of the Jews. Nehemiah brusquely rejected their charge, and his fellow Jews did not doubt his integrity. Finally, a false prophet tried to discredit him by urging him to avoid a supposed assassination plot by hiding in the temple sanctuary. Nehemiah flatly rejected, knowing that under the Mosaic Covenant only priests were allowed to enter the sanctuary (Num. 1:51).

In spite of opposition from without and within, it took the community a mere 52 days to complete the walls. What joy, what relief, when the last gate was hung on its hinges! They were safer now than they had been since the destruction of the city by Nebuchadnezzar. Furthermore, they had demonstrated that together they could accomplish major achievements. They could hold their heads up high! A grand dedication service was in order!

Nehemiah recruited Levites from all over Judah to lead the celebration and worship. First they and the people purified themselves. Then two choirs, one walking clockwise and the other counter clockwise walked around the top of the wall singing to the accompaniment of cymbals, harps and lyres. When the two choirs met, they joined many officials and priests in the temple courtyard giving thanks and offering sacrifices to God. The joyful noise rising from the city could be heard far and near. People were so delighted with the ministry of the priests and Levites that they began supporting them financially, as had been the custom back in the days of David and Solomon.

Dismayed by this turn of events, Israel's enemies were forced to acknowledge that the people's accomplishments in the face of opposition could only have been achieved with divine help. They were a small, remnant community but behind them stood the powerful Jehovah God.

▪ 188 ▪ The Jewish Community Restored

Nehemiah 8-13   *Date: 444-432 B.C.*

REBUILDING THE wall was only the first stage of Nehemiah's over-all goal of seeing the Jews fully re-established in their Promised Land. The next thing on his agenda was to reinstate the full-orbed pattern of worship as spelled out in the Torah. He had a wooden podium built in the Public Square and invited Ezra, still active as the spiritual leader, to read the Mosaic Law out aloud to the people. The community's leaders stood with him, and everyone listened reverently as he opened the scroll and began to read. Then Levites explained what was read clearly to the people. Deeply moved many began to weep, but Nehemiah and the Levites urged them to rejoice in the Lord because of their new understanding of His words.

The next day the people again gathered around Ezra to continue their study of the Torah. When they got to Leviticus 23, which described how the Feast of Booths was to be celebrated, they determined to do so properly. There was a lively, happy bustle as families went into the countryside, collected branches, erected shelters on the flat roofs of their houses and celebrated the thanksgiving feast together. The community was growing in spiritual unity and social cohesion.

Later that month the people separated from all foreigners, regathered in Jerusalem to confess their sins, to listen to the Word of God and to worship. A genuine revival had broken out. Leading Levites exhorted the people to stand up and praise their everlasting God. Their lengthy prayer began by exalting God as the creator, and then remembered His gracious election and covenant with Abraham. It reviewed the miraculous exodus from Egypt and the giving of law at Mount Sinai. God had led, protected and provided for them in the desert. In spite of their recurring disobedience and rebellious spirit, He had enabled them to take possession of the land, blessed them richly and made them "as numerous as the stars in the sky". In contrast to His faithfulness to covenant promises they had continued in their disobedience and rebellion. They had "put Jehovah's law behind their backs", killed His prophets and committed appalling blasphemies so that, in the end, He handed them over to their enemies. Whenever they cried out to Him for help, however, He had responded with compassion and raised up leaders to deliver them from their enemies. But as soon as the land was at rest they had again done evil in God's sight. They had stubbornly refused to listen and finally He had sent them into exile.

The Levites acknowledged that God had been righteous, just, patient, gracious and merciful in His dealings with them. "But Lord," they concluded, "today we are like slaves in our own land. We are taxed so heavily that the abundant harvests You grant go to the kings who rule over us... We are in great distress..." Their ongoing bondage to the kings of Persia made it clear that the postexilic restoration had not ushered in the glorious future of which prophets like Isaiah and, more recently, Zechariah had spoken. Nevertheless they now wanted to affirm their renewed commitment to place the service and worship of God at the center of their national life. They even composed a charter that spelled out their commitment to obeying the Mosaic Law, not to intermarry with the surrounding people, to keep the Sabbath and the sabbatical year, to tithe, to give their first fruits to God, and to diligently maintain the temple.

Nehemiah's next goal was to repopulate the city that, with its fully functioning temple and brand new wall, had suddenly become a viable place in which to live. Some moved to the city voluntarily, while every family living in the countryside and surrounding towns volunteered to send one family member in ten to live in the city.

Now that all seemed to be in order, Nehemiah returned to King Artaxerxes in Babylon. It was 432 B.C. and he had been gone for 12 years.

Nehemiah's thoughts were with the people in Judah, and sometime later he received permission to revisit Jerusalem. On arriving he was shocked by the degeneration of the people's zeal for the things of God while he had been gone. First of all, he discovered that the high priest had converted one of the temple's storerooms into an apartment for his relative Tobiah, who had opposed the building of the walls. Nehemiah was furious to discover that an enemy of the restoration community was living in the temple, and quickly moved the man out.

Furthermore, things at the temple were in disarray because people had failed to honor their pledge to keep tithing. As a result the Levites who had served there had been forced to return to their villages to work the land.

People were also failing to observe the Sabbath, trading and selling on it as on a normal workday. Nehemiah forcefully reminded them of calamities the nation had brought upon itself in the past because it had failed to honor the Ten Commandments. He then proceeded to lock the city's gates on the Sabbath, keeping any traders bringing their goods to market locked outside the walls.

Next Nehemiah had to deal with the same problem Ezra had confronted: intermarriage with non-Jews. He dealt very harshly with these compromisers, purifying them of everything foreign. The small community had to maintain its religious and social purity at all costs if it was to continue as God's covenant people! Compromise was not an option if it was to survive as a distinct nation.

Building on the work of Zerubbabel and Ezra, and the prophets Haggai and Zechariah, Nehemiah led the post-exilic community through some of its most difficult times. When he finally returned to Persia, however, he left a community with the necessary infrastructure in place to resume full-orbed national and religious life. It was still a small, struggling remnant of monotheists in a sea of polytheism, but God had preserved them as He had promised at Sinai. They were still His chosen people and He was still their covenant-keeping God.

▪ 189 ▪ Malachi: God's Final Exhortations

Malachi   *Date: circa 445-420 B.C.*

The prophet Malachi ministered after the temple had been rebuilt and addressed the same issues that Nehemiah confronted. In spite of their firm monotheism and the earlier Ezra-led revivals, and in spite of the lofty visions of a glorious future portrayed by the prophets, Jerusalem remained an impoverished backwater struggling to survive on the crumbling edges of the declining Persian Empire. There was nothing glorious about their existence and people once again became apathetic and skeptical. It was during this dreary period that Malachi, like all the prophets before him, evaluated Israel's spiritual life by the Law of Moses. His messages were short, sharp, and specific, and made extensive use of questions and answers.

Before chiding the Jews for breaking the covenant, however, Malachi comforted the people by reminding them that the Lord loved them. "But how has the Lord loved us?" the people asked despondently. They saw little of God's love in their current situation.

The prophet reminded them that, at the beginning of their history, God had chosen to set his affections on Jacob and not on his older twin Esau. Esau's descendants the Edomites had had to settle in the wasteland of Seir while Israel, the descendants of Jacob, had received the land of milk and honey. The Edomites were objects of God's wrath, not of His covenant relationship. By observing how Jehovah had dealt with their "twin nation" the people of Israel could grasp something of God's unusual and undeserved love for them. In spite of appearances God had neither forgotten them nor His covenant promises to them!

Malachi's second message was leveled at Israel's priests. He rebuked them for dishonoring and showing contempt for God.

"How have we shown contempt for God?" the priests asked unctuously.

"By offering animals that are sick, crippled and diseased," Malachi retorted. "Try giving those animals to the governor and see what he would do," he said pointedly. It would be better to shut the temple doors altogether than offer second-rate animals to the Lord Almighty. Then, looking forward to the time when the Messiah will rule the nations, Malachi predicted: "A time is coming when the Lord will exalt His name among the nations, a time when incense and pure offerings will be offered to Him all day long!" Then he continued vehemently, "Curses on you swindling priests for accepting healthy animals and sacrificing sick ones in their place! How can you expect God to bless if you behave like that?"

God had made a covenant with their tribe of Levi, and down through the ages had blessed the priests who revered His name. But now they had strayed from the truth and caused others to stumble. Because they had despised the Lord, the Lord had caused them to be despised by the people.

Malachi began his next indictment in response to another question: "Are we not all the children of one Father? How do we profane the covenant of our fathers by breaking faith with each other?" God had brought the nation into being and as sons of Jehovah they were duty-bound to honor and obey Him and support each other. Instead, they were breaking faith with each other, and then they would bring their offerings to the temple where they would weep and wail because they were not experiencing God's blessing! Malachi plainly explained that they were unfaithful on two accounts. Not only had they married women who served foreign gods, but they had also divorced their own Jewish wives.

Next Malachi declared, "You are tiring the Lord with your words."

"How have we tired the Lord?" they asked.

"By suggesting that all who do evil are good in God's eyes! By questioning God's justice!" the prophet responded. Although they paid lip service to Jehovah their lifestyles reflected their cynicism and disillusionment. After all, the glorious future Zechariah had envisioned when they were building the temple decades earlier had not happened. They had come to believe that they could basically live as they pleased and it would not make any difference. Malachi told them that the Lord would indeed come suddenly to his temple as Ezekiel and Zechariah had also prophesied. "But who can stand on the day he comes?" Malachi cried out. "He will be like a refiner's fire, like a launderer's soap! He will purify the Levites (i.e. the priesthood) like one purifies gold and silver. At that time people will come before Him in righteousness of heart, as in the days of old, and offer Him acceptable sacrifices!"

God did care about the details of their lives and would come to judge those who were engaged in sorcery, adultery, false witnessing, defrauding laborers, oppressing widows and orphans and depriving foreigners of justice. It was only because the Lord does not change,

Malachi reminded them, that they had not been destroyed. Only because He remained faithful to His covenant promises that they, "the sons of Jacob" had not been annihilated: "From your inception you have failed to keep my decrees. Return to me and I will return to you, says the Lord!"

"How should we return to the Lord?" the people asked.

Malachi responded by highlighting the area of tithing. Their failure to fully keep the Mosaic Law's injunctions on tithing had led to a breakdown of temple activities, and as a result the whole nation was cursed. "Bring the whole tithe into the storehouse and test me,' says the Lord. 'See how I will throw open the windows of heaven and pour out so much blessing that you won't be able to contain it!'"

"You have said many harsh things against me," Malachi reported the Lord as saying.

"What have we said against the Lord," the people asked importunately.

"You have said that serving Him is futile, that you gained nothing by mourning in His presence. You have said that evildoers prosper and that those who challenge God get away with it," the prophet replied. For most of them life was all about material well being, to be attained in whatever way was necessary.

The small remnant of people who remained faithful to the Lord responded positively to the prophet's stinging rebukes. They even wrote a "scroll of remembrance"—essentially a "covenant renewal pledge"—recommitting themselves to honor the Lord's name. This pleased the Lord. "They will be my treasured possession," He said. "On the day of judgment I will spare them. You will see the distinction I will make between the righteous and the wicked, between those who serve Me and those who do not." Evildoers will burn like stubble but for those who fear the Lord it will be a day when "the sun of righteousness will rise with healing in its wings". The wicked will perish but the righteous will be overwhelmed with joy.

Many centuries earlier, when Israel was just beginning its covenant relationship with Jehovah God, Moses had exhorted the people in his farewell address never to stray from the framework of the divine law they had received from His hands. Malachi, the last of the Old Testament prophets, concluded by reminding the nation that the old Sinaitic Covenant was still in operation and that they were obligated to abide by it. He also promised them that before the great and dreadful day of the Lord's judgement God would send an Elijah-like prophet who would prepare the people for His coming. This prophet would step onto the stage of history about four hundred years later. His name was John the Baptist, the forerunner of Jesus Christ, the long-awaited and promised Messiah.

Jesus Christ, the suffering Saviour, eventually fulfilled all the Old Testament laws, prophecies, types and covenants about an atonement which would crush the serpent's head and reconcile God with His people, as well as the promise of an eternal heir to David's throne. These truths would be divested of their narrow, national character and presented to the whole world as universally valid, spiritual truths made real in His life, teachings, death, resurrection and ascension. And when He comes again, He will gloriously conclude this epic story of God and man.

Bibliography

Arnold, TB, Beyee, B 1999. *Encountering the Old Testament*. Grand Rapids, MI. Baker Books.

Baxter, JS. 1965. *Explore the Book.* 6 vols. London. Marshall, Morgan, and Scott.

Benjamin, DC. 2004. *The Old Testament Story*. London, SCM Press.

Birch, BC, Breuggeman, W, Fretheim,TE. 1999. *A Theological Introduction to the Old Testament*. Nashville, Abingdon Press.

Boice, JM 2001. *An Expositional Commentary* (entire series on the Old Testament). Grand Rapids, MI. Baker Books.

Boyd, GA 1997. *God at War*. Downers Grove, IL. IVP Academic

Constable, TL. Dr. Constable's Expository Bible Study Notes. Retrieved from: http://www.soniclight.com/constable/notes.htm

France, RT 1971. *Jesus and the Old Testament: His Application of Old Testament Passages to Himself and His Mission*. London. Tyndale Press.

Gaebelein, FE (Editor). 1984. *The Expositor's Bible Commentary* (entire series). Grand Rapids, MI. Zondervan Publishing House.

Goldingay, J 1995. *Theological Diversity and the Authority of the Old Testament*. Grand Rapids, Wm. B. Eerdmans Publishing Co.

Goldsworthy, G. 1991. *According to Plan: The Unfolding Revelation of God in the Bible*. Downer Grove, Illinois. IVP Academic.

Hindson, E, Yates, G. eds. 2012. *The Essence of the Old Testament: A Survey*. Nashville, B & H. Publishing Group.

Kaiser, WC., Jr. 1978. *Toward and Old Testament Theology*. Grand Rapids: Zondervan Publishing House.

LaSor, WS, Hubbard, DA, Bush, FW 1996. *Old Testament Survey: The Message, Form and Background of the Old Testament*. Grand Rapids, MI. Eerdmans Publishing Company.

McFall, L. "A Translation Guide to the Chronological Data in Kings and Chronicles," *Bibliotheca Sacra* 148:589 (January-March 1991):3-45.

Miller, JM, Hayes, JH, 2006. *A History of Ancient Israel and Judah, 2nd. Ed.* London, SCM Press.

Ogilvie, LJ (General Editor) 1987. *The Communicator's Commentary.* W Publishing Group.

Pawson, D. 2007. Unlocking *the Bible: A Unique Overview of the Whole Bible.* London, Harper Collins.

Payne, JB. 1982. *The Theology of the Older Testament.* Grand Rapids, MI. Zondervan Publishing House.

Pink, AW. n.d. *Gleanings in Exodus.* Chicago, Moody Press.

_____. 1950. *Gleanings in Genesis.* Chicago, Moody Press.

Provan, I, Long, VP, Longman III, T. 2003. *A Biblical History of Israel.* Louisville, Westminster John Knox Press.

Sailhamer, JH. 1992. *The Pentateuch as Narrative.* Grand Rapids, MI. Zondervan Publishing House.

Smith, GA. 1974. *The Historical Geography of the Holy Land.* London, U.K. Collins, The Fontana Library

Routledge, R. 2008. *Old Testament Theology: A Thematic Approach.* Notthingham, Apollos.

Taylor, JB. 1969. *Ezekiel: An Introduction and Commentary.* Tyndale Old Testament Commentaries Series. Leicester and Downers Grove, Inter-Varsity Press.

Thiele, E. 1983. *The Mysterious Numbers of the Hebrew Kings.* Grand Rapids, MI, The Zondervan Corporation.

Voss, G. 1985. *Biblical Theology, Old and New Testaments.* Carlyle, PA. Banner of Truth.

von Rad, G. 1965. *Old Testament Theology. 2 vols.* Translated by D. M. G. Stalker. New York and Evanston, Harper & Row.

Waltke, BK, Yu C. 2007. An *Old Testament Theology: an exegetical, canonical, and thematic approach.* Grand Rapids, Zondervan.

Walton, JH. 1994. *Chronological and Background Charts of the Old Testament.* Grand Rapids, MI. Zondervan Publishing House.

Dr. P. Pikkert has spent much of his life in the Middle East working as a pioneer missionary, Bible teacher, writer, and translator with WEC International.

His previous books include several novels, descriptive grammars of Kurdish and Turkish, *The Fall of Christendom and the Rise of the Church*, and *Protestant Missionaries to the Middle East: Ambassadors of Christ or Culture?*

He has studied at Prairie Bible Institute, the Universities of Jordan, Istanbul, Syracuse and South Africa. He now teaches Theology, Missiology and Bible at Cornerstone Bible College, WEC's school for mission training in The Netherlands.

He is married to Anna, and they have two children, Owen and Rita.

Printed in Great Britain
by Amazon

The World of Wade® Whimsies

Ian Warner
& Mike Posgay

Schiffer Publishing Ltd®

4880 Lower Valley Road, Atglen, Pennsylvania 19310

Dedication

This book is dedicated to the memory of the late Margaret B. Wowra, a collector and Wade researcher of renown and to our dear friend and fellow Wade collector, the late Harriet Kellman.

Copyrights

The authors encourage Wade collectors to send information and color photographs of items not listed or illustrated in this book.
To contact the authors, write:

P.O. Box 93022
499 Main Street South
Brampton, Ontario, Canada L6Y 4V8
or
www.theworldofwade.com

Other books by the authors:
Swankyswigs. A Pattern Guide and Check List
The World of Wade
The World of Wade, Book 2
The World of Head Vase Planters
Wade Price Trends
The World of Wade Figurines and Miniatures
The World of Wade Ireland

Schiffer Books are available at special discounts for bulk purchases for sales promotions or premiums. Special editions, including personalized covers, corporate imprints, and excerpts can be created in large quantities for special needs. For more information contact the publisher:

Published by Schiffer Publishing Ltd.
4880 Lower Valley Road
Atglen, PA 19310
Phone: (610) 593-1777; Fax: (610) 593-2002
E-mail: Info@schifferbooks.com

Please visit our web site catalog at
www.schifferbooks.com

We are always looking for people to write books on new and related subjects. If you have an idea for a book, please contact us at the above address.

This book may be purchased from the publisher.
Include $5.00 for shipping.
Please try your bookstore first.
You may write for a free catalog.

In Europe, Schiffer books are distributed by:
Bushwood Books
6 Marksbury Ave.
Kew Gardens
Surrey TW9 4JF
England
Phone: 44 (0)208 392-8585
Fax: 44 (0)208 392-9876
E-mail: Info@bushwoodbooks.co.uk

Website: www.bushwoodbooks.co.uk
Free postage in the UK. Europe: air mail at cost.
Try your bookstore first.

Other Schiffer Books by Ian Warner & Mike Posgay
The World of Wade Figurines and Miniatures
The World of Wade Ireland

Other Schiffer Books on Related Subjects
Wade Miniatures: An Unauthorized Guide to Whimsies, Premiums, Villages, and Characters. Donna S. Baker.

Copyright © 2008 by Ian Warner & Mike Posgay
Library of Congress Control Number: 2008923275

Designed by Mark David Bowyer
Type set in University Roman Bd BT / Aldine 721 BT

ISBN: 978-0-7643-3077-3
Printed in China

Contents

Introduction

As with many Wade collectors, our first interest in Wade was through the Red Rose Tea figurines. This was in the 1970s when we were writing articles for *The Depression Glass Daze*, a monthly Michigan based newspaper specializing in the field of Depression Era Glassware. Although *The Daze*, the name by which it was commonly known, was primarily focused on glassware of the twentieth century, there were however, many readers with interests in pottery and porcelain. When letters from readers started to appear on the editor's desk asking questions about the little Canadian Red Rose Tea figurines, we were asked to investigate and write articles on the subject.

The late Derek Dawe was our first contact with Wade and he was of tremendous help with our research. Derek explained to us how Wade manufactured the miniature figurines and helped greatly with "all things Wade." Our research took us all over England and Northern Ireland, where we met and became friends with numerous Wade collectors. The days spent at the Newspaper Library in London, England, the New York Public Library, New York, and the Rakow Library in Corning, New York, were days of many surprises as we gradually uncovered details of Wade products, such as years of issue and interesting articles reporting on the various Wade potteries.

This, the sixth book in the World of Wade series, deals with the ever popular Wade Whimsies and related "pressed" figurines. Some of the figurines illustrated in this book are not, technically, Whimsies but are either extensions of the Whimsies or have been used as premiums or promotions, so we have included these and related figurines. A typical example of this is the Dogs and Puppies series, which was originally marketed under the Whimsies label but half way through the promotion dropped the Whimsies name. Recently a number of slip cast figurines have been produced and referred to as "Whimsies" and these have also been included in this book. Generally though, with a few exceptions, we have included only the "pressed" figurines in this book.

We have listed the size of the figurines as accurately as possible but with the newer method of manufacture – solid casting – measurements may vary considerably as only thirty to thirty-five figurines can be made from one mold. With this method of manufacture, numerous molds are used so the difference in size of figurines is not uncommon.

Also listed are a number of color variations of mass produced figurines. In recent years these color variations have become quite collectable and values have risen accordingly.

Acknowledgments

Through the many years that we have been writing about and researching Wade products, Jenny Wright, of Wade Ceramics Limited, has been of tremendous help answering numerous questions. We sincerely thank Jenny for her continued help and support and taking time from her very busy schedule to assist us.

Our good friends, Mary Ashby and Alan Clark, have once again been of great help with contents of this book. Thank you, Mary and Alan, we treasure your friendship and support.

Peg and Roger Johnson have been good friends for many years and we thank them, both for their friendship, and for welcoming us to their home to photograph their collection of Wade pottery.

Our very sincere thanks go to David Chown and Russell Schooley of C&S Collectables. David and Russell have always been helpful and supportive of our books. The time they spent from their busy schedule to answer our many questions is most appreciated.

We would like to thank Tess Contois for inviting us to her home in Massachusetts to photograph her superb collection of Wade Leprechauns and Minikins. Tess has to be the preeminent collector of the Wade "little people." Thank you Tess!

We are most grateful to Naseem Wahlah who invited us to her home to photograph her fabulous collection. Naseem, it was such a delight to get to know you. Part of the joy of working on books is to meet and become friends with people like yourself.

We thank Ed and Bev Rucker for inviting us to their home in Kansas and allowing us to photograph items from their collection. Ed's and Bev's joy in all things "Wade" is catching.

We sincerely thank Pat and Gary Keenan for both their help and interest in our books and for promoting the ever popular and exciting Summer Wade Fest. Long may it continue.

We extend our gratitude to Ben Dawson, Derbyshire, U.K. for his continued help with photographs.

We sincerely thank Fay Thompson for her help with this book. Fay has been a friend and supporter of our books for many, many years and we value her friendship.

We also thank Kim Rowley of Wade Ceramics Limited for her help over the years.

The staff at Redco Foods, Inc. have always been very supportive with supplying information for our books and we sincerely thank them. Special thanks go to Douglas Farrell, Leigh Ann Lowe, and Mary Register of Redco Foods, Inc.

We would like to thank John Rigg (former President of Brooke Bond in Canada) for his help with the Red Rose Tea premiums sold on the Canadian market.

We would like to thank Thomas J. Lipton Inc. for their help with their Canadian Red Rose Tea promotion, especially for their letter of January 17, 1986, where they listed and described the figurines in the series.

We thank the staff of Trebor Bassett for their help with the Sharps Easter Egg promotion.

Following are just some of the many collectors and friends to whom we owe thanks for sending pictures and for their encouragement. We also thank those of you who preferred to remain anonymous:

Caryl Alcock, Yorkshire, U.K.
Bob and Gail Barnhart, Michigan, U.S.A.
Regan Brumagen, The Corning Glass Museum, Corning, New York, U.S.A.
Ralph Brough, Yorkshire, U.K.
Fred and Gail Davidson, South Carolina, U.S.A.
The late Derek Dawe
Iris Lenora Carryer, California, U.S.A.
Caroline and Dennis Clarke, Isle of Wight, U.K.

Joyce and David Divelbiss, Pennsylvania, U.S.A.
Betty and Denny Hannigan, New Jersey, U.S.A.
John Eglinton, Pennsylvania, U.S.A.
Sharon Garwood, U.K.
William Harper, Staffordshire, U.K.
Rosie Heisey, Pennsylvania, U.S.A.
Sue and Brian Hunter, Manchester, U.K.
Beth Hylen, The Corning Glass Museum, Corning, New York, U.S.A.
Esther Kramer, Pennsylvania, U.S.A.
Thomas J. Lipton Inc.
Dianne LeBlanc, Ontario, Canada
Wanita May, Ontario, Canada
Karyl Miles, New Hampshire. U.S.A.
John A. Miller, Connecticut, U.S.A.
Jan and Gene Miszkowski, New York, U.S.A.
Valerie and Wayne Moody, Colorado, U.S.A.
Brian and Judi Morris, Kansas, U.S.A.
Carole and John Murdock, Colorado, U.S.A.

Wendy Murray, Massachusetts, U.S.A.
Keith Percival, Cheshire, U.K.
Redco Foods Inc.
William L. Read, Washington, U.S.A.
Marge and Bob Rolls, New York, U.S.A.
Nancy Rougvie, Rhode Island, U.S.A.
Michelle Tenty, The Netherlands.
Val Tolfrey, West Sussex, U.K.
Trudi Walton, Ontario, Canada
John and Beatrice Warren, Ontario, Canada
Jane and Paul Watson, Massachusetts, U.S.A.
Janice Weaver, Cheshire, U.K.
Jean Whittington, Maryland, U.S.A.
Nina and Richard Wilson, South Yorks, U.K.
Juanita & Erick Wowra, North Carolina, U.S.A.
The late Margaret B. Wowra
Jo-Ann Yadrow, Oregon, U.S.A.
Mary Yager, Kansas, U.S.A.

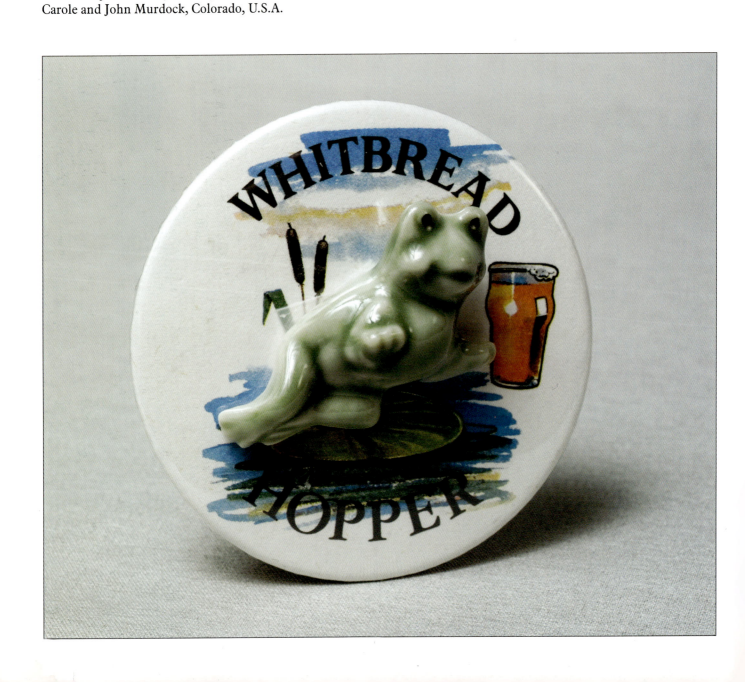

Development of the Wade Potteries

T he Wade family of potters was first heard of in 1867 when Joseph Wade (1833-1881), along with his brother John Wade (1836-1902), and a partner named Myatt, opened their first pottery in 1867 in Burslem, Staffordshire. The new pottery was given the name Wade and Myatt. In late 1867, John Wade and two partners, James and Henry Colclough, formed another pottery in Burslem, Staffordshire. The pottery went through a number of name changes, eventually settling on Wade & Co. In the 1890s, John Wade took one of his nephews, William Wade, into partnership forming J. & W. Wade & Co. Finally, another nephew, Albert Joseph Wade, who had started out as a schoolteacher, also joined the business. By the early twentieth century, both businesses had developed into two highly successful concerns.

In June 1927, J. & W. Wade & Co. was formed into a private company to be known as A. J. Wade & Co., and in the following December Wade & Co. was also formed into a private company taking the name of Wade, Heath & Co. Ltd.

Flaxman Tile Works (now demolished) from Greenhead Street, circa late 1990s. This was the home of A. J. Wade & Co., and later was the location of the first Wade Factory Shop.

Flaxman Tile Works (now demolished) from a 1949 drawing by Robert Barlow. This drawing was made just prior to the demolition of the old bottle ovens.

A. J. Wade (1866-1933)

Royal Victoria Pottery circa late 1990s. This was the home of Wade, Heath & Co. Ltd. and later the home to Wade Ceramics Limited. At the time of writing, Wade Ceramics Limited is once again moving to a new location.

In 1889, George Wade (1864-1938), elder brother of A. J. Wade and William Wade, took over another family owned pottery by the name of Wade and Sons. The major product of this endeavor was the manufacture of pottery fittings for the textile industry. George Wade soon became strong competition for the Henry Hallen pottery, which had been in business for many years, as both potteries were producing similar products for the textile industry.

In the 1900s, George Wade changed the name of the pottery to George Wade and finally bought out the Hallen pottery and combined the two businesses which were to be located at the Manchester Pottery on Greenhead Street. George Wade had a number of other business interests besides his pottery. One major interest was in the Chromo Transfer Company of Burslem, of which he was the joint Managing Director. He also held a position of Secretary of the Earthenware Manufacturer's Association, a post he held for a number of years.

George Wade
(1864-1938)

In 1906, George Wade's son, George Albert Wade (better known as Sir George Wade (1891-1986)), joined his father at the George Wade pottery and one of his first jobs was to oversee the move to the new premises, namely the Manchester Pottery. With the outbreak of World War I in 1914, G. A. Wade enlisted and was commissioned in the South Staffordshire Regiment. He saw active service in both France and Egypt and was awarded the MC and Bar. In 1915, he married Miss Florrie Johnson, the daughter of a local area pottery manufacturer. They had two daughters, Iris (who later married Straker Carryer of Wade (Ulster) Ltd. fame) and Cynthia, and a son, G. Anthony J. Wade (1924-1987), who also eventually joined the family business.

Manchester Pottery (now demolished) in the late 1990s looking across the car park from Greenhead Street.

An informal Sir George Wade (circa 1959)

On June 24, 1919, the original firm of George Wade was incorporated into George Wade and Son Ltd. to carry on the business of pottery fittings for the textile industry, electrical porcelain insulators, and other porcelain articles for industrial purposes. By the late 1920s, the company had also added decorative figurines of ladies and animals to their range of products, which were produced until the outbreak of WW II.

With the outbreak of World War II in 1939, work at the various Wade potteries gradually slowed down with eventually all work coming to a halt at both the Flaxman Tile Works (A. J. Wade & Co.) and at the Manchester Pottery. The production of pottery continued throughout the war at the Royal Victoria Pottery (Wade, Heath & Co. Ltd.) but with certain restrictions as directed by the Board of Trade under the Domestic Potters (Manufacture and Supply) Order. This order designated that all items manufactured for domestic consumption were to be plain, white, undecorated ware. However, items manufactured for the export market, which was still required to help finance the war effort, were given a license to be produced with full decoration.

It wasn't until August 6, 1952, that the Board of Trade Order was rescinded and Wade, Heath & Co. Ltd. was allowed to manufacture and sell decorated ware to the home market. George Wade and Son Ltd. was also back in business by 1946 but still unable to produce any items for decorative purposes. The pottery was being kept busy manufacturing electrical porcelain insulators for use in the home-building program, a program desperately needed to help rebuild the major cities devastated by the bombing of WW II. It was to be some years before the Manchester Pottery returned to the manufacture of decorative ware. In 1947, G. Anthony J. Wade joined the company and in 1948 became a Director and then Joint Managing Director in 1949. It was not too long before the pottery began producing the soon to be world famous Whimsies.

In 1946, as part of the post war rebuilding program, Col. G. A. Wade (later Sir George Wade), along with his son-in-law H. Straker Carryer, acquired and converted to a pottery an old linen mill in Portadown, Northern Ireland. This was incorporated as Wade (Ulster) Ltd. on January 2, 1950, as a subsidiary of George Wade and Son Ltd. The purpose of the Irish based pottery was to produce much wanted die-pressed insulators and other industrial ceramics.

On March 7, 1958, at a shareholders meeting of the Wade Potteries held in Burslem, Directors of the company announced they had entered into a contract to acquire the whole of the issued share capital of George Wade and Son Ltd. and its subsidiary Wade (Ulster) Ltd. With the formation of a new Board of Management, the Directors of both the Wade Potteries Limited and the Directors of George Wade and Son Ltd. were to remain unchanged but with the addition of H. Straker Carryer, Joint Managing Director of the Irish pottery and one other Hubert Thurman Robinson, the technical Director of the Manchester Pottery. The group of potteries was now to be known as Wade Potteries Limited.

Sadly, Sir George Wade died in 1986 at the great age of ninety-four, followed one year later, in 1987, with the death of his son, G. Anthony J. Wade. With these unfortunate deaths, the long run of the Wade Potteries with a family member at its helm came to an end. In 1989, the company was taken over by Beauford PLC, which gave the potteries a new name – Wade Ceramics Limited. At that time the company names of George Wade and Son Ltd. and Wade, Heath & Co. Ltd. ceased to exist. Wade (Ireland) Ltd., whose name had changed from Wade (Ulster) Ltd., remained as such until 1990 when the company changed its name to Seagoe Ceramics and by 1992, although still a member of Beauford PLC, the Irish pottery was no longer connected directly to Wade Ceramics Limited. In 1999, Wade Ceramics Limited was sold to the Wade management and is now a privately owned company.

At the time of writing, Wade Ceramics Limited was in the process of vacating The Royal Victoria Pottery and relocating to new premises on the outskirts of Burslem.

G. Anthony J. Wade (1924-1987) circa mid-1950s.

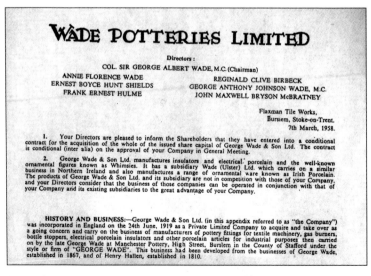

Extract from a notice to shareholders of Wade Potteries Ltd. on the takeover by that company of George Wade & Son Ltd. March 1958.

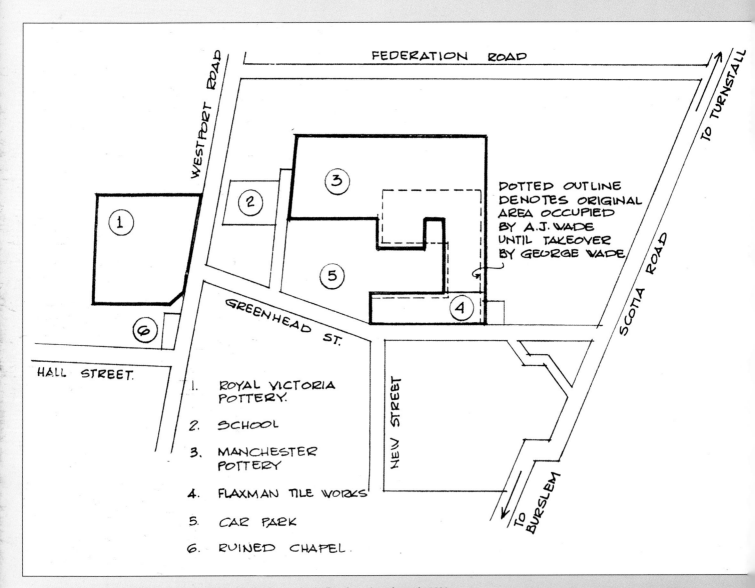

Location diagram of the Wade Ceramics Limited potteries in Burslem circa the early 1980s.

Wade exhibit at the 1954 British Industries Fair. Note the display of the boxed Whimsies Set No. 1 on the left hand side of the picture.

Wade Potteries
Marks & Back Stamps

Since the early 1980s we have been researching Wade and the company marks and back stamps. This search has taken us from Burslem to the Newspaper Library in London, to the Rakow Library in New York State, and The New York Public Library in New York City. These research trips have resulted in the most comprehensive listing and record of Wade marks and back stamps.

WADE & CO.

Mark Type 04
1893
Ink Stamp

Mark Type 03
1899
Ink Stamp

Mark Type 02
1900
Ink stamp

Mark Type 01
1901
Ink Stamp

Wades'
England

Mark Type 0
Late 1900s - mid-
1920s
Ink Stamp

WADES
ENGLAND

Mark Type 1
Mid 1920s - 1927
Ink Stamp

WADES
ORCADIA
WARE
BRITISH MADE

Mark Type 1A
Mid 1920s - 1927
Ink Stamp

WADE HEATH & CO. LTD.

Mark Type 2
1928 - 1937
Ink Stamp

WADEHEATH
ORCADIA
WARE
BRITISH MADE

Mark Type 2A
1928 - 1934
Ink Stamp

WADEHEATH WARE
MADE IN ENGLAND
MANUFACTURED BY PERMISSION
DISNEY MICKEY MOUSE LTD.

Mark Type 2B
1934 - Late 1930s
Ink Stamp

WADEHEATH
BY PERMISSION
WALT DISNEY
ENGLAND

Mark Type 2C
Mid 1930s - Late 1930s
Ink Stamp

Mark Type 2D
1934 - Late 1930s
Ink Stamp

WADEHEATH
B
ENGLAND

Mark Type 3
1939 - 1942
Ink Stamp

Flaxman Ware
Hand Made Pottery
BY WADEHEATH
ENGLAND

Mark Type 4
Circa 1936
Ink Stamp

Wadeheath
Ware
England

Mark Type 5
Circa 1937
Ink Stamp

Mark Type 6
Circa 1937 - 1938
Ink Stamp

Mark Type 7
Circa 1938 - 1950
Ink Stamp

Mark Type 7A
1942 - mid-1940s
Ink stamp

WADE
MADE IN ENGLAND

Mark Type 10A
Late 1940s
Ink Stamp

EMERALD
GOLD
WADE
ENGLAND

Mark Type 12B
Circa mid-1950s -
Late 1950s
Ink Stamp

Mark Type 17
Circa 1953+
Transfer

WADE
HEATH
ENGLAND
J

Mark Type 7B
Circa 1945 (?)
Ink Stamp

WADE
ENGLAND
A

Mark Type 10B
Circa 1945 - Late 1940s
Ink Stamp

"BLACK-VELVET"
WADE

Mark Type 12C
Circa Late 1950s
Ink Stamp

Mark Type 17A
1953 - Early 1960s
Ink Stamp

WADE
HEATH
ENGLAND

Mark Type 8
Circa 1938 - 1950
Ink Stamp

WADE
ENGLAND
"GOTHIC"

Mark Type 11
Circa 1948 - 1954
Ink Stamp

"HARVEST"
WARE
WADE
ENGLAND

Mark Type 13
Circa 1947 -
Early 1950s
Ink Stamp

Mark Type 18
Circa 1953+
Transfer

WADE
HEATH
ENGLAND
A

Mark Type 8A
Circa 1942 - Late 1940s
Ink Stamp

Mark Type 11A
1947 - mid-1950s
Transfer

WADE
ENGLAND

Mark Type 14
Circa 1947 - Early
1950s
Ink Stamp

Mark Type 18A
Circa mid-1950s - 1960s
Transfer

"GOTHIC"
WADE
HEATH
ENGLAND

Mark Type 9
Circa Late 1930s - 1950
Ink Stamp

WADE
Bramble
ENGLAND

Mark Type 12
Circa 1950 - 1955
Ink Stamp

WADE
ENGLAND

Mark Type 15
Circa 1947 - 1953
Ink Stamp

Mark Type 18B
Circa mid-1950s - 1960s
Transfer

WADE
ENGLAND

Mark Type 10
Circa Late 1940s
Ink Stamp

Mark Type 12A
Circa mid-1950s - Late 1950s
Ink Stamp

Mark Type 16
Circa 1953+
Transfer

Mark Type 18C
Circa mid-1950s
Ink & Transfer

WADE
ENGLAND

Mark Type 19
Circa 1953+
Transfer
(George Wade & Son Ltd.
also used this mark
from circa 1953 on)

Mark Type 19B
1956 - Early 1960s
Transfer

Mark Type 19C
Circa 1956 - Early 1960s
Transfer

Mark Type 19A
Late 1950s
Transfer

Mark Type 20
1985+
Transfer

Mark Type 23A
1947+
Ink Stamp

WADE
Porcelain
Made in England

Mark Type 24
1958+
Molded

WADE
PORCELAIN
MADE IN ENGLAND

Mark Type 25
1957 - 1981
Molded

WADE
MADE IN
ENGLAND

Mark Type 26
1959+
Molded

WADE
MADE IN ENGLAND

Mark Type 27
1958+
Molded

GENUINE
WADE
PORCELAIN

Mark Type 27A
Mid 1980s
Transfer

GEORGE WADE & SON LTD.

Mark Type 20A
1931 - mid-1930s
Ink Stamp

Mark Type 21A
Late 1930s
Ink Stamp

Mark Type 20B
Early 1930s - Late 1930s
Ink Stamp
(Usually found with the name
of the figurine)

WADE
MADE IN ENGLAND

Mark Type 22
Circa Early 1930s - Late
1930s
Hand Painted Ink

Mark Type 21
Circa Early 1930s - Late 1930s
Ink Stamp

Mark Type 23
Circa 1939
Ink Stamp

WADE CERAMICS LIMITED

Mark Type 27B
1990+
Transfer

Mark Type 27B2
2001
Transfer

Mark Type 27B1
2001+
Transfer
(Appears with or without:
Est. 1810 England)

OIWCC Logo
Transfer
(Appears in conjunction
with other Mark Types)

WADE (ULSTER) LTD. 1950 - 1966
&
WADE (IRELAND) LTD. 1966 - 1990

Mark Type 27C
Circa 1950+
Ink Stamp

Mark Type 27D
Circa 1952 - 1953
Ink Stamp

Mark Type 27E
Circa mid-1950s
Impressed

Mark Type 28
1953+
Impressed

Mark Type 29
1954+
Impressed

Mark Type 30
1954+
Transfer

Mark Type 31
Mid 1950s+
Molded

Mark Type 32
1955+
Impressed

Mark Type 32A
Circa Early 1960s -
1967
Transfer

Mark Type 32B
Circa Early 1960s -
1967
Transfer

Mark Type 32C
Circa 1963 - 1964
Transfer

Mark Type 33
1962
Molded
(Included the name of the
modeler/designer)

Mark Type 33A
1962
Molded

Mark Type 33B
1962 - 1986
Transfer

Mark Type 34
Mid 1960s
Molded

Mark Type 34A
Circa mid-1960s +
Impressed

Mark Type 35
1970
Impressed

Mark Type 36
1973
Impressed

Mark Type 36A
1974 - 1975
Impressed

Mark Type 37
1970+
Transfer

Mark Type 38
Mid 1970s
Impressed

Mark Type 39
1965 - 1968
Impressed

Mark Type 39A
Mid 1970s +
Molded

Mark Type 39B
Mid 1970s +
Molded

Mark Type 40
1977+
Molded

Mark Type 40A
Late 1970s
Molded

Mark Type 40C
Late 1970s+
Molded and Transfer

Mark Type 40B
Late 1970s
Molded

Mark Type 41
1980+
Molded and Transfer

SEAGOE CERAMICS LTD. 1990 - 1993

Mark Type 41A
1991
Ink Stamp

Mark Type 41D
1992 - 1993
Transfer

Mark Type 41B
1991+
Transfer

Mark Type 41E
1992 - 1993
Transfer

Mark Type 41C
1992 - 1993
Transfer

WADE HEATH & CO. LTD.
&
REGINALD CORFIELD (SALES) LTD.

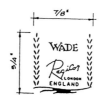

Mark Type 42
1950 - 1957
Transfer

Mark Type 43A
Circa Early - mid-1960s
Transfer

Mark Type 43
1957 - 1966
Transfer

(Note: Mark Type 43
similar to
Mark Type 42 but with
heavier lettering.)

Mark Type 44
1962 - 1968
Transfer

Mark Type 45
1968 - 1970
Transfer

WADE (PDM) LTD.

Mark Type 46
1970 - 1980
Transfer

Mark Type 48
1980
Transfer

Mark Type 47
1980+
Transfer

Mark Type 49
1990+
Transfer

SPECIAL BACKSTAMPS

S1
Ringtons Rose Bowl
and Plant Trough
1990

S2
Ringtons Backstamp

S3
Williamson and
Magor Elephant Tea Caddy
1990 - 1993

S4
Open Range (Various Shapes)

S5
Open Range (Various Shapes)

S6
Santa's Grotto Teapot (First
produced Christmas 1989)
1989+

S7
Open Range (Various
Shapes)

S8
Myrna Coffee Pot

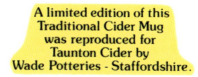

S9
Small Size Cider Mug (Taunton Cider)

S10
Small Size Teapot, Royal Society for the
Protection of Birds 1988)

S11
Standard Fine Bone China Backstamp
(Royal Victoria Pottery)

S12
Old Parr Flagons

S13
Gardner Merchant
1986

S14
Open Range (Various Shapes)

S15
No Record

S16
Irish Distillers Backstamp

S17
Belfry Hotel Coaster Dish

S21
Gordon Highlander Backstamp for Highland
Wildlife Decanter
Early 1990s

S25
Open Range (Various Shapes)

S26 to S35
Taunton Cider Mug Backstamps
1977 - 1989

S18
Whyte & Mackay Flagon Backstamp

S26

S22
Gordon Highlander Backstamp for Highland
Wildlife Decanter
Early 1990s

S19
Open Range (Various Shapes)

S27

20
No Record

S23
One Cup China Teapots, Open Range.
(Three Shapes)
Mid 1980s - Early 1990s

S28

S24
No Record

S29

S30

S31

S32

S33

S34

S35

S36
Boston Tea Party Teapot, Sugar and
Creamer Backstamp
Circa mid-1970s

S37
Wilton Castle Dish

S38
English Life Mug Backstamp
1988 - Early 1990s

S39
English Life Teapot Backstamp
1988 - Early 1990s

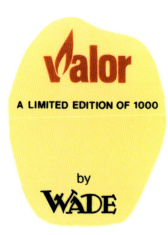

S40
Valor Teapot Backstamp
1990

S41 to S45
Gallery Collection Flower Jugs
1995

S41

S45

S50
Ringtons Ltd
Willow Range Backstamp
1994 - 1996

S42

HOUSE OF STRAW
1995

S46
The International Wade Collectors
Club Backstamp
Typical backstamp of early Club items

SPIRIT
of
ROBYN HOODE
Aged Malt Whisky

•

SPECIALLY SELECTED FOR
ROBYN HOODE DISTILLERIES
ELSTON, NEWARK, NOTTINGHAMSHIRE NG23 5PG.

40% vol   70cl ℮

Produced in the U.K. Registered design.

S51
Robyn Hoode Malt Whisky
1993

S43

HOLLY HEDGEHOG
C & S Collectables

S47
Holly Hedghog Backstamp
1994

S48
Wimbles Backstamp

Designed for
FINDLATER'S
Scotch Whisky

Hand Crafted Porcelain
by
WADE
Ceramics

S52
Findlaters Scotch Whisky

S44

S49
Punch and Judy Backstamp

S53
Bear Ambitions Teapots
1994 - 1995

S57
Lady and the Tramp Sweet Tray
Circa 1956

S61
Cockleshell Cove Collection
1990 - 1993

S54
The Christmas Collection
1991 - mid-1990s

S58
The Ringmaster Teapot
1990

S62
White Rabbit Teapot (Boots)
1992

S55
London Life Teapots
1994 - 1995

S59
Cat Burglar Teapot
Late 1980s

S63
Dressage Teapot (Boots)
1992

S56
Feline Collection Teapots
1989 - 1990

S60
Noah's Arc Teapot
1990

S64
Fish Collection
1992

What to Look for When Purchasing Wade Items for Personal Collections

All prices are for items in excellent condition. We prefer not to use the overworked expression "mint," as this would refer to unused items still contained in the original, unopened packaging. Of course it is also possible for so-called "mint" items to be damaged between final glazing and the original packaging.

It is advisable for collectors to remember a few tips when looking for Wade at flea markets, car boot sales, etc. It is often quite an exciting experience to find unusual or rare Wade items at the types of locations listed above. To avoid disappointment when unpacking a "find" on arriving home, bear in mind the following suggestions:

1) Check for defects such as cracks or chips, either minor or extensive. It is amazing how easy it is to overlook damage of many sorts on dirty, unwashed items.

2) If, by any chance, there are two similar items on a table, compare them for any damage, missing glaze, chips, etc. If there are rare or unusual items in large numbers, beware of reproductions!

3) Always buy what you really want and at prices that are realistic and also at prices that suit your pocketbook. As a collector, do not buy purely for investment.

Method of Establishing Prices

The suggested prices in *The World of Wade Whimsies* are derived from prices submitted to us by advisers and contributors from both the United Kingdom and the United States of America and from online antique markets.

It must be pointed out that the prices quoted are average prices.

Remember, this is a suggested price guide only. Prices suggested are not to be interpreted literally as final dealer prices; rather it is an indication of the range around which collectors might expect to pay.

Neither the authors nor the publisher are responsible for any outcomes resulting from consulting this reference.

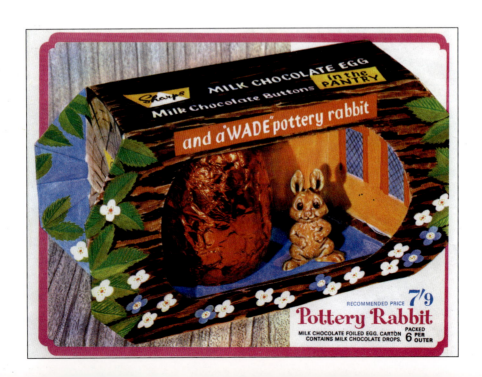

The Official International
Wade Collectors Club

The Official International Wade Collectors Club, usually referred to as OIWCC in this book, was launched in 1994. The club was formed with the intention to unite Wade collectors throughout the world in their common enthusiasm for Wade products, both new and old.

Collectors who join the club receive a quarterly magazine. Issue No. 1 was published in September 1994. *The Official Wade Club Magazine* contains notices of new figurines to be released, interesting articles, letters from club members, and Wade fair/show dates and reviews in both the U.K. and the U.S.A.

Although the Wade potteries no longer have a direct connection with the Wade family, the OIWCC does. The president of the club is Jeremy Wade, the eldest son of the late Anthony Wade and grandson of the late Sir George Wade.

Members of the OIWCC receive a free exclusive figurine each year. These figurines are available only to club members. Throughout each membership year special limited edition figurines are offered to club members.

To become a member of the OIWCC, write to:

The Official International Wade Collectors Club,
P.O. Box 3012, Stoke-on-Trent, ST3 9DD, England
UK

The email address for the club is:
club@wadecollectorsclub.co.uk
The website for the club is:
www.wadecollectorsclub.co.uk

Chapter 1

Whimsies, 1953 - 2007

Whimsies, 1953 - 1959

In the early 1950s, the Wade Group of potteries was badly hit by the cancellation of several large government contracts for electrical insulators, and the demand for industrial ceramics dropped considerably. The Royal Victoria Pottery (Wade Heath & Co. Ltd.), after wartime restrictions, was returning to the manufacture of tableware and certain ornamental lines so were fully occupied. However, the Manchester Pottery (George Wade and Son Ltd.) and the Portadown Pottery (Wade (Ulster) Ltd.) were experiencing a big drop in their industrial orders. To keep the potteries in production, the idea of producing attractive, inexpensive porcelain miniatures was devised.

With Wade's pre-World War II experience in the design and production of miniature ceramic animal figurines, it was a natural step to try and re-create their prewar success in this field. At a Wade management meeting in Burslem, ideas for new products were fielded around but it wasn't until Iris Carryer looked at some complicated, pressed porcelain switches sitting on a mantle shelf that a truly inspired thought came to her. "I was thinking of my childhood 'Noah's Ark.' All the little animals, two by two. If we can press small insulators why can't we press small animals instead?" So, from the agile brain of Iris Carryer, this was how the world famous "Whimsies" were born.

Planning for the figurines began in early 1953. Each figurine was to be modeled by William Harper, then a top modeler for Wade. Requirements for the new figurines were that the figurines had to appear "alive" either by expression or posture. This effect was made easier by the use of true porcelain as the body, thus enabling the designer to use a high degree of detail.

Tool room circa mid-1950s.

Pressing Operation circa mid-1950s.

William Harper (Spring 1990).

Pressers at work circa mid-1950s.

After detailed modeling of the figures, the next stage of production was the "forming" of the item. Forming was done by a then revolutionary process using hardened steel forming tools which were part cast and part hand engraved, and using "wet-pressed" porcelain dust that was pressed in a machine, under considerable pressure, to form the figurine. Using this forming process, it was possible to make up to 30,000 figurines per day, a much cheaper and speedier method of manufacture than using the more usual slip-cast system of forming.

Fettling Process circa early 1950s. From the December 1951 issue of *The Jolly Potter*.
Top left. Freda. (Fettler). Center left. Ada. (Glazing Dept.). Bottom left. Margaret. (Grinder). Top right. Jean. (Fettler). Center right. Nora. (Fettler). Bottom right. Betty. (Grinder).

The miniature figurines were then dried and "hand-fettled" by operatives sitting on either side of a slow-moving conveyor belt. The fettling process involved the delicate use of a sharp tool to remove all rough edges and surplus pieces of clay left from the forming process. Next came the decorating, also done by operatives sitting on each side of the conveyor belt. Each person had one particular job to do such as applying the eyes or one other small area of decoration. The piece then went on to the next operative for further decoration.

After decorating, the pieces – again on a slow-moving conveyor belt – went through a glaze spraying machine. The individual pieces were then placed on a trolley on batts set twelve tiers high. The trolleys, holding around 12,000 miniatures, were then rolled into the tunnel oven where they were fired at around 1250 degrees Celsius.

"Whimsical Production Line." Cartoon from the Summer 1954 issue of *The Jolly Potter*.

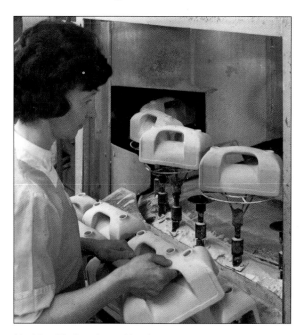

Machine Glazing circa mid-1950s.

The firing temperature imposed some limitations on the type of colors available. The single firing process, where the glaze was applied directly to the clay article, was less expensive than the traditional potting which separates bisque and glost firings. Finally, each item was inspected and boxed. It was this method of manufacture of the small ceramic figurines that George Wade and Son Ltd. was able to develop into a profitable business in the lean years after the war.

When first shown to wholesalers, the Whimsies as they were then called, proved a hard sell. Retailers did not appear interested so Wade management decided to package the figurines in presentation boxes of five models each and feature them at one of the major trade exhibitions. The boxed figurines were almost an instant success and orders for the Whimsies were soon mounting up.

plus higher quality of workmanship, the result being a very successful series of figurines.

In the later years of production, the availability of the various sets of Whimsies was varied. In a 1957 Price List, only Sets 3, 4, 5, 6, 7, and 8 were listed as available. Then in the 1958 Price List, all Sets were once again available. The January 1959 Price List noted only Sets 6, 7, 8, 9, and 10 being available. The January 1960 Price List had Sets 6, 8, 9, and 10 available. The Spring 1961 Price List had Sets 6, 8, and 9 available and in the Fall 1961 Price List only Set 9 was available. None of the Whimsies were listed in the Spring 1962 Price List. It would appear that Set 10 did not have a very long production run.

Wade exhibit at the 1956 British Industries Fair.

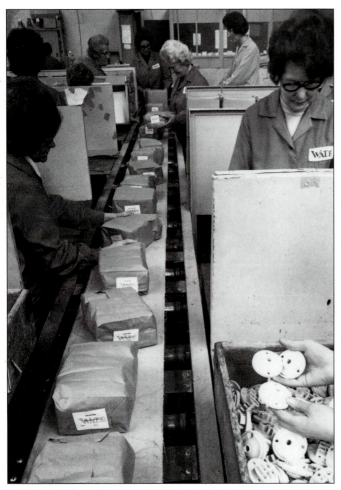

A packing line.

Due to the necessity of keeping both the Manchester and the Portadown potteries in production, the manufacture of the new Whimsies was divided between the two potteries with George Wade and Son Ltd. producing the odd numbered sets, i.e. Sets 1, 3, 5, 7, and 9, and the Irish pottery producing the even numbered sets, i.e. Sets 2, 4, 6, 8, and 10. From all reports, this decision to make the Whimsies in the two potteries caused quite some competition for both, faster production

Whimsies Set 1, *1953 - 1958*
Leaping Fawn measures 1-7/8" high by 1-1/2" overall and is mold marked Wade ($44, £22). **Spaniel** measures 1" high by 1-3/4" long and is unmarked ($34, £17). **Horse** measures 1-1/2" high by 2-1/8" overall and is mold marked Wade ($42, £21). **Squirrel** measures 1-1/4" high by 1-7/8" overall and is unmarked ($28, £14). **Poodle** measures 1-1/2" high by 1-3/4" overall and is unmarked ($42, £21).

Presentation box for Whimsies Set 1.

Presentation box for Whimsies Set 2. Version 1.

Whimsies Set 2, *1954 - 1958*
Dachshund measures 1-1/8" high by 1-1/2" overall and is unmarked ($88, £44). **Bull** measures 1-3/4" high by 2-1/8" overall and is transfer stamped Wade Made in England ($76, £38). **Lamb** measures 1-7/8" high by 1-1/4" overall and is transfer stamped Wade Made in England ($48, £24). **Kitten** measures 1-3/8" high by 1-3/4" overall and is unmarked ($90, £45). **Hare** measures 1-1/8" high by 1-3/4" overall and is transfer marked Wade Made in England ($42, £21).

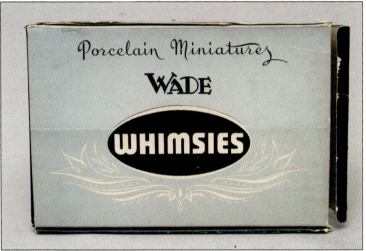

Presentation box for Whimsies Set 2. Version 2 closed.

Advertisement for Whimsies Set 2 from the Winter 1954 issue of *The Jolly Potter.*

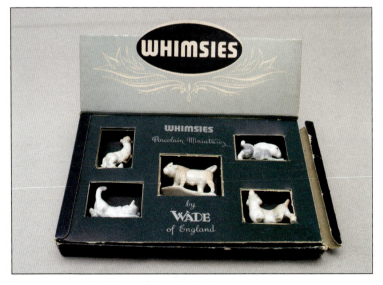

Presentation box for Whimsies Set 2. Version 2 open.

Whimsies Set 3, *1955 - 1958*
Badger measures 1-1/4" high by 2" overall and is unmarked ($42, £21).
Shetland Pony measures 1-3/8" high by 2" overall and is mold marked
Made in England ($36, £18). **Fox Cub** measures 1-3/8" high by 1-5/8" over-
all and is unmarked ($72, £36). **Stoat** measures 1-1/8" high by 1-3/4" overall
and is unmarked ($52, £26). **Retriever** measures 1-1/4" high by 1-7/8"
overall and is mold marked Wade Made in England ($34, £17).

Shetland Pony *(Set 3)*
Color variations ($36 each, £18 each).

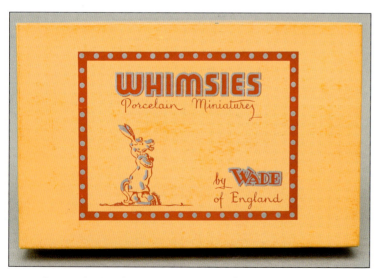

Presentation box for Whimsies Set 3.

Advertisement for Whimsies Set 3 & 4 from the November 1955 issue of
Pottery and Glass.

Whimsies Set 4, *1955 - 1958*
Monkey measures 1-7/8" high by 1-5/8" overall and is unmarked but has been found marked with an ink stamp ($34, £17). **Crocodile** measures 3/4" high by 1-5/8" overall and is ink stamped Made in England ($68, £34). **Rhinoceros** measures 1-3/4" high by 2-3/8" overall and is transfer stamped Wade Made in England ($40, £20). **Lion** measures 1-1/4" high by 1-5/8" overall and is unmarked ($50, £25). **Baby Elephant** measures 1-1/4" high by 1-7/8" overall and is ink stamped Made in England ($50, £25).

Advertisement for Whimsies Set 4 from the July 1955 issue of *Pottery and Glass.*

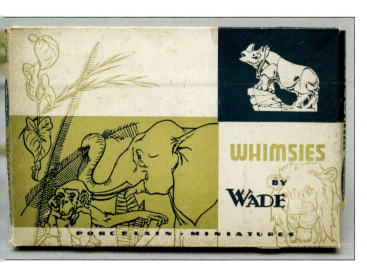

Presentation box for Whimsies set 4.

Left. Prototype Monkey and Baby. This figurine, modeled by William Harper, measures 3-1/2" high and is unmarked ($960, £550). Right. Monkey and Baby production model shown for size and color comparison.

Advertisement for Whimsies Set 5 and Minikins from the February 1956 issue of *Pottery Gazette and Glass Trade Review*.

Whimsies Set 5, *1956 - 1958*
Mare measures 1-7/8" high by 2" overall and is mold marked Wade ($44, £22). **Colt** measures 1-7/16" high by 1-5/8" overall and is mold marked Wade ($46, £23). **Beagle** measures 3/4" high by 1" overall and is unmarked ($62, £31). **Foal** measures 1-1/4" high by 1-3/4" overall and is mold marked Wade ($46, £23).

Mare *(Set 5)*
Color variations ($44 each, £22 each)

Presentation box for Whimsies Set 5.

Foal *(Set 5)*
Color variations ($46 each, £23 each)

Advertisement for Whimsies Set 6 from the December 1956 issue of the
Pottery Gazette and Glass Trade Review.

Colt *(Set 5)*
This figurine is a hollow prototype ($200, £100)

William Harper's sketch for figurines to be used in the Polar Set of Whimsies. Note his signature between the Baby Seal and the Husky.

Whimsies Set 6, *1956 - 1961*
(Polar Set)
Set No. 6, was officially announced in the August 1956, Wade Wholesalers Newsletter No. 1.
Baby Seal measures 7/8" high by 1-1/8" overall and is unmarked ($30, £15).
King Penguin measures 1-3/16" high by 5/8" dia. base and is unmarked ($46, £23).
Baby Polar Bear measures 7/8" high by 1-1/8" overall and is unmarked ($38, £19).
Husky measures 1-1/4" high by 1-1/8" overall and is unmarked ($46, £23).
Polar Bear measures 1-3/4" high by 1-3/4" overall and is unmarked ($42, £21).

Presentation box for Whimsies Set 6 (closed).

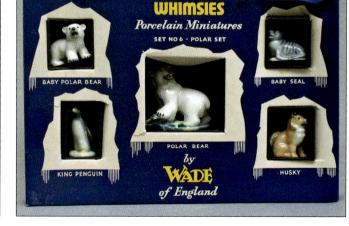

Presentation box for Whimsies Set 6 (open).

Whimsies Set 7, *1957 - 1959 (Pedigree Dogs)*
Set No. 7 was officially announced in the January 1957, Wade Wholesalers Newsletter No. 2.
Boxer measures 1-3/8" high by 1-1/2" overall and is unmarked ($38, £19). **West Highland Terrier** measures 1" high by 1-1/4" overall and is unmarked ($46, £23). **Alsatian** measures 1-3/8" high by 1-5/8" overall and is unmarked ($32, £16). **Corgi** measures 1" high by 1-1/4" overall and is unmarked ($38, £19). **St. Bernard** measures 1-1/2" high by 1-7/8" overall and is unmarked ($56, £28).

Alsatian *(Set 7)*
Top left. Production model ($32, £16). Top right. Prototype model ($60, £30).
Corgi *(Set 7)*
Bottom left. Production model ($38, £19). Bottom right. Prototype model ($60, £30).

Presentation box for Whimsies Set 7.

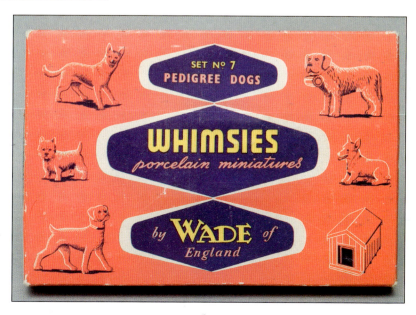

Whimsies Set 8, *1957 - 1961 (Zoo Set)*
Set No. 8, was officially announced in the August 1957, Wade Wholesalers Newsletter No. 3.
Giant Panda measures 1-1/4" high and is unmarked ($46, £23). **Bactrian Camel** measures 1-1/2" high by 1-5/8" overall and is unmarked ($40, £20). **Llama** measures 1-3/4" high by 1-1/8" overall and is unmarked ($42, £21). **Cockatoo** measures 1-1/8" high by 1-1/4" across the wings and is unmarked ($52, £26). **Lion Cub** measures 1" high by 1" overall and is unmarked ($34, £17).

Giant Panda
Left. **Panda** measures 1-1/2" high by 1" across the base and is unmarked. This was the early premium figurine and is shown for size comparison ($34, £17). Right. **Giant Panda** (Set 8) measures 1-1/4" high and is unmarked ($46, £23).

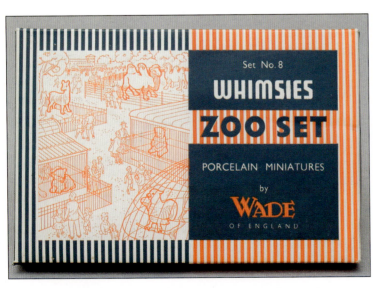

Presentation box for Whimsies Set 8.

Advertisement for Whimsies Set 8 from the January 1958 issue of *Pottery and Glass.*

Left. Prototype Cockatoo. The figurine, modeled by William Harper, measures 2-7/8" high by 2-3/4" across and is unmarked ($420, £280). Right. Production model shown for comparison.

Prototype Zebra. The figurine measures 1-5/8" high and is unmarked. This figurine, modeled by William Harper, was proposed for the 1958 Whimsies Zoo Set but never went into production ($310, £175).

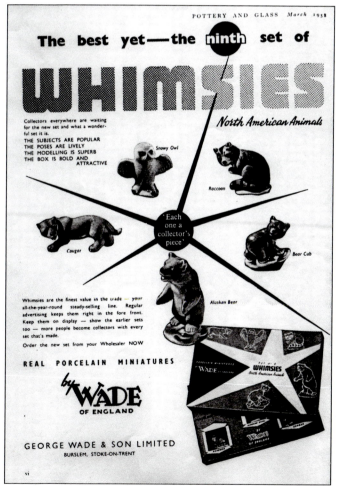

Advertisement for Whimsies Set 9 from the March 1958 issue of *Pottery and Glass.*

Whimsies Set 9, *1958 - 1961 (North American Animals)*
Set 9, was announced in the January 1958, Wade Wholesalers Newsletter No. 4.
Bear Cub measures 1-1/8" high by 1-1/8" overall and is unmarked ($38, £19). **Cougar** measures 3/4" high by 1-7/8" overall and is unmarked ($50, £25). **Grizzly Bear** measures 1-7/8" high on a 7/8" dia. base and is unmarked ($54, £27). **Snowy Owl** measures 1-1/8" high by 1-3/16" across the wings and is unmarked ($50, £25). **Raccoon** measures 1-1/8" high by 1-1/8" overall and is unmarked ($38, £19).

Grizzly Bear *(Set 9)*
This figurine is a hollow prototype ($300, £150)

Bear Cubs *(Set 9)*
Color variations ($38 each, £19 each).

Presentation box for Whimsies Set 9.

Whimsies Set 10, *1959 - 1960 (Farm Animals)*
In the August 1958 *Wade Wholesalers Newsletter No. 5,* it was announced that Set 10 would be delayed as Wade wanted to market Sets 6, 7, 8, and 9, especially for the Christmas trade. Set 10 was officially announced in the January 1959 *Wade Wholesalers Newsletter No. 6.*
Fox Hound measures 1" high by 1-3/4" overall and is unmarked ($68, £34). **Italian Goat** measures 1-3/8" high by 1-1/2" overall and is unmarked ($68, £34). **Piglet** measures 7/8" high by 1-1/2" overall and is unmarked ($70, £35). **Swan** measures 7/8" high by 1-1/2" overall and is unmarked ($190, £95). **Shire Horse** measures 2" high by 2-1/8" overall and is unmarked ($232, £116). Note. For Shire Horse and Swan reproductions see Chapter 11.

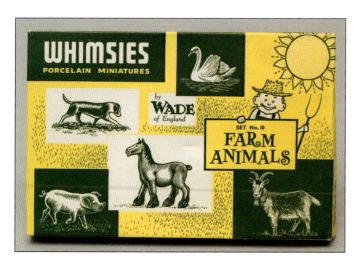

Presentation box for Whimsies Set 10.

Shire Horse *(Set 10)*
Left. William Harper prototype model ($400, £200). Right. Color variation ($250, £125).

Advertisement for Whimsies Set 10 from the March 1959 issue of *Pottery and Glass.*

William Harper prototype models of owls. The pair of owls ($520, £260) single owl ($220, £110). These owls show a remarkable similarity to the 1972 Whimsie owl. As William Harper had left Wade by the time of the 1971-84 Whimsies were produced, it is possible that the 1972 Whimsie owl was based on an earlier William Harper model.

William Harper's sketches for a dog series that never went into production. Note that the sketches are signed by William Harper.
Top row from left: Scotch Terrier pup. Poodle pup. Pomeranian dog.
Middle row: Boxer pup. Dalmatian pup. Pug dog.
Bottom row: Dachshund pup. Basset Hound pup. Beagle pup. Golden Spaniel pup.

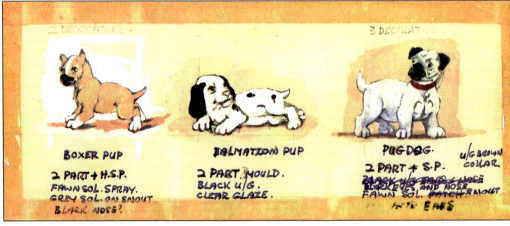

Whimsies, 1971 - 1984

After the success of the ten sets of Whimsies issued between 1953 and 1959, and the popularity of the miniature figurines used as premiums for party crackers and boxes of tea bags, George Wade and Son Ltd. decided to extend the line of the miniature porcelain figurines used as premiums into a full fledged retail line to be, once again, marketed under the name of Whimsies.

Advertisement for Whimsies from the June 1971 issue of *Tableware International*.

The new line of Whimsies was introduced as a retail line in 1971, with a first set of five figurines boxed either individually or as packages containing the complete set of five but with each figurine in its own box. Over the next few years the range was extended, at various intervals, with the issue of further sets of five figurines until the complete range comprised sixty porcelain miniatures. Each set of five figurines was issued in different colored boxes. Starting from the first set of five, the color of the boxes were dark blue, red, green, yellow, dark red, light blue, orange, magenta, medium blue, light green, brown, and dark blue again.

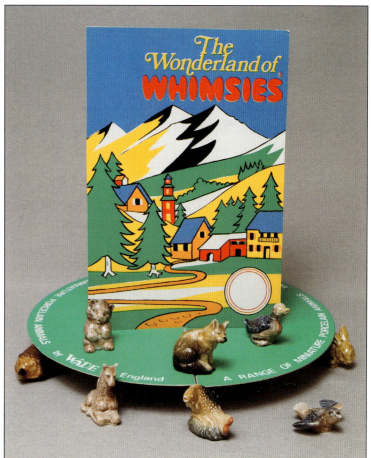

Whimsie display stand.

This second retail line of Whimsies was a great success and was eventually withdrawn from the Wade giftware range in 1984. Wade felt that after thirteen years the popularity of the Whimsies had run its course and should be replaced by a new line of miniature figurines, the form of which, at that time, had yet to be decided upon.

Obviously, due to the length and enormous amount of figurines manufactured during the run of the second set of Whimsies, many variations had appeared. These occurred either as a result of a worn mold being replaced by a new mold that had slight differences from the original or the retooling of an existing mold due to production problems. The latter is very apparent with the Hippo, Pig, and Bison figurines. These three figurines are to be found in various sizes as the molds had to be remade due to production problems caused by the bulky shape of the animals. It was found that the seams were splitting when the figurines were in the clay state and the only way to resolve the problem was to reduce the bulk. Due to the excellent workmanship of the toolmakers, the difference between the various sizes of figurines was minimal.

The pressed Whimsies are easily identified by the parallel molded lines on the underside of the base. The reason for the lines is to make it easier to remove the figurine from the steel tool.

A number of the 1971-84 Whimsies are to be found with the Wade England mold mark either around the base or in a recess under the base. In the early days of the production of the Whimsies, a number of the figurines were pressed with a two-part steel die with the underside forming the embossed part of the tool. This process resulted in the Wade mark appearing in a recessed base of the figurines. These molds were later replaced by new molds with the Wade name around the outside of the base.

Left. **Beaver** with recessed base. Right. **Field Mouse** with recessed base.

Trout with recessed base.

Hedgehog with base tab variations. A number of variations of the hedgehog base are to be found with varying depth of the recess and varying number of tabs.

Whimsies Set 1, *1971*
Top row.1. **Fawn** measures 1-3/8" high by 1-1/4" long ($6, £3). 2. **Rabbit** measures 1-1/8" high by 1-7/8" overall ($6, £3). 3. **Mongrel Pup** measures 1-3/8" high by 1-1/2" overall ($6, £3). 4. **Kitten** measures 1-3/8" high by 1-3/8" overall and is marked "England" only ($6, £3). 5. **Spaniel** measures 1-3/8" high by 1-3/8" overall and is marked "Wade" on the front and "England" on the back ($6, £3).

Whimsies Set 2, *1972*
Bottom row. 6. **Duck** measures 1-1/4" high by 1-1/2" overall and is marked "Wade" on one side of the base and "England" on the other ($6, £3). 7. **Corgi** measures 1-1/2" high by 1-1/2" overall and is marked "Wade" on the front and "England" on the back ($10, £5). 8. **Beaver** measures 1-1/4" high by 1-1/4" overall ($4, £2). A variation in the mold mark occurs on this figurine. Along with the usual "Wade England" mold mark around the base it is also found with "Wade England" molded into a recess on the underside of the base. 9. **Bush Baby** measures 1-1/4" high by 1-1/8" overall ($4, £2). 10. **Fox** measures 1-3/8" high by 1-1/2" overall ($8, £4).

Dark blue presentation box for Set 1.

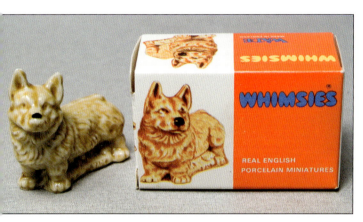

Red presentation box for Set 2.

Kitten *(Set 1)*
Above. **Kitten**. Color variation ($28, £14). Left. **Kitten** illustrates the production model from the 1971 Whimsies Set 1 ($6, £3). Right. **Kitten** illustrates the prototype model.

Rabbit *(Set 1)*
The rabbit is found in two variations. Left. **Rabbit Ears Apart,** which was the later version ($6, £3). Right. **Rabbit Ears Together,** which was the earlier version ($12, £6).

Beaver *(Set 2)*
Left. **Beaver** illustrates the production model ($4, £2). Right. **Beaver** illustrates the prototype model.

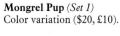

Mongrel Pup *(Set 1)*
Color variation ($20, £10).

Whimsies Set 3, *1972*

Top row. 11. **Bear Cub** measures 1-3/8" high by 7/8" across ($4, £2). A variation in the mold mark occurs on this figurine. The earlier models were marked "Wade England" molded into a recess on the underside of the base. The later models were mold marked "Wade" at the front in between the feet and "England" on the back to the left of the tail. 12. **Otter** measures 1-1/4" high by 1-1/2" overall ($4, £2). 13. **Setter** measures 1-3/8" high by 1-7/8" overall ($6, £3). 14. **Owl** measures 1-1/2" high by 7/8" across the base ($6, £3). A variation in the mold mark occurs on this figurine. Along with the usual "Wade England" mold mark around the base it is also found with "Wade England" molded into a recess on the underside of the base. 15. **Trout** measures 1-1/8" high by 1-3/8" overall. A variation in the mold mark occurs on this figurine. Along with the usual "Wade England" mold mark around the base, it is also found with "Wade England" molded into a recess on the underside of the base ($6, £3).

Whimsies Set 4, *1973*

Bottom row. 16. **Lion** measures 1-3/8" high by 1-3/4" overall ($6, £3). 17. **Elephant** measures 1-3/8" high by 1-3/4" overall ($12, £6). 18. **Giraffe** measures 1-1/2" high by 1-1/2" overall ($4, £2). 19. **Chimp** measures 1-1/2" high by 1-3/8" across ($4, £2). 20. **Hippo** measures 1-1/16" high by 1-3/4" overall - large ($12, £6).

Bush Baby *(Set 2)*
Color, mold, size, and base variations ($4 each, £2 each).

Dark green presentation box for Set 3.

Fox *(Set 2)*
Color variation ($20, £10).

Yellow presentation box for Set 4.

Above. **Dark Brown Trout.** Left. **Grey Trout.** Right. **Honey Trout.** All figurines are from the 1972 Whimsies Set 3. Color variations ($24 each, £12 each).

Owl *(Set 3)*
Color variation ($24, £12).

Otter *(Set 3)*
Color variation ($24, £12).

Elephant *(Set 4)*
Color variations. Left ($20, £10). Center and right ($12, £6).

Elephant *(Set 4)*
White undecorated version ($24, £12).

Hippo *(Set 4)*
Size Variations. Left. **Hippo** measures 15/16" high by 1-1/2" long ($6, £3). Center. **Hippo** measures 1" high by 1-5/8" long ($6, £3). Right. **Hippo** measures 1-1/16" high by 1-3/4" long ($12, £6).

Dark red presentation box for Set 5.

Chimp *(Set 4)*
Color variations ($20 each, £10 each).

Whimsies Set 5, *1974*
Top row. 21. **Squirrel** measures 1-3/8" high by 1-3/8" overall ($4, £2). 22. **Hedgehog** measures 7/8" high by 1-3/4" overall and is mold marked "Wade England" in a recess on the underside of the base ($6, £3). 23. **Pine Marten** measures 1-3/8" high by 1-1/2" overall ($4, £2). 24. **Field Mouse** measures 1-1/2" high by 3/4" across the base and is mold marked "Wade" on one side and "England" on the other side of the base. A variation in the mold mark occurs on this figurine. Along with the usual "Wade England" mold mark around the base it is also found with "Wade England" molded into a recess on the underside of the base ($12, £6). 25. **Alsatian** measures 1-1/4" high by 1-7/8" overall ($6, £3).

Whimsies Set 6, *1975*
Bottom row. 26. **Collie** measures 1-1/4" high by 1-3/8" overall ($8, £4). 27. **Cow** measures 1-1/4" high by 1-1/2" overall ($10, £5). 28. **Pig** measures 13/16" high by 1-1/2" overall ($16, £8). 29. **Horse** measures 1-5/8" high by 1-3/8" overall ($16, £8). 30. **Lamb** measures 1-3/8" high by 1-1/8" overall ($10, £5).

Light blue presentation box for Set 6.

Pine Marten
(Set 5)
Color variations
($24 each, £12
each).

Hedgehog *(Set 5)*
Color variations. The dark brown hedgehog is 7/8" high by 1-3/4" long, has two riser tabs and is mold marked: Wade England. The medium brown hedgehog is 7/8" high by 1-3/4" long, has three riser tabs, and is mold marked: Wade England in a deep recess on the underside of the base. The light brown hedgehog is 15/16" high by 1-3/4" long, has larger ears and face, two riser tabs and is mold marked: Wade England in a shallow recess on the underside of the base.

Pig (*Set 6*)
Size Variations. Left. **Pig** measures 1" high by 1-3/4" long ($24, £12). This was the first version. Right. **Pig** measures 13/16" high by 1-1/2" long ($16, £8). This was the second version.

Collie (*Set 6*)
Color variations. Left. White undecorated version ($24, £12).
Right. Production Model.

Horse (*Set 6*)
Color variation ($16, £8).

Whimsies Set 7, *1976*
Top row. 31. **Rhino** measures 7/8" high by 1-5/8" overall ($6, £3). 32. **Leopard** measures 7/8" high by 1-7/8" overall ($8, £4). 33. **Gorilla** measures 1-1/2" high by 1-1/4" overall ($6, £3). 34. **Camel** measures 1-3/8" high by 1-5/8" overall ($8, £4). 35. **Zebra** measures 1-5/8" high by 1-1/2" overall ($8, £4).

Whimsies Set 8, *1977*
Bottom row. 36. **Donkey** measures 1-1/4" high by 1-5/8" overall ($16, £8). 37. **Barn Owl** measures 1-1/2" high by 1" across the base ($16, £8). 38. **Cat** measures 1-1/2" high by 7/8" dia. base ($18, £9). 39. **Mouse** measures 1-1/2" high by 1" dia. base ($14, £7). 40. **Ram** measures 1-3/16" high by 1-3/8" overall ($14, £7).

Orange presentation box for Set 7.

Magenta presentation box for Set 8.

Zebra *(Set 7)*
Color variation ($28, £14).

Barn Owl *(Set 8)*
Color variation ($24, £12).

Whimsies Set 9, *1978*
Top row. 41. **Dolphin** measures 1-1/8" high by 1-3/4" overall ($30, £15). 42. **Pelican** measures 1-3/4" high by 1-3/8" overall ($20, £10). 43. **Angel Fish** measures 1-3/8" high by 1-1/4" overall ($12, £6). 44. **Turtle** measures 9/16" high by 2" overall ($8, £4). This figurine is mold marked "Wade England" in a recess on the underside of the base. 45. **Seahorse** measures 2" high by 3/4" dia. base ($24, £12).

Whimsies Set 10, *1979*
Bottom row. 46. **Kangaroo** measures 1-5/8" high by 1-1/8" along the base ($12, £6). 47. **Orangutan** measures 1-1/4" high by 1-1/4" across ($6, £3). 48. **Tiger** measures 1-1/2" high by 1-1/8" overall ($12, £6). 49. **Koala Bear** measures 1-3/8" high by 1-1/8" overall ($20, £10). 50. **Langur** measures 1-3/8" high by 1-1/2" overall ($4, £2).

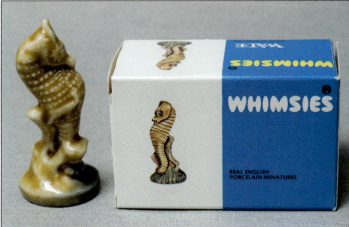

Cat *(Set 8)*
Left. Color variation ($28, £14).
Right. Prototype model.

Medium blue presentation box for Set 9.

Light green presentation box for Set 10.

Angel Fish *(Set 9)*
Color variations. Left ($24, £12). Center and Right ($12, £6).

Turtle *(Set 9)*
Color variations. Left ($24, £12).
Right ($8, £4).

Whimsies Set 11, *1979*

Top row. 51. **Bison** measures 1-1/8" high by 1-5/8" overall – small ($6, £3). 52. **Blue Bird** measures 5/8" high by 1-1/2" across the wings and is marked "Wade England" in a recess on the underside of the base ($8, £4). 53. **Bull Frog** measures 7/8" high by 1" across the base and is marked "Wade England" in a recess on the underside of the base ($24, £12). 54. **Wild Boar** measures 1-1/8" high by 1-5/8" overall ($10, £5). 55. **Raccoon** measures 1" high by 1-1/2" overall ($14, £7).

Whimsies Set 12, *1980*

Bottom row. 56. **Penguin** measures 1-5/8" high by 3/4" dia. base and is marked "Wade" at the front and "England" at the back of the base ($24, £12). 57. **Seal Pup** measures 1" high by 1-1/2" overall ($20, £10). 58. **Husky** measures 1-7/16" high by 1-1/8" overall ($20, £10). 59. **Walrus** measures 1-1/4" high by 1-1/4" overall ($10, £5). 60. **Polar Bear** measures 1-1/8" high by 1-5/8" overall ($20, £10).

Brown presentation box for Set 11.

Dark blue presentation box for Set 12.

Bison *(Set 11)*
Size variations. Left. **Bison** measures 1-3/8" high by 1-3/4" long, which is the earlier model ($10, £5). Right. **Bison** measures 1-1/8" high by 1-5/8" long, which is the later model ($6, £3).

Bison *(Set 11)*
Color variation ($24, £12).

Top. **Bluebird.** This figurine with painted black eyes is from the 1979 Whimsies Set 11 ($14, £7). Bottom. **Bluebird.** Color variation ($38, £16).

Blue Bird and Swallow
Comparison. Left. **Blue Bird** is the Whimsie bird from Set 11 and is also found in an all over blue color variation ($20, £10). Right. **Swallow** is the bird usually found on the Tree Trunk Posy Vase and Swallow Dish of the late 1950s ($30, £15).

Bull Frog *(Set 11)*
Color variations ($24 each,
£12 each).

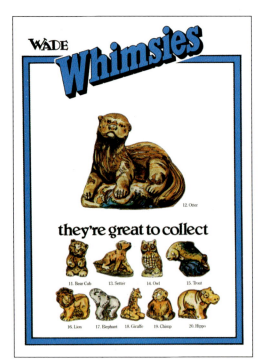

Wade flyer for
Whimsies Sets
3 & 4.

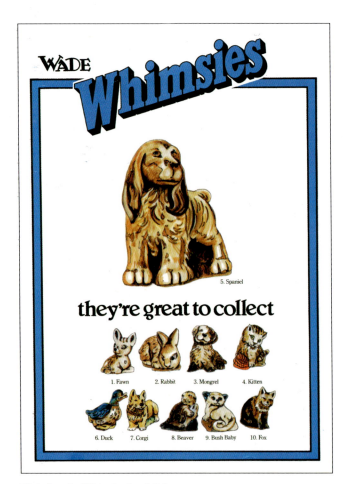

Wade flyer for Whimsies Sets 1 & 2.

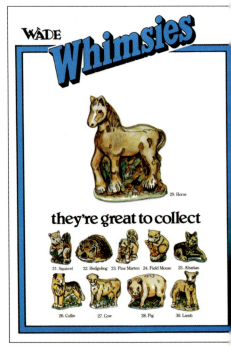

Wade flyer for Whimsies
Sets 5 & 6.

Wade flyer for Whimsies Sets 7 & 8.

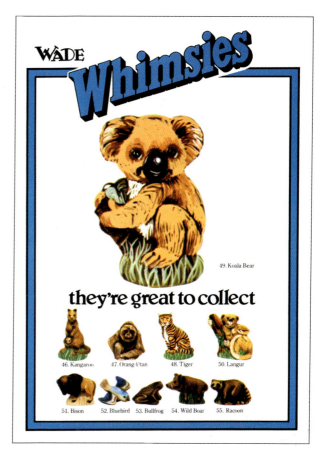

Wade flyer for Whimsies Sets 10 & 11.

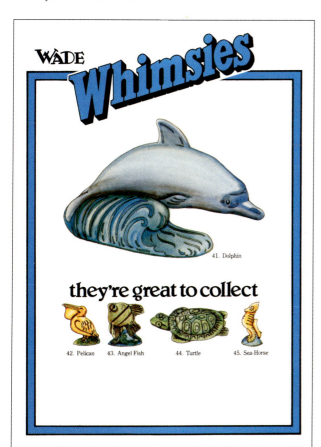

Wade flyer for Whimsies Set 9.

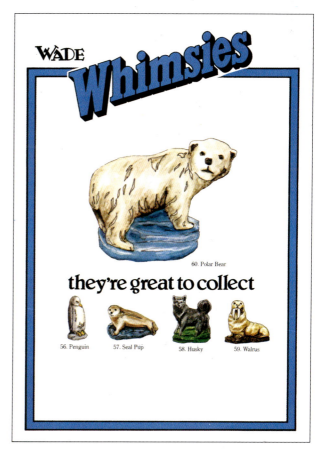

Wade flyer for Whimsies Set 12.

Whimsies, 1998 - 2007

In 1998, after a lapse of fourteen years, Wade reintroduced a new series of Whimsies. A number of molds from the earlier series of Whimsies were reused and some molds from premium promotions were used. Whether from new or reused molds, the color ways of the figurines were different, thus making it easy to differentiate the new sets from earlier sets. From 1998 onwards, the new Whimsies were sold either individually boxed or gift packed in hexagonal boxes containing the complete set of six figurines. Further sets of six figurines were issued at various intervals.

The method used by Wade Ceramics Limited for categorizing the new Whimsies can be somewhat confusing for new Wade collectors. Some sets were named by letters, such as Set "A" etc. and some were given numbers such as Set 1 etc. Here we have listed them as Set 1, Set 2, etc. along with the year of issue and the original Wade nomenclature.

Whimsies Set 1, *1998 – Set "A"*
When Wade reintroduced the Whimsies in 1998, a set of six figurines was produced utilizing four molds from the 1971-84 Whimsies and two molds from the Tom Smith Party Crackers Safari Set series. Although the molds were similar, the color ways were different.
Lion from Tom Smith Party Crackers Safari Set. **Raccoon** from Whimsies Set No.11. **Leopard** from Whimsies Set No. 7. **Hippo** from Whimsies Set No. 4. **Mole** from Tom Smith Party Crackers Wildlife Set. **Gorilla** from Whimsies Set No. 7 ($6 each, $36 set, £3 each, £18 set).

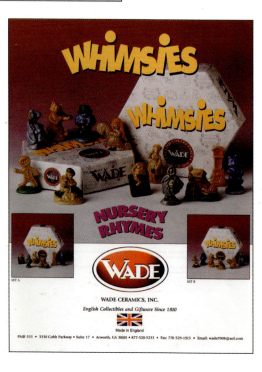

Hexagonal presentation box.

Starting in 2007, a new method of producing Whimsies was developed by Wade. Instead of the pressed method using steel dies, the new method is described as "solid casting." In this process the slip is poured into the mold and is left to solidify rather than the more usual method where extra slip is poured off. With this method of manufacture about thirty-five to forty figurines can be made from each mold. Due to the number of molds used for this type of production, there is more possibility of variations occurring.

Whimsies Set 2, *2000 – Set "B"*
A second set of six figurines was issued in 2000. Once again molds from the 1971-84 Whimsies were reused along with one mold from a Tom Smith Party Cracker promotion.
Polar Bear from Whimsies Set No. 12. **Beaver** from Whimsies Set No. 2. **Zebra** from Whimsies Set No. 7. **Kitten** from Whimsies Set No. 1. **Elephant** from Whimsies Set No. 4. **Pup** from Tom Smith Party Crackers Your Pets Set ($6 each, $36 set, £3 each, £18 set).

Wade Advertisement for Whimsies Set A and B.

Whimsies Set 3, *2001 – "Nursery" Set 1.*
In early 2001, Wade issued a new set of six Whimsies, this time reusing molds from the 1971-79 Canadian Red Rose Tea promotion. **Hickory Dickory Dock. Little Red Riding Hood. Puss'n Boots. Humpty Dumpty. Queen of Hearts. Old Woman in a Shoe** ($6 each, $36 set, £3 each, £18 set).

Wade advertisement for the New Whimsies.

Whimsies Set 4, *2001 – "Nursery" Set 2.*
The second set of six Whimsies issued in 2001 comprised four figurines from the 1971-84 Whimsies and two from a Tom Smith Party Cracker promotion.
Cat and the Fiddle. Tom the Piper's Son. Little Boy Blue from Tom Smith Party Crackers "Tales from the Nursery." **Little Bo-Peep. Ride a Cock Horse** from the Tom Smith Party Crackers Tales from the Nursery. **Gingerbread Man** ($6 each, $36 set, £3 each, £18 set).

Whimsies Set 5, *2003 – "Farmyard Whimsies"*
In 2003 a new set of Whimsies was issued using the molds previously used in earlier sets but with different color ways.
Cow. Rooster from the 1985 Whimsie-Land Set 3. **Pony** from the 1984 Whimsie-Land Set 1. **Pig. Duck. Goat** from the 1985 Whimsie-Land Set 3 ($7 each, $42 set, £4 each, £20 set).

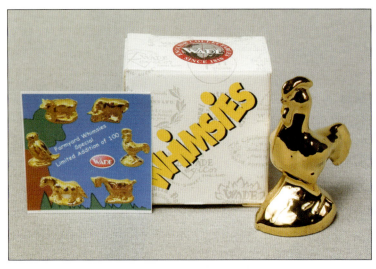

Individual box with certificate for the gold Farmyard Whimsies.

Whimsies Set 6, *2004 – Set "C"*
Wade produced a brand new set of six Whimsie figurines in February 2004 to help celebrate the 50th anniversary of the Whimsie.
Fox. Standing Cat. Sitting Cat. Puppy. Penguin. Duck ($7 each, $40 set, £3.5 each, £20.5 set).

Whimsies Set 5A, *2004 – "Farmyard Whimsies – Gold"*
In 2004 Wade reissued the six figurines from the Farmyard Set in an all-over gold version. This was a limited edition of 100 sets.
Cow. Rooster from the 1985 Whimsie-Land Set 3. **Pony** from the 1984 Whimsie-Land Set 1. **Pig. Duck. Goat** from the 1985 Whimsie-Land Set 3 ($60 each, £30 each).

Whimsies Set 7, *2005 – "Family Pets – Dogs"*
The year 2005 saw the introduction of the first Family Pets range of six dogs.
Setter. Boxer. Bull Terrier. Bassett Hound. Spaniel. Great Dane ($7 each, $40 set, £3.5 each, £20.5 set).

Whimsies Set 8, *2006 –*
"Family Pets – Cats"
The second set of Family Pets
Whimsies was introduced in
2005 with cats as the theme.
Standing Cat. Cat and
Kitten. Persian Cat. Lying
Cat. Brown and White Cat.
Tabby Cat ($7 each, $41 set,
£3.5 each, £21 set).

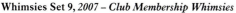

Whimsies Set 9, *2007 – Club Membership Whimsies*
Starting in February 2007, The Wade Collectors Club began issuing three
new Whimsie figurines with each quarterly magazine. These were solid
cast rather than the more usual pressed figurines. All dimensions are ap-
proximate as with solid casting the size of the figurines vary.
Set 1. February 2007.
Top row. **Snowy Owl** measures 1-5/8" high. **King Cobra** measures 1-5/8"
high. **Brown Hare** measures 1-5/8" high. All figurines are mold marked:
Wade ($52 set, £28 set).
Set 2. May 2007.
Bottom row. **Toco Toucan** measures 1-1/2" high by 2-1/2" overall. **Palm
Cockatoo** measures 2" high. **African Lion** measures 1-5/8" high by 2"
overall. All figurines are mold marked: Wade ($52 set, £28 set).

Set 3. August 2007.
Top row. **Eurasian Lynx** measures 1-1/4" high by 2-1/4" overall. **Polar Bear**
measures 2-1/2" high. **Grey Wolf** measures 1-7/8" high by 2-1/2" overall. All
figurines are mold marked: Wade ($52 set, £28 set).
Set 4. November 2007.
Bottom row. **Bengal Tiger** measures 1-7/8" high by 2-1/2" overall. **Wilde
Beest** measures 1-1/4" high by 2" overall. **Frilled Lizard** measures 1-3/4"
high by 2-1/4" overall. All figurines are mold marked: Wade ($52 set, £28).

Whimsie-Land Series, 1984 - 1988

When the second series of the popular Wade Whimsies was withdrawn in early 1984, a large gap was left in the Wade giftware line of small, inexpensive figurines. Due to the enormous success of the Whimsies, George Wade and Son Ltd. decided to introduce a new retail line of miniature animals to fill the gap.

After much consideration, it was decided that the new line should continue with a series of small porcelain animal and bird figurines which again would be issued in sets of five figurines per set. The new series was given the name Whimsie-Land. The hand-decorated, under glaze figurines were slightly larger and more detailed than the 1971-84 Whimsies.

The complete Whimsie-Land range was dropped in 1989 when Wade temporarily went out of the giftware market. The last five figurines in the Wildlife Set were in production for a short time only in 1987 and are therefore proving to be much harder to find than the other figurines in the series. As with earlier versions of the Whimsies, many of the remaining Whimsie-Land figurines were used to decorate a new line of Whimtrays.

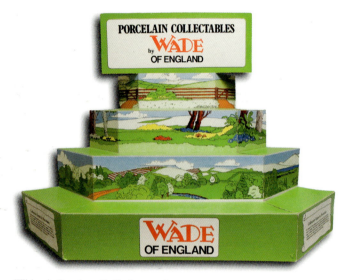

Whimsie-Land retail display stand.

Whimsie-Land Set 1, *1984 (Pets)*
1. **Retriever** measures 1-1/4" high by 1-5/8" along the base ($16, £8). 2. **Puppy** measures 1-3/8" high by 1-3/8" along the base ($12, £6). 3. **Rabbit** measures 2" high by 7/8" dia. base ($24, £12). 4. **Kitten** measures 1" high by 1-5/8" along the base ($14, £7). 5. **Pony** measures 1-1/2" high by 1-1/2" along the base ($18, £9).

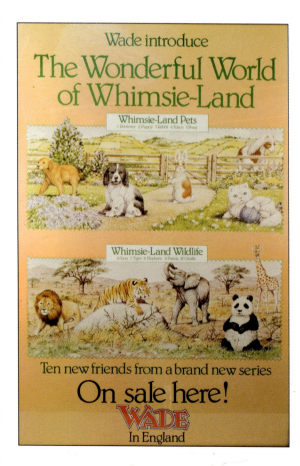

24" by 16-1/2" poster promoting the Whimsie-Land figurines.

Presentation box with rabbit.

Whimsie-Land Pony *Set 1 (Pets)*
Color variation ($24, £12).

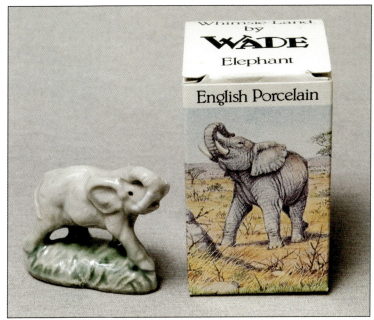

Presentation box with elephant.

Whimsie-Land Pony *Set 1 (Pets)*
Pony on Whimsie-Land display stand.

Whimsie-Land Set 2, *1984* (Wildlife)
6. **Lion** measures 1-1/4" high by 1-7/8" along the base ($16, £8). 7. **Tiger** measures 3/4" high by 1-3/4" along the base ($14, £7). 8. **Elephant** measures 1-3/8" high by 1-3/8" along the base ($18, £9). 9. **Panda** measures 1-3/8" high by 7/8" dia. base ($20, £10). 10. **Giraffe** measures 2" high by 1-1/4" along the base ($20, £10).

Whimsie-Land Tiger *Set 2*
(Wildlife)
Left. Prototype model.
Right. Color variations ($20,
£10).

Whimsie-Land Set 3,
1985 (Farmyard)
11. **Rooster** measures
2" high by 1-1/8" along
the base ($20, £10). 12.
Duck measures 1-5/8"
high by 1" along the
base ($20, £10). 13.
Cow measures 1-1/4"
high by 1-1/4" along
the base ($38, £19). 14.
Pig measures 1-1/8"
high by 1-1/4" along the
base ($16, £8). 15. **Goat**
measures 1-1/4" high
by 1-1/8" along the base
($16, £8).

Presentation
box with goat.

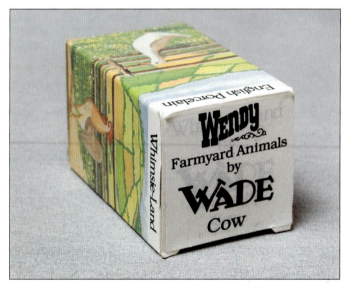

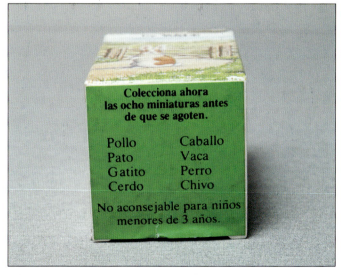

Top. Top of Wendy Farm Animals presentation box. Bottom. Bottom of
Wendy Farm Animals presentation box.

Top. Top of Wendy Farm Animals presentation box. Spanish version. Bottom. Bottom of Wendy Farm Animals presentation box. Spanish version.

Whimsie-Land Set 4, *1986 (Hedgerow)*
16. **Fox** measures 1-3/8" high by 1-1/4" along the base ($46, £23). 17. **Owl** measures 1-1/2" high by 7/8" along the base ($16, £8). 18. **Hedgehog** measures 7/8" high by 1-1/4" along the base ($16, £8). 19. **Badger** measures 1" high by 1-3/8" along the base ($14, £7). 20. **Squirrel** measures 1-1/2" high by 3/4" along the base ($12, £6).

Whimsie-Land Fox *Set 4 (Hedgerow)*
Prototype model.

Presentation box with badger.

Whimsie-Land Set 5, *1987 (British Wildlife)*
21. **Pheasant** measures 1-1/4" high by 2" long ($42, £21). 22. **Field Mouse** measures 1-1/4" high by 1-1/2" long ($44, £22). 23. **Golden Eagle** measures 1-1/8" high by 1-3/4" long ($40, £20). 24. **Otter** measures 1-1/2" high by 1-5/8" long ($18, £9). 25. **Partridge** measures 1-1/2" high by 1-3/4" long ($26, £13).

Presentation box with pheasant.

Whimsie-Land Otter *Set 5 (British Wildlife)*
Left. Prototype model. Right. Production model.

Whimsie-Land Pheasant *Set 5 (British Wildlife)*
Left. Prototype model. Right. Production model.

Whimsie-Land Field Mouse *Set 5 (British Wildlife)*
Left. Prototype model. Right. Production model.

Whimsie-Land Key Rings, 1988

Illustration of Whimsie-Land key rings.

When Wade discontinued the Whimsie-Land series, much of the remaining stock was made available as key rings. The illustration shows the Duck, Puppy, Kitten, Panda, and Badger in the key ring format ($20 each, £10 each).

Whimtrays, 1958 - 1965

The Whimtrays were developed as a way of using up odd, leftover stock from the popular Whimsies. At the end of the run of the various Whimsies, Wade was left with large quantities of figurines. As there were not enough figurines available to form quantities of complete sets, a decision had to be made as to the best way of clearing these "left over" figurines. The idea of producing a small round "Pin Tray" with a small ledge incorporated into the dish was decided upon. This would create a new giftware item, which would also use up the spare Whimsies figurines. The figurines were mounted onto the flat ledge and with the addition of the figurines to the trays the obvious name for the tray was "Whimtray."

The first Whimtrays were officially announced in the January 1958 Wade Wholesalers Newsletter No. 4. In the August 1958 Wade Wholesalers Newsletter No. 5, it was reported that all stocks had been sold out, including all stocks of the Zoolights. New trays were to be produced with figurines from Set 8 of the Whimsies, the Zoo Set.

These early Whimtrays, 3" in diameter and 5/8" high, were produced in a variety of colors, yellow, green, black, blue/green (dark turquoise), and pink. The first trays were manufactured in the Burslem potteries and had a ledge resembling the segment of an intersecting circle measuring 2-1/8" across by 3/4" at its widest point. (See Whimtray Type "A.")

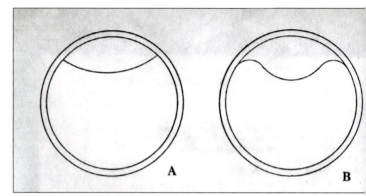

Whimtray Types
Left. Type A. Right. Type B.

These trays were all mold marked Whimtrays Wade Porcelain Made in England on the underside of the base. Sometime during the period of production, the manufacturing of the Whimtrays was transferred to Wade (Ireland) Ltd. in Portadown. With the change in location of manufacture also came a change in the shape of the ledge supporting the figurine. The ledge on the Irish made trays is in the shape of a half circle with the edges curved back to blend in with the upturned edge of the tray. (See Whimtray Type "B."). The mold mark on the underside of the Irish made Whimtray was changed to Mark Type 41.

Left. **Cockatoo** on "Type A" tray made in England. Right. **Penguin** on "Type B" tray made in Ireland ($30 each, £15 each).

WHIMTRAYS

Animal figures, delightfully detailed and coloured, on brightly glazed trays.

Only 2/6d. each—they can be bought from your shopkeeper singly or in cartons of 1 dozen.

Wade advertisement for Whimtrays from the Spring and Summer 1960 Price List.

Left. **Llama** on "Type A" tray made in England. Right. **Panda** on "Type A" tray made in England ($30 each, £15 each).

Husky on "Type B" tray made in Ireland. **Monkey and Baby** on "Type A" tray made in England. **Camel** on "Type A" tray made in England. **Polar Bear Cub** on "Type B" tray made in Ireland ($30 each, £15 each).

Left. **Swan** on "Type A" tray made in England. Right. **Boxer** on "Type A" tray made in England ($30 each, £15 each).

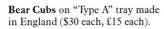

Bear Cubs on "Type A" tray made in England ($30 each, £15 each).

Left. **Owl** on "Type A" tray made in England. Right. **Rabbit** on "Type A" tray made in England ($30 each, £15 each).

Raccoon on "Type A" tray made in England ($30, £15).

Seal Pup on "Type A" tray made in England ($30, £15).

Whimtrays, 1971 - 1987

After a lapse of a few years, Whimtrays were reintroduced but this time with figurines from the 1971-84 series of Whimsies. Only three figurines were used on either black, green or blue trays, giving a limited variety of choices. The majority of the newer Whimtrays were made in Ireland and had a molded "Made in Ireland" mark. However, a few Whimtrays in the shape Type "B" have been found with a "Wade Made in England" mold mark.

The shape of the ledge on which the figurines are mounted is similar to the earlier Irish made Whimtrays, but there is a slight variation with the addition of a raised rim around the curved ledge. This would imply that a new mold must have been made for the 1971 reissue.

Left. **Trout** on made in Ireland tray. Top Center. **Fawn** on made in Ireland tray. Bottom Center. **Trout** on made in England tray. Right. **Duck** on made in Ireland tray ($20 each, £10 each).

Whimtrays, 1987 - 1988

The new Whimtrays, introduced in 1987, replaced the long-running round shaped trays first manufactured in 1958. The new Whimtrays were oval in shape and utilized figurines from the Whimsie-Land series. The new Whimtrays measured 4-1/2" long by 3-1/2" wide and were mold marked: Wade England.

Top row. **Owl, Pony**. Center. **Squirrel**. Bottom row. **Duck, Puppy**. ($24 each, £12 each).

Whoppas, 1976 - 1981

Starting in 1976, Wade introduced three sets of five animals each, which were marketed under the name of "Whoppas." The series remained in production until 1981. The fifteen figurines are all marked "Wade England" on the side of the base, even though the figurines comprising Set 1 were manufactured by Wade (Ireland) Ltd. in Portadown, Northern Ireland.

When the "Whoppas" were discontinued as a retail line, surplus stock was used for the short lived 1981 Canadian Red Rose Tea premium promotion.

Orange presentation box from Set 1 with Hippo.

Set 1, *1976*
1. **Polar Bear** measures 1-1/2" high by 2-1/4" overall ($20, £10). 2. **Hippo** measures 1-3/8" high by 2-1/4" overall ($20, £10). 3. **Brown Bear** measures 1-1/2" high by 1-3/4" overall ($20, £10). 4. **Tiger** measures 1-1/8" by 2-1/2" overall ($20, £10). 5. **Elephant** measures 2-1/8" high by 2" overall ($20, £10).

Whoppas Elephant
Left. Production model ($20, £10). Right. Prototype ($50, £25).

Set 2, *1977*
6. **Bison** measures 1-3/4" high by 2-1/4" overall ($30, £15). 7. **Wolf** measures 2-1/4" high by 1-3/4" overall ($20, £10). 8. **Bobcat** measures 1-1/2" high by 1-7/8" overall ($30, £15). 9. **Chipmunk** measures 2-1/8" high by 1" dia. base ($30, £15). 10. **Raccoon** measures 1-1/2" high by 2-1/4" overall ($30, £15).

Whoppas Bobcat
Prototype model ($50, £25).

Green presentation box from Set 2 with Bison.

Set 3, *1978*
11. **Fox** measures 1-1/4" high by 2-1/2" overall ($36, £18). 12. **Badger** measures 1-1/2" high by 1-7/8" overall ($32, £16). 13. **Otter** measures 1-1/4" high by 2" overall ($36, £18). 14. **Stoat** measures 1-1/2" high by 2-1/8" overall ($32, £16). 15. **Hedgehog** measures 1-1/4" high by 1-7/8" overall ($38, £19).

Brown presentation box from Set 3 with Badger.

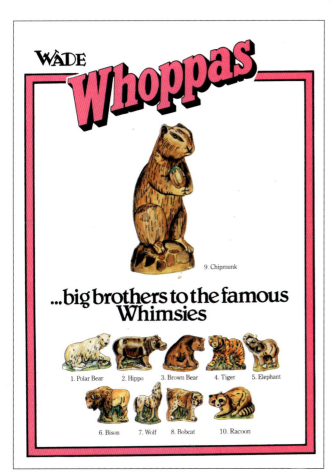

Wade flyer for Whoppas Sets 1 - 10

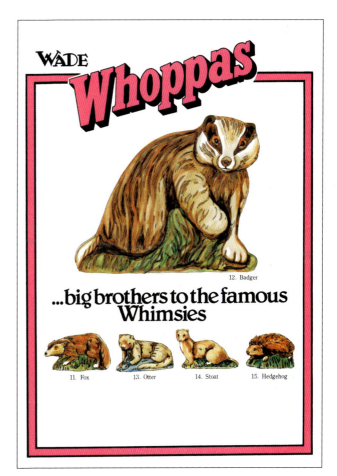

Wade flyer for Whoppas Sets 11 - 15

Zoolights, 1957 - 1960

Although the Zoolights were officially launched with an announcement in the January 1958 Wade Wholesalers Newsletter No. 4., they had already been marketed, unofficially, in the latter part of 1957. A note in the January 1958 newsletter reported "These [Zoolights] were designed for 1958, but being (for once in our lives) ahead of ourselves we couldn't resist the temptation of putting a few of them on the market before Christmas (entitled Animal Candlesticks).

That was our intention but repeats [repeated requests] flowed in so fast and furiously that we ended up by selling a very large quantity indeed prior to Christmas."

The August 1958 Wade Wholesalers Newsletter No. 5, reported that "...all stocks had been sold out in early 1958 so new ones with animals from Set 8, Zoo Whimsies were issued." However, in the January 1960 Wade Wholesalers Newsletter No. 8, it was reported that production was to end that year.

Although the birds and animals mounted on the Zoolights were made in Ireland, the base of the Zoolight was manufactured in Burslem.

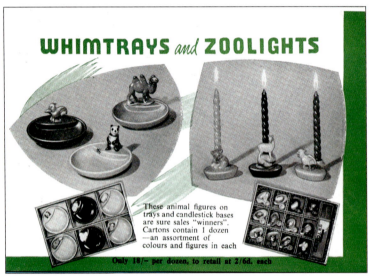

Whimtrays and Zoolights shown in the Autumn & Winter 1959 Wade Price List.

From left. **Baby Polar Bear** from the 1956 Polar Set (Set 6). **Corgi** from the 1957 Pedigree Dogs (Set 7). **Hare** from the 1954 (Set 7). **Llama** from the 1958 Zoo Set (Set 8). ($30 each, £15 each).

From left. **Boxer** from the 1957 Pedigree Dogs (Set 7). **Snowy Owl** from the 1958 North American Animals (Set 9). ($30 each, £15 each).

Top Left. **Rabbit** from the 1954 Whimsies (Set 2). Top Right. **Bear Cub** from the 1958 North American Animals (Set 9). Center. **Penguin** from the 1956 Polar Set (Set 6). Bottom. **Squirrel** from the 1953 Whimsies (Set 3). ($30 each, £15 each).

From left. **Camel** from the 1958 Zoo Set (Set 8). **Husky** from the 1956 Polar Set (Set 6). **West Highland Terrier** from the 1957 Pedigree Dogs (Set 7). **Baby Polar Bear** from the 1956 Polar Set (Set 6). ($30 each, £15 each).

Spaniel from the 1953 Whimsies (Set 1). ($30, £15).

Alsatian from the 1957 Pedigree Dogs (Set 7). **Husky** from the 1956 Polar Set (Set 6) ($30 each, £15 each).

Alsatian from the 1957 Pedigree Dogs (Set 7). **West Highland Terrier** from the 1957 Pedigree Dogs Set (Set 7) ($30 each, £15 each).

Horse from the 1956 Horse Set (Set 5). ($30, £15).

West Highland Terrier from the 1957 Pedigree Dogs Set (Set 7). ($30, £15).

Zoolight with Baby
2" high with Mark Type 25
($90, £45).

Seal from the 1956 Polar
Set (Set 6). **Panda** from
the 1957 Zoo Set (Set 8).
($30 each, £15 each).

Zoolights with Metal Figurines
Horse measures 2-3/4" high. **Pelican** measures 2-1/4" high. **Rooster** measures 2" high. **Cat** measures 2-1/2" high.
Horse measures 2-3/4" high ($20 each, £10 each).

Angel Figurines, 1959 - 1960s

The Angel figurines set consisted of three miniature angels in various poses, either standing, sitting or kneeling. The figurines were sold either separately, applied to dishes similar to the Whimtrays or attached to miniature candle holders. The Angel figurines have been found with green, pink, yellow, and blue glazes. All figurines are unmarked.

Although, technically, the Angel figurines were not retailed as Whimsies, they are small pressed figurines so we have included them here.

Angel Candle Holder
Above. The standing Angel candle holder measures approx. 2-1/4" high on a black, triangular base, 2" each side, and is mold marked Wade on the underside. Right. The kneeling Angel candleholder measures approx. 2-1/8" high on a similar base as above ($88 each, £44 each).

Angelic! A George Wade & Son Ltd. advertisement as it appeared in the September 1963 issue of *Tableware*. Note the Horse and Foal dish in the bottom right hand corner.

Left. **Kneeling Angel Figurine** measures 1-3/8" high ($80, £40). Center. **Sitting Angel Figurine** measures 1-3/8" high ($80, £40). Right. **Standing Angel Figurine** measures 1-1/2" high ($80, £40).

Angel Dish
Above. **Kneeling Angel** on Type "B" tray. Bottom Left. **Sitting Angel** on Type "B" tray. Bottom Right. **Standing Angel** on Type "B" tray. The dishes measure 2" high (including the figurine) and are mold marked "Angel Dish" Wade Porcelain Made in England ($80 each, £40 each).

Chapter 2
Fair Special Issues

I t has been the custom, at recent Wade Fair events to give out free figurines in special color ways to paying attendees of the events. The free figurines are usually, but not always, from the Whimsie or Whimsie-Land series.

The following illustrations not only show figurines given out for free but also figurines sold at the various fairs which in some way are connected to the free issues.

Wade Collector Fairs, 2000 - 2007

The biannual Wade Collectors Fairs are held in the spring and autumn of the year. The spring Fair is held in or around Stoke-on-Trent and the autumn Fairs are held in Dunstable, Bedfordshire.

Pearlized Duck (from the 1985 Whimsie-Land Set 3) given at the October 2001 Wade Collectors Fair, Trentham Gardens ($20, £10). **Pearlized Bunny** (from the 1988-89 Tom Smith, Your Pets Animates Crackers) given at the April 2002 Wade Collectors Fair, King's Hall, Stoke-on-Trent ($20, £10). **Pearlized Polar Bear** (from the 1980 Whimsies Set 12) given at the September 2002 Dunstable Wade Collectors Fair ($20, £10). **Pearlized Seahorse** (from the 1978 Whimsies Set 9) given at the April 2003 Wade Collectors Fair, North Stafford Hotel, Stoke-on-Trent ($20, £10).

Gold Bear Cub (from the 1972 Whimsies Set 3) given at the October 2000 Wade Extravaganza, Trentham Gardens, Stoke-on-Trent ($20, £10). **Gold Owl** (from the 1986 Whimsie-Land Set 4) given at the April 2001 Wade Collectors Fair, Trentham Gardens ($28, £14).

Silver Bluebird Whimsie was a limited edition of 25 ($50, £25). **Bluebird** Whimsie given at the April 2007 Wade Collectors Fair held at Discover Trentham ($16, £8). The **Gold Bluebird** Whimsie was a limited edition of 25 ($50, £25). This 1" high figurine was from a new mold and is mold marked Wade on one wing.

Pearlized Snail (originally from the 1975-80 Aquarium Set) given at the September 2003 Dunstable Wade Collectors Fair ($16, £8). **Pearlized Dolphin** (from the 1978 Whimsies Set 9) given at the April 2004 Wade Collectors Fair, North Stafford Hotel ($20, £10). **Pearlized Penguin** (from the 1980 Whimsies Set 12) given at the September 2004 Dunstable Wade Fair ($16, £8). Above. **Gold Penguin** (from the 1980 Whimsies Set 12) was given as draw or bran tub prizes ($50, £25).

Pearlized Boxer (from the 2005 Family Pets Dogs Whimsies) given at the September 2007 Dunstable Wade Collectors Fair ($12, £6).

Pearlized Puppy (from the 1988-89 Tom Smith, Your Pets Animates Crackers) given at the April 2005 Wade Collectors Fair, King's Hall ($18, £9). **Pearlized Giraffe** (from the 1973 Whimsies Set 4) given at the September 2005 Dunstable Wade Collectors Fair ($18, £9). **Pearlized Bull Terrier** (from the 2005 Family Pets Dog Whimsies) given at the April 2006 Wade Collectors Fair, King's Hall ($18, £9). **Pearlized Basset Hound** (from the 2005 Family Pets Dog Whimsies) given at the September 2006 Dunstable Wade Collectors Fair ($18, £9).

Wade Collectors Meet, 2000 - 2007

Established in 1986 by David Chown and Russell Schooley, C&S Collectables has become one of the major businesses to produce figurines made especially for them by Wade Ceramics Limited.

The Wade Collectors Meets are held in July or August of each year in Arundel, West Sussex. The Meets, sponsored by C&S Collectables, began in August 1997 and were originally named Wade Swap Meets but the name was changed to Wade Collectors Meet in 2001. C&S Collectables is also present at all other annual Wade Fairs in both the U.K. and the U.S.A.

Top row. **Grey Badger** (from the 1986 Whimsie-Land Set 4) given at the July 2003 Wade Collectors Meet ($10, £5). **Apricot Fox** (from the 1986 Whimsie-Land Set 4) given at the July 2004 Wade Collectors Meet ($10, £5). **Gold Fox.** This was a limited edition of 20 that was mixed in with the regular issue of the apricot foxes (N.P.A.). Bottom row. **Black Pig** (from the 1985 Whimsie-Land Set 3) given at the July 2005 Wade Collectors Meet ($16, £8). **Gold Pig.** This was a limited edition of 10 that were sold as part of a set that included both the black and the silver pigs (N.P.A.). **Silver Pig.** This was a limited edition of 20, which was mixed in with the regular issue of the black pigs (N.P.A.).

Top row. **Pink Salmon** (from the 1972 Whimsies Set 3) given at the August 2000 Arundel Swap Meet ($12, £6). **Beige Otter** (from the 1987 Whimsie-Land Set 5) given at the August 2001 Wade Collectors Meet ($12, £6). Bottom row. **Grey Otter** (from the 1987 Whimsie-Land Set 5) given at the August 2001 Wade Collectors Meet ($16, £8). **Honey Pony** (from the 1988-89 Tom Smith, Your Pets Animates Crackers) given at the July 2002 Wade Collectors Meet ($16, £8).

Gold Bear. This was a limited edition of 100, which were given to collectors who bought the Wade's Animaland Giant Panda 'Ping Ping.' (N.P.A.). **Beige Bear** (from the 1984 Whimsie-Land Set 2) given at the July 2006 Wade Collectors Meet ($16, £8). **Silver Bear.** This was a limited edition of 20, which was mixed in with the regular issue of the beige bears (N.P.A.).

Pearlized Great Dane (from the 2005 Family Pets Dogs Whimsies) given at the July 2007 Wade Collectors Meet ($10, £5).

Christmas Bonanza, 1999 - 2007

As well as sponsoring the Wade Collectors Meet, C&S Collectables also holds the Christmas Bonanza each December. The Bonanza is held at the C&S Collectables headquarters in Arundel, West Sussex.

Arthur Hare Teenies *1999-2000*
These figurines, produced by C&S Collectables, were miniature versions of the larger Arthur Hare series and were issued in limited edition. Each figurine measures approx. 2-1/4" high and is mold marked "Wade" on the base.
From left. **Teenie Jesthare. Teenie P.C. Gotchare.** The first three figurines were a limited edition of 300 each and sold at the 1999 Wade Christmas Bonanza. **Teenie Harestronaut. Teenie Sharehiff. Teenie Chief Bravehare.** The last two figurines were a limited edition of 250 figurines each and sold at the 2000 Wade Fest in Harrisburg, Pennsylvania ($36 each, £18 each).

Cobalt Blue Partridge given at the December 2003 Christmas Bonanza. The Burgundy, Pink, and Blue Partridges were a limited edition of 200 ($18 each, £9 each). **Pink Partridge** given at the December 2003 Christmas Bonanza. **Burgundy Partridge** (from the 1987 Whimsie-Land Set 5) given at the December 2003 Christmas Bonanza. **Gold Partridge** was a limited issue of 20 ($70, £35). **Silver Partridge** was a limited issue of 20 ($70, £35).

Green Robin (from the 1997 Set 11 Whimsies) given at the December 2006 Christmas Bonanza. **Burgundy Robin** (from the 1997 Set 11 Whimsies) given at the December 2006 Christmas Bonanza ($16 each, £8 each). The robins were a limited edition of 100 in each color of which 50 were given away free to the first 50 visitors to the Bonanza. The remaining robins were sold during the Bonanza. The **Silver Robin** was a limited edition of 25 and the **Gold Robin** was a limited edition of 25 ($50 each, £25 each).

Christmas Robin Whimsie was a Wade Ceramics special sold at the December 2007 Christmas Bonanza ($16, £8). This 1" high figurine was from the same mold as the one used for the April 2007 Trentham Collectors Fair. The figurine is mold marked Wade on one wing.

Betty Boop Whimsies *2004-2007*
C&S Collectables have long been known for their superb large and midsize Betty Boop figurines. In 2004, the company produced a Whimsie version of Betty Boop, which was modeled by Ken Holmes. The first Betty Boop Whimsies were given to paying visitors to the 2004 Christmas Bonanza followed by other figurines given at other Wade events. Finally a number of figurines were sold as a retail line.
Green Betty Boop Whimsie and **Burgundy Betty Boop Whimsie** were given to the first 100 visitors to the December 2004 Christmas Bonanza ($20 each, £10 each). **Orange Betty Boop Whimsie** was given to the first 50 visitors to the December 2005 Christmas Bonanza ($40, £20). **Dark Blue, Pink, White, and Beige Betty Boop Whimsies** were a retail line of 500 sets sold in 2004 ($16 each, £8 each). **Light Green and Light Blue Betty Boop Whimsies** were a retail line with approximately 3,500 made in each color ($12 each, £6 each). **Gold Pearlized Betty Boop Whimsie** was a limited edition of 50 figurines ($100, £50).

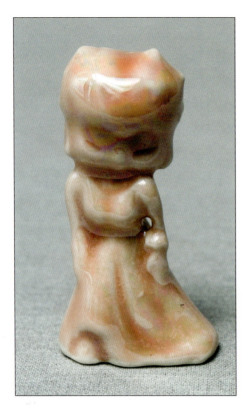

Betty Boop Pretty in Pink. This new model of the Betty Boop Whimsie was modeled by Cyril Roberts. The figurine measures 1-1/2" high and is a limited edition of 250 ($16, £8). This figurine is the first of a series. Other figurines will have different color ways.

Showtime Betty Boop. This third Whimsie version of the popular Betty Boop series was issued in 2008. ($16, £8).

Summer Wade Fest, 1999 - 2007

The Summer Wade Fest is organized by Patty and Gary Keenan of Keenan Antiques. The first fair was described as a Mini Fair, which was held in York, Pennsylvania, in 1999. The success of the Mini Fair resulted in a move to a larger facility in Camp Hill/Harrisburg where it has continued to be a very popular fair, with both dealers and collectors attending from all over the U.S.A., Canada, and England.

As well as promoting the Fair, Keenan Antiques also commissioned special Whimsies, some of which were given as free gifts with the Fair package or as door prizes. Complete sets were also sold at the Wade Fest.

Jenny the Black Poodle *1999*
This figurine was commissioned for the 1999 Mini Fair held in York, Pennsylvania. The poodle is from the same mold as the 1967-73 Canadian Red Rose Tea promotion. The black Poodle was a limited edition of 2,000 pieces ($14, £7). Jenny, as well as being retailed, was also given as gifts in the Fair package.

Harrisburg Kitten *2000*
These color variations of the Kitten from the 1988-89 Tom Smith set Your Pets were produced for the 2000 Summer Wade Fest. The black and white kittens as well as being given as gifts in the Wade Fest package were sold during and after the Fair. **Black Kitten** *(Thunder)* was issued in an edition of 1,200 pieces ($8, £4). **Gold Kitten** was a limited issue of 100 and was only given as gifts and door prizes and was never retailed ($40, £20). **White Kitten** *(Lightning)* was issued in a limited number of 800 pieces ($10, £5).

Harrisburg Mongrel Pup *2002*
These color variations of the Mongrel Puppy from the 1971 Whimsies were produced for the 2002 Summer Wade Fest. The black and white puppies, as well as being given as gifts in the Wade Fest package, were sold during and after the Fair. **Gold Mongrel Puppy** was a limited edition of 100 and given away as door and draw prizes and never retailed ($40, £20). **White Mongrel Puppy** was a limited edition of 550 ($6, £3). **Black Mongrel Puppy** was a limited edition of 550 ($10, £6).

Harrisburg Guinea Pigs *2001*
These color variations of the Guinea Pig from the 1988-89 Tom Smith Party Cracker set Your Pets were produced for the 2001 Summer Wade Fest. The black and white guinea pigs as well as being given as gifts in the Wade Fest package were sold during and after the Fair. **Black Guinea Pig** was a limited edition of 500 ($10, £5). **White Guinea Pig** was a limited edition of 1,000 ($8, £4). **Gold Guinea Pig** was a limited edition of 100 and given away as door and draw prizes and never retailed ($40, £20).

Harrisburg Reindeer *2003*
These color variations of the Reindeer are from the Tom Smith 1992-97 Snow Life set and were produced for the 2003 Summer Wade Fest. The honey and white reindeer, as well as being given as gifts in the Wade Fest package, were sold during and after the Fair. **Honey Reindeer** was a limited edition of 600 ($14, £7). **White Reindeer** was a limited edition of 600 ($6, £3). **Gold Reindeer** was a limited edition of 100 and given away as door and draw prizes and never retailed ($40, £20). **Honey Reindeer with Red Nose** (not shown) was a limited edition of 70 and given away as prizes (no price available).

Harrisburg Rabbit *2005*
These color variations of the Whimsie-Land Set 1, Rabbit was produced for the 2005 Summer Wade Fest. The honey and blue/grey rabbits, as well as being given as gifts in the Wade Fest package, were sold during and after the Fair. **Honey Rabbit** was a limited edition of 600 ($8, £4). **Blue/Grey Rabbit** was a limited edition of 600 ($8, £4). **Gold Rabbit** was a limited edition of 100 and given away as door and draw prizes and never retailed ($40, £20).

Harrisburg Wren *2004*
These color variations of the Wren are from the Tom Smith 1992-93 Bird Life set and were produced for the 2004 Summer Wade Fest. The blue/grey and white wrens, as well as being given as gifts in the Wade Fest package, were sold during and after the Fair. **White Wren** was a limited edition of 600 ($8, £4). **Gold Wren** was a limited edition of 100 and given away as door and draw prizes and never retailed ($40, £20). **Blue Wren** was a limited edition of 800 ($8, £4.).

Harrisburg Bulldog *2006*
These color variations of the Bull Dog are from the Tom Smith 1990-91 World of Dogs set and were produced for the 2006 Summer Wade Fest. The honey and white bull dogs, as well as being given as gifts in the Wade Fest package, were sold during and after the Fair. **Honey Bull Dog** was a limited edition of 600 ($6, £3). **White Bull Dog** was a limited edition of 600 ($6, £3). **Gold Bull Dog** was a limited edition of 100 and given away as door and draw prizes and never retailed ($40, £20).

Harrisburg Rabbits *2007*
This completely new mold was commissioned by Keenan Antiques for the 2007 Summer Wade Fest. This new rabbit figurine was produced using the solid cast method of production. Left. **White Rabbit** was a limited edition of 450 ($6, £3). Center. **Gold Rabbit** was a limited edition of 100 ($40, £20). Right. **Grey Rabbit** was a limited edition of 450 ($6, £3). The rabbits measure 1-7/8" high and are mold marked Wade.

Lil' Bits Figurines, 2001 - 2007

Starting in 2001, Keenan Antiques have issued miniature figurines for the Summer Wade Fest. As well as being given as free gifts in the Fair Package, the mini figurines are sold in sets. The gold version is given as prizes in lucky draws.

Lil' Bits Rabbits *2001*
These 1" high, pressed and unmarked miniature Bunnies were sold at the 2001 Wade Fest in Harrisburg, Pennsylvania. **Pink Rabbit** was a limited edition of 450. The intended color for the pink was cotton candy but this did not produce well and only 200 figurines were made in the cotton candy glaze ($10, £5). **Green Rabbit** was a limited edition of 430 ($10, £5). **White Rabbit** was a limited edition of 500 ($10, £5). **Blue Rabbit** was a limited edition of 500 ($10, £5). The pink, green, white, and blue bunnies were retailed and given as gift items in the Wade Fest package. **Gold Rabbit** was a limited edition of 50. This figurine was given as door and draw prizes only and never retailed ($50, £25).

Lil' Bits Mice *2002*
These 3/4" high, pressed and unmarked miniature mice were first made available at the 2002 Summer Wade Fest in Harrisburg, Pennsylvania. **Grey Mouse** was a limited edition of 500. A grey figurine was also included in the Wade Fest Goodie Bag ($8, £4). **Blue Mouse** ($8, £4), **Beige Mouse** ($8, £4), **White Mouse** ($8, £4). The blue, beige, and white mice were a limited edition of 500 pieces each and were originally sold as a set along with the grey mouse ($32 set, £16 set). **Gold Mouse** was a limited edition of 50 and given as draw prizes ($50, £25).

Lil' Bits Elephants *2003*
These 3/4" high, pressed miniature elephants were sold at the 2003 Summer Wade Fest and were mold marked Wade Eng. **Blue Elephant** was a limited edition of 500 ($8, £4). **Green Elephant** was a limited edition of 500 ($8, £4). **White Elephant** was a limited edition of 500 ($8, £4). **Grey Elephant** was a limited edition of 770. A grey figurine was also included in the Wade Fest Goodie Bag ($8, £4). These were originally sold as a set ($32 set, £16 set). **Gold Elephant** was a limited edition of 100 and given away as draw prizes ($40, £20).

Lil' Bits Ducks *2004*
These 3/4" high, pressed miniature ducks were sold at the 2004 Summer Wade Fest and were unmarked. **Green Duck** was a limited edition of 550 ($8, £4). **White Duck** was a limited edition of 550. A white figurine was also included in the Wade Fest Goodie Bag ($8, £4). **Honey Duck** was a limited edition of 500 ($8, £4). **Gold Duck** was a limited edition of 60 and given away as draw prizes ($24, £12). **Blue Duck** was a limited edition of 500 ($8, £4). The green, white, honey, and blue ducks were originally sold as a set ($32 set, £16 set).

Lil' Bits Pigs *2005*
These 1/2" high, pressed figurines were sold at the 2005 Summer Wade Fest and were mold marked Wade. **Blue Pig** was a limited edition of 500 ($8, £4). **Yellow Pig** was a limited edition of 500. A yellow figurine was also included in the Wade Fest Goodie Bag ($8, £4). **Pink Pig** was a limited edition of 575 ($8, £4). **Gold Pig** was a limited edition of 100 and given away as draw prizes ($24, £12). **Green Pig** was a limited edition of 500 ($8, £4). The blue, yellow, pink, and green pigs were originally sold as a set ($32 set, £16 set).

Lil' Bits Cats *2006*
These 7/16" high, pressed figurines were sold at the 2006 Summer Wade Fest and were unmarked. **Apricot Cat** was a limited edition of 495 ($8, £4). **Black Cat** was a limited edition of 500 ($8, £4). **White Cat** was a limited edition of 580 ($8, £4). A white figurine was also included in the Wade Fest Goodie Bag. **Gold Cat** was a limited edition of 100 and given away as draw prizes ($24, £12). **Grey Cat** was a limited edition of 458 ($8, £4). The apricot, black, white, and grey cats were originally sold as a set ($32 set, £16 set).

Lil' Bits Terriers *2007*
These 7/8" high solid cast and unmarked figurines were sold at the 2007 Summer Wade Fest. The **Honey Terrier** was a limited edition 400. The **Grey Terrier** was a limited edition of 300. The **White Terrier** was a limited edition of 450. This figurine was also included in the Wade Fest Goodie Bag. The **Black Terrier** was a limited edition of 450. The **Gold Terrier** was a limited edition of 100 and were given as draw prizes ($24, £12). The white, black, grey, and honey terriers were sold as a set ($30 set, £15 set).

PA Budgies *2003*
For the 2003 Summer Wade Fest, C&S Collectables produced special versions of their retail line of Budgies. The color ways were similar to the retail line but for this issue had the budgies perched on a silver branch and were issued in a limited edition of 100 sets.
White Budgie ($20, £10). **White/Gold Budgie** ($20, £10). **Orange Budgie** ($20, £10). **Green Budgie** ($20, £10). **Blue Budgie** ($20, £10). The figurines measure 1-3/4" high and are mold marked: Wade C&S.

Summer Wade Fest and Red Rose Tea Fair Special Issues, 2001 - 2007

For some years a number of companies such as Wade Ceramics or C&S Collectables and recently, Happy Wade-ing, have issued special sets of figurines to be sold at the Summer Wade Fest. In many cases, a number of the figurines were held back to be sold to collectors unable to attend the fairs.

The first annual Red Rose Tea Fair was organized by the Windsor Chamber of Commerce and held on the weekend of November 3 - 5, 2006 at the Hilton Garden Inn, Windsor, Connecticut. Redco Foods issued a special figurine for the 2006 Fair. Both Wade Ceramics and C&S Collectables issued special figurines to be sold at the Red Rose Tea Fairs in 2006 and 2007 and The Windsor Chamber of Commerce issued a special figurine for the 2007 Fair.

Arthur Hare "Wizhared" Whimsies *2001*
C&S Collectables produced special versions of their Arthur Hare series in a Whimsies size for the 2001 Wade Fest at Harrisburg, Pennsylvania. **"Wizhared" Whimsie** (blue). This figurine was a limited edition of 250 figurines ($20, £10). **"Wizhared" Whimsie** (green). This figurine was a limited edition of 1,750 figurines sold during April 2001 ($18, £9). **"Wizhared" Whimsie** gold/silver ($50, £25). The figurines measure 1-1/2" high and are mold marked Wade/C&S. The figurines were modeled by Simon Millard.

Gingerbread Girls *2005*
For the 2005 Summer Wade Fest, Keenan Antiques commissioned Wade to produce a set of Whimsie Gingerbread Girls from a new mold, which were sold at the Wade Fest. The pressed figurines measure 1-3/4" high and are mold marked: Wade Eng.
Terra-cotta/Red Skirt was a limited edition of 600 ($12, £6). **Gold Skirt** was a limited edition of 200 ($40, £20). **Green Skirt** was a limited edition of 600 ($12, £6). **Yellow Skirt** was a limited edition of 600 ($12, £6). **Blue Skirt** was a limited edition of 200 (although this color does not look too much like blue, that is the official color of the figurine) ($12, £6). The green, yellow, red, and blue skirt figurines were originally sold as a set ($50, £25).

Harrisburg Eagles *2006*

For the 2006 Summer Wade Fest held in Harrisburg, Pennsylvania, Wade Ceramics Ltd. produced a set of four Whimsie eagles in different color ways. There was also a special multi colored version, a gold version, and a special silver version issued in limited editions. These figurines were produced from a completely new mold.

The eagles measure 1-3/4" high by 2-3/4" across the wings and are mold marked Wade Eng on the front of the base. **Grey Eagle** was a limited edition of 100. **Silver Eagle** was a limited edition of 20. **Brown Eagle** was a limited edition of 100. **Multicolored Eagle** was a limited edition of 100. **White Eagle** was a limited edition of 100. **Gold Eagle** was a limited edition of 20. The white, grey, and brown eagles were sold as a set of three ($90, £45). The multicolored eagle was sold as a separate item. The gold and silver eagles were given as draw prizes (N.P.A.).

Harrisburg Rabbits *2007*

For the 2007 Summer Wade Fest Wade Ceramics Limited produced a set of rabbits, in a limited edition of 150 sets, using a completely new mold and made using the solid casting system of production.

Grey Rabbit was a limited edition of 100. **Gold Rabbit** was a limited edition of 20 and given as draw prizes. **Black and White Rabbit, Beige Rabbit** and **Honey Rabbit** were a limited edition of 100 each. The figurines measure 2" high and are mold marked: Wade. The grey, black and white, beige, and honey rabbits were sold as a set ($68 set, £34 set).

Alpaca Whimsie *2007*

For the 2007 Summer Wade Fest, C&S Collectables commissioned Wade Ceramics Ltd. to produce a Whimsie size alpaca figurine. The alpaca measures 2" high and is mold marked: Wade.

Top. A prototype **Alpaca**. Bottom. Production models which were produced in a limited edition of 250 pairs. The figurines were sold in pairs only, one **White Alpaca** and one **Brown Alpaca**. ($50 pair, £25 pair). The two brown versions show the color variation of the figurine.

Alpaca. This special color way alpaca was issued by C&S Collectables for the 2007 Red Rose Tea Fair in a limited edition of 100 pieces ($30, £15).

The Cow That Jumped Over The Moon *2007*

Happy Wade-ing first introduced this solid cast Whimsie figurine at the 2007 Red Rose Tea Fair held in Windsor, Connecticut. The figurine measures 1-5/8" high, is solid cast and is mold marked Wade at the edge of the base.

Left. **Blue Moon with Silver Cloud** was a limited issue of 100 ($28, £14). **Gold Moon with White Cloud** was a limited edition of 10 ($176, £88). Right. Rear view of The Cow That Jumped Over The Moon.

Leprechaun Riding a Duck *2007*
For the 2007 Summer Wade Fest, Happy Wade-ing introduced a completely new mold of a leprechaun riding a duck. The figurine was made using the solid casting system of manufacture. This, the first figurine of a series, was sold at the 2007 Summer Wade Fest. Variations of this figurine were sold at other Wade Fairs and via the Internet during 2007. The figurine measure 1-7/8" high and are mold marked: Wade.
Top row. **Red Hat Leprechaun** was a limited edition of 75 issued for the 2007 West Coast Fair ($76, £38). **Brown Hat Leprechaun** was a limited edition of 100. This was sold via the Happy Wade-ing Internet list ($30, £15). **Gold and White Leprechaun.** This was a limited edition of 10 and given as draw prizes ($176, £88). **Green Hat Leprechaun** was a limited edition of 150 ($30, £15).
Bottom row. **Yellow Hat Leprechaun** was a limited edition of 150 ($30, £15). **Orange Hat Leprechaun** was a limited edition of 150 ($36, £18). **Brown with Gold Hat Leprechaun.** This was a limited edition of 50 and was enclosed randomly in the "Gold Hat Goodie Box." **Blue Hat Leprechaun.** This was a limited edition of 100 and was sold at the 2007 Summer Wade Fest ($76, £38).

Flamingo *2006*
C&S Collectables produced a special color way Flamingo Whimsie for the first Red Rose Tea Fair. This figurine was from the same mold as the retail Flamingoes which were issued in a set of three. The retail line of flamingos is illustrated in Chapter 5.
This special color way Flamingo was issued for the November 2006 Red Rose Tea Fair ($20, £10).

Blow-Up Gingerbread Man *2006*
For the 2006 Red Rose Tea Fair Special Redco Foods issued this slip cast figurine of a blow-up Gingerbread Man. The figurine measures 3" high and is transfer marked Red Rose on the front of the base, 2006 Figurine Fair on the rear of the base, and Wade Made in England on the underside of the base. This was a limited edition of 300 ($30, £15). Although not a pressed figurine, it is included here for clarity.

Squirrel Whimsies *2006*
In November 2006, Wade Ceramics Ltd. produced a set of four different color way Squirrels, from the 1974 Whimsie mold, especially for the first Red Rose Tea Fair which was held on the weekend of November 3 - 5 in Windsor, Connecticut. A gold and a silver squirrel were also made available as prizes or for winners of lucky tickets in the Bran Tub draws.
All-over **Gold Squirrel** was a limited edition of 20 ($110, £55). **Squirrel with Black Nut** was a limited edition of 70. **Squirrel with Green Nut** was a limited edition of 70. **Squirrel with Brown Nut** was a limited edition of 70. **Squirrel with Gold Nut and Gold Base** was a limited edition of 70. The squirrels with brown, black, green, and gold nuts were sold as a show special set ($90 set, £45 set).

Blow-Up Three Bears *2007*
For the 2007 Red Rose Tea Fair, The Windsor Chamber of Commerce issued a blow-up figurine of the three bears in a limited edition of 100. The figurine measures 2-3/4" high by 2-1/2" across and is transfer marked Wade on the underside of the base. The front of the base reads: 2nd Red Rose Tea Fair Windsor CT. ($44, £22).

Dove Whimsies *2007*
For the 2007 Red Rose Tea Fair, Wade Ceramics issued a set of four Whimsie Doves. The figurines were solid cast and measure 1-3/4" high and are mold marked Wade on the front of the base. From the left: **Grey and White Dove.** This was a limited edition of 125. **Silver Dove.** This was a limited edition of 20 ($50, £25). **Honey Dove, Blue Dove.** These were a limited edition of 125 each. **Gold Dove.** This was a limited edition of 20 ($60, £30). **Grey Dove.** This was a limited edition of 125. The grey and white, honey, blue, and grey doves were sold as a set of four ($76 set, 38 set).

Kansas City Wade Fair, 2000 - 2001

In 2000, Ed and Beverly Rucker organized and promoted the first Kansas City Wade Fair, which was held at the Armadillo Antique Mall in Grain Valley, Missouri. For the 2001 Kansas City Wade Fair held in Kansas City, Missouri, Ed and Beverly went into partnership with Brian and Judi Morris and formed KSWader. Ed & Bev Rucker formed KSWader West and Brian & Judi Morris formed KSWader East.

Y2K Elephants *2000*
U. S. Wade dealers Peg and Rog Johnson of Illinois and Father Cox of Missouri, commissioned Wade to produce figurines for the year 2000 Wade Fair in Kansas City and for the Wade Fest 2000 in Pennsylvania. The figurine was a pink version of the 1973 Whimsie elephant with the letters Y2K on the side of the body. The letters appeared on one side only of the figurine, some on the left side and some on the right side.

Left. **Y2K Pink Elephant** was issued in a limited number of 500 figurines with the wording on the right hand side. These figurines were sold at the 2000 Wade Fest in Harrisburg, Pennsylvania ($20, £10). Right. **Y2K Pink Elephant** was issued in a limited number of 1,500 figurines which were made with the wording on the left hand side and were sold at the 2000 Kansas City Wade Fair ($10, £5).

Green Armadillo color variations ($10 each, £8 each).

Armadillo *2000*
As the 2000 Kansas City Wade Fair was held at the Armadillo Antique Mall the item chosen for the Fair Special was the Armadillo from the 1984-85 Tom Smith set The World of Survival. Two color ways of the Armadillo were produced. **Brass Armadillo** was a limited edition of 1,000 pieces ($8, £4). **Green Armadillo** was a limited edition of 927 pieces ($10, £8).

West Coast Wade Fair, 2000 - 2007

The West Coast Wade Fairs are organized and promoted by Reva and Michael Matthew. The first fair was held in Kalama, Washington, in 2000 and the 2001 and 2002 fairs were held in Vancouver, Washington. In 2003, the fair was held in Portland, Oregon. After a break of three years, the 2007 fair was again held in Portland, Oregon.

Patriot Eagles *2002*
The Fair Specials for 2002 were based on the Tom Smith Eagle from the 1984-85 World of Survival series and the 1992-93 Birdlife series. The Eagles measures 1-3/4" high and is marked Wade England. From left. **Red Eagle. White Eagle. Blue Eagle. Gold Eagle. Black Eagle.** There were 300 sets of the Red, White and Blue Eagles sold as sets of three, one of each color ($30 set, £20 set). The Black Eagle was a limited edition of 100 pieces packed in Goodie Bags and given away as prizes ($50, £25). The gold eagle was a limited edition of 10 given away as prizes ($100, £50).

Whimsical Whales *2003*
The Fair Specials for 2003 were based on the Tom Smith Whale from the 1998 - Sealife series. Top row. **Black/White Whale** with black base ($18, £9), **Gold Whale** was a limited edition of 9 ($100, £50) and **White Whale** was a limited edition of 100 ($30, £15). Bottom row. **Black/White Whale** with blue base ($18, £9) and **Black Whale** with blue base ($18, £9). The black, and black/white whales were a limited edition of 300.

Armed Forces Whimsies *2007*
The Fair Specials for 2007 were based on the various wings of the U.S. armed forces. The figurines are mold marked: Wade around the base of the figurine and are approximately 2" high.
Top. **Army, Navy, Marine, Air Force.** The regular glaze figurines were a limited edition of 250 sets ($60 set, £30 set).
Middle. **Army, Air Force, Marine, Navy.** The all-over gold figurines were a limited edition of 10 sets. These were draw prizes (N.P.A.)
Bottom. **Army, Marine, Navy, Air Force.** The figurines with the gold hat were a limited edition of 25 sets. ($80 set, £40 set).

Flying Flowers *2004*
The Fair Specials for 2004 were based on the Butterfly from 1967-73 Canadian Red Rose Tea promotion.
From top left. **Red/White/Blue butterfly** was a limited edition of 125 ($40, £20). **Orange/Black butterfly** was a limited edition of 125 ($40, £20). From middle left. **Burgundy butterfly** was a limited edition of 220 ($16, £8). **Gold butterfly** was a limited edition of 10 ($100, £50). From bottom left. **Cobalt Blue butterfly** was a limited edition of 220 ($16, £8). **Yellow butterfly** was a limited edition of 220 ($16, £8). **Black/White butterfly** was a limited edition of 125 ($40, £20).

Bran Tub Issues

At the various fairs in the UK and the U.S.A., Wade Ceramics Ltd. has been awarding prizes, usually a "One of a Kind" figurine, to collectors who buy a ticket for the lucky dip. For tickets not matching the prizes, a Whimsie figurine is given out as a consolation prize. The consolation Whimsie figurines are most often in a different color way to the regular issues and are referred to as "Bran Tub Issues."

Poodle. This poodle was a limited edition of 100 and was a bran tub prize at an Alton Towers Wade Fair ($30, £15).

Admiral Sam. This all-over light blue model of Admiral Sam from the Bear Ambitions series was issued for a 1998 Trade Exhibition in the U.K. The figurine was also used for the Bran Tub at the 1998 San Antonio Jim Beam/Wade Fair ($12, £6).

The **Frog, Terrapin,** and **Crocodile** were special color ways from existing molds and given as bran tub drawings at various Wade Fairs in 2003 ($8 each, £4 each).

Poodles. Left. The poodle with the pink skirt was a limited edition of 100 and was a bran tub prize at an Alton Towers Wade Fair ($30, £15). Right. The poodle with the gold skirt was a limited edition of 100 and was a bran tub prize at an Alton Towers Wade Fair ($30, £15).

Top row. **Black Kitten** with green eyes and pink ears was first issued in 2005. **Grey Pony.** Bottom row. **Blue Cock-a-teel, Orange Puppy.** These figurines were special color ways from existing molds and given as bran tub drawings at various Wade Fairs in 2006 and 2007 ($4 each, £2 each).

Mouse Whimsies. These prototype Whimsies are planned for the 2008 bran tub and as Wade Fair door prizes.

Chapter 3

Tea Figurines, 1967 - 2007

For many years it has been proven by manufacturers of products as diverse as cigarettes, party crackers, and packaged foods that the inclusion of a "give away item" or "premium" was a great incentive for the public to purchase that product. Needless to say, the manufacturing of the actual premiums has become, over the years, a very profitable sideline to industries specializing in plastic, paper, metal, and porcelain products.

In the mid-1960s, George Wade and Son Ltd. decided to enter the manufacturing side of the premium business by producing a series of miniature porcelain animals at a low enough production cost that they could compete in the premium market. The entire production of these miniature figurines was done by Wade. The process used to manufacture the premium figurines was similar to that used to produce the Whimsie figurines so popular in the 1950s and described elsewhere in this book.

At first twenty different figurines were produced, but by 1968 this number had increased to over forty models. It was from this range that Brooke Bond Foods Ltd. of Canada, which had been established in 1946, selected their first series of premiums to be included in their boxes of Red Rose Tea bags to be sold on the Canadian market starting in 1967. This promotion proved to be such a success that the British parent company, Brooke Bond Oxo Ltd. followed suit and released a promotion on the U.K. market between 1969 and 1970.

Trade Literature from the early 1960s illustrating the early range of 20 premium figurines.

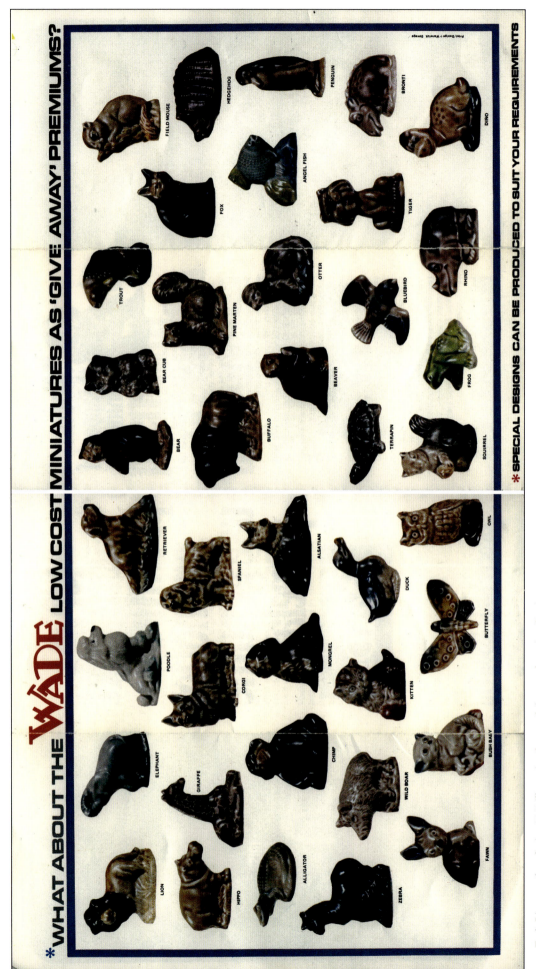

Trade Literature from Spring 1969 illustrating the extended range of premium figurines.

The first Canadian promotion comprised thirty-two miniature porcelain animals and proved to be such a success that Wade went on to develop the Red Rose Tea premiums into a full retail line of sixty animals marketed under the trade name of "Whimsies." Premium figurines continued to be packed in boxes of the Red Rose Tea sold on the Canadian market up until 1986. In June 1985, Brooke Bond of Canada was taken over by Thomas J. Lipton, Inc., who at that time became the Canadian distributor of Red Rose Tea. The new owners followed in the footsteps of Brooke Bond and introduced the last series of tea premiums to the Canadian market between 1985 and 1986.

After a hiatus of ten years, starting in or around 1997, Red Rose Tea in Canada began issuing a series of miniature teapots in the form of stoves and buildings in boxes of tea bags. None of these miniature teapots were made by Wade.

Starting in 1983, boxes of Brooke Bond (U.S.A.) Red Rose Tea sold in the United States began to appear with the Wade miniatures included as free premiums. In 1988, John Edwards, former President of Brooke Bond (U.S.A.), and John Rigg, former President of Brooke Bond (Canada), joined forces and founded Redco Foods Inc., and continued with the tradition of including premium figurines in their boxes of Red Rose Tea bags. Although management of Redco Foods has changed over the years, the company, to this day, includes Wade miniatures

in their boxes of Red Rose Tea bags. In November 2006 the company, along with the Windsor Chamber of Commerce, held the first Red Rose Tea Fair in Windsor, Connecticut, which proved to be a great success.

We have taken the numbering of the various series of U.S. promotions from literature supplied by Redco Foods, Inc.

Canadian Red Rose Tea Promotion No. 1, 1967 - 1973

This first Canadian Red Rose Tea promotion consisted of thirty-two figurines chosen from the range of stock premium models that Wade had developed. These small porcelain animals proved to be an instant success with the public and from their introduction in 1967 to 1973 when the series was discontinued, Wade supplied many millions of figurines to Brooke Bond. Twenty-five of these premiums went on to become part of the Wade retail line of 1971-84 Whimsies, but seven figurines, Green Frog, Butterfly, Poodle, Seal, Angel Fish, Terrapin, and Alligator used in the promotion were never sold in a retail line.

Fawn measures 1-3/8" high ($5, £2). **Rabbit** measures 1-1/8" high ($5, £2). **Mongrel** measures 1-3/8" high ($6, £3).
Kitten measures 1-3/8" high ($6, £3). **Spaniel** measures 1-3/8" high ($5, £2). **Duck** measures 1-1/4" high ($6, £3).
Corgi measures 1-1/2" high ($10, £5). **Beaver** measures 1-1/4" high ($4, £2).

Bush Baby measures 1-1/4" high ($4, £2). **Fox** measures 1-3/8" high ($8, £4). **Bear Cub** measures 1-3/8" high ($4, £2). **Otter** measures 1-1/4" high ($4, £2). **Setter** measures 1-3/8" high ($6, £3). **Owl** measures 1-1/2" high ($6, £3). **Trout** measures 1-1/8" high ($6, £3). **Lion** measures 1-3/8" high ($6, £3).

Giraffe measures 1-1/2" high ($4, £2). **Chimp** measures 1-1/2" high ($4, £2). **Hippo** measures 1" high ($6, £3). **Squirrel** measures 1-3/8" high ($4, £2). **Hedgehog** measures 7/8" high ($6, £3). **Alsatian** measures 1-1/4" high ($6, £3). **Bison** measures 1-1/8" high ($6, £3). **Blue Bird** measures 5/8" high ($8, £4). **Wild Boar** measures 1-1/8" high. This figurine has an all-over light brown glaze and has no green on the base as with the retail Whimsie version ($16, £8).

Frog non-retail measures 7/8" high ($10, £5). **Butterfly** non-retail measures 1/2" high by 1-3/4" across wing span ($8, £4). **Poodle** non-retail measures 1-5/8" high by 1-5/8" long ($8, £4). **Seal** non-retail measures 1-1/2" high by 1-1/4" along the base ($8, £4). **Fantail Goldfish** non-retail measures 1-1/4" high by 1-3/8" long ($12, £6). **Terrapin** non-retail measures 3/8" high by 1-5/8" long ($8, £4). **Alligator** non-retail measures 1/2" high by 1-1/2" long ($8, £4).

Terrapin.
Above. Four color variations ($12 each, £6 each).
Right. Color variation ($20, £10).

Seal (with black eyes) from the 1967-73 Red Rose Tea promotion. Color variation ($14, £7).

Alligator.
Variation of the molded mark types.

Canadian Red Rose Tea Promotion
No. 2, 1971 - 1979

Due to the outstanding success of the 1967-73 promotion of miniature animals, Brooke Bond Foods Ltd. decided to launch a second series of promotional figurines in their boxes of Red Rose Tea sold in Canada. Various ideas were submitted to Wade by Brooke Bond and by mutual agreement a new line of twenty-four porcelain figurines based upon characters from popular children's nursery rhymes was chosen for the new promotion.

The new line of premiums was first marketed in various parts of Canada during 1971, and became nationally distributed by 1973. Wade supplied approximately 100 million pieces of these attractive figurines to Brooke Bond by the time this second series of premiums was discontinued in 1979.

Although there was no official name given to the series, it has become known as "Nurseries." This name came about when Wade launched a short-lived line of figurines from the tea promotion that was named "Nurseries." The retail line was not a success and only five figurines in a presentation box were marketed.

Old King Cole measures 1-1/2" high by 1-1/4" long ($8, £4). **Little Jack Horner** measures 1-3/8" high by 1" across the base ($6, £3). **Jack** measures 1-1/4" high by 1-1/4" long ($6, £3). **Jill** measures 1-1/8" high by 1-1/4" long ($6, £3). **Humpty Dumpty** measures 1-1/2" high by 7/8" long ($6, £3). **Tom the Piper's Son** measures 1-5/8" high by 1-3/8" long ($8, £4). **Little Boy Blue** measures 1-5/8" high by 1" across the base ($8, £4). **The Pied Piper** measures 1-3/4" high by 1-1/8" long ($6, £3).

Red Rose Tea box cover of the 1971-1979 Canadian promotion.

Old King Cole.
Mold variations. Left. Space between feet. Right. No space between feet ($8 each, £4 each).

Little Jack Horner.
Color variation ($20, £10).

Little Boy Blue.
Rare, undecorated figurine ($30, £15).

Mother Goose.
Rare, undecorated figurine ($30, £15).

Doctor Foster.
Rare, undecorated figurine
($30, £15).

Little Miss Muffet measures 1-1/2" high by 1-3/8" long ($8, £4). **Doctor Foster** measures 1-3/4" high by 7/8" dia. base ($6, £3). **Mother Goose** measures 1-5/8" high by 1-1/4" long ($10, £5). **Old Woman Who Lived in a Shoe** measures 1-3/8" high by 1-5/8" long ($6, £3). **Goosey-Gander** measures 1-3/8" high by 1" long. The Red Rose Tea figurine has an orange/red beak ($6, £3). **Wee Willie Winkie** measures 1-3/4" high by 1" long ($8, £4). **Little Bo-Peep** measures 1-3/4" high by 3/4" dia. base ($6, £3). **The Three Bears** measures 1-3/8" high by 1-1/2" long ($22, £11).

Puss in Boots measures 1-3/4" high by 3/4" dia. base ($10, £5). **The House That Jack Built** measures 1-1/4" high by 1-1/4" long ($12, £6). **Little Red Riding Hood** measures 1-3/4" high by 7/8" long ($8, £4). **Queen of Hearts** measures 1-3/4" high by 1" across the base ($12, £6). **Baa Baa Black Sheep** measures 7/8" high by 1-1/8" long ($16, £8). **Hickory Dickory Dock** measures 1-3/4" high by 3/4" square base ($8, £4). **Ginger Bread Man** measures 1-5/8" high by 1-1/16" across ($28, £14). **Cat and the Fiddle** measures 1-7/8" high by 1" across ($20, £10).

Queen of Hearts.
Variations of heart design. Left. Multiple hearts ($60, £30). Center. Two small hearts ($16, £8). Right. Two large hearts ($16, £8).

Gingerbread Man.
Color variation ($28, £14).

Canadian Red Rose Tea Promotion
No. 3, 1981

In 1981, after a hiatus of just over a year, when the nursery figurine promotion was discontinued, Brooke Bond Foods Ltd. introduced their third series of Wade figurines to promote the sale of their boxes of Red Rose Tea bags. Unlike the previous two promotions this third set of premium figurines was of very short duration, from early 1981 to the late Fall of the same year.

For the 1981 promotion, the complete set of the fifteen Wade retail line of Whoppas was used as tea premiums. The Whoppas had been a Wade retail line since 1976, and discontinued as such in 1981, so presumably, this series of premiums was an ideal solution to clear left over stock.

With the previous Red Rose Tea premiums the figurines were enclosed in the boxes of tea bags without charge. However, this third series was a "mail-in offer" which meant that collectors had to send in a premium tab, cut from the box, along with $1.00 to claim the figurine. This promotion was not a great success due either to the fact that collectors had to mail-in a claim along with $1,00 or due to the small amount of figurines left over from the retail line. Either way, the promotion lasted only a few short months.

Advertisement from the April 1981 issue of Today magazine illustrating the Red Rose Tea "mail - in" offer for the Wade Whoppa figurines.

Polar Bear measures 1-1/2" high by 2-1/4" overall. **Hippo** measures 1-3/8" high by 2-1/4" overall. **Brown Bear** measures 1-1/2" high by 1-3/4" overall. **Tiger** measures 1-1/8" by 2-1/2" overall. **Elephant** measures 2-1/8" high by 2" overall ($20 each, £10 each).

Bison measures 1-3/4" high by 2-1/4" overall ($30, £15). **Wolf** measures 2-1/4" high by 1-3/4" overall ($20, £10). **Bobcat** measures 1-1/2" high by 1-7/8" overall ($30, £15). **Chipmunk** measures 2-1/8" high by 1" dia. base ($30, £15). **Raccoon** measures 1-1/2" high by 2-1/4" overall ($30, £15).

Fox measures 1-1/4" high by 2-1/2" overall ($36, £18). **Badger** measures 1-1/2" high by 1-7/8" overall ($32, £16). **Otter** measures 1-1/4" high by 2" overall ($36, £18). **Stoat** measures 1-1/2" high by 2-1/8" overall ($32, £16). **Hedgehog** measures 1-1/4" high by 1-7/8" overall ($38, £19).

Canadian Red Rose Tea Promotion No. 4, 1982 - 1984

In the Fall of 1982, Brooke Bond Foods Ltd. began marketing their fourth series of Wade miniature porcelain premium figurines. This new series comprised twenty-three miniature animals selected from the Wade line of Whimsies.

Of the twenty-three animals in the promotion, six of them – rabbit, corgi, beaver, bush baby, fox, and giraffe – had also been used in the 1967-73 promotion, and two – the turtle and angel fish – although similar in names, were from different molds.

Red Rose Tea box cover of the 1982-1984 Canadian promotion.

Rabbit measures 1-1/8" high ($5, £3). **Corgi** measures 1-1/2" high ($10, £5). **Beaver** measures 1-1/4" high ($4, £2). **Bush Baby** measures 1-1/4" high ($4, £2). **Fox** measures 1-3/8" high ($8, £4). **Giraffe** measures 1-1/2" high ($4, £2). **Pine Marten** measures 1-3/8" high ($4, £2). **Collie** measures 1-1/4" high ($8, £4).

Cow measures 1-1/4" high ($10, £5). **Pig** measures 13/16" high ($16, £8). **Horse** measures 1-5/8" high ($16, £8). **Lamb** measures 1-3/8" high ($10, £5). **Rhino** measures 7/8" high ($6, £3). **Leopard** measures 7/8" high ($8, £4). **Gorilla** measures 1-1/2" high ($6, £3). **Camel** measures 1-3/8" high ($8, £4).

Leopard.
Color variation ($8, £4).

Zebra measures 1-5/8" high ($8, £4). **Pelican** measures 1-3/4" high ($20, £10). **Angel Fish** measures 1-3/8" high ($12, £6). **Turtle** measures 9/16" high ($8, £4). **Seahorse** measures 2" high ($24, £12). **Orangutan** measures 1-1/4" high ($6, £3). **Langur** measures 1-3/8" high ($4, £2).

Canadian Red Rose Tea Promotion No. 5, 1985 - 1986

In June 1985, Brooke Bond Foods Ltd. was taken over by Thomas J. Lipton Inc. who, therefore, became the new Canadian distributor of Red Rose Tea. As did the previous distributor of Red Rose Tea, the new owners decided to follow their lead and introduce another series of Wade porcelain premium figurines to be included in their boxes of tea bags. For this promotion, the premiums were offered only in the boxes of Red Rose "Premium Blend" tea bags. The fifteen figurines used in this promotion were similar to the first fifteen figurines offered in the 1985 U.S.A. Red Rose Tea promotion.

Red Rose Tea box cover of the 1985-1986 Canadian promotion.

Koala Bear measures 1-3/8" high ($4, £2). **Giraffe** measures 1-1/2" high ($4, £2). Pine Marten measures 1-3/8" high ($4, £2). **Langur** measures 1-3/8" high ($4, £2).
Gorilla measures 1-1/2" high ($4, £2). **Camel** measures 1-3/8" high ($4, £2). **Kangaroo** measures 1-5/8" high ($6, £3). **Tiger** measures 1-7/16" high ($4, £2).

Zebra measures 1-5/8" high ($4, £2). **Polar Bear** measures 1-1/8" high ($4, £2). **Orangutan** measures 1-1/4" high ($4, £2). **Raccoon** measures 1" high ($4, £2).
Rhino measures 7/8" high ($4, £2). **Beaver** measures 1-1/4" high ($4, £2). **Leopard** measures 13/16" high ($4, £2).

U.S.A. Red Rose Tea Promotion
No. 1, 1983 - 1985

U.S. Animals Series No. 1.

After the successful completion of market testing in two areas of the U.S.A. (Pittsburgh and the Pacific Northwest), Red Rose Tea in the U.S.A. was ready to launch their first major distribution of Wade miniature animal figurines as premiums to be offered in boxes of Red Rose Tea sold on the U.S. market. The series comprised fifteen figurines, thirteen were chosen from the 1971-84 Wade Whimsies line and two were similar to Tom Smith figurines from the 1980-81 Wildlife Set. For economic reasons, all the figurines had a single glaze rather than the hand painted glazes as on the original Whimsies retail line.

Prior to this promotion, Red Rose Tea sold in the U.S.A. had used tea cards as premiums so this new venture was quite a change for the company.

As mentioned before, we have taken the numbering of the various series of U.S. promotions from literature supplied by Redco Foods, Inc.

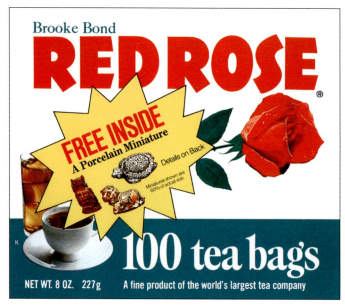

Red Rose Tea box cover of the 1983-1985 U.S. promotion.

Chimp measures 1-1/2" high ($4, £2). **Lion** measures 1-3/8" high ($6, £3). **Bison** measures 1-1/8" high ($6, £3). **Bush Baby** measures 1-1/4" high ($4, £2). **Owl** measures 1-1/2" high ($6, £3). **Bear Cub** measures 1-3/8" high ($4, £2). **Rabbit** measures 1-3/4" high ($8, £4). This figurine is sometimes referred to as Hare and was used in the 1980-81 Tom Smith Cracker set but with a different glaze. **Squirrel** measures 1-1/2" high ($6, £3). This figurine was used in the 1980-81 Tom Smith Cracker set but with a different glaze.

Bird measures 5/8" high ($8, £4). **Otter** measures 1-1/4" high ($4, £2). **Hippo** measures 1" high ($4, £2). **Seal** measures 1-1/2" high ($6, £3). **Turtle** measures 9/16" high ($6, £3). **Wild Boar** measures 1-1/8" high ($8, £4). **Elephant** measures 1-3/8" high ($8, £4).

U.S.A. Red Rose Tea Promotion
No. 2, 1985 - 1996

U.S. Animals Series No. 2.

With the success of the 1983-85 U.S.A. Red Rose Tea promotion, a new series of figurines was introduced in mid-1985. Once again this set of premiums consisted of miniature animals taken from the 1971-84 Wade Whimsies retail line, the only difference being the single glaze color, consistent with the first U.S.A. series. All figurines are mold marked "Wade England" around the base.

Wooden Shadow Box illustrated in the Fall 1987 Red Rose Tea Lover's Club Newsletter. This shadow box was not produced by Wade and is shown here for interest.

Red Rose Tea box cover of the second U.S. promotion with the full range of 20 figurines.

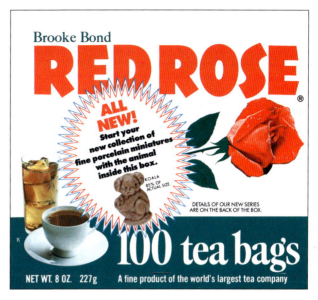

Red Rose Tea box cover of the second U.S. promotion with the first 15 figurines. The design of the box was changed when the final five figurines were added in 1990.

Back of Red Rose Tea box of the second U.S. promotion with the full range of 20 figurines.

Back of Red Rose Tea box of the second U.S. promotion with the first 15 figurines.

The first fifteen figurines in this series were issued between 1985 and 1995 with five more figurines added to the series in 1990 so that a full set of twenty figurines was on the market between 1990 and 1996. The five figurines added to the promotion in 1990 were previously used in the Tom Smith Party Crackers series, "Your Pets."

In 1992, this series was also used for a "mail-in" offer with boxes of decaffeinated tea but was not regarded, by Redco Foods, as a separate promotion.

Koala Bear measures 1-3/8" high ($4, £2). **Giraffe** measures 1-1/2" high ($4, £2). **Pine Marten** measures 1-3/8" high ($4, £2). **Langur** measures 1-3/8" high ($4, £2). **Gorilla** measures 1-1/2" high ($4, £2). **Camel** measures 1-3/8" high ($4, £2). **Kangaroo** measures 1-5/8" high ($6, £3). **Tiger** measures 1-7/16" high ($4, £2).

Zebra measures 1-5/8" high ($4, £2). **Polar Bear** measures 1-1/8" high ($4, £2). **Orangutan** measures 1-1/4" high ($4, £2). **Raccoon** measures 1" high ($4, £2). **Rhino** measures 7/8" high ($4, £2). **Beaver** measures 1-1/4" high ($4, £2). **Leopard** measures 13/16" high ($4, £2).

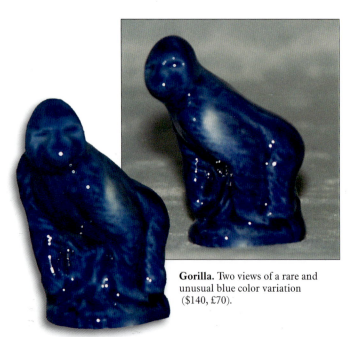

Gorilla. Two views of a rare and unusual blue color variation ($140, £70).

In 1990, the following five figurines were added to the original fifteen figurines of the second U.S. Red Rose Tea promotion. These figurines were similar to those used in the 1988-89 Tom Smith Your Pets series. All figurines are mold marked "Wade England" except for the Cock-a-Teel which is marked "Wade Eng."
Puppy measures 1" high ($6, £3). **Rabbit** measures 1-1/8" high ($6, £3). **Kitten** measures 1" high ($6, £3). **Pony** measures 1" high ($6, £3). **Cock-a-Teel** measures 1-3/8" high and is referred to as Parrot in the Tom Smith series ($4, £2).

U.S.A. Red Rose Tea Promotion
No. 3, 1994 - 1999

Circus Figurine Series.

The Circus Figurines Series, the third U.S. Red Rose Tea promotion, revisited the previously used Tom Smith Party Crackers series of 1978-79. There was very little difference in the glaze of these figurines, except for the two monkey figurines that had an all-over brown glaze, and the seal that had a light grey glaze as opposed to the greenish/grey glaze of the Tom Smith seal. The two Red Rose Tea elephants are often found with a lighter blue glaze than the Tom Smith elephants but this is hard to judge unless the figurines are set side-by-side.

The first fifteen figurines in this series, all mold marked "Wade England," were issued between 1993 and 1998, with a further five figurines added to the series in 1996 so that a full set of twenty figurines ran between 1996 and 1999. The five additional figures were all new molds and had not been used before.

Red Rose Tea box cover for the Circus Figurine Series.

Back of Red Rose Tea box for Circus Figurine Series.

Red Rose Tea box for the Circus Animal Series.

Seal measures 1-5/8" high ($6, £3). **Sitting Elephant** measures 1-1/4" high ($8, £3). **Bear** measures 1-3/16" high ($6, £3). **Poodle** measures 1-3/4" high ($6, £3). **Male Monkey** measures 1-5/8" high ($6, £3). **Standing Elephant** measures 1-3/16" high ($6, £3). **Tiger** measures 1-5/8" high ($8, £4). A mold variation of this tiger exists with a small "ruff" under the jaw. **Lion** measures 1-5/8" high ($6, £3). **Female Monkey** measures 1-1/2" high ($6, £3). **Horse** measures 1-3/4" high ($6, £3).

In 1996, Redco Foods, Inc. added the following five figurines to the Circus Figurine Series. These were all new molds. The two Clowns and Ringmaster are marked "Wade Eng" and the Strongman and Human Cannonball are marked "Wade England."
Strongman measures 1-1/2" high ($8, £4). **Human Cannonball** measures 1-1/8" high ($8, £4). **Clown with Drum** measures 1-5/8" high ($8, £4). **Clown with Pie** measures 1-1/2" high ($8, £5). **Ringmaster** measures 1-3/4" high ($10, £5).

Tiger.
Mold variations. Left. **Tiger.** Note the "ruff," the additional hair on the belly, and smaller feet on the newer version of the tiger. Right. **Tiger.** This is the earlier version of the tiger ($8 each, £4 each).

Bear.
Color variation ($16, £8).

Clown with Pie. Color variation ($16, £8).

Above. **Clown with Pie.** Color variations. Front of figurines.
Below. **Clown with Pie.** Color variations. Back of figurines.
($24 each, £12 each).

Ring Master.
Color variations ($16, £8).

Human Cannonball.
Color variation ($16, £8).

U.S.A. Red Rose Tea Promotion
No. 4, 1999 - 2002

The Endangered North American Animal Series.

The fourth series of Red Rose Tea premiums, featuring endangered North American animals, ran between 1999 and 2002. Of the ten figurines, three of them, the eagle, owl, and polar bear, had been used before. The remaining seven figurines were new models for this promotion. All are mold marked "Wade England" except for the Peregrine Falcon, which is marked "Wade Eng."

Red Rose Tea box cover for the Endangered North American Animal Series.

Exciting New Series!
Endangered North American Animals.
Collect all 10 Wade Porcelain Miniatures.

FLORIDA PANTHER — PEREGRINE FALCON — GREEN SEA TURTLE — HUMPBACK WHALE — SPOTTED OWL — STURGEON — MANATEE — TIMBER WOLF — BALD EAGLE — POLAR BEAR

Each porcelain animal miniature has been exclusively designed for Red Rose to help focus attention on conservation efforts to protect these treasured animals. Hand craft- ed by Wade of England, these genuine English porcelain miniatures are only avail- able in specially marked boxes of Red Rose Tea. Start your collection today.

LOOK FOR ONE OF THESE 10 MINIATURES INSIDE THIS PACKAGE

he "RIGHT" way o make tea.

water. Brew 3 to 5 minutes, or until desired strength. For tea by the pot: Rinse teapot with hot water. Place Red Rose Tea Bags in teapot, using one bag per cup. Pour boiling water into teapot and brew 3 to 5 minutes, or until desired strength. Add sugar, milk or lemon to taste.

Iced Tea: Follow hot tea directions: Use 3 Red Rose Tea Bags for every 2 glass- es. Pour into ice-filled glasses. Add lemon, sugar or mint as desired. If tea appears cloudy after refrigeration, clear by adding

a little boiling water.

By the Glass—for every 2 glasses of iced tea pour 2 cups of boiling water over 3 Red Rose Tea Bags. Brew 3 to 5 minutes or to desired strength. Remove tea bags and pour into ice-filled glasses. Add lemon, sugar, or mint as desired. If tea appears cloudy after refrigeration, clear by adding a little boiling water.

By the Quart—pour 1 quart boiling water over 6 Red Rose Tea Bags. Brew and pre- pare as directed above.

Hot Tea: For tea by the cup: Place 1 Red se Tea Bag in cup and pour in boiling

D ROSE BLENDS ONLY THE FINEST TEA LEAVES GROWN THROUGHOUT THE WORLD. TASTE THE RED ROSE DIFFERENCE!

Back of the Red Rose Tea box for the Endangered North American Animal Series.

Red Rose Tea box containing the figurines for the Endangered North American Animal Series.

Join America's most successful tea promotion!
Help protect the Endangered Animals of North America.

FLORIDA PANTHER — PEREGRINE FALCON — GREEN SEA TURTLE — HUMPBACK WHALE — SPOTTED OWL — STURGEON — MANATEE — TIMBER WOLF — BALD EAGLE — POLAR BEAR

xclusively in specially marked boxes of Red Rose ea Bags...10 Porcelain Endangered Animals are the ewest series in this time-proven promotion.

d Rose is one of North America's best-loved teas. e Red Rose Porcelain Miniature Promotion is a ven success in developing consumer interest and nd loyalty. Over 260 million of these genuine glish porcelain collectibles have been given away date. Think of it. That is the equivalent of one iature for every man, woman and child in erica!

ly inside specially marked packages Red Rose!

r customers can now collect all ten imported celain Endangered Animal Miniatures. Hand fted by Wade of England, these figurines have n designed exclusively for Red Rose Tea to help

focus attention on conservation efforts to protect these treasured animals.

More profits for you!
This series is destined to be one of the most popular ever offered. Both loyal Red Rose consumers and new collectors will treasure them, and continue to buy more Red Rose Tea. The Red Rose Porcelain Miniature Promotion is a proven success. Now the new Endangered Animal series offers you a sure-fire way of growing your tea category sales and boosting your profits!

RED ROSE

Redco Foods, Inc., P.O. Box 589, 100 Northfield Drive, Windsor, CT 06095 • Tel.: (860) 688-2121 • Fax: (860) 688-7844

Green Sea Turtle measures 1-1/4" high by 1-3/4" long. **Wolf** measures 1-3/4" high. **Spotted Owl** measures 1-1/2" high. This was originally issued as part of the 1971-84 "Whimsies." **Sturgeon** measures 1-1/8" high by 2" long. **Bald Eagle** measures 1-1/8" high. This was originally used in the Whimsie-Land British Wildlife Set. ($4 each, £2 each).

Red Rose Tea Advertisement for the Endangered North American Animal Series.

Manatee measures 1" high by 2" long. **Peregrine Falcon** measures 1-3/4" high by 7/8" across the base. **Polar Bear** measures 1" high. This was originally used in the Tom Smith Survival Set. **Hump Backed Whale** measures 5/8" high by 2" long. **Florida Panther** measures 1-3/8" high by 1-3/4" long ($4 each, £2 each).

Sea Turtle. Color variations ($16, £8).

Sturgeon. Color variation ($16, £8).

U.S.A. Red Rose Tea Promotion
No. 5, 2002 - 2006 and 2007

Noah's Ark Series.

In May 2002, Redco Foods introduced a new series of premium figurines to be packaged in their boxes of Red Rose Tea bags. The theme for the new series was based on the biblical story of Noah's Ark and comprised seven pairs of male and female animals and a combination figure of Noah and his wife. Also available was a large display piece of the Ark, which was large enough to hold all the figurines on the deck. All figurines for this series were new models. The larger scale Ark was only available by special order and was not included with any of the bags of tea.

The Noah's Ark series of figurines was reissued for a short time in the Spring of 2007 but in boxes of 100 tea bags only.

Red Rose Tea box cover for the Noah's Ark Series.

Back of Red Rose Tea box for the Noah's Ark Series.

Noah and his Wife measures 1-1/16" high and is mold marked Wade Eng. Although not mentioned in the Bible, according to Jewish tradition, the wife of Noah was named Na'amah ($6, £3). **Lioness** measures 7/8" high and is mold marked Wade England. **Lion** measures 1-1/8" high by 1-3/8" long and is mold marked Wade England. **Female Elephant** measures 1-1/8" high by 1-3/8" long and is mold marked Wade Eng. **Male Elephant** measures 1-1/2" high by 1-1/2" overall and is mold marked Wade Eng. **Goose** measures 1-3/8" high by 1-3/8" overall and is mold marked Wade Eng. **Gander** measures 1-1/4" high by 1-1/2" overall and is mold marked Wade England. **Ram** measures 1" high by 1-1/8" long and is mold marked Wade Eng. **Ewe** measures 7/8" high by 1-1/8" long and is mold marked Wade England. **Rooster** measures 1-1/2" high by 1" across and is mold marked Wade Eng. **Hen** measures 1-1/8" high by 1-1/8" overall and is mold marked Wade England. **Male Zebra** measures 1-1/8" high by 1-1/4" overall and is mold marked Wade Eng. **Female Zebra** measures 1-1/8" high by 1-1/4" overall and is mold marked Wade England. **Male Rhino** measures 1-1/4" high by 1-5/8" overall and is mold marked Wade England. **Female Rhino** measures 1-1/8" high by 1-3/8" overall and is mold marked Wade England. ($4 each, £2 each).

Noah's Ark. The ark measures 4-3/4" high by 10-3/4" long by 6-3/4" wide and is mold marked Wade England ($28, £14).

Top Row. **Noah and his Wife.** Mold variation showing base from above. Bottom Row. **Noah and his Wife.** Mold variation showing underside of the base. ($6 each, £3 each).

Lioness from the Red Rose Tea Noah's Ark series. Color variations ($4, £2).

U.S.A. Red Rose Tea Promotion No. 6, 2006 - present

Pet Shop Friends.

Late in 2005 Redco Foods introduced a new series of premium figurines to be included in their boxes of Red Rose Tea bags. This promotion comprised a series of ten animals and birds along with a large-scale porcelain "Pet Shop" on an oval base to be used as a display for the figurines.

Although the Noah's Ark series was reissued for a short time in the Spring of 2007, the Pet Shop Friends series continued to be marketed in the forty-eight and forty boxes of tea bags.

The Pet Shop figurines are produced using the solid casting method, therefore variations in size will occur more frequently. Only a small number of figurines can be made from one mold so new molds have to be produced more often and this is where variations can occur.

Red Rose Tea box cover for the Pet Shop Friends series.

Open box of the Red Rose Tea Pet Shop series showing the Wade figurine offer.

Insert of Wade figurine offer from inside of the boxes of Red Rose tea.

Budgie measures 1-3/4" high and is mold marked: Wade Eng. **Cat** measures 1-1/2" high and is mold marked: Wade England.
Kittens measure 1-1/4" high and is mold marked: Wade England. **Tropical Fish** measures 1-1/4" high and is mold marked:
Wade England. **Labrador** measures 1-1/2" high and is mold marked: Wade England. **Puppies** measure 1-1/8" high and is mold
marked: Wade Eng. **Turtle** measures 1" high and is mold marked: Wade Eng. **Pony** measures 1-1/4" high and is mold marked:
Wade England. **Rabbit** measures 3/4" high and is mold marked: Wade Eng. **Duck** measures 1-1/2" high and is mold marked:
Wade Eng. ($3 each, £2 each).

Pet Shop Display. The oval base measures 9-3/4" long by 6-1/8" across by 3/4" high. The height from bottom of base to top of chimney measured 5". The base is mold marked Wade on the far side. ($46, £23).

Goldfish.
Mold variations. Left. The figurine measures 1-5/16" high and has larger space between the bottom finn and rocks and the "Wade England" mold mark is stretched vertically. Right. The figurine measures 1-1/4" high. The "Wade England" mold mark is stretched horizontally and the middle rock below the fish is larger. ($3 each, £2 each).

Duck.
Mold and color variations. The figurines on the left and right measure 1-7/16" high and have the "Wade Eng" mold mark stretched horizontally and positioned low on the base. The duck in the center measures 1-1/2" high and has the "Wade Eng" mold mark stretched vertically and positioned higher on the base. ($3 each, £2 each).

Kittens.
Color and mold variations ($3 each, £2 each).

Rabbit.
Color variations ($3 each, £2 each).

Cat.
Color and mold variations. Left. The cat has no bags under the eyes and the "Wade England" mold mark is stretched horizontally and is well defined. Right. The cat has bags under the eyes, is fatter and the "Wade England" mold mark is stretched vertically. ($3 each, £2 each).

Budgie.
Color and mold variations. The figurines on the left and right measure 1-3/4" high and the figurine in the center measures 1-11/16" high. Beside the visible color differences, the figurine on the left has the "Wade Eng" mold mark stretched vertically and is positioned higher on the base. ($3 each, £2 each).

Puppies.
Color and mold variations ($3 each, £2 each).

Dogs.
Color and mold variations ($3 each, £2 each).

Ponies.
Color and mold variations ($3 each, £2 each).

Brooke Bond Oxo Ltd. England
Tea Promotion, 1969 - 1970

Brooke Bond was founded by Arthur Brooke in 1869. There never was a Mr. Bond. The word Bond was added to Brooke purely for the sound of the name. In 1968 Brooke Bond merged with Liebig Company to form Brooke Bond Oxo. In 1988, Brooke Bond Oxo merged with Bachelors to form Brooke Bond Foods, which is now part of Unilever Bestfoods UK.

During the 1950s and 1960s, Brooke Bond was most famous for including illustrated tea cards in their boxes of tea. Most of the series featured various animal life and wild flowers.

However, following the success of the promotion of the ceramic tea figurines in Canada, Brooke Bond Oxo Ltd. decided to launch a similar promotion in the U.K. The sixteen figurines in the U.K. promotion were issued over a one-year period utilizing similar figurines as used in the earlier Canadian promotion.

Top row. **Bear Cub** measures 1-3/8" high ($4, £2). **Fantail Goldfish** measures 1-1/4" high by 1-3/8" long ($12, £6). **Corgi** measures 1-1/2" high ($10, £5). **Bush Baby** measures 1-1/4" high ($4, £2).
Bottom row. **Butterfly** non-retail measures 1/2" high by 1-3/4" across wing span ($8, £4). **Duck** measures 1-1/4" high ($6, £3). **Beaver** measures 1-1/4" high ($4, £2). **Bison** measures 1-1/8" high ($6, £3).

Top row. **Seal** measures 1-1/2" high by 1-1/4" along the base ($8, £4). **Frog** measures 7/8" high ($10, £5). **Trout** measures 1-1/8" high ($6, £3). **Pine Marten** measures 1-3/8" high ($4, £2).
Bottom row. **Fox** measures 1-3/8" high ($8, £4). **Setter** measures 1-3/8" high ($6, £3). **Owl** measures 1-1/2" high ($6, £3). **Otter** measures 1-1/4" high ($4, £2).

Canadian Salada*

Tea Promotion, 1984

(*Registered Trade Mark of Kellogg Salada Canada, Inc.)

From September to December of 1984, Kellogg Salada Canada, Inc. began a "mail-in" offer for a series of premiums based upon six miniature houses from the popular "Whimsey-on-Why" village sets.

Along with the promotion of miniature houses was a tea caddy based on the tea caddy from The Wade "Village Stores" canister set. The design was identical to the original tea caddy except for a revised decal above the store front door. The decal has the word "Salada" in the center with "Salon de thé" on the left and "Ye Olde Tearoom" on the right. The decal was in both French and English to satisfy the bilingual requirements of the Canadian Government.

Back of box for the Salada* Tea promotion.

Box cover for the Salada*
Tea promotion.

Top Row from left. **Tobacconist's Shop** from "Whimsey-on-Why" set one ($10, £5). **Whimsey Station** from "Whimsey-on-Why" set three ($18, £9). **Antique Shop** from "Whimsey-on-Why" set two ($18, £9). Bottom Row from left. **Post Office** from "Whimsey-on-Why" set two ($16, £8). **Pump Cottage** from "Whimsey-on-Why" set one ($10, £5). **Greengrocer's Shop** from "Whimsey-on-Why" set two ($10, £5).

Canadian Salada* Tea Caddy.
The Salada* Tea Caddy measures 7-1/2" high by 3-5/8" square ($65, £38).

(*Registered Trade Mark of Kellogg Salada Canada, Inc.)

Chapter 4

Party Crackers Figurines, 1965 - 2007

The development and manufacture of "give away" tea premium figurines as described in Chapter 3 also applies to the small porcelain figurines packed in Christmas party crackers illustrated in this chapter.

In the mid-1960s, George Wade and Son Ltd. was approached by Balding and Mansell to supply figurines to be packaged in their boxes of Christmas crackers and in the early 1970s, Tom Smith & Co. Ltd. followed by including Wade figurines in their party crackers.

In 2001, Wade Ceramics Ltd. issued their first set of Christmas party crackers. Also in 2001, Absolutely Crackers began issuing boxes of party crackers that included Wade figurines as incentives.

to be included as prizes in their boxes of party crackers. The figurines were chosen from the early range of Wade premiums.

The Flintstones Party Crackers, 1965

In 1965, Balding and Mansell produced The Flintstones Party Crackers which comprised a set of eight Wade miniature figurines. The last four figurines were to be used in future promotions but Rhino, Tiger, Dino, and Bronti were only used once again.

Balding and Mansell, mid - late 1960s

During the 1960s, Balding and Mansell commissioned Wade to produce a number of miniature figurines

The Flintstones Party Crackers
Top row. **Rhino** measures 1" high ($26, £12). **Dino** measures 1-3/8" high ($26, £12). **Bronti** measures 1" high ($26, £18). **Tiger** measures 1-1/2" high ($28, £14). Bottom row. **Bluebird** measures 5/8" high ($8, £4). **Hedgehog** measures 7/8" high ($6, £3). **Terrapin** measures 3/8" high ($8, £4). **Crocodile** measures 1/2" high ($8, £4).

Color variations of figurines from the Balding and Mansell Party Crackers set. Top row. **Rhino** and **Tiger** ($40 each, £20 each). Bottom row. **Dino** and **Bronti** ($40 each, £20 each).

Wade Animal Party Crackers, late 1960s

In the late 1960s, another set of eight party crackers was issued by Mansell reusing some of the figurines from the earlier set.

Wade Animal Party Crackers
Top row. **Hippo** measures 1" high by 1-5/8" long ($6, £3). **Giraffe** measures 1-1/2" high by 1-1/2" overall ($4, £2). **Tiger** measures 1-1/2" high ($28, £14). **Rhino** measures 1" high ($26, £12). Bottom row. **Dino** measures 1-3/8" high ($26, £12). **Bronti** measures 1" high ($26, £12). **Zebra** measures 1-5/8" high by 1-1/2" overall ($20, £10). **Wild Boar** measures 1-1/8" high by 1-5/8" overall ($10, £5).

Tom Smith & Co. Ltd. Party Crackers, 1973 - 1998

For a number of years, George Wade & Son Ltd. supplied miniature figurines to be enclosed along with party hats, snaps, and mottos to Tom Smith & Co. Ltd., manufacturers of Christmas party crackers. It was the custom for the sets of figurines to be used for a period of two years with each set having a theme that was characterized by the type of figurine used. In some cases figurines from the "Whimsies" retail line were chosen, but in many cases special figurines were molded exclusively for Tom Smith & Co. Ltd.

In late 1998, the company was bought out by Napier Industries Ltd. who, to date, has not produced any new sets of promotional figurines.

Fire Cracker Pig, mid - 1970s

This pig was issued in a very limited quantity around the mid-1970s. The hole in the rear end of the pig was meant to hold firecrackers. Also in the mid-1970s, an elephant was produced with a small hole in the trunk to hold the firecracker.

Top left. **Fire Cracker Elephant.** The elephant measures 1" high by 1-1/2" overall and is unmarked ($60, £30). Top right. **Fire Cracker Pig.** The pig measures 1" high by 1-7/8" long and is unmarked ($45, £22). Bottom. This illustrates the rear end of the firecracker pig, which was meant to hold the firecrackers.

Animates Crackers, 1973 - 1975

The fantailed goldfish, bullfrog, butterfly, and terrapin were used in the 1967-73 Red Rose Tea promotion. All other figurines in this set were from the retail "Whimsies" line. All figurines are marked: WADE ENGLAND.

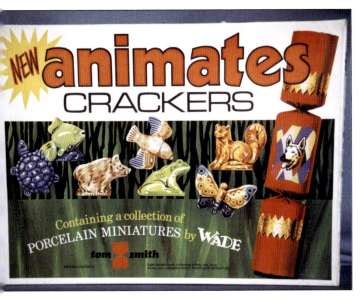

Animates Crackers presentation box closed.

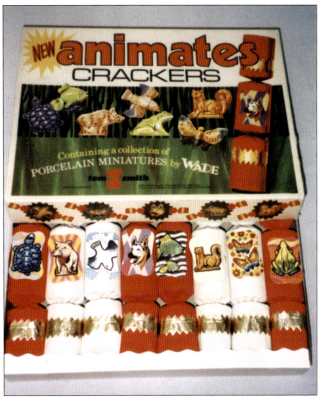

Animates Crackers presentation box open.

Alsatian measures 1-1/4" high by 1-7/8" overall ($6, £3). **Terrapin** measures 3/8" high by 1-5/8" long ($8, £4). **Butterfly** measures 1/2" high by 1-3/4" across the wings ($8, £4). **Pine Marten** measures 1-3/8" high by 1-1/2" overall ($4, £2). **Fantail Goldfish** measures 1-1/4" high by 1-3/8" long ($12, £6). **Bluebird** measures 5/8" high by 1-1/2" across the wings ($8, £4). **Bullfrog** measures 7/8" high by 1-1/8" across ($10, £5). **Wild Boar** measures 1-1/8" high by 1-5/8" overall ($10, £5).

Safari Park, 1976 - 1977

All figurines, other than the Musk Ox and Lion, were similar to the 1971-84 retail "Whimsies." The polar bear, although from the original Whimsie mold, is beige on a blue base rather than the original white on a blue base. The koala bear is dark grey and honey. The Musk Ox and the Lion were newly designed figurines for this series. All figurines are marked: Wade England.

Koala Bear measures 1-1/4" high ($24, £12). **Raccoon** measures 1" high ($14, £7). **Walrus** measures 1-1/4" high ($10, £5). **Kangaroo** measures 1-5/8" high ($12, £6). **Langur** measures 1-3/8" high ($4, £2). **Polar Bear** measures 1-1/8" high ($24, £12). **Orangutan** measures 1-1/4" high ($6, £3). **Tiger** measures 1-3/8" high ($12, £6). **Musk Ox** measures 1" high by 1" long ($18, £9). **Lion** measures 1-1/8" high by 1-3/4" long ($18, £9).

Circus Animals, 1978 - 1979

All figurines were new for this series and were marked Wade England on the drum type base. This set was reissued in 1993 as a Red Rose Tea premium series. Although the figurines were identical in design, there were slight color differences.

Sitting Elephant measures 1-1/4" high by 1" long. **Tiger** measures 1-5/8" high. **Standing Elephant** measures 1-3/16" high. **Lion** measures 1-9/16" high. **Bear** measures 1-3/16" high by 1" long. **Male Monkey** measures 1-5/8" high. **Poodle** measures 1-3/4" high. **Seal** measures 1-5/8" high by 1-1/8" long. **Horse** measures 1-3/4" high. **Female Monkey** measures 1-1/2" high (all figurines $8 each, £4 each).

Poodle.
Of these poodle color variations only the far right poodle with the blue skirt was used in the 1978-79 Tom Smith Circus Animals promotion ($10 each, £5 each).

British Wildlife, 1980 - 1981

All figurines were new for this series and are mold marked: Wade England. The Hare and the Squirrel are similar to the Rabbit (Hare) and Squirrel in the 1983-85 U.S.A. Red Rose Tea promotion but with different color glazes.

Squirrel measures 1-1/2" high by 3/4" dia. base. **Badger** measures 1-1/16" high by 1-1/4" long. **Weasel** measures 1-3/8" high by 1-1/2" long. **Hare** measures 1-3/4" high by 7/8" long. **Mole** measures 7/8" high by 1-9/16" long. **Fox** measures 1-3/8" high by 1-3/8" long. **Partridge** measures 1-1/8" high by 1-1/8" long. **Field mouse** measures 1-1/16" high by 1-1/8" long (all figurines $14 each, £7 each).

Squirrel from the Tom Smith 1980-81 British Wildlife set. Color variation ($20, £10).

Farmyard Animals, 1982 - 1983

The pig in this set is similar to the "Whimsies" retail line figurine but without the green base. The goose is similar to the "Goosey Gander" figurine from the 1971-79 Red Rose Tea promotion. All figurines in this set were mold marked: Wade England.

Duck Color Variations.
Of these three Duck color variations only the blue and white figurine on the left was used for the 1982-83 Tom Smith Farmyard Animals promotion ($14, £7). Center. Beige duck ($20, £10). Right. all-over blue duck ($28, £14).

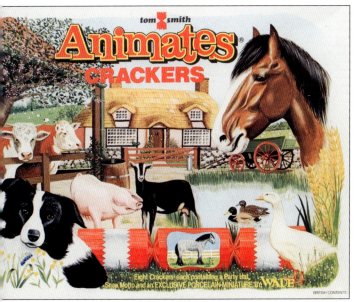

Presentation box for Farmyard Animals party crackers.

Dog.
Color variations ($14 each, £7 each).

Dog measures 1" high by 1-3/4" long ($14, £7). **Bull** measures 1-1/8" high by 1-1/4" long ($14, £7). **Horse** measures 1-1/2" high by 1-1/4" long ($14, £7). **Duck** measures 15/16" high by 1-1/4" long ($14, £7). **Goose** measures 1-3/8" high. The goose in this set does not have the orange/red beak as in the Red Rose Tea version. ($12, £6). **Goat** measures 1-1/2" high by 1-1/8" long ($14, £7). **Pig** measures 7/8" high ($14, £7). **Cow** measures 1-1/8" high by 1-1/8" long ($14, £7).

Goat.
Color variations.
Left. ($14, £7).
Right. ($20, £10).

Horse.
Color variations ($14 each, £7 each).

Wildlife, 1986 - 1987

All the figurines in this set were from the 1971-84 retail line of Whimsies. The models used for this promotion were all single glazed. All figurines were mold marked: Wade England.

Koala Bear measures 1-3/8" high ($8, £4). **Rhino** measures 7/8" high ($8, £4). **Kangaroo** measures 1-5/8" high ($10, £4). **Orangutan** measures 1-1/4" high ($6, £3). **Dolphin** measures 1-1/8" high ($20, £10). **Penguin** measures 1-5/8" high ($14, £7). **Leopard** measures 7/8" high ($6, £3). **Wild Boar** measures 1-1/8" high ($10, £5).

World of Survival, 1984 - 1985

The North American Bison in this set is similar to the "Whimsies" retail line figurine but with a different color way and the Harp Seal is similar to the Seal figurine from the 1967-73 Red Rose Tea promotion but in a different color way. All figurines in this set were mold marked: Wade England.

Gorilla measures 1-1/2" high by 1-3/8" across ($12, £6). **Sea Lion** measures 1-1/2" high ($6, £3). **Green Sea Turtle** measures 1-1/4" high by 1-1/4" long ($16, £8). **North American Bison** measures 1-1/8" high ($6, £3). **Blue Whale** measures 7/8" high by 1-1/4" long ($16, £8). **Armadillo** measures 1" high by 1-3/8" long ($16, £8). **Polar Bear** measures 1" high by 1-1/4" long ($16, £8). **Golden Eagle** measures 1-3/4" high by 7/8" across ($16, £8).

Nursery Rhyme Crackers, 1988

In 1988, Tom Smith and Co. Ltd. issued a set of party crackers with six nursery rhyme figurines. The colors were similar to those used in the 1971-79 Red Rose Tea promotion.

Bo-Peep ($6, £3). **Humpty Dumpty** ($6, £3). **Hickory Dickory Dock** ($8, £4). **Old Woman Who Lived in a Shoe** ($6, £3). **Wee Willie Winkie** ($8, £4). **King Cole.** Note the figurine in this series is the figurine with a space between the feet ($8, £4).

Village of Broadlands, 1988

This short-lived series issued between January 1988 and March 1988 was based on houses from the Whimsey-on-Why Village sets. Originally, there were to have been two sets in this series but, due to high costs, the second set was never produced. The buildings scheduled for the second set were: The Bank, The Duck Inn, The Post Office, The Thatched Cottage, and Broadlands Village School.

The Coach House Garage is the same model as Whimsey-on-Why No. 18 ($65, £32.50). **Rose Cottage** is the same model as Whimsey-on-Why No. 1 ($98, £49). **The Chapel** is the same model as Whimsey-on-Why No. 13 ($78, £39). **The Village Store** is the same model as Whimsey-on-Why No. 9 ($68, £34). **The Pink House** is the same model as Whimsey-on-Why No. 22 ($65, £32.50). These five miniature houses are becoming extremely hard to find and values are rising accordingly.

Village of Broadlands presentation box of crackers.

Village of Broadlands display card with buildings placed according to the layout.

Your Pets, 1988 - 1989

This set of eight party cracker miniature birds and animals was designed exclusively for Tom Smith. In 1990, after the exclusivity lapsed, five of the figurines (parrot, kitten, rabbit, and pony) were released for use as premiums for the 1990-96 U.S. Red Rose Tea promotion. The figurines are mold marked either Wade England or Wade Eng.

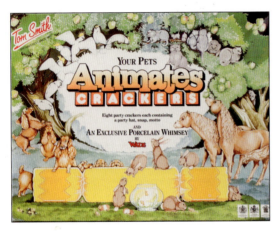

Presentation box for Your Pets party crackers.

Parrot measures 1-3/8" high by 1-3/4" overall ($4, £2). **Mouse** measures 1/2" high by 1-1/4" overall ($28, £14). **Puppy** measures 1" high by 1-1/4" overall ($4, £2). **Rabbit** measures 1-1/8" high by 1-1/4" overall ($8, £4). **Pony** measures 1" high by 1-7/8" overall ($8, £4). **Fish** measures 1" high by 1-1/2" overall ($20, £10). **Kitten** measures 1" high by 1-3/8" overall ($6, £3). **Guinea Pig** measures 3/4" high by 1-1/4" overall ($28, £14).

Kitten Color Variations.
These kittens from the 1988-89 Tom Smith Your Pets series show a variety of glazes. The white and black figurines on the right top row were chosen for the 2000 Summer Wade Fest and given the names Thunder for the black kitten and Lightning for the white kitten ($6 each, £3 each). The all-over blue kitten second from left at top ($28, £14).

Kitten from the Tom Smith 1988-89 Your Pets set. Color variations. Left ($6, £3). Right ($12, £6).

World of Dogs, 1990 - 1991

Other than the West Highland Terrier and the Bull Dog which were new designs for this set and the Poodle which was from the 1967-73 Red Rose Tea promotion, all figurines were from the 1971-84 retail line of Whimsies. All figurines are mold marked: Wade England.

Presentation box for World of Dogs party crackers.

Poodle measures 1-5/8" high ($12, £6). **West Highland Terrier** measures 1-1/4" high by 1-1/4" overall ($10, £5). **Bulldog** measures 1" high by 1-1/4" overall ($10, £5). **Spaniel** measures 1-3/8" high ($8, £4). **Alsatian** measures 1-1/4" high ($10, £5). **Husky** measures 1-7/16" high ($14, £7). **Mongrel** measures 1-3/8" high ($10, £5). **Corgi** measures 1-1/2" high ($10, £5).

Husky from the Tom Smith 1990-91 World of Dogs set. Left. Husky with black ear and nose ($20, £10). Right. Production model shown for comparison.

Eagle from the Tom Smith 1992-93 Bird Life set. Color variations ($14 each, £7 each). The eagles on the left and right are color variations. The eagle in the center is the production model shown for comparison.

Birdlife, 1992 - 1993

In this set, only the Wren was a new design. The Duck, Partridge, and Cockerel were from the Whimsie-Land series, the Barn Owl and the Pelican were from the 1971-84 Whimsies retail line, and the Goose was from both the 1971-79 Canadian Red Rose Tea promotion and the Tom Smith Farmyard set.

Duck from the Tom Smith 1992-93 Bird Life set. Color variation ($20, £10).

Cockerel measures 2" high by 1-1/4" long. Partridge measures 1-1/2" high by 1-3/4" long. Goose measures 1-3/8" high by 1" long. Pelican measures 1-3/4" high by 1-3/8" overall. Eagle measures 1-3/4" high by 7/8" across the base. Barn Owl measures 1-1/2" high by 1" across the base. Duck measures 1-5/8" high by 1" along the base. Wren measures 1-1/2" high by 1" overall (all figurines $14 each, £7 each).

Color variations from the Tom Smith 1992-93 Bird Life set. Pelican left ($14, £7). Pelican center ($28, £14). Barn Owl right ($20, £10).

Snow Life, 1992 - 1997

In this set, only the Reindeer was a new design. The Owl and Fox were from the Whimsie-Land series and the Penguin, Polar Bear, Seal, and Walrus were from the 1971-84 Whimsies retail line. The Whale and Hare were previously used in Tom Smith sets and the Goose was from both the 1971-79 Canadian Red Rose Tea promotion and the Tom Smith Farmyard set.

The Snow Goose and the Whale were added to the original set in 1995.

Reindeer from the Tom Smith 1992-97 Snow Life set. Mold variations ($18 each, £9 each).

Seal Pup from the Tom Smith 1992-97 Snow Life set. Color variations ($20 each, £10 each).

Presentation box for the Snow Life party crackers.

Walrus from the Tom Smith 1992-97 Snow Life set. Color variation ($28, £14).

Penguin from the Tom Smith 1992-97 Snow Life set. Color variation ($20, £10).

Fox measures 1-3/8" high by 1-1/4" along the base ($12, £6). **Reindeer** measures 1-3/8" high by 1-3/8" overall ($18, £9). **Polar Bear** measures 1-1/8" high by 1-5/8" overall ($8, £4). **Hare** measures 1-3/4" high by 7/8" along the base ($10, £5). **Walrus** measures 1-1/4" high by 1-1/4" overall ($10, £5). **Owl** measures 1-1/2" high by 7/8" along the base ($10, £5). **Whale** measures 7/8" high by 1-1/4" long ($12, £6). **Penguin** measures 1-5/8" high by 3/4" dia. base ($10, £5). **Seal Pup** measures 1" high by 1-1/2" overall ($18, £9). **Goose** measures 1-3/8" high by 1" long ($12, £6).

Owl from the Tom Smith 1992-97 Snow Life set. Color variations ($10 each, £5 each).

Tales from the Nursery, 1994 - 1997

Other than Little Boy Blue and Ride a Cock Horse, which were new designs for this set, all other figurines were taken from the 1971-79 Canadian Red Rose Tea promotion. All figurines are mold marked: Wade England.

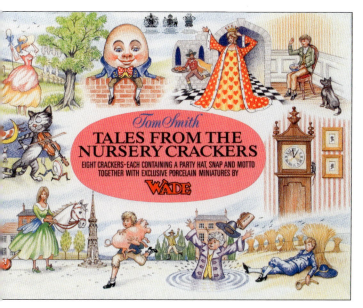

Presentation box for the Tales from the Nursery party crackers.

Queen of Hearts measures 1-3/4" high by 1" across the base. **Little Bo-Peep** measures 1-3/4" high by 3/4" dia. base. **Cat and Fiddle** measures 1-7/8" high by 1" across the base. **Little Boy Blue** measures 1-3/4" high by 1" dia. base. **Dr. Foster** measures 1-3/4" high by 7/8" dia. base. **Little Jack Horner** measures 1-3/8" high by 1" across the base. **Ride a Cock Horse** measures 1-1/2" high by 1-5/8" overall. **Hickory Dickory Dock** measures 1-3/4" high by 3/4" square base. **Humpty Dumpty** measures 1-1/2" high by 7/8" base. **Tom the Piper's Son** measures 1-5/8" high by 1-3/8" across the base (all figurines $6 each, £3 each).

Cat Collection, 1996 - 1997

The Standing and Stalking Cats were new designs for this set. The Sitting Cat, Sitting Kitten, Tiger, Lion, and Leopard were from the 1971-84 Whimsies retail line. The Lying Kitten was from the Whimsie-Land series and the Cat and Fiddle was from the 1971-79 Canadian Red Rose Tea promotion. All figurines are mold marked: Wade England.

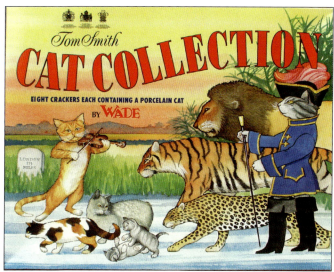

Presentation box for the Cat Collection party crackers.

Cat and Fiddle measures 1-7/8" high by 1" across the base ($8, £4). **Kitten Lying** measures 1" high by 1-5/8" along the base ($8, £4). **Lion** measures 1-3/8" high by 1-3/4" overall ($6, £3). **Stalking Cat** measures 7/8" high by 1-3/4" long ($8, £4). **Puss in Boots** measures 1-3/4" high by 3/4" dia. base ($8, £4). **Kitten** measures 1-3/8" high by 1-3/8" overall ($8, £4). **Tiger** measures 1-1/2" high by 1-1/8" overall ($4, £2). **Leopard** measures 7/8" high by 1-7/8" overall ($4, £2). **Sitting Cat** measures 1-1/2" high by 7/8" dia. base ($8, £4). **Standing Cat** measures 1-7/8" high by 1-3/8" overall ($8, £4).

Cat Collection.
Color variations.

Christmas Time Crackers, 1996 - 1997

The six bears in this set are from the Bear Ambitions retail line but in different color ways.

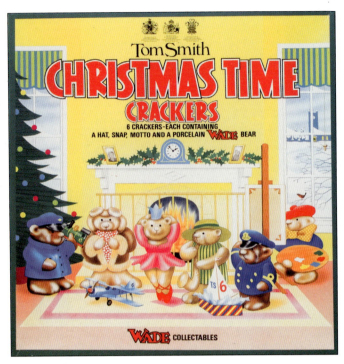

Presentation box for Christmas Time Crackers.

Admiral Sam measures 1-5/8" high. **Artistic Edward** measures 1-1/2" high. **Locomotive Joe** measures 1-5/8" high. **Beatrice the Ballerina** measures 1-3/4" high. **Alex the Aviator** measures 1-5/8" high. **Musical Marco** measures 1-5/8" high (all figurines $8 each, £4 each).

Hedgerow, 1998 - 1999

All figurines in this set had been used previously. The Rabbit, Squirrel, Mouse, and Otter were from the 1971-84 Whimsies retail line. The Hare, Mole, and Badger had been used by Tom Smith in earlier issues and the Butterfly was from the 1967-73 Canadian Red Rose Tea promotion.

Presentation box for Hedgerow party crackers.

Badger measures 1" high by 1-3/8" along the base. **Rabbit** measures 1-1/8" high by 1-7/8" overall. **Otter** measures 1-1/4" high by 1-1/2" overall. **Hare** measures 2" high by 7/8" dia. base. **Mouse** measures 1-1/2" high by 1" dia. base. **Mole** measures 7/8" high by 1-9/16" long. **Butterfly** measures 1/2" high by 1-3/4" across wingspan. **Squirrel** measures 1-3/8" high by 1-3/8" overall (all figurines $8 each, £4 each).

Sealife, 1998 - 1999

All figurines in this set had been used previously. The Angel Fish, Dolphin, Seahorse, Turtle, and Walrus were from the 1971-84 Whimsies retail line. The Whale had been used by Tom Smith in an earlier set, the Snail was from the 1975-80 Aquarium Set and the Seal was from the 1967-73 Canadian Red Rose Tea promotion.

Presentation box for Sealife party crackers.

Seal measures 1-1/2" high by 1-1/4" along the base ($10, £5). **Snail** measures 1-1/4" high ($12, £6). **Dolphin** measures 1-1/2" high by 1-3/4" overall ($10, £5). **Walrus** measures 1-1/4" high by 1-1/4" overall ($10, £5). **Whale** measures 7/8" high by 1-1/4" along the base ($12, £6). **Angel Fish** measures 1-3/8" high by 1-1/4" overall ($12, £6). **Turtle** measures 9/16" high by 2" overall ($10, £5). **Seahorse** measures 2" high by 3/4" dia. base ($10, £5).

Miscellaneous Tom Smith & Co. Ltd. Party Crackers, 1985 - 1993

Between 1985 and 1993, Tom Smith & Co. Ltd. packaged a number of Wade miniatures in various sets of party crackers along with other miscellaneous party gifts. No mention was made on the miscellaneous sets of cracker boxes that a Wade miniature was included as a prize.

Wade miniatures included in miscellaneous boxes of party crackers in 1987 included: beige **Hickory Dickory Dock** ($6, £3), honey **Hare** ($14, £7) (which was also used as a cracker gift in 1988), dark brown **Gorilla** ($4, £2), beige **Old Woman in a Shoe** ($10, £5), blue **Old King Cole** ($28, £14), blue **Wee Willie Winkie** ($28, £14). Also included in 1987 but not illustrated were a honey **Bo-Peep** and a brown **Humpty Dumpty**.

Wade miniatures included in miscellaneous boxes of party crackers in 1989 included: beige **Koala Bear** ($6, £3), **Little Bo-Peep** ($6, £3), **Wee Willie Winkie** ($8, £4), **Hickory Dickory Dock** ($8, £4) (similar in colors as the Red Rose Tea Nurseries), honey **Kangaroo** ($10, £5).

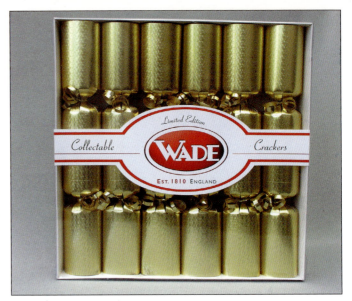

Wade miniatures included in miscellaneous boxes of party crackers in 1990 included: **Old King Cole** ($8, £4) (similar in colors as the Red Rose Tea Nurseries), blue **Squirrel** ($6, £3), brown **Hare** ($8, £4).

Presentation box for the Nursery Christmas Crackers.

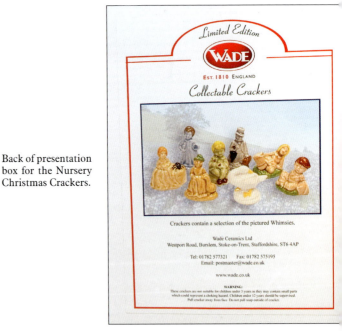

Back of presentation box for the Nursery Christmas Crackers.

Wade miniatures included in miscellaneous boxes of party crackers in 1992 included: blue **Blue Bird** ($20, £10), honey **Koala Bear** ($6, £3). These two figurines in similar glazes were also used in 1993 along with a blue **Mongrel**, not illustrated ($28, £14).

Wade Ceramics Limited
Christmas Crackers, 2001 - 2003

In 2001, Wade Ceramics Limited introduced their first set of Christmas party crackers followed, in 2003, by a second set. The figurines used for these party crackers were from both previously used molds and new molds.

Whimsies "Nursery"
Christmas Crackers, 2001

All figurines in the 2001 set of crackers were from the 1971-79 Canadian Red Rose Tea series but with different color ways.

Top Row from left. **Dr. Foster. Little Miss Muffet. Mother Goose. Wee Willie Winkie.**
Bottom row from left. **Jill. Jack. Little Jack Horner. Goosey Gander** ($48 set, £24 set).

Whimsies "Safari Set" Christmas Crackers, 2003

Only two figurines in this set were from new molds, the crocodile and the giraffe. All other figurines were from the 1984 Whimsie-Land Set 2 but with different color ways.

Top Row. **Tiger. Panda** and **Lion.** Bottom row. **Elephant. Crocodile** and **Giraffe** ($30 set, £15 set).

Back of presentation box for the Safari party crackers.

Snowmen with Red Hats. These are prototype figurines and are to be used in Wade party crackers in 2008.

Front of presentation box for the Safari party crackers.

Absolutely Crackers, 2001 - 2007

For the Christmas season 2001-02 Absolutely Crackers Ltd. issued a set of eight bird figurines, randomly placed in their boxes of Christmas crackers. Seven of the figurines used were similar to the models used for the 1992-93 Tom Smith promotion but in different color ways. The owl was the same model as used for the Whimsie-Land Hedgerow Set 4.

In 2003 Absolutely Crackers issued a set of Christmas crackers featuring the Wade Safari Whimsies and the 2001 Set 2 Wade dinosaurs are currently being used as inserts for Absolutely Crackers.

Absolutely Crackers - Bird Whimsies *2001 - 2002*
Cockerel measures 2" high. **Eagle** measures 1-3/4" high. **Duck** measures 1-5/8" high. **Pelican** measures 1-3/4" high. **Wren** measures 1-1/2" high. **Owl** measures 1-1/2" high. **Partridge** measures 1-1/2" high. **Goose** measures 1-3/8" high (all figurines $10 each, £5 each).

Absolutely Crackers - Safari Whimsies *2002 - 2003*
Top Row. **Panda. Tiger** and **Giraffe.** Bottom row. **Elephant. Crocodile** and **Lion** ($30 set, £15 set).

Absolutely Crackers - Dinosaurs *2005*
Wade advertising flyer for Dinosaur set 2 illustrating the figurines used by Absolutely Crackers in this promotion. ($36 set, £18 set).

Chapter 5

Retail and Commissioned Whimsies, Early 1960s - 2007

Miscellaneous Wade Retail and Collectors Club Whimsies

Over the years, Wade has issued a number of Whimsies to be sold either to retail stores, at Wade Fairs, or produced for sale to members of The Official International Wade Collectors Club. Special Whimsies have also been commissioned by various companies and individuals over the last few years and retailed either at Wade Fairs or by mail order.

Nursery Favourites, 1972 - 1981

This retail giftware line of Nursery Rhyme figurines was marketed at approximately the same time period as the miniature nursery figurines used for the Red Rose Tea promotion. A number of the Nursery Favourites were similar in design to their smaller, premium counterparts, and others, although similar in characters, were of a different design.

Three of the twenty characters (Mary Lamb, Polly Kettle, and Tommy Tucker) did not appear in the premium nursery series. The Nursery Favourites were issued in four sets of five over a period of nine years, each set having a distinctive colored box containing the figurine. All figurines are mold marked "Wade England" at the back of the base.

Set 1, *1972 (green box)* Top Row. 1. **Jack** measures 2-7/8" high ($50, £25). 2. **Jill** measures 2-7/8" high ($48, £24). 3. **Little Miss Muffet** measures 2-5/8" high ($48, £24). Bottom Row. 4. **Little Jack Horner** measures 1-7/8" high ($40, £20). 5. **Humpty Dumpty** measures 1-3/8" high ($34, £17).

Green presentation box for Set 1.

Blue presentation box for Set 2.

Set 2, *1973 (blue box)*
Top Row. 6. **Willie Winkie** measures 1-3/4" high ($28, £14). 7. **Mary Lamb** measures 2-7/8" high ($44, £22). 8. **Polly Kettle** measures 2-7/8" high ($50, £25). Bottom Row. 9. **King Cole** measures 2-1/2" high ($52, £26). 10. **Tom Piper** measures 2-3/4" high ($52, £26).

Purple presentation box for Set 4.

Yellow presentation box for Set 3.

Set 4, *1976 (purple box)*
Top Row. 16. **Puss-in-Boots** measures 2-7/8" high ($64, £32). 17. **Three Bears** measures 2-7/8" high ($66, £33). 18. **Goosey Gander** measures 2-5/8" high ($162, £80). Bottom Row. 19. **Bo-Peep** measures 2-7/8" high ($120, £60). 20. **Old Woman in the Shoe** measures 2-1/2" high ($130, £65).

Set 3, *1974 (yellow box)*
Top Row. 11. **Little Boy Blue** measures 2-7/8" high ($56, £28). 12. **Mary Mary** measures 2-7/8" high ($76, £38). 13. **Cat & Fiddle** measures 2-7/8" high ($50, £25). Bottom row. 14. **Queen of Hearts** measures 2-7/8" high ($64, £32). 15. **Tommy Tucker** measures 3" high ($50, £25).

Three Bears.
Brown color variation from the Nursery Favorites
Set 4 ($66, £33).

Gold Star Gifthouse
backstamp.

Nursery Favourites, 1990 - 1991

A limited reissue of five of the Nursery Favourite figurines was made by Wade for the U.S. based Gold Star Gifthouse. These figurines, although from the same molds as the original issue, are all marked with the year of manufacture, thus enabling collectors to differentiate between the originals and the reissues. The figurines issued in 1991 may also be found with a diamond shaped ink stamp on the underside of the base enclosing the letters GSG.

Retail Nurseries, 1979 - 1980

A short-lived line of five figurines was offered as a retail line as a boxed set under the name of "Nurseries." The molds for these figurines had previously been used in a Canadian Red Rose Tea promotion.

The figurines used for this retail line were Little Jack Horner, Woman in the Shoe, Old King Cole, Little Bo Peep, and Cat and the Fiddle. These figurines did not prove popular with the public and were soon withdrawn from the market. For designs and measurements, see the 1971-79 Canadian Red Rose Tea promotion.

Wade Giftware flyer illustrating the retail nurseries.

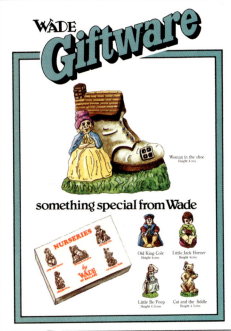

Top Row 1. **Polly Kettle** measures 2-7/8" high and is mold marked: Wade England 90 ($40, £20). 2. **Tom Piper** measures 2-3/4" high and is mold marked: Wade England 90 ($40, £20). 3. **Mary Mary** measures 2-7/8" high and is mold marked: Wade England 90 ($40, £20). Bottom Row. 4. **Old Woman in the Shoe** measures 2-1/2" high and is mold marked: Wade England 91. Note that the little dog is not colored as is the dog in the original 1976 issue ($70, £35). 5. **Goosey Gander** measures 2-5/8" high and is mold marked: Wade England 91 ($70, £35).

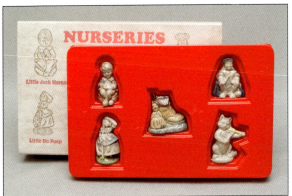

Boxed set of five Nurseries issued in 1979 ($60, £30).

Whimsie Special Issues, 1996 - 1999

For the membership years 1996 and 1998, the O.I.W.C.C. issued new color way Whimsie figurines to members of the club renewing their membership.

OIWCC White Seal *1996 - 1997*
This color variation of the 1980 Whimsie Seal from Set 12 was issued to members renewing or joining The Official International Wade Collectors Club for the membership year 1996-97 ($20, £10).

OIWCC Blue Angel Fish *1998 - 1999*
This color variation of the 1978 Whimsie Angel Fish from Set 9 was issued to members renewing or joining The Official International Wade Collectors Club for the membership year 1998-99 ($16, £8).

Dog Key Chains, 2003 - Present

Starting in August 2003, Wade Ceramics Ltd. began producing a series of key chains with a small ceramic dog attached to the chain. These key chains were sold from the Factory Shop via mail order and at various Wade Fair events.

Dalmatian Key Chain. This was issued in May 2003 and was the first dog key chain issued in the new series. The Dalmatian key chain was dropped from the Wade Price List in 2007 ($16, £8).

Bulldog Key Chain. This was issued in August 2003 ($16, £8).

Left. **Spaniel Key Chain.** This was issued in February 2004. The Spaniel key chain was dropped from Wade Price Lists in the summer of 2007 ($16, £8). Right. **St. Bernard Key Chain.** This was issued in August 2004. The St. Bernard key chain was dropped from Wade Price Lists in 2006 ($16, £8).

Australian Kangaroo, 2004

This special color way of the Whimsie kangaroo from the 1979 Whimsies Set 10 was given to attendees at a meeting with Wade personnel in Australia in 2004.

Australian Kangaroo. This was a limited edition of 80 figurines complete with certificate ($80, £40).

Billy Bottle Oven, 2004

Billy Bottle Oven was originally produced for sale by Ceramica, a pottery related visitor attraction located in Market Street, Burslem. Later the Whimsie bottle oven was sold at the Wade Factory Shop. In 2005 Billy Bottle Oven was sold at the Summer Wade Fest and later via mail order.

Billy Bottle Oven.
Top left. This figurine is the original 2004 version ($20, £10). Top right. This figurine is the version sold at the Summer Wade Fest and is marked in gold: Summer Fest 2005 ($26, £13). Above. This "One of a Kind" figurine was won in a draw at the 2006 Summer Wade Fest. (N.P.A.). The figurines measure 2-1/4" high and are mold marked: Ceramica Wade Eng.

Billy Bottle Oven. This prototype figurine measures 2-1/4" high and never went into production with this color glaze ($90, £45).

Nativity Set Whimsies, 2005

Wade Ceramics Ltd. produced a range of Nativity Whimsies based on the larger regular series issued in 2001. This set of Whimsies was sold in retail stores and via mail order and also at Wade Fairs. Each figurine was individually boxed and was a limited edition of 1,000.

Top row: **Mary and Child** measures 1-5/8" high. **Angel** measures 2-1/4" high. **Wiseman** measures 1-5/8" high. Second row: **Shepherd** measures 1-3/4" high. **Donkey** measures 1-7/16" high. **Wiseman** measures 1-5/8" high. **Wiseman** measures 1-5/8" high. ($86 set, £43 set). All figurines are solid cast and are marked with a gold colored Wade transfer on the back of the figurines.

Tetley Tea Whimsies, 2006 - 2007

In 2006, for the first time since 1997, the membership pieces given to continuing and new members of The Official International Wade Collectors Club were Whimsies. In this case the Whimsies were based upon the popular Tetley Tea characters, Gaffer and Gordon.

Wade Ceramics Limited also produced Whimsie versions of the popular Tetley Tea figurines, Maurice and Sidney. These figurines were Fair Specials at two Wade Collector Fairs in 2006 and 2007.

Maurice Gold and Sidney Gold.
Bottom Left. Maurice measures 2-1/4" high. Right. Sidney measures 2-3/8" high ($60 each, £30 each). The figurines are solid cast and transfer marked: Wade England Tetley. These figurines were sold at the April 2007 Wade Collectors Fair, Trentham Gardens in a limited edition of 75 pieces each.

Gaffer and Gordon.
Gaffer measures 2-1/8" high. Gordon measures 2-1/8" high. Each figurine is solid cast and is transfer marked: Wade England Tetley. Membership Pieces for 2006 ($30 each, £15 each).

Maurice and Sidney.
Left. Maurice measures 2-1/4" high. Right. Sidney measures 2-3/8" high. ($30 each, £15 each). The figurines are solid cast and transfer marked: Wade England Tetley. These figurines were sold at the April 2006 Wade Collectors Fair, Stoke-on-Trent.

Felix the Cat Whimsie, 2006

In 2006, Wade Ceramics, under a new license agreement, began producing figurines of Felix the Cat. The first Felix the Cat figurine was launched at the April 2006 Wade Collectors Fair. The first Whimsie size Felix the Cat was announced in the November edition of The Official Wade Collectors Club Magazine.

Felix Whimsie. The figurine measures 2-3/8" high and is solid cast. This figurine is a prototype only.

Felix the Cat Whimsie measures 3" high and is slip cast. This figurine was a limited edition of 100 ($30, £15). This figurine was produced in 2006 and was available through the Wade Club or via the internet.

Felix the Cat prototypes. These figurines are prototypes only and are therefore hollow and unmarked. The production pieces are planned with a base to help stabilize the figurine.

Snow People Whimsies, 2007

These prototypes were on view at the 2007 Summer Wade Fest in Pennsylvania. The figurines are based on the popular larger size retail figurines. The final production models were advertised in the November 2007 edition of *The Official Wade Collectors Club Magazine* in a limited edition of 2,000 sets.

Snow People. The figurines are hollow and unmarked and measure between 1-5/16" high and 1-5/8" high. The final production models will be solid and were scheduled to be on sale in late Novemeber 2007 ($40 set, £20 set).

Peacock Whimsies, 2007

These prototype peacock Whimsies were shown at the November 2007 Red Rose Tea Fair.

Peacock Whimsies. The four Whimsie size peacocks are prototypes only and the color and decoration may change when the figurines are officially issued. The peacocks measure 1-1/2" high, are slip cast and are mold marked Wade around the base.

C&S Collectables, 2003 - 2007

C&S Collectables has commissioned Wade Ceramics Limited to produce a number of figurines which are sold either via retail or over the Internet. Many figurines were issued specially for Wade Fairs and these are featured in Chapter 2.

Budgies, 2003

These budgies, modeled by Cyril Roberts, were commissioned by C&S Collectables in a limited edition of 500 sets which were sold via the Internet or mail order. The pink budgie was commissioned by Wade Watch. All figurines were mold marked: Wade C/S.

See Chapter 2 for Summer Wade Fest Special Budgies.

Budgies.
Top row. **Blue Budgie. Pink Budgie** was a limited edition of 300 commissioned by Wade Watch ($12, £6). **White** and **Gold Budgie** was a limited edition of 50 and given as prizes and for lucky ticket winners in draws at various Wade Fairs ($50, £25).
Bottom row. **Green Budgie, White Budgie, Orange Budgie.** The blue, orange, white, and green budgies were commissioned by C&S Collectables in a limited edition of 500 sets which were sold via the internet or mail order ($60 per set, £30 per set).

Flamingos, 2006

These figurines were sold as a retail line and at various Wade Fairs throughout 2006. A special color way flamingo was produced for the 2006 Red Rose Tea Fair and is shown in Chapter 2. The flamingos were modeled by Cyril Roberts.

Flamingos. The figurines with the bronze, silver, and gold base measure 1-3/4" high ($56 per set, £28 per set).

Gingie Bear, 2006 - 2007

The C&S Collectables' Gingie Bear is based on a figurine developed by Little Words Ltd. In 2006, C&S Collectables commissioned Wade Ceramics Ltd. to produce the figurine in ceramic, which proved to be very popular with collectors. Gingie Bear has been produced in a number of configurations in both larger size and Whimsie size.

The Gingie Bear Whimsie was first produced in February 2006 in a limited edition of 500 and sold via the C&S Collectables online shop. Further variations of the Gingie Bear Whimsie were produced as specials for various Wade Fairs but are shown here in order to show them as a group.

Gingie Bear.
Gingie Bear Whimsie. A limited edition of 500 ($20, £10). **Gingie Bear Uncle Sam.** This was a limited edition of 100 sold at the 2006 Summer Wade Fest and at the 2006 Red Rose Tea Fair ($30, £15). **Gingie Bear Uncle Sam Gold.** This was a limited edition of 20 ($110, £55). **Gingie Bear Uncle Sam Silver.** This was a limited edition of 20 ($110, £55). **Gingie Bear Halloween.** This was a limited edition of 100 sold at the 2006 Red Rose Tea Fair ($80, £40). **Gingie Bear Christmas Time.** This was a limited edition of 100 and sold at the 2006 Christmas Bonanza ($80, £40).

Snoopy Whimsies, 2005 - 2007

C&S Collectables first introduced the Snoopy Whimsie in July 2005 and sold the figurine via mail order. Variations of the original Snoopy Whimsie were issued at various times and at various Wade events. The Snoopy figurines were modeled by Cyril Roberts.

Snoopy Whimsies.
Snoopy with Black Collar was a limited edition of 400 and sold at the 2005 Summer Wade Fest ($30, £15). **Snoopy Christmas Time** was a limited edition of 100 and sold at the December 2006 Wade Christmas Bonanza ($90, £45). **Snoopy with Red Collar** was first issued as a retail item in July 2005 ($30, £15). **Snoopy with Silver Collar** and **Snoopy with a Gold Collar** were included in the Treasure Chest sold at the July 2007 Wade Collectors Meet ($70 each, £35 each). **Snoopy Witch Halloween.** This was a limited edition of 100 ($80, £40).

Animal Bust Whimsies, 2007

C&S Collectables first showed these Whimsie size figurines in late 2007. This will be the first set of a series. These prototype figurines, modeled by Cyril Roberts, feature the busts of an Alsatian, Horse, and Eagle. When issued the actual colors may change.

Animal Bust Whimsies. The figurines measure 1-1/2" high and are mold marked Wade around the base. When issued the set will be $50 set, £24 set.

Arundel Town Mouse Whimsie Family 2008

Due to the popularity of the large size Town Mouse figurines, C&S Collectables decided to introduce a set of Whimsie size figurines in April 2008.

Arundel Town Mouse Whimsie Family. These figurines are approximately half the size of the regular Town Mouse Family and were issued in a limited edition of 1000 sets ($60 set, £30 set).

Cricket Design Incorporated of Costa Mesa, California, circa 1980

Cricket Design Incorporated (CDI Imports), a California based import company, purchased a number of Wade products for distribution under the CDI name. The original names of the series imported were changed somewhat from the original Wade titles. Nursery Favourites became "Fairytale Friends," the Dogs and Puppies series became "Doggy Family," and the Puppy Dish line became "Pups in a Basket."

Fairytale Friends, circa 1980

CDI Imports marketed the complete series of the Wade retail line of Nursery Favourites under the new name of Fairytale Friends. The figurines were similar in every way to the original Wade line except for the packaging and a few changes in the name of figurines.

Presentation box for Fairytale Friends complete with Polly Kettle ($60 with box, £30 with box).

The
Fairytale Friends
Series:

1. Jack
2. Jill
3. Miss Muffett
4. Jack Horner
5. Humpty Dumpty
6. Willie Winkie
7. Mary Lamb
8. Polly Kettle
9. King Cole
10. Tom Piper
11. Blue Boy
12. Mary Mary
13. Cat and Fiddle
14. Queen of Hearts
15. Tommy Tucker
16. Puss-in-Boots
17. Three Bears
18. Goosey Gander
19. Bo Peep
20. Old Woman in Shoe

CDI IMPORTS
WADE in England

Back of presentation box for Fairytale Friends.

Fairytale Friends
Collectible Miniatures
Fine English Porcelain

Who are your Fairytale Friends? Can you remember those wonderful tales of fantasy from yesteryear? Now 20 nursery rhyme characters in real English porcelain are yours to possess. Each miniature individually gift boxed – the ideal gift for mother or child. Start a collection now.

1. Jack
2. Jill
3. Miss Muffett
4. Jack Horner
5. Humpty Dumpty
6. Willie Winkie
7. Mary Lamb
8. Polly Kettle
9. King Cole
10. Tom Piper
11. Blue Boy
12. Mary Mary
13. Cat and Fiddle
14. Queen of Hearts
15. Tommy Tucker
16. Puss-in-Boots
17. Three Bears
18. Goosey Gander
19. Bo Peep
20. Old Woman in Shoe

CDI IMPORTS WADE in England
Cricket Design Incorporated
3333 South Bristol
Costa Mesa, California 92626

Collect our additional porcelain miniatures:
Happy Family
Doggy Family
Pup-In-A-Basket
Turtle Family
Whoppas

Advertising flyer for Fairytale Friends.

Top Row. 1. **Jack** ($50, £25). 2. **Jill** ($48, £24). 3. **Miss Muffet.** Little Miss Muffet in the Nursery Favourites. ($48, £24). Bottom Row. 4. **Jack Horner.** Little Jack Horner in the Nursery Favourites. ($40, £20). 5. **Humpty Dumpty** ($34, £17).

Top Row. 6. **Willie Winkie** ($28, £14). 7. **Mary Lamb** ($44, £22). 8. **Polly Kettle** ($50, £25). Bottom Row. 9. **King Cole** ($52, £26). 10. **Tom Piper** ($52, £26).

Top Row. 16. **Puss-in-Boots** ($64, £32). 17. **Three Bears** ($66, £33). 18. **Goosey Gander** ($162, £80). Bottom Row. 19. **Bo-Peep** ($120, £60). 20. **Old Woman in the Shoe** ($130, £65).

Happy Family, circa 1980

CDI Imports marketed four of the Wade retail line of the Happy Families series. The figurines were similar to the original Wade retail line.

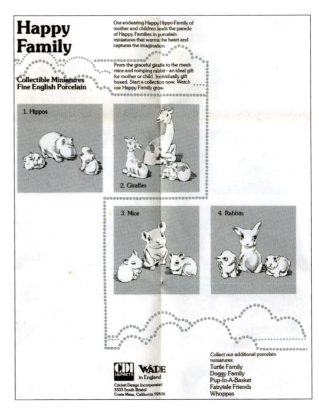

Advertising flyer for the CDI Imports Happy Family.

Top Row. 11. **Boy Blue.** Little Boy Blue in the Nursery Favourites. ($56, £28). 12. **Mary Mary** ($76, £38). 13. **Cat & Fiddle** ($50, £25). Bottom row. 14. **Queen of Hearts** ($64, £32). 15. **Tommy Tucker** ($50, £25).

Hippo Family
Baby Hippo Sleeping is 5/8" high ($10, £5). **Mother Hippo** is 1-1/8" high ($30, £10). **Baby Hippo Sitting Up** is 1" high ($10, £5).

Giraffe Family
Baby Giraffe Sleeping measures 5/8" high ($10, £5). **Mother Giraffe** measures 2-5/16" high ($30, £15). **Baby Giraffe Sitting Up** measures 1-9/16" high ($10, £5).

Mouse Family
Baby Mouse Sleeping measures 1-1/16" high ($10, £5). **Mother Mouse** measures 2" high ($30, £15). **Baby Mouse Eyes Open** measures 1" high ($10, £5).

Rabbit Family
Baby Rabbit Sitting Up measures 1-1/4" high ($10, £5). **Mother Rabbit** measures 2" high ($30, £15). **Baby Rabbit Lying Down** measures 1-1/8" high ($10, £5).

Animal Families, circa 1980

CDI Imports marketed three of the Wade retail line of the Dogs and Puppies Sets and five of the puppy dishes under the general name of Animal Families. The Dogs and Puppies were renamed Doggie Family and the Puppy Dishes were renamed Pup-in-a-Basket.

The Wade retail line of three tortoise figurines was also marketed by CDI Imports under the name Turtle Family. CDI advertising also mentions that the company marketed the Wade Whoppas but no records have been found to confirm that they actually were distributed by the import company.

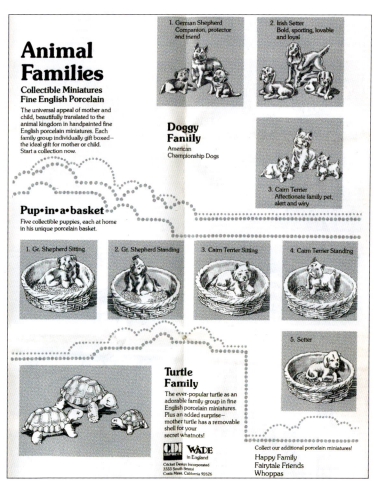

Advertising flyer for the CDI Imports Animal Families.

Doggie Family

The dogs and puppies imported by CDI Imports were similar to the original Wade retail line, however the name of the Alsatian was changed to German Shepherd and the Red Setters were renamed Irish Setters.

Pup-in-a-Basket

CDI Imports marketed five of the Wade retail line of Puppy Dishes under the name of Pup-in-a-Basket.

Mother German Shepherd measures 2-1/2" high. **German Shepherd Puppy** measures 1-1/4" high. **German Shepherd Puppy Sitting Up** measures 1-3/4" high ($36 set, £18 set).

German Shepherd Puppy Dishes ($16 each, £8 each).

Mother Irish Setter measures 2-1/4" high. **Irish Setter Puppy Sitting Up** measures 1-1/2" high. **Irish Setter Puppy** measures 1-1/2" high ($48 set, £24 set).

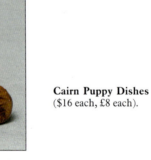

Cairn Puppy Dishes ($16 each, £8 each).

Mother Cairn measures 2-1/2" high. **Cairn Puppy** measures 1-3/8" high. **Cairn Puppy Standing** measures 1-1/2" high ($52 set, £26 set).

Irish Setter Puppy Dish ($16, £8).

Turtle Family

CDI Imports marketed the Tortoise Family of papa and the two babies but renamed them the Turtle Family.

Turtle Family ($60 set of three, £30 set of three).

KSWader, 2000 - 2007

As well as producing figurines specifically for their fairs, KSWader also commissioned Wade to produce figurines which were sold either via "mail order" or at other U.S. Wade fairs. In early 2007, KSWader was dissolved.

Horse Whimsies, 2003

A set of four horses based on the 1982-1983 Tom Smith Farmyard Animals set was commissioned by KSWader in 2003.

Horse of a Different Color Whimsies
Top row. **Blue Horse** ($14, £7), **Green Horse** ($14, £7), and **Orange Horse** ($14, £7). Bottom row. **Maroon Horse** ($14, £7). These were a limited edition of 250 sets. **White/gold Horse** ($40, £20). The white and gold horse was a limited edition of 100 given as prizes and offered to members of the KSWader e-mail list of members.

Dragon Whimsies, 2004

In July 2004, KSWader released a set of new Whimsie dragons in a limited edition of 500 sets. The silver dragon was sold to members of the KSWader mailing list and the gold dragon was given as prizes and for promotions. Each pressed figurine is mold marked: Wade Eng. 2004.

Dragon Whimsies.
Top row. **Burgundy Dragon. Grey Dragon. Orange Dragon.** Bottom row. **Cobalt Dragon.** The cobalt, burgundy, grey, and orange figurines were sold as a set in a limited edition of 500 sets ($56 set, £28 set.). **Silver Dragon** was a limited edition of 100 ($70, £35). **Gold Dragon** was a limited edition of 25 ($100, £50).

Cat Whimsies, 2005

KSWader issued a set of four cats in early 2005 using the 1977 Whimsie cat mold. The cats were from the same mold as the 1977 Whimsie cat. The Cobalt cat was a special issue for the 2005 Summer Wade Fest and the Black cat with Gold base was a limited edition of 100 and given as draw prizes and sold to members of the KSWader mailing list.

Cat Whimsies.
Gold Cat. This was a limited edition of 25 and given as draw prizes ($150, £75). **Cobalt Cat.** This was a limited edition of 100 ($46, £23). **Calico Cat. Tuxedo Cat. Siamese Cat** ($20 each, £10 each). **Ginger Cat** ($8, £4). These were a limited edition of 400 and sold in sets. **Black and Gold Cat.** This was a limited edition of 100 ($76, £38).

Rabbit Whimsies, 2005

KSWader issued a set of four rabbits in 2005 using the 1971 Whimsie rabbit mold. The rabbits, one calico, one pink, one lavender were issued in a limited edition of 250. The Dutch Rabbit was a limited edition of 300.

Rabbit Whimsies.
Top row. **Lavender Rabbit** was a limited edition of 250 ($12, £6). **Pink Rabbit** was a limited edition of 250 ($12, £6). **White Rabbit** ($30, £15). **Calico Rabbit** was a limited edition of 250 ($26, £13). **Gold and White Rabbit** ($224, £112). **Black and White Rabbit** (Dutch) was a limited edition of 300 ($30, £15).

Unicorn Whimsies, 2006

In 2006, KSWader issued a set of three Whimsie size unicorns, using a completely new mold, in a limited edition of 150 sets. In December 2006 two more unicorns were issued in green and red in a limited edition of 100. The unicorns are solid cast and measure 1-3/4" high and are mold marked: Wade.

Unicorn Whimsies.
Back row. **Green Unicorn, Red Unicorn.** These were a limited edition of 100 sets and sold as a pair at Christmas 2006 ($42 pair, £21 pair). **Gold Unicorn** was a limited edition of 25 and given as prizes and promotions ($50, £25). Front row. **Cobalt Unicorn** was limited edition of 100 ($30, £15) **Brown Unicorn, Black Unicorn, White Unicorn** were a limited edition of 150 sets ($60 set, £30 set).

Happy Wade-ing, 2007

After KSWader was dissolved in early 2007, Ed and Bev Rucker formed Happy Wade-ing. The new business continues to commission figurines manufactured by Wade Ceramics Limited with Whimsie type figurines being the primary feature of their products.

Angel Fish Whimsie, 2007

Happy Wade-ing issued a cobalt angel fish with silver eyes which was sold to members on their e-mail announcement list. The figurine was from the same mold as the 1978 Whimsie Angel Fish.

See Chapter 2 for further Happy Wade-ing issues sold at various Wade Fairs and over the Internet.

Cobalt and Silver Angel Fish.
The angel fish, based on the 1978 Whimsie Angel Fish is highlighted with silver eyes and base and was a limited issue of 125 pieces ($22, £11).

Wade Watch Limited

In 2001, the long established Wade Watch Limited, publishers of the quarterly newsletter, *The Wade Watch*, collaborated with C&S Collectables of England to commission Wade to produce a set of five miniature teapots. The die pressed teapots were designed in such a way that they could be used as Christmas ornaments, key chains, or to be placed in shadow boxes. Three of the teapots used the Wade chintz pattern. The teapots measure 1" by 1-1/2" and are transfer marked: Wade England.

Top row from left. **Chintz Butterfly, Gold, Chintz Thistle.** Bottom row from left. **Chintz Sweet Pea, Silver.** The teapots were sold in boxed sets of five. In the U.S.A. Wade Watch Limited sold 250 sets ($48 set). In the U.K. C&S Collectables sold 250 sets (£24 set).

Sherwood Forest Series, 1989 - 1998

These limited edition figurines were produced by George Wade & Son Ltd. and Wade Ceramics Ltd. for Mianco Partners of Canada (formerly POS-NER Associates) in quantities of 5,000 figurines per model. Each of the die cast figurines is mold marked MIANCO®, year of issue, and Wade England.

Friar Tuck was issued in 1994 and the grey/green Friar Tuck in 1998 in a limited edition of 450. Although The Sheriff of Nottingham was sampled, it never went into production.

Robin Hood. Prototype figurines. **1. Robin Hood** measures 5-1/8" high and is unmarked. Figurines in this size have been produced in other color ways and have appeared on the secondary market ($120, £60). **2. Robin Hood** measures 2-7/8" high and is unmarked.

1. Robin Hood measures 2-3/4" high and was issued in 1989 ($30, £15).
2. Maid Marian measures 2-5/8" high and was issued in 1990 ($30, £15).
3. Friar Tuck measures 1-3/4" high and was issued in 1994 ($30, £15).
4. Friar Tuck measures 1-3/4" high and was issued in 1998. Only 450 figurines were issued in this color way ($50, £25).

Robin Hood. Prototype figurine measures 5-1/8" high and is unmarked ($160, £80).

Robin Hood. Prototype figurines.

Top row. **Friar Tuck.** Color variations. Left. Unpainted tree trunk. Right. Painted tree trunk. Bottom row. **Friar Tuck.** Color variations. Left. Unpainted mug. Right. Painted mug. ($30 each, £15 each).

Maid Marian. Color variations. All figurines measures 2-5/8" high and are unmarked.

Friar Tuck. Prototype and color variations. All figurines measures 1-3/4" high and are unmarked except for the figurine in the top left hand corner which is 2" high.

Sheriff of Nottingham. Prototypes and color variations. All figurines measure 2" high and are unmarked.

Above. **Friar Tuck.** Color variation ($40, £20). Right. Base for Friar Tuck.

Black West Highland Terrier, 2000

Sharon Latka, a U.S. based Wade collector and dealer, commissioned Wade to produce 2000 black glazed figurines utilizing the West Highland Terrier mold from the 1990-91 Tom Smith crackers, The World of Dogs Set.

Right. **Friar Tuck.** Color variation ($40, £20). Below. Base for Friar Tuck.

Friar Tuck. Color variation ($60, £30).

Black West Highland Terrier measures 1-1/4" high and is mold marked: Wade England ($10 , £5).

Key Kollectables, 1998 - 2006

Key Kollectables is run by the husband and wife team of Andrew and Mandy Key. During a tour of the Wade factory Andrew expressed a wish to have his own pieces made by Wade. This was realized soon afterwards by the birth of the Straw Family series. This was soon followed by train sets and other items produced under license.

Key Kollectables ceased business in 2006 with the Fireman and Usherette from The Whimsey-on-Why People series being the last figurines commissioned.

Summer Train *2000*
The engine measures 2" by 1" by 1-1/8" and the carriages measure 1-3/4" by 3/4" by 1" and all pieces are mold marked: Wade England Key. The Summer Train was issued in 2000 in a limited edition of 500 sets ($74, £37).

Spring Train *2001*
The engine measures 2" by 1" by 1-1/8" and the carriages measure 1-3/4" by 3/4" by 1" and all pieces are mold marked: Wade England Key. The Spring Train was issued in October 2001 in a limited edition of 400 sets ($74, £37).

Spring Train Special *2001*
The engine measures 2" by 1" by 1-1/8" and the carriages measure 1-3/4" by 3/4" by 1" and all pieces are mold marked: Wade England Key. The Spring Train Special was issued in October 2001 in a limited edition of 100 sets ($100, £50). In order to purchase the gold version Spring Train, collectors had to also purchase the standard version Spring Train.

Autumn Train *2002*
The engine measures 2" by 1" by 1-1/8" and the carriages measure 1-3/4" by 3/4" by 1" and all pieces are mold marked: Wade England Key. The Autumn Train was produced in a world wide limited edition of 200 sets with standard lettering and 100 sets with gold colored lettering ($74, £37).

Fred Figurines, 2001

The figurine of the Home Pride® Fred character was produced by Wade Ceramics Ltd. exclusively for Key Kollectables under license from Campbell Grocery Products Limited. Each figurine was issued with a color postcard/certificate signed personally by Andrew Key of Key Kollectables. Under terms of the License Agreement the figurines were sold only in the United Kingdom.

The illustrations of the Fred figurine are reproduced by permission and ©2002 and Trademarks licensed by Campbell Grocery Products Limited. All rights reserved.

Advertisement for the Mini Freds.

Mini Home Pride Fred.
The mini Freds measure approximately 2-1/8" high and are marked: "Homepride Fred"© 2004 TM CGPL Wade made in England ($28 each, £14 each).

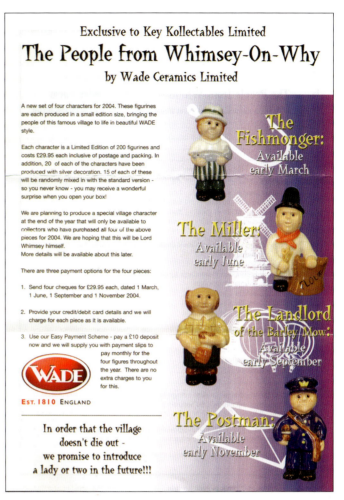

Advertisement for the People from Whimsey-on-Why.

Whimsie Freds.
A set of Whimsie Freds was produced in 2004. The figurines measure 1-3/4" high. The figurines are marked: Wade CPGL. (Homepride Fred © 2004 & TM Campbell Grocery Products Limited.) ($12 each, £6 each).

The People from Whimsey-on-Why, 2003 - 2006

Starting in 2003, Key Kollectables began issuing a series of miniature ceramic character figurines based on people who would have inhabited the Whimsey-on-Why village. The first figurine to be issued was the Butcher who was first announced in the February 2003 *Wade Collectors Club Magazine*. Further figurines were issued in 2004, 2005, and the final figurines appeared in 2006. The figurines were also issued with a certificate of authenticity.

Left. **Butcher.** The figurine was issued in 2003 in a limited edition of 250 and measures 2-1/2" high and is marked: Wade ($84, £42). Above. **Butcher gold.** This figurine was issued in a limited edition of 20 (N.P.A.).

Doctor. The figurine was issued in 2003 in a limited edition of 250 and measures 2-5/8" high ($74, £37). Not illustrated is the Doctor issued in a limited edition of 20.

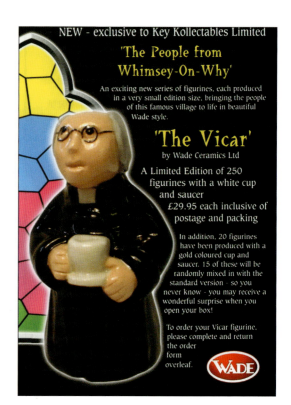

Advertisement for the Vicar of the People from Whimsey-on-Why.

Left. **Blacksmith gold anvil.** This figurine was issued in 2003 in a limited edition of 10 (N.P.A.). Center. **Blacksmith silver anvil.** This figurine was issued in a limited edition of 20 (N.P.A.). Right. **Blacksmith grey anvil.** This figurine was issued in a limited edition of 250 ($74, £37). The figurines measure 2-5/8" high and are marked: Key Kollectables Ltd. Limited Edition Wade England Vicar Whimsey-on-Why.

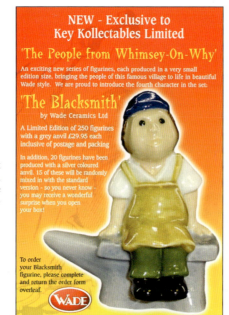

Advertisement for Blacksmith of the People from Whimsey-on-Why.

Top. **Whimsey-on-Why Church** was issued in 2003 in a limited edition of 125 ($70, £35). Bottom. **Whimsey-on-Why Church gold** was issued in 2003 in a limited edition of 25 ($100, £50).

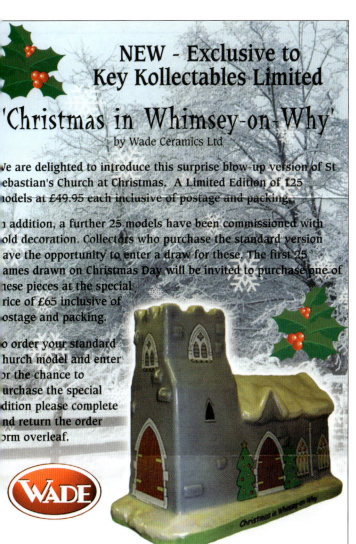

NEW - Exclusive to
Key Kollectables Limited

'Christmas in Whimsey-on-Why'
by Wade Ceramics Ltd

We are delighted to introduce this surprise blow-up version of St
Sebastian's Church at Christmas. A Limited Edition of 125
models at £49.95 each inclusive of postage and packing.

In addition, a further 25 models have been commissioned with
gold decoration. Collectors who purchase the standard version
have the opportunity to enter a draw for these. The first 25
names drawn on Christmas Day will be invited to purchase one of
these pieces at the special
price of £65 inclusive of
postage and packing.

To order your standard
church model and enter
for the chance to
purchase the special
edition please complete
and return the order
form overleaf.

Advertisement for the Church of Whimsey-on-Why.

Fishmonger was issued in 2004 in
a limited edition of 200 ($84, £42).
Not illustrated is a Fishmonger
gold which was issued in a limited
edition of 20 (N.P.A.). The figurines measure 2-3/4" high and are
marked: Wade Made in England.

Right. **Miller** was issued in
2004 in a limited edition of
200 ($74, £37). Below. **Miller
gold** was issued in 2004 in a
limited edition of 20 (N.P.A.).
The figurine measures 2-3/4"
high and is marked: Key Kollectables Ltd. Miller Wade
Made in England.

Left. **Vicar.** The figurine in a black cassock and white cup was issued in
2004 in a limited edition of 250 ($74, £37). Center. **Vicar.** The figurine with
the burgundy cassock and gold cup was issued in 2004 in a limited edition
of 20 (N.P.A.). Right. **Vicar.** The figurine with the black cassock and gold
cup was issued in 2004 in a limited edition of 20 (N.P.A.). The figurines
measure 2-5/8" high and is marked: Key Kollectables Limited edition
Wade England Vicar Whimsey-on-Why.

Landlord was issued in 2004
in a limited edition of 200 and
measures 2-3/8" high and is
marked: Wade Made in England
($74, £37). Not illustrated is a
Landlord gold which was issued
in a limited edition of 20.

Postman was issued in 2004 in a limited edition of 200 and measures 2-3/4" high and is marked: Wade Made in England ($78, £39). Not illustrated is a Postman gold which was issued in a limited edition of 20.

Lord Whimsie was issued in 2004 to those who had bought the Fishmonger, the Miller, the Landlord, and the Postman during 2004 ($96, £48).

Above. **Headmistress with red skirt** was issued in 2005 in a limited edition of 100 ($86, £43). Right. **Headmistress with white skirt** was issued in 2005 in a limited edition of 20 (N.P.A.).

Fireman. This figurine was issued in 2006 in a limited edition of 100 ($88, £44).

Above left. **Farmers Wife with blue striped apron** was issued in 2005 in a limited edition of 100 ($88, £44). Above. **Farmers Wife with red striped apron** was issued in 2005 in a limited edition of 20 (N.P.A.). Left. **Farmers Wife with gold striped apron** was issued in 2005 in a limited edition of 10 (N.P.A.).

Usherette. This figurine was issued in 2006 in a limited edition of 100 ($86, £43).

Your Miniatures, 2007

After KSWader was dissolved in early 2007, Brian and Judi Morris formed Your Miniatures, a business which features various miniatures, including some special commissions from Wade Ceramics Limited. The first Wade figurines to be produced for Your Miniatures is a series of mini goldfish with applied decals similar in theme to the Wade Minikins.

Mini Gems, 2007

These 1" high by 1-1/4" long, hand-painted miniature fish are solid cast and mold marked: Wade. Each fish has small differences due to the hand painting and are sold individually packaged in an Italian Jewelry Box.

The Exclusive Wade Whimsies Collection, 2007

This short lived, limited distribution magazine *The Exclusive Wade Whimsies Collection*, featured Wade Whimsies and offered a free Whimsie with each magazine, except for the second issue which offered two Whimsies. To date, only four magazines have been issued. The figurines were based on similar molds to Whimsie-Land and Tom Smith figurines but were solid cast rather than pressed. The figurines are mold marked around the base: Wade England.

Top row. **Heart Fish** is a limited edition of 125 ($20, £10). **Gold Fish** is a limited edition of 25 (N.P.A.). **Shamrock Fish** is a limited edition of 125 ($20, £10). Bottom row. **Flower Fish** is a limited edition of 125 ($20, £10). **Orange Fish** is a limited edition of 25 (N.P.A.). **Green "W" Fish** is a limited edition of 50 ($50, £25).

Top row. **Farm Duck.** This figurine is from a mold similar to the 1985 Whimsie-Land Duck. **Woodland Badger.** This figurine is from a mold similar to the Badger of the Tom Smith 1980-81 British Wildlife Set and the 1998 Hedgerow Set. **Farm Cockerel.** This figurine is from a mold similar to the 1985 Whimsie-Land Cockerel. Bottom row. **Golden Retriever Pup.** This figurine is from the 1972 Whimsies Set 3. **Farm Cow.** This figurine is from a mold similar to the 1985 Whimsie-Land Cow. ($16 each, £8 each).

Chapter 6
Minikins and Dinosaurs

Minikins, 1955 - 1959

After the success of the Wade Whimsies, the name of George Wade and Son Ltd. had become synonymous with miniature porcelain figurines. Due to the increased demand for porcelain miniatures, Wade devised a new, low-priced series of items comprising mini animals and birds to meet this demand and gave the series the name Minikins.

Due to the 3/4" or less overall height of the Minikins, a new style of glazing machine had to be developed. The fettlers sat at a large turntable, each doing their appointed tasks. The miniatures were then carried by a belt through the glazing machine and then fired at a temperature of 1,300 degrees Celsius in batches of 12,000 animals.

These miniature animal and bird figurines were designed and modeled by William Harper and were issued in three series with four figurines per series. Series "A" was issued in 1955, Series "B" in 1956, and Series "C" in 1957.

Illustrations from trade literature for Minikins Sets "A," "B," and "C."

The Minikins were marketed in decorative presentation boxes containing forty-eight figurines. The August 1956 issue of The Wade Wholesalers Newsletter No. 1, noted that for Series "B" there were "... four entirely new animals but with even gayer treatment than before. A wide range of fantastic decorations will ensure a choice of over 100 different items. The box, too, will be gayer than ever and is being modified to make it suitable for display purposes." This statement would imply that the decoration variations were not confined to one box of forty-eight models and that various boxes had varying decorations. The newsletter went on to mention that a show card would be included in each box of Minikins to remind people that the Minikins would make ideal Christmas gifts.

When Series "C" was issued in August 1957, The Wade Wholesalers Newsletter No. 3. reported: "... Minikins "C" – consisting of a dog, donkey, pelican and fawn is proof of our contention [value for money]! At 1/-d (one shilling) each they cannot help but sell and, although we have already produced well over a million Minikins, we have high hopes that Series "C" will break all records."

Series "A," "B," and "C" of the Minikins were marketed to wholesalers in tea chests with each tea chest containing six dozen boxes of figurines.

Minikins Series "A," 1955 - 1956

The four figurines in the first series of Minikins consisted of a series of cats and rabbits, some only highlighted with shading and well defined eyes and ears while others had highlighting along with line decoration. The figurines ranged from approximately 3/4" high to 1-1/4" high. None of the figurines were marked with either a mold mark or back stamp.

Minikins Series "A" was dropped from the George Wade and Son Ltd. giftware range in 1956 and did not appear in the Wholesale Price List for January 1957.

Left. Retail display plaque with price omitted from the plaque ($200, £100). Below. Retail display plaque showing price ($230, £115).

SERIES "A" *1955*
The series consisted of four shapes of cats and rabbits and for each of these shapes there were two different pairs of eyes and expressions, and two different styles of decoration ($20 each, £10 each).

Series "A" Cats. Decoration variations ($20 each, £10 each).

Series "A" Rabbits. Decoration variations ($20 each, £10 each).

Series "A" Rabbits. Unusual color variations ($50 each, £25 each).

Series "A" Rabbits. Ears and eyes decoration variations ($20 each, £10 each).

Series "A" Rabbits. Eyes and mouths decoration variations ($20 each, £10 each).

Series "A" Cats. Eye decoration variations ($20 each, £10 each).

Series "A" Cat. Color variation ($20 , £10).

Minikins Series "B," 1956 - 1959

The second series of Minikins once again comprised four miniature animals – a cow, bull, kitten, and rabbit. Series "B" had highly decorated figurines with hearts, flowers, and musical notes along with the well-defined eyes. As with Series "A," the figurines in Series "B" ranged from approximately 3/4" high to 1-1/4" high. None of the figurines were marked with either a mold mark or back stamp.

In the January 1959 issue of The Wade Wholesalers Newsletter No. 6., it was reported that Minikins Series "B" was to be discontinued.

SERIES "B" *1956*
The second series consisted of a kitten, rabbit, bull and a cow. They were decorated with either areas of shading applied to the beige body or with flowers, hearts and arrows or musical notes ($20 each, £10 each).

Series "B" Kittens. Decoration variations ($20 each, £10 each).

Series "B" Rabbits. Decoration variations ($20 each, £10 each).

Series "B" Bulls. Decoration variations ($20 each, £10 each).

Series "B" Cow. All over white variation ($20, £10).

Series "B" Cows. Decoration variations ($20 each, £10 each).

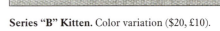

Series "B" Kitten. Color variation ($20, £10).

Minikins Series "C," 1957 - 1958

The four figurines in Series "C" were: pelican, fawn, dog, and donkey. As with the first two series, the figurines in the final series had a wide variety of decorations and were of similar sizes and, again, with no mold marks or back stamps.

In the August 1958 issue of The Wade Wholesalers Newsletter No. 5., it was announced that Minikins Series "C" was to be discontinued.

Series "C" Dogs and Pelicans. Decoration variations ($20 each, £10 each).

Presentation box for Series "C" Minikins. This box is extremely rare.

SERIES "C" *1957*
The third series comprised a pelican, dog, donkey and a fawn. The figurines were decorated with bright colors and motifs such as anchors and flowers ($20 each, £10 each).

Series "C" Donkey and Fawn. Decoration variations ($20 each, £10 each).

Dinosaurs, 1993 - 2001

Although not strictly Whimsies, the miniature dinosaurs have been categorized as such on the Wade Ceramics Limited "Online Shopping" section of their web site. We have therefore included them here.

The first set of five die-pressed dinosaurs was issued in 1993. Each figurine is mold marked: Wade England.

Dinosaurs Set 1, 1993

A set of five die-pressed figurines was produced by Wade Ceramics Ltd., designed by Barbara Cooksey, and modeled by Ken Holmes. All figurines are mold marked: Wade England. In 2001 a number of color variations appeared on the secondary market.

Dinosaur Set 1 display box.

Top from left. **Protoceratops** measures 1-1/8" high by 2-3/8" long ($8, £4). **Tyrannosaurus Rex** measures 1-3/4" high by 2-3/8" long ($8, £4). Bottom from left. **Camarasaurus** measures 2" high by 1-3/4" long ($8, £4). **Euoplocephalus** measures 1" high by 2-1/4" long ($8, £4). **Spinosaurus** measures 1-5/8" high by 2-3/8" long ($8, £4).

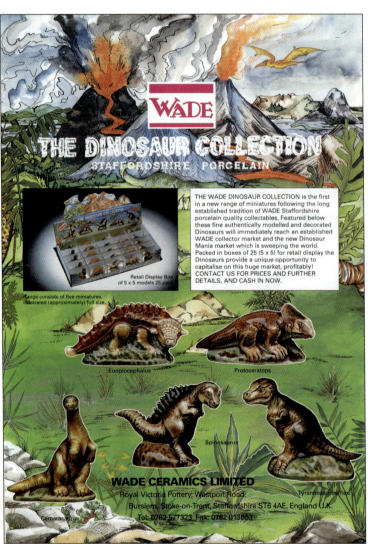

Dinosaur Set 1. Advertisement.

Tyrannosaurus Rex. Color variations ($70 each, £35 each).

Spinosaurus. Color variations ($70 each, £35 each).

Dinosaurs Set 2, 2001

This second set of die-pressed dinosaur figurines was issued in 2001. Five of the figurines were new models but one, the Protoceratops, was from the same mold as the figurine in Set 1, but in a slightly different color way.

Top from left. **Vulcanodon** measures 2" high by 2-3/8" long ($6, £3). **Saurolophus** measures 1-7/8" high by 2" long ($6, £3). **Corythosaurus** measures 2" high by 2-1/4" long ($6, £3). Bottom from left. **Scutellosaurus** measures 1-1/4" high by 2-3/8" long ($6, £3). **Protoceratops** measures 1-1/8" high by 2-1/4" long ($6, £3). **Nodosaurus** measures 1-1/8" high by 2-3/8" long ($6, £3).

Camarasaurus. Color variations ($70 each, £35 each).

Protoceratops. This illustrates the color variation between the figurine from Set 1 (left) and Set 2 (right).

Euoplocephalus. Color variations ($70 each, £35 each).

Protoceratops. Color variations ($70 each, £35 each).

Corythosaurus. Color variation ($70, £35).

Dinosaurs Set 3, 2008

Dinosaurs. These figurines are prototype dinosaurs to be issued in 2008. The colors may vary from those illustrated here.

Happy Families, 1961 - 1965 and 1978 - 1987

The Happy Families series, designed by Leslie McKinnon, was first issued starting in 1961. Each set features a large size parent figurine accompanied by two baby figurines. In a three year period, 1961-65, five sets were issued. These were the Hippo, Tiger, Giraffe, Rabbit, and Mouse families. The series was reintroduced starting in 1978 and ran to 1987.

Of the five original families, four were reissued but the Tiger family was dropped from the line. The last two families to be added to the line were the Dog and Cat families which were available for one year only in 1987. Most figurines are found with a red or black transfer back stamp: "Wade Made in England." Some of the figurines, usually the babies, can be found unmarked unless noted otherwise.

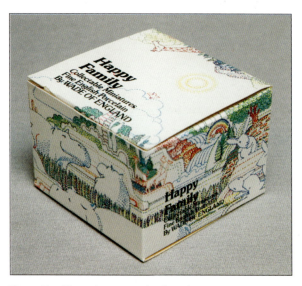

Happy Families early presentation box circa 1961.

Hippo Family *1978 - 1987*
Parent Hippo is 1-1/8" high ($30, £10). **Baby Hippo** is 5/8" high ($10, £5). **Baby Hippo** is 1" high ($10, £5).
Tiger Family *1961 - 1965*
Baby Tiger is 1/2" high ($60, £30). **Parent Tiger** is 1-3/4" high ($84, £42). **Baby Tiger** is 1/2" high ($60, £30).

Giraffe Family *1978 - 1987*
Parent Giraffe measures 2-5/16" high ($30, £15). **Baby Giraffe** measures 5/8" high ($10, £5). **Baby Giraffe** measures 1-9/16" high ($10, £5).
Mouse Family *1978 - 1987*
Baby Mouse measures 1-1/16" high ($10, £5). **Parent Mouse** measures 2" high ($30, £15). **Baby Mouse** measures 1" high ($10, £5).

Rabbit Family *1963 - 1965*
Parent Rabbit measures 2" high ($70, £35). **Baby Rabbit** measures 1-1/4"
high ($50, £25). **Baby Rabbit** measures 1-1/8" high ($50, £25).

Rabbit Family *1978 - 1987*
Parent Rabbit measures 2" high ($30, £15). **Baby Rabbit** measures 1-1/4"
high ($10, £5). **Baby Rabbit** measures 1-1/8" high ($10, £5).
Frog Family *1984 - 1987*
Baby Frog measures 1" high ($10, £5). **Parent Frog** measures 7/8" high
($30, £10). **Baby Frog** measures 5/8" high ($10, £5).

Elephant Family *1984 - 1987*
Baby Elephant measures 1-3/4" high ($18, £10). **Parent Elephant** measures
1-1/4" high ($25, £12). **Baby Elephant** measures 1" high ($18, £10).

Dog Family. Prototype figurines.

Dog Family *1987*
Puppy measures 1-1/4" high ($20, £10). **Parent Dog** measures 2" high ($40,
£20). **Puppy** measures 1-1/4" high ($20, £10).
Cat Family *1987*
Kitten measures 1-3/8" high ($20, £10). **Parent Cat** measures
1-7/8" high ($80, £40). **Kitten** measures 1-1/4" high ($20, £10).

Owl Family *1984 - 1987*
Parent Owl measures 1-3/4" high ($30, £15). **Baby Owl** measures 1" high
($10, £5). **Baby Owl** measures 7/8" high ($10, £5).
Pig Family *1984 - 1987*
Parent Pig measures 1-1/8" high ($30, £15). **Baby Pig** measures 9/16" high
($10, £5). **Baby Pig** measures 5/8" high ($10, £5).

Zebra Family
This prototype Zebra Family was designed and modeled by
Wm. Harper but never went into production (N.P.A.).

Pocket Pals, 1999

Pocket Pals were launched in late 1999 as a new retail
line. The figurines were based on the adult figurines from
the Happy Families series first seen in the 1960s, and again
in the 1970s. Each figurine in the new series was given a new
color and name, easily distinguishing them from the earlier
models.

At the time of the launch of the new range of the Wade
Pocket Pals, three special limited editions were also issued.
Two were available through the magazine *Collect it!* and one
was available from C&S Collectables. As these three figurines
were issued as "promotional" items, we are including the
Happy Family series and the Pocket Pal series here.

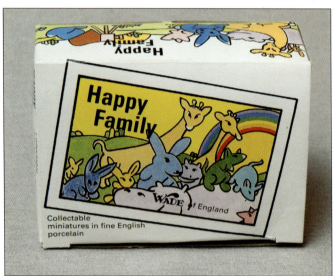

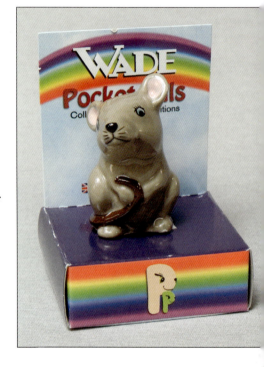

Typical packaging for
Pocket Pals.

Top. White presentation box used for the dog and cat families issued
in 1987. Bottom. Blue presentation box used for the figurines issued
between 1978-87.

1. **Waggs the dog** measures 2" high ($10, £6). 2. **Truffle the pig** measures
1-1/8" high ($10, £6). 3. **Cheesy the mouse** measures 2" high ($10, £6). 4.
Tusker the elephant measures 1-1/4" high ($10, £6). 5. **Stretch the giraffe**
measures 2-5/16" high ($10, £6). 6. **Slinky the cat** measures 1-7/8" high
($10, £6). 7. **Hip Hop the frog** measures 7/8" high ($10, £6). 8. **Paddles the
hippo** measures 1-1/8" high ($10, £6). 9. **Bounce the rabbit** measures 2"
high ($10, £6). 10. **Specs the owl** measures 1-3/4" high ($10, £6).

Paddles the hippo. Color variation.

Slinky the cat. Left. Production model with presentation box. Right. Color variation.

Pocket Pal Frog prototypes *1999*
These decorated frogs were proposed for *Collect it!* magazine but never went into production.

Pocket Pal Specials, 1999

At the time of the launch of the new range of the Wade Pocket Pals, three special limited editions were also issued. Two were available through the magazine *Collect it!* and one was available from C&S Collectables.

1. Tango was based on the Pocket Pals cat Slinky, was issued in a limited edition of 1,000, and was available only from C&S Collectables ($15, £10). **2. Hopper** was based on the Pocket Pals frog Hip Hop, was available free only to subscribers of *Collect it!* magazine and those magazines sold through W. H. Smith ($16, £10). **3. Woofit** was based on the Pocket Pals dog Waggs and was available only from Wade via a special "mail in" offer through *Collect it!* magazine ($25, £14).

Bear Ambitions, 1995 - 1998

Each of these die-pressed miniature teddy bear figurines has its own distinctive decoration signifying the artistic talent or hobby of the particular bear. All figurines are mold marked "Wade Eng" on the back.

The six bears in this set were used in the 1996-97 Tom Smith Christmas Time Crackers Set but in different color ways. We are therefore including the original set here.

Artistic Edward with presentation box.

Admiral Sam *1998*
This hand painted multi color variation was a
"One of a kind." (N.P.A.)

Top Row. **Artistic Edward** measures 1-1/2" high. **Locomotive Joe**
measures 1-5/8" high. **Alex the Aviator** measures 1-5/8" high. Bottom
Row. **Beatrice the Ballerina** measures 1-3/4" high. **Admiral Sam**
measures 1-5/8" high.
Musical Marco measures
1-5/8" high ($6 each, £3
each).

Bisque Bear Ambitions.
Top row. Musical Marco
and Locomotive Joe. Bot-
tom row. Beatrice the Ballerina and Artistic Edward
($70 each, £35 each).

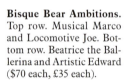

Beatrice the Ballerina.
Color variations ($60
each, £30 each).

Admiral Sam. Color variations.

Green Bear Ambitions, 1998

A reissue of the 1995 Bear Ambitions in an overall green glaze was made for The Teddy Bears' Picnic held at Ripley Castle, England. These green Bear Ambitions were also sold in the Factory Shop.

Beatrice the Ballerina with presentation box.

Top Row. **Artistic Edward** measures 1-1/2" high. **Locomotive Joe** measures 1-5/8" high. **Alex the Aviator** measures 1-5/8" high. Bottom Row. **Beatrice the Ballerina** measures 1-3/4" high. **Admiral Sam** measures 1-5/8" high. **Musical Marco** measures 1-5/8" high ($6 each, £3 each).
This picture illustrates the variation of the green glaze found on these figurines from light green to dark green.

The Tortoise Family, 1958 - 1988

This series of various sized tortoises, from tiny baby figurines to large jumbo sizes, were extremely popular and had a long production life. With the introduction of "Papa" tortoise in 1958, a new type of glaze finish was used by Wade and given the name "Scintillite." This type of finish was achieved by using a soluble blue color under an amber glaze. The "Scintillite" type finish was also used for many other lines of giftware.

The three smaller tortoises were modeled by William Harper, who told us that these were his favorite pieces of all the figurines he modeled for Wade. Although all figurines are marked Made in England, production of the Tortoise Family began in Ireland at the Wade (Ulster) Ltd. pottery.

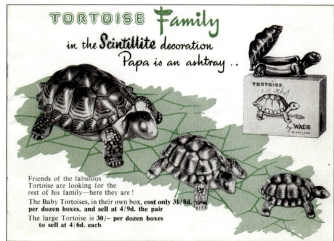

The Tortoise Family shown in the 1959 Autumn & Winter Wade Price List.

"Papa" Tortoise was introduced in the January 1958 Wade Wholesalers Newsletter No. 4. The figurine has a removable shell/lid and was first advertised as an ash tray. The tortoise measures 4" from head to tail by 2-3/4" wide at the feet by 1-5/8" tall. It has an impressed mold mark "Wade Porcelain Made in England" along with the figure 1 which would indicate the mold number ($30, £15). This size tortoise is to be found in two versions. One version has a recess in the back of the base and the lid has a tab extension which fits into the recess and the second version has a plain base with no recess.

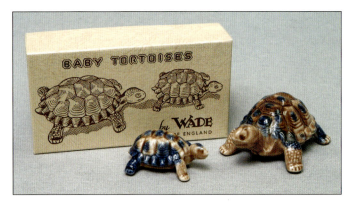

Left. **Baby Tortoise,** along with its larger partner, was first announced in the January 1959 Wade Wholesalers Newsletter No. 6. The figurine measures 2" from head to tail by 1-1/2" wide at the feet by 7/8" high and is mold marked: Wade Porcelain Made in England ($10, £5). Right. **Baby Tortoise** (sometimes referred to as "Mama Tortoise") measures 3" from head to tip of tail by 2-1/8" wide at the feet by 1-1/4" high and is mold marked: Wade Porcelain Made in England ($20, £10).

Jumbo Tortoise was introduced to the tortoise line in 1973. The shell forms a removable lid exposing a good-sized dish. The overall size with shell/lid in place measures 6" from head to tail by 4" wide by 2-3/8" high and is mold marked: Wade Porcelain Made in England on the base ($90, £45). Although advertised as a tortoise, this figurine more closely resembles a sea turtle rather than a tortoise which lives on land.

Slow K and Slow Fe Tortoise, circa 1969 - 1970

These figurines were produced for the pharmaceutical firm Ciba Geigy to promote their products and given as gifts to members of the medical profession.

Left. **Slow K** measures 1-1/4" high by 3" long. This figurine was used to promote the Ciba Geigy slow release potassium product ($90, £45). Right. **Slow Fe** measures 1-1/4" high by 3" long. This figurine was produced as a promotional item for the Ciba Geigy slow release iron product ($70, £35).

Devil's Hole Bermuda Tortoise, circa late 1960s

In the late 1960s, Wade (Ireland) Ltd. began exporting a number of souvenir items to A.S. Cooper & Sons of Bermuda. Most well know of these items were the small and large egg coddlers. As the tortoises were being made in Ireland, it was easy to amend the tortoise mold to feature wording to help advertise some of Bermuda's attractions.

Bermuda's Devil's Hole is a water-filled sinkhole which forms a natural aquarium and has been a tourist attraction since the 1830s. Various species of reef fish are found in this natural aquarium, including Moray Eels and the Green Bermuda Turtle, which has become a protected species.

Devil's Hole Bermuda Tortoise. The figurine measures 1-1/4" high by 3" long ($90, £45). Other figurines with Bermuda area names were also produced at that time.

Green Tortoise, circa late 1960s

These hard to find, green tortoises were issued by Wade in a very limited quantity. This green color version of the popular tortoise range did not sell well and was soon withdrawn from production. It is possible that these green tortoises were produced for A.S. Cooper & Sons of Bermuda to advertise the Green Bermuda Turtle.

Baby Tortoise measures 1-1/4" high by 3" long and is mold marked: Wade Porcelain Made in England ($50, £25). **Baby Tortoise** measures 7/8" high by 2" long and is mold marked: Wade Porcelain Made in England ($30, £15).

Baby's Tooth Brush Holder. It is not clear why or for what reason this figurine was produced but it has been described as a toothbrush holder. The figurine, which has a removable lid, measures 4" long by 2-3/4" wide by 1-5/8" tall and is mold marked "Wade Porcelain Made in England" ($50, £25).

Prototype **Tortoise** measures 3-1/2" high by 6-1/2" overall. The figurine is transfer marked: Wade ($120, £60).

Chapter 7
Whimsies Series 2

In the early 1960s with the success of the Whimsies, Wade decided to launch a second set of miniature figurines under the name of Whimsies Series 2. These were to be a series of figurines in the human form. This was to be followed by Series 3, which would feature a series of dogs and puppies.

Unfortunately these later sets of Whimsies were not as well received as the first sets of miniature animals and birds. Half way through the promotion of the dogs and puppies sets, the name Whimsies was dropped from the promotion.

Whimsies Series 2
"The British Character," 1963

A set of four figurines based on typical characters, merchants, and professionals found in the city and East End of London was issued as Whimsies Series 2. The figurines have applied circular black/gold labels marked "Genuine Wade Porcelain Made in England." Over the years, many of the labels have been removed; however, this does not reflect on the value of the figurine.

Until recently it had been reported that this set of figurines had been issued in or around 1959 but when we were researching Wade we discovered that the figurines had actually been introduced in 1963. In the May 1963 issue of *Tableware*, it was reported, "The theme of this entirely new series is the BRITISH CHARACTER.... First deliveries will soon be leaving the factory and an attractive show card will be enclosed with each initial supply..."

Retail 'show card' for "The British Character."

Advertisement for the launch of "The British Character" series from the May 1963 edition of *Tableware*.

From left: **Lawyer** measures 2-7/8" high ($220, £110). **Pearly King** measures 2-3/4" high ($180, £90). **Pearly Queen** measures 2-7/8" high ($150, £75). **Billingsgate Porter** measures 3-1/8" high ($220, £110).

Pearly Queen. Color variations.

Billingsgate Porter. Color variations.

Presentation box for Billingsgate Porter.

Dogs and Puppies Sets, 1969 - 1982

Starting in 1969, a retail line of miniature dogs accompanied by two puppies of the same breed made its appearance in the Wade range of giftware. Five sets of dogs and puppies were issued in a total of ten boxes. The first six boxes were colored blue with the wording of "Whimsies" above the breed name. The remaining four boxes were colored red but this time the word "Whimsies" was replaced by "Dog Series." Unless noted otherwise, all figurines had a Wade paper label with the wording "Wade Made in England."

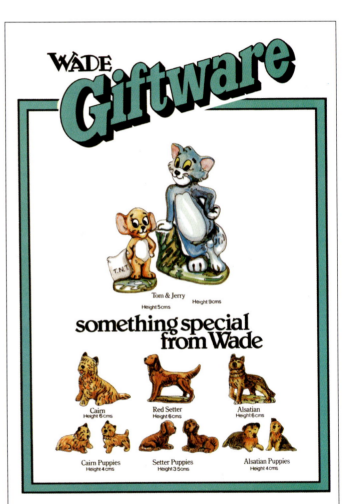

Wade Giftware flyer illustrating the dogs and puppies series.

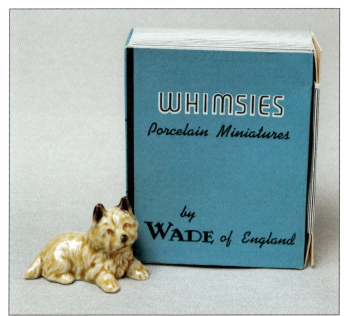

SET 2, *1969*
Adult Cairn measures 2-1/2" high. **Cairn Puppy** measures 1-3/8" high.
Cairn Puppy Standing measures 1-1/2" high ($52 set, £26 set).

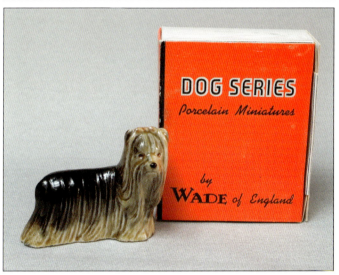

Above. Blue presentation box for the early Dogs and Puppies sets.
Below. Red presentation box for the later Dogs and Puppies sets.

Typical label found on the dogs and puppies.

SET 1, *1969*
Adult Alsatian measures 2-1/2" high. **Alsatian Puppy** measures 1-1/4"
high. **Alsatian Puppy Sitting Up** measures 1-3/4" high ($36 set, £18 set).

SET 3, *1973*
Adult Red Setter measures 2-1/4" high. **Red Setter Puppy Sitting Up** measures 1-1/2" high. **Red Setter Puppy** measures 1-1/2" high ($48 set, £24 set).

SET 4, *1979*
Adult Corgi measures 2-1/4" high and is mold
marked: Wade England. **Corgi Puppy** measures
1-1/8" high and is mold marked: Wade England.
Corgi Puppy Sitting Up measures 1-5/8" high
and is mold marked: Wade England ($100 set,
£50 set).

SET 5, *1979*
Adult Yorkshire Terrier measures 2-1/8" high and is
mold marked: Wade England. **Yorkshire Terrier Puppy**
measures 1-1/2" high. **Yorkshire Terrier Puppy Standing**
measures 1-3/8" high ($168 set, £84 set).

Cat and Puppy Dishes, 1974 - 1981

During the run of the Dog and Puppy sets, an addition
was made to this line of giftware by the manufacture of basket shaped dishes into which the ten puppies were mounted.
These dishes were given the name "Puppy Dishes." During
the same period, a figurine of a cat, larger in size than the
puppies, was also made and mounted in a similar basket. This
was known as the "Cat Dish." For the size of puppies refer to
the "Dogs and Puppies" sets. The size and shape of the dishes
is similar for all puppies and the cat, being oval shaped and
measuring 2-7/8" long by 2-1/2" across. All dishes are mold
marked: "Wade England."

Ginger and White Cat.
This was a prototype cat
for the Cat Dish figurine
($128, £64).

Top. **Cat Dish and Box.** The cat measures 2-3/8" high ($56 incl. box,
£28 incl. box). Bottom. **Whimsie Kitten Dish.** This was not a production piece. The attempt to develop a Cat and Kitten dish series using the
Whimsie kitten never materialized.

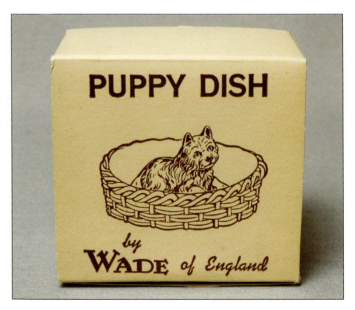

Presentation box for Puppy Dishes.

Red Setter Puppy Dishes
($16 each, £8 each).

Yorkshire Terrier Puppy Dish ($30 each, £15 each).

Dog Pipe Rests, 1973 - 1981

In 1973, Wade introduced a set of five pipe rests featuring large dogs from the "Dogs and Puppies" series. The pipe rests had slightly "off" circular bases measuring 3-1/4" in dia. by 3/4" deep. Each pipe rest bears the wording "Wade England" molded onto the underside of the base.

Alsatian Puppy Dishes
($16 each, £8 each).

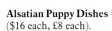

Top row. **Cairn Terrier** ($24, £12). **Corgi** ($24, £12). Bottom row. **Red Setter** ($24, £12). **Alsatian** ($24, £12).

Cairn Puppy Dishes
($16 each, £8 each).

Yorkshire Terrier pipe rest with presentation box ($50 incl. box, £25 incl. box).

Horse Sets, 1974 - 1981

In 1974, Wade introduced a set comprising a farm cart horse along with two foals. None of the figurines were mold marked but were issued with paper labels. A second set, again comprising a farm cart horse with two foals, was issued in 1978. This second set is mold marked "Wade England" around the base.

SET 1, *1974*
Left. **Foal** measures 1-7/8" high by 2" overall. Center. **Horse** measures 2-3/4" high by 3" overall. Right. **Foal** measures 1-3/8" high by 2" overall ($60 boxed set, £30 boxed set).

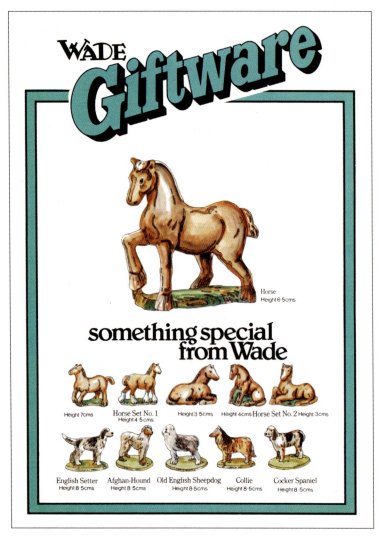

Wade Giftware flyer illustrating the Horse sets.

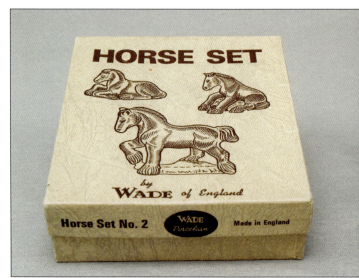

Presentation box for the Horse Set 2.

Presentation box for the Horse Set 1.

SET 2, *1978*
Left. **Foal** measures 1-1/2" high by 1-5/8" overall. Center. **Horse** measures 2-1/2" high by 2-3/4" overall. Right. **Foal** measures 1-1/4" high by 1-7/8" overall ($60 boxed set, £30 boxed set).

Championship
Dogs, 1975 - 1981

In 1975, Wade introduced a set of five mid-size, quality, underglaze colored figurines based on purebred dogs. Each dog was mounted on an oval shaped base measuring 3-1/2" long by 2-1/4" wide. The front face of the base is mold marked "Championship Series" and "Wade England" on the back face. Originally each figurine also had an applied orange-colored paper label marked "Championship Series" and "Wade England" along with the appropriate breed of dog.

Top row. **English Setter** measures 2-3/4" high by 4-1/8" long ($90, £45). **Afghan Hound** measures 3" high by 3-3/8" long ($90, £45). **Collie** measures 3-1/4" high by 4" long ($90, £45). Bottom row. **Cocker Spaniel** measures 2-7/8" high by 3-5/8" long ($90, £45). **Old English Sheep Dog** measures 3-1/4" high by 3" long ($90, £45).

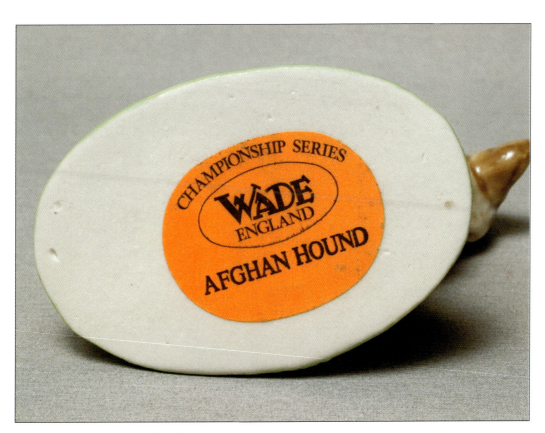

Original paper label on base of the Afghan Hound.

Chapter 8.

Miniature Village Sets
1980 - 1993

In 1984, Kellogg Salada Canada, Inc. used six models from the Wade retail line of miniature village sets, as a promotion to help sell their tea. In 1988 Tom Smith & Co. Ltd. also used models from the Wade retail line as a promotion for their party crackers. We are therefore including the complete line of Wade miniature village sets here.

Whimsey-on-Why, 1980 - 1987

Whimsey-on-Why is the name given to a mythical English village made up of a series of miniature houses and buildings found in a typical English village.

The sets, the first of which was issued in 1980, were issued with eight models in each set except Set 5 which had only four models. Along with the miniature houses, Wade also published four issues of the *Whimsey-on-Why Chronicle*. This was a "spoof" newspaper as Wade felt that a true village should have its own paper. As well as introducing the latest "Whimsey-on-Why" village set, the *Chronicle* also announced a number of additions to the Wade giftware line.

All models are mold marked "Wade England" on the base. The exceptions to this are: No. 16 the Windmill and No. 32 the Market Hall, which are not marked. Each model is numbered to identify its position in the series. A number of models were designed by Richard Wade who based the designs on existing buildings in villages near his home. The model of Bloodshot Hall was based on Brand Hall the home of Sir George Wade from 1952 until his death in 1986.

Brand Hall - Home of Sir George Wade and model for Bloodshot Hall.

Front page of Whimsey-on-Why *Chronicle* No.1.

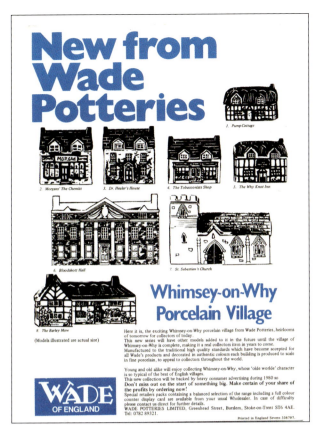

Back page of *Chronicle* No.1.

Chronicle No.2.

Chronicle No.4.

Chronicle No.3.

SET 1, *1980*

Top row. 1. **Pump Cottage** measures 1-1/8" high by 1-1/4" long ($10, £5). 2. **Morgan's the Chemist** measures 1-3/4" high by 1-1/2" long ($15, £7.50). 3. **Doctor Healer's House** measures 1-3/4" high by 1-1/2" long ($18, £9). 4. **Tobacconist's Shop** measures 1-1/2" high by 1-1/2" long ($10, £5). Center row. 5. **Why-Knot Inn** measures 1-3/8" high by 1-1/2" long ($12, £6). 6. **Bloodshott Hall** measures 2" high by 3-1/8" long ($22, £11). Bottom row. 7. **St. Sebastian's Church** measures 2-1/8" high by 3" long ($30, £15). 8. **The Barley Mow** measures 1-1/2" high by 3" long ($28, £14).

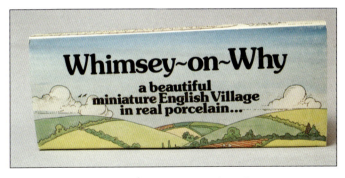

Typical presentation box for Whimsey-on-Why Sets 1&2.

Back of presentation box for Sets 1&2.

SET 2, *1981*

Top row. 9. **Greengrocer's Shop** measures 1-1/2" high by 3/4" deep ($10, £5). 10. **Antique Shop** measures 1-1/2" high by 3/4" deep ($18, £9). 11. **Whimsey Service Station** measures 1-1/2" high by 1-1/2" long ($18, £9). 12. **Post Office** measures 1-1/2" high by 1-1/2" long ($15, £7.50). Center row. 13. **Whimsey School** measures 1-5/8" high by 1-7/8" long ($30, £15). 14. **Water Mill** measures 1-3/4" high by 2-1/2" long ($15, £7.50). Bottom row. 15. **The Stag Hotel** measures 1-7/8" high by 2-1/2" long ($20, £10). 16. **Windmill** measures 2-1/4" high by 1-3/16" dia. base ($85, £42.50).

SET 3, *1982*

Top row. 17. **Tinker's Nook** measures 1-3/8" high by 1" long ($10, £5). 18. **Whimsey Station** measures 1-1/2" high by 1-1/2" long ($18, £9). 19. **Merryweather Farm** measures 1-7/8" high by 1-7/8" long ($35, £17.50). Center row. 20. **The Vicarage** measures 1-5/8" high by 2" long ($75, £37.50). 21. **Broomyshaw Cottage** measures 1-5/8" high by 1-1/2" long ($15, £7.50). 22. **The Sweet Shop** measures 1-5/8" high by 1-1/2" long ($12, £6). Bottom row. 23. **Briar Row** measures 1-3/8" high by 3" long ($32, £16). 24. **The Manor** measures 1-7/8" high by 2-1/2" long ($20, £10).

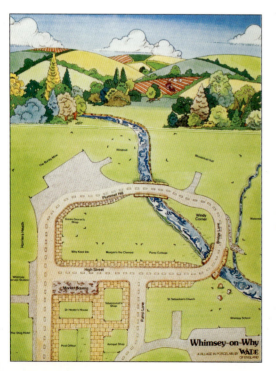

Whimsey-on-Why Display Sheet for Sets 1 and 2.

Whimsey-on-Why Display Sheet for Set 3.

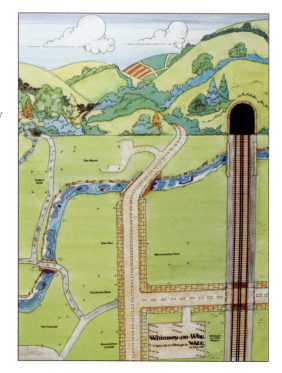

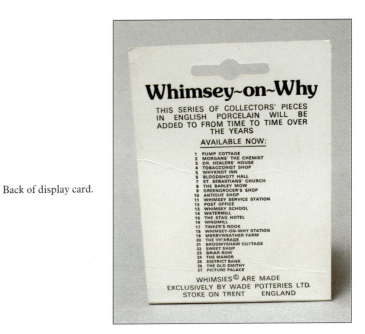

Back of display card.

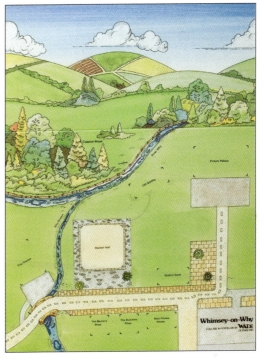

Whimsey-on-Why Display Sheet for Set 4.

SET 4, *1984 -1985*
Top row. 25. **District Bank** measures 1-7/8" high by 1-1/2" long ($22, £11). 26. **Old Smithy** measures 1" high by 1-3/4" long ($18, £9). 27. **Picture Palace** measures 2-1/8" high by 2-1/2" long ($25, £12.50). Center row. 28. **Butcher's Shop** measures 1-5/8" high by 1" square ($30, £15). 29. **The Barber's Shop** measures 1-5/8" high by 1" square ($48, £24). 30. **Miss Prune's House** measures 1-1/2" high by 1-1/2" long ($18, £9). Bottom row. 31. **Fire Station** measures 1-5/8" high by 1-3/4" long ($28, £14). 32. **Market Hall** measures 1-7/8" high by 2" square ($20, £10).

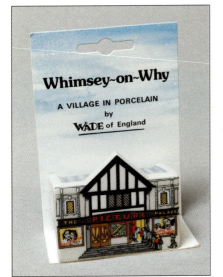

Picture Palace mounted on display card. Most models were sold individually on display cards rather than as a complete boxed set.

SET 5, *1987*
33. **School Teacher's House** measures 1-3/4" high by 1-1/2" long ($75, £37.50). 34. **Fish Monger's Shop** measures 1-5/8" high by 1" long ($85, £42.50). 35. **Police Station** measures 1-5/8" high by 1" long ($110, £55). 36. **Library** measures 2" high by 1-1/2" long ($55, £27.50).

Whimsey-in-the-Vale Village, 1993

In February 1993, Wade Ceramics Ltd. introduced a new line of miniature houses. The new models utilized the same molds as those used for some of the Whimsey-on-Why Village houses. The applied decals were newly designed by Judith Wooten. Unlike the Whimsey-on-Why houses, the Whimsey-in-the-Vale houses are not numbered. After each model, the corresponding model from the Whimsey-on-Why series is listed.

Top row. 1. **St. Lawrence Church** is the same model as No.7, Set 1 ($32, £16). 2. **Town Garage** is the same model as No.32, Set 4 ($20, £10). 3. **Vale Farm** is the same model as No.15, Set 2 ($22, £11). Center row. 4. **Boar's Head Pub** is the same model as No.8, Set 1 ($22, £11). 5. **St. John's School** is the same model as No.31, Set 4 ($35, £17.50). 6. **Jubilee Terrace** is the same model as No. 23, Set 3 ($28, £14). Bottom row. 7. **Antique Shop** is the same model as No. 5, Set 1 ($30, £15). 8. **Whimsey Post Office** is the same model as No. 9, Set 2 ($22, £11). 9. **Rose Cottage** is the same model as No. 11, Set 2 ($28, £14). 10. **Florist's Shop** is the same model as No. 11, Set 2 ($22, £11).

Although the models are not numbered, the order in which they were listed on the presentation pack is as follows: 1. Boar's Head Pub, 2. St. John's School, 3. Jubilee Terrace, 4. Town Garage, 5. Antique Shop, 6. St. Lawrence Church. 7. Post Office, 8. Florist's Shop, 9. Vale Farm, 10. Rose Cottage.

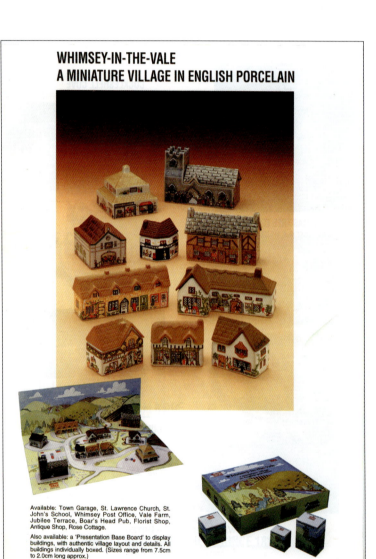

Advertisement for Whimsy-in-the-Vale.

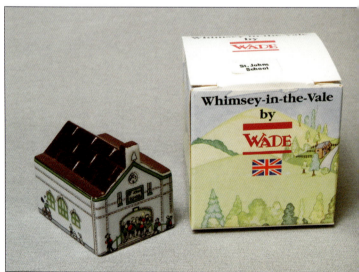

St. John's School with display box.

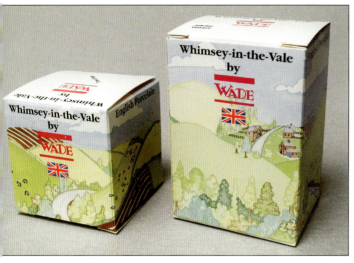

The small and medium presentation boxes for Whimsey-in-the-Vale models.

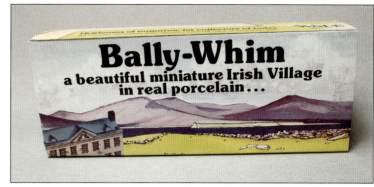

Presentation box for the Bally-Whim village.

Whimsey-in-the-Vale Display Card with buildings.

Top row. 1. **Undertaker's House** measures 2" high by 1-1/2" long ($32, £16). 2. **Moore's Post Office** measures 1-1/2" high by 1" long ($28, £14). 3. **Barney Flynn's Cottage** measures 1-1/8" high by 1-3/4" long ($32, £16). 4. **Kate's Cottage** measures 1-1/8" high by 1-3/4" long ($25, £12.50). 5. **The Dentist's House** measures 2" high by 1-3/4" long ($22, £11). Bottom row. 6. **Mick Murphy's Bar** measures 1-3/4" high by 1-1/2" long ($28, £14). 7. **W. Ryan's Hardware Store** measures 1-1/2" high by 1-1/2" long ($32, £16). 8. **Bally-Whim House** measures 2" high by 3-1/4" long ($30, £15).

"Bally-Whim" Village, 1984 - 1987

With the popularity of the English village series "Whimsie-on-Why," Wade (Ireland) Ltd. introduced a series of miniature houses typical of those found in an Irish Village. The Irish village was given the name of "Bally-Whim." Each miniature house is mold marked Wade Ireland and each model bears its number in the series.

Bally-Whim village display card with buildings.

"Painted Ladies" Series, 1984 - 1986

This short-lived "San Francisco Mini Mansions" set is similar in theme to the Whimsey-on-Why village sets but on a slightly larger scale. A companion piece to the Mini Mansions was a miniature Cable Car so typical of San Francisco. All models, including the Cable Car, are marked "Wade Porcelain England SF/1 through SF/6." This mark is located on the sidewall of the Mini Mansions and on the back end of the Cable Car.

This series was designed and produced by Sir George Wade's daughter, Iris, and her husband, Straker Carryer.

Front of presentation box for the Mini Mansions.

Back of presentation box for the Mini Mansions.

Top row. 1. **Pink Lady** measures 2-1/4" high by 1" wide ($125, £63). 2. **White Lady** measures 2-1/4" high by 1" wide ($95, £48). 3. **Brown Lady** measures 2-1/2" high by 1-1/4" square ($135, £68). Bottom row. 4. **Yellow Lady** measures 2-1/2" high by 1-1/4" square ($68, £34). 5. **Blue Lady** measures 2-7/8" high by 1-1/2" square ($75, £38). 6. **Cable Car** measures 7/8" high by 1-1/2" long ($135, £68).

SPECIAL CABLE CAR
This miniature cable car is based on the cable car from the "Painted Ladies" series. One side of the car advertises White Label whisky and the other side advertises Dewars whisky. Other design variations exist ($140, £70).

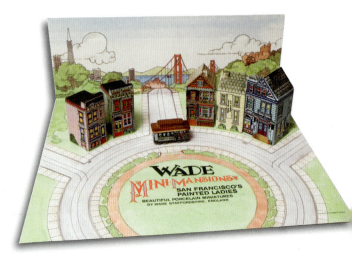

San Francisco Mini Mansions Display Card with Buildings.

Granada Television Promotions,
1988 - 1989

Between 1988 and 1989 Granada Television commissioned George Wade & Son Ltd. to produce three miniature die pressed houses based on the popular and long running British Television series "Coronation Street." The three houses were all mold marked: Wade England.

In 1999, two popular characters from Coronation Street were produced by Wade in the form of salt and pepper shakers. Each figurine is transfer marked: ©GTV Ltd. '99. Wade England.

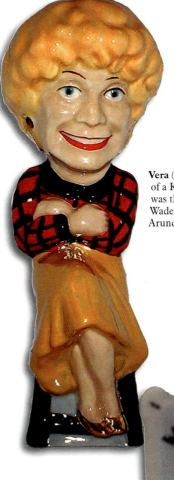

Vera (pepper shaker). One of a Kind. This figurine was the Bingo Prize at the Wade Event of July 2003 at Arundel.

Left. **The Rover's Return** measures 1-7/8" high ($24, £12). Center. **The Duckworths** measures 1-5/8" high ($22, £11). Right. **The Corner Shop** measures 1-5/8" high ($20, £10).

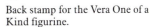

Back stamp for the Vera One of a Kind figurine.

Left. **Jack** (salt shaker) measures 4-1/4" high ($20, £12). Right. **Vera** (pepper shaker) measures 4-3/4" high ($20, £12) and presentation box.

Chapter 9

Miscellaneous Premium and Promotional Figurines

Miscellaneous Promotional Figurines, circa early 1960s - 1970s

Over the years that Wade has produced promotional figurines, a number of color variations of Whimsies and other miniature figurines have surfaced. Little is known about their origin other than that they were proposals for various promotions or just experimental.

Illustrated here are a number of figurines that have no recorded history in as much that they do not appear in any regular set or promotion.

Kodiak Brown Bear *circa early 1960s*
This figurine first appeared in the original range of twenty premium figurines of the early 1960's. This bear has been found in two versions. Left. **Bear** measures 1-1/2" high, is mold marked Wade England and is the later version ($36, £18). Center. **Bear** measures 1-5/8" high, is unmarked and is the earlier version ($100, £50). Right. **Grizzly Bear** from the 1958 Early Whimsie Set 9 (North American Animals). This figurine is shown for comparison to the Kodiak Brown Bears.

Panda and Zebra
This panda figurine first appeared in the original range of twenty premium figurines of the early 1960's and is often mistaken for the 1958 Early Whimsie Zoo Set.
Left. **Panda** measures 1-1/2" high by 1" across the base and is unmarked. This was the early premium figurine ($50, £25). Right. **Zebra.** This is the zebra from the Spring 1969 range of premiums ($20, £10).

Black Glazed Whimsies
These figurines from the 1971-84 Whimsies with a thick black glaze are difficult to explain. The dark glaze completely covers and hides any detail or mold definition. There is no record of the original use for these figurines but they are found quite often.
Top row. **Ram** from the 1977 Set 8. **Lamb** from the 1975 Set 6. Bottom row. **Zebra** from the 1976 Set 7. **Gorilla** from the 1976 Set 7. ($10 each, £5 each).

Lion from the 1976-77 Tom Smith Safari Park set. **Hedgehog** from the 1974 Whimsies Set 5. **Gorilla** from the 1984-85 Tom Smith World of Survival. Color variations ($20 each, £10 each).

Green Glazed Whimsies

Top Row. **Koala Bear** from the 1979 Whimsies Set 10. **Sea Turtle** from Tom Smith Crackers 1984-1985 World of Survival. **Gorilla** from the 1976 Whimsies Set 7.
Middle Row. **Elephant** from the 1973 Whimsies Set 4. **Dolphin** from the 1978 Whimsies Set 9. **Bison** from the 1979 Whimsies Set 11.
Bottom Row. **Tiger** from the 1984 Whimsie-Land Wildlife Set. **Panda** from the 1984 Whimsie-Land Wildlife Set. **Rhino** from the 1976 Whimsies Set 7. ($20 each, £10 each).

Corgi from the 1972 Whimsies Set 2. **Husky** from the 1980 Whimsies Set 12. **Langur** from the 1979 Whimsies Set 10. Color variations ($20 each, £10 each).

Bear Cub with recessed base. From the 1972 Whimsies Set 3. **Beaver** with recessed base. From the 1972 Whimsies Set 2. **Bison** from the 1979 Whimsies Set 11. **Butterfly** from the 1967-73 Canadian Red Rose Tea series. **Hedgehog** from the 1974 Whimsies Set 5 ($20 each, £10 each)

Duck from the 1972 Whimsies Set 2. **Trout** from the 1972 Whimsies Set 3. **Goose** from the 1971-1979 Canadian Red Rose Tea promotion ($20 each, £10 each).

Miscellaneous Color Variations

Top row. **Trout** from the 1972 Whimsies Set 3. **Eagle** from the 1984-1985 Tom Smith Crackers World of Survival. **Setter** from the 1972 Whimsies Set 3. **Duck** from the 1972 Whimsies Set 2. Bottom row. **Hedgehogs** from the 1974 Whimsies Set 5 ($20 each, £10 each).

Miscellaneous Premiums and Promotions, circa late 1950s - 2005

Many companies, over the years, have approached Wade to produce ceramic figurines to help promote their products. Following are just some of those companies who chose Whimsies or Whimsie-size figurines as promotional items.

Arthur Price of England, circa late 1970s - early 1980s

Circa late 1970s - early 1980s Wade supplied Arthur Price of England, distributors of silver-plated ware, with a number of figurines taken from the 1971-84 line of Whimsies to be added to presentation boxes of children's giftware.

On The Farm
This set included the collie, cow, horse, lamb, pig from the 1975 Set 6 and the ram from the 1977 Set 8 of the 1971-84 Whimsies ($64, £32).

Jungle Babies
This set included the fawn from the 1971 Set 1, the bush baby from the 1972 Set 2, the chimp from 1973 Set 4, the pine marten from the 1975 Set 5, and the langur and koala bear from the 1979 Set 10 of the 1971-84 Whimsies ($64, £32).

Pets and **Companions**
This set included the kitten, mongrel and spaniel from the 1971 Set 1, the alsatian and donkey from the 1974 Set 5, and the cat and donkey from the 1977 Set 8 of the 1971-84 Whimsies ($64, £32).

Jungle Kings
This set included the lion from the 1974 Set 4, the gorilla and leopard from the 1976 Set 7, the orang-utan and tiger from the 1979 Set 10, and the polar bear from the 1980 Set 12 of the 1971-84 Whimsies ($64, £32).

King British Aquarium Accessories Ltd., circa 1976 - 1980

A set of six die cast figurines produced by George Wade & Son. Ltd. for King British Aquarium Accessories Ltd. with the intention that the items would be used as decorative ornaments to be placed in aquariums. The Lighthouse, Seahorse, Mermaid, and Bridge were purchased in September 1976 and the Diver and Snail in February 1977. Equal quantities of each model were produced over a period of three to four years. Of the six figurines, the Seahorse and Snail (in this order) are the most difficult to find. All items are mold marked: WADE ENGLAND.

Lighthouse. Color variation ($70, £35).

Mermaid measures 2-1/2" high ($60, £30). **Diver** measures 2-3/4" high ($30, £15). **Lighthouse** measures 3" high ($60, £30). **Seahorse** measures 3" high ($190, £95). **Bridge** measures 1-3/4" high by 3-1/4" overall ($120, £60). **Snail** measures 1-1/4" high ($120, £60).

Cadbury World

For a number of years, Wade Ceramics Limited has produced promotional items for Cadbury, producers of the world famous chocolate. In 2002 Wade produced the first Cadbury Whimsie, the "Chuckle Bean."

"Chuckle Bean" Whimsies *2002*
The Chuckle Beans measure 1-1/2" high and are mold marked: Wade England. The beans were produced with either green, black or yellow feet ($4 each, £2 each).

Babycham, circa late 1950s

Babycham was a low alcohol drink very popular in the 1950s. The Trade Mark was a small deer with a bow around its neck. The deer Trade Mark was very visible in the 1950s, both in magazines and on television advertisements. Babycham is now making quite a comeback in towns around Europe. Babycham is a Constellation Europe Brand.

"Chuckle Bean" Key chain *2005*
The Chuckle Bean Key Chain measures 1-1/2" high and is mold marked: Wade England ($4, £2).

Babycham prototype figurine. The figurine measures 2-7/8" high by 1-3/8" across the base and is unmarked. This figurine was modeled by William Harper and it is not known to have been produced ($450, £225).

"Hazelnut" Whimsie and **"Raisin"** Whimsie *2005*
Left. Cadbury Hazel Nut measures 1-3/4" high and is mold marked: Wade Eng. Right. Cadbury Raisin measures 1-5/8" high and is mold marked: Wade England ($6 each, £3 each).

Collect it! Magazine, 2000

Collect it! is advertised as "The World's No. 1 Glass Collecting Title." The magazine has sponsored numerous fairs in the UK where products of Wade Ceramics Ltd. have been in the forefront. *Collect it!* has also commissioned Wade to produce figurines for sale through the magazine.

Collect it! **Bear Cub** *2000*
This figurine was an all-over honey glaze version of the Whimsie Bear Cub and was given away in October 2000 to U.K. subscribers of the magazine ($10, £5).

General Foods, circa 1990

There was a proposed promotion for General Foods in the early 1990s and although a number of figurines were produced, the promotion never went ahead. Many of the figurines have now found their way onto the secondary market.

Whimsie figurines
Top row. **Badger** from the 1980-1981; Tom Smith British Wildlife. **Elephant** from the 1973 Whimsies Set 4. **Lion** from the 1973 Whimsies Set 4. Bottom row. **Panda** from the 1984 Whimsie-Land Set 2 (Wildlife). **Zebra** from the 1976 Set 7 Whimsies. **Owl** from the 1986 Whimsie-Land Set 4 (Hedgerow). Above. **Monkey** from the 1973 Whimsies Set 4. Right. **Penguin** from the 1980 Whimsies Set 12 ($50 each, £25 each)

Miniature Nursery Rhyme Figurines
These single color glazed figurines were sampled for the General Foods promotion. Dr. Foster, Pied Piper, Little Bo-Peep, Red Riding Hood, Miss Muffet, and Queen of Hearts ($28 each, £14 each).

Miniature Nursery Rhyme Figurines
These single color glazed figurines were sampled for the General Foods promotion. Tom Piper, Old King Cole, Cat and Fiddle, Wee Willie Winkie, House that Jack Built, and Little Boy Blue ($28 each, £14 each).

Miniature Nursery Rhyme Figurines
These single color glazed figurines were sampled for the General Foods promotion. Old Woman in a Shoe, Jill, House that Jack Built ($10 each, £5 each), Puss in Boots ($28, £14), Jack ($10, £5), and Hickory Dickory Dock ($28, £14).

Guinness Promotional Figurines, 1968

In December 1968, Guinness Brewing commissioned George Wade & Son Ltd. to produce four promotional figurines based on characters featured in the "Guinness Book of Advertising." The order was for 3,000 sets of the four figurines and 8,000 singles, (2,000 each of the four figurines). These figurines have proven to be highly collectable and, due to the limited issue, hard to find, thus commanding a high price.

None of the figurines are marked with a Wade back stamp but all have "Guinness" mold marked on the front of the base. However, the hand-painted under glaze finish is unmistakably "Wade." The illustrations of the figurines and the reproduction of excerpts from the *Guinness Book of Advertising* are "Reproduced by kind permission of Guinness Brewing."

"Wellington Boot" Extract from *The Guinness Book of Advertising* (reproduced by permission).

Tony Weller measures 3" high. **Tweedledum & Tweedledee** measures 2-7/8" high. **Madhatter** measures 3-1/4" high. **Wellington Boot** measures 3-1/2" high ($190 each, £85 each).

"Tweedledum and Tweedledee" Extract from *The Guinness Book of Advertising* (reproduced by permission).

KP Foods Limited Promotion, 1983

This 1983 promotion comprised six miniature "Friars" and was limited to the United Kingdom only. The first figurine of the set was free but the remaining five could only be obtained by submitting proof of purchase of a certain number of potato chip packages. This is most probably the reason that the first figurine (Father Abbot) is the most easily found. The last three figurines, Brother Crispin, Brother Angelo, and Brother Francis are the most difficult to find.

All the figurines have the name of the character marked on the front of the base. All figurines are mold marked "Wade" on the back of the base.

Advertising flyer for K.P. Friars inserted in packets of potato chips (crisps).

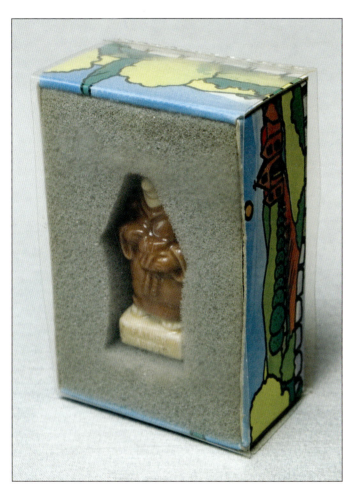

Presentation box for Father Abbot.

Presentation box for K.P. Friars.

Early presentation box for K.P. Friars.

Presentation box for K.P. Friars of a later date.

My Dog Skip, 2001

This solid-pressed figurine was modeled after "Skip" from the Warner Bros. film *My Dog Skip*. The figurine was given away with the purchase of the video only in the UK. This was an issue of fifty thousand but a small number were sold at the 2001 Summer Wade Fest in Harrisburg, Pennsylvania.

Brother Benjamin. Color variation ($40, £20).

Skip measures 1-5/8" high and is mold marked Wade Eng. around the base ($16, £8).

Top row from left: **Brother Crispin** who "Makes Sure KP are the Crispiest Crisps ever Created" measures 1-5/8" high ($44, £22). **Brother Crispin** measures 1-3/4" high and is a prototype figurine. **Brother Francis** who "Delivers KP Fast and Fresh from the Friary" measures 1-5/8" high ($44, £22). **Brother Francis** measures 1-3/4" high and is a prototype figurine. **Brother Angelo** who is the "Keeper of the Good Book of Delicious KP Recipes" measures 1-7/8" high ($44, £22). Bottom row from left: **Brother Peter** who "Tends the KP Friary Potato Patch" measures 1-5/8" high ($18, £9). **Father Abbot** who is the "Founder of the Famous KP Friary" measures 1-3/4" high ($20, £15). **Father Abbot** measures 1-7/8" high and is a prototype figurine. **Brother Benjamin** who "Bags the Best Foods in the Land" measures 1-5/8" high ($14, £7).

Memory Jars™, 1999

The first hand-painted Memory Jars™ were produced in 1999 by Wade Ceramics for Memory Jars™ located in Highnam, Gloucestershire, UK. The purpose of the jars is to be a "safe place" in which to store memories such as baby pictures, locks of hair etc.

The first Memory Jar™ was produced in the Chinese Year of the Rabbit so the jar was issued along with a blue rabbit and a gold rabbit from the same mold as the 1971-84 Whimsies. Every Memory Jar™ carries the genuine Elephant Hallmark.

The blue Whimsie rabbit issued with the Memory Jars™ was a limited edition of 450 ($50, £25). The gold rabbit (not illustrated) was a limited edition of 50.

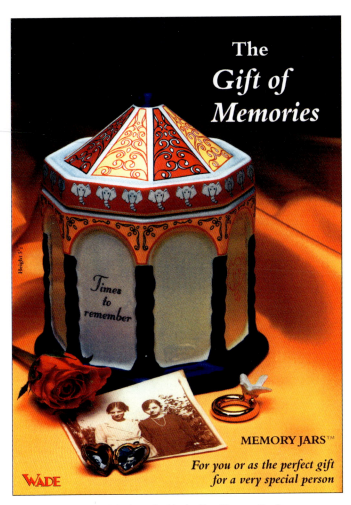

The advertising pamphlet issued with the first Memory Jars™. The jars are 5-1/2" high.

Ridgways of London

This mini teapot key ring was used as a promotional item for Ridgways Tea. The mini teapots, produced for Wade Watch Ltd. of Colorado, were produced from the same mold as the Ridgways mini teapot.

Ridgways Tea Teapot measures 1" by 1-1/2" and is unmarked ($46, £23).

James Robertson & Sons, early – mid-1960s

A set of porcelain figurines known as Robertson's Gollies was produced by George Wade & Son Ltd. The Gollies feature the Robertson's marmalade Trade Mark figurine playing various musical instruments. Each figurine has "Robertson" mold marked on the front of the base. None of the figurines were marked Wade. Later, less expensive versions of the Robertson's "Gollies" were produced in Europe and added to the set. The Wade figurines can be differentiated from the later models by the white porcelain base.

In the early 2000s, a number of unfinished Gollies were taken from the site of the demolished Manchester Pottery and sold on the secondary market. See Chapter 11 for a description of the unlawfully refinished figurines.

All figurines are 2-5/8" high. **Saxophone Player. Trumpet Player. Accordion Player. Clarinet Player. Bass Player** ($220 each, £110 each). Not shown are the Guitar Player and the Vocalist.

Robertson's Gollies Band Stand
This circular Band Stand was produced by Wade to display the "Gollies" and is hard to find (N.P.A.).

Presentation box for Robertson's Gollies.

Trebor Bassett Ltd.

Trebor Bassett Ltd., formed in 1990, is the UK's largest producer of mint sweets, Licorice Allsorts, Wine Gums, and numerous other sweet candies. Trebor was founded in 1907 as Robertson & Woodstock but acquired the name Trebor from a house in London used as the company's headquarters. Bassett's origins began in 1842 when it was founded by George Bassett who, quite accidentally, in 1899, discovered Licorice Allsorts. The story is, whilst showing a customer a tray of samples, a salesman knocked the tray over and the customer was so impressed with the resulting mixed-up confectionaries, he immediately placed an order. Thus Licorice Allsorts were born.

Sharps was founded in 1880 and became a successful manufacturer of toffee and fudge. The company gained Royal Patronage and was awarded Warrant in 1947 and 1955. Sharps was an independent company until 1981 when it became part of Trebor. Today, Trebor Bassett is part of the Cadbury Schweppes Group.

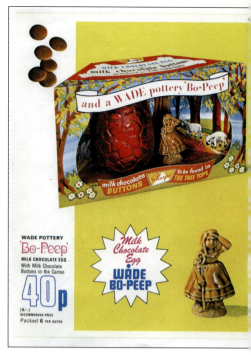

Advertisement for Sharps Bo-Peep.

Sharps Easter Egg Promotions, 1970 - 1971

Between March 27 and March 30, 1970, Sharps, an English manufacturer of candies and sweets, used a porcelain Easter Bunny manufactured by George Wade & Son Ltd. as a promotional item. Between April 9 and April 12, 1971, the company used a porcelain figure of Bo-Peep as a promotional item. The Bo-Peep figurine was also made by George Wade & Son Ltd.

Easter Bunny measures 2-1/2" high and is unmarked ($40, £20). **Bo-Peep.** This undecorated version measures 2-5/8" high and is mold marked: Wade England ($30, £15). **Bo-Peep.** This decorated version measures 2-5/8" high and is mold marked: Wade England ($40, £20). See Reproductions in Chapter 11 for the smaller, unauthorized reproductions of both these figurines.

Advertisement for Sharps Easter Bunny. Note that the egg cups at the top of the advertisement were not made by Wade.

Trebor Murray Mints Promotion, circa mid - 1970s

Trebor, as part of Trebor Bassett, has a long history of producing mints, one of which is the Trebor Murray Mint. The Murray Mint Cowboy, modeled by Wade, has a vague history as an advertising item and dates of issue are approximate.

Murray Mints Cowboys. These prototype figurines are not known to have been in full production. Both figures measure 3-1/4" high by 2-1/4" overall. Only the figure on the left has Murray Mint molded on to the front of the base ($1200 each, £600 each).

Simons Associates, circa mid - 1970s

In the mid-1970s, Simons Associates, Inc. of Los Angeles marketed twenty-four selected Whimsies which were individually shrink packed on decorative cards. For the list of figurines in this promotion refer to the illustration on the back of the display card.

Whimsie Elephant from Set 4. ($16, £8).

Whimsie Alsatian from Set 5. ($16, £8).

Whimsie Spaniel from Set 1. ($16, £8).

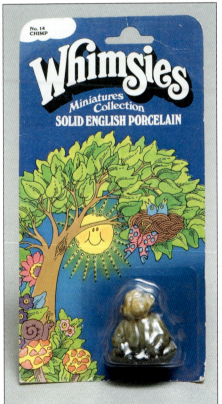

Whimsie Chimp from Set 4. ($16, £8).

Illustration of the back of Simons Associates, Inc. display card.

Imperial Tobacco Limited, 1986

In 1986, Imperial Tobacco Limited commissioned Wade to produce an appropriate figurine as a premium to help promote their brand of St. Bruno tobacco. The premium was a miniature figurine of a St. Bernard dog to be used as a key chain with the chain portion attached to the back of the head.

St. Bernard Dog Key Chain measures 1-1/4" high by 7/8" along the base and is unmarked ($30, £15).

Spillers Foods Ltd., 1991

In 1991 Wade produced a single figurine in the form of a retriever dog which was used as a promotional item for the pet food supplier Spillers Foods Ltd. Purchasers of Spillers Foods could claim the figurine after submitting a "proof of purchase" tokens.

Spillers Retriever measures 1-1/8" high by 2-1/8" long and is mold marked: Wade England ($24, £12).

Field Mouse
A shrink packed field mouse on original display card. This was not issued by Simons Associates but issued by an unknown firm circa 1975 ($20, £10).

Black Zebra
A shrink packed black zebra on original display card ($70, £30). This was not issued by Simons Associates but issued by an unknown firm circa 1975.

"Signal" Toothpaste Promotion, circa late 1960s - early 1970s

The twenty-four figurines used in this Lever Rexona New Zealand Limited toothpaste promotion were similar to those used in the 1971-79 Canadian Red Rose Tea Promotion. One figurine was offered free with each carton of "Signal 2" toothpaste.

Original carton for the tube of toothpaste which would also include one figurine from the promotion.

Whitbread Hopper, 1987

Enterprise Products, a company specializing in button badge assembly equipment, commissioned Wade in 1987 to produce a ceramic frog to be attached to a metal pin badge by means of a double sided tape as an advertisement for Whitbread beers. Records indicate that only a few thousand frogs were produced. Due to the method of attachment of the two items, the frog is most often found alone. The full value of the pin badge is only realized when both the pin and the frog are found together.

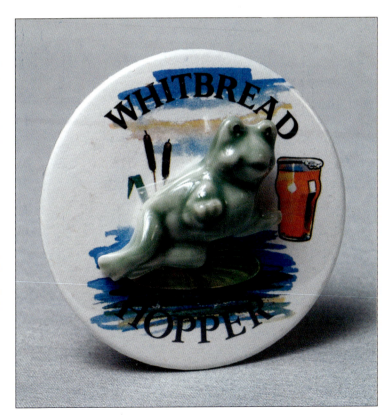

Whitbread Hopper. The pin badge measures 2-1/4" dia. and the ceramic frog measures 1-1/2" long. The frog is unmarked ($40 complete, £20 complete. Frog only $24, £12).

Chapter 10

Quick Figurine Comparison Guide

Illustrated in this chapter are a number of figurines with similar names or from similar molds but in different sets and color ways. The set or sets in which these figurines appear is noted along with the year of issue. Some of these figurines were also issued with an all-over gold or silver glaze but are not illustrated here.

Angel Fish

From left. (1). 1978 Whimsie Set 9. Angel Fish and 1982-84 Can. Red Rose Tea. (2). 1998-99 OIWCC membership figurine. All-over dark blue. (3). 1998-99 Tom Smith Sealife. All-over light green. (4). 2007 Happy-Wading. All-over dark blue with silver eyes and base.

Badgers

From left. (1). 1980-81 Tom Smith British Wildlife. All-over greenish grey. (2). 1998-99 Tom Smith Hedgerow. All-over light grey. (3). 2007 The Exclusive Whimsies Collection magazine. Multi-colored with green base.

Beavers

From left. (1). 1972 Whimsie Set 2 . Also 1967-73 and 1982-84 Canadian Red Rose Tea. (2). 1985-95 U.S. Red Rose Tea. All-over dark brown. (3). 2000 New Whimsie Set "B." Blue/grey with brown tree truck.

Cock-a-Teel/Parrot

From left. (1). 1985-96 U.S. Red Rose Tea (added to the set in 1990) and 1988-89 Tom Smith Your Pets. All-over green. (2). 2006+ Bran Tub Parrot. All-over blue.

Ducks

From left. (1). 1985 Whimsie-Land Set 3 (Farmyard). Grey back. (2). 2003 Whimsie Farmyard Set. Blue back. (3). 1992-93 Tom Smith Bird life. All-over white. (4). 2001-02 Absolutely Crackers. All-over beige/brown. (5). 2007 The Exclusive Whimsies Collection magazine. Orange/brown back.

Elephants

Top row from left. (1). 1983-85 U.S. Red Rose Tea. All-over blue/grey. (2). 1973 Whimsie Set 4. All-over light blue/grey. (3). 2000 New Whimsie Set "B." Orange/brown with green base.
Bottom row. (4). 1984 Whimsie-Land Set 2 (Wildlife). Grey with green base. (5). 2003 Christmas Crackers Safari Set. Grey with brown base.

Frogs

From left. (1). 1979 Whimsies Set 11. Two tone brown. (2). 2003 + Bran Tub. All-over light green. (3). 1967-73 Can. Red Rose Tea and 1973-75 Tom Smith Animates Crackers. All-over yellow/green.

Geese

Top row from left. (1). 1982-83 Tom Smith Farmyard Animals. The glaze is brown and beige and the beak is not colored. (2). 2001 Whimsie "Nursery" Christmas crackers goose which has a white body glaze with yellow beak and feet. (3). 1971-79 Canadian Red Rose Tea goose. Again this is a brown and beige glaze similar to the Tom Smith Farmyard goose but this one has an orange beak which helps to differentiate the two figurines.

Bottom row from left. (4). 1992-93 Tom Smith Bird Life goose which has an all-over honey glaze including the beak. (5). 1992-97 Tom Smith Snowlife goose which has an all-over white glaze. (6). 2001-02 Absolutely Crackers goose which has an all-over dark brown glaze.

Kangaroos

From left. (1). 1979 Whimsie Set 10 and 1976-77 Tom Smith Safari Park. Dark brown with light beige base. (2). 1985-96 U.S. Red Rose Tea and 1986-87 Tom Smith Wildlife. All-over honey. (3). This special color way of the Whimsie kangaroo from 1979 Whimsies Set 10 was given to attendees at a meeting with Wade personnel in Australia in 2004. Honey and white body on green base.

Kittens

Top row from left. (1). 1971 Whimsie Set 1 and 1967-73 Canadian Red Rose Tea. (2). 2000 Whimsie Set "B."
Bottom row. (3). 2000 + Bran Tub. Green eyes and pink ears. (4). 1988-89 Tom Smith Your Pets. All-over grey/blue. (5).
1985-96 U.S. Red Rose Tea. All-over blue (added to the set in 1990). (6) and (7). 2000 Summer Wade Fest. White Kitten
(Lightning). Black Kitten (Thunder).

Koala Bears

From left. (1). 1979 Whimsie Set 10. (2). 1986-87 Tom Smith Wildlife. All-over light beige. (3). 1985-96 U.S. Red Rose Tea.
All-over dark beige. (4). 1976-77 Tom Smith Safari Park. Charcoal body with light beige base.

Owls

Top row from left. (1). 1972 Whimsie Set 3, and 1967-73 Canadian Red Rose Tea. (2). 1983-85 U.S. Red Rose Tea. All-over dark brown glaze.

Bottom row from left. (3). 1986 Whimsie-Land Set 4 (Hedgerow). White body, black eyes, orange beak, and green base. (4). 1992-97 Tom Smith Snow Life. All-over white glaze. (5). 2001-02 Absolutely Crackers. All-over light brown glaze.

Partridges

From left. (1). 2001-02 Absolutely Crackers. All-over blue (2). 1992-93 Tom Smith Bird Life. All-over honey. (3). 1987 Whimsie-Land Set 5 (British Wildlife). White body, black eyes and green base. (4) and (5). 2003 Christmas Bonanza. All-over burgundy and all-over cobalt blue (also gold and silver).

Pelicans

From left. (1). 1978 Whimsie Set 9 also 1982-84 Canadian Red Rose Tea. (2). 2000-02 Absolutely Crackers. All-over white. (3). 1992-93 Tom Smith Bird Life. All-over dark brown.

Polar Bears

Top row from left. (1). 1984-85 Tom Smith World of Survival. All-over dull white. (2). 1998-02 U.S. Red Rose Tea. All-over bright white.
Bottom row. (3). 1985-96 U.S. Red Rose Tea and 1992-97 Tom Smith Snow Life. All-over white. (4). 2000 New Whimsie Set "B." White body on a blue base. (5). 1980 Whimsie Set 12. Dull white body with black nose and blue base. (6). 1976-77 Tom Smith Safari Park. Beige or light beige body on a blue base.

Rabbits

(1) and (2). 2005 Summer Wade Fest. All-over grey and all-over honey. (Also in all-over gold). (3). 1984 Whimsie-Land Set 1 (Pets). Brown and honey.

Rabbit/Hare

From left. (1). 1983-85 U.S. Red Rose Tea. All-over dark brown. (2). 1980-81 Tom Smith British Wildlife. All-over honey. (3). 1992-97 Tom Smith Snowlife. All-over white. (4). 1998-99 Tom Smith Hedgerow. All-over beige.

Raccoons

From left. (1). 1979 Whimsie Set 11. Honey body on a green base. (2). 1998 Whimsie Reissue Set "A."
Blue/grey body with black highlights. (3). 1985-96 U.S. Red Rose Tea. All-over dark brown.

Retriever/Setter

Top row from left. (1). 2007 The Exclusive Whimsies Collection magazine. White body with brown highlights on a green base. (2). 1972 Whimsies Set 3. Honey body on a grey/blue base.
Bottom row. (3). 1984 Whimsie-Land Set 1 (Pets). Yellow/honey body on a light green base. (4). 1991 Spillers Foods Ltd. Retriever. Light and dark honey on a green base.

Rooster/Cockerel

From left. (1). 2003 Whimsie Farmyard Set. White and blue body with red wattles on a pale blue base (also in all-over gold). (2). 2007 The Exclusive Wade Whimsies Collection magazine. White and blue/grey body with orange wattles on a dark blue base. (3). 1985 Whimsie-Land Set 3 (Farmyard). White and grey body, red wattles on a green base. (4). 2001-02 Absolutely Crackers. All-over grey. (5). 1992-93 Tom Smith Bird Life. All-over green.

Seal Pups

From left. (1). 1980 Whimsies Set 12. Beige body on blue base. (2). OIWCC membership figurine 1996-97. White body on a blue base. (3). 1992-97 Tom Smith Snow Life. All-over grey.

Shetland Pony

From left. (1). 2006-07 Bran Tub. All-over grey. (2). 1988-89 Tom Smith Your Pets. All-over beige/pale honey. (3). 2001 Wade Collectors Meet. All-over honey.

Squirrels

From left. (1). 1980-81 Tom Smith Wildlife. All-over dark brown. (2). 1983-85 U.S. Red Rose Tea. All-over dark blue.

Wild Boars

From left. (1). 1979 Whimsie Set 11. Beige with green base. (2). 1973-75 Tom Smith Animates Crackers. and 1986-87 Tom Smith Wildlife. All-over dark beige. (3). 1967-73 Canadian Red Rose Tea and 1983-85 U.S. Red Rose Tea. All-over light beige (no green base).

Wrens

From left. (1). 2001-02 Absolutely Crackers. All-over light green. (2). 1992-93 Tom Smith Bird Life. All-over brown. (3) and (4). 2004 Summer Wade Fest. All-over white and all-over blue (also in all-over gold.)

Chapter 11

Reproductions

O ver the past twenty years or so, there have been a number of reproductions of Wade figurines appearing on the market. For some reason, Canada appears to be the source of many of these reproductions. Regardless of the origin of these reproductions, the fact that they are out there must be recorded if only to alert new collectors of Wade to be careful and informed.

Swan and Shire Horse Reproductions, 1992

In 1992, a reproduction of the early Whimsie Swan appeared on the market. The reproduction Swan has a shorter, thicker, and straighter neck with a smooth transition from head to beak. The wings are more rounded and lumpier than the original and it has shorter, more rounded tail feathers and a lack of detail between the wings.

In the same year, a reproduction of the Shire Horse also appeared on the market. The reproduction horse is crude and is taller than the original, measuring 2-1/16" high. The reproduction has a decidedly backward slant and appears as if the horse were about to fall backwards. It also has large, clumsy, and poorly formed hooves.

SHIRE HORSE (*Set 10*)
Left. Shire Horse is the production model. Right. Shire Horse is the unauthorized reproduction.

Hand Painted Red Rose Tea Figurines

These four enamel finished figurines from the Canadian Red Rose Tea promotion were not produced by Wade in this finish. The bright colors were added by an outside party.

SWAN (*Set 10*)
Left. Swan illustrates a black version of the unauthorized reproduction. Center. Swan illustrates the white version of the unauthorized reproduction. Right. Swan is the production model.

Old Woman in the Shoe. Little Red Riding Hood. Little Bo-Peep, and Humpty Dumpty ($8 each, £4 each).

Brass Whimsies, circa early 1980s

In the early 1980s, brass reproductions of the Wade Whimsies began appearing on the market. Wade manufactured none of these but we are including them here to alert collectors so that they can be informed on reproductions.

In 1982, the brass figurines were being imported into the U.S. by A. A. Importing Company, a wholesale catalog for decorative accessories and giftware for dealers only. A. A. Importing Company, Inc. was founded in 1934 by A. A. Gralnick in the Gas Light Square area in St. Louis, Missouri. The company was heavily involved in the importation of fine crystal, art glass, and fine porcelain from Europe. By the mid-

1970s, A. A. Importing was the leading company in the world in the field of antique reproductions.

The A. A. Importing catalog listed two sets of brass figurines. The "Fairy Tale Set" included Old Woman in a Shoe, Ginger Bread Man, Cat and Fiddle, Puss in Boots, Irish Leprechaun, and Hickory Dickory Dock. The "Gentle Creatures Set" comprised Owl, Rabbit, Squirrel, Turtle, Duck, Blue Bird, Frog, and Butterfly.

Some figurines are found with paper labels reading either Canadianna Brass Inc. Chatham, Ont., or Riverside Brass, New Hamburg, Ontario. Some just had a paper label reading Canada. Riverside Brass, a family owned company founded in 1966, is still in business in New Hamburg, Ontario.

A selection of brass reproduction Whimsies.

A selection of brass reproduction Nurseries.

Reproduction Sharps' Bo-Peep and Easter Bunny, circa early 1990s.

These fake Bo-Peep and Easter Bunny figurines first appeared in Canada in the early 1990s. It would appear that both fake figurines were made from molds using the original figurines as models. Reasoning for this assumption is that the fakes are about twelve percent smaller than the original figurines. This would be consistent with a "one size shrink" when making a new mold from an original figurine. The reproductions also have similar detailing as the originals, including the Wade mold mark of Wade England on the Bo-Peep figurines.

Poodle with Red Skirt, circa 1990s

This poodle with the red enamel finished skirt is vague in its origins. From all reports it appears that it was not produced by Wade in this finish. The bright red enamel on the skirt was added by an outside party.

Left. Original Sharps Bo-Peep shown for comparison. Right. Reproduction Bo-Peep. The reproduction Bo-Peep measures 2-5/16" high.

Robertson's Gollies, circa early 2000s

Left. Original Sharps Easter Bunny shown for comparison. Right. Fake Easter Bunny. The reproduction Easter Bunny measures 2-1/8" high.

The back of the original and reproduction Easter Bunny.

When the Manchester Pottery was demolished in 2002 it was discovered that many damaged figurines such as the Whimsies, Disney Figurines and the Robertson Gollies had been thrown away and used as the base for building expansions. Unfortunately a number of these figurines were taken from the site and repainted and sold. The genuine Robertson Gollies had printed eyes applied as a transfer, the illegally restored figurines have painted eyes. It is not easy to differentiate the genuine models from the restored figurines but generally the eyes on the genuine figurines are round and the restored figurines with painted eyes are more oval and poorly painted.
The figurines illustrated here are the illegally restored figurines with painted eyes.

Bibliography

Baker, Donna. *Wade Miniatures 4th Edition*. Atglen, Pennsylvania: Schiffer Publishing Ltd., 2007.

Carryer, the late H. Straker. Personal communication.

Carryer, Iris Lenora. Personal communication.

Carryer, Iris Lenora. "Searching for the Pony." Privately published.

Lee, Dave. *The Wade Dynasty*. Woking, Surrey, UK: The Kudos Partnership Limited, 1996.

Dawe, the late Derek. L. J. Personal communication.

Harper, William. K. Personal communication.

Collect it! Finchampstead, Berkshire, UK. Collect it Ltd. May 2000 Issue.

Collect it! Finchampstead, Berkshire, UK. Collect it Ltd. March 2001 Issue.

Murray, Pat. *Wade Whimsical Collectables Eighth Edition*. Toronto, Ontario: The Charlton Press, 2007.

The Exckusive Wade Whimsies Collection, London, England, Hachette Paperworks Ltd. Issues 1, 2, 3, and 4.

The Wade Watch. Arvada, Colorado. Wade Watch Ltd. Various Issues.

The Official Wade Club Magazine. Burslem, Stoke-on-Trent, UK. Wade Ceramics Limited. Various Issues.

Wade's World. Burslem, Stoke-on-Trent, UK. Wade Ceramics Limited. Various Issues.

Warner, Ian and Mike Posgay. *The World of Wade*. Marietta, Ohio: The Glass Press, Inc., dba Antique Publications, 1988.

Warner, Ian and Mike Posgay. *The World of Wade Book 2*. Marietta, Ohio: The Glass Press, Inc., dba Antique Publications, 1994.

Warner, Ian and Mike Posgay. *Wade Price Trends First Edition*. Marietta, Ohio: The Glass Press, Inc., dba Antique Publications, 1996.

Warner, Ian and Mike Posgay. *The World of Wade Figurines and Miniatures*. Atglen, Pennsylvania: Schiffer Publishing Ltd., 2003.

Warner, Ian and Mike Posgay. *The World of Wade Ireland*. Atglen, Pennsylvania: Schiffer Publishing Ltd., 2007.

Wade Wholesalers Newsletters, issues 1 through 10.

Web Sites of Interest

http://www.theworldofwade.com

http://www.wadecollectorsclub.co.uk

http://www.cscollectables.co.uk

http://www.wadeusa.com

http://www.redrosetea.com

http://www.wadeattic.com

http://www.happywadeing.com

http://www.benswade.co.uk

Resource Centers

The Rakow Library, Corning Museum of Glass, Corning, New York, USA.

Toronto Reference Library, Toronto, Ontario, Canada.

The New York Public Library, Science and Technology Division, New York, New York, USA.

Ohio State University, Columbus, Ohio, USA.

The British Library, Newspaper Library, London, England.

The Patent Office, Public Record Office, Richmond, England.

Index